D1480531

REFERENCE
DISCARD

HISTORICAL DICTIONARIES OF RELIGIONS, PHILOSOPHIES, AND MOVEMENTS
Edited by Jon Woronoff

HISTORICAL DICTIONARY OF ECUMENICAL CHRISTIANITY

by
Ans Joachim van der Bent

Historical Dictionaries of Religions, Philosophies, and Movements, No. 3

The Scarecrow Press, Inc.
Metuchen, N.J., & London
1994

R
270
.8203
V228

British Library Cataloguing-in-Publication data available.

Library of Congress Cataloging-in-Publication Data

Van der Bent, A. J. (Ans Joachim)
  Historical dictionary of ecumenical Christianity / Ans
Joachim van der Bent.
    p.   cm.—(Historical dictionaries of religions, philoso-
phies, and movements ; no. 3)
  Includes bibliographical references.
  ISBN 0-8108-2853-7 (alk. paper)
  1. Ecumenical movement—Dictionaries. 2. Ecumenists—
Biography—Dictionaries. 3. Christian union—Dictionaries.
I. Title. II. Series.
BX6.3.V36 1994
270.8'2'03—dc20   94-494

Copyright © 1994 by Ans Joachim van der Bent
Manufactured in the United States of America

Printed on acid-free paper

CONTENTS

EDITOR'S FOREWORD

One of the most extraordinary movements of this century is the movement for unity within the Christian Church. Not even imagined, and hardly imaginable until after the Second World War, it has flowed strongly and constantly over the years, bringing the various churches closer together, sometimes even uniting them, and affecting the lives of hundreds of millions of people. While certainly of greatest interest to church leaders, it has also been of considerable interest to the laity and has been supported directly or indirectly by countless concerned laypersons. Moreover, while dealing primarily with "church" matters, such as ecclesiology and theology, it has also been amazingly active in other fields, most notably service, health, refugee work, and international affairs (economic development, racism and apartheid, ecology, peace, and justice).

The Christian Church has occasionally been accused by outsiders of being parochial. Often enough, Christian leaders have themselves lamented a lack of interest in the outside world. Yet, as just noted, the ecumenical movement has taken up any number of issues that affect not only Christians but all men and women. Indeed, to be perfectly fair, the outside world has often been more "parochial" by ignoring these substantial efforts. Outsiders do not know much, and certainly not enough, about the ecumenical movement. That was partly because they lacked a handy primer such as this *Historical Dictionary of Ecumenical Christianity*. It fills the gap by providing short and readable entries on significant persons, events, institutions, and activities. It also includes a helpful chronology and comprehensive bibliography.

This book could only have been written by an insider. In this case, it is the work of an exceptional insider who was not only an observer but a participant as well. Having studied theology and librarianship, Ans Joachim van der Bent was most prominent as director of the library and archives of the World Council of

Churches in Geneva from 1963–1989. From 1985–1989 he also served as its ecumenical research officer because of his vast ecumenical memory. During this time, he wrote and lectured about the ecumenical movement, producing numerous books, reference works and survey articles. Only such experience could have culminated in a historical dictionary of this scope and depth.

Series Editor
Jon Woronoff

ABBREVIATIONS AND ACRONYMS

AACC	All Africa Conference of Churches
ACAT	Action of Christians for the Abolition of Torture
AGEM	Advisory Group on Economic Matters
ARC	Action for Renewal of the Churches
ARCIC	Anglican-Roman Catholic International Commission
BCC	British Council of Churches
BEM	*Baptism, Eucharist and Ministry,* WCC, 1982
BFBS	British and Foreign Bible Society
CADEC	Christian Action for Development in the Caribbean
CBC	church-based community
CCA	Christian Conference of Asia
CCBI	Council of Churches for Britain and Ireland
CCC	Caribbean Conference of Churches
CCIA	Commission of the Churches on International Affairs
CCLA	Committee on Cooperation in Latin America

CCPD	Commission on the Churches' Participation in Development
CEC	Conference of European Churches
CELA	Latin American Protestant Conference (Conferencia Evangelica Latina Americana)
CELAM	Council of Latin American Bishops (Consejo Episcopal Latino Americano)
CICARWS	Commission of the Churches on Inter-church Aid, Refugee and World Service
CIM	China Inland Mission
CIMADE	Comité intermouvement auprès des évacués
CLAI	Latin American Council of Churches (Consejo Latino Americano de Iglesias)
CLF	Christian Literature Fund
CLS	Christian Literature Society (Madras)
CMC	Christian Medical Commission
CMS	Church Missionary Society
COCU	Consultation on Church Union (USA)
CPC	Christian Peace Conference
CSI	Church of South India
CWCs	Christian World Communions
CWME	Commission on World Mission and Evangelism
CWS	Church World Service

DECC	Disciples Ecumenical Consultations Council
DFI	Dialogue with People of Living Faiths and Ideologies
EACC	East Asia Christian Conference
FAO	Food and Agriculture Organization
F&O	Faith and Order
FRG	Federal Republic of Germany
GDR	German Democratic Republic
ICC	International Congregational Council
ICCC	International Council of Community Churches
ICYF	International Catholic Youth Federation
IFR	International Fellowship of Reconciliation
ILO	International Labour Organisation
IMC	International Missionary Council
IMF	International Monetary Fund
IRM	*International Review of Mission* (WCC, quarterly, 1912–)
ISAL	Church and Society in Latin America (Iglesia y Sociedad en America Latina)
JPIC	Justice, Peace and the Integrity of Creation
JPSS	Just, Participatory and Sustainable Society
JWG	Joint Working Group

LMF	London Missionary Society
L&W	Life and Work
LWF	Lutheran World Federation
MECC	Middle East Council of Churches
MIT	Massachusetts Institute of Technology
NCCs	National Councils of Churches
NCCCUSA	National Council of the Churches of Christ in the USA
NEB	New English Bible
NECC	Near East Council of Churches
NGOs	Non-Governmental Organizations
NRMs	New Religious Movements
NT	New Testament
OP	Dominican Order
OSA (OESA)	Augustinian Order
OSB	Benedictine Order
OT	Old Testament
PCC	Pacific Conference of Churches
PCR	Program to Combat Racism
PTE	Program on Theological Education
RC	Roman Catholic

RCC   Roman Catholic Church

RCL   Renewal and Congregational Life

RSV   Revised Standard Version

SA   Salvation Army

SCM   Student Christian Movement

SDA   Seventh-Day Adventists

SEDOS   Servizio de Documentazione e Studi (RC)

SODEPAX   Committee on Society, Development and Peace

SPCK   Society for Promoting Christian Knowledge

SPCU   Secretariat for Promoting Christian Unity

SYNDESMOS   World Fellowship of Orthodox Youth

TEF   Theological Education Fund

TNCs   transnational corporations

UBS   United Bible Societies

UIM   Urban Industrial Mission

UK   United Kingdom of Great Britain and Northern Ireland

ULAJE   Ecumenical Youth Union in Latin America (Union Latina Americana de Joventud Ecumenica)

UN   United Nations

UNCTAD   United Nations Conference on Trade and Development

UNDP	United Nations Development Program
UNELAM	Movement for Evangelical Unity in Latin America (Movimento pro Unidad Evangélica Latinoamericana)
UNESCO	United Nations Educational, Scientific, and Cultural Organization
UNHCR	United Nations High Commissioner for Refugees
UNICEF	United Nations Children's Fund
UP	University Press
URM	Urban Rural Mission
US, USA	United States of America
USSR	Union of Soviet Socialist Republics
WACC	World Association for Christian Communication
WARC	World Alliance of Reformed Churches
WCC	World Council of Churches
WCCE	World Council of Christian Education
WCFs	World Confessional Families
WCRP	World Conference on Religion and Peace
WEF	World Evangelical Fellowship
WMC	World Methodist Council
WSCF	World Student Christian Federation
YCS	Young Christian Students (RC)

YCW	Young Christian Workers (RC)
YFCI	Youth for Christ International
YMCA	Young Men's Christian Association
YWCA	Young Women's Christian Association

CHRONOLOGY OF ECUMENICAL CONFERENCES AND EVENTS

1846 Foundation of the World's Evangelical Alliance.

1855 Foundation of the World's Young Men's Christian Association.

1894 Foundation of the World's Young Women's Christian Associations.

1895 Foundation of the World Student Christian Federation.

1910 World Missionary Conference in Edinburgh, Scotland.
      Eight commissions dealt with (1) carrying the gospel to all the non-Christian world, (2) the church in the mission field, (3) education in relation to the Christianization of national life, (4) the missionary message in relation to non-Christian religions, (5) the preparation of missionaries, (6) the home base of missions, (7) missions and governments, (8) cooperation and the promotion of unity.

1914 Foundation of the World Alliance for Promoting International Friendship through the Churches in Constance, Switzerland.

1920 Encyclical letter of the ecumenical patriarch of Constantinople to "all the churches of Christ for closer intercourse and mutual co-operation".

1921   Creation of the International Missionary Council.

1925   First Universal Christian Conference on Life and Work in Stockholm, Sweden.

Main subjects were (1) the purpose of God for humanity and the duty of the church, (2) the church and economic and industrial problems, (3) the church and moral and social problems, (4) the church and international relations, (5) the church and Christian education, (6) methods of cooperation and federative efforts by the Christian communions.

1927   First World Conference on Faith and Order in Lausanne.

The sections considered (1) the call to unity, (2) the church's message to the world: the gospel, (3) the nature of the church, (4) the church's common confession of faith, (5) the church's ministry, (6) the sacraments, (7) the unity of Christendom and the relation thereto of existing churches.

1928   Meeting of the International Missionary Council in Jerusalem.

Sections dealt with (1) the Christian message in relation to non-Christian systems of thought and life, (2) religious education, (3) the relation between the younger and the older churches, (4) the Christian mission in relation to the race conflict, (5) the Christian mission in relation to industrial problems, (6) the Christian mission in relation to rural problems, (7) international missionary cooperation.

1937   Second World Conference on Life and Work in Oxford.

Sections were (1) church and community, (2) church and state, (3) church, community and state in relation to the economic order, (4) church, community and state in relation in education, (5) the universal church and the world of nations.

Second World Conference on Faith and Order in Edinburgh.

Four sections considered (1) the grace of our Lord Jesus Christ, (2) the church of Christ and the word of God, (3) the church of Christ: ministry and sacraments, (4) the Church's unity in life and worship.

1938 Meeting of the provisional committee in Utrecht, the Netherlands, laying the foundation of the World Council of Churches "in process of formation"; appointment of W. A. Visser 't Hooft as general secretary.

Meeting of the International Missionary Council in Tambaram, India.

Sections comprised (1) the authority of the faith, (2) the growing church, (3) evangelism, (4) the life of the church, (5) the economic basis of the church, (6) the church and the state.

1939 First World Christian Youth Conference in Amsterdam, the Netherlands. Main theme: Christus Victor.

1947 Meeting of the WCC provisional committee, Buck Hill Falls, Pennsylvania, USA.

Second World Christian Youth Conference in Oslo, Norway. Main theme: Jesus Christ is Lord.

Meeting of the International Missionary Council in Whitby, Canada. General theme: Christian witness in a revolutionary world. Subjects treated were (1) partners in obedience, (2) the "supranationality" of missions, (3) the functions of the IMC.

1948 First assembly of the World Council of Churches in Amsterdam, the Netherlands.

Main theme: Man's disorder and God's design. Sections: (1) the universal church in God's design, (2) the church's witness to God's design, (3) the church and the disorder of society, (4) the church and the international disorder.

1950   Meeting of the WCC central committee in Toronto, Canada. Issues: The church, the churches, and the World Council of Churches: The ecclesiological significance of the World Council of Churches.

1952   Meeting of the International Missionary Council in Willingen, Germany.

     Major themes were (1) the missionary obligation of the church, (2) the indigenous church—the universal church in its local setting, (3) the role of the missionary society, (4) reshaping the pattern of missionary activity.

     Third World Conference on Faith and Order in Lund, Sweden. Section titles were (1) Christ and his church, (2) continuity and unity, (3) ways of worship, (4) intercommunion.

1952   Third World Christian Youth Conference in Kottayam, India. Main theme: Jesus Christ the answer—God was in Christ reconciling the world unto himself.

1954   Second assembly of the World Council of Churches in Evanston, Illinois, USA.

     Main theme: Christ—the hope of the world, Sections: (1) our oneness in Christ and our disunity as churches, (2) the mission of the church to those outside her life, (3) the responsible society in a world perspective, (4) Christians in the struggle for world community, (5) the churches amid racial and ethnic tensions, (6) the laity: the Christian in his vocation.

1958   Meeting of the International Missionary Council in Accra, Ghana.

     Group discussions pondered (1) Christian witness in society and nation, (2) the Christian church facing its calling to mission, (3) the Christian church and non-Christian religions, (5) what "partnership in obedience" means.

1959 Meeting of Church and Society in Thessalonica, Greece.
 Culmination of an international ecumenical study: The common responsibility toward areas of rapid social change.

1960 Creation of the Vatican Secretariat for Promoting Christian Unity.

1961 Third assembly of the World Council of Churches in New Delhi, India.
 Main theme: Jesus Christ—the light of the world. Sections: (1) witness, (2) service, (3) unity.

1962–1965 Second Vatican Council.
 Significant ecumenical documents were: Decree on Ecumenism (*Unitatis redintegratio*), Pastoral Constitution on the Church in the Modern World (*Gaudium et spes*), Declaration on the Relationship of the Church to Non-Christian Religions (*Nostra aetate*), Declaration on Religious Freedom (*Dignitatis humanae*).

1963 Fourth World Conference on Faith and Order, Montreal, Canada.
 Three sections studied (1) Christ and the church, (2) worship, (3) Tradition and traditions.

 WCC Division on World Mission and Evangelism meeting in Mexico City.
 Sections dealt with (1) the witness of Christians to men of other faiths, (2) the witness of Christians to men in the secular world, (3) the witness of the congregation in its neighborhood, (4) the witness of the Christian church across national and confessional boundaries.

1965   Creation of the Joint Working Group between the Roman Catholic Church and the World Council of Churches.

1966   World Conference on Church and Society in Geneva.
Sections considered (1) economic development in a world perspective, (2) the nature and function of the state in a revolutionary age, (3) structures of international cooperation—living together in peace in a pluralistic world society, (4) man and community in changing societies.

Eugene Carson Blake appointed general secretary of the World Council of Churches.

Meeting of the Division of Inter-Church Aid, Refugee and World Service in Swanwick, England.
The sections were (1) development aid, (2) uprooted people, (3) the role of ICA in the use and training of the churches' manpower, (4) criteria for inter-church aid projects (the so-called Herrenalb categories of 1956).

1967   Meeting of the Commission on Faith and Order in Bristol, England.
The five sections dealt with (1) creation, new creation and the unity of the church, (2) the eucharist, a sacrament of unity, (3) ministry, church union negotiations, (4) tradition and traditions, (5) general faith and order problems.

1968   Fourth assembly of the World Council of Churches in Uppsala, Sweden.
Main theme: "Behold, I make All Things New". Sections: (1) the Holy Spirit and the catholicity of the church, (2) renewal in mission, (3) world economic and social development, (4) toward justice and peace in international affairs, (5) worship, (6) toward new styles of living.

1969   Pope Paul VI visits the Ecumenical Center in Geneva.

1970   Ecumenical Consultation on Ecumenical Assistance to Development Projects in Montreux, Switzerland.

               The working groups discussed (1) the debate about development, (2) policy and procedures for church support to development projects, (3) structure and organization of ecumenical assistance to development projects, (4) technical assistance for church-sponsored development, (5) the mobilization of funds.

1971   Meeting of the Commission on Faith and Order in Louvain, Belgium.

               The committees were (1a) authority of the Bible, (1b) "giving account of the hope that is in us", (2a) catholicity and apostolicity, (2b) worship today, (2c) participation in and methods of Faith and Order, (3a) "baptism, confirmation and eucharist", (3b) "beyond intercommunion", (3c) the ordained ministry, (4a) study on the council of Chalcedon, (4b) common witness and proselytism, (4c) conciliarity and the future of the ecumenical movement, (5) church union negotiations and bilateral conversations.

          Meeting of the World Council of Christian Education in Lima, Peru.

               The union of the WCC and the WCCE was consummated.

1972   Philip A. Potter appointed general secretary of the World Council of Churches.

1973   Meeting of The Commission on World Mission and Evangelism in Bangkok, Thailand.

               Main theme: Salvation today. Sections considered (1) culture and identity, (2) salvation and social justice in a divided humanity, (3) churches renewed in mission.

1974   World Conference on Science and Technology for Human Development in Bucharest, Romania.

Sections: (1) the significance for the future of pressures of technology and population on environment, and of natural limits to growth, (2) self-reliance and the technical options of developing countries, (3) quality of life and the human implications of further technological change, (4) human settlement as a challenge to the churches, (5) world social justice in a technological age, (6) the theological understanding of humanity and nature in a technological era.

Meeting of the Commission on Faith and Order in Accra, Ghana.

The two main themes were giving account of the hope that is within us, and the unity of the church.

1975   Fifth assembly of the World Council of Churches in Nairobi, Kenya.

Main theme: Jesus Christ frees and unites. Sections: (1) confessing Christ today, (2) what unity requires, (3) seeking community, (4) education for liberation and community, (5) structures of injustice and struggles for liberation, (6) human development.

1977   World Consultation of the WCC Sub-unit on Dialogue with People of Living Faiths and Ideologies.

Main theme: Dialogue in community.

1978   Meeting of the Commission on Faith and Order in Bangalore, India.

The themes were (1) a common account of hope, (2) growing together in unity. Subjects of discussion groups were (1) the meaning of "conciliar fellowship'', (2) toward communion in one faith, (3) growing into one eucharistic fellowship, (4) the discipline of communion in a divided world, (5) new ecumenical experiences and existing ecumenical structures.

1979   World Council of Churches' Conference on Faith, Science and the Future at the Massachusetts Institute of Technology in Cambridge, Massachusetts, USA.

Sections: (1) the nature of science and the nature of faith, (2) humanity, nature and God, (3) science and education, (4) ethical issues in the biological manipulation of life, (5) technology, resources, environment and population, (6) energy for the future, (7) restructuring the industrial and urban environment, (8) economics of a just, participatory and sustainable society, (9) science/technology, political power and a more just world order, (10) toward a new Christian social ethic and new social policies for the churches.

1980   Meeting of the Commission on World Mission and Evangelism in Melbourne, Australia.

Main theme: Your kingdom come. Sections: (1) good news to the poor, (2) the kingdom of God and human struggles, (3) the church witnesses to the kingdom, (4) Christ—crucified and risen—challenges human power.

1982   Meeting of the Commission on Faith and Order in Lima, Peru.

Sections: (1) the work of F&O, (2) F&O and the WCC, (3) the Latin American context, (4) baptism, eucharist and ministry, (5) toward the common expression of the apostolic faith today, (6) steps toward visible unity, (7) the unity of the church and the renewal of human community, (8) the community of women and men in the church.

1983   Sixth assembly of the World Council of Churches in Vancouver, Canada.

           Main theme: Jesus Christ—the life of the world. Issue groups: (1) witnessing in a divided world, (2) taking steps toward unity, (3) moving toward participation, (4) healing and sharing life in community, (5) confronting threats to peace and survival, (6) struggling for justice and human dignity, (7) learning in community, (8) communicating credibly.

1984   Pope John Paul II visits the Ecumenical Center in Geneva.

1985   Emilio Castro appointed general secretary of the World Council of Churches.

           Meeting of the Commission on Faith and Order in Stavanger, Norway.

           The three program areas were (1) baptism, eucharist and ministry, (2) apostolic faith, (3) unity and renewal.

1986   Meeting of the Commission on Inter-Church Aid, Refugee and World Service in Larnaca, Cyprus. The theme was: Called to be neighbors.

1987   Meeting on the ecumenical sharing of resources in El Escorial, Spain. The theme was: Koinonia: sharing life in a world community.

1989   Meeting of the Commission on World Mission and Evangelism in San Antonio, Texas, USA.

           Theme: Your will be done: Mission in Christ's way. Sections studied the topics (1) turning to the living God, (2) participating in suffering and struggle, (3) the earth is the Lord's, (4) toward renewed communities in mission.

           Meeting of the Commission on Faith and Order in Budapest, Hungary. The major item on the agenda was the responses to BEM, the 1982 F&O text on baptism, eucharist and ministry.

World Convocation on Justice, Peace and the Integrity of Creation in Seoul, Korea. This convocation completed the first stage of a process initiated by a decision at the Vancouver assembly in 1983 "to engage member churches in a conciliar process of mutual commitment (covenant) to justice, peace and the integrity of all creation (JPIC)."

1991   Seventh assembly of the World Council of Churches in Canberra, Australia.

Main theme: Come, Holy Spirit—renew the whole creation. Sections/sub-themes: (1) giver of life—sustain our creation, (2) Spirit of truth—set us free, (3) Spirit of unity—reconcile your people, (4) Holy Spirit—transform and sanctify us.

1993   Konrad Raiser appointed general secretary of the World Council of Churches.

Fifth World Conference on Faith and Order in Santiago de Compostela, Spain.

Theme: Toward koinonia in faith, life and witness. Sections: (1) the understanding of koinonia and its implications, (2) confessing the one faith to God's glory, (3) sharing a common life in Christ, (4) called to common witness for a renewed world.

Ecumenical Global Gathering of Youth and Students in Mendes, Brazil.

INTRODUCTION

Christianity finds its origin in the humble ministry of Jesus Christ and his simple message that the kingdom of God is at hand. St Paul wrote that "he has broken down the wall of hostility, by abolishing in his flesh the law of commandments and ordinances, that he might create in himself one new man in place of the two, so making peace . . ". (Ephesians 2:14–15). Yet, in the course of its history, Christianity has created many walls of division. Within Judaism, to be sure, there are Orthodox and liberal Jews; Sunnites and Shiites claim a different adherence to Islam; and Buddhism developed the Mahāyāna and Hīnayāna ways to salvation. But Christianity has produced far more separations and schisms than any other world religion.

When Martin Luther pinned his Ninety-Five Theses to the door of the chapel of Wittenberg Castle in 1517, he had no idea that the solid stem of the church he challenged would soon be split into many branches. Reforming the church in Geneva, John Calvin was unable to anticipate the schism ahead between the Church of England and the Roman Catholic Church in 1570 Still less could he foresee the formation of Baptist, Congregational and Methodist churches in Great Britain, let alone Mennonites, Brethren, Quakers, Disciples of Christ and Old Catholic churches in Europe and North America.

But the divisions in the church had begun long before the Reformation. Five centuries earlier a first great schism between Greek and Latin churches had already taken place. From 1054 onward Eastern churches celebrated the divine liturgy according to the Byzantine rite and rejected the authority of the pope in Rome. Orthodoxy became a self-contained world of its own and almost nine hundred years were to pass before Western theologians began to take serious notice of Orthodox theology. Only after the Second World War did churches in the West start to care

1

about the life of millions of Orthodox Christians in Central and Eastern Europe and in other parts of the world.

In fact, church concern of any sort that crossed confessional and denominational lines was in short supply. Until the beginning of the 20th century, nearly all Christian communities lived in self-centered isolation. Each church, small or large, pointed to its own tradition, celebrated its own liturgy, shepherded the needs of its own flock and was preoccupied with its own identity. The idea of churches together rendering witness and service to the world was foreign. Theology was carried on in the form of confessional monologues. Individual Christians who dared to refer to the church of Jesus Christ as one family, with a common history and a common destiny, were classified as utopian and odd, or simply ignored.

The church's habit of branching out (and breaking off) in all directions was not simply a matter of the Western hemisphere. Divisions were soon transplanted in mission lands, from the 17th century onward, as the growth of colonies and church expansion went hand in hand. After the founding of the Baptist Missionary Society in 1792 and the London Missionary Society in 1795 many other national denominations and free churches followed suit by creating their own missionary agencies. As at home the First Presbyterian Church stood next to the First Baptist Church and opposite the Second Methodist Church in the same street of the city, so new churches and mission posts were created next to one another in the same way in numerous places in Asia, Africa and Latin America. There were a few exceptions: J. H. Taylor, for example, founder of the China Inland Mission, was resolutely non-denominational by refusing connections with any one particular church.

The Origin of the Ecumenical Movement

By the beginning of the 20th century, Christianity was a genuinely international religion and had decisively broken out of its Western boundaries. In many parts of the world missionaries (some 50,000 by the end of the 19th century) had created schools and colleges, championed native peoples in fights against white exploitation, played an important role in the legal abolition of slavery, pioneered medical services, helped to check cannibalism and infanticide, and made notable translations of the Bible. Through all this they had contributed to the transformation of countless lives by the power of Jesus Christ. However, the patterns of teaching, catechizing and including the new faithful in each local denominational church were the same; regardless of the culture, the unspoken assumption was that Western standards of literate faith were the norm. Not only was there often a sharp rejection of indigenous culture wherever it impinged on religion, but the converted natives had to conform strictly to the traditions, doctrines and ethical standards of each mother church engaged in the missionary enterprise.

Slowly but ever more deeply the disgrace of disunity was being felt. It was the missionary expansion, notably in Africa and Asia, that gave birth to the 20th-century ecumenical movement. This movement is generally reckoned to have begun at the World Missionary Conference in Edinburgh in 1910. The event had been preceded by the formation of several transdenominational bodies during the 19th century, in particular the Evangelical Alliance (1846), dedicated to promoting the interests of a "Scriptural Christianity", the oppressed religious minorities in the West and the observance of an annual week of prayer, and the World Student Christian Federation (1895), formed to draw together the student Christian movements in various countries. Important were also the creation of the Young Men's Christian Associations (1855) and the World Young Women's Christian Associations (1898).

The Edinburgh conference led to the International Missionary Council in 1921, created "to help coordinate the activities of the national missionary organizations of the different countries and to unite Christian forces of the world in seeking justice in international and inter-racial relations". To achieve this lofty goal a whole series of world missionary conferences followed. From 1939 onward the International Missionary Council worked closely with the World Council of Churches (while the latter was "in process of formation"). Then, in 1961, after the third assembly in New Delhi, the Missionary Council became the Division of World Mission and Evangelism of the WCC. It had taken several decades to realize that the unity of the church and the mission of the church are but two sides of the same coin.

The Faith and Order and Life and Work Movements

The ecumenical movement as it developed during the 20th century flowed through two other streams of international Christian endeavor. Bishop Charles Brent, an American Episcopalian who attended the Edinburgh conference, launched a proposal for a conference on Faith and Order to include representatives of "all Christian communions throughout the world which confess the Lord Jesus Christ as God and Savior". The first fully constituted world conference on Faith and Order took place in Lausanne in 1927, but other meetings followed in Edinburgh (1937), Lund (1952) and Montreal (1963). All these Faith and Order gatherings were not only concerned with ways to organic church union but also with seeking together a common mind on various matters of Christian theology, tradition and renewal. From the very beginning numerous discussions took place on whether the Faith and Order movement sought a federation of independent churches, based on doctrinal compromise, or whether it should tackle something more innovative and far-reaching.

The third channel of 20th-century ecumenism had a service aspect and was of ethical significance. This movement came to be known as Life and Work and it was decisively influenced by Archbishop Nathan Söderblom of Sweden. His enthusiasm for Christian unity, kindled in his youth, made him another outstanding leader of the ecumenical movement. In 1925, on his initiative, the Universal Christian Conference on Life and Work was convened at Stockholm in order to study the application of Christian principles to international relations and to social, industrial and economic life.

The movement went forward under the slogan "service unites, doctrine divides", and hence in the early stages avoided too much discussion of a doctrinal nature. The report of the Oxford Life and Work Conference (1937) remains to this day the most comprehensive ecumenical statement on problems of church and society and Christian social responsibility. It was the impetus of this Life and Work movement that helped develop the ecumenical quest for a responsible world community expressed so often in WCC gatherings since 1948. This quest has often led to controversy. The Third World Conference on Church and Society, for example, held in

Geneva in 1966 and involving 400 lay experts and theologians, saw a sharp confrontation of the technological expertise of the Western industrialized world with the revolutionary politics of the Third World, particularly Latin America.

The Birth of the World Council of Churches

It soon became evident that if the churches were to give adequate support to the ecumenical cause, both Faith and Order and Life and Work (and later World Mission and Evangelism) ought to join together in a single movement. A provisional committee, meeting in Utrecht in 1938, laid the first solid foundation on which the more permanent structure of the World Council of Churches was built over the next two decades. The most important constitutional questions concerned the authority and the Basis of the Council. There is no doubt, however, that the disastrous effects of the Second World War determined the main course of the ecumenical movement. In spite of the isolation and hatred of nations, many churches remained in contact through the Geneva office, under the leadership of W.A. Visser 't Hooft, the general secretary of the Council. Chaplaincy service, work amongst prisoners of war, preparation for reconstruction after the war and the reconciliation with the Evangelical Church in Germany constituted a vital contribution to the supranational witness of the church.

The words "We intend to stay together" provided a moving testimony from all representatives participating in the first assembly of the World Council of Churches in Amsterdam in 1948. Never before had so many Christians from so many different traditions and backgrounds prayed the Lord's Prayer together, everyone in his or her own language. Never before had there been such a shared enthusiasm and conviction among Anglicans, Baptists, Congregationalists, Calvinists and Lutherans, Methodists, Mennonites, Quakers, Moravians, Disciples, Old Catholics, members of the Salvation Army and of the Orthodox churches. The Church of Jesus Christ was finally marching on the road to visible unity, empowered to give a joint witness and engaged in a common service to the world. An organic union of all Protestant churches was envisaged within the next 15 years.

From 1948 to 1993

With its first assembly in Amsterdam, the World Council of Churches began a growing process, which has continued ever since. The chain of conferences and consultations—ever more numerous and ambitious in their undertakings—has not been interrupted. At the assemblies since 1975 there were almost 4,000 people, including delegates, consultants, observers, staff, visitors and a press corps large enough to stage a conference of its own.

The variety of churches and Christians gathered in the Council is ever more unlimited. Friends worshipping in silence and Orthodox churches celebrating their exuberant divine liturgy seem worlds apart. Salvationists singing hymns in the slums seem to have very little in common with the Old Catholics' emphasis on the mystical Body of Christ. The Church of Christ on Earth begun by the prophet Simon Kimbangu in Zaire can hardly be compared with the Lutheran Church of Sweden. But churches not only differ in confessional and theological positions. Some have millions of members, others only a few thousand. Some Christian communities live and witness in authoritarian states of the political left or the political right. Many are burdened with the problems of affluence, others live among the poorest of the poor. Yet, all these churches attach great value to a place in the ecumenical fellowship. At Amsterdam in 1948, 147 churches officially constituted the World Council of Churches. At that time only 30 churches came from Asia, Africa and Latin America. At the Canberra assembly in 1991, 317 churches from every continent, first world, second and third, were members of the Council.

This impressive membership is no chance collection. It reflects a trust in the World Council as an agent of Christian unity and action. The following brief sampling of highlights since 1948 serves to illustrate the breadth and complexity of the WCC during the last 45 years. The second assembly in Evanston, Illinois, in 1954 reflected many of the tensions of the Cold War rampant at that time. It was not accidental that the assembly's theme was "Jesus Christ-the Hope of the World". Delegates resolved to dedicate themselves to God anew, "that He may enable us to grow together". Two years before Evanston, the Third World conference on Faith and Order in Lund was largely concerned with clarifying the differences that existed between churches and comparing the traditions out of which these differences had emerged. The aim of the Lund report was "to penetrate behind the divisions of the church on earth to our common faith in the one Lord". The Phrase "non-theological factors" commanded increasing attention as it was realized that not only questions of doctrine but social, political and cultural factors played their part in dividing the churches.

The third assembly in New Delhi in 1961 was marked by two major new events. The 20th-century missionary movement became fully integrated in the World Council's concerns. And, after long deliberations, the Orthodox churches in the socialist countries joined the Council. At the fourth world conference on Faith and Order in Montreal in 1963 the full effect of Orthodox participation and the presence of Roman Catholic observers in the theological discussions was felt. Thorny questions of Scripture, tradition, worship, unity, and the nature of ministry were tackled.

The main shift of emphasis illustrated at the WCC's Division of World Mission and Evangelism meeting in Mexico City (1963) carried with it a new insight into the nature of the church's missionary task. *Mission to Six Continents* was the title of the published report. The assumption that the Western world itself no longer needed to be evangelized was radically challenged. All continents need to receive the gospel anew and come to terms with its demands and promises. In 1966 the world conference on Church and Society was held in Geneva. Concentrating on such concrete issues as world economics, development, responsible participation in political life and structures of international cooperation, the conference had a great impact on the fourth assembly in Uppsala in 1968.

More than other assemblies, the Uppsala gathering faced squarely the conflicts of this world: the growing gap between rich and poor nations, the disastrous effects of white racism, the ambiguity of new scientific discoveries, the tensions between generations and the student revolts. Youth participants in great numbers were very articulate and often critical of what went on in the sessions.

The triennial meeting of the Faith and Order Commission in Louvain in 1971 had different concerns. It dealt with a number of ongoing studies on such subjects as baptism, confirmation and the eucharist, ordination, worship and the nature of scriptural authority. All these were received alongside the main theme, "The Unity of the Church and the Unity of Mankind". In the same year as the Louvain meeting, in Lima, Peru, ten years of debates ended with the integration into the WCC of two important ecumenical organizations—the World Council of Christian Education and the World Sunday School Association.

The Commission on World Mission and Evangelism conference in Bangkok (1972–1973) on "Salvation Today" was another landmark meeting. It refused to separate the human being into body and soul or to resolve the tension between personal and social aspects of salvation. Though this position gave rise to misunderstanding and criticism, the meeting brought new insight into the comprehensiveness of God's will for the salvation of all humankind in all its cultural and religious diversity. The WCC's fifth assembly in Nairobi in 1975 showed that the ecumenical movement had reached a new level of maturity. At this very representative gathering, an impressive range of issues was covered with a degree of understanding few observers had thought possible. The list of the six sections into which that assembly's main business was divided illustrates something of the ambitious scope of that meeting.

In 1979 the WCC Sub-unit on Church and Society convened a world conference on "Faith, Science and the Future" at the Massachusetts Institute of Technology in Boston. The two volumes of *Faith and Science in an Unjust World* coming out of the MIT conference had wide distribution and influenced theological discussions and programs of churches in various nations. Some of the themes promoted the present WCC program on Justice, Peace and the Integrity of Creation. An international public hearing on Nuclear Weapons and Disarmament, jointly organized by Church and Society and the Commission of the Churches on International Affairs, took place in Amsterdam in· 1981. The purpose of the hearing—which heard testimony from 37 expert witnesses from various fields, different political perspectives, and all parts of the world—was to consider the problems posed by the escalation of the nuclear arms race and changing concepts of nuclear war.

At the Faith and Order Commission meeting in Lima, Peru, in

1982 the final text of *Baptism, Eucharist and Ministry* was unanimously approved as having reached "such a stage of maturity that it is now ready for transmission to the churches". Quickly acquiring the shorthand title BEM, the document has become the most widely translated and distributed publication of the WCC. Celebrating with great enthusiasm the eucharist according to a new order of worship (the Lima liturgy), reflecting the Faith and Order convergence statement on BEM, the Vancouver assembly in 1983 recommended as a WCC priority the engagement of member churches "in a conciliar process of mutual commitment (covenant) to justice, peace and the integrity of creation", whose foundations were "confessing Christ as the life of the world and Christian resistance to the demonic powers of death in racism, sexism, caste oppression, economic exploitation, militarism, violations of human rights, and the misuse of science and technology".

At El Escorial 1987 the central theme was that the resources to be shared ecumenically are not only the material wealth and power that a few control but also the churches' rich theological understandings, spiritualities, cultures, expressions through music, prayer, song and dance, and perhaps most important of all, the testimonies of those who are suffering. The world convocation on Justice, Peace and the Integrity of Creation (JPIC) in Seoul in 1990 stated that ten affirmations provide a basic direction for Christian commitment to JPIC: power as accountable to God, God's option for the poor, the equal value of all races and peoples, the creation of male and female in God's image, truth as the foundation of community, the peace of Jesus Christ, creation as beloved of God, the earth as the Lord's, the dignity and commitment of the younger generation, and human rights as given by God.

War in the Gulf broke out just three weeks before the seventh assembly in Canberra began. Discussion about a statement on the war revealed the deep differences within the WCC over classic questions about the justifiability of war. Moreover, despite significant ecumenical theological convergence in recent years, assembly discussions and worship made clear that eucharist, ordained ministry and views about the nature of the church remained painful stumbling blocks to full communion.

Other Ecumenical Bodies

Only churches are eligible for membership in the WCC. But three types of ecumenical organizations whose work is related to that of the Council may participate (though not vote) in assemblies and central committee meetings. Some are organized geographically (national councils of churches and regional ecumenical organizations), others are international organizations of one confessional tradition (Lutheran World Federation, World Alliance of Reformed Churches), others are world ecumenical organizations that focus on a specific issue (United Bible Societies) or a specific constituency (World Student Christian Federation).

There are regional organizations in Africa, Asia, the Caribbean, Europe, Latin America, the Middle East and the Pacific. No regional body exists in North America, where one of the three major countries (the United States) has ten times the population of another (Canada), which would create an inevitable imbalance if a regional ecumenical organization were set up. The oldest regional body is the East Asia Christian Conference (now the Christian Conference of Asia).

National councils of churches have been formed in about 90 countries, such as the National Council of the Churches of Christ in the USA (1950), the British Council of Churches (1942) and the National Christian Council of India (1947). Some relate to the WCC as "associated councils", entitled to nonvoting representation at assemblies and central committee meetings. Others are "affiliated" with the WCC's Commission on World Mission and Evangelism but not directly with the WCC as a whole. A third category is Christian councils "in working relationship" with the WCC—often functioning as a channel of communication and cooperation with the WCC's Commission on Inter-Church Aid, Refugee and World Service. The Roman Catholic Church has become a full member of well over 20 national councils of churches and also of the Caribbean and Pacific regional councils. The decision for membership in each case is made by the national or regional conference of bishops, but the Vatican has spoken positively of the councils as one of the more important forms of ecumenical cooperation.

There are 12 international confessional organs of which the World Alliance of Reformed Churches, the Lutheran World Federation and the World Methodist Council have their offices with the WCC in the Ecumenical Center of Geneva. The Center also provides offices to the Conference of European Churches, and representatives of the Russian Orthodox Church and the Ecumenical Patriarchate in Constantinople. In a strict sense the 12 confessional organizations are not "ecumenical", since their member churches come from a single confessional tradition. But many are partners in theological dialogues across confessional lines; and the situations of their own member churches may lead them to share many of the concerns on the ecumenical social agenda.

WCC relations with a variety of other global ecumenical organizations are not as deliberately structured as contacts with regional and national councils or with Christian world communions. Among the oldest links are those with the worldwide associations for the YMCA and the YWCA and the World Student Christian Federation. The WCC may collaborate on particular programs or activities with organizations like the United Bible Societies, the World Association for Christian Communication or the International Fellowship for Reconciliation. The focus of these organizations on one issue or constituency and the fact that they may have individual as well as corporate members may enable them to be more effective than the WCC in certain circumstances.

In addition to all these bodies, there are almost 200 ecumenical institutes around the world with a great variety of programs. European institutes, grouped together by the Societas Oecumenica, have made scholarly contributions to ecumenical theology, social ethics and spirituality, while Asian and African study and dialogue centers have deepened the understanding of the Christian faith in a multi-religious environment.

Local-Ecumenism and New Forms of Fellowship

It is probably on the very local level in many places that the ecumenical movement has progressed more than anywhere else.

Joint catechetical classes are conducted by Roman Catholic priests and Protestant ministers. Mixed-marriage groups are alive and actively reminding the respective ecclesiastical hierarchies of their pastoral responsibility. Ecumenical baptisms and marriages are ever more frequently celebrated. New church buildings serve several denominations under one roof. Ecumenical groups share everything from Bible study to sponsorship of a development project in a Third World country. This all goes considerably beyond the once-in-a-year coming together for the Week of Prayer for Christian Unity and an occasional exchange of pulpits. That sort of ecumenism is now increasingly seen as old and timid. Hesitant church authorities cannot slow down any more the pace of ecumenism, precisely because too many local congregations have joined the march.

Besides local manifestations for unity the ecumenical movement is still further propelled by less formalized Christian communities and groups, trying out spontaneous or experimental forms of worship, common life and service, and witness and social action. Protesting against the complacency of the institutional churches and the bureaucracy of their ecumenical organs, these groups often provide a creative challenge to traditional church life and status quo ecumenical attitudes. The variety of these groups is enormous, as the following sampling shows.

More than four centuries after Luther's attack on monasticism, the first Protestant Taizé brothers said their regular "offices" together in the cathedral of St Peter in Geneva where Calvin (who also condemned the monastic vows and life) had preached. The brothers' life of prayer, which sustains their life of service, has not been a mere imitation of the ancient monastic centers, such as Cluny, although this historic site lies near Taizé in Burgundy. When the *Office de Taizé* was published in 1962, its careful balance of old and new aroused the attention of many who were concerned for the renewal of Christian worship. The establishment of this charitable and liturgical community has challenged Protestants and Catholics together to reconsider their past rejection of each other. Hundreds of thousands of young people have made a pilgrimage to Taizé and celebrated the eucharist with the brothers, all of whom have taken the traditional vows of lifelong poverty, chastity and obedience.

Evangelical academies and lay training centers provide another challenge to established ecumenism. The work in these places has been formed not so much around the traditional order of common prayer or the free worship of Spirit-filled groups of believers, as around the contemporary disorder of life in the world. These academies and centers were born in Germany as a result of ruin in the 1940s. The academies of Bad Boll, Arnoldshain, Loccum, Tutzing, the Sigtuna Foundation above Lake Mälar in Sweden, the Kerk en Wereld Institute at Driebergen near Utrecht, and several other communities have been effective in meeting people's spiritual and intellectual needs, running conference retreats, specializing in courses for politicians and trade unionists, discussing the life problems of industrial workers and training lay people for parishes and schools. Lay institutes have spread outside Europe, in Japan, Korea, India, Zambia, Australia, Canada, the United States and many other countries. They have all helped to bring a renewed Christianity to grips with the secular world. Particular mention should be made of church-based communities for which the cornerstone is the word of God. They have been seedbeds of many popular organizations and continue to provide them with active participants and support, especially in Latin America. Church-based communities are of ecumenical significance by the mere fact that they re-create the church on the pattern of the early church and not as reproduction of the prevailing type of church.

In France radically minded Christians responded to their country's political drama back in 1939 by creating the CIMADE (Comité Inter-Mouvement auprès des Evacués). Old people, the chronically unemployed, discharged prisoners, foreign students and thousands of migrant workers and helpless refugees have been given friendship and some security by the workers of this two-thirds French, one-third international volunteer organization. In Germany, the *Kirchentag* every two years brings Christians together in their tens of thousands for several days of intensive Bible study, education and argument. These rallies, which make special provision for many international visitors, owe their existence to the vision and courage of one man, the late Reinhold von Thadden-Trieglaff. The Kirchentag has crossed the political barriers dividing Germany. Collaboration with Roman Catholics has grown. The massive efficiency and success of the rallies continue to attract many ecumenical visitors and provide a meeting point for Christians in Germany from the East and the West.

Evangelicals and Charismatics

An important category of "non-members" with whom the WCC has sought to cultivate relationships is groups that define themselves as "evangelical". There are, however, two qualifications that complicate any discussion of "evangelicals and the WCC": 1) the word "evangelical" has no precise agreed-upon definition; 2) within the WCC member churches there is a large number of people, and some organizations, who would describe themselves as "evangelical".

Historically, it has been in the area of mission and evangelism that the WCC and evangelical organizations have had the greatest communality of interests. Not surprisingly, it has also been the area where significant controversies have arisen. Evangelicals have charged the WCC with too much concern for social action and too little for evangelism. Ecumenical dialogue with people of living faiths has been regarded in evangelical quarters as dulling the edge of evangelism, if not abandoning the historic Christian claim about the salvation in Jesus Christ. What the multi-religious world needs more than ever before is the verbal proclamation of this fact and the conversion to its Savior.

Since the 1974 Lausanne Congress on World Evangelization, sponsored by a number of evangelical organizations, there has been a global "evangelical" mission conference at about the same time as each of the WCC's world mission conferences. A few people have typically attended both conferences, but it is clear that a large number of each would consider the gulf between them too wide to be bridged by holding a single conference.

A continuing source of tension within the WCC constituency is the way in which wealthy and independent evangelical mission, relief and development agencies headquartered in North American and Western Europe operate in countries in the Third World. Local churches there, often representing an ancient but struggling minority of Christians, sometimes charge that evangelical organizations from abroad show little respect for the culture and traditions of the area and that, despite their strictures against "the church getting involved in politics", they themselves support a particular political line.

The growth of Pentecostalism has been phenomenal during the last few decades. Its manifestations—speaking in tongues (*glossolalia*), divine healing and prophecy—are parts of a charismatic renewal that has affected all the traditional Protestant and Roman Catholic churches in Europe, North and South America. Attaching great value to the simplicity and fervor of the Acts of the Apostles, the strength of Pentecostal communities lies in the warmth of their worship. They are in this sense ecumenical, believing that the baptism of the Holy Spirit is available to believers in all ages. A number of Pentecostal churches have joined the WCC, and some of their leaders have shared in its meetings. But there are still many Pentecostal groups that remain suspicious of the official ecumenical movement.

The WCC has begun to intensify contacts with African independent churches (a handful of these churches are members of the Council). Allowing for the diversity among these churches, most share a strong sense of the local congregation as a charismatic, healing community and a vivid belief in a spiritual world in which God's power confronts and overcomes the powers of darkness. Their rootedness in their own culture enables them to contextualize the Christian message in a way that missionaries from outside have never managed. Their priorities, however, may not fit closely with the traditional agenda of the WCC and the ecumenical movement. In turn, many feel unfairly snubbed ecumenically for what is seen as a lack of theological depth and training, authoritarian charismatic leadership accountable to no one, inadequate recognition of the social causes of the poverty of many of their members, orientation to the life-to-come as an escape from the miseries of the present, excesses of ecstatic enthusiasm.

It is still unclear how all these new forms of Christian fellowship have affected the churches around the world. Such terms as "revival", "renewal", "radical change", and "revolutionary commitment" prove elusive when it comes to surveys of ecumenism. Various new initiatives have been domesticated by official acceptance. Others wear their unorthodoxy with pride. Many lay people and clergy ask whether renewal can come, but the call to the churches by the first assembly of the WCC nevertheless remains valid: "Our first and deepest need is not new organization, but the renewal, or rather the rebirth, of the actual churches". There is indeed an intimate relation between unity and renewal. The greatest contribution to unity will be made by the church in each place, and in all places, that is most ready to let itself be thoroughly renewed by the Holy Spirit.

The Roman Catholic Church

For all its ecumenical service for more than 40 years, the World Council of Churches is not itself the ecumenical movement, but only a privileged instrument of that movement. Other forces and other churches, in particular the Roman Catholic Church, not yet belonging to the World Council, also strive for the unity of all Christians. Roman Catholicism has radically changed its attitude toward the ecumenical movement during the last 30 years. The decisive turning point came with the Second Vatican Council, 1962–1965, and the great influence of Pope John XXIII. Before that time the official position of the Vatican was negative toward rapprochement with other churches. It is very difficult to answer the question whether the Second Vatican Council was a greater breakthrough in the Roman Catholic Church than the first assembly of the World Council of Churches within the Protestant churches.

In 1961 Rome at last agreed to the participation of official observers in the New Delhi assembly, while in return a great number of delegated observers from various denominations were invited to attend the Vatican Council. The Council's Decree on Ecumenism praised "the ecumenical sincerity and energy of the separated brethren". Pope John XXIII created in 1960 a Secretariat for Promoting Christian Unity, which coordinates all ecumenical relations with non-Roman Catholic churches. From 1965 onward a Joint Working Group—its members are appointed by the Vatican Secretariat for Christian Unity and the World Council of Churches—has met annually to discuss common problems and concerns among their members. But collaboration goes much further. The Week of Prayer for Christian Unity is annually prepared by a group of World Council and Roman Catholic representatives. The Commission on Faith and Order now includes a considerable number of Roman Catholic members. Every major WCC conference and consultation has been attended by fully participating Catholic delegates.

It was with this spirit of cooperation in mind that Pope Paul VI, visiting the World Council in Geneva in 1969, called the occasion "a prophetic moment and truly blessed encounter". Pope John Paul II, visiting the Council in 1984, expressed the wish of growing collaboration between the WCC and Roman Catholic constituencies.

Yet, most observers doubt that the issue of Roman Catholic membership in the WCC will be on the agenda any time soon. A Roman Catholic application for membership would present some formidable problems. The Roman Catholic Church is very different from the member churches of the WCC. Because of its size, Roman Catholic membership of the WCC would make the already delicate questions of balanced representation on the WCC governing bodies even more difficult. Moreover, WCC member churches are self-governing and in general nationally organized. The organization of the Roman Catholic Church, by contrast, as a worldwide body with a central church government that has universal jurisdiction, would greatly complicate its participation in the WCC.

Also, in international relations, the WCC's status is quite different from that of the Holy See. The WCC relates to governments through the national churches and to the United Nations and its agencies as an accredited nongovernmental organization; the Vatican is itself a state, with diplomatic ties with many governments and membership of several UN agencies. The difference of status makes it difficult for the WCC and the Roman Catholic Church to act jointly. For example, the WCC's established practice of making public statements on current issues is quite foreign to the Vatican.

Above all this it remains extremely complicated to remove remaining obstacles on the road to doctrinal agreement and visibly restored unity, in particular theological differences with regard to the place of Mary and the role of the pope. The ecumenical problem in both of these cases is complicated by how the Roman Catholic Church understands itself and the authority of its teachings. In the ethical field, there are significant differences on how to approach questions such as abortion, birth control and euthanasia, or questions of just war and nuclear deterrence.

Whatever the ultimate shape of the greater unity the churches seek to manifest—many Christians pray for a eucharistic unity of all in each place—it will certainly not be any expansion or imitation of that kind of unity currently existing within the Roman Catholic Church. This largest Christian community, as it is freely acknowledged, is also called to radical renewal, like the rest of the Christian denominations.

Differing Interpretations of the Ecumenical Movement

Within the brief compass of this introduction one person's selection of highlights, based on printed sources that themselves reflect the individual points of view of only some of the events of the ecumenical movement, can in no way be represented as an "official" account. Indeed this introduction cannot and should not be seen as an objective ecumenical history. From the dizzying variety of events and interpretations of these events, others would accent different themes—perhaps things ignored in the official records. Ten, 20 or 100 years from now different moments will seem to have been important and will be interpreted in differing ways. Moreover, if the ecumenical insight into the importance of the unity of "all in each place" is taken seriously, it is obvious that an account of the whole ecumenical movement and particularly the life and work of the WCC (even with brief references to regional and national events) excludes a larger part of the ecumenical story.

Some will be quick to point out that the perfect unity for which Jesus prayed is not to be expected in this world, for the forces of sin and division will continue until the final consummation. Yet, especially the WCC represents the enduring conviction, never entirely absent in church history but particularly flowering in the 20th century, that neither the elusiveness of ultimate success nor the recognition of unity as a gift and not as an achievement exempts us from working for it. In their message to the churches delegates to the first assembly of the WCC expressed this eloquently:

"It is not in man's power to banish sin and death from the earth, to create the unity of the Holy Catholic Church, to conquer the hosts of Satan. But it is within the power of God. He has given us at Easter the certainty that his purpose will be accomplished . . . By our acts of obedience and faith, we can on earth set up signs which point to the coming victory".

This introduction should have made clear that the portrait of the ecumenical movement and its agencies cannot be a finished one. When dramatic events shake the life of the world and of the church, ecumenical organizations may act boldly and significantly, perhaps in radical new ways. Much of the time, though, the earthshaking importance of their pronouncements and actions is not evident. Still, the faithful and unspectacular work of encouraging the churches to grow in unity, witness, service and renewal goes on, equipping them to face the next unexpected crisis.

Is the ecumenical movement moving? If so, some may be tempted to say, it moves very slowly. Thus, paradoxically, the WCC calls for both patience—recognition that, in ecumenism as in mountain climbing, progress is slower the closer one gets to the top—and a constant renewal of the "holy impatience" with the status quo that led to its formation in the first place.

THE DICTIONARY

ABORTION see SEXUAL ETHICS

ABRECHT, PAUL (1917–). After having pursued theological studies at Berkeley Baptist Divinity School and studies on Christian ethics under Reinhold Niebuhr and John Bennett (qq.v.) at Union Theological Seminary in New York, Abrecht joined the staff of the WCC (q.v.) in 1949 until his retirement. After having functioned as secretary for the study program on Christian Action in Society, he was appointed director of the Department (later Sub-unit) on Church and Society, 1954–1983. He was responsible for three ecumenical study programs: "The Responsible Society", 1949–1954, "The Common Christian Responsibility towards Areas of Rapid Social Change", 1955–1961, and "The Future of Humanity and Society in a World of Science-based Technology", 1969–1979. He edited *Background Information,* 1959–1969, and *Anticipation,* 1969–1983. He wrote *The Churches in Rapid Social Change* and was the editor of *Fifty Years of Ecumenical Social Thought.*

ACADEMIES, LAY see ECUMENICAL INSTITUTES

ACCRA 1958 see INTERNATIONAL MISSIONARY COUNCIL

AINSLIE, PETER (1867–1934). As moderator of the national convention of the Disciples of Christ (q.v.), he led this church in 1919 to renew its commitment to Christian unity. Ainslie shared the Faith and Order (q.v.) vision of Bishop Charles H. Brent (q.v.) and served in key positions of the Faith and Order movement, including the first world conference in Lausanne (1927). Ainslie also served the Federal

Council of Churches in the USA (q.v.) and was active in the American Conference on Organic Union (the Philadelphia Plan), and Disciples bilaterals with Episcopalians, Presbyterians, Congregationalists and Baptists (qq.v.). Traveling widely and often to Europe he was a delegate to the Stockholm conference in 1925 and a member of the Church Peace Union and of the World Alliance for Promoting International Friendship through the Churches (q.v.), attending conferences in Constance (1914), The Hague (1919), Geneva (1920) and Copenhagen (1922). In 1927 he organized the Christian Unity League, which called upon Christians to affirm "the quality of all Christians" and promised to work for a "co-operative united Christendom". He was editor of *The Christian Union Quarterly,* 1911–1934.

ALEXIS (SIMANSKY). Patriarch of Moscow and all Russia (1877–1970). Alexis studied first law and later theology. In 1902 he became a monk, in 1903 he was ordained a priest, and in 1913 he was made bishop of Tikhvin. Following his exile from 1922 to 1926, he became the leader of the diocese of Novgorod in 1926, metropolitan of Leningrad (where he suffered with his people the horrors of the German blockade) and in 1945 patriarch. After several conversations with leaders of the ecumenical movement (in particular W. A. Visser 't Hooft [q.v.]) he decided in 1960 that the Russian Orthodox Church should become a member of the WCC (qq.v.). He was the only patriarch who sent observers to the Second Vatican Council (q.v.).

ALIVISATOS, HAMILKAR SPIRIDONOS (1887–1969). After having studied from 1904 onward theology in Athens, Alivisatos continued his studies of church history and canon law in Berlin and Leipzig and in 1918 became professor of canon law (q.v.) and pastoral theology in Athens. He was greatly concerned with the renewal of the Orthodox church, the training of priests and the promotion of Christian social activities. From 1948 until his death he was a member of the WCC (q.v.) central committee and the Commission on Faith and Order (q.v.), and other ecumenical committees. He often criticized the WCC for its one-sided Protestant position, pleaded for a significant Orthodox (q.v.) contribution to the ecumenical movement and was keen to be involved in effective interchurch aid (q.v.).

ALL AFRICA CONFERENCE OF CHURCHES (AACC). It was to the beating of African drums that the All Africa Conference of Churches came into existence in 1963 in Kampala, Uganda. As with the East Asia Christian Conference (q.v.) there had been an earlier period of preparation, and the decision to create the regional organization had been taken at a widely representative meeting in Ibadan, Nigeria, in 1958. In the brief period between 1958 and 1963 about 20 African nations had achieved political independence, and this phenomenon, with all the turbulence and high expectations that accompanied it, inevitably colored the thought and the definition of dominant concerns of the new all-Africa organization.

The historical and cultural background of the church in Africa gives a particular direction to the ecumenical thinking and possibilities in this continent. The stress is on practice rather than theory, on experience rather than intellectual debate. The political situation, with a great emphasis on independence and liberation, and on the rejection of all traces of colonialism, brings special problems and opportunities for the movement for Christian unity (q.v.). The independent churches offer a special vision of Christianity, posing many questions to traditional mainstream churches.

The AACC is made up of almost 150 member churches and associated councils in 33 countries. It represents over 50 million African Christians, which is more than one-third of the total Christian population in Africa. The AACC headquarters are located in Nairobi. The main concern of the AACC at present is to keep before the churches and national Christian councils the demands of the gospel pertaining to their life and mission, for witness in society, for service and unity, and to this end to promote consultation and action among the churches and councils. The hope is that the diverse peoples of Africa will share information from their respective spiritual and cultural resources, learn from one another's knowledge and experience, identify common problems and participate in finding possible solutions.

AMERICAN COUNCIL OF CHRISTIAN CHURCHES *see* ANTI-ECUMENISM

AMMUNDSEN, OVE VALDEMAR (1875–1936). President of the World Alliance for Promoting International Friendship through the Churches (q.v.), 1935–1936, and joint president of the Universal Christian Council for Life and Work. Ammundsen was professor of church history in Copenhagen, 1923–1936, and Bishop of Haderslev, 1935–1936.

AMSTERDAM 1939 *see* YOUTH

AMSTERDAM 1948 *see* WORLD COUNCIL OF CHURCHES ASSEMBLIES

ANGLICAN CHURCH. The Church of England separated from Rome in the 16th century after Henry VIII's quarrel with the papacy over the question of his divorce from Catherine of Aragon. The Act of Supremacy in 1534 rejected the authority of the pope. The establishment of a new national church was completed by the Act of Uniformity during the reign of Elizabeth I, and by the issue of Archbishop Cranmer's *Book of Common Prayer* in 1549 and the publication of the King James Authorized Version of the Bible in 1611. Both the beliefs and organization of the Church of England represent a blend of Protestant and Roman Catholic (qq.v) traditions and teachings. The Protestant principles of the Reformation (q.v.) were introduced through a gradual process. Doctrine and ritual were laid down in the *Thirty-nine Articles of Faith,* finally promulgated in 1571, and in the revised *Book of Common Prayer* of 1559. The Bible was the final authority and was available to all men and women. Ritual was simplified, the sacraments reduced in number. The cult of the Virgin and the saints and the insistence on the celibacy of the clergy were rejected. Services were held in English instead of Latin.

On the other hand, Anglicanism laid great stress on the continuity of its faith. It maintained all the creeds (q.v.) and doctrines of the early church, and its bishops are claimed to be ordained in direct succession from the first apostles. This inclusiveness has left room for all shades of opinion within the Church. It absorbs both Evangelicals, with their emphasis on simple faith and personal salvation (q.v.), and Anglo-Catholics with their high view of the sacraments (q.v.) and their emphasis on ritual.

The spread of Anglicanism was due partly to migration and partly to missionary effort by the Society for the Propagation of the Gospel and the Church Missionary Society. The Anglican churches overseas are all independent national churches. The Church of England no longer exercises authority over them. They are held together by a common faith and doctrine, common liturgy (q.v.) and common episcopal policy. Bishop Ralph S. Dean, secretary of the Advisory Council on Missionary Strategy, pointed out in 1968 that "the Anglican Communion is not a confessional body in the ordinary sense of the term", but that Anglican churches "are bound together chiefly by the fact that each is in communion with the see of Canterbury and with each other, that there is no specifically Anglican confession of faith, no central authoritative structure, no longer even one Book of Common Prayer, for at least eight different rites now obtain, though all partake of a common shape of the liturgy". There are some 396 dioceses in the Anglican communion. The number increases by about eight a year. They exist in all continents. The number of members, in terms of those who describe themselves as Anglicans, is about 61 million.

The Lambeth conferences, in which all bishops participate, began in 1867. The conference is presided over by the Archbishop of Canterbury. A second field of communication has been the Pan-Anglican congresses. These have been held in London in 1908, in Minneapolis, USA, in 1954, and in Toronto, Canada, in 1963. The congress, though like the Lambeth conference in having no executive authority, is distinguished from it by the presence of clerical and lay representatives from all the dioceses in the communion. Since 1971 the Anglican Consultative Council—its headquarters are in London—has met every two or three years in different parts of the world; its standing committee meets in the intervening years. The Council has no legislative powers, but fills a liaison role, consulting and recommending, and at times representing, the Anglican communion. Its ecumenical functions are:

—to encourage and guide Anglican participation in the ecumenical movement and the ecumenical organizations; to cooperate with the World Council of Churches and the Christian World Communions (qq.v.) on behalf of the Anglican communion; and to make arrangements for the conduct of Pan-Anglican conversations with the Roman Catholic Church, the Orthodox (qq.v.) churches and other churches;

—to advise on matters arising out of national or regional church union negotiations or conversations and on subsequent relations with united churches.

The Anglican communion faces contemporary problems of unity, identity and calling. The lack of central authority means, e.g., that the ordination of women (q.v.) to the presbyterate or episcopate is practiced in one part of the communion and not in another. Liturgical revision is pursued on a province-by-province basis. Reunion with other Christian communities, which is central to the calling of Anglicans, creates complications when it actually becomes imminent. The Anglican communion, moreover, wrestles with the problem of its cultural conditioning, which arises from its English heritage, its conservatism in relation to distinctively Anglo-Saxon ways and the ambiguous role for the see of Canterbury.

ANNUAL PRAYER FOR CHRISTIAN UNITY *see* **WEEK OF PRAYER FOR CHRISTIAN UNITY**

ANTI-ECUMENISM. Even though the ecumenical movement grew out of a ground swell of commitment to church unity, it has always had its critics. In the second half of the 20th century, the WCC (q.v.) has become the most visible expression of the ecumenical movement. It should not come as a surprise, therefore, that the Council, ever since its foundation in 1948, has been the target of constant criticism, both inside and outside of its constituencies. Besides the ban on Roman Catholic (q.v.) attendance and the decision of several Orthodox (q.v.) churches not to join, delegates of 58 conservative Protestant (q.v.) churches, also meeting in Amsterdam just a week before the first assembly, formed an International Council of Christian Churches "to stand against the WCC". In 1941 the American Council of Christian Churches was organized to provide organized evangelical opposition to the liberal policies of the Federal Council of Churches (q.v.). Carl McIntire, the leader of the council and a veteran WCC critic, has been a visible adversary at many of the WCC meetings.

Criticisms of the WCC may be summarized under four headings: political, theological, ecclesiological and institutional.

1) Although it is often said that the WCC has more and more subordinated church unity to socio-political issues, its involvement in international affairs and the negative reactions to it go back to the very beginning. With a skillful use of innuendo and quotations taken out of context, *Reader's Digest* and the network television program *60 Minutes* focused on the charge that ecumenical bodies like the WCC and the National Council of the Churches of Christ in the USA (q.v.) support radical, revolutionary and often-violent Marxist-inspired liberation movements with money given by sincere members of Christian churches. But political criticism has not been only Western. Beijing's *People's Daily* saw the 1961 integration of the International Missionary Council (q.v.) with the WCC as "a new strategy of American imperialist missionary enterprise". Soviet media attacked the WCC's human rights (q.v.) stand at the fifth assembly of the Council in Nairobi in 1975. Brazilian landowners described in the 1980s the WCC's support for the land rights of indigenous people there as a conspiracy with US interests to violate the country's sovereignty. And, in the tangle of Middle Eastern politics, the WCC has been attacked from all sides, often taking the blame for activities of Christian groups with which it has no connection whatever.

2) Theological criticisms of the WCC also vary according to who is making them. The tensions between "doctrinal" concerns of Faith and Order and the "social" concerns of Life and Work (qq.v.) remained despite their merger in the WCC. In the face of unceasing insistence on holding the two together, churches and Christian groups have often objected

that the Council is giving too much attention to one or the other. The lack of the WCC's seriousness about mission (q.v.) and evangelism is another source of misgiving and criticism. Even the explicit pronouncements of the 1982 central committee statement *Mission and Evangelism: An Ecumenical Affirmation* have not stilled objections from those who say social concerns obscure WCC concern for verbal proclamation of the gospel to millions of people who have never been invited to accept Jesus Christ (q.v.) as personal Savior. Questions about the commitment to evangelism have taken on a new dimension with growing WCC involvement in the dialogue with people of other living faiths (q.v.), which some say dulls the edge of Christian witness and leads to syncretism (q.v.). Others have criticized the WCC for a view of human nature that is too optimistic, a view of sin that focuses too much on evil social structures and not enough on personal evil, and too uncritical a faith in human potential for inaugurating the kingdom of God. Some churches in the Reformed (q.v.) tradition have seen in the document *Baptism, Eucharist and Ministry* (q.v.) a "catholicizing" tendency that they say subordinates the Word to the sacraments (q.v.) or downplays the ministry of all believers in favor of a clerical hierarchy. Orthodox member churches sometimes object that the WCC is still a largely Protestant-inspired council promoting essentially Protestant concerns.

3) A fundamental critique of the WCC comes from those traditions that place the accent on their conviction that the body of Christ becomes visible from below, as the local congregation gathers around Word and sacrament, whereas international ecumenical structures, including the WCC, take national churches as the basic building block of ecumenism. The national structure, some representatives of the "historic peace churches" have argued, explains why the WCC has never taken up a theologically consistent stand against war. Some complain that the WCC Basis is too minimal, that it does not specify enough of the nonnegotiable elements of the Christian faith. Others object to the fact that although a WCC member church must express agreement with the Basis, there is no provision for verifying that the affirmations implied in

the Basis in fact function in its life. Still others argue that the WCC is too "church-oriented" and does not do justice to the contribution of Christian groups and movements for social justice.

4) As the ecumenical movement has progressed, some say, institutionalization has created a bureaucracy that is rigid, unimaginative and preoccupied with self-preservation. Others point out that in the face of so many human needs, the WCC too reflexively begins new programs, sometimes ill considered, making it a far too complicated organization with little coordination. WCC ethical positions on current issues are sometimes criticized as "idealistic" or ignorant of the complicated technicalities of the subjects they address. Finally, the relevance of the WCC's methods of work has been questioned, in particular, the numerous international conferences and consultations that produce many long documents in an ecumenical jargon that appeals to a very limited audience, even if it makes an effort to take advantage of them.

All this criticism, even when it is painful, can be very salutary, pointing out and helping to correct ecumenical blind spots, challenging some of its myths and clichés. It is especially indispensable for the health of an organization that draws on highly committed people from all over the world, for their dedication to the cause may cause them to lose perspective. Unfortunately, the most widely publicized criticism of the WCC is not of this constructive kind. Often ideologically based, it may trade on stereotypes that are reinforced by deliberate and effective campaigns to misrepresent and discredit the Council. Recognition of the WCC's vulnerability to unfair criticism, especially from governments or mass media that have far more resources than the WCC has for answering them, should be balanced by the acknowledgment that the WCC, as any other body, is a human organization. Neither the nobility of its cause nor the breadth of participation in its deliberation and decision-making exempts it from wavering and error.

ANTI-SEMITISM. Anti-Semitism is a grave prejudice that must be examined in the framework of the Jewish-Christian dialogue (q.v.). During the Nazi period, 1933–1945, anti-Semitism made Christianity particularly susceptible to the racialist doctrine of a total war against the Jews, which used Luther and other Christian theologians by quoting selectively from them. This modern anti-Semetism resulted in the Nazi holocaust of 6 million Jews. The first WCC assembly (q.v.) in Amsterdam in 1948 issued a Resolution on Anti-Semitism and stated the following: ''We call upon all the churches we represent to denounce anti-Semitism, no matter what its origin, as absolutely irreconcilable with the profession and practice of the Christian faith. Anti-Semitism is sin against God and man''. In a Statement on the Hope of Israel, made by the second WCC assembly in Evanston, Illinois, in 1954, the following was expressed: ''The New Testament speaks also of the 'fulness' of Israel, when God will manifest His glory by bringing back His 'eldest son' into the one fold of His grace (Rom. 11:12–36; Matt. 23:29). This belief is an indispensable element of our one united hope for Jew and Gentile in Jesus Christ . . . We cannot be one in Christ nor can we truly believe and witness to the promise of God if we do not recognize that it is still valid for the people of the promise made to Abraham''.

In a Resolution on Anti-Semitism, the third WCC assembly in New Delhi in 1961 said: ''. . . The assembly urges its member churches to do all in their power to resist every form of anti-Semitism. In Christian teaching the historic events which led to the Crucifixion should not be so presented as to fasten upon the Jewish people of today responsibilities which belong to our corporate humanity and not to one race or community. Jews were the first to accept Jesus and Jews are not the only ones who do not yet recognize him''. Also the Declaration on the Relationship of the Church to Non-Christian Religions (*Nostra aetate*) of the Second Vatican Council (q.v.), despite its controversial debate and general reservations, calls forth commendation and gratitude. It sternly rebukes any effort to make of Christianity an indictment of the Jewish people, and removes the major blocks in the way of cordial and dignified dialogue between Catholics and Jews. It provides the basis for a united and thoroughgoing Christian campaign against anti-Semitism. The *Ecumeni-*

cal Considerations on Jewish-Christian Dialogue, a document recommended to the churches by the WCC central committee in 1982, provides detailed guidelines for Jewish-Christian dialogue and takes a strong stand against anti-Semitic theological teachings.

APOSTLES' CREED *see* CREEDS

APOSTOLICITY/APOSTOLIC SUCCESSION. Besides unity, holiness and catholicity (qq.v.), apostolicity is one of the criteria for the legitimacy of the church as the community of faith. Although the term is not found explicitly in the New Testament, it is connected with the sending of the apostles by Jesus Christ (Luke 10:16), the normative proclamation of the faith (e.g., I Cor. 14:37ff.), and the life of the church (Acts 4:32ff.). By the end of the 4th century the concept was contained in the Apostles' Creed (q.v.), which is of special (ecumenical) value to all Christian confessions. Roman Catholicism (q.v.), more than other churches, has strongly emphasized the apostolicity of and the apostolic succession in its communion of faith. Vatican II (q.v.) restressed the apostolicity of the church in the *Dogmatic Constitution on the Church* (12, 31, 35) and the *Decree on the Apostolate of the Laity* (2).

As the church is the personal communion of the faithful, so the personal succession of the ministry of the bishops is the necessary expression of the pneumatological (q.v.) tradition initiated by Jesus Christ (q.v.), and the sacramentality of his Body. Apostolicity characterizes Orthodoxy, Anglicanism and the Old Catholic Church (qq.v.), although Roman Catholicism does not recognize the Anglican orders. Protestantism (q.v.) simply adheres to the doctrine: apostolicity is provided when the witness of the church and its life according to that witness is grounded in the New Testament. The relationship between apostolic succession and apostolic witness has been debated by the Commission on Faith and Order (q.v.), particularly in the drafting of the consensus document *Baptism, Eucharist and Ministry* (q.v.), published in 1982.

It is now admitted in the still divided churches that what

has traditionally been called apostolic succession does not necessarily guarantee faithfulness to apostolic faith and practice, though the recovery of the traditional threefold ministry (including bishops) could well be regarded as a sign that apostolic continuity as been preserved in practice. The role of prophetic and charismatic leadership is also stressed. The uncontroversial aspects of apostolicity have been summarized by a consultation, organized by Faith and Order in Chantilly in 1985, as part of the study "Towards the Common Expression of the Apostolic Faith Today".

APPASAMY, AIYADURAI JESUDASEN (1891–1975). Appasamy as an Indian Christian underlined the native tradition of Bhakti in Hinduism, devotion to a personal "lord", as entry point for Christian insight. Without necessarily denying the identification of Jesus Christ (q.v.) with the relational form of the divine, he concentrated on how that form generates individual love and devotion in the believer. He was ordained in 1930 and was involved in the negotiations leading to the establishment of the Church of South India (1947). He was the first bishop of this church from 1950 to 1957. On his consecration, he felt guided by God to call for a year of prayer (q.v.) in his diocese in preparation for its missionary outreach.

ASMUSSEN, HANS (1898–1968). He was involved in the drafting of the Barmen declaration of 1934 and in many synodal meetings of the Confessing Church (q.v.) struggling against National Socialism and its ideology. Asmussen again played a key role in drafting the Stuttgart declaration (1945). His conviction was that Christians are called to stand together before God and make their confessions of sins to Him and to one another. He knew that this kind of confession could be misunderstood, but instead of opting for clever diplomacy he chose the expression the "foolishness in Christ". Asmussen was the vice-chairman of the theological group working on "Ways of Worship" in preparation for the second world conference on Faith and Order (q.v.), in Lund, 1952.

ASSEMBLIES *see* WORLD COUNCIL OF CHURCHES ASSEMBLIES

ATHEISM. The doctrine that denies the existence of deity in its various forms and expressions is a rather recent phenomenon, except that Sankhya Hindu thought, Buddhism and Jainism have long been described as atheistic, since they deny a personal God. With the increase in scientific knowledge and the consequent scientific explanation of phenomena formerly considered supernatural, atheism has become a more natural and less despised philosophical trend. Belief in the theory of evolution or in such philosophies as materialism, rationalism, monism or existentialism, with their stress on the human being, machine and the material world, virtually precludes belief in an omnipotent, omnipresent God and an unquestionable divine law. Karl Marx was the defender of a practical atheism as denial of God for the sake of human beings and the well-being of their society.

The ecumenical movement has been mainly concerned with a Marxist-Leninist understanding of atheism. Discussing communism and capitalism (q.v.), the first WCC assembly (q.v.) in Amsterdam in 1948 stated: "Christians should recognize with contrition that many churches are involved in the forms of economic injustice and racial discrimination which have created the conditions favorable to the growth of Communism, and that the atheism and the anti-religious teaching of Communism are in part a reaction to the chequered record of a professedly Christian society; . . . Communism has for many filled a moral and psychological vacuum".

Although Vatican II (q.v.) still condemned atheism because it "casts man down from the noble state to which he is born" (*Guadium et spes* 21), thinking on atheism has advanced in two directions: toward a greater sensitivity for the elements of unbelief in the lives of believers, and toward the possibilities of dialogue and rapport with professed unbelievers. A more authentic and honest understanding of the demands of faith has led to the discovery of subtle and usually undeclared forms of disbelief, which afflict even sincerely held faith. This is one of the reasons why the Marxist-Christian dialogue (q.v.) flourished during the 1960s and the early 1970s.

ATHENAGORAS I (ARISTOKLES PYROU) (1886–1972). Athenagoras was ecumenical patriarch of Constantinople from 1949 until his death and a leading figure in the contemporary development of Orthodoxoy (q.v.) and the ecumenical movement. In 1922 he became bishop of Corfu and Paxos, and in 1931 was named archbishop of the Greek church in America. He instituted biennial meetings of clergy and laity to define the main directions of pastoral work. He was determined "to set aside all the cares of the world" to serve Christian unity by gathering all the Orthodox churches in conciliar fashion. Athenagoras led his see into active participation in the WCC (q.v.) and in closer relations with the Roman Catholic Church (q.v.). In events of historic importance, he sent observers to Vatican II (q.v.), exchanged the kiss of peace with Pope Paul VI (q.v.) at the Mount of Olives in 1964, joined with the pope the following year in simultaneously nullifying the anathemas pronounced by their predecessors in 1954, received Paul at the Phanar in July 1967, and visited him at the Vatican the following October. Seeking to advance unity among the Orthodox churches, Athenagoras convened a Pan-Orthodox conference in Rhodes in 1961 to begin preparations for an ecumenical council that would be the first in the Orthodox world since the 11th-century division between East and West. He also encouraged theological dialogues with the Anglican Communion (1966), the Old Catholic Church (1966) and the Oriental Orthodox churches (1968) (qq.v). The relationship with the WCC was strengthened by setting up a permanent representation of Constantinople in 1955 and by visiting the WCC in 1967.

ATHENAGORAS (KONNINAKIS). Archbishop of Thyateira and Great Britain (1912–1979). As a member of the delegation of the Ecumenical Patriarchate Athenagoras attended the first four WCC assemblies (qq.v.) and was a member of the central committee, 1961–1975. He presented the message of the Ecumenical Patriarchate on the occasion of the 25th anniversary of the WCC in 1973. He was actively involved in the 1963 Faith and Order (q.v.) meeting in Montreal and in several bilateral dialogues, particularly between the Anglicans (q.v.) and Orthodox, functioning as copresident of the bilateral commission. He served as metropolitan of Greek churches in Canada, 1961–1963, and then became archbishop of Thyateira and Great Britain.

ATKINSON, HENRY AVERY (1877–1960). Atkinson was general secretary of the Church Peace Union and the World Alliance for Promoting International Friendship through the Churches (qq.v.), 1918–. He was also co-general secretary of the Continuation Committee on Life and Work (q.v.), responsible for the preparation of the Stockholm conference, 1925, and for the conference itself. Atkinson was secretary of the special service commission of the Congregational Churches in the United States, 1911–1918.

ATONEMENT FRIARS *see* WATTSON, PAUL JAMES FRANCIS

AUTHORITY. It is useful to distinguish between external and internal authority. External authority is that attaching to a person as an official or to an office as an office. Internal authority is the authority residing in convincing argument or weighty moral or spiritual example or experience. In the New Testament almost all authority is internal. The ultimate authority, which is the word of God, is expressed through preaching or through miraculous occurrences, or found in meditation or in the reading of the Old Testament Scripture. Even the twelve apostles do not hold authority because they have been invested with an office but because they are in a position to bear witness to what Christ did in the days of his flesh and to his appearances as risen Lord. But as the church gradually became a fixed and relatively uniform institution, official, external authority inevitably came to play an ever greater part. By the 4th century Christian writers are appealing to earlier authors as "the tradition of the Fathers", having regard rather to who they were than to what they said. The advent of the Reformation (q.v.) with its emphasis on the response of the individual person in faith to the demand of the word of God, and the divisions of the church that resulted from it, assisted by the many impulses created by the

Renaissance toward individualism and the rejection of established authority in metaphysics and theology, gradually brought about an entire change of attitude toward authority in the minds of Christians.

Today the pendulum of opinion has swung to the other extreme. Internal authority is now widely regarded as the only authority in religious matters. Contemporary ecumenical debates have paid increasing attention to the problem of authority in the church, examining it in particular in relation to the question of ministries, which still constitutes a crucial item for ecumenical progress. The most advanced dialogue on the problem of authority is undoubtedly the conversations of the Anglican-Roman Catholic Commission (ARCIC). The first Venice document (1976) begins with the Christian authority, which is at work in the church through the action of the Holy Spirit. The Windsor document (1981) studied four especially difficult topics: the interpretation of the Petrine passages in the New Testament, divine right, jurisdiction, and infallibility (q.v.). All church traditions have a tendency to emphasize particularly one of the three aspects of authority—personal, collegial and communal—whose complementarity was already recognized at the first world conference on Faith and Order (q.v.) in Lausanne in 1927.

In the field of Christian ethics claims to authority on the basis of revelation or religious faith have been very much under fire in modern times. Standards of conduct can no longer be upheld by a simple appeal to the authority of the church or the Bible. In modern secular societies, Christian ethicists agree that it is unreasonable to try to legislate Christian standards for the whole body of citizens, for example, in such matters as marriage and divorce. Even faithful members of the churches do not always follow the teaching of their communities on particular matters. If therefore we can still talk of an "authority" in Christian ethics, it can hardly be thought of as an authority that is imposed, for it rests on the voluntary acceptance of those who profess themselves to be Christians. The ultimate authority for all Christian ethics is Jesus Christ (q.v.) himself. But this statement is not very helpful when it comes to deciding about some actual situation, for we have to find some way of relating that situation to Christ. It would seem that the most indisputably authoritative statements in Christian ethics are also the most general, and the more specific we become, the more careful we must be about laying claim to "authority". Amid the complexities of contemporary society, a certain degree of modesty is desirable, and moral pronouncements by the churches should have some flexibility and be open to revision. *See also* INFALLIBILITY; PAPACY/PRIMACY.

AZARIAH, VEDANAYAGAM SAMUEL (1874–1945). As a champion of the ecumenical movement among the younger churches and as YMCA secretary for South India, Azariah initiated in 1903 the Indian Missionary Society of Tirunelveli. At the missionary conference in Edinburgh in 1910 he pleaded for friendship between foreign and national missionary workers. In 1912 he was consecrated as the first Indian bishop of Dornakal of the Anglican Church (q.v.), and later assistant bishop of the diocese of Madras, where he stressed discipline, witness, Christian education, proper instruction of converts and more Indian clergy. He also promoted Indian cultural forms in church services, evangelism, teaching and architecture, while repudiating syncretism (q.v.). Prominent in national and international Christian forums, he worked incessantly for church union. Azariah was chairman of the National Christian Council of India, an influential participant in the International Missionary Council (q.v.), and one of the leaders in the movement that led to the formation of the Church of South India in 1947.

- B -

BAILLIE, DONALD MACPHERSON (1887–1954). Baillie was active in ecumenical work, especially in the Faith and Order (q.v.) movement. He was the chairman of a committee that produced a volume on *Intercommunion* for the world conference of Faith and Order in Lund, 1952. After theological studies in Edinburgh, Marburg, and Heidelberg, he became professor of systematic theology at St. Andrews University from 1935. His best-known work was *God Was in Christ*

(1948). He occupied a mediating position between old liberalism and modern neoorthodoxy.

BAILLIE, JOHN (1886–1960). Baillie was moderator of the Church of Scotland general assembly in 1943, and made a Companion of Honour by Queen Elizabeth in 1957—a rare distinction for a churchman. He was an early supporter of the WCC (q.v.) and one of its presidents, from 1954 until his death. He was also involved in an unsuccessful move in 1957 to advance the cause of union with the Church of England. From 1934 onward he was professor of divinity at Edinburgh University. Baillie combined traditional liberalism and orthodox Barthianism with a pronounced mystical tendency. He published many works.

BANGKOK 1973 *see* MISSION

BAPTISM. One of the most important of the controversies that have agitated Christianity has been whether baptism should be administered to adults only, or to infants also. Some maintain that it was the practice of the time of the apostles to baptize the infants of Christians. Others say that at first only adult converts who made a conscious decision to join the church were baptized. They allege that infant baptism arose only when conscious choice ceased to be regarded as a necessary condition for sacramental efficacy. Two modes of baptism are practiced, one by immersion and another by aspersion, or sprinkling. The advocates of sprinkling universally admit the validity of baptism administered by immersion, but the advocates of immersion generally refuse to acknowledge that baptism by sprinkling is adequately grounded in Scripture. The greatest controversy on baptism is probably, however, between those who insist that baptism is a unique action of grace on the part of God himself and those who maintain that it is an act of obedience on the part of the human being. It should be admitted, however, that in baptism the grace of God and the faith of the human being meet each other.

The Roman Catholic Church (q.v.) teaches that one of the effects of baptism is birth into a supernatural order. Particularly, the Lutheran (q.v.) churches teach a similar doctrine of baptismal regeneration. But the Reformed (q.v.) Protestant churches in general hold that baptism is a sign and seal of regeneration by grace (q.v.) and of God's assurance that the sins of the penitent will be forgiven, an act of consecration and dedication upon the part of parents or sponsors in behalf of infants and children, and a profession of faith on the part of adults indicating their desire to be initiated into the community of Christ and his church. The Commission on Faith and Order (q.v.) has attached an increasing importance to a common recognition of baptism by all the churches, in particular in the 1960s and at its meetings in Louvain in 1971 and in Accra in 1974. Recognition of baptisms in other churches amounts already to recognition of a degree of ecclesiality of the different Christian communities; it amounts to recognizing a fundamental community of faith in Christ as unique Lord and Savior and in the Trinity of the Father who sent his Son into the world for its salvation (q.v.), which is bestowed by the Holy Spirit. It is the recognition of a measure of communion in the one Body of Jesus Christ. The document on *Baptism, Eucharist and Ministry* (1982) (q.v.) expresses the conviction that the need to recover baptismal unity is at the heart of the ecumenical task. ". . . Our one baptism into Christ constitutes a call to the churches to overcome their divisions and visibly manifest their fellowship" (B6).

BAPTISM, EUCHARIST AND MINISTRY (THE "LIMA TEXT"). In Lima, Peru, in 1982 the Commission on Faith and Order (q.v.) produced in a final form a text entitled *Baptism, Eucharist and Ministry,* often referred to under the acronym BEM. The three statements of this ecumenical consensus document are the fruit of a 50-year process of study and discussion stretching back to the first Faith and Order conference in Lausanne in 1927. The material has been discussed and revised by the Faith and Order commission in Accra (1974), Bangalore (1978) and Lima (1982). Between the plenary commission meetings, a steering group on baptism, eucharist and ministry (qq.v.) has worked further on the drafting, especially after September 1979 under the presidency of Frère Max Thurian of the Taizé community (qq.v.). The documents also reflect ongoing consultation and collaboration between the commission members (approved by the churches) and with the local churches themselves. The WCC's fifth assembly (qq.v.) in Nairobi in 1975 authorized the distribution for the churches' study of an earlier text (Faith and Order Paper, no. 73). Most significantly, over one hundred churches from virtually every geographical area and ecclesiastical tradition returned detailed comments. These were analyzed at a 1977 consultation in Crêt-Bérard, Switzerland (Faith and Order Paper, no. 84). Meanwhile particularly difficult problems were also examined at special ecumenical consultations held on the themes of infant and believers' baptism in Louisville, 1978 (Faith and Order Paper, no. 97), on *episkopé* (oversight) and the episcopate in Geneva (Faith and Order Paper, no. 102). The draft text was also reviewed by representatives of the Orthodox churches in Chambésy, Switzerland, 1979. In conclusion, the Faith and Order Commission was again authorized by the WCC's central committee (Dresden, 1981) to transmit its finally revised document (the ''Lima text'' of 1982) to the churches, along with the request for their official response as a vital step in the ecumenical process of reception.

Baptism, Eucharist and Ministry (the most widely distributed document in more than 40 translations) represents the significant theological convergence that Faith and Order has discerned and formulated. Since the churches have greatly differed in doctrine and practice on baptism, eucharist and ministry, the importance of the large measure of agreement can be appreciated. Virtually all the confessional traditions are included in the commission's membership. That theologians of such widely different backgrounds should be able to speak so harmoniously about baptism, eucharist and ministry is unprecedented in the modern ecumenical movement. The agreed text purposely concentrates on those aspects of the theme that have been directly or indirectly related to the problems of mutual recognition leading to unity. The main text demonstrates the major areas of theological convergence; the added commentaries either indicate historical differences that have been overcome or identify disputed issues still in need of further research and reconciliation. Particularly noteworthy is the fact that the commission also includes among its full members theologians of the Roman Catholic (q.v.) and other churches that do not belong to the WCC. Almost 190 official responses of the churches were received and published in six volumes, *Churches Respond to BEM* (1986–1988). Reactions were also received from several councils of churches and numerous groups of theologians. *Baptism, Eucharist and Ministry 1982–1990* (Faith and Order Paper, no. 149) is the report on the process and responses. *See also* BAPTISM; EUCHARIST; FAITH AND ORDER; LIMA LITURGY; MINISTRY.

BAPTIST CHURCHES. The modern Baptist Church was founded in Holland in 1609 by John Smyth, a clergyman who had broken away from the Church of England. He maintained that the church should receive its members by baptism (q.v.) after they had consciously acknowledged their faith and, since a child is unable to do this, he opposed infant baptism. Some of his followers established a Baptist church in London in 1612, its pastor being Thomas Helwys, who believed in religious toleration for all men and women, including atheists and pagans as well as Christians. The spread of Baptist churches was greatly influenced by revival movements during the following two centuries. In 1891 the General and Particular Baptists were united in the Baptist Union of Great Britain and Ireland. The Baptists are the largest denomination in the USA. There are significant Baptist communities in the Soviet Union, Romania, Sweden and Germany. But it is a world church, and Baptists witness in many other countries as well. Interpreting the New Testament, Baptists stress that the church as the body of Christ is a communion of the faithful who have made personally and voluntarily a decision for Christ, and because of their personal confession of faith have become, through baptism, members of Christ's church. Baptists recognize only the Bible (no creed) as binding authority. Under the guidance of the Holy Spirit (q.v.) each church may interpret the Scriptures and design the life of its community. The pronounced congregational constitution does not allow for a centralized church structure but promotes unions and conventions of individual churches.

The Baptist World Alliance is a voluntary association among Baptists in unions and conventions of churches, with a total membership of over 34 million. There are several millions of other Baptists who belong to churches that are not members of the Alliance. The preamble of its constitution reads: "The Baptist World Alliance, extending over every part of the world, exists as an expression of the essential oneness of Baptist people in the Lord Jesus Christ, to impart inspiration to the brotherhood, and to promote the spirit of fellowship, service and cooperation among its members; but this Alliance may in no way interfere with the independence of the churches or assume the administrative functions of existing organizations".

The First Baptist World Congress was held in London in 1905. A Baptist world congress is held every five years, attended by thousands from all continents. These congresses set the theme and programs of the Alliance for the next five years. Every Baptist member body can send council members, who have equal voice and vote. An executive committee governs the Alliance between congresses. A large part of the budget of the Baptist World Alliance comes from the over 13 million member Southern Baptist Convention (USA), whose only official ecumenical relationship on a membership basis is with the Alliance. The Southern Baptist Convention was organized in Augusta, Georgia, in 1845. It holds a more conservative Calvinistic theology than Baptists in the north. Regional sub-organizations of the Alliance exist in North America and in Europe. The Alliance, with headquarters in Washington, D.C., has study commissions working on various concerns, themes and programs.

BAPTIST WORLD ALLIANCE *see* BAPTIST CHURCHES

BARMEN DECLARATION *see* GERMAN CONFESSING CHURCH

BAROT, MADELEINE (1909–). Member of a Huguenot family, Barot early became involved in the Student Christian Movement in France while she studied at the University of Paris. She learned how to be in dialogue with Roman Catholics,

Orthodox and later also Muslims (qq.v.), preparing for a leading ecumenical career in the ecumenical youth, student and women's movements. From 1935–1940 she was archivist at the French archaeological school in Rome. Appointed general secretary of the CIMADE (Comité intermouvement auprès des évacués) she shared in the deplorable condition of French and foreign refugees (q.v.) in an interment camp at Gurs, near the Pyrenees. When the deportation of Jews, Communists and gypsies began in 1942, she joined the resistance movement and worked clandestinely, risking her life to help many to escape across the borders into Spain and Switzerland (in the latter case in liaison with the WCC [q.v.]). Having attended the two world conferences of Christian youth in Amsterdam in 1939 and in Oslo in 1947, Barot was elected moderator of the Committee of the WCC Youth Department. She directed the WCC Department on Cooperation of Men and Women in Church, Family and Society from 1953 to 1966. Throughout the world—especially in Africa, India and the Pacific—Barot has helped many women (q.v.) to prepare for ecumenical responsibilities. After 1966 she was appointed to the WCC Department on Development Education. After her retirement she worked for the French Protestant Federation, the ecumenical anti-torture organization ACAT and, once again, CIMADE.

BARROW, NITA (1916–). Barrow was a president of the WCC (q.v.) (1983–1991), and associate director of the WCC Christian Medical Commission in 1971 and its director (1975–1981). She was an expert in advising church-affiliated health (q.v.) agencies throughout the world on new developments in health care. She was a pioneer in studying and working with alternative forms of health care for the underprivileged. Barrow served as president of the YWCA (q.v.) and as president of the International Council for Adult Education, and was permanent representative and ambassador of Barbados at the United Nations (q.v.). She was the convener at the Nairobi meeting (1985), which marked the close of the UN Decade for Women. Barrow graduated from the University of Toronto School of Nursing and from Columbia University, New York.

BARTH, KARL (1886–1968). Preeminent proponent of neo-orthodox theology, Barth studied at the universities of Bern, Berlin, Tübingen and Marburg. He was an initial adherent of the liberal Protestant theology of teachers such as Adolph von Harnack and Wilhelm Hermann. He soon questioned the adequacy of liberal theology and lost confidence in the ultimate perfectibility of the human being. In 1919 he published *The Epistle to the Romans*. This powerful commentary, especially the completely rewritten second edition of 1922, launched a fresh theological movement dedicated to the recovery of a theology of the Word of God. Barth emphasized the sinfulness of humanity, God's absolute transcendence, and the inability of human beings to know God except through mediation. Called to a professorship in 1921, Barth taught systematic theology at the Universities of Göttingen (1921–1925), Münster (1925–1930), Bonn (1930–1935) and Basel (1935–1962). His illustrious career included theological leadership of the Confessing Church (q.v.) against Nazi influence in the German Protestant Church, chief authorship of the Barmen Declaration of 1934, expulsion from Germany by the Nazi government in 1935, participation in the Amsterdam assembly of the WCC (qq.v.) and in the meetings of a committee of 25 outstanding personalities preparing for the Evanston assembly theme: "Christ—the Hope of the World". For a long time Barth was critical of both the WCC and the Roman Catholic Church (q.v.), but after Vatican II (q.v.) he felt urged to lift the dialogue between Protestants and Roman Catholics to a higher level.

BAUM, GREGORY (1923–). Since 1966 Baum has been professor of theology and religious studies at St Michael's College of the University of Toronto. He is also consultant to the Secretariat for Promoting Christian Unity (q.v.) and editor of *The Ecumenist*. An expert in Christianity and other religions, in particular Jewish-Christian dialogue (q.v.), he came to Canada in 1940. His Ph.D. dissertation at the University of Fribourg, Switzerland, was: *That They May Be One*. He joined the Augustinian order in 1947 and was ordained a priest in 1954.

BEA, AUGUSTIN (1881–1968). Bea was president of the Vatican Secretariat for Promoting Christian Unity (q.v.), 1960–1968. He served on many Roman congregations such as the Pontifical Biblical Commission and the Congregation for the Doctrine of the Faith, and presided over the drafting of three documents of the Second Vatican Council (q.v.): the *Dogmatic Constitution on Divine Revelation,* the *Declaration on the Relationship of the Church to Non-Christian Religions* and the *Decree on Religious Freedom.* He served as confessor to Pius XII, 1945–1958. In 1966 he received, together with W. A. Visser 't Hooft (q.v.), the peace price of the Frankfurt Book Fair. From 1917 to 1921 he taught Old Testament in the German theologate at Valkenburg. He went to Rome in 1924 to take charge of Jesuits assigned to graduate studies and taught in the Pontifical Biblical Institute, of which he was rector from 1930 to 1949. The list of his publications is lengthy and impressive. His ecumenical achievements in the cause of Christian unity (q.v.) stemmed directly from his talents for friendship and his interest and competence in biblical scholarship.

BEAUDUIN, LAMBERT (1873–1960). In 1924 Pope Pius XI requested the Benedictine congregations to foster the healing of the schism between the church of Rome and the churches of the East. In response Dom Beauduin founded a new priory at Amay-sur-Meuse, and in 1939 the "monks of unity" moved to their present site at Chevetogne in Belgium. They celebrate alternatively every other week the divine Orthodox liturgy and the Roman Catholic liturgy (qq.v.), from the beginning in the tentative use of the vernacular but eventually permanently. In 1926 Beauduin founded the ecumenical journal *Irénikon.* In a 1925 memoir he had formulated the then controversial conversations between Anglicans (q.v.) and Roman Catholics in similarly controversial words: "the Anglican church united to Rome, not absorbed". His bold views in liturgy and ecclesiology (q.v.) shocked many Roman Catholics. In 1931 he was condemned before a Roman tribunal and sent to the abbey of En-Calcat in southern France. He was able to return to Chevetogne in 1951.

BEGUIN, OLIVIER (1914–1972). Béguin directed from 1941 onward, on behalf of the WCC (q.v.), the Ecumenical Commission in Geneva for the distribution of Bibles to prisoners of war and refugees (q.v.). He was general secretary of the United Bible Societies (q.v.), an international interconfessional organization grouping together a great number of national Bible societies. He was influenced by Suzanne de Diétrich, Reinhold von Thadden-Trieglaff and W. A. Visser 't Hooft (qq.v.), considering Bible societies to be vital instruments of the ecumenical movement.

BELL, GEORGE ALLEN KENNEDY (1883–1958). Bell was a leading English ecumenist and the first moderator of the WCC (q.v.) central committee from 1948 to 1954, and afterward honorary president of the WCC. He was chaplain to Randall Davidson (q.v.), archbishop of Canterbury, 1914–1924, then for five years Dean of Canterbury and for 27 years bishop of Chichester, 1928–1957. He acted as secretary of the Lambeth conference of 1920, was one of the initiators of the "Appeal" and edited four volumes of *Documents on Christian Unity.* He was also greatly active as chairman of the Universal Christian Council on Life and Work preparing for the Oxford conference in 1937. He maintained close relations with the Confessing Church (q.v.) in Germany, stressed that not all Germans were National Socialists and opposed the British "area bombing" of German cities as incompatible with the doctrine of just war (q.v.). He continued to be prominent in the reconstruction of the German churches after the war and was a witness to the Stuttgart Declaration of Guilt of the German Evangelical Church in October 1945. In preparation for the Evanston assembly (q.v.) he wrote *The Kingship of Christ,* in which he saw the church as an instrument of the kingdom, the "sustaining, correcting and befriending opposite of the world". He was a spiritual father to Dietrich Bonhoeffer (q.v.), who informed him about tragic developments in Germany and who, before his execution, said: "Tell him [Bell] that for me this is not the end but the beginning. With him I believe in the principle of our universal Christian brotherhood, which rises above all national interests".

BENNETT, JOHN COLEMAN (1902–). Bennett was secretary of the section on church and economic order at the Oxford conference on Church, Community and State in 1937, and was coeditor of *Christianity and Crisis.* Ordained to the ministry in 1939 in the Congregational church, he became a Reinhold Niebuhr (q.v.) professor of social ethics (q.v.) at Union Theological Seminary, New York, and taught at various other universities and seminaries. He edited *Man's Disorder and God's Design,* an outline of preparation for the first assembly of the WCC (qq.v.) in Amsterdam. The author of many books, he was from 1943 on an officer and participant in numerous national and international ecumenical conferences on social and ethical concerns.

BERDYAEV, NICOLAS (1874–1948). Because of his strong spiritual resistance to the communist regime, he was exiled from the Soviet Union in 1923 and spent the rest of his life in Berlin. He studied science at the University of Kiev and philosophy at Heidelberg. Originally a Marxist, Berdyaev soon abandoned this position under the influence of Kant and idealistic philosophy. Later an added influence was the mysticism of Jacob Boehme. He interpreted the Christian religion in the light of modern intellectual interests, expounding a "spiritual Christianity" that has no need of doctrinal definitions. His main focus was always the problem of the human being, and his main emphasis on human freedom. He can be called a "Christian existentialist". He wrote many books in Russian, but most of his works were available in various translations.

BERGGRAV, EIVIND (1884–1959). Attending the Universal Christian Conference on Life and Work in Stockholm in 1925, he became a friend of Archbishop Nathan Söderblom (q.v.) and rapidly won leadership in the ecumenical movement, being elected president of the World Alliance for Promoting International Friendship through the Churches (q.v.) in 1938 and calling a conference of Scandinavian church leaders on the outbreak of war in 1939. After the occupation of Norway by the Nazis—he became the primate of the Church of Norway in 1937—Berggrav took an active part in organizing resistance to the Quisling government. With six other Norwegian bishops he resigned on 24 February 1941. Arrested on 9 April, he remained a solitary prisoner in his log cabin in Asker/Oslofjord on the outskirts of Oslo until he fled to Sweden in February 1945. He retired in 1951 but remained active in founding, with Oliver Beguin, the United Bible Societies (q.v.), of which he became president. Berggrav was influential in the founding of the WCC (q.v.), addressed its first two assemblies, and also the assembly of the Lutheran World Federation (q.v.) in Hannover in 1952. He served as WCC president, 1950–1954.

BERKHOF, HENDRIKUS (1914–). Berkhof was an outspoken member of the WCC (q.v.) central committee, 1954–1975, and had a major part in the Faith and Order (q.v.) study on "God in Nature and History", 1963–1968. He addressed Uppsala 1968 (q.v.) on "The Finality of Jesus Christ", another Faith and Order study. On the staff of the "Church and World" Institute at Driebergen, he was from 1960 onward professor of dogmatics and biblical theology at the University of Leiden. As of 1975 Berkhof was president of the Ecumenical Council of the Netherlands. Several of his works are the fruit of his ecumenical reflections.

BIBLE IN THE ECUMENICAL MOVEMENT. The fact that a historical-critical examination of the Bible started within Protestantism (q.v.) should not come as a surprise, and that this process did not stop at the frontiers of all Christian confessions is an ecumenical phenomenon. Conservative groups, however, have resisted this kind of dealings with the Bible. As they were often most active in missions, they tried to protect the younger churches against such "misuse" of Scriptures. Historical-critical hermeneutics (q.v.) have contributed to a rapprochement between confessions. The Life and Work (q.v.) movement, e.g., came into being because of a liberal and moral understanding of the Bible. Afterward there was a turn to the emphasis of more central theological themes in the Bible. Church-based communities (q.v.) that sprang up in Latin America and have spread worldwide since the 1960s are a contemporary phenomenon. In these communities the Bible is always read face-to-face with the actual life of the people. This is a Bible/life method, a procedure that obviates any spiritualizing tendency of fundamentalism. It sets the word in the real living conditions of the people: a struggle for survival and for social change. From 1946 onward the question was repeatedly raised in the ecumenical movement: "What is the authority of the Bible?". Susanne de Diétrich (q.v.) became a widely recognized expert in biblical exegesis, and courses at the Ecumenical Institute of Bossey were influenced by it. Is it possible to understand the Bible as an ongoing process of "salvation history", or should the trinitarian understanding of history of the ancient church be stressed, or should an existential approach, leading to the "demytholization" of Scriptures, be favored? With regard to the historical-critical method a Christocentric-salvation history view prevailed in ecumenical conversations until the early 1970s.

Although an awareness of the role of the Bible for the ecumenical movement continued through the creation within the WCC (q.v.) of a small Biblical Studies Secretariat in 1971, which until 1988 was directed by H.-R. Weber (q.v.), the interest in biblical theology diminished in the churches in the West. Christians in Latin America became suspicious that the historical-critical method in the North diverted from burning sociopolitical problems. The Commission on Faith and Order (q.v.) meeting in Bristol in 1967 stressed the necessity of a thoroughly scientific biblical exegesis with an indispensable knowledge of Hebrew and Greek. The authors of the Bible express themselves in different situations, which condition their witness and which should not be prematurely harmonized; on the contrary, they make us better understand the present divisions. It is not accidental that in 1961 the Christological Basis of the WCC was enlarged with the words: "according to the Scriptures". All exegesis of the Bible serve the purpose to witness clearly to Christ's liberating invitation to follow him. Yet it must be admitted that different church traditions and different historical situations lead to different interpretations of the person and work of Jesus Christ (q.v.). Exegesis alone cannot solve this problem as long as there is not an ecumenical willingness to let one's own traditional understanding of Christ be corrected by the biblical witness. Much work remains to be done. Ecumenical reflection about the authority and interpretation of the Bible needs to be continued, taking account especially of new insights of feminist and other contemporary ways of reading the Bible outside the North Atlantic world. There is no doubt that corporate Bible studies in ecumenical gatherings will be maintained. *See also* HERMENEUTICS; TRADITION AND TRADITIONS.

BIBLE SOCIETIES. In several countries the Bible societies are a privileged place of ecumenical encounter and cooperation, because these societies make an effort to involve all Christian communities in their work. Since Vatican II, also the Roman Catholic Church (qq.v.) seeks cooperation with various Bible societies, and many of their staff are Roman Catholics. This is also true for Orthodox (q.v.) churches, which show an increasing interest in the translation and distribution of Bibles. In 1968 the Vatican Secretariat for Promoting Christian Unity (q.v.) endorsed the publication *Guiding Principles for Interconfessional Cooperation in Translating the Bible,* together with the United Bible Societies (UBS), which came into existence in 1946. Since then, the larger societies have withdrawn from direct control of work in other countries and encouraged the development of autonomous national societies. The UBS provides information and technical assistance to all member societies and administers a world budget through which the richer societies support the less rich.

The modern Bible society movement began in 1804 with the establishment of the British and Foreign Bible Society. In that year it was reckoned that the Bible or some parts of it had been translated into 67 languages. Largely through the work of the Bible societies, that number rose to 200 by 1850, to 500 by 1900 and to 1,000 by 1950. The following statistics are provided for the distribution of Bibles in 1984 (in millions):

	Bibles	NT	Biblical books	Selected Texts
Africa	2.9	1.9	3.3	5.5
America	4.4	4.8	8.7	230.0
Asia	2.7	5.0	11.1	166.0
Europe	1.9	1.3	2.3	3.0

The United Bible Societies invested approximately US $27 million in this enterprise. Bible translating and publishing agencies not linked to the UBS include the International Bible Society, Living Bibles International, the Gideons, the Trinitarian Bible Society, the Scripture Gift Missions, the World Home Bible League and Wycliffe Bible Translators. By the end of 1989 some portions of the Bible had been published in 1,928 languages and dialects by all these agencies.

BILATERAL DIALOGUES. In the beginning of this century bilateral dialogues took place between Anglicans and Roman Catholics (1921–1926), Anglicans and Orthodox (1930ff), Anglicans and Old Catholics (1931), and Lutherans and Reformed (1947ff.) (qq.v.). Subsequently bilateral dialogues for a while receded into the ecumenical background. Multilateral encounters prevailed, particularly in the realm of the WCC (q.v.). In the 1960s, however, there was a new interest in bilateral dialogues on both international and national levels, in which almost all churches and church traditions are involved. The bilateral dialogues have again become a main focus within the modern ecumenical movement. The following dialogues have taken place:
    Anglican-Lutheran dialogue
    Anglican-Methodist dialogue
    Anglican-Oriental Orthodox dialogue
    Anglican-Orthodox dialogue
    Anglican-Reformed dialogue
    Anglican-Roman Catholic dialogue
    Baptist-Lutheran dialogue
    Baptist-Reformed dialogue
    Baptist-Roman Catholic dialogue
    Disciples of Christ-Reformed dialogue

Disciples of Christ-Roman Catholic dialogue
Disciples of Christ-Russian Orthodox dialogue
Lutheran-Methodist dialogue
Lutheran-Orthodox dialogue
Lutheran-Reformed dialogue
Lutheran-Roman Catholic dialogue
Methodist-Orthodox dialogue
Methodist-Reformed dialogue
Methodist-Roman Catholic dialogue
Old Catholic-Orthodox dialogue
Oriental Orthodox-Orthodox dialogue
Oriental Orthodox-Roman Catholic dialogue
Orthodox-Reformed dialogue
Orthodox-Roman Catholic dialogue
Pentecostal-Roman Catholic dialogue
Reformed-Roman Catholic dialogue

Two factors contributed especially to the flourishing of bilateral dialogues. The multilateral encounters of the early ecumenical movement and later within the WCC, particularly in the setting of its Commission on Faith and Order (q.v.), had both spiritually and theologically prepared the ground for a more direct encounter between the individual churches. Secondly, as the Roman Catholic Church entered into the ecumenical arena, it developed a natural and strong preference for bilateral dialogues, which was matched by other churches wishing to enter into dialogue with the largest church and affirm their identity. The subjects of discussion have been manifold, such as the eucharist (q.v.), Scripture and Tradition (q.v.), creeds (q.v.) and councils, Christology (q.v.), Holy Spirit, ecclesiology (q.v.), the role of Mary, ministry and ordination (q.v.), apostolic succession (q.v.), church and society, mission and evangelism (q.v.) and proclamation today.

There are several reasons why the bilateral form of dialogue has gained a renewed emphasis. Theological divergencies rooted in the historical heritage of each confession must be overcome if a lasting and true fellowship is to be established. Since the dialogues are official they help to enhance the authenticity of their results. And, since a detailed study and exchange of the specific issues that separate two traditions is made, it becomes possible to bring out the principles that, despite separation, the traditions have in common. A disadvantage of bilateral dialogues is the danger of losing sight of the indivisibility of the whole ecumenical movement. To this effect the WCC has sponsored five forums on bilateral dialogues in 1978, 1979, 1980, 1985 and 1990. *See also* MULTILATERAL DIALOGUES.

BILHEIMER, ROBERT S. (1917–). An ordained minister of the Presbyterian Church (USA), Bilheimer served the WCC (q.v.) from 1948 to 1963. He was involved in the final preparations for Amsterdam (1948), in the organization of Evanston (1954), and was associate general secretary and director of the WCC Division of Studies, also responsible for preparing New Delhi (1961). He visited South Africa in 1960 in preparation for a meeting of representatives of the WCC and South African member churches, which issued the Cotteslee declaration. Bilheimer was administrative secretary of the World Student Service Fund (1940–1941), and national secretary of the Interseminary Movement (1945–1948). For ten years he served as executive director of the Institute of Ecumenical and Cultural Research, from 1963 onward. His book *Breakthrough* (1989) is an insightful personal account of the ecumenical movement.

BIOTECHNOLOGY AND BIOETHICS. Belief in divine creation and redemption (q.v.) of human beings carries with it the responsibility to God for one's own life and the life of others and for the created order itself. The recent emphasis of the WCC (q.v.) on the integrity of creation is a reminder of the human obligation before God. Consequently, bioethics implies for Christians a strong sense of fidelity to God's design of creation, however controversial and debatable such perceptions may be. In 1973 the Sub-unit on Church and Society sponsored a consultation on "Genetics and the Quality of Life"; and "ethical issues in the biological manipulation of life" was one of the sections of the world conference on Faith, Science and the Future in Boston, in 1979. Later, a Church and Society study group produced a report entitled *Manipulating Life,* summarizing the debate through the early 1980s and reporting unanimous agreement on the need for systematic monitoring genetics. A report on *Biotechnology—Its Challenges to the Churches and the World,* presented to the WCC central committee in 1989, set the ethical issues raised by biotechnology in the context of the ecumenical discussion on the theology of creation. It stated: "... The advent of biotechnology calls the churches to reexamine the fundamental Christian understanding of the relationship between God, humanity and the created world".

The report identifies six areas of ethical concern: human genetic engineering, reproductive technology, intellectual property, environmental effects, military applications and the impact of biotechnology on the Third World. Especially in the first two of these areas, the knowledge and possibilities made available by scientific techniques already being used can confront individuals with agonizingly difficult choices, adding complex new dimensions to the church's pastoral role as well. Ethical issues raised by developments in some of these areas seemed clear enough to the central committee to warrant absolute prohibitions. Genetic testing should not be used (as it often is) for sex selection (statistics from various countries indicate that a far greater number of female than male fetuses are aborted). "Commercialized childbearing" (surrogate motherhood, commercial sale of ova, embryos and sperm) should be banned.

Genetic engineering that enables greatly increased production of chemical or biological warfare agents should be prohibited. Research to develop new kinds of warfare agents (for example, by genetically increasing the virulence of infectious micro-organisms or cloning "selective toxins" that target specific racial or ethnic groups) should be halted. In other areas the committee's recommendations took the form of warnings about potential or unpredictable consequences of scientific developments. It noted that testing of a person's genetic makeup—which some corporations already do—can be the basis of unfair discrimination (for example, refusing to hire someone with a predisposition to a certain disease in order to reduce insurance costs). Genetic diagnosis to detect handicapping conditions in fetuses could lead to a kind of "social engineering" in which parents who give birth to a child with a disability are considered to impose a "preventable burden" on society and public support for disabled (q.v.) people is reduced.

Because genetic materials can reproduce, mutate and migrate, their release into the environment raises special concern. Since industrialized countries are likely to set strict guidelines on this, the Third World, already a dumping ground for toxic chemical wastes, may also bear the unforeseeable consequences of experiments releasing genetically altered organisms into the environment if international controls are not adopted. The report further offers a sobering corrective to the idea that biotechnology is an unalloyed benefit for agriculture and food production. Scientific developments may soon make it possible to produce crops and livestock that are better adapted to less favorable climatic and soil conditions. But the report warns that "in a context of gross social, economic and political inequality, technological innovations cannot automatically bring radical transformation in the quality of life". For example, biotechnical development of "natural" vanilla flavor in the laboratory could eliminate the need for cultivating the vanilla bean—which could result in the loss of US $50 million a year to Madagascar, which now grows three-quarters of the world's vanilla beans.

More dramatically, the report suggests that "the whole future of seeds is at stake". Patenting of seeds cloned in First World laboratories to be high-yielding and disease-resistant would give transnational agribusinesses control of genetic variety. Instead of saving some of each year's harvest for the next year's planting, small farmers whose economic situation is already precarious could be forced to pay fees to corporations every time they reproduce a patented plant.

With the multiplication of centers for research in the fields of biotechnology and medical technology, as well as the formation of ethics committees in hospitals, it is evident that persons having theological expertise and religious commitment are playing important roles. There is an implicit ecumenism expressed in these institutions, which is also revealed in publications devoted to ethics in the life sciences.

BIRCH, L. CHARLES (1918–). Birch was vice moderator of the WCC (q.v.) Sub-unit on Church and Society, 1970–1983, during which time the Council was initially involved in issues of science, technology and environment (qq.v.). He attended the second world conference of Christian youth in Oslo in 1947 and became a leader of the Australian Student Christian Movement. He is Challis professor of biology, University of Sydney, and was a fellow of the Australian Academy of Science, 1954–1984. A member of the Club of Rome, Birch was visiting professor at various universities in the USA as well as the University of São Paulo in Brazil. He has written several works on contemporary problems of population ecology and evolutionary biology.

BIRTH CONTROL *see* SEXUAL ETHICS

BLACK THEOLOGY *see* THEOLOGY, LATE 20TH CENTURY TRENDS IN

BLAKE, EUGENE CARSON (1906–1985). After studying theology at Princeton Theological Seminary, Blake became pastor of a large parish in Pasadena, California. In 1951 he was elected stated clerk of the Presbyterian Church in the USA (later the United Presbyterian Church in the USA). In a sermon at Grace Cathedral in San Francisco in 1960, he made a proposal for church union of several churches in the USA, which developed into the Consultation on Church Union (q.v.). He was president of the National Council of the Churches of Christ in the USA (q.v.), 1954–1957, and continued as a member of the general board until 1966. Blake was elected second general secretary of the WCC (q.v.), 1966–1972, while he was earlier a member of its central and executive committees, 1954–1961, and chairman of the Division of Inter-Church Aid, Refugee and World Service, 1961–1966. He was instrumental in increasing Roman Catholic (q.v.) participation in the ecumenical movement, received Paul VI (q.v.) in the Ecumenical Center in Geneva in 1969, and was personally involved in setting up the Program to Combat Racism (earlier he was in his own country a leader in antisegregation demonstrations). He had considerable administrative skills and guided the WCC in a period of expansion and reconstruction.

BLISS, KATHLEEN (1908–1992). Bliss entered the ecumenical movement through the World Student Christian Federation (q.v.) and edited the *Christian News Letter* (1939–1949). At the first WCC assembly (qq.v.) in Amsterdam in 1948 she spoke significantly about the unsolved problem of the control of power (q.v.) and drafted the phrase ''we intend to stay together'' for the assembly message. Based on a questionnaire to women in some 50 countries she wrote in 1952 *The Service and Status of Women in the Churches*. From 1954 to 1968 she was a member of the WCC central committee and was moderator of the board of the Ecumenical Institute in Bossey (q.v.), supporting the ecumenical education of the laity (q.v.). In New Delhi 1961 she became the moderator of the Division of Ecumenical Action. She served on the British Council of Churches, 1942–1967, and was general secretary of the Board of Education of the Church of England, 1957–1966. Unfortunately she was unable to finish an extensive biography of J. H. Oldham (q.v.) before her death.

BOEGNER, MARC (1881–1970). After studying law and theology, Boegner served a Reformed congregation in Passey, 1918–1954. Because of his outstanding intellectual and diplomatic qualifications he became, as the first Protestant theologian, a member of the Académie Française in 1962. He was president of the Protestant Federation of France, 1928–1961, the Reformed Church of France, 1938–1950, the Student Christian Movement in France, 1920–1939, and the CIMADE (Comité inter-mouvements auprès des évacués), 1945–1960. Participating actively in Oxford and Edinburgh 1937, he was one of the founders of the WCC (q.v.) and became a president of the Council in 1948. He was an official observer at the Second Vatican Council (q.v.) and in 1965 addressed the gathering at the WCC headquarters when Cardinal Bea (q.v.) announced the creation of the Joint Working Group (q.v.). Boegner had a profound ecumenical influence in his country and is remembered as a champion trying to come to the rescue of the persecuted Jews.

BONHOEFFER, DIETRICH (1906–1945). After successful theological studies Bonhoeffer became pastor of a German congregation in London, 1933–1935, devoting much of his energy to making known the fate of the Confessing Church (q.v.) in Germany and informing bishop George Bell (q.v.) about the tragic developments in his country. Earlier in 1931 he was appointed one of the three part-time youth secretaries for the World Alliance for Promoting International Friendship through the Churches (q.v.) and for the Ecumenical Council of Life and Work. He did not convince leaders in the ecumenical movement to abandon the official church in Germany and to recognize the Confessing Church as the true community of Jesus Christ. After a short stay in the USA in 1939 he decided to return to his country and to join the resistance movement preparing a plot against Hitler. He visited church leaders in occupied Norway, W. A. Visser 't Hooft (q.v.) and Hans Schönfeld in Geneva and met with bishop Bell in Stockholm to appeal for support of the plotters. Arrested in April 1943, he was executed in April 1945 in Flössenberg, Bavaria. His spiritual and theological inspiration shines through his life and work, in particular in his *Letters and Papers from Prison* and the biography of his close friend Eberhard Bethge. His notions of "God, the beyond in the midst", "the world come of age", "the non-religious interpretation of Christianity", and "the secret discipline of the church" were new and original. Bonhoeffer had a great influence on theologians, Christians and churches in North and South America as well as in parts of Africa and Japan.

BOROVOY, VITALI (1916–). Borovoy served as a staff member and assistant director of the Secretariat for Faith and Order (q.v.), 1966–1972, and afterward as a member of the WCC (q.v.) central committee and the Faith and Order standing committee. He was an observer at the Second Vatican Council, 1962–1965, a member of the Joint Working Group, 1965–1972, and of the annual meeting of the Christian World Communions (qq.v.), 1962–1985. Commenting on the Toronto statement (q.v.) Borovoy said: "For the Orthodox it is the great charter of the WCC". He was quite outspoken on the role of the laity (q.v.) in the ecumenical movement: "The laymen can be, must be and are, by what they say and by the example they give, the best witnesses of

Christ to non-Christians and non-believers''. He was vice dean of the Minsk Theological Seminary, 1944–1954, professor of ancient church history at the Leningrad Theological Academy, 1954–1962, and dean of the Moscow Patriarchal Cathedral and professor of Byzantine church history at the Moscow Theological Academy, 1973–1978. He has served as deputy chairman of the department for external church relations of the Moscow patriarchate since 1985.

BOSSEY, ECUMENICAL INSTITUTE OF. Situated in the foothills of the Jura mountains, half an hour's drive from the WCC's (q.v.) headquarters in Geneva, the Ecumenical Institute in Bossey is a symbol of what the Council is: an organization enabling people to work for unity (q.v.) in their own contexts. Bossey's initial emphasis was on the ecumenical training of laypeople for whom traditional parish life was no longer enough after their experiences of the Second World War. "An energizing center and laboratory for the whole ecumenical movement" is how W. A. Visser 't Hooft (q.v.) described the Institute. It stood for "reawakening the church through the spiritual mobilization of the laity". Two gifted lay theologians, Hendrik Kraemer and Suzanne de Diétrich (qq.v.), gave it early and inspired leadership. In 1951 Bossey added to its program an annual Graduate School of Ecumenical Studies, organized in collaboration with the theological faculty of the University of Geneva. Some 60 students from all over the world participate in these graduate studies and several of them later hold key ecumenical positions in churches and organizations. Hundreds of people come to Bossey each year for conferences and courses, which expand their understanding of what churches around the world are doing together. Ecumenical learning through the action/reflection method and the equipment of lay and clergy leaders for local ministries remain the Institute's aim, which is achieved through study, worship (q.v.) and community living in an international, transconfessional and intercultural setting. *See also* ECUMENICAL INSTITUTES.

BOYER, CHARLES (1884–1980). Promoter of an ecumenical climate in Rome, Boyer's principles were loyalty to the holy see, willingness to repent, mutual information and prayer (q.v.). On the request of G. B. Montini (Paul VI [q.v.]), in 1945 he changed a community of learning and unity between the Russian Orthodox Church and the Roman Catholic Church into an ecumenical group, called Unitas. Beginning in 1946 he edited a journal *Unitas.* Despite many difficulties he made contact with the WCC Amsterdam assembly (qq.v.) in 1948. In 1950 Boyer organized a Catholic ecumenical conference at Grottaferrata, Italy, a center for information for non-Catholic Christians visiting Rome. During the Second Vatican Council (q.v.) it became a meeting point for guests and observers of other churches. A member of the Jesuit order in 1907, he was ordained a priest in 1916, and was professor of philosophy and theology at the Gregorian University in Rome, 1922–1969, and general secretary of the Academy of St. Thomas Aquinas.

BRENT, CHARLES HENRY (1862–1929). Born and raised in Canada, Brent became a pastor in the Protestant Episcopal Church in the USA (Buffalo and Boston), 1888–1891. Consecrated as Protestant Episcopal bishop of the Philippines in 1901 he was greatly committed to the promotion of health and the combat of the opium traffic. In 1909 he was president of the opium conference in Shanghai, and in 1923 he represented the USA at an international opium conference of the League of Nations. After having attended the World Missionary Conference in Edinburgh 1910, he stressed the need for church unity (q.v.) and expressed at the general convention of the Protestant Episcopal Church his conviction that "a world conference on Faith and Order should be convened". Traveling widely and addressing many ecumenical gatherings he had a great influence on the early developments of the Faith and Order (q.v.) movement and was the first president of the first Faith and Order World Conference in Lausanne in 1927.

BRETHREN. The Church of the Brethren in the USA, among several Brethren communities, is the only one to be involved in the ecumenical movement. It joined the Federal Council of the Churches of Christ in America in 1941 (since 1950 the National Council of the Churches of Christ in the USA) and was a founding member of the WCC (qq.v.) in 1948. It has most actively participated in the activities of these councils, always contributing an unusually large number of leaders and dollars in proportion to its size. The Brethren have a strong sense of mission (q.v.). This missionary spirit led to the development of home missions from the early beginnings; missionary activity developed outside the USA in the mid-19th century. The major Brethren missionary areas were Puerto Rico, Ecuador, Nigeria, Sudan, India, China and Indonesia. From the beginning, the Brethren embodied a high doctrine of the church as a close-knit community whose life together is a means of grace (q.v.), not a loose association of like-minded believers. They stress obedience to the teachings of Jesus and conformity to the life of early Christian communities. They practice adult baptism (q.v.) by immersion, celebrate the love feast, with foot washing according to John 13, a common meal, and the bread and the cup, and teach nonresistance. A Brethren Service Committee (1939) focused during the Second World War on civilian public service, a cooperative program of the Brethren, Mennonites and Friends (qq.v.) with the federal government. The comprehensive three-volume *Brethren Encyclopedia* is a basic reference work.

BRILIOTH, INGVE TORGNY (1891–1959). Brilioth was involved in Edinburgh 1937, Amsterdam 1948, and Evanston 1954 (qq.v.). As chairman of the Commission on Faith and Order (q.v.), 1947–1957, succeeding Archbishop William Temple (q.v.), he oversaw the work of the theological commissions as they prepared for the Lund conference in 1952. He became professor of church history in Aebe (Finland) in 1925, professor in Lund in 1929, bishop of Väzjö in 1939, and archbishop of Uppsala in 1950. He was a scholar in Anglicanism.

BRITISH COUNCIL OF CHURCHES *see* COUNCIL OF CHURCHES FOR BRITAIN AND IRELAND

BROWN, ROBERT McAFEE (1920–). Brown was Protestant observer at the Second Vatican Council, 1963 and 1965, representing the World Alliance of Reformed Churches, and has been a member of the Institute for Advanced Theological Studies, Tantur (qq.v.) (near Jerusalem), 1965–1973, and of the United States Holocaust Memorial Council, 1978–1986. He was a keynote speaker at Nairobi 1975. Brown was Auburn professor of systematic theology, Union Theological Seminary, New York, 1953–1962, professor of religious studies, Stanford University, California, 1962–1976, professor of ecumenies and world Christianity, Union Theological Seminary, 1976–1979, and professor of theology and ethics, Pacific School of Religion, California, 1979–1986.

BROWN, WILLIAM ADAMS (1865–1943). A leader in Stockholm 1925 and Lausanne 1927, in 1937 Brown chaired the meetings of the US delegation to the Oxford conference and helped finalize the report of the Edinburgh assembly (qq.v.). In 1938 he cosigned the invitation to the churches to join the WCC (q.v.). Brown was chairman of the department of relations with churches abroad of the Federation of the Churches of Christ in America (q.v.), professor at Union Seminary in New York, and president of the committee on educational policy at Yale University, 1919–1930. Among several works he wrote *Toward a United Church: Three Decades of Ecumenical Christianity.* See also *The Church through Half a Century: Essays in honor of William Adams Brown.*

BUDDHIST-CHRISTIAN DIALOGUE *see* DIALOGUE WITH PEOPLE OF LIVING FAITHS

BÜHRIG, MARGA (1915–). Bührig was a president of the WCC (q.v.), 1983–1991, and during this period greatly involved in the WCC program on "Justice, Peace and the Integrity of Creation" (q.v.), particularly in the world convocation at Seoul in 1990. From 1946 she was engaged in ecumenical women's (q.v.) work in Switzerland and Germany, and since 1954 in the international ecumenical movement through the WCC Department on the Cooperation of Men and Women in Church, Family and Society. She was co-president of the Women's Ecumenical Liaison Group (Vatican, Consilium de Laicis, and the WCC), 1968–1972, director of the Boldern Academy (near Zurich), 1971–1981, and president of the Ecumenical Association of Academies and Laity Centers in Europe, 1976–1982. She wrote *Women Invisible* (1993).

BULGAKOV, SERIUS (1870–1944). Bulgakov began as a Marxist, but soon abandoned this position and gradually came back to the faith of the Eastern Orthodox Church. He was an active member of the All-Russian Church Council and was elected to the Supreme Church Board in 1917. Ordained to the priesthood in 1918, he was expelled from Russia in 1923, left for Prague, where he taught political economy at the Russian Graduate School of Law, and then moved to Paris, where he was dean of the Russian Orthodox Theological Institute, 1925–1944. Bulgakov had a considerable influence on the ecumenical movement despite his frequent criticism. He was actively involved in the Anglo-Russian Fellowship of St. Alban and St. Sergius (q.v.). His ambition was to give an inclusive and comprehensive interpretation of all main traditional Christian doctrines in light of *sophia* (holy wisdom). His ideas met with strong opposition and his orthodoxy was challenged, though no close examination of his views was ever made. Several of his books were translated into English.

BUTHELEZI, MANAS (1935–). Bishop of the Central Diocese of the Evangelical Lutheran Church in Southern Africa. Buthelezi was a member of the Commission on Studies of the Lutheran World Federation, and a member of the WCC Commission on World Mission and Evangelism (qq.v.), 1975–1983. He currently is a member of the standing committee of the Faith and Order (q.v.) Commission, a member of the International Commission on Lutheran-Roman Catholic Dialogue (q.v.) and president of the South African Council of Churches. In 1968 he received a Ph.D. from Drew University, New Jersey.

- C -

CAMARA, HELDER (1909–). Archbishop of Olinde and Recife, 1964–1985, afterward emeritus archbishop. Camara participated actively in the first general conference of the Latin American episcopate (1955), which resulted in the founding of CELAM. He was Brazilian delegate to CELAM and second vice president, 1958–1964, and delegate of the Brazilian episcopate to the second general assembly of the Latin American episcopate (Medellin 1968). He addressed the conference of the WCC (q.v.) Commission on the Churches' Participation in Development (Montreux 1970) and several other major ecumenical gatherings. As a priest-counselor at the Second Vatican Council (q.v.), he aligned himself unreservedly with the group of bishops advocating reform. He urged the Council fathers to ease off the outward trappings of their office—the episcopal ring, the mitre and other signs of splendor. Camara has constantly born witness to the principle of nonviolence, taking as his model Martin Luther King, Jr., (q.v.) in the USA. In 1955 he was the organizer and general secretary of the 36th International Eucharistic Congress, and in 1959 he founded the Bank of Providence (providing aid to the poor). His works have been translated into many languages.

CANBERRA 1991 *see* WORLD COUNCIL OF CHURCHES ASSEMBLIES

CANON LAW. Canon law is the body of rules that the Christian community makes for the government of its internal affairs and the conduct of its members. The Greek word *kanon*, meaning a rule, is used by St Paul. No one can deny that the church, like any other corporate body, needs some basic rules to function. The earliest example of the enactment of canon law appears in Acts 15:6–29, in which the council of elders at Jerusalem framed rules of discipline for the Gentile converts to Christianity. As time went by, the number of rules multiplied, and in the Middle Ages they were codified in the Western church in the *Corpus Iuris Canonici*. When the Roman Catholic Church (q.v.) revised its canon law in

1918, there were no less than 2,414 canons. The *New Code of Canon Law* consists of five books. The first book consists of general rules; the second, rules regarding ecclesiatical persons; the third book deals with sacred objects and rites, such as altars and sacramentals; the fourth, with canonical trials; and the fifth with crimes and punishments. Following Vatican II (q.v.), there was a further revision, effective in 1983.

In the Greek Orthodox Church (q.v.) canon law is composed of a small number of homogeneous, ancient regulations, which have remained unchanged. The Church of England adapted the medieval canons to its own needs. Its canon law dates from 1604, revised in 1969. The expression "canon law" is not used among Protestants, though of course they have their own regulations. Much of canon law is concerned with ecclesiatical questions that have no particular ethical significance, e.g., rules about ordination and admission to the sacraments (qq.v.). But there are areas where canon law and ethics overlap, e.g., marriage discipline. In earlier times, when church and state (q.v.) were intimately bound up with each other, the canon law relating to marriage and sexual conduct was similar to that of the state. But with the separation of church and state, either in law or in fact, canon law has likewise become separated from civil law. A fundamental ecumenical experience has been the rediscovery of canon law both as intrinsic to the Trinitarian communion, which gives the church a structure as a confessing church, and also expressing itself in sacramental processes with an instituting function. The last function is subordinated to the first.

CAPITALISM. The term "capitalism" is of recent origin. Karl Marx called his three volume analysis of capitalism *Das Kapital;* in it he spoke of capitalists and the capitalist mode of production but does not use the abstract noun *capitalism.* The Marxist labor movement and its propaganda freely used the word. In 1902 Werner Sombart (1863–1941) published his work *Modern Capitalism,* and a few years later Max Weber (1864–1920) wrote his monumental work *The Protestant Ethic and the Spirit of Capitalism,* in which he sought to demonstrate that Protestantism (q.v.), especially the Puritan ethic and Calvinism, laid the foundation for the emergence of modern Western capitalism. This gave the term capitalism academic respectability. Thereafter R. H. Tawney (1880–1962), a philosopher of history, and others accepted it. Capitalism as a historical phenomenon has its cycle of birth, growth and decline. It began in Great Britain and spread to the European continent and the USA, achieving in England the status of a fully developed system in only about the middle of the 19th century. But an uncontrolled capitalism in which there is exploitation of workers and consumers by a few powerful profit seekers is largely a thing of the past. State regulation of industry and commerce, and many labor unions, protect both workers and consumers, as well as the community at large. Competition and incentives within a system of free enterprise provide built-in controls against some evils, such as the production of inferior goods. Capitalism, moreover, has its own virtues, for it requires the diligence and concern associated with risk and encourages care for property.

Nevertheless the first WCC assembly (qq.v.) at Amsterdam in 1948 felt it necessary to draw attention to the conflict between Christianity and capitalism. It argued that capitalism tends to subordinate what should be the primary task of any economy—the meeting of human needs—to the economic advantages of those who have most power over its institutions. The report of the assembly concluded that laissez-faire capitalism, like communism, makes promises that it cannot redeem. Capitalism falsely claims that by stressing freedom, it can be presumed that justice (q.v.) will follow as a by-product of free enterprise. Christians are not committed to any particular economic system. They must seek the economic well-being of all and fight against injustice, poverty and waste. The Evanston assembly (1954) was concerned with the problem of the appropriateness of the capitalist system as a model for Third World development (qq.v.). But it also criticized the Western system itself, warning against the accumulation of riches for their own sake, pressing for equity in distribution, urging more responsibility on the part of trade unions and drawing attention to the need for national policies to be aware of the international consequences of their actions. The rich countries particularly must remember that one test of their policies is their effect on the underdeveloped areas of the world. The New Delhi assembly (1961) argued that the pursuit of maximum production for maximum consumption is no longer acceptable. It also criticized the role of the welfare state in Western capitalist societies for providing too much affluence and security. The assembly at Nairobi (1975) noted that "many often erroneously associate the term 'ideology' only with Marxism. Christians in the West, as elsewhere, ought to scrutinize sensitively and critically their own, perhaps unconscious, ideological perspectives." The assembly also considered proposals for a new international economic order as an alternative way of ordering both national and international economic structures and systems.

The Vancouver assembly (1983) stated: "We need ethical guidelines for a participatory society which will be both ecologically responsible and economically just, and can effectively struggle with the powers which threaten life and endanger our future". This led the assembly to ask the WCC "to engage member churches in a conciliar process of mutual commitment (covenant) to justice, peace and the integrity of creation" (JPIC) (q.v.). Economic issues were high on the agenda of the world convocation of JPIC in Seoul 1990. The convocation affirmed God's preferential option for the poor (q.v.) and resisted the idea that anything in creation is merely a resource of capitalist exploitation. One of the covenants adopted was for a just economic order on local, national, regional and international levels for all people, and for liberation from the foreign debt bondage that affects the lives of hundreds of millions of people. These calls were echoed by the Canberra assembly (1991), which said that "flagrant international inequality in the distribution of income, knowledge, power and wealth persists", and the "totally irresponsible exploitation of the created world continues", and that "the market economy is in need of reform". The present situation, with its confused response to the problems of capitalism, offers ecumenical social thought an unparalleled opportunity and a crucial test. To seize the opportunity and to meet the test it must reassess the application of its principles to the historic, contingent and changing facts. Here lies its challenge. *See also* DEVELOPMENT; SOCIALISM.

CARIBBEAN CONFERENCE OF CHURCHES (CCC). As regards ecumenical relations and actions, the Caribbean churches, including the Roman Catholic Church and a few evangelical churches (qq.v.), have come a long way in the past twenty years. The Caribbean Conference of Churches, with its twin agencies CADEC (Christian Action for Development in the Caribbean) and ARC (Action for Renewal of the Churches), has carved out a place and a role for the regional ecumenical movement in the ongoing struggles of Caribbean peoples for unity (q.v.), identity, change, justice (q.v.) and development (q.v.). It is deeply aware of the racial and religious pluralism of the region, as well as of the ideological pluralism (q.v.).

The inaugural assembly of the CCC was held in Kingston, Jamaica, in 1973. The main offices of the CCC are in Bridgetown, Barbados. The membership spans the four major languages of the region: Dutch, Spanish, French and English. Membership in 1990 stood at 34 churches from 37 countries. The Antilles Episcopal Conference of the Roman Catholic Church was a founding member. The search for greater Christian unity is consciously charted via common participation in the human struggles of society, as evidenced in the preamble of the CCC. "We are deeply concerned to promote the human liberation of our people, and are committed to the achievement of social justice and the dignity of man in our society". In the process toward these goals, the churches' understanding of the dimension of mission has expanded and their experience of "community" has become a greater reality.

CASTRO, EMILIO ENRIQUE (1927–). Castro was the fourth general secretary of the WCC (q.v.), 1985–1993. He studied theology in Buenos Aires, 1944–1950, and one year with Karl Barth (q.v.) in Basel, 1953–1954. He received a doctor's degree from the University of Lausanne in 1984; the title of his dissertation was *Freedom in Mission in the Perspective of the Kingdom of God.* Before his appointment as director of the WCC Commission on World Mission and Evangelism, 1973–1983, he was a pastor of Methodist parishes in Uruguay and Bolivia. He was vice president of the Christian Peace Conference (q.v.), 1964–1968, coordinator of the Commission for Evangelical Unity in Latin America (UNELAM), 1965–1972, executive secretary of the South American Association of Theological Schools, 1966–1969, president of the Evangelical Methodist Church of Uruguay, 1970–1972, and chairman of the Agency for Christian Literature Development, 1970–1972.

CATECHISMS. Until modern times a catechism was any compendious system of teaching drawn up in the form of question and answer, especially one for religious instruction. During the first centuries the word "catechism" referred to the method of instruction for catechumens preparing for their baptism (q.v.); later it was extended to mean religious instruction in general. In the 16th century catechism became identified with manuals of instruction in the tenets of the Christian faith. Two classic catechisms of Martin Luther— small catechism, 1529; large catechism, 1530—became the most important ones among catechetical manuals. The context of Luther's catechisms was clearly homiletical: they grew out of his preaching and were supposed to be used for and in connection with the Sunday sermon. His two catechisms became the model for many others. Reformed catechisms followed soon after, among them those of Martin Bucer (1537), John Calvin (1537, 1541–42) and Heinrich Bullinger (1561). The Heidelberg, or Palatinate catechism was compiled by Caspar Olevianus and Zacharias Ursinus, at the request of the Elector Frederick III, of the Palatinate. It was published in 1563 and has been translated into all the languages of Europe:

In the Roman Catholic Church (q.v.) the first official catechism, prepared by the Council of Trent and published in 1566, was known as the *Roman Catechism.* It was not a textbook, but a compendium of doctrine for the guidance of pastors and teachers. A popular catechism was written by the

German Jesuit Peter Canisius and published in 1555. The catechism of the Church of England in the smaller form, published in the *Book of Common Prayer,* is in two parts: the first contains and explains baptismal covenant, the creed (q.v.), the ten commandments and the Lord's Prayer (q.v.); the second explains the two sacraments, baptism and the Lord's Supper.

During the 20th century a new approach and orientation in the nature and use of catechisms developed. New catechisms have taken into account the anthropological foundations and the cultural context of faith (q.v.); most have moved away from the standard question-and-answer method to a more narrative, participatory and situation-orientated approach. A clear example was the so-called Dutch catechism, published in 1966. The new world catechism of the Roman Catholic Church takes its structure from the traditional division into doctrine, sacraments (q.v.) and commandments. It is intended as a reference book for national and diocesan catechisms. *The Common Catechism: A Christian Book of Faith,* edited by J. Feiner and Lukas Vischer (q.v.) and published in 1973, is an ecumenical Protestant-Catholic undertaking; but joint catechisms on the whole have not been a favorite area of ecumenical initiative. Perhaps the Faith and Order documents *Baptism, Eucharist and Ministry* (qq.v.) and *Towards the Common Expression of the Apostolic Faith* could become a basic ecumenical catechism that would inspire denominational catechisms. The question is still open as to what kind of instruction could best serve the transmission of faith in the diversity of different church traditions (q.v.). *See also* CREEDS.

CATHOLICITY. The word "catholic" is the transliteration of the Greek term *katholikos,* meaning "general" or "throughout the whole". It was first used by Christian writers to distinguish the entire body of believers from individual bodies. Later it was applied to faith, tradition (qq.v.), and doctrine; it was understood to express the universality of the church. After the separation of the Greek and Latin churches, the epithet "catholic" was assumed by the latter, as "orthodox" was by the former. At the Reformation (q.v.) the term was claimed by the Church of Rome, in opposition to the Protestant churches. In England the national church was said to be the truly catholic church of the land, and the expression "Roman Catholic" came into use for the sake of distinction. Protestants have generally interpreted the term to mean the entire community of the saved at all times and in all places. The word "catholic" in the phrase "the one, holy, catholic church" of the Apostles' Creed (q.v.) indicates that the church is to be disseminated through all nations, that it contains all necessary truths, exacts absolute obedience from human beings to the commands of Christ, and furnishes all with all graces (q.v.) necessary to make them acceptable and their actions well-pleasing to God.

The Second Vatican Council (q.v.) approached the understanding of Catholicism by the Counter-Reformation in a new way. Catholicity in *Lumen Gentium* (8) is no longer assumed to be exclusively Roman catholicity. It is now treated primarily as an attribute of the church of Christ. It *subsists in* the Roman Catholic Church. Although the fullness of catholicity can be obtained only in full communion with Rome, this does not imply that other churches not in communion with Rome have not preserved at least some of the essential qualities of catholicity. The Joint Working Group (q.v.) published in 1968 a document on "Catholicity and Apostolicity" in which the most important emphases are on Christology and pneumatology (qq.v.). The church attains catholicity to the degree that it expresses the truth and love of Christ and the Holy Spirit (q.v.). The full dimensions of catholicity will not be manifested, moreover, until the return of Christ in glory. This notion adds an important eschatological dimension to the notion of catholicity.

Since the fourth WCC assembly (qq.v.) at Uppsala in 1968 produced a section report ón "The Holy Spirit and the Catholicity of the Church" there is now much less disagreement between Catholics and Protestants than there was in 1948. Catholicity is defined as "the quality by which the church expresses the fullness, the integrity, and the totality of life in Christ". It is argued that catholicity cannot be separated from the marks of unity (q.v.), holiness, and apostolicity (q.v.). Furthermore, there must also be a balance between continuity and renewal. The church involved in the ecumenical advance can achieve an even broader catholicity.

CAVERT, SAMUEL McCREA (1888–1976). As a member of the Committee of 35 at Westfield College in 1937, Cavert suggested the name "World Council of Churches". In 1938 he participated in the Utrecht conference, which laid the foundations of the WCC (q.v.). He was a member of the provisional committee of the WCC, 1938–1948, and organizing secretary of Amsterdam 1948. In 1919 Cavert joined the staff of the Federal Council of the Churches of Christ (q.v.), and in 1921 was elected general secretary serving through 1950, when it united with other agencies to form the National Council of the Churches of Christ in the USA (q.v.), of which he became the first general secretary until 1954. He served as a member of the Geneva staff in connection with the Stuttgart declaration, 1945, and was Protestant liaison officer for the US government in Europe. Head of the US Conference for the WCC, 1954–1957, Cavert attended the North American Conference on Faith and Order at Oberlin, 1957. Among several works he wrote *On the Road to Christian Unity.*

CHAKKO, SARAH (1905–1954). Born in a Syrian Orthodox family Chakko was educated in Madras and undertook further studies in the USA (universities of Chicago and Michigan). In 1945 she was named principal of Isabella Thoburn College in Lucknow. Attending the first WCC assembly (qq.v.) in Amsterdam in 1948 she was made the moderator of the WCC Commission on the Life and Work of Women in the Church, and the first woman elected as a WCC president, 1951–1954. At her invitation the central committee met in Lucknow in 1953.

CHARISMATIC MOVEMENT. The expression "charismatic movement" refers to a worldwide phenomenon whose distinctive stress on experience, action and behavior contrasts with the traditional Western Catholic and Protestant emphases on administering the sacraments (q.v.) and on preaching the word of God. Its common characteristics of baptism (q.v.) in the Spirit, speaking in tongues, direct revelations from God, and divine intervention in response to prayer for well-being (conversion, physical and emotional healing, exorcism, and deliverance from evil) have formed a distinctive common culture. This culture is enjoyed not only by charismatics who maintain or have some link with historic churches, but also by millions of Christians whose charismatic churches have arisen in the 20th century on all continents. Participants in the charismatic movement commonly see the movement as a second wave of the Spirit. It extends the first wave of the Pentecostal (q.v.) movement, but differs in its refusal to be organized into separate Pentecostal denominations and in its generally less dogmatic formulation of the core experience of the baptism in the Holy Spirit.

The charismatic movement should be seen as a recapturing on a large scale of ecumenical elements that had been in some origins of the Pentecostal movement but were later eclipsed. In this perspective, the Holy Spirit was poured out to revive various Protestant churches in several countries. The advent of Roman Catholic (q.v.) charismatic renewal also dramatically advertised the movement's ecumenical character and potential. Catholics saw their Pentecostal experience as a providential result of the renewal thrust and ecumenical openings of Vatican II (q.v.).

The Vatican Secretariat for Promoting Christian Unity (q.v.) planned in 1971 a series of dialogues on charismatic renewal with representatives of Pentecostal churches and charismatics in Protestant, Orthodox and Anglican (q.v.) churches. The first dialogue was cochaired by David du Plessis (q.v.) and Kilian McDonnell. In the 1970s several charismatics saw their movement as a means of healing denominational divisions. Underlying their hopes was the ease with which Catholic and Protestant charismatics worshipped and ministered together. The overtures of David du Plessis led to a mutual understanding between the WCC and several Pentecostal churches, and to "charismatic events" at WCC meetings. As the movement has progressed, however, charismatics have tended to strengthen their ties with their own communities. Others have left their churches to join new "restorationist" churches, which hold that the recovery of spiritual life requires the foundation of new institutions, not the reform of existing ones. *See also* PENTECOSTAL CHURCHES.

CHO, KIYOKO TAKEDA (1917–). Cho was a president of the WCC (q.v.), 1971–1975, and previously a delegate to the first world conference on Christian youth, Amsterdam, 1939, she participated in the WCC commissions on humanum studies, education and international affairs. In Tokyo she was professor of intellectual history of Japan and comparative culture at the International Christian University, Tokyo, 1961–1988, and has served as director of the Institute of Asian Cultural Studies, 1975–1976, and a member of the board of trustees, United Board for Christian Higher Education in Asia, 1974–1979. She has lectured on Christianity and Japanese (and Asian) indigenous cultures at various universities in the West and in Asia.

CHOISY, JACQUES EUGENE (1866–1949). Choisy participated as a Swiss delegate in the preparation of Stockholm 1925, and also attended Lausanne 1927. He was a frequent lecturer, together with Adolf Keller (q.v.), at the annual ecumenical seminar in Geneva, sponsored by the Universal Christian Council, 1934–1939. Actively involved in the founding of the Federation of Protestant Churches in Switzerland, and its president, 1930–1941, he was professor of church history at the University of Geneva, 1909–1939, and moderator of the Compagnie des pasteurs. He founded the Reformation Museum, with an important library and archives on John Calvin.

CHRISTIAN CHURCH (DISCIPLES OF CHRIST). Early in the 19th century several groups separated themselves from the Presbyterian Church (q.v.) in North America, because of their preference for the forms of the church during New Testament times. Now that they were in a new country, these groups desired to overcome the old church divisions, and soon called themselves "Christians", "Christian Churches", "the Church of Christ" or "Christian Disciples". Groups around Burton W. Stone, Thomas and Alexander Campbell joined together in one Church: Christian Churches (Disciples of Christ). Soon sister churches were established in England, Australia and New Zealand. Missionary churches were founded, in particular in some countries of Africa and in the Pacific.

Christian Churches follow a congregational pattern of church polity, which they regard as being in accordance with New Testament teaching. One of the major goals is to align all church practice and belief with the Scriptures. Nothing is to be accepted as an article of faith or as a condition of communion but "what is expressly taught and enjoined . . . in the word of God", which is "the perfect constitution for the worship, discipline and government of the New Testament church". The Bible (q.v.) is the best source of information about God, far better than creeds (q.v.) or statements of dogma. The Disciples of Christ affirm their belief in the Trinity (q.v.), the virgin birth, the vicarious atonement, the necessity of spiritual birth, and the need for believers' baptism (q.v.) by immersion. The Christian Church (Disciples of Christ) in the USA, with 1,200,000 members, is the largest church within the family of Christian churches. It has been greatly active in the ecumenical movement. As early as 1910 a Council of Christian Unity was created that participated actively in the early Faith and Order (q.v.) movement. From 1961 onward the ecumenical journal *Midstream* has been published regularly.

The World Convention of the Churches of Christ (Disciples) was started in 1930 in the United States. Each convention elects an executive committee to which the executive secretary is responsible. Between conventions, work is carried on through committees on study, finance, program and interfaith relations. The preamble to the constitution of the World Convention says: "The World Convention of Churches of Christ exists in order more fully to show the essential oneness of the churches in the Lord Jesus Christ; impart inspiration to the world brotherhood; cultivate the spirit of fellowship; promote the unity of the church upon the basis of the New Testament Scriptures. The World Convention may in no way interfere with the independence of churches or assume the administrative functions of existing ongoing organizations or institutions among us''.

The Disciples Ecumenical Consultative Council (DECC) was created in Nairobi in 1975 during the fifth assembly of the WCC (qq.v.). It held its first international conference in Kingston, Jamaica, in 1979. It intends to nurture and to challenge the Disciples of Christ, from the beginning of the ecumenical movement, to commit themselves to the church's ecumenical future with intelligence and firmness. A second international conference took place in 1985 in Des Moines, Iowa. The three current dialogues of the Disciples Ecumenical Consultative Council are with the Roman Catholic Church (1977), the Russian Orthodox Church (1987) and the World Alliance of Reformed Churches (1987) (qq.v.). The DECC includes membership of Disciples of Christ churches (and united churches that have former Disciples ties) in Argentina, Australia, Canada, Jamaica, Mexico, New Zealand, Paraguay, Puerto Rico, Southern Africa, the United Kingdom, the USA, Vanuatu and Zaire. The total membership of the Christian Church is approximately 1,350,000.

CHRISTIAN CONFERENCE OF ASIA (CCA). The East Asia Christian Conference (EACC), now called the CCA, was the first institutionalized expression of regional ecumenism. When Rajah Manikam (q.v.) began his work as secretary in East Asia for the World Council of Churches and the International Missionary Council (qq.v.), he was surprised to discover how little the Asian churches knew of one another. Many of them were well-informed about the churches in Europe and America, and some of them had strong links with Christian communities in these continents. Yet, these churches were often unaware of vital happenings within their own neighboring churches in Asia; sometimes they were even totally ignorant of one another's existence. Three principle motives lay behind the creation of the East Asia Christian Conference. First, there was the desire of Asian Christian leaders to develop closer and more regular contacts with one another. Second, there was the concern for common enrichment and the strengthening of a common witness throughout the continent. Third, there was the expressed desire that ways should be found for channeling more effectively the contribution of the Asian churches to the ecumenical understanding of faith (q.v.), and of the life and witness of the church universal.

In 1973 the East Asia Christian Conference became the Christian Conference of Asia. There are almost 100 member churches and over 15 national councils within the CCA fellowship today. Besides the two preparatory meetings in Bangkok, and the planning meeting in Prapat, Indonesia, 1957, assemblies were held in Kuala Lumpur, Malaysia, 1959, Bangkok, 1968, Singapore, 1973, Penang, Malaysia, 1977, Bangalore, India, 1981, Seoul, 1985, and Manila, 1990. Each assembly had a special theme. The CCA was expelled by the government of Singapore in 1987 and operates since then from offices in Osaka (Japan), Hong Kong, Manila and Chiang Mai. Its main concerns relate to evangelism, dialogue, communication, women, youth, education, laity, development (qq.v.), international affairs, urban and rural mission (q.v.), medical service and theology.

CHRISTIAN EDUCATION *see* EDUCATION, ECUMENICAL

CHRISTIAN LITERATURE FUND (CLF). The idea of a world fund for the development of Christian literature grew out of recommendations made at successive ecumenical meetings, from Tambaram (1938) onward. Discussions took place between the literature societies and agencies in Europe and North America; regional literature conferences were held in Hakene, Japan, in 1958, and Mindolo, Zambia, in 1961. Also a worldwide gathering was held in Bethel, Germany, in 1962. At the meeting of the WCC Division on World Mission and Evangelism in Mexico, 1963, the CLF was established, analogous to the Theological Education Fund (q.v.), to act not as an operating agency but to dispense funds for schemes to be carried out by agencies of the churches in Asia, Africa, Latin America, Oceania and the Caribbean. After a mid-term review (1968) it was followed in 1970 by the Agency for Christian Literature Development, which merged with the World Association for Christian Communication (q.v.) in 1975. From 1965 to 1968 grants and allocations totaled US

$1,887,000 and at the end of the mandate more than US $2.5 million had been disbursed in addition to further sums by many participating societies. The aim of the Fund was the growth of well-coordinated and indigenous Christian literature of considerable quality, largely self-sustaining and capable of spontaneous growth. At least 25 percent of the fund went into the training of qualified personnel in printing, publishing and distribution as well as regional and local workshops for writers, translators and salespersons.

CHRISTIAN PEACE CONFERENCE (CPC). This conference was founded in 1958, at the instigation of the Comenius Faculty of Theology of the University of Prague, to bring together Christian churches in Eastern Europe in their search for peace. From the outset it was made clear that it would not compete with the WCC (q.v.) but would complement its activities. The CPC has played a significant role in the East-West dialogue of Christian communities and peace groups. At its second assembly in 1964 there was already a large number of representatives from Africa, Asia and Latin America and the discussion of Third World issues shaped the CPC into a truly worldwide movement. At its six assemblies it influenced the thinking and life of churches and individual Christians in around 90 countries (including Vietnam and North Korea). Its president and undisputed leader was Josef L. Hromádka (q.v.), who resigned his position in 1969 over alleged curtailment of the freedom and sovereignty of "a body of devout Christians" who act "in the perspective and under the guidance of the gospel". Since then the leadership of the Russian Orthodox Church (q.v.) has had a distinct impact on the CPC.

The Christian Peace Conference has championed the Marxist-Christian dialogue (q.v.), sought to be "an apostle of the pilgrim church moving through a revolutionary age", and faced the challenge that Christians must abandon the notion of just war (q.v.) and advance just peace. Foremost on the agenda in the 1980s were three issues: imperialism, anticommunism and the nuclear problem. The recent radical changes in Central and Eastern Europe question the existence, structures and decision-making process of the CPC. In view of its past one-sided position and faltering credibility, it has become an open question whether it can recuperate its effectiveness and deal with the urgent problem of global economic justice.

CHRISTIAN WORLD COMMUNIONS (CWCs). The term "Christian World Communions" came into common use only in 1979. They used to be known as "world confessional church groups", "world confessional groups", or "world confessional bodies" until 1967 when, at a meeting of secretaries of such bodies in Geneva, the term "world confessional bodies" was adopted. At that time these church families were described as consisting of "the various Christian traditions taken as a whole. Each world confessional family consists of churches belonging to the same tradition and held together by this common heritage; they are conscious of living in the same universal fellowship and give to this consciousness at least some structured visible expression". The designation "world confessional families" is not entirely satisfactory. Several communions of churches (Orthodox, Anglican [qq.v.] and others) do not understand themselves as a particular confession, that is, as churches marked by ties to particular creeds (q.v.). They are built on different ecclesiological assumptions. Yet, all the participants in the 1967 meeting accepted the collective term "world confessional families".

The forms of structured visible expressions of confessional organizations vary greatly. One Christian world communion has many employees and a large annual budget. Several have small staffs and moderate budgets. Some had origins that preceded the modern ecumenical movement by several decades. Others were formed or assumed their present level of activities since the WCC (q.v.) was officially launched in 1948. Difficult as they are to define and varied as they are in their structure and purpose, the Christian World Communions are very much alive, and must be studied in their relationship with the ecumenical movement. In their beginnings they were in fact the principal existing forms of the ecumenical movement, giving the members of their churches a new consciousness of universality through an understanding of the worldwide dimensions of their own fellowships. Many of their leaders participated in the formation of the WCC and today hold positions of leadership in it. During the last three decades confessional groupings have increased in strength and their scope of work. At the same time, their status, paradoxically, has become limited by the growth of the ecumenical movement. Shorn of any claim to absolutism, confessional organizations today seek and generally find constructive roles, or they examine reasons for separate existence even as they pursue their steadily expanding and deepening relations with other Christian world communions. Even in their totality, the Christian world communions do not represent all branches of Christianity. Two groups of churches in particular exist outside a worldwide confessional framework: the independent or indigenous churches, especially in Africa, and the united and uniting churches (q.v.), which came into existence from the 1920s onward.

Since 1957 the conference of secretaries of world confessional families has met annually, normally in Geneva. (No meetings were held in 1960, 1961 and 1975.) It has discussed various concerns, like Corpus Confessionum, relationship with the Roman Catholic Church (q.v.), the place and task of confessional families in the ecumenical movement, national loyalties: a help or hindrance to world fellowship, bilateral dialogues (q.v.), the relationships between Bible societies (q.v.) and the CWCs, religious liberty and human rights (q.v.), the CWCs' commitment to the future of the ecumenical movement. Since 1968 the Secretariat for Promoting Christian Unity (q.v.) has been regularly represented at the conference. It has therefore been unnecessary to keep the question of the relationship between the CWC conference and the Roman Catholic Church on subsequent agendas. The fact that an important network of interconfessional conversations has developed in recent years, in which the Roman Catholic Church is involved at the world level, reveals how seriously the Roman Catholic Church is taking the role of the various CWCs. In this field too the WCC and the CWCs complement each other on the ecumenical scene.

Confessions in Dialogue, in its third, revised and enlarged edition published by the WCC in 1975, contains accounts of various bilateral, international, regional and national dialogues between CWCs that have taken place from 1959 to 1974. The volume discusses the methods and procedures of the consultations, presents the important subjects of discussion—gospel, Scripture and tradition, creeds and confessions, eucharist and intercommunion, ministry, unity and mission, worship (qq.v.)—and concentrates on the problems and possibilities of bilateral conversations, shifts in self-understanding, wider relationships, a permanent forum and the challenge of the bilaterals to churches and Christian World Communions. After the publication of *Confessions in Dialogue* three forum meetings on bilateral conversations were held, with the participation of representatives of the world confessional bodies engaged in bilateral dialogues and members of the Faith and Order (q.v.) secretariat. These were the first steps toward integrating the bilateral and multilateral levels of ecumenical dialogue. The first forum was held in Bossey in 1978 on the theme "Concepts of Unity"; the second met in Geneva in 1979 on the theme "Joint Statements of Consensus"; the third took place in Glion in 1980 on the theme "Reception".

Besides the Eastern Orthodox churches, the Oriental Orthodox churches, the Anglican Church, Baptist churches, Christian Church (Disciples of Christ), Lutheran churches, Mennonites, Methodist Church, Old Catholic churches, Pentecostal churches, Presbyterian and Reformed churches, Religious Society of Friends and United churches, a representative of the Salvation Army (qq.v.), the General Conference of Seventh-Day Adventists and the Reformed Ecumenical Synod participate in the discussions of the conference of secretaries of Christian World Communions. *See also* MULTILATERAL DIALOGUES.

CHRISTOLOGY *see* JESUS CHRIST

CHURCH *see* ECCLESIOLOGY

CHURCH AND STATE. The complex relationship between church and state has been a significant part of human history from the 1st century to the present day. Christianity has been from the beginning a missionary and, hence, a world-transforming movement. Because of its proclamation of a coming new order, it has been essentially a dynamic force in society and, consequently, has never been at peace with the world around it. This has led to continuous tension and conflict. The state is concerned with temporal life as an end in itself; the church is concerned with temporal life as a means to spiritual ends.

There is an increasing need in the ecumenical movement to examine afresh the whole field of church-state relations. For many years, the question has not been a focus of attention. "Church, community and state" was extensively discussed at the World Conference of the Life and Work (q.v.) movement in Oxford (1937). At that time the churches faced the threat of totalitarian regimes. Common reflection on the witness of the church in such societies was therefore urgently called for. The Oxford conference provided the guidance many had hoped for. The report had an enormous influence even in the period after the Second World War.

At a conference at the Ecumenical Institute of Bossey (q.v.), in 1976, organized by Faith and Order (q.v.), it was repeatedly emphasized that attention should not concentrate too exclusively on the two concepts: "Church" and "State". This could easily lead to too narrow a discussion. It is much better to discuss "Church, State and Society" or "Church, People and State". The church's first question should not be about its due rights in the political system. It should primarily be concerned with the question of how, as a Christian community, it can serve the wider community. (*Church and State: Opening a New Ecumenical Discussion.* Faith and Order Paper, no. 85). Worldwide trends in church-state relations continue to be toward separation of the two authority structures. As in the past, this has been for a variety of reasons, but predominantly in order to keep the church out of the affairs of the state. In this respect the trend has been increasingly toward unfriendly separation. Today even the Western countries are faced with the question of religious pluralism (q.v.). The state is called upon to become the instrument and expression of a national community and a national ethos in which many religions and ideologies are free to enter into dialogue with one another for the common good. The relation of Christian ecumenism to this larger ecumenism has yet to be worked out.

CHURCH-BASED COMMUNITIES. Through efforts at pastoral renewal church-based communities sprang up in Latin America in the 1950s and then spread to all continents. One can speak of a truly ecumenical-ecclesiastical renewal under the influence of the Holy Spirit (q.v.). Several reasons can be given for the establishment of church-based communities: the bureaucracy and the clericalization of churches, critique of their hierarchies and an advocacy of democratization of church life, the reading together of the Bible (q.v.) without interference of the magisterium or some particular theology, and the consciousness of the necessity of political engagement of the Christian community. The Latin American Conference of Bishops in Medellin in 1968 and in Puebla in 1979 furthered the growth and impact of church-based communities.

The Bible is always read face-to-face with the actual life of the people. This is the Bible/life method, a procedure that obviates spiritualizing fundamentalism. It sets the Scriptures in the real living conditions of the people: a struggle for survival and social change. The Bible leads to vital commitment, and vital commitment to a better understanding of the Bible. As in the New Testament the term "laity" (q.v.) does not exist, all people are competent and have gifts to interpret the gospel, are subject of their own history, and called to be responsible members of the Christian community and society. Church-based communities are particularly numerous in Brazil, Bolivia and Chile, as well as in Central America and Mexico. They are further found in several countries in Africa, Asia, Western and even Eastern Europe (Hungary and Poland) as well as in the USA and Canada.

The ecumenical significance of church-based communities lies in the fact that they re-create the church on the pattern of the early Christian community and are not a reproduction of the prevailing type of church. They stress not the denominational characteristics but rather the common Christian elements of the centrality of a faith in Jesus Christ (q.v.), the Scriptures, baptism (q.v.), the Lord's supper (q.v.), witness, charity, etc. They exist, moreover, at the church-based level and not in the upper reaches of the hierarchy and the theologians. As simple believers, especially when they are poor, they are freer and have a greater interest in ecumenical dialogue. Although many Protestants and Roman Catholics (q.v.) feel at home in this style of grass-roots Christianity, other groups of Christians resist and oppose the church-based communities because of their biblical fundamentalism and political conservatism.

CHURCH OF ENGLAND *see* ANGLICAN CHURCH

CHURCH WORLD SERVICE (CWS). This body, a relief, rehabilitation and resettlement agency of the American Protestant and Orthodox churches, was founded in 1946 by the Federal Council of Churches (q.v.), the Foreign Missions Conference and the American Committee of the WCC (q.v.). When the National Council of Churches (q.v.) was formed in 1950, CWS became a department, and in 1965 joined the Council's Division of Foreign Missions to form the Division of Overseas Ministries. During its separate existence, CWS received cash contributions of almost US $20 million directly and through Protestant and Orthodox denominations, and contributions and relief supplies valued at US $36,505,000. It disbursed these in relief activities in Europe and Asia, and also in its program for the resettlement of 51,000 Protestant and Eastern Orthodox displaced persons in the USA. It further pioneered in the development of long-range programs designed to help people to help themselves. Whenever possible, it works through national Christian councils in host countries and in close cooperation with the WCC Commission of Inter-Church Aid, Refugee and World Service.

COCU *see* CONSULTATION ON CHURCH UNION

COLLEGIALITY. The term is derived from the Latin word "collegium", which indicates a group of persons who gather together with a common purpose. In Acts 8:1 the apostles are described as a group or community with seat in Jerusalem; through their proclamation of the gospel various churches came into being. At the end of the 2nd century a synodal praxis was instituted through which the bishops decided on important matters. From the 11th century onward until the Second Vatican Council (q.v.) the college of cardinals, with the pope as its head, replaced the college of bishops. From the 17th century onward the Roman curia exercised a decisive role in the leadership of the Roman Catholic Church (q.v.). In the Dogmatic Constitution on the Church (*Lumen Gentium*) of Vatican II the notion of the hierarchy as collegial opens a new era in Roman Catholic conceptions of church order. Now once again, as in the patristic period, it is to be understood that the entire episcopacy (q.v.), under the presidency of the bishop of Rome, shares in the leadership of the entire church. This is a striking advance beyond the extremes of traditional "ultramontanism" on the one hand, and traditional "conciliarism" on the other. No one any longer has to choose between the primacy of the Petrine office and the authority of the episcopal "college".

This implies important developments in the responsibility and effectiveness of episcopal conferences and of local ordinaries, without any corresponding loss of unity among the bishops or in their communion with the head of the college. The bishops collectively are seen to constitute a "stable body" or "college" that is collectively responsible for the ruling of the universal Christian community. The Latin American conference of bishops (CELAM) meeting in Medellin (1868) and in Puebla (1979) is an example of the revival of former regional councils. In the East the synodal structure of the church through which the bishops exercise their authority has remained a pillar of the Orthodox conception of the church. In Anglicanism (q.v.), the Lambeth conferences, which take place every ten years, have preserved the element of collegiality. Within the churches of the Reformation, congregationalism (q.v.) has particularly emphasized the dimension of collegiality in church affairs. The question still remains whether the principle of collegiality can bear fruit for the communion of the churches involved in the ecumenical movement, whether the pope can exercise a ministry acceptable to other churches, and how collegiality relating to conciliarity (q.v.) can lead to a future truly ecumenical council. *See also* CONCILIARITY; EPISCO-PACY.

COMMITTEE ON SOCIETY, DEVELOPMENT AND PEACE *see* SODEPAX

COMMUNICATION. The Reformation (q.v.) profited successfully from Johannes Gutenberg's discovery of the printing press, and Martin Luther himself was a master in promoting publicity. Pope Pius XII (1939–1958) was one of the first church leaders of the 20th century to speak positively about the potential value of the mass media for the church. Although recognizing the ambiguities of values of the secular press, he emphasized that they should be used to propagate Christian teaching. The first council of a church to address communication as an area of Christian concern was Vatican II (q.v.) in its Decree on the Instruments of Social Communication (*Inter Mirifica*). It recommended that national offices should be set up everywhere for "affairs of press, motion pictures, radio and television". Such offices would have "the special obligation of helping the faithful to form a true conscience about the use of these media and of fostering and co-ordinating Catholic activities directed to this end". Following the reorganization of the Roman curia in 1989, the new Pontifical Council for Social Communication became responsible for the use of all media.

Concentrating on the theme of mass communication the first WCC assembly (qq.v.) in Amsterdam in 1948 enunciated that "the right to determine faith and creed (qq.v.) becomes meaningful when man has the opportunity of access to information . . . This right requires freedom from arbitrary limitation of religious expression in all means of communication, including speech, press, radio, motion pictures and art". The assembly urged that further research in the realm of media should be undertaken. The Uppsala assembly in 1968 issued a major statement on "The Church and the Media of Mass Communication", being well aware that "the world of the media of mass communication is so new and often so bewildering to the churches that we are only starting to probe its significance, possibilities, perversions and use for good''. Nevertheless, the statement was too optimistic in outlook, reflecting the theological mood of the 1960s in its affirmation of the presence of God in the secular world of the media, which can help to shape a new, universal human society. The pastoral instruction *Communio et progressio* of Pope Paul VI (q.v.), issued in 1971, struck a similar optimistic note. It stressed the need for a more affirmative attitude to the media. The pope saw modern developments as making it possible to multiply contacts within human society and to deepen social consciousness, which would contribute to the growth of human unity. The issue ''Communicating Credibly'' of the Vancouver assembly, raising questions about the pastoral, evangelical and prophetic functions of the churches in relation to the media, was not a strong and helpful document. Theology has not yet corrected its traditional considerations of communication. Its systematic theological examination has only started recently. The demands for a New World Information and Communication Order, whereby people would affirm their own values, assert their own cultures and determine their own priorities, is still largely ignored.

Many churches in many countries run a professional communication office. The World Association for Christian Communication (WACC) (q.v.), with headquarters in London, continues to develop and to cooperate with other organizations involved in Christian communication. The majority of its members that support the world association are deeply rooted in the ecumenical movement as it has developed in the Protestant and Orthodox (qq.v.) churches. In 1975 the Agency for Christian Literature Development, a program of the WCC Commission on World Mission and Evangelism, was merged with the WACC. UNDA is an international Roman Catholic association with headquarters in Brussels. Cooperation between the WACC and UNDA is particularly close in Latin America. The Center for the Study of Communication and Culture in London is devoted to research in the field of international communication.

The WCC Department of Communication has been concerned from its very beginning in 1948 with problems of ecumenical communication and different styles of work. The Information Department Committee in its first report in 1955 said that ecumenical information must not be thought of as "an expensive sideshow in which we commit ourselves to the distasteful work of popularizing what cannot be popularized". Its Ecumenical Press Service (1933 to 1947, the International Christian Press Information Service), which is published weekly by the WCC, the World Student Christian Federation, the World Association of YMCAs and the World YWCA (qq.v.), has become less a house organ and more a press service, less North Atlantic, and less interested in "ecumenical greats".

CONCILIARITY. This concept is contained in the doctrine that an ecumenical council is the highest authority in the church and limits the ultimate authority of the pope. Conciliarism and the theory of conciliarity appeared during the time of the schism in the Roman Catholic Church (q.v.) during the Middle Ages, when two popes laid claim to the legitimate exercise of the papacy. The council of Constance (1415) declared in its decree *Haec Sancta* that "all persons of whatever rank or dignity, even a pope, are bound to obey [a general council] in matters relating to faith and the end of the schism". From the time of the council of Florence (1438–39), however, this conciliar doctrine was greatly opposed and later came to symbolize the so-called Gallicanism, which was contested by the First Vatican Council (q.v.) in 1870.

The Second Vatican Council has taken up the matter of conciliarity in the context of understanding the church as the people of God and the collegiality of the bishops. The WCC assembly (qq.v.) in Uppsala in 1968 suggested that its member churches should "work for the time when a genuinely universal council may once more speak for all Christians and lead the way into the future". The meeting of the Commission on Faith and Order (q.v.) in Louvain in 1971 stated: "The Church imperatively needs conciliar forms if it wishes to maintain and constantly renew the universal communion. The word 'conciliarity' is used to denote the communion in which the different local churches are joined

. . . Examples of conciliarity are found in various forms throughout the entire history of the church''. A consultation of Faith and Order in Salamanca in 1973 declared: ''The one church is to be envisioned as a conciliar fellowship of local churches which are themselves truly united. In this conciliar fellowship, each local church possesses, in communion with others, the fullness of catholicity (q.v.), witnesses to the same apostolic faith, and, therefore, recognizes the others as belonging to the same church of Christ and guided by the same Spirit''. The WCC assembly in Nairobi in 1975 continued to say: ''True conciliar fellowship presupposes the unity of the Church . . . The source of the Church's unity, as of her faith and her joy, is the meeting of the Apostles with the risen Christ who bears the marks of the cross, and the continued encounter with the disciples today with his living presence in the midst of the eucharistic fellowship. He brings its members into the communion of the Holy Spirit, and makes them children of the Father''. This theme is pursued in the recent work of Faith and Order. *See also* COLLEGIAL-ITY.

CONFERENCE OF EUROPEAN CHURCHES (CEC). In 1939 Europe once again became the battlefield of the world. Contrary to the experience in the 1914–1918 war, however, in the Second World War the fellowship of Christians never ceased, and the WCC in process of formation played no small role in maintaining contacts. The story of the church struggles in Europe, of the various church renewal movements that sprang from them, and the remarkable saga of interchurch aid in postwar Europe, belong to the general ecumenical history. The largest operation of the WCC, the Division of Inter-Church Aid and Service to Refugees, worked almost exclusively for Europe until 1955.

The task of the Conference of European Churches in trying to comprehend in one overall pattern the many differences, geographical, cultural, linguistic and ecclesiastical, is enormous. That task has become still more complicated because of the political and socioeconomic differences between Western and Eastern Europe. A first unofficial conference of European churches was held in Liselung, Denmark, in 1957. Because the initiative came mainly from Reformed and United churches, many large Lutheran (qq.v.) churches were cautious about committing themselves. Also the Anglican and Orthodox (qq.v.) were not yet represented, except by a delegate of the Ecumenical Patriarchate. At a following meeting in Nyborg, Denmark, in 1959, a number of the larger Lutheran, Anglican and Orthodox churches were represented. For the participants of the small Protestant minority churches in the USSR, Poland, Czechoslovakia, Hungary, Yugoslavia and Greece, as well as for the Latin countries of Europe, the first two gatherings were of great importance.

Organizationally things remained open, but the CEC had become a fact. The series of "Nyborgs" in the now famous hotel at Nyborgstrand continued: 1960, 1962, 1964, 1967, 1971. The last three assemblies were held at Engelberg, 1974, in Crete, 1979, and in Prague, 1992. At the meeting in 1971, all countries in Europe were represented with the single exception of Albania. Today over 120 churches are members of the European Conference of Churches. Its offices are located at the Ecumenical Center in Geneva. The main concerns are ecclesiological questions bearing on church unity, peace questions in Europe, human rights (qq.v.) in the area of Helsinki signatory states, interchurch aid in Europe, the churches and the Muslim communities in Europe, European responsibility in the divisions and tensions of the contemporary international situation and European responsibility toward the developing nations.

CONFESSIONS OF FAITH *see* CREEDS

CONFESSING CHURCH *see* GERMAN CONFESSING CHURCH

CONFIRMATION. The baptism (q.v.) of infants can be justified only if baptism and confirmation are looked upon as together making up the one act of Christian initiation, even though they are separated in time by several years. Baptism in infancy, if it is not followed at the age of discretion by a personal confession of faith (q.v.), is not Christian initiation in the New Testament sense; a good work has been begun but it has not been completed. In the Eastern tradition baptism and confirmation (chrismation) are administered in immediate succession even when the recipient is an infant. The initiation is then complete. The person baptized is at once admitted to the eucharist (q.v.) without further ceremony. Here the question must be asked whether children are given sufficient opportunity of making for themselves the confession of faith made on behalf of their baptism.

In the Western tradition, baptism and the laying on of hands (confirmation) were separated at quite an early date. Whereas baptism could be performed by the priest, the laying on of hands was reserved for the bishop. This meant that usually some time elapsed between baptism and confirmation. Where the person was an infant, the time interval could be of several years. Confirmation thus gradually became independent of baptism although the close connection between the two was never completely forgotten. Confirmation came to mean strengthening by the gift of the Holy Spirit (q.v.). Admission to eucharistic fellowship could take place either before or after confirmation. All Western churches face the problem of refusing to admit children to the eucharist even though they have been baptized. The Western practice of initiation is to be found particularly in the Roman Catholic Church (q.v.). Recently this church has been more willing to admit confirmation by a priest in certain special cases, and to emphasize, especially in the case of adults, the unity of the process of initiation.

Western practice prompts the question whether the division of initiation into two related yet distinct sacramental acts does not prejudice the unique once-for-all character of baptism. The churches of the Reformation (q.v.) sought to reassert the sufficiency of baptism. Since they found no basis in Scripture for confirmation as a sacramental act, it was abandoned. Other reasons, however, led the churches of the Reformation to adopt an act similar to the sacramental act of confirmation. Baptized children are not admitted to the eucharist until they are able to make for themselves the profession of faith made for them at baptism. Confirmation furnishes the occasion for this act: a service of worship is held in which baptism is recalled and the persons previously baptized make a public confession of faith and are consecrated for service. From then on they are admitted to the eucharist. This tradition shares the difficulty common to all the Western traditions. But the practice of this kind of confirmation presents a special problem. Confirmation normally takes place when children reach a given age. This frequently turns confirmation into a social formality in practice. Many Protestant churches have consequently begun to change their practice in this matter, some even going so far as to drop insistence on confirmation as an essential condition for the admission to the eucharist.

In Anglicanism (q.v.) the practice of episcopal confirmation was retained. It has always involved both the personal ratification by the candidate of the promises made on his or her behalf at baptism, and the laying on of hands with prayer for the strengthening of the gift of the Holy Spirit. It is regarded as the way of entrance into the communicant status. The churches of the Baptist (q.v.) tradition administer baptism only to those who make profession of faith. They have no rite of chrismation or confirmation, but in some churches there is a laying on of hands upon those who have been baptized. In all cases those who have been baptized are admitted at once to the eucharist. Often the children of baptized parents are dedicated at a special service of worship (q.v.).

After having taken up a special study within Faith and Order (q.v.) on the admission of children to the eucharist, the Vancouver assembly (1983) outlined the following: " 'Do not hinder the children', says Jesus. Everything we do in the name of Jesus Christ needs to be seen in the light of this demand". The assembly recommended "to review church structures, worship and related activities in order to give room for the participation of children". *See also* BAPTISM.

CONGAR, YVES MARIE-JOSEPH (1904–). Congar is one of the most outstanding Roman Catholic (q.v.) ecumenical theologians. He entered the Dominican order in 1930 and became professor of ecclesiology in Le Saulchoir, 1931–1954. He also taught at Strasbourg, 1955–1968, and afterward again in Le Saulchoir. After being forbidden to teach and to have contacts with Protestants in 1954, Pope John XXIII rehabilitated Congar by placing him on the preparatory commission for Vatican II (q.v.), which drafted various documents. His book *Principes d'un oecuménisme catholique* (Paris, 1937) was the first volume in an impressive series "Unam Sanctam", which Congar founded. In his book *Lay People in the Church* he rendered a precious service in outlining a theology of the laity (q.v.). His further concerns were Jesus Christ (q.v.), Mary, the local church, the relation of the church to the world, the Eastern Orthodox churches, collegiality and the papacy (qq.v.), all in an ecumenical context. He criticized his church for not incorporating valid principles of the Reformation (q.v.) in its theology and insisted that Orthodoxy (q.v.) has particular insights in the mystery of the church, the sacraments (q.v.) and monasticism, which are complementary to the Western tradition. Although afflicted already in the mid-1930s by a chronic and painful neurological disease, Congar has been indefatigable his entire life.

CONGREGATIONALISM. Congregationalism was born when, in 1582, the English parliament considered it treason to worship apart from the Church of England. Congregationalists were called "Separatists", "Non-conformists" and "Puritans". The 16th-century leader in separatism, Robert Browne, described the qualities of the congregationalists as follows: 1) they are a company of true believers who confess Christ alone as Savior and Lord; 2) authority in the church rests solely in Christ as the head; 3) teachings from the Bible as the Scriptures are perspicacious; 4) the church is to be self-disciplining with pastors, elders, deacons and members keeping watch over the conduct of the church; 5) all congregational churches are interdependent and should seek fellowship for mutual benefit.

The spread of congregationalism to many parts of the world was the result of the evangelical awakening during the second half of the 18th century. The International Congregational Council first met in London in 1891, obtained its constitution in 1948, and united with the World Presbyterian

Alliance to form the World Alliance of Reformed Churches (q.v.) in 1970. Congregationalism maintains its lively heritage and historical diversity—from independent churches and interdependent fellowship to a more presbyterian form with denominational authority, from no creeds (q.v.) to Westminster and Savoy, from fellowshipping in conciliar movements to no ecumenical attachments. Because of their inherent Catholicity (q.v.) many Congregationalists, however, have been ecumenically inclined. Congregationalism continues as a pluralistic movement, sometimes proud and sometimes frustrated by that fact. In 1984 the United Church of Christ listed 6,419 churches with some 1,694,000 members. Smaller Congregational churches, not members of the WCC (q.v.), are the National Association of Congregational Christian Churches and the Conservative Congregational Christian Conference.

CONSCIENTIOUS OBJECTION *see* PACIFISM

CONSULTATION ON CHURCH UNION (COCU). COCU is a venture in reconciliation by nine American churches exploring the formation of a united church. The original impetus for this formation came from a sermon, "A Proposal Toward the Reunion of Christ's Church", delivered by Eugene Carson Blake (q.v.), then stated clerk of the United Presbyterian Church in the USA, in Grace (Episcopal) Cathedral, San Francisco, on 4 December 1960, the eve of the fifth triennial assembly of the National Council of Churches (q.v.). Blake proposed that his own church enter discussions with the Methodist Church (q.v.), the Episcopal Church and the United Church of Christ in view of uniting in a church "truly catholic, truly evangelical, and truly reformed". His proposal envisaged a union of churches of widely different theological and historical traditions; in contrast, previous church unions in the United States involved churches of the same confessional families.

By the late 1960s COCU had grown to include nine US communions, among them the African Methodist Episcopal Church (1965), the (Southern) Presbyterian Church in the U.S., the African Methodist Episcopal Zion Church (1966) and the Christian Methodist Episcopal Church (1967). During its first five years, COCU was primarily concerned with theological issues, which were resolved, after long discussions, with widely accepted consensus. Subsequent plenaries focused on practical problems in structuring the proposed united church. A definitive statement on covenanting was agreed upon by the 17th plenary of COCU in 1988. This proposal is being voted upon by the member churches for possible implementation in the mid-1990s. The intention of covenanting is to enable organic unity without organizational merger and while providing for considerable diversity in retaining the ethos of each community.

CONTEXTUALIZATION *see* GOSPEL AND CULTURE

CONVERSION. In the Old Testament the call to be converted was repeatedly sounded by the prophets. It was a call to return to the Lord, and to the obligations of his covenant. In the New Testament the call to be turned to Jesus Christ (q.v.) signified a personal relation to him, a visible community and a new pattern of behavior. The same three elements are to be seen in the early beginnings of apostolic preaching. The relation of the first to the other two requirements is a complex one. From the very beginning it has been a source of controversy. There was no agreement on whether the Gentile converts were to be totally incorporated in Judaic Christianity, being circumcised like Jewish proselytes. The decision not to do this was a radical break with precedent; converts were not to be mere proselytes. Conversion was a new work of Holy Spirit (q.v.), establishing new patterns of life (Acts 11:15–18). The Bible knows of no conversion that is an internal emotional experience apart from a turning round to behave in a different way. But conversion does not mean the imposition of a new law—on the contrary, the gift of the Holy Spirit is freedom from law to serve God as he directs. Conversion is urgent, yet, in calling others to conversion, Christians must learn to ''move into the space of others'' and ''recover the delicacy of touch'' of God's dealing with humankind.

There is no concept of conversion in the Bible so clearly

defined as to lend itself to doctrinal use, and there is no past or present theology of conversion that is generally accepted. Many Christians will agree that conversion is primarily linked with the kingdom of God rather than with entry into a church or mere individual decision. Conversion always implies a reorientation to God and to fellow human beings at the same time. This is as true for the missionary period of previous centuries as for the ecumenical movement in this century. The ecumenical discussion, however, indirectly exposed Western individualistic anthropology, deeply connected with the traditional concept of conversion—a personal acceptance of faith by each human being—and the various contents, meanings and consequences of conversion. Conservative evangelicals who often claim to be the champions engaged in Christian mission leading to conversion should be surprised to hear that the WCC (q.v.) has often dealt with the issue of conversion. Whole numbers of the *Ecumenical Review* (July 1967 and October 1992) and of the *International Review of Mission* (July 1983) were devoted to the topic.

The first preparatory volume published for the world conference on Church and Society in Geneva in 1966, *Christian Social Ethics in a Changing World,* includes a long contribution by Emilio Castro (q.v.) entitled "Conversion and Social Transformation". In preparation for the Uppsala assembly (1968), Paul Löffler wrote a study document *Conversion to God and Service to Man.* The WCC's Commission on World Mission and Evangelism in Bangkok in 1973 devoted a subsection to "On Conversion and Cultural Change". For the first time it was stated: "Conversion as a phenomenon is not restricted to the Christian community; it finds its place in other religions as well as in certain political and ideological communities". Section I of the Nairobi assembly (1975), "Confessing Christ Today", rejected various forms of cheap and doubtful conversion. The last paragraph in the section on conversion, *Mission and Evangelism: An Ecumenical Affirmation* (1982), said: "The experience of conversion gives meaning to people in all stages of life, endurance to resist oppression, and assurance that even death has no final power over human life because God in

Christ has already taken our life with him, a life that is 'hidden with Christ in God' '' (Col. 3:3).

The various traditional experiences, formulations and outlooks of conversion can be supplemented and combined in the ecumenical movement and consequently become enlarged and enriched in unexpectedly new ways. The awareness of belonging to God's kingdom makes all the difference. The maturity of the World Council of Churches depends on its ability to stress the necessary inter-relationship between various conversion traditions— Orthodox, Roman Catholic, Protestant, Free Church, Evangelical, Pentecostal charismatic (qq.v.) and others. The time should be ripe to move beyond ecumenical discussions of conversion to a greater emphasis on living out together our individual and collective conversions, so that the creative tension between the renewal of human beings and the renewal of structures of society may illuminate God's own unswerving design of salvation (q.v.).

This implies that conversion is still more than the impact of the gospel on individual human beings, convincing their reasoning, warming their emotions and causing their will to act with decision. We would still not have a different world overnight. This further implies that a pooling of ecclesiastical and confessional resources pertinent to conversion is still not sufficient. All Christian traditions do not suffice to proclaim fully salvation to the world. It also implies that the exchange of conversions between Christians and people of other living faiths cannot render God's love for the whole of humanity totally transparent. The opening of individual hearts to God, the obedient mission and ministry (qq.v.) of the churches and the liberating search for a pluralistic theology of faiths are but adumbrations of the one God who is the author and completer of all salvation (q.v.). *See also* PROSELYTISM; RENEWAL.

COUNCIL OF CHURCHES FOR BRITAIN AND IRELAND. Formerly known as the British Council of Churches, this council was founded in 1942, amalgamating the Council on the Christian Faith and the Common Life (1937), the Commission for International Friendship and Social Responsibility (1937) and the British section of the World Conference on Faith and Order. The purposes of the Council are the advancement of the Christian religion, the relief of poverty (q.v.) and the promotion of education and any other purposes that are charitable according to the law of England and Wales. It assists the growth of ecumenical consciousness in the members of all churches. It meets twice annually in an assembly (the policy-making body) whose members include representatives of the member churches, associate members and bodies in association. The Council's work is done through a wide variety of committees, consultations, conferences and working parties. The Council is related to over 700 local councils of churches (q.v.).

COUNCILS OF CHURCHES, LOCAL, NATIONAL, RE-GIONAL. Councils of churches are important and widespread expressions of the ecumenical movement. They vary greatly in size, program and impact. The first local councils of churches, bringing churches officially into a common framework for joint action and the eventual achievement of full unity (q.v.), sprang up in Britain in 1918 and 1919. In 1946 there were 126 local councils in this country in association with the British Council of Churches. The 1960s saw a new boost in local ecumenical activities. More and more countries were experimenting with local councils of churches, the Netherlands and the USA perhaps preeminent. The goal of the pilgrimage remains that "all in each place who confess Christ as Lord and Savior are brought into one fully committed fellowship" (New Delhi Assembly), or as refined in the 1975 Nairobi assembly: "The one church is to be envisioned as a conciliar fellowship of local churches which are themselves truly united".

Early national councils of churches (NCCs) have been the Protestant Federation of France (1905) and the Federal Council of the Churches of Christ in America (1908) (q.v.). Many national councils around the world were rooted in the efforts begun between 1900 and 1930 to strengthen the identity and independence of missionary-founded churches. The International Missionary Council (q.v.) greatly supported this development. It was also important in providing the newly formed councils with access to international ecumenical structures. The number of national councils has grown steadily from only two in 1910 to twenty-three in 1928 and at least thirty by 1948. Today there are some ninety national councils, including almost twenty-five in Africa, more than fifteen in Asia, ten in the Caribbean and Central America, almost twenty in Europe, two in North America, four in Latin America and eight in the Pacific.

The WCC assembly (qq.v.) in Evanston in 1954 made provision for a more formal working relationship of national Christian councils with the World Council by creating a category "associated councils". The difference between "associated councils" and "affiliated councils" is that associated councils are formally related to the WCC as a whole. They are represented by fraternal delegates at WCC central committee meetings and assemblies. "Affiliated councils" are legally members of the Conference on World Mission and Evangelism and support the work of the WCC Commission on World Mission and Evangelism. Some of these councils do not wish to become directly associated with the WCC because of certain conservative-evangelical reasons. A third category of 35 Christian councils are in a working relationship, though not in association, with the WCC. These councils frequently function as a channel of communication and cooperation with the WCC Commission on Inter-Church Aid, Refugee and World Service and the Commission on World Mission and Evangelism.

Today there are 35 associated councils. They have made a significant contribution to the ecumenical movement. They have served as vital channels for interpretation, support, and implementation of the work of the World Council of Churches. Some councils have reproduced in their own structures some parts of the organizational pattern of the WCC. This development not only indicates the growing commitment of national councils to the life and work of the ecumenical movement; it has meant a progressive involvement on their part in the work of the WCC itself and in ecumenical activities in their own areas.

The Montreal meeting of the Faith and Order Commission (1963) made "the ecclesiological significance of councils of churches'' an important item on its agenda. A world consultation on Christian councils was held in Geneva in 1971. The report recommends that councils must think of themselves as ''temporary'' servants of the movement toward visible unity. The participants affirmed that unity, renewal and mission are inseparable parts of a council's agenda. Churches in a council should not hesitate to examine questions of faith and order (q.v.) alongside their efforts to render cooperative service. The report asserts that ''even now, when churches share in some common life, and witness together, a new ecclesiastical reality appears''. This ecclesiastical reality, however, inheres not in the councils themselves but in the bonds of fellowship that binds member churches. The report calls further on councils to give greater attention to ''spiritual ecumenism'', especially through the search for sharing eucharistic (q.v.) communion; to promote development (q.v.), social justice (q.v.) and racial understanding; to enlarge their fellowship (especially by encouraging Roman Catholic participation) and to reach out in dialogue (q.v.) and cooperation with other faiths and radical movements; to move toward financial self-support; to improve communications, including those with the WCC; and to pioneer in controversial areas as both servant and leader of the churches.

Two other international consultations of NCCs took place in Geneva in 1986 and in Hong Kong in 1993. At the last meeting it was stressed that it would be a serious mistake to think of councils simply as associations founded on mutual goodwill, on the recognition of the need for organization or even on a feeling akin to that which creates all sorts of coalitions in our society with a view to greater efficiency. The members of councils of churches must see the councils as a crucible in which God prepares in one place or another the visible and canonical communion of all those communities that are faithful to his Son Jesus Christ (q.v.).

Since 1972 the Joint Working Group (JWG) between the Roman Catholic Church (qq.v.) and the World Council of Churches has on several occasions given attention to the issue of councils. One of the results of this collaboration was the April 1972 issue of *One in Christ,* in which a series of papers and documents dealing with councils of churches was published. In 1975 the Secretariat for Promoting Christian Unity (q.v.) published *Ecumenical Collaboration at the Regional, National and Local Levels*. Councils, this document stressed, are not churches, nor the beginning of a new church. Their significance derives from the churches that take part in them, but they are, nonetheless, "very important instruments of ecumenical collaboration, both for expressing the unity existing already among the churches and also advancing towards a greater unity and a more effective Christian witness". The pamphlet makes clear the Roman Catholic position that councils do not have responsibility for church union negotiations, but it does note that they are in a position to give important material help to union conversations and can, upon request, give consultative and organizational assistance.

By the time the world consultation on Christian councils took place in 1971, ten national councils had within them full Roman Catholic membership. Catholics now belong to nearly half of the 90-plus NCCs around the world, and to three of the seven regional councils. It is up to the Catholic bishops conferences in a country to decide whether or not to join an NCC. But participants are assured that the Vatican sees such membership as "an important opportunity for cooperation and witness"; and a ten-member official delegation was present at the Hong Kong meeting in 1993. The Secretariat for Promoting Christian Unity is in touch with councils, especially those that have Roman Catholic membership, by means of correspondence and staff visits. A consultation was held in 1982 between the Secretariat for Promoting Christian Unity (through the Joint Working Group) and the WCC. The findings of this consultation were reported to the Vancouver assembly in 1982 through the JWG.

What has been said about national councils of churches applies to a considerable extent to the regional associations of churches. They are the All Africa Conference of Churches, the Caribbean Conference of Churches, the Christian Conference of Asia, the Conference of European Churches, the Latin American Council of Churches, the Middle East

Council of Churches and the Pacific Conference of Churches (qq.v.). In this dictionary an entry is made for each individual regional council or conference. Also the Federal Council of the Churches of Christ in America, the National Council of the Churches of Christ in the USA and the Council of Churches for Britain and Ireland (qq.v.) have separate entries.

Recently it has been recommended that churches, coming together in national or regional councils, should move from *cooperation with* one another to *commitment to* one another. This is a significant shift in emphasis. Commitment to one another in the search for the unity Christ prayed for requires that churches accept for themselves the goal of reaching that unity, that they pursue it and in so doing help, stimulate and challenge one another. It implies therefore that the goal of unity is indeed at the very heart of the raison d'être of the council to which the churches have chosen to belong. It has other consequences as well. The council is no longer there to do things on behalf of the churches, but as the place where churches do things together, as an exercise in and a foretaste of the unity to come. Thus cooperation requires a new quality. Programs of the council become the joint responsibility of the churches working together instead of being run by the council as a body distinct from the churches.

COUTURIER, PAUL-IRÉNÉE (1881–1953). Couturier was a priest of the archdiocese of Lyons. Since 1920 he was concerned with the condition of Russian emigrants to France, and in 1932 became familiar in Amay-sur-Meuse (Chevetogne, Belgium) with Roman Catholic-Anglican efforts to work for Christian unity (q.v.). He saw the dilemma that the Octave of Prayer for Unity, 18–25 January, as then observed, created for non-Roman Christians. He sought a formula of prayer (q.v.) in which all might join without any wounding of denominational loyalties, and he found it in the Roman Missal. With the encouragement of the archbishop of Lyons, he advocated the Octave of Prayer on the inclusive basis that "our Lord would grant to His Church on earth that peace and unity which were in His mind and purpose when, on the evening of His Passion, He prayed that all might be one". The success of this was immediate; it was a basis on which all could unite, Protestants, Orthodox, Anglicans and Roman Catholics (qq.v.). His main motive was the mutual sharing in the various spiritual riches. His efforts were continued by the Association interconfessionelle Unité Chrétienne. *See also* WEEK OF PRAYER FOR CHRISTIAN UNITY.

COVENANT, THEOLOGY OF. The concept of the covenant relationship between God and Israel is fundamental to the theology of the Old Testament. It is also basic for the theological reflection in the New Testament. Jesus Christ (q.v.) adopted the idea of the covenant and fulfilled it, and the NT writers both used it and developed it. The covenant with Israel is based on God's gracious and sovereign will; only his free decision constituted Israel as the people of God, not to be made undone by the apostasy and disobedience of Israel. The prophets pictured a different and better covenant in all kinds of symbols: a more consummated marriage (Hos. 2:22); as realized in a more faithful servant of a higher kind (Isa. 42:18ff; 52:13ff); a new covenant written on the heart (Jer. 31; Ezek. 36–7). This prophetic hope is of great importance to the Christian interpretation of the covenant. For St. Paul the covenant is fulfilled by Jesus sealing it with his death through which the sins of humankind are forgiven. Human beings are won over to God at the cost of Christ's supreme sacrifice without any claim or merit.

The terms "to covenant" and "covenant" were used in the ecumenical movement to express the will of those who came together at the Amsterdam assembly (q.v.). In spite of all their differences, they found one another in Jesus Christ. In committing themselves afresh to him they committed themselves to one another ("covenanted with one another") in constituting the World Council of Churches (q.v.). Before the formation of the WCC, in an encyclical issued in 1920, the Ecumenical Patriarchate of the Greek Orthodox Church in Constantinople proposed "to the churches of Christ everywhere the formation of a *koinonia* of churches". While the *koinonia* given in Jesus Christ makes possible the coming together of the churches, the *koinonia* as demonstrated by the early church is broken. Given the present situation of divided churches, such *koinonia* has to be actively sought as a goal of the fellowship that is the WCC. The Third Assembly in New Delhi (1961) spoke of the unity (q.v.) that the churches are seeking as a "fully committed fellowship", thus reemphasizing the idea of a covenant relationship indicated in Amsterdam. The Louvain meeting of Faith and Order (1971) (q.v.) with its statement on "Conciliarity (q.v.) and the Future of the Ecumemical Movement" brought into ecumenical prominence the conciliar character of the church, which can be explained as the periodic meeting of the church in councils, throughout its long history, to resolve disputes regarding the understanding and practice of the Christian faith and to take common positions regarding its mission (q.v.)—its responsibility to the world.

In his general secretary's report to the Nairobi assembly (1975) (q.v.), Philip Potter (q.v.) reflected this concern of conciliarity when he placed the following challenge before the participants: "This assembly will have failed in its purpose if we do not advance to a new covenant relationship between the member churches at all levels of their life and the World Council at all levels of its activities". The assembly then stated itself: "All programs of the WCC should be conceived and implemented in a way which enables the member churches to grow towards a truly ecumenical, conciliar fellowship. In this respect the programs of the WCC should become living expressions of the covenant relationship among the churches within the WCC and foster growth towards fuller unity".

Eight years later, the Vancouver assembly (1983) (q.v.) restated the same thrust more tersely in these words: "To engage member churches in a conciliar process of mutual commitment (covenant) to justice, peace and the integrity of creation should be a priority of World Council programs". There has been much debate about the use of the concept of covenant both during and in the years following the assembly. Nevertheless, the world convocation on "Justice, Peace and the Integrity of Creation" (q.v.) in Seoul in 1990 made several major affirmations "in responding anew to God's covenant".

On the one hand, the concept of covenant provides both

the reference for understanding theologically justice, peace and the integrity of creation and the framework within which their interdependence can be grasped. God's covenant with the whole of creation not only affirms the integrity of creation but also defines the parameters and conditions for human interaction with the rest of creation. In the context of covenant, justice is not a forensic term having to do with our rights and privileges. Rather, it has to do with the right behavior of the covenant community. The acid test of right behavior is whether or not the justice due to the poor and oppressed is secured. Peace is not merely the absence of war, but the security and welfare of all—the vision of *shalom*—that is promised in God's covenant of peace. On the other hand, the precise theological meaning of the terms "covenant" and "covenanting" in ecumenical discussions is not clear. There is the *conditional* type, where the covenant loyalty of the suzerain (Yahweh) to the vassal (Israel) is assured, provided the vassal does not behave in a way that is contrary to the covenant agreement; the covenant at Sinai is the major example of this type. There is the *unconditional, promissory* type where the one who initiates the covenant undertakes to maintain the covenant in perpetuity. Should the lesser (human) partner be unfaithful to the covenant, punishment would ensue, but the covenant itself would not be abrogated. A good example of this type is the covenant with David. So far there is no definitive ecumenical understanding of what biblical concept of covenant can be imported into the discussions to fix the meaning of covenant. *See also* JUSTICE, PEACE AND THE INTEGRITY OF CREATION.

CRAGG, ALBERT KENNETH (1913–). Cragg was professor of Arabic and Islamic studies at Hartford Theological Seminary, 1951–1956, study secretary of the Near East Council of Churches, 1956–1966, and visiting professor at Union Theological Seminary, New York, 1965–1966, and the University of Ibadan, Nigeria, 1968. He has written several scholarly works and made a significant contribution to the interfaith dialogue, in particular the Muslim-Christian dialogue (q.v.).

CREEDS. The principle and authoritative articles of faith of various churches are called creeds. As religions develop, originally simple doctrines are subjected to elaboration and interpretation that, in turn, give rise to differences of opinion. Detailed creeds therefore become necessary to emphasize the differences between the tenets of schismatic branches of the church and to serve as formulations of belief when liturgical usage, as in the administration of baptism (q.v.), requires a profession of faith (q.v.). In the Christian church, the Apostles' Creed was the earliest summation of doctrine; it has been used with only minor variations since the 2nd century. In addition to the Apostles' Creed, the Nicene Creed and the Athanasian Creed are in common use in various churches, including the Roman Catholic Church (q.v.). In the Orthodox (q.v.) churches the only creed formally adopted was the Nicene Creed, without the insertion of "filioque" (q.v.) in connection with the procession of the Holy Spirit.

With the Reformation (q.v.), the establishment of various Protestant churches necessitated the formulation of new creeds that, because of the many differences in theology and doctrine, were considerably longer than the creeds of the ancient church. The Augsburg Confession is accepted by Lutherans (q.v.) throughout the world, as is the Smaller Catechism of Martin Luther. The Formula of Concord, accepted by most early Lutherans, is now more limited in acceptance. The doctrines of the Church of England (q.v.) are summarized in the Thirty-nine Articles and those of the Presbyterians (q.v.) in the Westminster Confession. Most of the Reformed churches (q.v.) in Europe subscribe to the Second Helvetic Confession, of the Swiss reformer Heinrich Bullinger, and Calvinists generally accept as authoritative the Heidelberg Catechism.

For the restoration of the full communion of Christians, a common confession of the faith is an essential prerequisite. From the very beginning of the ecumenical movement the Apostles' Creed and the Nicene-Constantinopolitan Creed have been recognized as the most common ecumenical statements of faith. As the WCC (q.v.) is not authorized by its member churches to write or propose an ecumenical creed, present Faith and Order (q.v.) studies "Towards the Common Expression of the Apostolic Faith Today" assist the churches in their manifestations to full unity. In various bilateral dialogues (q.v.) and in church union negotiations, the classic credal affirmations and their use in worship have been a significant element in the progress toward reconciliation. *See also* CATECHISMS.

CRITICISM OF THE ECUMENICAL MOVEMENT AND OF THE WCC *see* ANTI-ECUMENISM

CULLMANN, OSCAR (1902–). As an observer at Vatican Council II (1962–1965) and active in promoting relationships between Roman Catholics and Protestants (qq.v.) in Europe, Cullmann believed that Christian tradition embodies a permanent spiritual gift, which it should preserve, purify and deepen, and which should not be given up for the sake of mutual agreement. He was a cofounder of the Ecumenical Institute for Higher Theological Studies at Tantur near Jerusalem, and director of an Ecumenical Institute in Heidelberg, attached to its university. He taught both at Strasbourg (1927–1938) and Basel (1938–1972), the latter paralleled by teaching at the Sorbonne (1951–1972). For almost 40 years he was the leading advocate of the salvation-historical (q.v.) interpretation of the New Testament and a major opponent of the existentialist school led by Rudolf Bultmann. He contended that the foundation and unifying theme of the whole Bible (q.v.) is *Heilsgeschichte,* that is, the history of the self-disclosure and saving action of God in the events that lead up to and follow the Christ event. The life, death and resurrection of Jesus Christ (q.v.) constitute the midpoint and consummation of this saving history and determine its meaning from the beginning to the end. He insisted that every attempt to isolate the biblical message from its salvation-historical context inevitably ends in a dangerous Docetism. One of his latest books *Unity through Diversity* (1986) aroused considerable controversy.

CULTURE *see* GOSPEL AND CULTURE

- D -

DAVIDSON, RANDALL THOMAS (1848–1930). Consecrated bishop of Rochester in 1891 and transferring to Winchester in 1895, Davidson became archbishop of Canterbury in 1903. Presiding over the Lambeth conference of 1908, he requested the appointment of a permanent committee to deal with relations of the Anglican Communion with the Orthodox (qq.v.) East, and suggested that certain forms of intercommunion could be brought into effect at once (e.g., in cases of emergency). By attending the world missionary conference in Edinburgh in 1910, he represented the conservative wing of the Church of England. At the Lambeth conference of 1920, he encouraged closer contacts with the Church of Sweden and the Ecumenical Patriarchiate of Constantinople. Davidson was much involved in the long preparations for the Stockholm conference on Life and Work (q.v.) in 1925, and insisted that if the conference was to be genuinely ecumenical, invitations should be sent to the Roman Catholic (q.v.) and the Orthodox churches to participate. As the 1920 Lambeth conference had issued its "Appeal to All Christian People", the way was open for archbishop Davidson and cardinal Merciér (q.v.) to start the Malines conversations (q.v.) in 1921. Contacts between the Old Catholic Church (q.v.) and the Church of England led in 1925 to the formal acceptance of the Anglican orders by the Old Catholic Church. Davidson did not manage in 1928 to convince the British Parliament to undertake a revision of the *Book of Common Prayer.*

DAVIS, JOHN MERLE (1875–1960). Davis was the first director of the department of Economic and Social Research and Counsel of the International Missionary Council (q.v.) 1930–1946. In that position he made extensive surveys of labor conditions, modern industry, social and economic conditions of churches in Central Africa, East Asia, Latin America and the Caribbean, and of the effects of the European impact on African marriage and family life. A large volume on *The Economic Basis of the Church* examined the problem of how younger churches will eventually be able to maintain themselves financially without assistance from the older churches. Son of an American missionary, Davis was educated in Oberlin and Hartford Theological Seminary. He was director of the Institute of Social and Religious Research of New York City, 1925–1930, and the first general secretary of the Institute of Pacific Relations.

DEBT PROBLEM. Within no more than two decades, many of the poorer nations have found themselves trapped in a permanently crippling condition of foreign debt, from which there is no prospect of release anywhere in sight. This is the "black hole" of the world economy today, whose incalculable and disastrous ramifications stretch far into the future. The debt problem arises from a complicated development. It began when banks and governments in the North encouraged governments and leaders in the South to accept loans in the 1970s—often of speculative capital deriving from oil sales in those days. These were used for various purposes, often for military equipment and arms, often for large-scale roads or dams designed to enable much of the "new development", but often also for purposes of the private interests of the elite. It is reckoned that leaders of several developing nations have placed in banks in Europe and North America money equivalent to their countries' entire debt. If the "owners" would repatriate it, the debt could immediately be paid. But there is no way in current economic relationships that those people could be made to use it constructively for their nation. Meanwhile the banks in the First World use the deposits very profitably.

The problem took a further twist when interests rates in the USA were greatly increased in the early 1980s so as to counter the effects of that nation's huge continuous trade and federal budget deficits. Overnight the poor countries found themselves liable to "service" their debts by far higher annual interest payments than before, often amounting to a large proportion of their entire production, let alone of their export earnings for the hard currency in which the debt had to be paid. Appeals to the World Bank and the International Monetary Fund (IMF) for rescheduling and other palliative help have led to "structural readjustment programs" designed to allow governments to earn more and spend less. These nearly always involved cuts in public spending by which the already low levels of medical care, education and nutrition deteriorate further. Diseases such as cholera and polio, thought to have been rooted out, have reappeared in some places. Moreover the implementation of these programs can require highly unpopular, even dictatorial measures, which pose a dangerous threat to social peace, let alone to fragile democratic patterns of governments. The impact of the debt crisis comes close to a new version of slavery.

It has been calculated that between 1982 and 1990 the underdeveloped countries have remitted to the North in debt service alone US $1,345 billion (interest and principal), which is US $418 billion more than the total resource flow in those years to those countries, much of which has anyway been in the form of new loans. For purposes of comparison, the US Marshall Plan transferred US $14 billion to war-ravaged Europe—about US $70 billion in 1991 values. Thus, in the eight years from 1982, the poor have financed six Marshall Plans for the rich through debt service alone. The human side of all this beggars the imagination. It includes the irresponsibility of the lenders, the cynicism of many borrowers immediately misusing what they now expect their compatriots to slave to pay back, the callousness of IMF officials insisting on the execution of "structural adjustment", and the willful blindness of the "world economic summit" of Northern political leaders in refusing to consider new mandates to the International Monetary Fund. The debt has by now already been more than paid, though the idea of simply cancelling it leaves many intricate questions hanging. It has become the prime example of an economic system that grinds tragically on for sheer lack of the political, indeed, the spiritual imagination and will to devise a way through and out.

The WCC's (q.v.) Advisory Group on Economic Matters (AGEM) spoke of the need to reform the international financial system. This calls for a restatement of values and goals, stressing the priority of equality, justice and sustainability. At the same time, this involves the need for systematic reforms in the operations of the IMF, the World Bank and national governments. On the basis of several studies, the WCC central committee called in 1985 for creditors to cancel the debts. *See also* DEVELOPMENT.

DECREE ON ECUMENISM *see* VATICAN COUNCIL II

DEISSMANN, ADOLF (1866–1937). After his studies at Tübingen and Berlin, 1885–1988, he presented his dissertation to the University of Marburg in 1892 and taught there until 1895. In 1897 he became professor of New Testament in Heidelberg, and in 1908 assumed the same post in Berlin. His books remain authoritative studies in the biblical field. Already during early travels to the Middle East, England and Sweden, Deissmann discovered the necessity and the possibility of reconciliation between churches and nations. From 1914 onward he issued many *Evangelische Wochenbriefe,* which were sent to addresses in the USA, Great Britain and other European countries. These letters were intended primarily as a means of breaking through the spiritual isolation with which Germany was threatened in consequence of the wartime blockade. He presented the German churches at the meeting of the International Committee of the World Alliance for Promoting International Friendship through the Churches (q.v.) (Oud Wassenaar 1919) and at the Universal Christian Conference on Life and Work (Stockholm 1925). He was one of the writers of the Stockholm message and of the Lausanne 1927 declaration on "The Gospel" and in 1926 published the inclusive report of the Stockholm conference in German.

DEVANANDAN, PAUL DAVID (1901–1962). Devanandan was a pioneer in the realm of interfaith dialogue and had many friends among adherents of other faiths. Theologians and church leaders in India looked to him for personal guidance, wisdom and counsel. He studied at Madras University and the Pacific School of Religion in Berkeley, California, and obtained his Ph.D. degree in religion from Yale University. He was William Paton lecturer at Selly Oak, Birmingham, Henry Luce visiting professor at Union Theological Seminary, New York, and Teape lecturer at Cambridge University. From 1957 to 1962 Devanandan was director of the Christian Institute for the Study of Religion and Society in Bangalore, and in 1961 he addressed the New Delhi assembly.

DEVELOPMENT. Hardly any theme and concern in official ecumenical statements has been so inadequately handled during the period 1948–1965 as that of economic development. A naïve and romantic conviction prevailed that once poor peoples in the Third World obtain a minimum of technology and are profiting from ''the benefits of more machine-production'', the living standards of a large part of the population will be raised. The ecumenical concept of the ''responsible society'' was indiscriminately applied to developed and underdeveloped nations. The capability and the willingness of the affluent West to send generous aid to the rest of the world and the harmful effects of that aid were not questioned. There was an undue optimism that the Christian churches can play an important role in assisting disrupted peoples with technical and welfare services and thus will enable them to help themselves.

Only in 1966 did the Geneva world conference on Church and Society make a serious attempt on the part of the WCC (q.v.) to understand the revolutionary realities that shape the modern world. It made the issue of world economic development a major concern of the churches and stressed that large contributions from the rich nations are needed and deep changes in economic and political structures required if global economic growth is to be achieved. Development continued to be a major ecumenical concern since the WCC assembly at Uppsala in 1968, which did more than make declarations to the world at large. It made specific recommendations to the churches everywhere, in rich countries and poor ones. It spoke of the educational and prophetic tasks, as well as of the service functions of the Christian communities. To determine how the WCC could carry out its mandate a world consultation on Ecumenical Assistance to Development Projects was held in Montreux in 1970, which recommended the creation of a new WCC Commission on the Churches' Participation in Development (CCPD). This commission and its constituency have engaged in reflection and action of worldwide development ever since.

The reports of the conferences that SODEPAX (q.v.) (the joint Roman Catholic-WCC committee on Society, Development and Peace) sponsored from 1968–1971 displayed penetrating insight and great analytical quality. Yet, they were also too optimistic, as was the WCC, that the prosperity so far enjoyed by a minority of humanity would eventually be shared by the majority of the human race. From 1975 onward the CCPD has attempted to make contributions to the WCC's search for a just, participatory and sustainable society (q.v.), to the concern for people's participation as a social phenomenon in history, which poses challenges to socioeconomic structures as to the church, to people's technologies, which fit in with their culture and values, to a deeper analysis of the crushing economic power of the transnational corporations, to various aspects of development education, and to "new life styles" (q.v.) in the churches. The CCPD also developed a theological concept of "the church of the poor"(q.v.). Still, during the last ten years a mood of impotence, resignation and even despair has often prevailed. In the international secular realm organizations like UNCTAD, UNESCO, FAO and others have experienced the crippling assumptions of prestigious development blueprints. In the religious realm the idea of the church of the poor has not reinforced the tremendous thrust and commitment of the Uppsala assembly (q.v.). Few consequences have been drawn by the churches from their new insight in God's preferential option for the poor and exploited.

The two percent appeal for development aid as an action model has been accepted and practiced by few Christian communities. And only the governments of the Netherlands, Norway and Sweden have spent between 1.2 and 0.8 percent of their GNP on development aid. Foreign assistance itself remains a controversial issue. Its critics believe that it is either often badly administered, or that it is harmful in principle. Following centuries of colonialism and neo-colonialism the era of aid prolongs dependency, poverty and underdevelopment. Unless there is a much deeper awareness among the churches about the world disparities and the reasons for their existence, the opportunities they have to change the structures of their own existence and to contribute to the establishment of a new international economic order will remain unused. Engagement in development education at the grass roots is surely necessary. But the whole church, particularly its hierarchy, needs to become aware that it lives in a world that is totally different from the world 50 years ago.

DIAKONIA. Diakonia, or the "responsible service of the gospel by deeds and by words performed by Christians in response to the needs of people", is rooted in and modelled on Christ's service and teachings. Because Christ has served human beings, human beings as Christians do their diakonia. The permanence of diakonia on the churches' agenda and the desirability of ecumenical service are two convictions that have always undergirded WCC (q.v.) involvement in interchurch aid. About the continuing call for diakonia there can hardly be any doubt, as the interminable chronicle of human tragedy brought into people's homes by the mass media attests only too well. As to the second condition, however, despite the substantial sharing the churches undertake together through the WCC, ecumenical diakonia represents a relatively small part of the total aid given by Christians.

Christian service has its highest profile in emergency relief. Since disasters often elicit immediate aid from many quarters—governments, United Nations bodies, the Red Cross and nongovernmental organizations—the churches locally and internationally try not to duplicate the efforts of these other agencies but to identify a specific role in the overall relief effort. In recent years there has been a growing ecumenical emphasis on the churches' part in emergency preparedness, especially in areas prone to seasonal natural disasters. Besides meeting material needs, the Christian communities have a pastoral task, responding to the shock and the sorrow of victims, and an advocacy role, seeing that the aid rendered does not pass by the most vulnerable. There will always be a need for a Christian response to human suffering; and in many cases the churches' initial response will be in the form of material aid. But not all human misery is the immediate consequence of a disaster; and aid sent to alleviate suffering may in fact work against removing the causes of suffering. An effective ecumenical diakonia must go beyond charity.

The Second World War and its aftermath challenged all philanthropic agencies and especially the relief organizations. In 1966 a world consultation on Inter-Church Aid (q.v.) was sponsored by the WCC in Swanwick, UK. To the prevailing concept of social relief work and service, the Swanwick consultation added the idea of social advancement or social action. Service to refugees (q.v.) developed into interchurch aid. In 1967, a diakonia desk was established by the WCC for research and study, and was attached to Inter-Church Aid. Swanwick contributed to the formation of the WCC Unit II, Justice and Service. In 1971, the diakonia desk was integrated into a new portfolio and became part of the Commission on Inter-Church Aid, Refugee and World Service. Questions related to the theology of diakonia and of the relationship to the churches belong more properly to Faith and Order (q.v.).

In the 1970s the ecumenical movement and many churches reflected the widespread enthusiasm for "development" (q.v.) as the new direction for diakonia, particularly in newly independent countries. By the 1980s optimism about development was waning. Awareness was growing that despite sizable investments in development projects the churches and the vulnerable people they sought to aid were losing the struggle for justice. The Vancouver assembly in 1983 reported: "The 'liturgy after the Liturgy' is diakonia. Diakonia as the church's ministry of sharing, healing and reconciliation is of the very nature of the church. It demands of individuals and churches a giving which comes not out of what they have, but what they are . . . Diakonia constantly has to challenge the . . . self-centered structures of the church and transfer them into living instruments of the sharing and healing ministry of the church". The WCC called a major consultation in 1986 on "Diakonia 2000" to find a new outlook for ecumenical commitment to the service of human need. The consultation suggested that an approach to diakonia that focuses on development projects should give way to an area-centered approach. By continuously enlarging and deepening its awareness of the total political, social, economic and church situation in each area of the world, the ecumenical community could respond more effectively to the range of its needs. In contrast to the current process of reacting—often slowly by the time all the procedures are followed—to requests for resources for projects, an area-centered approach would enable acting quickly and creatively. Still, the question is not answered as to what proportion of the church resources should go locally, nationally and internationally to emergency aid, prevention, rehabilitation, development and political change. Should churches practice complemetary diakonia? *See also* DEBT PROBLEM.

DIALOGUE, BILATERAL *see* BILATERAL DIALOGUES

DIALOGUE, MULTILATERAL *see* MULTILATERAL DIALOGUES

DIALOGUE WITH PEOPLE OF LIVING FAITHS. Christianity and non-Christian religions from the 1930s to the 1950s, and the Word of God and the living faith of men in the 1960s, have been specific concerns in the ecumenical movement, particularly in the work of the International Missionary Council (q.v.). In 1971 a new Sub-unit on Dialogue with People of Living Faiths and Ideologies was established in the WCC (q.v.), which sponsored many bilateral and multilateral dialogues (qq.v.) and issued a considerable number of publications. Note that in the title of the subunit the emphasis is on "people", not on religious systems, and that the word "living" has been added to "faiths" to indicate that they are not superstitious relics of the past. *Living Faiths and the Ecumenical Movement* lists the various meetings that took place from 1955 to 1970. The dialogues that were organized until 1980 are listed in *The Minutes of the Fifth Meeting of the Working Group, Bali, Indonesia, Dec.,–Jan., 1981–82.* The subunit published in 1979 *Guidelines on Dialogue.* The real breakthrough in the dialogue within the multi-religious, multicultural and multi-ideological world became visible in the late 1960s and the early 1970s. The statements issued and the convictions and concerns expressed during this period witness to the deep sensitivity and the daring insights of theologians and lay people, and have laid the basis for ongoing ecumenical reflection and activities in the realm of interfaith dialogue.

Yet, the practice of dialogue has raised inevitably and with greater intensity the controversial question of how Christians see the place of people of other faiths within the activity of God in human history. This is not an abstract, theoretical issue; it is asked, the *Guidelines* note, "in terms of what God may be doing in the lives of hundreds of millions of men and women who live in and seek together community with Christians, but along different lines". Although people of other faiths were invited officially as guests to the WCC Nairobi (1975) and WCC Vancouver (1983) assemblies (qq.v.), where they addressed plenary sessions and took part in the program for assembly visitors, the questions were repeatedly raised as to whether dialogue is not a betrayal of mission and leads to syncretism (qq.v.). Until now it is not sufficiently realized that it is mission in dialogue and dialogue in mission that should take place in our contemporary world. Mission has its justification in conversation because its absence would diminish the credibility of dialogue. At the same time witness is pointless if it is not shaped by the experience of dialogue. With regard to the danger of syncretism, it is seriously overlooked that the interreligious dialogues of the last few decades have amply proved that humanity is not on its way to produce a syncretistic world religion, a new normative faith for all the members of the world community. Such a combined faith is not only a poor alternative to religious search for truth and an impoverishment of the human race, but it is strongly resisted by any religion defending its own spiritual integrity.

A vital ecumenical issue today is the necessity of developing a pluralistic theological approach to the world religions that corrects the conservative "exclusivist" and the liberal "inclusivist" Christian approaches of the past. The first maintained that salvation (q.v.) can only be found in Jesus Christ (q.v.) and that, since all other religions are based on sheer human inspiration, they have no value and thus lead to perdition. The second position recognizes the salvific richness of other faiths but then it views this richness as the work of Christ's redemption. It speaks of Christ "in cognito" among people of other living faiths. The problem of the exclusivist and the inclusivist method is that they betray paternalism and condescension. A pluralistic view of religions, however, also has its pitfalls. The recognition of historical relativity easily leads to the quicksand of historical relativism in which no one is allowed to make "absolute" judgments on anyone else. Given the disjunctions and discontinuities existing between religious traditions, it is also impossible and imperialistic to subsume the religions under universal categories. Pluralism (q.v.) does not allow for a universal system. A pluralistic system would be a contradiction in terms. The incommensurability of ultimate systems is unbridgeable. Pluralism is, therefore, not an ultimate, but an immediate concern. For all religions, including Christianity, what is at stake is their view of their own place in history, and their understanding of God.

The process of starting a discussion on the issue of the theology of religions was started by the WCC with the launching of a study process that resulted in the publication *My Neighbor's Faith—and Mine: Theological Discoveries through Interfaith Dialogue* (1986). This study booklet was translated into 18 languages. It is intended to raise awareness of plurality in the churches and to explore how Christians today may look theologically at other traditions and expressions of faith.

The Vatican II (q.v.) Declaration on the Relationship of the Church to non-Christian Religions (*Nostra aetate*) spelled out the pastoral dimensions of this relationship. Other key Vatican II documents, including the Dogmatic Constitution on the Church (*Lumen gentium*) and the Decree on the Church's Missionary Activity (*Ad gentes*), contained important comments that pointed to a favorable dialogic attitude toward people of other religious traditions. Although the Second Vatican Council did not develop a clear theological position, it did, by opening up the issue in the direction of interfaith dialogue, mark a new phase in the relations of the Roman Catholic Church (q.v.), in all parts of the world, with people of other faiths. Pope Paul VI (q.v.) established in 1964 a Vatican Secretariat for Non-Christians (later the Pontifical Council for Interfaith Dialogue).

Jewish-Christian dialogue. The long history of anti-Jewish sentiment, the insidious teaching of contempt, legal discrimination and pogroms prepared the ground for 20th-century anti-Semitism (q.v.), which culminated in the Nazi tragedy. A recognition of this history has brought about a determination by many Christian bodies to oppose every form of anti-Semitism. This was expressed at the first WCC assembly in Amsterdam in 1948, and even more strongly at the third WCC assembly in New Delhi in 1961. *Nostra aetate* (1965) of Vatican II affirmed a common "spiritual patrimony" and stated that the passion of Christ "cannot be charged against all the Jews" and that the relationship between Christians and Jews "concerns the church as such". It further stressed that Jews are "very dear to God" and that "he does not take back the gifts he bestowed or the choice he made". The WCC's *Ecumenical Considerations of Jewish-Christian Dialogue* (1983) and especially statements by many of its member churches, most notably by the general synod of the Netherlands Reformed Church (1970) and the synod of the Evangelical Church in the Rhineland (1980), have developed even stronger affirmations of Israel and Judaism. The latter repudiated all attempts to convert Jews to the Christian faith, emphasizing the one hope for the kingdom, shared by Jews and Christians, the joint mission that God's name be hallowed, and the mutual witness of equal partners in the dialogue.

There is a general ecumenical agreement that the church of Jesus Christ has not directly replaced the people of Israel, and that God remains faithful to those with whom he has made a convenant (q.v.). There is, however, not a common mind yet on whether there is one covenant or two and, if two, how they are related. For some, faith (q.v.) in Christ points already to a relationship with God that Jews enjoy by virtue of their historic faith. The resurrection validates belief in the Father of Jesus, who was then, and is now, in a loving relationship to Jews. Jews, for their part, stress that Judaism must be defined in Jewish, not Christian, terms and that

Judaism is a living religion, people and culture through the centuries and should not be equated with the religion of the Hebrew Scriptures. For many Jews, the state of Israel is seen as fulfilling the old religious longing and as providing a homeland that has been denied them for 2,000 years. The unwillingness of the Vatican to recognize the state of Israel and what is seen as only a grudging recognition of it by other Christian communities is a source of resentment. Furthermore, the natural sympathy of WCC member churches for the Palestinian cause is a reason of disquiet for Jews.

Muslim-Christian dialogue. The multilateral dialogues in Ajaltoun, Lebanon (1970), and in Colombo, Sri Lanka (1974), with Buddhists, Hindus, Jews and Muslims gave an impulse to bilateral dialogues with Muslims in Cartigny, Switzerland, in 1969, in Broumana, 1972, in Legon, 1974, in Hong Kong, 1975, and in Chambésy, Switzerland, 1976. The Conference of European Churches sponsored on a regional level dialogues with Muslims in Salzburg in 1978 and in St. Pölten, Austria, in 1984. More recently, the Sub-unit on Dialogue has sponsored several regional colloquia on local themes to lay the groundwork for a document on ecumenical perspectives on Muslim-Christian dialogue: Porto Novo, Benin (1986), Kuta, Bali (1986), Kolymbari, Crete (1987), New Windsor, Maryland (1988), and Arusha, Tanzania (1989). Initiatives to engage in dialogue are not exclusively Christian. Muslim organizations have been the hosts of international dialogues, such as those held in Amman under the auspices of the Royal Academy for Islamic Affairs of the ones organized by the Center for Economic and Social Research at the University of Tunis. Representatives of the Muslim World Congress, the World Muslim League and the World Islamic Call Society have been meeting regularly with representatives from the Vatican and the WCC for several years to exchange information, encouragement and advice.

According to Muslim teaching both Jews and Christians have clear defects, Judaism errs in its ethnocentricity (Zionism), its exclusiveness (the chosen people) and its neglect of missionary work (lack of universalism). Christianity, asserts the Koran, is wrong on a number of points, most of which concern Jesus. Although Muslims believe that Jesus was sinless, born from the virgin Mary, a prophet powerful in word and deed, who raised the dead, healed the sick and taught the "gospel", he "was no more than a servant of God" (43.59). Because "Allah is one, the Eternal God", teaches the Koran, ". . . none is equal to him" (112.3). "Those who say, 'The Lord of Mercy has begotten a son', preach a monstrous falsehood", states the Koran (19.88). Abraham, it is affirmed, "was not a Jew nor a Christian but a true Muslim" (3.67).

By the late 1980s it was estimated that there were 1 billion Muslims, with an annual growth rate of almost 5 percent. By the start of the 21st century Islam may surpass Christianity as the world's largest religion.

Hindu-Christian dialogue. The Western discovery of India initiated an important missionary enterprise, first by the Roman Catholic Church and later by Protestant (qq.v.) communities, which led to the establishment of Indian Christian churches along Western denominational lines. The newly converted were forced to break all links with their Hindu past and to consider the religion professed by their ancestors as inferior. Hindus had a similar contempt for all non-Hindus and believed that contact with them would be harmful. Hinduism was first presented as an integrated universal faith as recently as 1893, when Swami Vivekananda (1863–1902) expounded his interpretation of *Advaita Vedanta* at the World Parliament of Religions in Chicago. This "Neo-Vedanta" espoused a combination of advaitic spirituality and social service, practiced by the Ramakrishna Mission. Other Hindu figures were Aurobindo Ghose (1872–1950), Ramana Maharshi (1879–1950) and Jiddu Krishnamurti (1895–1986). Sarvepalli Radhakrishnan in the early 1930s pleaded particularly for a dialogue of religions. Two Christians deserve special credit for the Hindu-Christian dialogue, Paul Devanandan (q.v.), the founder-director of the Christian Institute for the Study of Religion and Society in Bangalore, and Jacques-Albert Cuttat, Swiss ambassador to India. Both the Vatican Secretariat for Non-Christians and the WCC Sub-unit on Dialogue—under the leadership of the Indian scholar Stanley Samartha (q.v.)—promoted Hindu-Christian relations in significantly new ways. Both initiatives were largely ecumenical, with the Christian side usually represented by various denominations. Through the dialogue, modern Hinduism has interacted with the secularizing influences of nationalism, humanism, communism and the Western scientific outlook on religion. Still 80 percent of the population in India's half million villages have remained conservative, and only city dwellers have become more open to secularization.

Buddhist-Christian dialogue. Buddhism distinguishes between salvation through one's own strength and salvation through a foreign power. The first is represented by the Mahāyāna school, the latter by the Hīnayāna school, which believes that the merciful Buddha practices graceful assistance, comparable to the Christian understanding of grace (q.v.). The Amida piety, however, is grounded in the metaphysical philosophy of Mahāyāna, which is irreconcilable with the Christian believe in a Creator-God. A great contemporary pioneer in Buddhist-Christian relations was Thomas Merton (q.v.), although he followed the ancient tradition of dialogue through monasticism and mysticism in his plea for an international and interreligious monastic, spiritual encounter. In Sri Lanka a group of priests including Aloysius Pieris, Michael Rodrigo, Antony Fernando, Lynn de Silva (Methodist) and Yohan Devananda (Anglican) were studying Buddhism under Buddhists and searching for new forms of Buddhist-Christian community living and dialogue. Similar ventures can be cited in other countries. Also significant ventures are the activities of the Ecumenical Institute for Study and Dialogue in Sri Lanka (formerly the Center for Religion and Studies), the East-West religious project started by the University of Hawaii department of religion and the North American Buddhist-Christian theological encounter group under Masao Abe and John Cobb.

Three dialogues were sponsored by the WCC. In 1978 Christians and Buddhists met in Colombo to discuss the subject of "religious experience in humanity's relation to nature". The gathering in Hong Kong in 1984 brought together representatives of the two religion from North Asia-Japan, Korea, Taiwan and Hong Kong. In 1988 a Pan-Asian Buddhist-Christian meeting was held in Seoul; here Buddhists and Christians contributed on issues of justice and peace in the context of the WCC process of "Justice, Peace and the Integrity of Creation" (q.v.). During Vatican II specific mention was made of Buddhism as teaching a path by which humans "can either reach a state of absolute freedom or attain supreme enlightenment by their own efforts or by higher assistance". The Pontifical Council for Interreligious Dialogue and the WCC have closely collaborated in establishing closer relations with adherents of Buddhism, as of other religions. The meeting of Buddhist leaders in Rangoon, Burma, in 1954–1956, marked the 2000th anniversary of Gautama Buddha's final *nirvana* and planned a worldwide missionary program.

The WCC Sub-unit on Dialogue has also been concerned with traditional religions, particularly in Africa, and with Christian-Sikh relations, both in India and the West. *See also MISSION; PLURALISM, RELIGIOUS; SALVATION.*

DIASPORA CHURCHES. The multiplication of denominational or confessional diasporary churches has been a particular phenomenon of history, but especially of modern times. Practically all mainline churches have large or small affiliated communities scattered in various countries, sometimes without any direct link with the mother church. Demographic explosions, schisms, reform movements, political upheavals and voluntary emigration have led to many Christian diaspora churches. The concept of dispora can be used for various groups with a religious and/or ethnic identity. In the current ecumenical language the term "minority" is preferred. A minority can be defined as "a group numerically inferior to the rest of the population of a state, in a non-dominant position, whose members—being nationals of the state—possess ethnic, religious or linguistic characteristics differing from those of the rest of the population and show, if only implicitly, a sense of solidarity, directed towards preserving their culture, traditions, religion or language" (a working definition of the US subcommission on prevention of discrimination and protection of minorities).

As an example of churches that represent a minority among other Christians in their territory, the Orthodox Church of Czechoslovakia (some 350,000 faithful in 1950), the Orthodox Church of Poland (about 350,000) and the Orthodox Church of Albania (about 210,000 faithful in 1944) can be mentioned. There is further a widespread Orthodox diaspora in the USA as many different Orthodox Christians immigrated to that country for economic or political reasons. Some judge that many small national churches in a diaspora situation are unfairly excluded from the benefits of belonging to the WCC (q.v.) because they do not have enough members to be eligible for it. Others note that the WCC does not take sufficient account of the interests of diaspora Christians—these in a smaller jurisdiction of a church with its headquarters in another country.

It has been emphasized that the whole Christian church is today in a diaspora situation. The church no longer expresses the soul of a nation but has become a minority of believing Christians among a majority of indifferent and unbelieving human beings.

DIBELIUS, OTTO (1880–1967). Lutheran bishop of Berlin and Brandenburg, 1945–1967. He rose quickly in the German Protestant hierarchy, and in 1925 became bishop of East Prussia (Berlin) diocese. When Hitler came to power he was suspended from his office for refusing to concur in Nazi racial theories. Throughout World War II, he was an active member of the Confessing Church (q.v.) and joined in the drafting of the Barmen Declaration 1934. Again after the war Dibelius found himself laboring to build the church under another totalitarian regime. He worked indefatigably not only to reunite the church in Germany but worldwide. In 1948 he participated in the founding of the WCC (q.v.) and was instrumental in the formation of the Evangelical Church in Germany. He subsequently served as chairman of this church (1949–1961) and was a president of the WCC, 1954–1961.

DIÉTRICH, SUZANNE DE (1891–1981). De Diétrich obtained a degree in electronic engineering from the University of Lausanne in 1913. She joined the French Student Christian Movement and decided in 1914 to engage in student work, instead of returning to the family foundry in Alsace. She was active in the World Student Christian Federation, 1935–1946, and also collaborated with the World YWCA (q.v.). In spite of a severe walking handicap she traveled throughout the world. She was a leader of the Bible studies at the World Christian Youth Conference in Amsterdam in 1939 and participated in numerous ecumenical gatherings. She was assistant director of the Ecumenical Institute in Bossey (q.v.), 1946–1954, and worked from 1956 onward for the CIMADE in Paris. She was a greatly qualified interpreter of the Bible (q.v.) and made the theologians of her time, Karl Barth (q.v.), Emil Brunner and Eduard Thurneysen, accessible to laypeople. Several of her books were translated into other languages. De Diétrich was also interested in questions of liturgy and worship (q.v.).

DISABLED. It was only in 1971 that the WCC (q.v.) started to discuss seriously the problems of disability at the meeting of the Commission on Faith and Order (q.v.) in Louvain. The debate took place in the context of the unity of the church and the handicapped of society. The fifth assembly in Nairobi in 1975 issued a statement on ''The Handicapped and the Wholeness of the Family of God'' in which it was stated: ''The disabled are treated as the weak to be served, rather than as fully committed, integral members of the Body of Christ and the human family; the specific contribution which they have to give is ignored''. At the next assembly in Vancouver in 1983 the issue of persons with physical and mental disabilities was high on the agenda, resulting in the next year in the appointment of a full-time consultant (a disabled person) to coordinate work in the WCC and its member churches. Since then much has been done ecumenically in Europe and North America, although lack of funds and limited human resources have often made it difficult for significant progress to occur regionally in member churches. Also national councils of churches are challenged to incorporate concern for people with disabilities into their agendas. The United Nations (q.v.) estimated in 1989 that 7 to 10 percent of the world's population of 5.2 billion have some form of physical or mental disability due to malnutrition, famine, diseases, poor quality of health care, armed aggression, war, torture, accidents and violation of fundamental human rights (q.v.).

DISARMAMENT *see* PEACE AND DISARMAMENT

DISCIPLES OF CHRIST *see* CHRISTIAN CHURCH (DISCIPLES OF CHRIST)

DODD, CHARLES HAROLD (1884–1973). Dodd was a New Testament scholar and author of numerous works. He became particularly known for the concept of "realized eschatology". This theory emphasized the presence of the kingdom of God in the ministry of Jesus Christ (q.v.) and placed less emphasis on eschatology (q.v.) as events of the future. Dodd was also known for his theory of the New Testament *kerygma* (proclamation, preaching) set forth in *The Apostolic Preaching and Its Development* (1936). In 1950 he was appointed director of an ecumenical group that produced the translation of the Bible (q.v.) published in 1970 as the *New English Bible*. A participant in the ecumenical movement he addressed the 1948 founding assembly of the WCC (q.v.) on the biblical basis of Christian unity (q.v.).

DU PLESSIS, DAVID J. (1905–1987). Du Plessis was a leading figure in the Pentecostal churches (q.v.) and their relation to the ecumenical movement. Born of French Huguenot stock he emigrated to the USA in 1949. He participated in several conferences of the International Missionary Council (q.v.) and in numerous conferences and assemblies of the WCC (qq.v.) from Evanston 1954 to Vancouver 1983. He further attended the first Pentecostal World Conference in Zurich in 1947 and was organizing secretary for several subsequent ones. A promoter of the charismatic movement for renewal (qq.v.), which started in the USA in the 1960s, Du Plessis was looked on with suspicion and rejection in several Pentecostal communities because of his relations with the WCC and the Roman Catholic Church (q.v.). His contacts with the Vatican culminated in the Pentecostal-Roman Catholic dialogue (q.v.), which began in 1972.

DUN, ANGUS (1892–1971). Dun was an ardent advocate of ecumenism and peace (q.v.), serving both as chairman of the Federal Council of Churches (q.v.) and the Commission on Ecumenical Relations of the Protestant Episcopal Church. In addition he was a member of the WCC (q.v.) central committee from 1948 onward and served in this capacity for ten years. Ordained in 1917, he was professor of theology at the Episcopal Theological School, 1920–1940, and dean, 1940–1944. He served as bishop of Washington, D.C., 1944–1962, during which time he officiated at Franklin D. Roosevelt's funeral. He was afflicted his whole life with crippling injuries.

DUPREY, PIERRE (1922–). Duprey was appointed under secretary in 1963, and secretary in 1983, of the Secretariat For Promoting Christian Unity (q.v.). He has been a member of the Joint Working Group (q.v.) since 1965 and was liaison officer of the Secretariat and the Commission on Faith and Order, 1971–1983. He has been a member of the international joint commission between the Anglican communion and the Roman Catholic Church (qq.v.) since 1970. He was also president of the preparatory commission for the dialogue between the Roman Catholic Church and the Orthodox churches (q.v.) in 1975, and secretary of this commission from 1980 onward. He is also a member of the commission for dialogue with the Lutheran World Federation, the World Alliance of Reformed Churches, and the Pentecostal churches (qq.v.). He is a member of the executive committee of the Ecumenical Institute for Theological Research in Tantur (q.v.) (near Jerusalem). He was ordained a bishop in 1990.

- E -

EAST ASIA CHRISTIAN CONFERENCE *see* CHRISTIAN CONFERENCE OF ASIA

EASTERN CATHOLIC CHURCHES *see* UNIATE CHURCHES

EASTERN ORTHODOX CHURCHES. At present Eastern Orthodoxy consists of the following autocephalous and/or autonomous churches: the four ancient Patriarchates of Constantinople, Alexanderia, Antioch and Jerusalem; the four Patriarchates of more recent origin: Russia, Serbia, Romania, Bulgaria; the Catholicossate of Georgia; and the churches of Cyprus, Greece, Poland, Czechoslovakia, Albania and Finland. There is a strong Orthodox diaspora (q.v.) presence in the Americas, Australia and Western Europe. A section of the USA orthodox has been granted autocephaly, which nevertheless is not recognized by all Orthodox churches. The same applies for the Orthodox Church in Japan. The monastery of Sinai enjoys autonomy. All these churches are held together by a bond of unity in the faith and communion in the sacraments (qq.v.). The Patriarch of Constantinople is known as the Ecumenical Patriarch. He has a position of special honor, as ''first among equals'', with the right of convening, after consultation with primates of other Orthodox churches, Pan-Orthodox conferences, but not the right of interfering in the internal affairs of the other local Orthodox churches.

Orthodoxy claims to be the unbroken continuation of the Christian Church established by Christ and his apostles. Its faith is based primarily upon the dogmatic definitions of the seven Ecumenical Councils. The Orthodox do not recognize as ecumenical any council held since the Second of Nicea in 787. From the 9th century onward there developed an increasing estrangement between the two great sees of Rome and Constantinople. This led eventually to an open and lasting schism. The final breach between Greek and Latin Christendom is usually assigned to the year 1054. Two issues were at stake: the universal supremacy of the jurisdiction of the pope, which was rejected by the Orthodox, and the doctrinal issue of the Filioque (q.v.). The West had inserted a phrase into the Nicene-Constantinopolitan Creed: ''I believe in the Holy Spirit . . . who proceeds from the Father *and the Son''*.

Orthodox churches acknowledge the seven sacraments, or ''mysteries'' as they are termed. However, other sacramental actions are common in the liturgical praxis. Baptism (q.v.) is performed by immersion; chrismation (confirmation [q.v.]) is administered by the priest immediately after baptism, and children can partake of communion from infancy. The bread and the wine in the eucharist (q.v.) are considered to become, at the consecration, the true and real body and blood of Christ. The Orthodox commune after careful preparation and confession. Services are in principle held in national languages, but in Greece, Russia, Bulgaria and other places, an old liturgical language is used, not the modern vernacular. The veneration of icons plays a notable part in Orthodox worship, both public and private. Prayers to the Mother of God and the saints are common in liturgical texts. Monasteries have been highly influential throughout Orthodox history. From the 6th century onward bishops have been drawn from the ranks of the monastic clergy. Parish priests, on the other hand, are generally married. The Orthodox Church has never insisted upon the celibacy of the clergy.

The Patriarchate of Constantinople has from the start firmly supported the ecumenical movement. It appealed as early as 1920 in an Encyclical Letter to "all the churches of Christ" for "closer intercourse and mutual cooperation", and it became a founding member of the WCC (q.v.). The Ecumenical Patriarchate has had a permanent representative in the WCC since 1955, the Russian Orthodox Church since 1962. Both representatives participate regularly in the annual conference of representatives of the Christian World Communions (q.v.). The Orthodox churches mentioned above have a total membership of over 100 million. *See also* ORIENTAL ORTHODOX CHURCHES; ORTHODOXY.

ECCLESIOLOGY. The Toronto statement (1950) of the WCC (q.v.) central committee declares that the WCC has no ecclesiology of its own, therefore no church is obliged to change its own ecclesiology, nor to accept "a specific doctrine concerning the nature of church unity". The basis for fellowship in the WCC is merely "the common recognition that Christ is the divine head of the body". Admittedly the churches belonging to the WCC recognize "that membership of the Church of Christ is more inclusive than the membership of their own church body . . . The member

churches enter into spiritual relationships through which
they seek to learn from each other and to give help to each
other in order that the body of Christ may be built up and that
the life of the churches may be renewed''.

In his well-known book *Images of the Church in the New
Testament* (1960), Paul Minear (q.v.) considers some 96
analogies. Among the major images he lists several taken
from the covenant (q.v.) history of Israel (e.g., people of God,
holy nation, temple), several based on the universal cosmic
order (e.g., new creation, kingdom of God, communion in the
Holy Spirit), several referring to the mutual union of Christians in the faith (e.g., fellowship of saints, disciples, household of God) and several pointing to the organic relations
between God and his people (e.g., Body of Christ, fullness of
God). Patristic and medieval theology, while exploiting
these NT images of the church, tended to enrich them with
allegorical interpretations of biblical texts that did not refer
literally and immediately to the church.

Martin Luther and John Calvin developed a critical ecclesiology, resistant to what they considered as exaggerated
Roman Catholic (q.v.) claims. Both of them distinguished
sharply between the visible and invisible church, according
greater importance to the latter. Nevertheless, both of them
sought to defend, against outspoken spiritualism, the importance of the visible church as the community where the
gospel is preached and the sacraments (q.v.) are correctly
administered. The complex history of Protestantism since the
Reformation (qq.v.) precludes any easy ecclesiological im-
agery. Some Protestants have tended to look on the visible
church as a merely human organization having no necessary
relation to eternal life. The mainstream of Protestant thought,
however, has depicted the church as the place where the
saving word of God resounds and is accepted in faith (q.v.).
The historical sociological work of Max Weber and Ernst
Troeltsch has defined the church as a type of Christian social
organization, based on characteristic understandings of theological first principles as institutionalized in distinctive ways
in society to form a social ethic (q.v.). The Christian
community attempts to be a socially inclusive establishment
both in the sense that it tries to draw all human beings into

itself and in the sense that it tries to cooperate with and normatively inform all other sectors of social life—familial, economic, political, intellectual and social.

The Roman Catholic theologians of the Counter-Reformation reacted strongly against the Reformers. They preferred categories borrowed from Aristotelian philosophy and Roman law and to interpret the biblical data by means of these categories. Robert Bellarmine, for instance, portrayed the church as a universal society under the government of the pope as the vicar of Christ. This type of ecclesiology was still dominant at the time of Vatican I (1869–1870) (q.v.), which defined the powers of the pope as ''shepherd and teacher of all Christians''. With Vatican II (1962–1965) (q.v.) official Roman Catholic ecclesiology moved in a new direction. In the Dogmatic Constitution on the Church the mystery of the church as the new people of God was unfolded. Yet, it also emphasized that this people is a hierarchically structured society in which the pope and the bishops in union with him hold the plentitude of power. According to Orthodox (q.v.) teaching the church is neither fully described in the Bible nor in the Tradition (qq.v.). The church is a mystery grounded in the fullness of life of the holy Trinity (q.v.). The participation of the faithful in the life of the church is a participation in the body and life of Jesus Christ (q.v.). This participation starts with the hearing of the word of God, the response of faith, and in the subsequent incorporation in the divine human nature of Christ through the sacrament of baptism (q.v.); it grows through the descent of the pneumatological gift of unction (Myron) and finds its climax in the reception of the resurrected himself, in the body and blood of the eucharist (q.v.).

Another ecclesiological model has emerged in the late 20th century, ''secular theology''. The church, according to this view, has the task of pioneering the unity of the larger human society. It considers itself as a servant of the coming unity of the whole human race. In this perspective the internal unity of the church is not of primary importance. The main focus is on the goals of universal peace, justice (qq.v.) and solidarity, to which the service of the church is ordered. The various images of the church and models in ecclesiology have been intensively discussed within the ecumenical movement and the debates should continue. *See also* JESUS CHRIST; PEOPLE OF GOD; UNITY.

ECOLOGY/ENVIRONMENT. Among the ten affirmations of the world convocation on Justice, Peace and the Integrity of Creation (q.v.) in Seoul in 1990, the affirmation of "the creation as beloved of God" with "its own inherent integrity" stressed that "we will resist the claim that anything in creation is merely a resource for human exploitation". This WCC (q.v.) conference outlined the ecumenical program to preserve the human environment, recognizing that "the self-renewing, sustainable character of natural ecosystems" must be maintained. After a long past of ignorance and indifference it is only recently realized in Christianity that the technologized world has failed to control the hazardous by-products of its industries, with the result that water, soil and air are polluted around and beyond heavily industrialized areas. The effects of such pollution vary, but the consequences for human health and the delicate balance of the ecosystem are profound, in some cases irreversible.

In the report of the 1979 Church and Society conference at the Massachusetts Institute of Technology, which brought together scientists, technocrats, political leaders and theologians, a section report was devoted to "Technology, Resources, Environment and Population". Therein was stated: "Even if solutions to environmental problems are possible, they are often complex. They involve an inter-relation of industry, individuals, and the political system. Sometimes there appears as yet to be no solution". There are three positions on how an ecological theology should be developed.

1) A sacramental understanding of the world must be reinforced. In his book *The Human Presence: An Orthodox View of Nature*, Paulos Gregorios (q.v.) says that the two attitudes of "mastery and mystery" need to be reconciled. "A secular technology of mastery of nature for oneself is the 'original' sin, of refusing our mediatory position between God and the universe, for the sake of indulging in our own cupidity, avarice and greed . . . the loss of our proper

humanity caused by our technological civilization is greater than all the harm it has done through pollution, resource depletion, and all the rest''.

2) The understanding of the world through process theology. Charles Birch (q.v.), who addressed the Nairobi assembly in 1975, is an outspoken representative of this philosophy, initiated by Alfred North Whitehead. In the evolutionary ecological process of the world God, the human being and the earth cooperate together. Love for one's neighbor must be extended to the subhuman world in which nature has its own intrinsic value, because God has given it special value.

3) The third position stresses ''solidarity in conflict''. It presupposes that the ecological crisis cannot be overcome by living in harmony with nature or cooperating with nature. Although it is true that human beings are part of nature, the difference between God and human being/world cannot be ignored. The dualistic separation between the human being and God must be resisted as much as a monistic harmonization. The threat to the environment should serve human beings to become more deeply aware of their mortality.

The WCC created within the context of ecological ethics a program ''Energy for my Neighbor''. This action program was intended to sensitize churches about energy problems faced by developing countries and to activate practical steps to ameliorate the energy situation for the less privileged. Many churches took up this challenge. A number of ecumenical consultations were held on the subject in different developing countries. Increasingly, environmental issues are becoming limiting factors to continued industrial development. Climate change is already taking place. Forests are disappearing due to air pollution in the developed countries and to unsustainable overuse in the developing countries. In addition to helping to clarify the related social and ethical issues, the Christian communities also have a responsibility to act. The problem remains, however, what to do, and on what basis?

ECUMENICAL INSTITUTES. Various kinds of ecumenical institutes have arisen since the Second World War: lay academies, lay training centers, dialogue centers and scholarly theological institutes. The first evangelical academy was founded in Bad Boll, Germany. Other academies soon followed. Representative among these are Arnoldshain, Berlin, Erfurt, Hamburg, Bremen, Iserlohn, Magdeburg, Mühleim (Ruhr) and Tutzing. They all bring together Christian laypeople and theologians to address contemporary issues in church and society in the light of the gospel. Study sessions are arranged during vacation periods and on weekends to allow professionals from all walks of life to participate. Clergy and university professors often serve as resource persons. A typical session includes Bible study, theme addresses, and wide-ranging discussions on how to relate one's faith (q.v.) to daily responsibilities. Some 15,000 persons annually have become involved in academy-sponsored meetings since the inception of the movement.

Several dozens of lay academies and lay training centers spread outside Germany. Representative are the Iona Community (Scotland), Sigtuna (Sweden), Boldern (Switzerland), Mindolo (Zambia), Nippon Christian Academy (Japan), Five Oaks Christian Center (Canada), etc. There are further institutes in Asia (South Korea, Taiwan, Hong Kong, Indonesia) and in Africa (South Africa, Lesotho, Nigeria, Benin, Cameroon, Tanzania, Zambia, Kenya, Ethiopia, Madagascar). Particularly in Asia, study centers were founded that became known as dialogue centers or institutes for religion and culture. Most of them concentrate on research and dialogue (q.v.) in areas of religions and cultures and on social analysis for renewal in mission (qq.v.). Several of them publish journals in order to share their findings with the churches. Well-known institutes of this type are in Bangalore, Lucknow, Colombo, Batala, Hong Kong, Kyoto and Manila. They are in working relationship with the WCC Commission on World Mission and Evangelism (qq.v.). Consultations on the role of study centers were held in Kandy (1967), Hong Kong (1971) and Singapore (1980) in cooperation with the WCC. A Fellowship of Study Centers was organized in 1980.

A European association of academy directors was established in 1956 including about 45 member centers in various countries of Europe. At present the Ecumenical Association of Academies and Laity Centers in Europe includes some 90 centers in 16 continental countries. The majority are Protestant, but there are also a dozen Roman Catholic and two Greek Orthodox (qq.v.) member centers. Together with the European association the academies outside Europe formed the World Collaboration Committee for Christian Lay Centers, Academies and Movements for Social Concern. This came as a result of the first world conference of lay academies sponsored by the WCC in 1972 at the Orthodox Academy in Crete. Since 1980 a North American Retreat Directors' Association has been active in the USA and Canada, and it also regularly cooperates with centers in Latin America, the Caribbean, the Pacific and the Middle East. Some 600 centers around the world are related to the WCC Sub-unit on Renewal and Congregational Life and exchange information regularly. The Societies Oecumenica, the European Society for Ecumenical Research, was founded in 1978 and represents various Roman Catholic, Protestant and Orthodox ecumenical institutes, centers and professors of ecumenics at European theological faculties and seminaries. Several ecumenical themes, sometimes supplementing and deepening ongoing WCC theological programs, have been discussed during its meetings in 1980, 1982, 1984, 1986, 1988, 1989 and 1993. The Bossey Ecumenical Institute (q.v.) in Switzerland, an agency of the WCC, and the Ecumenical Institute in Chicago, a division of the Church Federation of Greater Chicago, belong to this last category of institutes.

More than 250 leaders from 72 countries gathered in Montreat, North Carolina, in September 1993, under the sponsorship of the World Collaboration Committee of Christian Lay Centers, Academies and Movements for Social Concern, which planned the meeting in cooperation with the WCC. The event, which had "Weaving Communities of Hope" as its theme, involved five regional organizations: Association of Christian Institutes for Social Concern in Asia, Association of Christian Lay Centers in Africa, Ecumenical Association of Academies and Laity Centers in Europe, Collaboration for Ecumenical Planning and Action in the Caribbean and Ecumenical Christian Association of Retreat and Renewal Centers and Leaders in North America.

ECUMENICAL PRAYER CYCLE. At the very heart of the ecumenical movement is the reality of prayer (q.v.). Jesus prayed that his followers may all be one, united in God in the mystery of the Trinity (q.v.). That is the basis and the goal of the search of Christians for unity (q.v.). Prayer is their pathway to unity. What they seek in and through the ecumenical movement is a communion that they cannot articulate in words because it belongs to their life in God. It is through prayer that Christians seek and celebrate that communion. Intercessory prayer is of the essence of the church's vocation. Like Abraham interceding for Sodom and Gomorrah, and following the example of Jesus' priestly prayer in the gospel of St John, Christians raise their hearts and minds to God in worship and adoration, and intercede on behalf of all with whom they share the world and all its joys and sorrows. Through the daily discipline of intercession they affirm their solidarity with fellow Christians all over the world, brothers and sisters living in diverse situations and experiencing diverse problems.

The first edition of the *Ecumenical Prayer Cycle, For All God's People,* published in 1978 and later translated into some 20 languages, was the first introduction to ecumenical prayer. The Vancouver assembly (q.v.) in 1983 reaffirmed the centrality of worship (q.v.). Participants there experienced the power of prayer. They interceded for churches everywhere and for the nations and peoples of the world. It is out of such ecumenical worship experience that the second edition of *With All God's People* (1989) has been prepared. It includes prayers from many countries, allowing us to journey in prayer through every region of the world and through every week of the year. It enables members of the various churches to pray together, *with* all God's people and *for* all God's people, from within concrete contexts. A separate volume contains various orders of worship for the church calendar year and for ecumenical concerns. *See also* PRAYER.

EDINBURGH 1910 *see* INTRODUCTION, INTERNATIONAL MISSIONARY COUNCIL

EDINBURGH 1937 *see* INTRODUCTION, FAITH AND ORDER

EDUCATION, ECUMENICAL. The late 19th and early 20th centuries saw the rise of a number of international Christian organizations, such as the YMCA, the YWCA, the World Student Christian Federation (qq.v.) and the World Sunday School Association, which were not only, in varying degrees, expressions of the ecumenical movement, but to a large extent concerned with Christian education, primarily with education of young people and students. There has been considerable interlocking between these organizations, especially in their leadership and sources of support, and with the formation of the WCC (q.v.) provision was made in the Council's constitution for the participation of fraternal delegates from these bodies. Right from the beginning in 1947, the World Council of Christian Education (q.v.) (continuing in part the work of the World Sunday School Association) was not only concerned with nurture in the Christian faith but with the more fundamental question of what ecumenical education is in the light of the Christian understanding of the meaning of life and the nature and destiny of human beings.

At the second assembly in Evanston (qq.v.) in 1954 the WCC Division of Ecumenical Action was established. This division included the Laity Department, the Department of Co-operation between Men and Women in Church, Family and Society, the Youth Department and the Ecumenical Institute in Bossey (q.v.). At the fourth assembly in Uppsala in 1968 the Office of Education was added to the division. After a process of restructuring the WCC, Unit III, Education and Renewal, was created in 1971, which includes Education, Women in Church and Society, Renewal and Congregational Life, Youth, Biblical Studies and Theological Education. It was in that same year that a joint negotiating committee at the last assembly in Lima, Peru, of the World Council of Christian Education decided to integrate with the

WCC. The International Missionary Council (q.v.) created in 1958 a Theological Education Fund (TEF). With headquarters in London it supported until 1977 theological schools in Africa, Asia and Latin America and strengthened their libraries through the provision of theological textbooks, commentaries and Bible dictionaries in indigenous languages. The example of TEF was followed by the creation in 1964 of a similar Fund for Christian Literature. The Theological Education Fund was continued in 1977 by the Program on Theological Education (PTE) whose programmatic emphasis since the Vancouver assembly (1983) is on theology by the people, spiritual formation and theological and ministerial formation. In 1992 the WCC set new priorities within the structure of four program units. The second unit is concerned with Life, Education and Mission.

Although the New Delhi assembly in 1961 distinguished between ecumenical education, Christian education and general education, it was only from the 1970s onward that the whole spectrum of education and learning of all age groups and social classes was discovered and followed through. The progress in the various fields of education has since then been described as "one of widespread change, trial and error, yet always open to new ideas and insights". The basic orientation has been increasingly toward people—women, youth, children, families, students, congregations, oppressed and poor—in order that each and all of them may be prepared for active engagement in renewing the life of the churches and for intelligent participation in God's work in a changing world. Within these new emphases the task of Christian educators has been approached from a holistic point of view. The report of a world consultation in Bergen, Holland, in 1970 was entitled *Seeing Education Whole.* The perspective has also been based on theological reflection, keeping in mind the two elliptical poles of general education and Christian education, world and worship (q.v.), liberation and community, education and renewal (q.v.).

Special mention must be made of the emphasis on adult education. In the early 1970s, Paulo Freire (q.v.), a Brazilian known for his work in literacy and author of *Pedagogy of the*

Oppressed, was invited to set up a desk of adult education within the WCC. From the beginning, the thrust of the desk was what he called "liberating education" as against "domesticating education". His insights can be summarized as follows: 1) education is never neutral; 2) learners should be involved in selecting the subject matter of learning; 3) pedagogy should be problem posing and not merely transfer of knowledge from those who know to those who do not know; 4) education is not an academic exercise but should contribute to the radical transformation of society so that people can take their destiny in their own hands; 5) learning takes place in dialogue situations. Another influential figure in the field of ecumenical adult education was Ernst Lange (q.v.), concerned during his short life with widening the horizon of the parochial church to a universal outlook.

In spite of the fact that throughout its recent history the WCC Program Unit III has tried to respond to the changing needs in ecumenical learning and that the Vancouver assembly in 1983 finally included a section on "Learning in Community", the importance of ecumenical education has not sufficiently drawn the attention of the established churches. Not only has funding been hard to find but Christian denominations have often not been able to seek ways of translating new insights gained in ecumenical debates into their own life and calling. It will take a long time, it seems, before the wealth of new ecumenical knowledge and experience will create and permeate inclusive Christian communities. Also within the WCC itself concerns for effective learning have remained to a large extent a separate pursuit, blessed but left alone by the much older and experienced movements of Faith and Order, World Mission and Evangelism (qq.v.), Church and Society, and Inter-Church Aid (q.v.). They have felt competent to deal with the proclamation of the apostolic faith, the fostering of growth to fully Christian unity and the facing of the brokenness of the human situation without being disturbed by the evidence of educational implications. As long as there is no deep interpenetration of ecumenical learning and unity, witness, dialogue and service, Unit III (now Unit II) will remain a sectarian enterprise. Summing up the progress in the ecumenical movement, W. A. Visser 't Hooft (q.v.) wrote in 1970: "In spite of all attempts made to educate church members for participation in the ecumenical enterprise the movement is still too much an army with many generals and officers, but with too few soldiers". Ernst Lange was right to recall that Jesus demonstrated that the large household of God was from the beginning oriented toward the whole human family.

EHRENSTRÖM, NILS (1903–1984). Ehrenström began his ecumenical career in 1930 with the Universal Christian Council for Life and Work, as staff member of the international Christian Social Institute. Greatly influenced by his fellow countryman Nathan Söderblom (q.v.), he helped to prepare the Oxford conference on "Church, Community and State" (1937). In that context he wrote *Christian Faith and the Modern State: An Ecumenical Approach,* which showed a rare combination of theological knowledge, sociological insight and ethical judgment. Ehrenström was director of the Study Department of the WCC, 1948–1955, responsible for an inquiry on "Christian Action in Society", and was secretary of the Study Commission on Institutionalism of Faith and Order. He moved to the USA where he taught at the Boston School of Theology and trained many students for service in the ecumenical movement. After his retirement he rendered several services to Faith and Order (q.v.) and continued his search for ways in which the churches and their various ecumenical institutions might develop forms of a more radical change toward a fully committed fellowship.

ELIADE, MIRCEA (1907–1986). As a Romanian scholar, Eliade gained worldwide fame for his studies of religious beliefs and practices and for his attempts to relate them to primordial myths and specific forms of the religious perception of humankind. He studied Sanskrit and Indian philosophy at the University of Calcutta, 1928–1931, before writing his doctoral dissertation on yoga. After serving as a visiting professor at the Ecole d'hautes études of the Sorbonne, 1945–1956, he joined the faculty at the University of Chicago until his retirement in 1985. In 1961 he founded the international journal *History of Religions* and was the editor in chief of the *Encyclopedia of Religion* (1986).

ELLUL, JACQUES (1912–). Ellul became professor of law at the University of Bordeaux in 1943 and was professor at the Institute of Political Studies in Bordeaux until his retirement. Active in the French resistance movement, 1940–1944, he was the secretary of the regional movement for liberation, 1944–1946. He was a member of the national council of the Reformed Church of France, 1951–1970, and of the national synod. Ellul participated in several conferences, organized by the WCC Department on Church and Society and in consultations at the Ecumenical Institute in Bossey (q.v.), where he frequently lectured. He was often critical of the ecumenical movement and missed a prophetic stance of the WCC (q.v.).

EMILIANOS (TIMIADIS) of Silivria (1917–). Emilianos studied theology at the Theological Faculty of Chalki until 1941 and in 1947 went to London where he was the personal secretary of the metropolitans of Thyateira, Germanos, 1947–1951, and of Athenagoras, 1951–1962. He continued his theological studies at Oxford and received a doctor's degree from the University of Thessaloníki. In 1952 he was the pastor of a Greek Orthodox congregation in Brussels and worked among dockers in Antwerpen and Rotterdam. He was permanent representative of the Ecumenical Patriarchate of Constantinople, 1959–1985, and in this capacity was one of the observers at the Second Vatican Council (q.v.), 1962–1965. He was the moderator on the Inter-Orthodox Commission for Dialogue with the Lutheran Churches (qq.v.).

ENCYCLICALS, PAPAL. Formal pastoral letters on doctrinal, moral or disciplinary matters are circulated by the pope as an activity proper to his offices of shepherd of the church and head of the episcopal college, and are thus a part of his ordinary magisterium in contrast to his extraordinary infallible magisterium, exercised in such solemn functions as the definition of dogma or the official approbation of the decrees of an ecumenical council. While these pastoral letters are not of themselves infallible pronouncements, and although their teachings are subject to change, nevertheless Roman Catholics are obligated to assent to their doctrinal and moral content. The following list includes more significant encyclicals of the popes since Pius XXI.

Encyclicals of Pius XII (1939–1958). Mystici corporis, 1943 (the church as the body of Christ); *Divino afflante Spiritu,* 1943 (biblical studies); *Humani generis,* 1950 (on subversive doctrines); *Fidei donum,* 1957 (present condition of Roman Catholic missions, especially in Africa); *Ad apostolorum principis,* 1958 (communism and the church in China).

Encyclicals of John XXIII (q.v.) (1958–1963). Princeps pastorum, 1959 (missions, native clergy and lay participation); *Mater et magistra,* 1961 (Christianity and social progress, reaffirming the fundamental social teachings of Leo XIII); *Pacem in terris,* 1963 (concerning the establishment of universal peace in truth, justice, charity and liberty).

Encyclicals of Paul VI (q.v.) (1963–1978). Ecclesiam suam, 1964 (the church's duty to other Christians and to nonbelievers, and its future development); *Myterium fidei,* 1965 (Holy Eucharist); *Popularum progressio,* 1967 (the development of peoples); *Sacerdotalis caelibatus,* 1967 (the necessity of priestly celibacy); *Humanae vitae,* 1968 (the regulation of birth, rejecting all artificial means of birth control).

Encyclicals of John Paul II (q.v.) (1978–). Redemptor hominis, 1979 (redemption and the dignity of the human race); *Dives in misericordia,* 1980 (the need to demonstrate the mercy of God in an increasingly threatened world); *Laborem exercens,* 1981 (the dignity of labor and the rights of workers); *Slavorum apostoli,* 1985 (commemorating the eleventh centennial of the deaths of St. Methodius and St. Cyril who evangelized the Slavs in the 9th century); *Redemptoris mater,* 1987 (announcing a holy year of the Virgin Mary); *Sollicitudo rei socialis,* 1987 (on creating a new order in human society).

A basic reference work with full documentation is *The Gospel of Peace and Justice: Catholic Social Teaching since Pope John* (1975).

ENVIRONMENT *see* ECOLOGY/ENVIRONMENT

EPISCOPACY. The system of church government whereby ultimate local church jurisdiction resides in the office of one person, the bishop, is called episcopacy. In the New Testament responsibility for *episkopé*(Greek) belongs to Christ (I Pet. 2:25), the Twelve (Acts 1:20) and presbyters (Acts 20:28; Titus 1:5–7; I Pet. 5:2). Whether a presbyter exercised oversight as part of a team or on individual initiative is not clear from Titus 1:7, nor is it clear that the overseeing group in a church was always presbyters (Phil. 1:1). Oversight was exercised in practice, if not especially described as such, by Paul and his delegates Timothy and Titus. The 2nd-century bishop was expected to guard the faith, give pastoral care to clergy and people, govern, discipline and administer the community of his see, and symbolize the unity of the church on behalf of Jesus Christ (q.v.). By the 3rd century ultimate jurisdiction by one bishop over a local church (a see) was the rule, and bishops as a group had collegial authority over the church while exercising independent authority within their sees.

Since the beginning of the ecumenical movement, the episcopacy proved a difficult theme to tackle, both in theory and practice. Concrete schemes for the unification of churches of different tradition and polity had to decide on what was to be done about the episcopate. The most significant ecumenical development was that of the Church of South India, which united several denominations after many years of preparation in 1947. This plan brought together the Anglican church and some non-episcopal churches in one episcopal church, but without calling into question the authenticity of the previous exercised ministry of the non-episcopal churches and without demanding re-ordination. In most other church unions the episcopal form of church government has prevailed over non-episcopal forms of leadership.

The section of *Baptism, Eucharist and Ministry* (BEM) on ministry (qq.v.) represents the theoretical foundations of recent ecumenical discussions and reflects a widely agreed upon policy, even if not to the satisfaction of all. In asking for the possible restoration of the episcopacy in churches that have not maintained it, as key to the tripartite forms of the ministries of bishop, presbyter and deacon, BEM presents it as a historical phenomenon of early origins and of some significance to the life of the church, rather than something that dates from the apostles or that is absolutely essential to the church. It also admits a possible diversity in the forms that episcopate would take. In official reactions to the BEM document, a number of churches ask for a clarification of the relation between *episkopē* and episcopacy. Reformation and Free churches continue to express a "functional" understanding of *episkopē* while the Roman Catholic and Orthodox (qq.v.) churches emphasize that "it is more than a function of oversight next to other functions and ministries"; it is also "a sacramental sign of integration and a focus of communion". Though they are prepared to widen the meaning and function of *episkopē*, they still value episcopacy as the supreme and indispensable sacramental form of such *episkopē*. Although greater understanding on episcopacy has been achieved through various dialogues, in conjunction with changes internal to participating churches, full agreement on the episcopacy is by no means an ecumenical reality in the present stage. *See also* MINISTRY.

ESCHATOLOGY. Since the traditional account of Jesus' life and ministry had no place for eschatology, except as a description of what is yet to happen at the end of history, the term eschatology was hardly used until the end of the first half of the 19th century. It was Albert Schweitzer who argued at the beginning of this century that a central, not a peripheral, position must be given to the eschatological teaching of Jesus (q.v.). He maintained that only by means of a consistent application of the eschatological category can we understand Jesus at all, because he came in order to proclaim the approaching eschatological climax. He believed that by sending out the Twelve he would bring the crisis to its consummation. When this failed to happen, Jesus decided that he must deliberately take upon himself the apocalyptic woes and offer himself as the ransom that would enable God to inaugurate the New Age. In the 1930s C. H. Dodd (q.v.)

reacted to the extreme position of Schweitzer and tried to restore the balance by speaking of a "realized exchatology". He argued that much of Jesus' teaching suggests a kingdom that is already present, as he brought the kingdom and is the kingdom. The whole complex of events comprising Jesus' ministry, teaching, death and resurrection themselves constitute the coming of the kingdom. Since then various mediating positions have been taken up by various New Testament theologians.

Eschatology as the starting point of theology inevitably affected the understanding of the gospel and consequently of the church's nature and mission. In the context of the ecumenical movement, this influence helped Orthodox and Protestant churches and the Roman Catholic Church (qq.v.) to understand themselves as dynamic communities of God's presence in the world that find their true nature and fulfilment in the coming reality of God's kingdom. During the years of preparation for the second WCC assembly (qq.v.) in Evanston in 1954, with its main theme "Christ the Hope of the World", there was a lively discussion concerning the meaning and relevance of eschatology. The advisory committee on the main theme, composed of theologians of extremely varied backgrounds, had a hard time arriving at a common document; but the assembly admitted that the report "exhibits a substantial ecumenical consensus" and that "it indicates the direction in which we all must move". Yet, the concept of Christian hope held by European churches still tended to be truly eschatological, whereas the concept of the American churches was still more optimistic and more concerned with the Christian hope in this world here and now. The assembly agreed that a genuine theology of mission must be related to eschatology. At the WCC assemblies in New Delhi and Uppsala it was suggested that the structures of the church should be conceived in an eschatological framework, but the Orthodox churches rejected this proposal as they conceive the structures of the body of Christ sacramentally as divinely ordained and therefore unchangeable.

In the Dogmatic Constitution on the Church of Vatican II (q.v.) the intrinsically eschatological nature of the church was also affirmed. It should be noted that although the WCC never ignored the weight of eschatological dimensions in theological discussions, it always avoided defining exactly the being of the church, which has resulted in only occasional and fragmentary presentations of how eschatological perspective affect the life and witness of the church and advances the cause of church unity (q.v.). *See also* HOPE; KINGDOM OF GOD.

ESPY, EDWIN R. H. (1899–1993). Espy was a leader of the ecumenical movement for more than forty years. He joined the National Council of the Churches of Christ in the USA (q.v.) in 1955 and was its general secretary from 1963 to 1973, a period when this ecumenical body's strong support for the civil rights movement provoked much controversy. Earlier he was the secretary of the study department of the American YMCA. Espy was the secretary of the first world conference of Christian youth in Amsterdam (1939), and edited a symposium in commemoration of this conference in 1979. He served, moreover, as the North American representative to the Joint Working Group (q.v.), which considered a broad range of religious issues and relationships.

ETHICS, SEXUAL *see* SEXUAL ETHICS

EUCHARIST. There is no doubt that since the beginning of the 2nd century, and possibly in the New Testament itself, the word *eucharistia* was used by Greek Christian writers to denote the rite that Jesus instituted at the Last Supper and that became the central observance of the church. The original word "eucharist" should in fact be preferred to other terms such as "holy communion", "the Lord's supper", etc. Whether the Last Supper was a Passover meal is disputed by biblical scholars, but there is little doubt that the accounts of the institution of the eucharist given in the synoptic gospels and in I Cor. 11 are not meant as a complete description of the rite but simply record, as handed down in the liturgical traditions, certain words that Jesus added to the accepted forms of blessing bread at the beginning, and a common cup at the end, of a solemn Jewish meal. Those words consist of: 1) a declaration that the bread was his body and the wine was his blood of the (new) covenant; and 2) a command to "do this" as his *anamnesis,* or "memorial".

At the time of the Reformation Protestants commonly believed that Roman Catholic (qq.v.) theologians held that the eucharist either repeated the sacrifice of the cross or else performed some further sacrificial function that the cross had been unable to perform, and medieval devotion and practice certainly gave some color to this impression, though whether medieval theology taught anything like this is doubtful and has been disputed. Protestantism in general has seen the presence of Christ as operative in the *action* of the eucharist rather than identified with the eucharistic *objects,* the bread and the wine. While the Roman Catholic Church has adhered firmly to the doctrine of transubstantiation, promulgated at the fourth Lateran Council in 1215 and reaffirmed by the Council of Trent in 1551, Protestant churches have tended toward "receptionism", i.e., the doctrine that Christ's body and blood are received by the devout communicant at the same time as the bread and the wine but are in no real sense identical with them.

In its Constitution on the Sacred Liturgy, Vatican Council II (q.v.) insists on the traditional teaching of the real presence of Christ in the eucharistic species (7). But it also enlarges that understanding by affirming the real presence of Christ in the minister, in the word of Scripture, in the praying and singing congregation. In every liturgical celebration, it is Christ who associates the church with himself in the everlasting worship that he offers to the Father. This statement shifts the focus of the point of departure for the theology of the eucharist from the really present body of Christ as both sign and reality in the eucharist to the really present body that is the church whose unity with its Lord is sacramentalized in the deepening of their mutual real presence in and by means of the entire eucharistic celebration.

The section on the eucharist in *Baptism, Eucharist and Ministry* (BEM) (q.v.) has been regarded by several responses of the churches as the most satisfactory of the three parts of the Lima text. It is admitted that it is irenic in approach and successfully transcends old divisive controversies, because it draws its inspiration from recent biblical, patristic and liturgical scholarship. In its reply the Roman Catholic Church stated: "If all the churches and ecclesial communities are able to accept at least the theological understanding and description of the celebration of the eucharist as described in BEM and implement it as part of their normal life, we believe that this would be an important development, and that these divided Christians now stood on a new level in regard to achieving common faith on the eucharist". Analyzing the official responses there is indeed a broad agreement or convergence concerning the Trinitarian structure and meaning of the eucharist, the inseparability of word and sacrament, the "real, living and active presence" of Christ and the commemoration of his sacrifice, the mutual reference of *anamnesis* and *epiklesis,* as well as the ethical, missionary and eschatological dimensions of the eucharist. Such convergence not only provides the framework for the settlement of remaining differences in eucharistic doctrine, but also suggests that the churches already share a largely common vision of the apostolic faith as a whole.

It is the official entry of the Roman Catholic Church into the ecumenical movement that caused to open the possibility of "eucharistic hospitality"—in fact a better word than "intercommunion" because increasingly "open" communion services were conducted. Vatican II recognized that other Christians, by virtue of baptism and faith in Jesus Christ (qq.v.), already enjoy a "certain, though imperfect, communion with the Catholic church" (*Unitatis redintegratio*) (3). The Roman Catholic emergency hospitality is offered to Protestants as individual Christians, while Catholics are still expected not to take communion in Protestant churches whose Lord's supper is marred by a "defect" at the level of ordination. The Methodists (q.v.) were perhaps the first to practice open communion. But the World Alliance of Reformed Churches (q.v.) recommended in 1975 the admission to the Lord's table of "any baptized person who loves and confesses Jesus Christ as Lord and Savior". The Orthodox (q.v.) still reject the notion of eucharistic hospitality on the grounds that there is either one communion in one church or no communion at all.

Since 1975 the clear constitutional goal of the WCC (q.v.) has been to help the churches to advance to "visible unity in one faith and in one eucharistic fellowship". This is still a difficult goal. A passionate paragraph in BEM should help Christians to move in the right direction. It states: "The eucharist involves the believer in the central event of the world's history. As participants in the eucharist, therefore, we prove inconsistent if we are not actively participating in those ongoing restoration of the world's situation and the human condition. The eucharist shows us that our behavior is inconsistent in face of the reconciling presence of God in human history: we are placed under continual judgment by the persistence of unjust relationships of all kinds in our society, the manifold divisions on account of human pride, material interest and power politics and, above all, the obstinacy of unjustifiable confessional oppositions within the body of Christ" (E207).

"As the eucharist celebrates the resurrection of Christ, it is appropriate", declares BEM, "that it should take place at least every Sunday" (E31). The Reformers stopped the "multiplication of masses", but they were unable to rees-tablish the regular weekly communion of the faithful, which most church leaders desired. Consequently, the normal Sun-day service in the Protestant churches became the service of preaching, prayers and hymn singing. Some Protestant com-munions have, however, recognized anew that the celebra-tion of the eucharist every Sunday corresponds with the biblical tradition of conducting a worship (q.v.) service of both word and sacrament.

EUTHANASIA. With the possible exception of emergency situa-tions, Christians have generally opposed any right to volun-tary euthanasia, i.e., the deliberate ending of life to enable the gravely sick person to die in dignity and peace. Euthanasia involves several practical legal and moral considerations. It is difficult to be absolutely sure that the patient has given his or her full consent. It is further impossible to devise laws that contain adequate safeguards to prevent misuse and abuse. Added to these facts are theological arguments centering on the belief that God is the creator, judge and redeemer, and that human beings, created in his image, have no right to choose the time of their death, but should accept the care of their fellow human beings. Yet, it is argued by the Voluntary Euthanasia Legalization Societies in Great Britain and America that, with various safeguards, the law should permit a human being in special circumstances to terminate his or her own life or request a doctor to do it for him or her. Euthanasia has hardly been a subject of searching ecumenical debate. Pope Pius XII rejected decidedly euthanasia in the 1940s and 1950s. It was condemned by the archbishops of Canterbury in 1936, and York in 1950, and by the Protestant Episcopal Church in America in 1952. A profound theological-ethical discussion in all confessions on this complex issue has become urgent.

EVANGELICAL ACADEMIES *see* ECUMENICAL INSTITUTES

EVANGELICAL ALLIANCE *see* WORLD EVANGELICAL FELLOWSHIP

EVANGELICALS. The term "evangelical" is derived from the Greek word for "gospel". The term first came into usage during the Reformation to distinguish Protestants from Roman Catholics, and it stressed the centrality of Jesus Christ, grace, faith (qq.v.) and Scripture. In Germany it gradually came to be applied collectively to Lutheran, Reformed (qq.v.) and Union communions, and even today evangelical is synonymous with "Protestant" in much of Europe. As much of the spiritual vigor of the Reformation eroded during the ensuing age of orthodoxy, three movements in the late 17th and 18th centuries—German pietism, Methodism and the Great Awakening—led to the renewal of the Protestant church. Common to these movements were a rather simplistic emphasis on a conversion experience of some kind, the need to live a "holy life" and personal evidence of newly found or renewed faith in good works of evangelism (q.v.) and social concern.

Around the time of the Second World War, some groups within the conservative and fundamentalist evangelical families grew dissatisfied with their isolation and wished to see a more broadly based cultural, theological and ecclesiastical engagement. Describing themselves as "evangelicals", they set out to build coalitions of cooperation in evangelism, missionary work and unity (q.v.) against liberalism as it affected the integrity of Scriptures. Consequently leaders of new evangelicalism rejected the separatism, anti-intellectualism, legalism and moralism that had come to be identified with the older fundamentalism. They endeavored to bring about renewal (q.v.) in the church through evangelism, built some ecumenical bridges and even manifested a renewed interest in the social dimension of the Christian message. The Billy Graham (q.v.) organization was the major catalyst for evangelical ecumenism, since it (in collaboration with *Christianity Today*) called the the World Congress on Evangelism (Berlin, 1966) and the International Congress on World Evangelism (Lausanne, 1974). The subsequent meetings sponsored by the Lausanne committee, including a second world congress in Singapore in 1989, together with the activities of the World Evangelical Fellowship (q.v.) and the regional organizations formed by evangelicals in Africa, Asia, Latin America and Europe have fostered closer relations and cooperative efforts in evangelism, relief work, and theological development.

More than one-fourth of the WCC (q.v.) member churches have the word "evangelical" in their name. Discussion with evangelicals on their relation to the WCC, however, generally refers to contacts with evangelicals just described briefly above. Although it is in the area of mission (q.v.) and evangelism that the WCC and evangelical organizations have the greatest communality of interests, it is precisely in this area that significant controversies arise. Evangelicals charge the WCC with too much concern for social action and too little for evangelism. Ecumenical dialogue with people of living faiths (q.v.) has been regarded in some evangelical quarters as dulling the edge of mission, if not abandoning the historic claims about the unique salvation in Jesus Christ (qq.v.). Since the 1974 Lausanne congress there has been a global "evangelical" mission conference at about the same time as each of the WCC's world mission conferences. Some people have attended both conferences, but it is clear that a large number at each would consider the gulf between them too wide to be bridged by holding a single conference.

A continuing source of tension within the WCC constituency is the way in which wealthy and independent evangelical mission, relief and development agencies headquartered in North America and Europe operate in countries of the Third World. Local churches there, often representing an ancient but struggling minority of Christians, sometimes charge that evangelical organizations from abroad show little respect for the culture and tradition of that area and that, despite their strictures against "the church getting involved in politics", they themselves support a particular political line. But it is important not to fall into stereotypes when talking about "evangelicals" and social or political involvement. Certain evangelical groups have a long heritage of costly and thoughtful engagement in society; and serious discussion of social justice (q.v.) issues has gone on among many evangelicals in recent years.

Because most evangelical groups are organized in a way that precludes the kind of direct relationships with the WCC that church-based ecumenical bodies have, WCC relations with evangelicals cannot be highly structured. Most effective in building understanding are "unofficial" contacts with individual evangelical leaders—always with the risk for both sides that such a contact may be looked askance among some of their own constituency.

EVANGELISM *see* MISSION AND EVANGELISM

EVANSTON 1954 *see* WORLD COUNCIL OF CHURCHES ASSEMBLIES

EVDOKIMOV, PAUL (1901–1970). Evdokimov studied in Kiev, and at St Sergius in Paris, and obtained a Ph.D. in philosophy at the University of Aix-Marseille in 1942. He left Russia for Constantinople and arrived in France in 1923. Teaching at the Orthodox (q.v.) faculty of theology of St Sergius from 1953 onward, he became involved in the activities of Faith and Order (q.v.). From 1943 he worked with the CIMADE, an ecumenical organization created to help refugees (q.v.)

and displaced persons. He directed a center for refugees in Bièvres, near Paris, 1946–1947. His works on Orthodox theology in an ecumenical context are widely known.

- F -

FAGLEY, RICHARD M. (1910–1993). Fagley retired from the WCC (q.v.) in 1975 after serving as executive secretary in the Commission of the Churches on International Affairs (CCIA) for 25 years at the United Nations (q.v.) headquarters liaison office in New York, having first joined the CCIA in 1951. A graduate of Yale University, he was ordained a minister of the Congregational Christian Churches (later part of the United Church of Christ) in 1939. He served from 1945–1947 as executive secretary of the Commission on Just and Durable Peace of the United States' Federal Council of Churches (q.v.), and from 1950–1951 as director of the department of International Justice and Goodwill of the National Council of Churches of Christ in the USA (q.v.).

FAITH. "Faith" in classical and modern biblical theology means trustful obedience toward God as he reveals himself in his Word. It is a human response to the divine forgiveness and grace (q.v.) contained in Scripture, as it was variously spoken to the fathers by the prophets, has become an incarnate expression in Jesus Christ (q.v.) and is addressed to Christians now by the Holy Spirit (q.v.) through the word and the sacraments (q.v.) of the gospel. The object of faith is never a set of doctrinal propositions, but the personal reality of God in Christ; faith therefore must be understood essentially in terms of a personal relationship. The gospel, to be sure, cannot be proclaimed without the use of propositional statements. But the gospel does not call for an assent to these propositions; it calls for faith in Jesus Christ and in God through him. In Roman Catholic (q.v.) theology, on the contrary, "faith" means essentially mental assent to divinely revealed truth, that is, to the faith of which the church is the custodian and the interpreter. The credibility of the truth as revealed to human beings is sufficiently attested by the authority of the church. There are clear arguments, which can be rational, philosophical and historical, for the existence of God, the fact of revelation, and the infallibility (q.v.) of the church as witness to this revelation.

Faith has been and remains the driving force and the common goal of the ecumenical movement. There are, however, still different understandings of the form and content of the Christian faith. This also pertains to the World Council of Churches (q.v.). Discussions continue about the nature of faith, both as a gift and as a task, about the authoritative teaching of the faith, the relation of personal faith to the faith of the church, the intermediary role of Scripture and the role of tradition (q.v.). A legitimate pluralism of faith has always been advocated in the ecumenical movement.

The Amsterdam assembly (1948) was preoccupied with modern unbelief. "A formidable obstacle to Christian faith is the conviction that it belongs definitely to a historical phase now past. To those who know little of it, it seems merely irrelevant. More thoughtful men, who hold that it enshrines some spiritual and cultural values, regard it as no longer honestly tenable as a system of belief". One of the reasons for this general world situation, particularly in the western hemisphere, is that "the church is accused by many of having been blind to the movement of God in history, of having sided with the vested interests of society and state, and of having failed to kindle the vision and to purify the wills of men in a changing world". The world conference on Church and Society in Geneva (1966) countered the Amsterdam statements as follows: "In secular technology and revolution, man in the context of faith differs fundamentally from man in a non-believing context, in his understanding of the power of God to whom he is responsible, to human sin with which he must reckon, and the vision of true humanity which he finds in Christ. He is by this very token a part of the struggle in our time to achieve a responsible society of justice and peace among men, and to discern and and realize relative meanings in history". The Humanum Studies of the WCC (1969–1975) emphasized the relationship of the claims of Christian identity to the agonies and struggles for human identity. There is "a necessary interaction between the area of faith and the areas of humanization and ecumenicity . . . The question of what faith recognizes, or whom faith seeks to obey and about whom the faith seeks to bear witness, remains necessary and central".

The WCC Sub-unit on Dialogue with People of Living Faiths (q.v.) has taken various initiatives from the 1970s onward for real dialogue (q.v.) and cooperation and has prepared the ground for a wider ecumenism and a more open, respectful and peaceful attitude of faith in many Christian churches today. A conference in Chiang Mai, Thailand, in 1977 stated: "Dialogue is between people of faith. Faith is no one's monopoly . . . The common ground in dialogue is Faith, which ought to be only one. And the goal of dialogue should be to discover the Faith in the mist of faiths". The WCC's *Guidelines on Dialogue with People of Living Faiths and Ideologies* (1979) formulated the same concern in the following words: "It is Christian faith in the Triune God— Creator of all humankind, Redeemer in Jesus Christ, revealing and renewing Spirit—which calls us Christians to human relationships with our many neighbors. It is Christian faith which sets us free to be open to the faith of others, to risk, to trust and to be vulnerable. In dialogue, conviction and openness are held in balance".

Since its meeting in Bangalore in 1978, the Commission on Faith and Order has embarked on a long-term study project "Towards the Common Expression of the Apostolic Faith Today". The study distinguished methodologically between common recognition, explication, and confession of the apostolic faith as expressed especially in the Nicene-Constantinopolitan Creed (381) and as related to contemporary challenges. Convinced that a short presentation of the goal and the contents of the study could help to broaden the discussion within the churches, Faith and Order revised *Confessing One Faith* and transmitted the text to the churches in 1991. The fifth world conference on Faith and Order in Santiago de Compostela, Spain, in 1993 expressed the hope that the document will prove to be an instrument capable of provoking the recognition of the faith and an instrument of passage that will lead Christians beyond recognition of the faith in their own lives and in one another to common confession. The wider perspective of confessing the faith today has been served by Faith and Order through its series of texts *Confessing Our Faith Around the World* in four volumes, covering the various continents and regions, published in 1984 and 1985. *See also* ATHEISM; BILATERAL DIALOGUES; CATECHISMS; CREEDS; DIALOGUE WITH PEOPLE OF LIVING FAITHS; MULTILATERAL DIALOGUES.

FAITH AND ORDER. Together with the movement for Life and Work (q.v.) and the International Missionary Council (q.v.), the Faith and Order movement was a major expression of ecumenism during the first half of the 20th century. Following the 1910 world missionary conference in Edinburgh, the convention of the Protestant Episcopal Church in the USA in the same year resolved "that a Joint Commission be appointed to bring about a conference for the consideration of questions touching Faith and Order". Several churches passed similar resolutions and others responded positively to the invitation to join in the preparation of such a world conference. Efforts to win the participation of the Roman Catholic Church (q.v.) met with a negative response. Thus, the Faith and Order movement was born, and after years of work and a preparatory meeting in Geneva in 1920, the first world conference on faith and order took place in Lausanne in 1927. It provided the first occasion in modern church history for representatives of Orthodox, Anglican, Reformation (qq.v.) and Free churches—more than 400 people—to come together to discuss their agreements in faith (q.v.) and the deep differences that had divided them for centuries. The conference met in the context of a new world situation: there was a growing awareness of an interdependent and "smaller" world in which the Christian churches were beginning to discover the need for common witness and service. From these early years onward Faith and Order has perceived its theological task as one of overcoming church-dividing differences and preparing the way toward visible unity (q.v.), thereby also supporting this common calling to mission (q.v.) and service.

The second world conference on faith and order in 1937 in Edinburgh was more systematically prepared by a number of commissions. It followed the same comparative methodology of registering agreements and disagreements, but was able to clarify several concepts of church unity with a certain preference for that of organic or corporate union. The conference also agreed, despite some opposing voices, to the proposal to unite the Faith and Order and Life and Work movements "to form a council of churches". This decision was implemented in 1948 in Amsterdam when the World Council of Churches (q.v.) was formed. Within the new structure of the WCC the tasks of the Faith and Order movement were carried on by the Commission on Faith and Order. But the idea of a movement was preserved and expressed in the form of a special constitution (later, by-laws), which provides for membership on the commission of representatives from churches that do not belong to the WCC, and for the commission to continue to organize world conferences from time to time. The aim of the commission, according to the by-laws, is "to proclaim the oneness of the church of Jesus Christ (q.v.) and to call the churches to the goal of visible unity in one faith and one eucharistic fellowship, expressed in worship (q.v.) and in common life in Christ, in order that the world may believe".

In 1952 the commission organized the Third World conference on faith and order in Lund, where it moved from the former comparative method to a form of theological dialogue that seeks to bring out agreements and convergences and to struggle with controversial issues by starting from a common biblical and Christological basis. The fourth world conference took place in 1963 in Montreal, and the fifth world conference was held at Santiago. While the first phase of the Faith and Order movement was marked by the world conferences in 1927 and 1937, since 1948 an increasingly broader program of studies has developed. These studies have been planned and discussed at regular commission meetings (every three or four years), while the standing committee (30 members) supervises and implements the study programs and ongoing work together with the secretariat, which is an integral part of the WCC structure in Geneva. Most Faith and

Order studies and reports have been published in Faith and Order Papers, nos. 1–103. 1910–1948, and in Faith and Order Papers, nos. 1–. 1948–. Two volumes include the major texts of studies and reports: *Documentary History of the Faith and Order Movement, 1927–1963* and *Documentary History of Faith and Order, 1963–1993.*

Consultations that Faith and Order sponsored were on a great variety of subjects, such as baptism, worship, ministry, the ordination of women, patristic studies, the week of prayer for Christian unity, bilateral dialogues, the "filioque" (qq.v.) controversy, eucharist with children and several other subjects. Also various study programs in between Faith and Order commission meetings were undertaken on such themes as The Finality of Jesus Christ in the Age of Universal History, Tradition and Traditions (q.v.), Institutionalism, Ways of Worship, God in Nature and History, Man in Nature and History, Giving Account of the Hope that Is in Us, How Does the Church Teach Authoritatively Today?. Two recent study projects are: Towards the Common Expression of the Apostolic Faith Today and The Unity of the Church and the Renewal of Human Community. Since 1978 the commission has organized five meetings of the forum on bilateral dialogues (q.v.). From 1982 onward Faith and Order has become even more widely known in connection with its consensus document *Baptism, Eucharist and Ministry* (BEM) (q.v.), to which a great number of churches inside and outside the WCC reacted.

The composition of the Faith and Order Commission, which now has up to 120 members, has considerably changed during the last decades. The formerly rather small number of Orthodox members has increased to over 20 percent, while representatives of churches from the southern hemisphere now make up nearly 50 percent. Women theologians, who were virtually absent from the commission, now represent 34 percent of its membership and include the present moderator, Mary Tanner. Since 1968 the Roman Catholic Church has been officially represented by 12 members and participates in and supports all Faith and Order studies and decisions. The moderators of the commission were: Ingve Brilioth (q.v.) (1947–1957), Douglas Horton (q.v,.) (1957–1963), Paul Minear (q.v.) (1963–1967), H. H. Harms (1967–1971), John Meyendorff (q.v.) (1971–1975), Nikos Nissiotis (q.v.) (1975–1983), John Deschner (1983–1991) and Mary Tanner (1991–).

There is no doubt that Faith and Order—both the movement and the commission—has been and is an appropriate and effective instrument of and within the ecumenical movement. It has challenged and assisted the churches to overcome the doctrinal differences, to share their diverse spiritual and theological insights and forms of life as a source of mutual enrichment and renewal (q.v.), and to reappropriate and express together their common heritage in faith, life and witness. All these efforts have had as their goal the manifestation of the visible unity of the church of Jesus Christ. This goal has been seen in the wider perspective of the calling of the churches, sustained and inspired by the Holy Spirit (q.v.), to become a credible sign and instrument of God's saving and transforming purpose for all humanity and creation.

A fifth world conference of Faith and Order took place in Santiago de Compostela in Spain in 1993. Its main theme was "Towards Koinonia in Faith, Life and Witness". The New Testament term *koinonia* is commonly translated as "communion" or "fellowship". In the final message, "On the Way to Fuller Koinonia", the world conference spoke of "deeper", "broader" and "greater" koinonia and "the conversion to Christ that true koinonia in our time demands". It was not the first time that reference was made to a "new ecumenical reality", which has created a new need for a new way of moving toward Christian unity. It had been noticed that the commission's work should be done in the context of the total ecumenical movement and inseparably related to the work of the WCC for mission and witness and for service and renewal. Others have argued that the traditional Faith and Order concentration on theological differences and issues of church structure has become too narrowly academic, a specialized interest of a minority of like-minded theologians and a program of little importance for the actual life of the churches. It was in particular the present WCC secretary who said in his address to the world conference that the intervening years have brought a new situation in which "the center of gravity of the Christian world" has shifted away from Europe and North America. The churches that founded the WCC "have been gripped by deep uncertainty and spiritual paralysis . . . They lack the spiritual strength to shake off the confessional identities that have been shaped by mutual differentiation and exclusion". Konrad Raiser (q.v.) further stated that "if the stalemate of the ecumenical process in the quest for visible unity is to be overcome, a new approach will have to be found". To meet the need of the new situation, he called for "an ecumenical intercultural hermeneutic" that would view unity as a fellowship among Christians who continue to be different. Looking toward the fiftieth anniversary of the WCC in 1998 and plans for an eighth general assembly that year, Raiser noted that the fiftieth year was a jubilee year in biblical terms, and suggested that an appropriate action for the churches to take that year would be lifting "the doctrinal anathemas of the past".

FAITH AND SCIENCE *see* SCIENCE AND RELIGION

FEDERAL COUNCIL OF THE CHURCHES OF CHRIST IN AMERICA. This council was of special importance in ecumenical history as being a pioneer among national councils. It made experiments and sometimes mistakes; it led to the formation of other councils and passed on the results of its experience to them; it finally initiated the greatest experiment yet made in cooperation between churches. The Council's main objects, as set forth when it was founded in 1908, were: "a) to express the fellowship and Catholic unity of the Christian Church; b) to bring the Christian body of America into united service for Christ and the world". It had "no authority to draw up a common creed (q.v.) or form of government or worship (q.v.) or in any way to limit the full authority of the Christian bodies adhering to it". As to its basis, the Constitution contained the clear requirement that the member denominations were to be those that recognize Jesus Christ as "Divine Lord and Savior".

The Council was an almost new departure in ecumenical history, an organization constituted by the definitely ecclesiastical action of the churches through their highest authorities. By 1910, 31 denominations had joined, including the great majority of American Protestants, exceptions at that time being the Southern Baptists, the Lutherans (qq.v.) and Protestant Episcopal churches. The latter came into full membership in 1940, at the same time as four Eastern Orthodox (q.v.) bodies. In spite of these additions, the number of churches within the council in 1948 was 29 in contrast to 31 in 1910, a reduction due to unions that had taken place between member churches. At the time of the merger of the Federal Council with other bodies to form the National Council of Churches (q.v.), the number of local congregations within the federated churches was 143,959, with a total membership in the neighborhood of 32 million.

The ultimate success of the Council was due in large measure to the leadership of its first general secretary, Charles S. Macfarland (q.v.). He was indefatigable in personal contacts with officials of churches and of nations and in service to the worldwide ecumenical movement. His audacity, aggressiveness, tenacity and willingness to take risks went far toward making the Council what it became. *See also* NATIONAL COUNCIL OF THE CHURCHES OF CHRIST IN THE USA.

FELLOWSHIP OF RECONCILIATION *see* INTERNATIONAL FELLOWSHIP OF RECONCILIATION

FELLOWSHIP OF ST ALBAN AND ST SERGIUS. The Anglo-Orthodox Fellowship of St Alban and St Sergius was founded at a conference at St Albans in England in 1928. Bishop Walter Frere, a well-known Anglican (q.v.) liturgist, was elected its first president. St Alban was the first martyr of Britain and St Sergius of Radonezh, patron saint of the Russian theological academy in Paris, with which many of the Orthodox (q.v.) founder members were connected. The Fellowship soon became a center of various ecumenical experiments. Besides its annual general conferences, it organized a number of local conferences, which usually began with an Orthodox eucharist (q.v.) celebrated in English, with a choir drawn from among Anglican and Free Church Christians. The service was followed by papers and discussions introducing the Eastern tradition of Christianity to the members of the local congregation, which had otherwise few opportunities to meet representatives of the Orthodox churches.

Another of the Fellowship's activities was the organization of short courses of lectures on the Eastern tradition in theological colleges in Great Britain. G. Florovsky and N. Zernov (qq.v.) did considerable work in this field. The Fellowship was also responsible for the exchange of students and professors, and for the organization of visits of English Christians to Orthodox centers. English theological students went to Romania before the war; Romanian, Serbian, Russian and Bulgarian students stayed for shorter or longer periods in England. Finally, the Fellowship started to publish a special form of reunion literature, which aimed at comparing various traditions of Christianity and was written by authors who were familiar with both the Eastern and the Western outlook. In 1943 the Fellowship acquired a permanent base in London. There were various discussions on ecumenical advances, in particular intercommunion between Anglicans and Orthodox, but these were not continued. After Vatican II, Roman Catholics (qq.v.) make up a significant minority of those who join. The inauguration of the Anglican-Orthodox Joint Doctrinal Discussions in 1973, involving several fellowship members, can be seen as an official continuation of the work carried on previously and unofficially by the Fellowship. It has today over 2,000 members, with half approximately in Britain and the other half spread over the rest of the world. The main event in the life of the Fellowship is still the annual conference, which brings together theologians and non-theologians, clergy and laity (q.v.) from a great number of countries.

FEMINISM *see* WOMEN IN CHURCH AND SOCIETY

FILIOQUE. The word is the Western insertion in the article on the Holy Spirit in the Nicene-Constantinopolitan Creed (qq.v.), "Who proceedeth from the Father *and the Son*", to express the doctrine of the double procession of the Holy Spirit. In the eyes of Eastern Orthodoxy (q.v.) the changing of the wording of the

Nicene Creed by any other authority than an ecumenical council is both canonically illegitimate and an offense against the Christian community. Doctrinally speaking, moreover, if the Spirit only proceeds from the Father he is operative in creation already from the very beginning. This is important in the contemporary dialogue with people of other living faiths (q.v.) and in the search for a pluralistic theology of religions. The Old Catholic Church erased the word from the creed (q.v.); the Lambeth conference of 1978 and the Church of Scotland suggested the same deletion. Celebrating the anniversary of the 381 creed in 1981, Pope John Paul II (q.v.) also did not cite the "filioque". Recently suggestions for alternative formulations, such as "from the Father through the Son" or "who proceeds from the Father and shines forth in the Son" have been made. It remains to be seen what kind of ecumenical theological agreement will relegate the filioque controversy to the past. *See also* TRINITY.

FISHER, GEOFFREY FRANCIS (1887–1972). Fisher became archbishop of Canterbury from 1945 onward, was chairman of the WCC (q.v.) at its inauguration in Amsterdam, 1948, and a president of the Council, 1948–1954. He met Pope John XXIII (q.v.) in 1960, the first archbishop of Canterbury to go to Rome since 1397. He also met in the same year with the Orthodox (q.v.) patriarch of Jerusalem and the ecumenical patriarch of Constantinople. He presided over the Lambeth conferences of 1948 and 1958, which owed their representative character to this careful preparation. From 1946 onward he devoted considerable time to the revision of canon law (q.v.).

FLOROVSKY, GEORGES VASILIEVICH (1893–1979). Florovsky initially studied philosophy, emigrated to Prague and in 1926 started teaching patrology at the Orthodox Theological Institute St Sergius in Paris. In 1948 he emigrated to the USA, taught at St Vladimir's Theological Seminary and from 1956 onward at Harvard University. After retirement he was active at Princeton Theological Seminary. In his works, mainly written in Paris, he showed himself to be self-critical of Orthodox renewal (qq.v.) and at the same time critical of the Western Christian tradition. Florovsky was an active, but difficult, participant in the ecumenical movement. He represented Orthodoxy at the Faith and Order Conference in Edinburgh in 1937. He became a member of the WCC central committee, 1948–1961, and continued his ecumenical engagements afterward.

FREIRE, PAULO REGLUS NEVES (1921–). Freire was a special consultant to the WCC Sub-unit on Education and professor at the Faculty of Education of the University of Geneva, 1970–1980. He was visiting professor at Harvard University and the Center for Studies in Development and Social Change, 1969–1970. From 1980 onward he taught at the Pontifical Catholic University in São Paulo, and was secretary of education of the municipality of the same city. He wrote numerous books in Portuguese, which were translated into many languages, including *Pedagogy of the Oppressed.* He is widely known for his use of the concept "conscientization" in education, meaning that "both teachers and pupils become knowing subjects, brought together by the object they are knowing". *See also* EDUCATION.

FREUDENBERG, ADOLF (1894–1977). Freudenberg was secretary of the WCC (q.v.) secretariat for non-Aryan refugees (q.v.) in Geneva, 1939–1947. He was pastor of a parish for refugees near Frankfurt, 1947–1960, and lived there until his death. After studying law, he was in the service of the German foreign office from 1922 to 1935, from which he was expelled because of his Jewish origin. After studying theology, he managed to escape to London and then came to Geneva in 1939.

FREYTAG, WALTER (1899–1959). Among the most important German representatives in theology and mission (q.v.) in the ecumenical movement, Freytag from 1928 onward was active in the International Missionary Council (IMC) (q.v.) and played a vital role in its conferences, and the last two years was its vice president. He was a member of the committee on the integration of the IMC and the WCC (q.v.), and chairman of the WCC division of studies from 1954 onward. Traveling widely throughout the world he also laid in his own country the foundations of a new missionary theology, complaining about the "lost directness" of earlier missionary strategy. He was preoccupied with the problem of indigenous theology, the growth of the younger churches, the question of conversion (q.v.) and the Christian attitude toward other faiths. He emphasized, together with Karl Hartenstein (q.v.), the eschatological aspect of mission and God's sovereignty over mission (*missio Dei* [q.v.]). In 1928 he became director of the Deutsche Evangelische Missions-Hilfe, in 1946 moderator of the Deutschez Evangelischez Missionsrat, and in 1953 professor of missions and ecumenical relations at the University of Hamburg.

FRIENDS, SOCIETY OF *see* RELIGIOUS SOCIETY OF FRIENDS

FRIES, HEINRICH (1911–). Fries was professor of fundamental and ecumenical theology at the Roman Catholic faculty of theology in Munich, and until 1979 directed the Institute for Ecumenical Theology in Munich. A consultant to the Vatican Secretariat for Promoting Christian Unity (q.v.) and a member of the ecumenical commission of the German bishops' conference, the international academy of religious sciences and the working group of Protestant and Roman Catholic theologians in the Federal Republic of Germany, he has participated in numerous conferences. Together with Hans Küng (q.v.) he wrote *Unity of the Churches: An Actual Possibility.*

FRY, FRANKLIN CLARK (1900–1968). Fry was president of the United Lutheran Church in America, 1944–1962, and one of the founders of the Lutheran World Federation (q.v.) in Lund in 1947, its treasurer, 1948–1952, its first vice president, 1952–1957, and its president, 1957–1963. A leading figure during his lifetime in the ecumenical movement in the USA—he was one of the founders of the National Council of the Churches of Christ in the USA (q.v.)—he was vice moderator of the WCC (q.v.) central and executive committees, 1948–1954, and moderator of both, 1957–1968. Fry was educated at Hamilton College, Clinton, New York, and the Philadelphia Lutheran Seminary. From 1929 to 1944 he served as a pastor of the Trinity Lutheran Church, Akron, Ohio. He had a reputation for being decisive and courageous, and was willing to make difficult and popularly inexplicable decisions for the sake of the right result.

- G -

GARDINER, ROBERT HALLOWELL (1855–1924). After law studies at Harvard University, Gardiner established himself in a law office in Boston, which he moved later to Gardiner, Maine. Appointed in 1910 as secretary of the Episcopal church commission on its constitution, he became an advocate of the Faith and Order movement (q.v.) until his death. He carried on his own work as a lawyer while acting as the leader of the ever-increasing work involved in assembling the world conference on Faith and Order for which he never received any payment. The movement was often financially in his debt, and the provision made for an office and staff seems to have been very meager in view of the huge correspondence and the amount of literature prepared and circulated. Gardiner was an understanding friend of all the churches. His contacts with the Protestant churches in Europe were especially appreciated. Continentals spoke of him as ''the noblest figure that American Christianity had produced''. It was due to his faith, insight, courage, patience and unceasing industry that the movement was built on a solid foundation. His conviction was firmly established that the laity (q.v.) plays a key role in the reunion of the churches.

GENEVA 1966 *see* INTRODUCTION, SOCIAL ETHICS

GERMAN CONFESSING CHURCH. The fight of the ''Confessing Church'' in Germany and its claim to be the true church of Jesus Christ (q.v.) from 1933 to 1945 presented a challenge that over the years profoundly affected the ecumenical movement, by raising critical questions about the nature of the true church and the requirements of ecumenical solidarity. Many, both Christians and non-Christians, who had thought little about the church, were brought to a new realization of its significance when it emerged as the impregnable bulwark against the onslaughts of a totalitarian pseudochurch, and as a witness to the meaning of true community. The first confessing synod of the German Evangelical (Protestant) Church in Wuppertal-Barmen in 1934 adopted unanimously a confession of Christian principles in the face of the ideology of National Socialism. The synod was convened to counter the growing Nazification of the church administration and the influence of pro-Nazi "German Christians" and it was a pivotal event in the unfolding church struggle. The original draft was penned by Karl Barth (q.v.). The document consists of six theses, each introduced by a biblical text and followed by an affirmation on this text and identification of a false doctrine that is rejected.

Doctrines condemned included teachings that there are other sources of revelation besides Scripture, that some areas of life are not under the lordship of Jesus Christ, that the church's message and order may be modified in response to political conditions, that special leaders may be appointed with ruling authority, that the German state was the single authoritarian order of human life, and that the Lord's word and work could properly serve human powers. The Barmen declaration became a model statement of Christian freedom and obedience and has inspired texts such as "A Message to the People of South Africa" (1968) and the Kairos document on the South African situation (1985). The new Council of the Evangelical Church of Germany issued in 1945 the Stuttgart declaration of guilt. This was possible because of the Confessing Church's ecumenical relations before and during the war with churches outside Germany. Later Confessing Church leaders—an example is Martin Niemöller (q.v.)—served as WCC (q.v.) leaders.

GERMANOS (STRENOPOULOS) (1872–1951). In 1922 Germanos was appointed archbishop of Thyateira, with seat in London, and exarch for West and Central Europe. He met John R. Mott and Nathan Söderblom at a conference of the World Student Christian Federation (qq.v.), in Constantinople in 1911, and started from that year onward his ecumenical career. He participated in the publication of the *Encycli-*

cal unto all the Churches of Christ, issued by the patriarchate of Constantinople in 1920, to which he referred during his lifetime. He insisted that unity (q.v.) does not imply uniformity and applied St Augustine's words "in dubiis libertes— in necessarris unitas" to the ecumenical movement. He was vice president of the first world conference of Faith and Order (q.v.) in Lausanne in 1927 and also vice president of the second world conference on Faith and Order (q.v.) in Edinburgh in 1937. Much involved in the final creation of the WCC (q.v.), he was named one of its presidents, 1948–1951.

GLADDEN, WASHINGTON (1836–1918). A Congregational minister, crusading journalist author and prominent early advocate of the social gospel movement, Gladden was dedicated to the realization of the kingdom of God (q.v.) in this world. As he said in his autobiography, he opposed both socialism and classical economic theory and sought to apply Christian law to social problems. He was one of the first clergymen of note to approve of unionization. An advocate of church union, in 1904 Gladden became moderator of the National Council of Congregational Churches and soon afterward made the startling proposal that the denomination's foreign mission board should reject John D. Rockefeller's gift of $100,000 on the ground that it was "tainted money". In some 40 books he stressed the simple and direct nature of the gospel as well as its practicality. His poem "O Master, Let Me Walk with Thee" became a familiar hymn.

GOLLWITZER, HELMUT (1908–1993). Gollwitzer participated in the world conference on Church and Society in Geneva, 1966, and Uppsala, 1968. Educated in Erlangen and Bonn, he was professor of systematic theology in Bonn, 1950, and professor at the Free University of Berlin, 1957. In the 1930s he supported the Confessing Church in Germany (q.v.) and served in the army, 1940–1945; he was then a prisoner of war in the Soviet Union until 1949. Involved in the student protests, 1967–1968, Gollwitzer had great interest in the progress of socialism (q.v.), the Marxist-Christian dialogue (q.v.), the dialogue between the church and the Jewish people and problems of disarmament and conscientious objection (q.v.). Among his numerous works should be mentioned *The Christian Faith and the Marxist Criticism of Religion.* Because of his leftist leanings, the authorities in Basel refused to appoint him as successor to Karl Barth (q.v.) in 1961. Christian Kaiser-Verlag in Munich is in the process of preparing ten volumes of Gollwitzer's selective works.

GOODALL, NORMAN (1896–1985). Goodall studied theology at Mansfield College, Oxford, until 1922 and became pastor of a Congregational parish in London. From 1936 onward he was foreign secretary of the London Missionary Society for India, secretary of the International Missionary Council (IMC) (q.v.), 1944–1955, and secretary of the Joint Committee of the IMC and the WCC (q.v.), 1955–1961, prior to the union of the two in New Delhi, 1961, assistant general secretary of the WCC, 1961–1963, chairman of a WCC structure committee, and secretary of the International Congregational Council, 1962–1968. He participated actively in the first four assemblies of the WCC and edited the report of the Uppsala assembly. He lectured widely (Selly Oak Colleges, Birmingham, the Jesuit College, Heythrop) and was author of several ecumenical publications.

GOSPEL AND CULTURE. Culture develops from the encounter of human beings with nature and depends on geographical conditions, climate, historical events and traditions and customs. Each culture contains good and evil elements as do human beings themselves. The strong and powerful shape the culture of a people. History shows that the conquerors impose their culture on others: the spread of Hellenistic culture by the conquest of Alexander the Great; the imposition of Western culture through colonialization. No culture can claim absolute value and continuation. Every culture is critically judged by the gospel.

The gospel concerns the whole of human life and promises liberation from all forms of slavery—spiritual, religious, social and political. In his well-known book *Christ and Culture* (1951) H. Richard Niebuhr developed five conceptual types of molds that have shaped our approach to Christ and culture: 1) Christ against culture; 2) the Christ of culture;

3) Christ above culture; 4) Christ and culture in paradox; and 5) Christ the transformer of culture. The question today is whether this typology does not restrict Christian thinking, particularly in the Third World, from coming up with new insights and developing a contemporary theology of cultures. All too often it has been overlooked that theology, which deals more with concepts than with people, is not equipped to grasp the relation between gospel and culture. Mission and evangelism (q.v.) as Christian monologues, instead of dialogues with people of living faiths (q.v.) and no faith, are depriving cultures of their promise and meaning. Concerns in the realm of church and society and of Christian service to the world are bypassing the traditional predicaments of cultures if they are not related to the struggles, sufferings and achievements of people. Ecclesiology (q.v.), proclamation and soteriology (q.v.), and the theology of culture, belong together and condition one another.

The pluralism of cultures is the pluralism of people. The incarnated Christ is neither above cultures, nor in paradox with cultures, as he is ceaselessly a part of the suffering and the well-being of people and manifests his redemptive love. His passion for people is their salvation (q.v.). His salvation takes place in and through culture. In the final report of the WCC (q.v.) *Humanum Studies, 1969–1975,* Canon (now bishop) David E. Jenkins (q.v.) wrote that "in the ecumenical movement we have only just begun to glimpse the implications and possibilities of cultural diversity taken absolutely seriously in the context of the ecumenical activity of God". The themes of "religion and culture", "Christianity and culture", "gospel and culture" and "Christ and culture" are related to one another in a dynamic and dialectical tension; we will never be able to deal with one or the other theme totally satisfactorily. As human beings we cannot exclusively concentrate on Christ and/or culture without taking peoples' traditions and beliefs into account.

For this reason terms such as "contextualization", "inculturation" and "acculturation" were used from the 1960s onward. The last word means to adapt Christian practices to local culture: the clergy in the pulpit wearing traditional clothing, the congregation using traditional music and indigenous instruments in worship services, incorporating local architectural styles into church buildings, developing Christian arts in native forms. To contextualize Christianity authentically a deep knowledge of both the Christian religion and culture and an intimate link between liberation and inculturation is required. The people must be fully involved in the entire process of doing theology in a new way. They need the necessary freedom to think and experiment, with the cooperation of church leaders at all levels and adequate teaching for active participation. Only in this way will new theological horizons be opened that will provide glimpses of the depth and breadth of the mystery of God's salvation of all nations and peoples. Only in this way can it be shown that Jesus Christ (q.v.) is the sovereign, unfathomable and uncontrollable Lord of all cultures.

It is important that today the gospel address particularly the poor, as a majority of the world's population, especially in the Third World, continues to live in poverty. Dependence, exploitation, oppression and fatalism are characteristics of the "culture of poverty". The poor (q.v.) need to hear the message of complete redemption through the struggle against want and injustice. A better understanding of the intimate relation of gospel and culture is more than before one of the primary thrusts of the WCC.

GOUNELLE, ELIE (1865–1950). Together with Wilfred Monod (q.v.), Gounelle was a leading personality in the Life and Work movement, and was also involved in the World Alliance for Promoting International Friendship through the Churches, and in the Faith and Order movement (qq.v.). A close friend of Nathan Söderblom (q.v.), he played a key role in Stockholm 1925. Gounelle attended Lausanne 1927, Oxford 1937, and other ecumenical gatherings, representing French Protestantism. The crusading watchword of the Oxford conference, "Let the church be the church", signaled for him, and others, the unfortunate triumph of ecclesiastical introversion. Looking to the future, Gounelle felt that the only hope for the ecumenical movement was "the alliance of the priestly and prophetic function of the church". He was editor of *Christianisme Social*, 1910–1945, and author of numerous articles on trends in the ecumenical movement and developments in Christian social ethics (q.v.).

GRACE. In Protestantism (q.v.), grace has mainly been understood in terms of God's favorable regard to the human being, communicated primarily by the word of Scripture, and with the accent on the forgiveness of sins and the restoration of the sinner to favor with God. In Roman Catholicism (q.v.), the main emphasis has been on grace as a power, conveyed primarily through the sacraments (q.v.), and often described in terms suggestive of a metaphysical substance. When the doctrine of grace was treated by Faith and Order (q.v.) in the 1930s, William Adams Brown (q.v.) recognized in his synthesis that, despite differences on justification, predestination, the church as locus of grace and the sacraments as means of grace, all bodies of Christians hold to "the conviction that man's welfare and happiness depend in the last analysis upon God and the conviction that God is moved to his gracious activity toward man by no merit on man's part but solely by a characteristic of his own nature which impels him to impart himself in free outgoing love".

The Third World conference on faith and order (q.v.) in Lund in 1952 stressed that "word and sacrament are both the gift of God. In the reading and preaching of the Word and the administration of the sacraments, God offers us his grace, imparts saving knowledge of himself and draws us into communion with himself". Speaking about "the whole gospel" the Nairobi assembly (1975) affirmed that "the gospel always includes: the announcement of God's kingdom and love through Jesus Christ (q.v.), the offer of grace and forgiveness of sins, the invitation to repentance and faith in him, the summons to fellowship in God's church, the command to witness to God's saving words and deed, the responsibility to participate in the struggle for justice and human dignity, the obligation to denounce all that hinders human wholeness, and a commitment to risk life itself". A new reading of Christian traditions (q.v.) in the light of the communication of the Bible brings all Christians together before God who has shown his utter grace in Jesus Christ.

GRAHAM, WILLIAM FRANKLIN (BILLY) (1918–). Ordained in 1940 by the Southern Baptist Convention, Graham graduated from Wheaton College, Illinois, and was a vice president of Youth for Christ International when a 1949 evangelistic mission in Los Angeles launched him into national and international prominence. He wrote many books, several of them best-sellers. He was criticized for seeking cooperation with a wide range of churches, including the Roman Catholic Church (q.v.) and for his personal friendship with several US presidents, particularly Richard Nixon. He attended several WCC assemblies (qq.v.) and meetings, such as a ten-day consultation on "A Theology of Evangelism" at the Ecumenical Institute in Bossey (q.v.) in 1958. During the 1980s Billy Graham was the promoter of two large international training conferences in Amsterdam for thousands of "itinerant evangelists" of several continents. He is honorary chairman of the Lausanne Committee for World Evangelization (q.v.).

GREGORIOS, PAULOS MAR (PAUL VERGHESE) (1922–). He studied in India, at Union and Princeton theological seminaries, Oxford University, Gregory of Nyssa Institute, Münster, and Serampore University, where he received a Ph.D. in 1975. He was personal adviser to Emperor Haile Selassie of Ethiopia and executive secretary of the Government Committee for Relief Aid, 1956–1959. He is principal of the Orthodox Theological Seminary in Kottayam and director of the Delhi Orthodox Center. Gregorios was director of the WCC (q.v.) Division of Ecumenical Action and associate general secretary, 1962–1967, observer at the Second Vatican Council (q.v.), 1962–1965, moderator of the WCC Working Committee on Church and Society, 1975–1983, and a WCC president, 1983–1991. He served as joint organizer of the Oriental Orthodox-Eastern Orthodox dialogue (qq.v.) as well as joint chairman of the Indian Orthodox-Roman Catholic Joint Commission.

GREMILLION, JOSEPH (1919–). Gremillion was cochairman and co-founder of the Committee on Society, Development and Peace (SODEPAX) (q.v.), 1968–1980, established by the WCC (q.v.) and the Roman Catholic Church to promote Orthodox-Protestant-Catholic (qq.v.) cooperation worldwide in social teaching and ministry. Pope Paul VI (q.v.) appointed him secretary of the Pontifical Commission for Justice and Peace, 1967–1974, and he was on the Catholic delegation at Uppsala 1968 and other WCC gatherings and a member of the Joint Working Group (q.v.) between the Roman Catholic Church and the World Council of Churches, 1968–1975. Gremillion directed the Muslim-Jewish-Christian Conference, Washington, D.C., 1975–1981, and the Institute for Pastoral and Social Ministry, Notre Dame University, 1983–1986. Since 1986 he has been professor emeritus and scholar in residence at Notre Dame, Indiana.

GRUBB, KENNETH (1900–1980). Sir Kenneth Grubb was an Anglican (q.v.) layman. As moderator of the foreign department of the British Council of Churches he participated in the creation of the Commission of the Churches on International Affairs (CCIA) in 1946 and was appointed its chairman until 1968, while O. Frederick Nolde (q.v.) functioned as its director. Grubb was member or officer of numerous church bodies, including the Church Missionary Society, the British Foreign Bible Society and the United Society for Christian Literature. He was the British representative at the general assembly of UNESCO in 1954, general secretary of the Hispanic Council, moderator of the parliament of the laity of the Church of England, director of *The British Weekly* and coeditor of the *World Christian Handbook* (1949, 1952, 1957, 1962). He wrote an autobiography: *Crypts of Power.* When he and Nolde left the CCIA in 1968, a period of English-American ecumenical diplomacy came to an end.

GUTIÉRREZ, GUSTAVO (1928–). Although a professional Roman Catholic theologian and priest, Gutiérrez is of "the people", born and raised in Peru. After a solid theological education in Europe, he returned to minister to working-class people in Lima and found that he had to start learning all over again, in the midst of his involvement with the people in Rimac, a slum area of Lima in which he still lives and works. One of his more recent works is *We Drink from Our Own*

Wells, while his previous works include *A Theology of Liberation* and *The Power of the Poor in History.* Gutiérrez can be called the founder of liberation theology (q.v.). His aim is to practice Christian theology, to spread the Christian message within a context of repression and oppression rather than in an abstract vacuum. In so doing he has not just introduced a new way of theologizing, but also a new spirituality, viz., the spirituality of solidarity with the poor (qq.v.). Gutiérrez is a pioneer in theological practice, which has mobilized an entire continent and opened the eyes of European and North American theologians to their unhistorical and often idealistic way of thinking. Although he has been criticized by political and theological conservatives for using Marxist analysis of society in his thought, he has avoided aggressive language and an elaboration of an outspoken leftist political theory, emphasizing his primary pastoral role in the service of a genuine church.

- H -

HANDICAPPED *see* DISABLED

HARTENSTEIN, KARL (1894–1952). Hartenstein played a key role in the world missionary conferences, Tambaram 1938, Whitby 1947, and Willingen 1952 and traveled widely in several countries. From 1938 onward he was a member of the committee on integration of the WCC and the International Missionary Council (qq.v.), and attended Amsterdam 1948. As a member of the Deutschez Evangelischez Missionsrat, he endorsed the Barmen declaration (q.v.) of 1934 but argued against political resistance and anticipated the suffering of the church in Germany. With Walter Freytag (q.v.), he was the spokesman of an eschatological perspective of mission (q.v.). In his early years influenced by Karl Barth (q.v.), he turned away from dialectical theology and followed more closely Karl Heim and Emil Brunner. Hartenstein was convinced that the ministry of the church and the ministry of mission form one single whole. He produced over 500 publications.

HEADLAM, ARTHUR CAYLEY (1862–1945). Ordained in the Church of England in 1889, Headlam held various posts at Oxford University, 1885–1896, then was appointed rector of Welwyn, 1896–1903, before serving as principal of King's College, London, 1903–1912, during which period he was also professor of dogmatic theology, 1903–1917. He then returned to Oxford as professor of divinity, 1918–1923, and finally was consecrated bishop of Gloucester, 1923–1945. He was a delegate at the first world conference on Faith and Order (q.v.) in Lausanne (1927) and continued to render great service to the Faith and Order movement as a man of considerable learning and of clear and strong convictions. After 1927 Headlam chaired the theological committee, which took as its first subject the doctrine of grace, and later dealt with difficult questions of the ministry and the sacraments (qq.v.). He also attended the second world conference of Faith and Order in Edinburgh (1937), and opposed the recommendation of the committee of thirty-five, which had met before at Westfield College in London in the same year, to integrate both the Faith and Order and Life and Work movements into a World Council of Churches (qq.v.). He expressed his fear that the new council would pass resolutions on public affairs and thereby do a great deal of harm.

HEALTH, HEALING AND WHOLENESS. The work of Christian missions was from the beginning closely linked to charitable service to human beings in need. Just as Jesus Christ (q.v.) made himself available to men and women in sickness and suffering, so must those who make it their aim to follow him direct their attention to those whom he has characterized as our neighbors. Since medical aid provided by colonial governments was in many areas insufficient, and the measures taken by independent governments failed to meet the need, medical missions in many countries took over representatively responsibility for social service in the form of care for the sick and dying. Exactly on the lines of the development that had taken place in the West, this was carried out mainly through the establishment of institutions such as hospitals and clinics. Doctors and nurses were sent out from Europe and North America, and rendered their service to the population. In the first half of the 20th century this service attained considerable proportions.

When countries became independent and younger churches were faced with the question of their responsibility of practical service, deep reflection as to the significance of Christian medical activity became inescapable. Not only did developments in the field of medicine make medical work increasingly costly; it was gradually realized that the large rural populations need far more mobile medical services than hospital care. Preventive medicine through adequate nutrition and hygiene became, moreover, the watchword of the modern times. Two ecumenical consultations, organized jointly by the WCC and the Lutheran World Federation (qq.v.) in Tübingen, Germany, in 1964 and 1968 concentrated on medical mission in the Third World and on the role of the church in healing. The Christian Medical Commission (CMC) was created within the WCC in 1968 to assist the member churches to deal with the various new problems and to encourage church-related health programs to develop ecumenical cooperation.

In 1978 the CMC embarked on a program to study "health, healing and wholeness". It recognized that service in institutions may actually hinder the development of genuine Christian communities with a right understanding of service, since the community may be led to delegate to specialists something that really belongs to every Christian by the fact of his or her being a Christian. This has led to a radical rethinking of the place of medical mission, which not only concerns congregations and churches in the developing world, but also Christian communities in the developed world. Last but not least, it is now accepted as a fact that most important to health is the spiritual dimension. Unresolved guilt, anger and resentment and meaninglessness are being found by medical science to be very potent suppressors of the body's health-controlling immune system, while loving relationships in community are among the strong augmenters. Since the wholeness of life is a central concern of the gospel, the churches must be involved in a comprehensive health care system in which all aspects of well-being have an appropriate place.

HEILER, FRIEDRICH (1892–1967). As a Roman Catholic (q.v.) Heiler studied theology, philosophy and oriental languages at Munich. Later, however, he came under the influence of Protestantism, especially through the Swedish theologian Nathan Söderblom (q.v.), and in 1919 he became a member of the Lutheran church (q.v.) in Uppsala. He was appointed professor of the comparative history of religions at Marburg. Influenced by the writings of Friedrich von Hügel (1853–1925), his development later took a more Roman Catholic line. Heiler became the organizer of a German high church movement and founded an evangelical order of Franciscan tertiaries. He played an interconfessional role in the ecumenical movement and later influenced the religious thought of the Second Vatican Council (q.v.). Through his works he became a sensitive interpreter of Catholicism and Orthodoxy (q.v.) as well as an authority on the history of religions.

HERMENEUTICS. The word "hermeneutics" is derived from the Greek *hermeneus,* meaning messenger and interpreter. Hermeneutics is the science and art of interpretation of ancient writings, which were considered to contain divine truth. It was held that human beings of the ancient world stood nearer to the truth than later generations, and consequently what has been handed down from their inspired sources is worthy of special attention and careful explication. An entirely new aim confronted biblical scholars in the 19th century with the rise of the critical-historical method of scriptural investigation. It became indispensable to understand what the author was saying against the background of his own unsophisticated and prescientific times. The conviction that the ancient writings were nearer to the truth was now contested as in contradiction to the facts. Exegesis became a matter of relating scriptural texts to their historical background and less a matter of asking about their truth as revelation.

During the middle of the 20th century there has been a return to classical Christian hermeneutics, which accepts the principle that the Bible contains the main principles of its own interpretation and that these principles are as authoritative and reliable as in the whole of biblical revelation. The interpreter's main task is therefore to discover and apply them. The way the New Testament interprets the Old Testament becomes the model. Karl Barth (q.v.) followed the principle that the Bible (q.v.) is itself interpreting when he endeavered to purge his theology of modern existentialism (Rudolf Bultmann and others). In every age of the life of the church the effects can be seen of getting one's hermeneutical bearings from the prevailing philosophy of the time rather than from the Bible itself. This does not imply that Scripture is to be treated in isolation from either the currents of thought or the world of its modern interpreters. But it does mean that the biblical concepts themselves are to furnish the interpreter with hermeneutical guidelines. The hermeneutic task is basically the same activity as that of the preacher: both presuppose historical, critical scholarship of high quality and also insight into our existential situation in the modern world.

At a Faith and Order (q.v.) conference held at Wadham College, Oxford, in 1949, the influence of Karl Barth and his defense of biblical theology was clearly in evidence. But soon it was recognized that the problem of correct hermeneutics is more complicated than Wadham had acknowledged. Discussions during the 1970s and 1980s centered on several specific issues; 1) the use of the Bible in the liturgy (q.v.) of the churches as well as in the devotional life of Christians, thereby counteracting a one-sided intellectual approach to Scripture; 2) the experience of Christians in Latin America, Asia and Africa emphasizing the contemporaneity of Bible interpretation in Third World contexts; 3) a greater variety of interpretive methods, such as political hermeneutics, which raise, in turn, questions for biblical interpretation. On the other hand, the increasing participation of representatives of the Orthodox churches (q.v.) since Montreal 1963 has led to a more balanced appreciation of Scripture and Tradition (q.v.). The ecclesial locus of hermeneutics has been even more strongly emphasized in the 1980s than in the Orthodox tradition. *See also* BIBLE IN THE ECUMENICAL MOVEMENT; TRADITION AND TRADITIONS; UNITY.

HIERARCHY OF TRUTHS. The term refers to the order and relationship that Christian doctrines have with one another. While the expression came into common theological usage at the Second Vatican Council (q.v.), the basic idea of differentiation in the scale and value of individual truths has been long recognized in various ways by Roman Catholic (q.v.) theologians. Reformation Christians do not use the term, but do also acknowledge that some doctrines are closer to the center of the gospel than others. At the uniquely authoritative summit, by common consent, are the classic Christological and Trinitarian credal affirmations that define the person of Jesus Christ (q.v.), i.e., true God and true man, second person of the Triune deity. Those who thus agree on who Jesus is and who God is can join together in what from the beginning of Christianity was the central community-forming acclamation—Jesus is Lord. They can hope to remove the incompatibilities of their dogmatic formulations at lower levels while returning an enriching diversity.

The *Decree on Ecumenism* advised theologians engaged in ecumenical dialogue: "when comparing doctrines, they should remember that in Catholic teaching there exists an order or hierarchy of truths, since they vary in their relationship to the foundation of the Christian faith" (ch. 2.11). Since Vatican II did not explain the meaning of hierarchy of truths, its usage has varied since the Council. The second part of the *Ecumenical Directory,* issued by the Secretariat for Promoting Christian Unity (q.v.) in 1970, identified the hierarchy of truths in terms of the relationship of a particular truth to the foundations of Christian faith, but also distinguished between "revealed truths" and "theological doctrines". It is undoubtedly because of the progressing ecumenical movement that, by better understanding the ways in which other Christians express and live their faith, the more the pluralistic unity of the church of Jesus Christ will be advanced.

HINDU-CHRISTIAN DIALOGUE *see* DIALOGUE WITH PEOPLE OF LIVING FAITHS

HODGSON, LEONARD (1889–1969). Hodgson was general secretary of Faith and Order (q.v.), 1932–1937, and organizer and general secretary of the Faith and Order conference in Edinburgh, 1937. Earlier he was a member of the research department of the Universal Christian Council for Life and Work, appointed in 1934, and then secretary of the WCC (q.v.) committee of fourteen at Utrecht, 1938, and a member of the WCC provisional committee and of the WCC secretariat on Faith and Order. He was professor of Christian apologetics at General Theological Seminary in New York, 1925–1931, Regius professor of moral and pastoral theology at Oxford, 1938–1944, Regius professor of divinity, University of Oxford, 1944–1958, and from 1954 Warden, William Temple College, Rugby.

HOEKENDIJK, JOHANNES CHRISTIAN (1912–1975). Hoekendijk was executive secretary of the WCC (q.v.) Department of Evangelism, 1949–1952, professor of biblical and practical theology at Utrecht, 1953–1965, and professor of missions at Union Theological Seminary, New York, 1965–1975. Informed by his studies on the development of 19th- and 20th-century missiological thinking, he tended to characterize these trends as having an undue emphasis on nationalism, confessionalism and church centrism, thereby deviating from the original missionary impulse in which the triad "heart, kingdom of God and world" is the basic pattern. (See particularly his book *The Church Inside Out*). One of his dictums was that the church is a function of the apostolate, the original missionary movement of God in the world, expressing itself in a variety of forms in witness, service and community. Hoekendijk exercised a major influence on various efforts of the WCC to deal with mission and evangelism (q.v.) in a period of developing worldwide ecumenical partnerships, in particular on the study project "The Missionary Structure of The Congregation" (q.v.), launched in 1961.

HOLINESS CHURCHES. Some smaller churches in the USA emphasize sanctification and/or such gifts of the Spirit as ecstatic utterance. They are largely a product of 19th-century revivalism. Holiness people accept John Wesley's teaching on "entire sanctification" as normative but not absolutely definitive. Charles G. Finney, a Congregational preacher and Arminian theologian, was one of the major popularizers of the movement. Following the Civil War, the national holiness movement gained a considerable following among several mainline churches (especially Methodist [q.v.]), and a number of small groups split off on holiness grounds: Nazarenes, Pentecostal denominations, International Church of the Four Square Gospel, Church of God and Saints of Christ, etc. In England the teaching of holiness was associated with the Keswick Convention. Most holiness groups celebrate both baptism and eucharist (qq.v.), but the Salvation Army and some Friends (qq.v.) celebrate neither. The Church of God advocates the term ordinances and celebrates three: baptism, the Lord's supper and foot washing. Some churches practice believer's baptism only.

The gift of speaking in tongues (*glossolalia*) is particularly valued, and has helped greatly to spread the movement to Latin America and West Africa. Holiness churches believe that the early church is normative and that the church afterward fell into corruption. They stress the recovery of the Spirit of inspiration that blessed the early church, and they are vigorous in him and foreign missions. Some are premillennialist, a number practice divine healing, temperance and nonresistance are often emphasized, and separation from the world is cultivated. Doctrinal understandings and ethical principles of the ecumenical and undivided church are considered their own; they also accept the history of the church catholic in their teachings. The work of the Salvation Army represents the strongest continuing expression of the Wesleyan emphasis on social as well as personal holiness, but also other holiness groups have recently shown revived concern for social witness reinforced by the consciousness of the past commitments of the movements.

HOLY SPIRIT. In the reports of major ecumenical conferences prior to the formation of the WCC (q.v.), references to the Holy Spirit were made along the lines of traditional Protestant theology of the past. The Holy Spirit was primarily understood as the divine power operating in the church and in the life of individual Christians. While the confession of the Trinitarian faith was not ignored, the affirmation of the Spirit as person in communion with the Father and the Son remained largely underdeveloped. In spite of efforts at giving the doctrine of the Holy Spirit a logical and permanent place in Christian theology, this doctrine has remained a puzzlement to the church. When the Spirit is spoken of as God in action, the power of God, the presence of God, and the like, it is hard to think of him as the third Person in the Trinity (q.v.). When he is referred to as the Spirit of Christ, the living Christ, or again as the presence of Christ, these affirmations make hardly any differences. When he is thought of in the analogy of the human spirit, or spirit in general, we are not nearer to the doctrine of the Trinity.

The more conventional reference to him as the immanence of God makes him hard to distinguish from God as the Spirit of God. When he is spoken of in terms of a metaphor such as wind, the mind is turned away from the church's teaching that he is a Person of the Godhead. When one tries to put all those designations of the Holy Spirit into a coherent conception with a proper referent, the task proves to be extremely difficult, if not impossible. This is the reason why Unitarianism (q.v.) cut the Gordian knot by questioning whether the Spirit is truly a third divine person, rather than a referring expression for God himself, especially in relation to his power at work in the world. As "Spirit" has come to be stressed as God's mode of immanence in creation in idealism and classic liberalism, theological studies in pneumatology have tended to go in pantheistic directions and have lost sight of the biblical focus on the Spirit as the redeeming presence of God in his chosen people.

The strength of Orthodox (q.v.) is that it does not isolate pneumatology from the doctrine of the Trinity, expounded in early patristic teaching. Orthodox theology avoids the pitfalls of "Christomonism" as well as "pneumatomonism" as it applies the terms "hypostasis" and "person" to the Holy Spirit. According to the Bible the Holy Spirit has personal characteristics, as for instance in Matt. 12:32, Mark 3:28–29 and Luke 12:10 a blasphemy against the Holy Spirit cannot be forgiven, which would make little sense if the Spirit is an impersonal power. The "comforter" and "paraclyte", according to John 14:16, has personal traits. In I Cor. 12:11 it is the personality of the Holy Spirit who distributes the "charismata" to whom he wills. For this reason, Orthodoxy insists that the "fioloque" (q.v.) has no place in the Nicene-Constantinopolitan Creed. As the Son has his personal existence in the Father and is true God, so the Holy Spirit proceeds from the Father and is true God. All the structures of the church are determined by the dual mediation of the Son in the Spirit and the Spirit in the Son, by that dual, real presence of the Lord Jesus and the Comforter, and in and through them by the encounter with the Father who is the source and term of the divine communion.

Recognizing in the ecumenical movement in the 1950s that the doctrine of the church must be treated in close relation both to the doctrine of Christ and to the doctrine of the Holy Spirit, the third WCC assembly (q.v.) in New Delhi in 1961 decided to set the Christocentric affirmation of the original WCC Basis into an explicitly Trinitarian setting by adding the doxological formula "to the glory of the one God, Father, Son and Holy Spirit". A fully developed exposition of this Trinitarian approach was presented in a plenary session of the assembly by Nikos Nissiotis (q.v.) on "The Witness and Service of Eastern Orthodoxy to the one Undivided Church". The fourth world conference of Faith and Order (q.v.) in Montreal in 1963 dealt extensively with the work of the Holy Spirit in ecumenical thought. It stated: "The community of the Church was founded to proclaim God's saving act to the world through all ages, and to be continually used by the Spirit to make Christ present again and again through the proclamation of the Word and the administration of the Sacraments (q.v.). Through these means Christ is always at work afresh through his Spirit, bestowing his salvation (q.v.) on man and calling him to obedient service". A deeper exploration of the relationship between ecclesiology and pneumatology (qq.v.) was afterward undertaken through the study on "Spirit, Order and Organization" and through a process of reflection on "The

Holy Spirit and the Catholicity of the Church'', leading up to section I of the Uppsala assembly in 1968.

This section was not only concerned with the unity (q.v.) of the church but with the quest for the unity of humanity. The Uppsala assembly stated: ''The church is faced by the twin demands, of continuity in the one Holy Spirit, and of renewal in response to the call of the Spirit amid the changes of human history''. It ''is bold in speaking of itself as the sign of the coming unity of mankind. However well founded the claim, the world hears it sceptically, and points to 'secular catholicities' of its own. For secular society has produced instruments of conciliation and unification which often seem more effective than the church itself. To the outsider, the churches often seem remote and irrelevant, and busy to the point of tediousness with their own concerns. The churches need a new openness to the world in its aspirations, its achievements, its restlessness and its despair''. The Faith and Order Commission meeting in Louvain (1971) brought together most of the studies initiated since Montreal 1963 and formulated more fully insights gained during the previous period concerning the various aspects of the work of the Holy Spirit.

This enabled the Nairobi assembly in 1975 to affirm confidently: ''We believe with certainty in the *presence and guidance of the Holy Spirit,* who proceeds from the Father and bears witness to Christ (John 15:26). Our witness to Christ is made strong in the Holy Spirit and is alive in the confessing community of the church''. For the first time the theme of a WCC assembly in Canberra in 1991 focused on the third person of the Trinity, and for the first time the theme took the form of a prayer: ''Come, Holy Spirit—Renew the Whole Creation''. The theme, however, raised a number of questions on which Christians have long disagreed, including: How do we discern the true activity of the Holy Spirit in the midst of the ''spirits'' of the world? This question became a focus of debate due to an electrifying presentation on the theme by Professor Chung Hyun Kyung of the Presbyterian Church in South Korea. Reactions to the address were, to say the least, mixed. There was as much passionate applause as passionate silence. Statements by

Orthodox and evangelical (qq.v.) participants in particular stressed the need for serious ecumenical study in order to develop criteria for determining the limits of theological diversity in this radically pluralistic age. "We must guard", said the Orthodox statement, "against a tendency to substitute a 'private' spirit, the spirit of the world or other spirits for the Holy Spirit who proceeds from the Father and rests in the Son. Our tradition is rich in respect for local and national cultures, but we find it impossible to invoke the spirits of 'earth, air, water and sea creatures' ".

The doctrine of the Holy Spirit has traditionally been tied to varieties of "enthusiasm", which have occurred in the history of the church, Enthusiasm has been expressed in visions, "speaking with tongues", energetic behavior, with extraordinary psychic and physical phenomena, which have rather annoyed the sober people of the church. Indeed, the identification of the work of the Spirit with enthusiasm is not justified. Faith, hope (qq.v.), and love, with peace and joy, and every good thing in the church are also the work of the Holy Spirit. It appears that from the very beginning Christians have hovered between assigning the receiving of the Spirit to baptism (q.v.) and dividing the gift between baptism and confirmation (q.v.). Similar positions are held today. The New Testament identifies the gift of the Spirit primarily and intrinsically with conversion-regeneration and secondarily with baptism. Sacramentalism tends to reverse the theological order to accord priority to baptism. In Pentecostalism and related charismatic movements the emphasis on the immediate experience of the Spirit accords with the NT, but when they require a second-blessing reception of the Spirit their views differ from Luke-Acts where the Pentecost gift is a sine qua non of authentic Christian existence—experienced initially with charismata, not as a secondary "empowering". *See also* TRINITY.

HOMOSEXUALITY *see* SEXUAL ETHICS

HOPE. The word figures prominently in the New Testament, and in many cases it signifies the hope of life continuing after death. This hope is based on the fact that Jesus Christ (q.v.)

rose from the dead. "If for his life only we have hoped in Christ, we are of all men most to be pitied" (I Cor. 15:19). Without God, a person is without hope (Eph. 2:12). Hope includes expectation (I Cor. 1:7), trust (Rom. 15:13) and patience (Rom. 8:25). It is inseparable from faith (q.v.). On the one hand, faith is the foundation upon which hope rests (II Cor. 5:7; Rom. 8:24); on the other hand, hope enlivens faith (Gal. 5:5; Col. 1:5). Christian hope directs present-day life. It is a stimulus to godliness (I John 3:5); it is essentially related to love (I Cor. 13:13; Col. 1:4–5). It matures in suffering (Rom. 5:1–5); it results in steadfastness (I Thess. 1:3, Heb. 6:11), in confidence (II Cor. 3:12) and in joy (Rom. 5:1–2; Heb. 3:6). Hope is the basis on which the believer labors for the Lord (I Cor. 15:58). The Christian hope is not hope in a divine transformation scene that alone enables Christians to tolerate life in this vale of tears. It is the inevitable consummation of the life lived in Christ on earth.

Hope has been a central and recurrent theme in the ecumenical movement. It was the main theme of the Evanston assembly (1954): "Christ—the Hope of the World". An advisory commission of 32 prominent theologians worked on a document that offered a searching discussion of the ultimate Christian hope and its relation to the more provisional hope of the present time. Because God's kingdom will come, the pilgrim people of God have realistic hope for their unity and mission (qq.v.). In the 1970s the Faith and Order (q.v.) Commission undertook an ambitious study on "Giving Account of the Hope That Is Within Us" (I Pet. 3:15). The title of the study had been chosen to avoid the false impression that the study aimed at writing a new ecumenical creed (q.v.) to take the place of the ancient creeds. It rather aimed at the kind of answer invited by the author of the Epistle. The study was carried out "from below"—that is, in groups formed by local churches and Christian communities in many parts of the world. It was made clear from the outset that the groups were not simply to produce documents for the commission but to wrestle with the question of how to give account of their Christian hope in their own social and political situations.

On the basis of the work done by these local groups, the

commission was able, at its 1978 meeting in Bangalore, to accept unanimously "A Common Account of Hope", which was also a call to Christians around the world to share their own accounts of hope. The hope study led intentionally and directly to the major new Faith and Order study of the 1980s, "Towards a Common Expression of The Apostolic Faith Today". The study document interprets the text of the Nicene creed, its biblical foundation and its significance for today. Over 70 reactions to the document were received from commissions, consultations, theological seminaries and individuals. Faith and Order organized four consultations with the goal of critically re-reading the main parts of the document. The wider perspective of confessing the faith today has been served by Faith and Order through publishing a series of texts on "Confessing Our Faith Around the World" (4 vols). *See also* ESCHATOLOGY; KINGDOM OF GOD.

HORTON, DOUGLAS (1891–1968). Horton was one of the chief architects of the United Church of Christ, uniting the Congregational churches with the Evangelical and Reformed Church (qq.v.) in 1957. A member of the WCC (q.v.) central committee, 1948–1954, he served on a WCC committee that investigated criticisms of the Basis laid down in Amsterdam in 1948. He was chairman of the Commission on Faith and Order, 1957–1963, moderator of the International Congregational Council (ICC) (q.v.) 1949–1953, delegate observer of the ICC at the Second Vatican Council (q.v.), 1962–1965, and involved in several programmes of the National Council of the Churches of Christ in the USA (q.v.). His several works include *Toward an Undivided Church*. Horton was dean of the Harvard Divinity School, 1955–1959.

HORTON, WALTER MARSHALL (1895–1966). Minister of the United Church of Christ and consultant to various ecumenical conferences between 1938 and 1954, Horton was attached to the study department of the WCC (q.v.) in 1947. His best-known book is *Christian Theology: An Ecumenical Approach*. He was professor of theology at Union Theological Seminary in New York, 1922–1925, and then professor at

Oberlin College, 1926–1961. As a "realist" in theology, he tried to purge liberal theology of idealistic illusions while retaining its valid insights.

HROMÁDKA, JOSEF LUKL (1889–1970). Hromádka was professor of systematic theology at the John Hus Faculty in Prague, 1920–1939, and at the Comenius Faculty of Protestant Theology, 1947–1969 (its dean from 1950 onward). Opposed to National Socialism, he taught apologetics and ethics at Princeton Theological Seminary, 1939–1947. His involvement in the ecumenical movement was long and varied. He attended conferences of the World Alliance for Promoting International Friendship through the Churches (1928) and Faith and Order (qq.v.) (1937, on whose commission he served until 1961). At the WCC's (q.v.) founding assembly in Amsterdam in 1948 (where he was elected to the first of his three terms as a member of the central committee; from 1954 onward also as a member of the executive committee), he defended the socialist revolution in an encounter with John Foster Dulles (later US secretary of state).

Convinced that "Western civilization" was a spent force in world history, Hromádka emphasized the socialist vision of society "in which man will be free of all external greed, mammon and material tyranny, and in which a fellowship of real human beings in mutual sympathy, love and goodwill will be established". When Warsaw pact troops invaded Czechoslovakia in 1968, crushing the "Prague spring" and its effort to build "socialism with a human face", he protested against the invasion and occupation by foreign troops. He was the founder of the Christian Peace Conference (q.v.) in 1957 and its president until he resigned in 1969. Warning that rigid anticommunism would lead to catastrophe, Hromádka was a leading figure in the Marxist-Christian dialogue (q.v.) in the 1960s, both in his own country and abroad, and sought to maintain contacts between Eastern and Western churches by inviting Christians from abroad to travel to Central and Eastern Europe. The theology of Hromádka was strongly Christocentric and he had a charismatic capacity for reconciliation.

HUMAN RIGHTS. Among the nine objectives for its work that the founding conference in 1946 had mandated the Commission of the Churches on International Affairs (CCIA) was the maintenance of contacts with international agencies, particularly with the United Nations (q.v.), for the "encouragement of, respect for, and observance of human rights, and fundamental freedoms, special attention being given to the problem of religious liberty" (q.v.). In the years following the adoption of the Universal Declaration of Human Rights, the CCIA was constantly present to advise and to lobby the UN on human rights matters and to promote the elaboration of the international covenants on human rights, as well as other human rights instruments. In the WCC (q.v.) understanding it is not appropriate to arrange rights in a hierarchy of importance. An international consultation in St. Pölten, Austria, sponsored by the CCIA in 1974, put it this way: "Individual rights and collective rights are not in flat opposition. They are related. It should be the aim of the community to secure the welfare of all its members, the aim of the individual to serve the general good. In both instances rights involve responsibilities".

The world conference on Church and Society in Geneva in 1966 called upon the churches "to urge their governments to ratify and enforce the various UN Covenants on Human Rights, not only as ends in themselves, but also as a stimulus to the evolution of an international moral ethos". Two years later the Uppsala assembly made another pressing appeal: "Human rights cannot be safeguarded in a world of glaring inequalities and social conflict. A deep change in attitude is now required. Christians and Christian churches should in their own relations set an example of respect for human dignity, equality and the free expression of thought even in print". The CCIA was directly responsible for the creation of the Churches' Human Rights Program for the Implementation of the Helsinki Final Act, a program cosponsored by the Conference of European Churches, the National Council of the Churches of Christ in the USA (qq.v.) and the Canadian Council of Churches. Since 1980, this program has worked to build awareness, established a network of communications, held workshops and consultations, monitored the further development of the "Helsinki process" and handled human rights complaints, both individual and collective, in numerous countries in the area.

At the Vancouver assembly (1983) human rights issues were high on the agenda and treated from many angles. Participants were greatly concerned over the increasingly sophisticated forms of physical and psychological torture, the denial of basic human rights on the basis of a doctrine of national security, the growing climate of religious fanaticism and the rise of political fundamentalism, the denial of the right of workers to establish and join trade unions that genuinely represent their interests, the predicament of refugees (q.v.) throughout the world and of migrant workers who face the problems of unemployment and the deprivation of civil liberties in their own countries or in their countries of adoption. They emphasized the right to know one's rights and to struggle for them, and the need to set individual rights and their violation in the context of society and its social structures. Churches were urged to examine and change their own structures and methods of operation, and to consider a variety of strategies in the advocacy of human rights.

The CCIA has brought out many documents on human rights matters during the last 15 years. *CCIA Background Information* has dealt with matters of human rights in Africa, the Middle East, Lebanon, the West Bank, Korea, Kampuchea and Vietnam, the Philippines, the Pacific, New Caledonia, El Salvador, and a number of other regions and countries. Readers may wish to consult *Human Rights on the Ecumenical Agenda* (1983), which not only traces new developments from the early 1970s onward; it also provides an assessment of the human rights policies of the WCC and its constituency. It deals in detail with basic methodological principles, the strengthening of the churches' instruments, responsible criteria for public communications, modes of action in human rights and the WCC's Human Rights Advisory Group.

Ecclesiastical structures on the whole do not permit participation and action at the levels of decision-making and power politics. Supporting the status quo, a number of churches still tacitly accept many forms of discrimination and inequality, in particular those of women, children, minorities and people of other races. Churches have been tempted to judge other societies more quickly than their own, and to see the problems of others through the lenses of their own histories, theologies and worldviews. Nevertheless, in many parts of the world there are hopeful signs that oppressed, intimidated and silent people apprehend the reality of their political, socioeconomic and personal predicament as they discover and live the liberating message of the gospel. The relation between true faith (q.v.) and genuine life becomes evident and leads to the courage to denounce systematically the many violations of human rights in spite of ever new threats of aggression and humiliation. In some nations active Christian communities are one of the voices of protest, sometimes the only one, against the insidious violation of human rights. Many national and international experiences have indicated that the ecumenical fellowship will have to achieve a greater political sophistication in dealing with the root causes of human rights abuse, causes that concern all nations and cannot be dealt with by humanitarian approaches within specific offending nations alone. *See also* RELIGIOUS LIBERTY; UNITED NATIONS.

HYMNOLOGY. Hymns are a balanced unity of words and music. The music is not a slave to the word while the word is not shackled. Both music and words are liberated by the gospel and become new means of human expression. Ecumenical hymns overcoming the barriers that can keep human beings apart express people's deepest and most genuine aspirations. All peoples in the world do sing as a part of their culture. So also Christians from the earliest times were hymn singing people (cf., Eph. 5, 19, the Magnificat, etc.). In the Western church the *Hymnarium* was the liturgical book containing sacred poetry (hymns) of the divine office, ordered for the particular seasons of the liturgical year. In 1737 John Wesley published the first modern hymnal. It is a collection of hymns, psalms and chorales for worship (q.v.), coming from a variety of traditions (q.v.), and can be considered ecumenical for that period.

Cantate Domino has served as the hymnbook of the ecumenical movement over many decades. Its first two editions were published by the World Student Christian Federation (q.v.). At the request of the Uppsala assembly (1968) the Faith and Order (q.v.) secretariat supervised the compilation of a third edition, which became available in 1974. The 200 hymns in several languages it contains, while including a number of "old favorites" of Western hymnody, represent musical and liturgical styles of different parts of the world in greater variety than ever before. At the Vancouver assembly (1983), forms of cultural doxological expression of Third World churches came to the forefront and innovations to the liturgy (q.v.) of churches in the northern hemisphere were introduced. The communities of Taize (q.v.) and Iona, Scotland, have also influenced the hymn singing ecumenical fellowship.

- I-

IBIAM, FRANCIS AKANU (1906–). Ibiam was a president of the WCC (q.v.), 1961–1968. He established the Student Christian Movement in Nigeria in 1937, was president of the Christian Council of Nigeria, 1955–1958, a member of the standing committee of the International Missionary Council (q.v.), 1957–1961, chairman of the provisional committee of the All African Conference of Churches (AACC) (q.v.) and AACC representative at the inaugural conference of the East Asia Christian Conference (q.v.) in Kuala Lumpur in 1959. He was a speaker at the New Delhi assembly in 1961, attended the Uppsala assembly in 1968 and was present as a guest at the Nairobi assembly in 1975. Identifying with his people, and in protest against the support by the British government of the central Nigerian regime against Biafra, Ibiam renounced in 1967 all honors that the United Kingdom had bestowed on him. He found himself in an extremely controversial position at the Uppsala assembly.

ICONOGRAPHY. After a period of iconoclasm, the veneration of icons (in Greek signifying "images") was allowed by the second ecumenical council in Nicea (787) and has ever since played a large part in the Orthodox (q.v.) devotion. Gradually the word "icon" came to denote a specific form of sacred painting on wood in the Byzantine tradition. The Trinity, Jesus Christ (qq.v.), Mary (*theotokos*), martyrs and saints have been represented by icons. The Eastern approach to reality is rather Platonic, not bound by the Aristotelian categories of the West. For Eastern Christians earthly reality is reflective of a higher reality, indeed, a heavenly reality, which can be communicated. The theology of icons is a typical example of this. The church is not perceived so much as a militant society but as a theophany, the coming of the eternal into time. Spirituality (q.v.) is defined in terms of *theosis* (divinization); grace (q.v.) is seen as the transforming action of God, and not as a means of living in this world. These differences are reflected in Eastern iconography.

The reasons for the veneration of icons is twofold: 1) It is a question of the relation that icons establish to the person portrayed—Jesus Christ, Mary, Saints—and finally to the triune God. They are the depicted persons full of grace and thus communicate their divine energy. The grace is not present in the icons but the divine efficacy. In this energy of the Holy Spirit (q.v.) the faithful is incorporated through his prayer (q.v.) and veneration into the illustrated. In other words, in the prayer of the faithful the icon is the bridge to God. 2) The contempt of icons is a disregard of the mirrored person in which God is delighted and through which his name is honored. Therefore, icons are indispensable in the life of the church because they are not only a question of obedience but belong by all means to the Christian faith, which expresses itself also outwardly through kneeling down, making the sign of the cross before icons or kissing them.

Icons are gaining momentum in the ecumenical context. They are present in many Roman Catholic (q.v.) places of worship and in homes; they also appear in some Anglican and even Protestant (qq.v.) churches; and they have begun to be a natural part of ecumenical gatherings and centers. Both within and outside the Orthodox world icon painting is practiced. With the aid of a film on Andrei Rublov's famous 15th-century icon of the Trinity, the Vancouver assembly (1983) was led in meditation on the triune God as the ultimate ground for both the unity of the church and the renewal of human community. *See also* WORSHIP.

IDEOLOGY AND IDEOLOGIES. From the 1930s to the 1960s the term "ideology" in the ecumenical movement was used in an exclusively pejorative sense. Ideologies, and particularly the revolutionary ideology of Marxist origin, were regarded as total systems of thought competing for the spiritual allegiance of humanity. As they are based on utter godlessness, the consequence of distorted social perspectives and surrender to utopian expectations, they must be unequivocally rejected. The second world conference on Church and Society in Oxford (1937) stated: "Every tendency to identify the kingdom of God with a particular structure of society or economic mechanism must result in moral confusion for those who maintain the system and in disillusionment for those who suffer from its limitations".

The contribution of the first two WCC assemblies (qq.v.) to the ecumenical analysis of ideologies carried the argument in a new direction. At Amsterdam (1948) the churches were admonished "to reject the ideologies of both Communism and laissez-faire capitalism (q.v.)", seeking "to draw men away from the false assumptions that these extremes are the only alternatives". The idea of the "responsible society" (q.v.) was proposed as an alternative to such ideological extremes and as a way of seeking "creative solutions which never allow either justice or freedom to destroy the other". Evanston (1954), reflecting the Cold War experiences, reiterated the main points of the first assembly on the conflict between Christian faith (q.v.), Marxist ideology and totalitarian practice. It also pointed, however, for the first time to the unfortunate effects that sterile anticommunism was producing in many Western societies. Nevertheless, until 1966 it was repeated several times that Christians must say a clear "no" to the communist state before they can begin to recognize positive aspects within the communist achievement. The churches must work to enlarge the area of freedom through "gradual and slow" reform.

At the world conference on Church and Society in Geneva in 1966, ideologies, like communism, were for the first time approached in a new non-Western context. The conference succeeded in defining ideology in a non-pejorative sense: "By ideology we mean a process quite different from a total system of ideas which is closed to correction and new insight. Ideology as we use it here is the theoretical and analytical structure of thought which undergirds successful action to realize revolutionary change in society or to undergird and justify its status quo. Its usefulness is proved in the success of its practice. Its validity is that it expresses the self-understanding, the hopes and values of the social group that holds it, and guides the practice of that group''. This new, positive understanding of ideology reflected the concern for open Christian thought to new ideological developments arising in the liberation struggles in Africa, Asia, Latin America and the Middle East. The gathering in Geneva admitted that ''theology reflects not only action but interaction between God's revelation and man's ideological understanding of his own condition and desires. Christians, like all other human beings, are affected by ideological perspectives''. In 1970 it was added that ''the relation of faith to ideology remains a question to be worked out in concrete situations''.

The working committee on Church and Society, meeting in Nemi, Italy, in 1971 compiled in its third report, entitled *Images of the Future,* a list of current ideologies describing briefly: 1) liberal ideology; 2) Marxist ideology; 3) social democratic ideology; 4) technocratism; 5) nationalism; 6) reactive ideologies; and 7) cultural traditionalism, adding to each characterization in a few sentences a critical evaluation and a healing vision of their future.

As the concern for a deeper analysis and a better understanding of the problem of ideology had to be inserted somewhere more officially into the WCC's program, the central committee in Addis Ababa in 1971 decided to add the two words ''and Ideologies'' to the phrase ''Dialogue with People of Other Faiths''. By doing so it indicated that the outreach of dialogue should include the proponents of both religious and ideological worldviews. No suggestions or recommendations, however, were made as to how to work out a combined dialogue between religions and ideologies or even how to conduct a bilateral Marxist-Christian dialogue (q.v.). While it was right not to put ideologies in a totally different category, because religions in dialogue are apt to defend their common religious front against a threatening secular world, and because all religions tend to deny forcefully any ideological infiltration or bias within their own system of faith, the follow-up of the 1971 mandate resulted in confusion and embarrassment.

On the one hand, a small Christian-Marxist consultation, sponsored by the WCC Department on Church and Society in 1968, remained a single and isolated event. One repeatedly emphasized the impossibility of finding sufficient and the right East-European Marxists and communists from Asia, Africa and Latin America willing to participate in an ongoing and meaningful dialogue; the old questions were also still raised as to what the purpose of such dialogue is, what specific issues are to be discussed and what method of approach at the ecumenical level should be recommended. On the other hand, in spite of a more positive view of ideology in theory and in practice, one of the conclusions of the 1966 Geneva conference remained valid: ''. . . there is no agreement among Christians themselves on the degree to which analysis and action in Christian ethics itself must wrestle with ideological bias''. Thus, the WCC continued to wonder how to face the task of defining the term ideology more precisely for its own use and of undertaking some inclusive studies of ideological presuppositions and perspectives implicit in the formulation and implementation of its own programs and activities.

The Sub unit on Dialogue with People of Living Faiths and Ideologies (DFI) sponsored a specific consultation on ideology and ideologies in Geneva in 1981. The theme was not churches and Christians *against* ideologies, but *among* ideologies. Using the working definition of the Geneva conference in 1966, the consultation added: ''The given definition needs one qualification. There are, on the one hand, comprehensive blueprints for the structure of society. On the other hand, there are to be found ideological elements or factors that might not be part of a well thought out system but are nevertheless of great influence on the behavior of human beings, perhaps without their conscious knowledge''. Receiving the report *Churches among Ideologies,* the central committee, meeting in Geneva in 1982, recommended: ''1)

That additional dialogue programs be developed by DFI which focus on: a) the so-called ideological captivity of the churches; b) the ideological elements in interfaith dialogue; and c) direct dialogue between and among Christians and persons for whom ideological convictions alone give meaning to their lives . . ''.. 2) ''That in order to implement this program on ideologies, the DFI sub-unit would require additional staff who possess competency in the field of ideologies and with sufficient financial resources to pursue the program with vigor''.

These recommendations have never been followed through. Even after the collapse of the communist ideology, a further inquiry into the relationship between faith and ideology is necessary. It is not enough to examine the economic rootedness of ideologies if the spiritual ground of faith is dualistically divorced from it. An increasing humanization of all ideological systems is required leading to the higher goal of enhancing human dignity, freedom, justice, creativity and wholeness. In Latin America Christians and Marxists have found themselves side by side in a common struggle against immediate and concrete cases of oppression and enforced dependency. These are situations in which Christianity and Marxism cannot be set over against each other as neat alternatives. See also MARXIST-CHRISTIAN DIALOGUE.

INCARNATION see JESUS CHRIST, SALVATION

INCULTURATION see GOSPEL AND CULTURE

INFALLIBILITY. The term refers to the quality of being divinely preserved from error. The general infallibility of the church in its enunciation of dogmas pronounced or endorsed by general councils, or in its teaching of the basic Christian truths, has for a long time been held by Roman Catholics, the Eastern Orthodox churches, and to some extent by the Church of England (qq.v.). In 1870 the First Vatican Council (q.v.) defined the infallibility of the pope as an expression of the infallibility of the church. It declared that when the pope speaks *ex cathedra*, when he defines a doctrine concerning faith (q.v.) or morals to be held by the universal church, he is then "endowed with that infallibility with which the Divine Redeemer has willed that his Church should be equipped", and it added that such decisions are "of themselves—and not by virtue of the consent of the Church—irreformable". Since the middle of last century, only two *ex cathedra* pronouncements have been made: the definition of the dogma of the Immaculate Conception in 1854 by Pope Pius IX and the definition of the Assumption of the Virgin in 1950 by Pope Pius XII.

Yet, in the ecumenical discussions between the Roman Catholic Church and other Christian communities, the question of infallibility remains one of the realms in which complete agreement appears an impossible achievement. The Orthodox churches disapprove of the Roman Catholic position because it defined the view of papal infallibility after the separation between East and West, and consequently it precluded the possibility of debate and decision by an authoritative ecumenical council in which all the apostolic traditions were represented. Anglicans also differ from Roman Catholics in their perception of the manner in which infallibility is exercised through the solemn definitions pronounced by the bishop of Rome. They are worried by the fact that Pius IX and Pius XII exercised their privilege to define two dogmas when the faith was not under threat. To Anglicans this prerogative is of such extraordinary importance that it should be asserted only in cases of extreme urgency or necessity. *See also* PAPACY/PRIMACY.

INTERCESSION *see* PRAYER

INTERCHURCH AID. A theology of interchurch aid and of the service of the church to the world has not been fully developed and spelled out. The insights of the Bible are accepted that the apostolate of the church includes *kerygma, koinonia* and *diakonia* (q.v.). All belong together and condition one another. The aim of all charity is to change the status quo of society in view of the kingdom of God breaking into history. All service is participation in the redeeming ministry of Jesus Christ (q.v.). According to the *Memoirs* of W. A.

Visser 't Hooft, the challenge of postwar reconstruction took up a very central place in the ecumenical movement. Unity and mission (qq.v.), to be sure, remain priorities, but the strengthening of human relations between churches and their faithful and all others in need, the expression of tangible love and generous care is the quintessence of world Christianity. Matt. 25:31–46 is a truly ecumenical text for all churches and Christians.

The history of interchurch aid, refugee and world service has often been difficult and complicated due to intricate ecclesiastical structures. It took a long time to combine the concerns of the Department of Inter-Church Aid and Service to Refugees, the International Missionary Council (q.v.), and later the Commission on Inter-Church Aid, Refugee and World Service, the Commission on World Mission and Evangelism, and the Commission on the Churches' Participation in Development into one meaningful whole. Yet CICARWS, the largest subunit of the WCC, has rendered continuous service throughout the years throughout the world. In many church circles, particularly in the Third World, the WCC (qq.v.) is first of all known through the activities of CICARWS.

From the 1960s onward the relation between giving and receiving churches has been increasingly questioned. Already in 1959 the East Asia Christian Conference (now the Christian Conference of Asia [q.v.]) was critical of the giving of ecumenical aid by rich churches to poor churches. In spite of the misgivings, it has been extremely difficult to change the structures of one-sided support and monological communication. The project system remained for years largely under control of the donor agencies. Bilateralism continued to flourish. A number of consultations in the 1960s on the role of institutional Christian service fed into an international interchurch aid gathering in Swanwick, UK, in 1966. The meeting was important for extending the idea of *diakonia* beyond "charitable" relief and service to programs of social advancement. Organizationally, it led to the establishment of a new desk on development education in the Division of Inter-Church Aid. Since 1971 it took several years to clarify the overall mandate of Unit II: Justice and Service. The long discussion to implement the sharing of ecumenical resources culminated in a global consultation in El Escorial, Spain, in 1987. The theme was "Sharing Life in a World Community". The commitments made by the participants highlighted identifying with the poor (q.v.) and oppressed, making marginalized people equal partners in decision-making, challenging the root causes and structures of injustice and overcoming the present divide between the churches' evangelistic work and their action in society. Although the WCC seldom operates relief and development (q.v.) programs itself, it does channel large sums of money every year, which means it is part of the system against which El Escorial put large question marks.

There has been an increasing awareness also of the complexity of the churches' involvement in their service in refugees (q.v.). To deal with the effects of various refugee situations is not enough. Refugees are victims of unjust social, economic and political structures of societies, of the consistent violation of their rights and their human dignity. Refugee assistance is valid only when it makes a contribution toward meeting overall community needs. Despite the difficulties of establishing human order in a disordered world, and of bringing new hope to refugees in despair, Christianity must express its determination not only to help ease but finally to bring the world refugee crisis to an end. Unfortunately, as the flow of refugees from other parts of the world has increased, the possibilities of finding refuge by resettling in Europe have been severely limited by restrictive government policies and a resurgence of xenophobia, fueled by political parties and movements that make little effort to conceal their racism. The sanctuary movement, in which churches sought to prevent the repatriation of undocumented people fleeing to the USA from civil war, death squads, detention without trial and torture in Central America, has received financial support of the WCC.

Due to the widespread sense that in the global struggle for justice (q.v.), the people and the churches were losing, a global ecumenical conference on interchurch aid, the first such meeting since Swanwick in 1966, took place in Larnaca, Cyprus, in 1986, a year before the El Escorial gathering. The theme "Called to be Neighbors: Diakonia 2000" pointed to the need felt by many in the ecumenical community for a new outlook for the churches' commitment in Christian service as the 21st century approaches. Insisting that poor and oppressed people, who are at the margins of the world's concern, should be the center of Christian service, Larnaca described diakonia as "liberating and transforming, suffering and empowering". Christian service cannot be separated from the struggle for justice and peace (q.v.). The ecumenical community, it added, must learn that advocacy, solidarity and sharing of skills are as essential to *diakonia* as money. In practical terms, Larnaca said, WCC interchurch aid should shift its style of work from evaluating applications and channeling funds for individual aid and development projects to an "area-centered" approach, in which ecumenical responses to human needs in a given country or region can be more effectively coordinated to make the most of the resources available. New challenges in interchurch aid are posed to both the local and the international ecumenical family.

INTERCHURCH WORLD MOVEMENT OF NORTH AMERICA. In 1918 a conference of executives of denominational boards—missionary, educational and benevolent—launched the movement. John R. Mott (q.v.) was appointed chairman of the executive committee. The Interchurch World Movement was not an effort to achieve organic unity among churches, nor was it intended to be like the Federal Council of Churches (q.v.). It was an effort of numerous interdenominational and denominational agencies to coordinate various home and foreign missions, Christian education and social services in the interests of greater efficiency. Projected hastily, under the impulse of enthusiasms generated by the war, the movement lacked clear delineation of its relationships. Whether it was to be temporary or permanent, whether it was to be promotional only or might assume certain administrative responsibilities, were unanswered questions. The Federal Council of Churches pursued an independent course, sympathetic with the aim of the movement but establishing no connection with it. The culmination of the movement was a simultaneous campaign for funds, totaling no less than US $336 million, in the spring of 1920. The participating agencies were to carry on their solicitations within their own constituencies. This proved to be a fateful miscalculation. The movement asked for itself US $40 million but received less than one-tenth of the amount. Having built up an extensive staff and conducted expensive surveys, mainly on borrowed money, it was left with a staggering debt of more than $6 million and collapsed in less than two years. Indirectly the Federal Council of Churches was strengthened in the eyes of its member denominations; the values of its constitutional structure now stood out in clearer light.

INTERCOMMUNION *see* EUCHARIST

INTERNATIONAL ASSOCIATION FOR LIBERAL CHRISTIANITY AND RELIGIOUS FREEDOM *see* UNIVERSALISM/UNITARIANISM

INTERNATIONAL CONGREGATIONAL COUNCIL (ICC). The first International Congregational Council was called in London in 1891. Subsequent meetings took place in 1908, 1920, 1930 and 1949 on an alternating basis on opposite sides of the Atlantic. In the beginning ecumenical questions as such did not figure largely in their programs, though inevitably they have been the background of much discussion. From 1949 onward the council met every four or five years, adopted a more formal organizational structure, appointed permanent leadership, and created a special service fund to finance interchurch visits, scholarships for foreign seminars and research projects. It also became increasingly involved in ecumenical ventures and engaged in social action linked with evangelism (q.v.). The 1966 assembly "agreed without dissent" to approve the proposed merger of the ICC with the World Alliance of Reformed Churches (q.v.), which took place in 1970.

INTERNATIONAL COUNCIL OF CHRISTIAN CHURCHES *see* ANTI-ECUMENISM

INTERNATIONAL COUNCIL OF COMMUNITY CHURCHES (ICCC). Community churches in the United States date from the mid-1800s. The earliest national organization began in 1923. The current one resulted from a 1950 merger of two previous councils, one comprised of churches with predominantly black and the other of churches with predominantly white membership. The ICCC is directly related to each community in which its local congregations are located and encourages each local church to take an active part in all ecumenical affairs within its community. It seeks to encourage every local church to share its faith with other Christians and people of other faiths. Its stance is that of representing ecumenical Christian religion in the local community. In concert with other mainline religious bodies it seeks to bring the light of Christian faith (q.v.) to bear upon all problems of society, political, social, cultural, etc. Its concept of the "people of God being one in the place where they are" is of great influence in drawing people of different backgrounds together in action to build the good community. Because it was the first significant merger of predominantly white and predominantly black religious bodies (1950) it has always had as one of its major emphases the overcoming of racism (q.v.). Increased effectiveness of the church in local as well as in international life is sought through annual conferences in which representatives of the churches come together to offer mutual support and encouragement. Among other major efforts are the upgrading of educational background for its ministers and laypeople and interpreting ecumenism and the World Council of Churches (q.v.).

INTERNATIONAL FELLOWSHIP OF RECONCILIATION (IFR). The Fellowship of Reconciliation was founded in Great Britain in 1914 by a group who saw in a pacifist direction the solution of problems raised by Christians by war. It spread to other countries, and in 1919 the International Fellowship of Reconciliation was organized. Its networks now exist in 27 countries. From the beginning it has brought Roman Catholics (q.v.) into cooperation with members of other churches. Thus, it has always been ecumenical in its effects. After both world wars the IFR organized work camps for young people in Europe in order to promote reconciliation and peace (q.v.) through service. By 1950 work camps were taken into the newly formed Youth Department of the WCC (q.v.). The international headquarters are in Alkmaar, the Netherlands. Its major journal, *Reconciliation Quarterly,* started in 1924. *See also* PACIFISM.

INTERNATIONAL MISSIONARY COUNCIL (IMC). The council sprang from the World Missionary Conference, Edinburgh, 1910, and had a continuous evolution through the First World War until its formal constitution in 1921 in Lake Mohonk, New York. It joined in an international federation the national Christian councils and councils of churches in Asia, Africa and Latin America with the mission councils of the West. It was the first worldwide ecumenical council of churches. Its purview included most of the problems confronting Protestant churches outside the western hemisphere. Among its larger accomplishments were the creation of a strong global network of national councils of churches, the convening of major missionary conferences, the formulation (chiefly through its member bodies) of significant policies for worldwide mission, stimulation of creative thought in the continuing development of a theology of mission (q.v.), support of "orphaned missions" during two world wars and a major contribution to the emergency of the WCC (q.v.). The movement enjoyed the able leadership of Joseph H. Oldham, John R. Mott and William Paton (qq.v.). A number of important conferences that facilitated the work of the IMC were held in Jerusalem (1928), in Madras (1938), in Whitby, Ontario (1947), in Willingen, Germany (1952), and in Ghana (1958).

Throughout its history of promoting Christianity in the multireligious and nonreligious world, the International Missionary Council has acknowledged the variety and complexity of belief of its constituent members. It has not insisted upon a single doctrinal statement but has emphasized the need for Christian fellowship and united action. Thus, it became a key element in the development of the ecumenical spirit among the main branches of the non-

Roman Catholic churches. Among its many publications that advocated fellowship and cooperation in missions the most important is the quarterly journal, *International Review of Mission.*

The chief objective of the meeting in Ghana was to proceed to the integration of the IMC and the WCC. The majority approved, yet the Orthodox equated mission with proselytism (q.v.). Latin American churches were uneasy about the WCC; the Norwegian Missionary Council feared that mission would be submerged in the WCC. Nevertheless, at the New Delhi assembly (q.v.) in 1961, the IMC became the WCC's Division of World Mission and Evangelism. The members of the division (now commission) meet every five years and establish policy. The structural rebirth of the IMC as CWME (Commission on World Mission and Evangelism) has had a profound theological significance. It demonstrates that world mission and mission to the world help constitute the essential life of the ecumenical community. *See also* MISSION.

INTERNATIONAL ORDER AND LAW. Relationships between nations are subject to God's judgment. In Christian perspective international order must be viewed as applying to the world criteria of justice (q.v.) and order similar to those traditionally assigned as functions to the national state. International order requires the adequate structuring of the relations of states and the harmonious and effective functioning of international processes toward desired goals. Under a sovereign God the world is to be regarded as a unity. Therefore, the need for principles and rules of conduct between independent states arises whenever such states develop mutual relations. The beginning of the modern system of internal law naturally coincided with the emergence of the sovereign state and was stimulated by interest in Roman law in the 16th century. Building largely on the work of previous legal scholars, the Dutch statesman Hugo Grotius can be called the founder of modern international law. In 1899 and 1907 the first and second peace conferences in The Hague resulted in agreements, signed by many nations, on the peaceful settlement of international disputes. The Convenant of the League of Nations, which was signed in 1919, provided for the submission to the League Council of all disputes likely to lead to the rupture of relations. The Council under this covenant could issue decisions that were legally binding upon the member states. In 1928 the Kellogg-Briand Pact, signed in Paris, made it obligatory upon nations to renounce war "as an instrument of policy". Finally, in 1945, the charter of the United Nations (q.v.) established an elaborate machinery for the growth of international law through international conventions, and for solving problems in international relations.

Since then a major and international order is the preservation of peace (q.v.), in the negative sense of the absence of war. In the words of the WCC assembly (qq.v.) in Amsterdam (1948), "War as a method of settling disputes is incompatible with the teaching and example of our Lord Jesus Christ". Yet, mere cessation from military conflict is not sufficient. Nations may refrain from physical aggression and yet not live in peace. In its fullest sense peace also involves cooperative pursuit of the common welfare. It is on the basis of the understanding of the development of the international law of cooperation that the WCC, through its Commission of the Churches on International Affairs (CCIA), has always strongly supported the activities of the United Nations as a forum and instrument of multilateral concerted action. Ecumenical endeavors include seeking a substantial role for the UN and demanding effective means of cooperation based on respect for the international law. This is also reflected in the by-laws of the CCIA, whose tasks include encouraging the development of international law and of effective international institutions.

The emerging crisis in international relations led in the ecumenical movement to a deeper awareness of the critical issues with regard to international order, such as development (q.v.), understood as the promotion of justice through self-reliance, economic growth and people's participation, and the guarantee of human rights (q.v.), a critical analysis of militarism, the transnationalization of capital and production and the monopoly of the power of science and technology (qq.v.). The earlier emphasis on order and freedom gave way to the struggle for justice and liberation. An international order based on the maintenance of the existing political, economic and financial structures was perceived as the primary obstacle to true liberation and peace. Thus, ecumenical thought and action have increasingly turned away from improving international structures to movements of people with the aim of building up a world of solidarity instead of a world of domination. This change was especially reflected in the recommendation of the Vancouver assembly (1983) to engage in a "conciliar process for justice, peace and the integrity of creation" (CPIC) (q.v.). Unfortunately, debates over the continuing validity of traditional principles continue in the face of claims that new principles, more just and appropriate to a changing world order, are required. The role of international adjudication, especially of the International Court of Justice in The Hague, has been largely modest to the point of near irrelevance.

For this very reason the international sphere in its full range is for the ecumenical movement an area of obedience to God. The Lord of the nations calls all human beings to repentance, faith (q.v.) and compassionate concern for fellow human beings everywhere. Both the biblical message and the historical experience of a worldwide church show the possibilities of a new fellowship of human beings. The church as the body of Christ has a ministry of reconciliation. In the light of God's love the limitations of political nationalism and economic selfishness become clearer manifestations of sinful pride and greed. An international ethos, therefore, oriented toward lasting peace, justice and respect for the world's environment (q.v.) becomes ever more urgent for those moved by the deeper dimensions of their faith (q.v.).

This does not imply that the ecumenical movement falls victim to pious illusions. International order does not necessarily mean the absence of all forms of conflict. Differences in policy or ideology may contribute to mutual enrichment rather than to physical hostility or destructive rivalry. Within a framework of basic agreements, procedures can be worked out for the creative handling of conflict and for deeper reconciliation after differences have been openly faced. Neither will coercion be totally absent from international order in a world of imperfect human beings. Given the power of self-interest and the lure of evil, order cannot rest on consent alone. Power is always necessary to implement purpose. That power can never be solely persuasive because of the irrational impulses of human beings. If human society is to continue substitutes for the grosser forms of violence available to the modern state must be found. Procedures of police power need to supersede reliance on international war. This involves both drastic disarmament as a goal and the development of more redemptive and less punitive forms of force. Spiritual factors in world order are fundamental. Without nonmaterial and noninstitutional foundations, even the best international political structures and economic practices are weak and transitory. A common groundwork of social understanding and ethical principles must strengthen every superstructure. Consequently, the full concept of international order based on international law requires also in the secular sphere a common basic ethos. *See also* HUMAN RIGHTS; UNITED NATIONS.

- J -

JACKSON, LADY (WARD, BARBARA) (1914–1981). Ward delivered a major speech on world development at Uppsala, 1968. She joined the staff of *The Economist* in 1939, was visiting professor and lecturer at Harvard University, 1957–1968, and professor of international economic development at Columbia University, 1968–1973. A member of the Pontifical Commission Justice and Peace (q.v.) in 1971, she was the first woman to address a Vatican assembly. Ward was a member of the Overseas Development Institute and president of the International Institute for Environment and Development from 1973 and its chairman from 1980. She skillfully assisted the churches in producing appeals based on sound economic ideas and exact facts and figures.

JENKINS, DAVID EDWARD (1925–). Jenkins served the WCC (q.v.) as director of the Humanum Studies, 1969–1975. This experience and the travel entailed developed his interest in problems of church and society, Marxism, liberation theology and health services. In 1973 he returned to England to be the director of the William Temple Foundation in Manchester. In 1979 he was appointed professor of theology at the University of Leeds. He became bishop of Durham in 1984. In spite of his doubts about and criticism of the vocabulary and concepts of traditional theology, in particular the teachings of the virginal conception and bodily resurrection of Jesus, he was consecrated and entered upon his episcopate. His way of presenting the Christian faith is more in terms of living with questions than living with certain truths.

JERUSALEM 1928 see INTRODUCTION, INTERNATIONAL MISSIONARY COUNCIL

JESUS CHRIST. The person and ministry of Jesus Christ has been discussed in the ecumenical movement under various headings: Jesus Christ, Finality; Jesus Christ, Incarnation; Jesus Christ, Lord and Savior; Jesus Christ, Lordship; Jesus Christ, the New Man; Jesus Christ, Resurrection; Jesus Christ, Unity Given in Him, and still other headings. The movement did not enter into debates about hermeneutical questions, such as historical criticism, Jesus as teacher and preacher, the ethical teachings of Jesus; nor did it evaluate the validity of the Christology of modern Protestant theologians, such as Karl Barth (q.v.), Rudolf Bultmann, Friedrich Gogarten, Paul Tillich, Ernest Käsemann or Roman Catholic (q.v.) theologians, such as Karl Rahner, Hans Küng (qq.v.) and Edward Schillebeeckx. The WCC (q.v.) Basis refers to the council as "a fellowship of churches which confess the Lord Jesus Christ as God and Savior according to the scriptures". Every major ecumenical conference since the first world conference on Faith and Order (q.v.) in Lausanne (1927) has included in its report some reference to a Christological agreement. The main theme of four WCC assemblies included the name of Jesus Christ: "Christ—The Hope of the World" (Evanston, 1954); "Jesus Christ, The Light of the World" (New Delhi, 1961); "Jesus Christ Frees and Unites" (Nairobi, 1975); "Jesus Christ—The Life of the World"

(Vancouver, 1983). In the earlier days from 1955 onward Faith and Order engaged in several study programs: "The Lordship of Christ over the World and the Church", "The Finality of Jesus Christ in the Age of Universal History", and "Christ and the Church".

The foundation of the ecumenical movement is grounded in the finality and universality of Jesus Christ. The universal significance of the life, death and resurrection of Jesus Christ is the fundamental conviction of the Christian community from the very beginning. "God our Savior desires all human beings to be saved" (1 Timothy 2:4). In Christ reconciliation with God and one another is offered to the whole of humanity. This universality of salvation (q.v.) in Christ is expressed in the Bible in different theological contexts. The incarnation of the Son of God is related to the cosmos (John 3:16) and seen in a universal historical connection (Luke 2). The exalted Christ is Lord over all principalities and powers. His rule will culminate in a new heaven and a new earth with God directly and universally present (Col. 1; Phil. 2:9ff; Eph. 1:10; Rev. 21:1–5). Together with the church the whole creation awaits the liberation and redemption through Christ. The universality of his message clearly corresponds to the oneness of salvation: There is only one God, he is the Father of all. There is only one Lord, Jesus Christ, in whom all will be saved. All who confess Jesus Christ as Lord, have the same faith and live the same hope. St Paul is convinced that there is only one gospel, or there is no gospel at all (Gal. 1:6). When Christ repeatedly stresses: "I and the Father are one" (John 10:30), then this implies that there is only one way, one door to salvation—Jesus, the Son of the Father.

The one church includes both the greatest diversity of spiritual forms of expression and the most different national and social human origins (1 Cor. 12; Gal. 3:28). The unity (q.v.) of the church is the unity of the local congregation (1 Cor. 1:10ff), but it is also the unity of congregations beyond geographical frontiers, as is shown by the council of the apostles and the collections for the church in Jerusalem. The unity of the church signifies different traditions (q.v.) that are, to be sure, held together by the one fundamental tradition: the apostolic attestation of the crucified and risen Christ. The church cannot claim to have lasting possession of the knowledge of Jesus Christ and his salvation and already now be leading a life of perfection. As a community of justified sinners, the church lives from the promise that with the universality and oneness of salvation in Christ it also will be revealed as the one and universal communion of saints. In this context the sentence: "I believe in the one, holy, catholic and apostolic church" of the Nicene-Constantinopolitan Creed (325) must be understood.

This article has so far made clear that the ecumenical movement from the very beginning was thoroughly oriented by a Christocentric universalism. Thanks to the central ecumenical vision of the given unity in Christ during the 1940s and the 1950s the old lines of demarcation and division in the realm of the unity of the church were slowly overcome. But from the 1960s onward the shortcoming in the classical Christological approach has been increasingly realized. It operated with a "Christology from the top" in which the humanity of Christ does not find sufficient significant development. The decisive change that has occurred from the 1970s onward is a new appreciation of the humanity of Christ, i.e., a transition from the classic perspective of the "kingship of Christ" over the church and the world to God's kingdom seen in messianic perspective, which takes its bearings from the Jesus of Nazareth, who in his solidarity with the poor and the marginalized and in his powerlessness on the cross, was acknowledged as the hidden Messiah, the embodiment of the promised kingdom of God (q.v.). This change of perspective from "above" to "below" has proved particularly resourceful in the exploration of Christology through the liberation theology (q.v.) of Latin America. Great emphasis is laid on the humanity of Jesus as the primary element of a theology of liberation. This stress is not a denial of the traditional confession of his divinity; it is experienced as a relocation of that confession as Christ judges the whole of human history. Following Jesus implies to share in the "failure" of the cross, walking in the way of justice (q.v.), being exposed to the power of oppression, even when there is no real hope of what could be considered a successful issue.

The double name Jesus Christ indicates a distinction that can be expressed as the "Jesus of history" and the "Christ of faith". The name Jesus, his own proper name, draws attention to the fact that he was a human being living in Palestine during the reign of Herod; the title Christ, or anointed one, indicates that he is honored much more than a key figure in history—in fact as eternal Lord. In the tension between these two the whole truth of the Christian faith is involved. It requires the conviction and the boldness of the contemporary church as a whole in attempting to interpret and to act in current history in the light of God's revelation in Jesus Christ. *See also* SALVATION; THEOLOGY, LATE 20TH CENTURY TRENDS IN; TRINITY.

JEWISH-CHRISTIAN DIALOGUE *see* DIALOGUE WITH PEOPLE OF LIVING FAITHS

JOHN XXIII (ANGELO GUISEPPE RONCALLI) (1881–1963). A "mere transitional pope" who initiated a new age in Roman Catholicism (q.v.). During the First World War he served as army chaplain. In 1925 he began a Vatican diplomatic career, and in 1927 he visited the patriarch of Constantinople. Roncalli was apostolic delegate to Turkey and Greece, 1934–1944. He served in postwar France as apostolic nuncio with the primary task of healing divisions between the victorious followers of De Gaulle and the discredited members of the Vichy regime. Three months into his pontificate in 1958, John XXIII announced his intention to convoke "an ecumenical council for the universal church", envisaging the event as "an invitation to the separated communities to seek again that unity for which so many are longing in these days throughout the world". He called for the council without prior consultation claiming that his idea was based on an inspiration of the Holy Spirit (q.v.). He set up the Secretariat for Promoting Christian Unity (q.v.) in 1960, invited Orthodox, Anglicans and Protestants as delegate observers to Vatican II (qq.v.) and approved the delegation of official observers to the third assembly of the WCC (qq.v.) in New Delhi in 1961. As bishop of Rome he restored the tradition of visiting parishes, charitable organizations, hospitals, schools and prisons of the city. He died of gastric cancer before the Vatican Council began its second session and was succeeded by Paul VI (q.v.). John XXIII issued seven encyclicals (q.v.). The most noteworthy were *Mater et magistra* (1961), on modern social questions in the light of Christian doctrine, *Pacem in terris* (1962), on peace among all nations based on truth, justice, charity, freedom and the right organization of society, and *Princeps pastorum* (1959), on updating Christian missions.

JOHN PAUL II (KAROL JOSEPH WOJTYLA) (1920–). John Paul studied philosophy and theology secretly in a seminary in Krakow from 1942 onward. In 1946 he was ordained and sent to Rome to study for a doctorate in philosophy. In 1953 he was appointed professor of ethics and moral theology at Krakow and the Catholic University in Lublin. He was named auxiliary bishop of Krakow (1958), later its archbishop (1964) and cardinal (1967). He attended the four sessions of Vatican II (q.v.) and strongly defended the draft document on religious freedom. He was elected pope in 1978. Against the background of Vatican II and the papacy of Paul II (q.v.), John Paul II has been trying to pull back in line the church that ''threatened to run away'' from what he understands were the contents and intent of Vatican II. His explicit ecumenical commitment has been questioned by some and lauded by others. He visited the WCC (q.v.) headquarters in Geneva in 1984. Some contend that despite his contacts with Anglicans and Protestants, he is more interested in healing the division between the Roman Catholic Church and the Orthodox churches (qq.v.). John Paul II is well-known for several of his encyclicals (q.v.), particularly the social encyclicals *Laborem exercens* (1981) and *Sollicitudo rei socialis* (1987).

JOINT WORKING GROUP (JWG). The JWG of the Roman Catholic Church and the World Council of Churches (qq.v.), established in 1965, is the highest-level continuing contact and collaboration between the Council and the Roman Catholic Church. Representatives appointed by the Vatican and the WCC meet annually at different places to assess the overall ecumenical situation and discuss theological and ethical issues related to the unity (q.v.) of the church, mixed marriages (q.v.), engagement in social issues, ecumenical formation and many other topics. It has submitted six official reports of its deliberations to its two authorities in 1966, 1967, 1971, 1975, 1982 and 1990, which were published in the *Ecumenical Review*. Keeping its structures to a minimum while concentrating on ad hoc initiatives in proposing new concerns and programs, the JWG has attempted to be flexible in styles of working together. It has assisted in the annual joint preparation of the liturgical materials for the Week of Prayer for Christian Unity (q.v.). It sponsored, moreover, several studies on its own initiative: "Catholicity and Apostolicity" (1968); "Common Witness and Proselytism" (1970); "Common Witness" (1980); "Hierarchy of Truths" (1990); and "The Church: Local and Universal" (1990). The initial field of social collaboration was the work of SODE-PAX (q.v.) (the joint WCC/RCC Committee on Society, Development and Peace, started in 1968), whose mandate was terminated in 1980 after difficult discussions. An interim structure was then formed: the Joint Consultative Group linking WCC subunits in Unit II was the corresponding dicasteries in the Roman Curia.

The sixth official report acknowledged difficulties that have been experienced in collaboration, particularly in the field of social thought and action, and indicated possible areas for future common work. It also made several proposals for strengthening the role of the JWG. The Canberra assembly (1991) suggested that a newly composed JWG should be requested to concentrate its attention on a substantive review of the relationship between the RCC and the WCC. It should, in particular, analyze more deeply the obstacles that have prevented the relationships from developing more fully. Therefore, it should not only be liberated from the task of monitoring ongoing collaboration, but should aim at a common acknowledgment of the ecclesial character of the relationship that has grown between the RCC and the fellowship of churches in the WCC, suggesting ways of giving more real expression to it and examining especially whether on the threshold to the next millennium a preconciliar conference could be held that would seek binding steps toward complete unity.

JUST, PARTICIPATORY AND SUSTAINABLE SOCIETY

(JPSS). The search for a "just, participatory and sustainable society" was a major focal point of the WCC's work between the fifth and sixth assemblies (qq.v.). One source of this new (and, some complained, unpronounceable) phrase was Church and Society's five-year study program on "The Future of Man and Society in a World of Science-Based Technology", which concluded just before Nairobi. The focal point in the new ecumenical program theme of JPSS became *justice* (q.v.). The other two elements, participation and sustainability, were seen as the necessary dimensions of the contemporary struggle for justice. From the point of view of the kingdom of God, justice is not a principle or an ideal value that can ever be fully realized. Rather, as the historical embodiment of love, it indicates a quality of relationships in community and a criterion for evaluating and changing social structures.

The biblical reality at the root of the idea of *participation* is fellowship (*koinonia*). Christians can and must work together in the realization that their faith (q.v.) is not a mere private affair between the individual and God. But how can participation be organized and guaranteed? How can people be freed from being at the mercy of "experts" and given greater control over the direction of developments in science and technology? How can human relationships and community be maintained in the struggle against impersonal structures of nationalism and internationalism? The concept of *sustainability* brings to the fore the critical problem that the achievement of a high level of consumption in developed countries is in many ways the result of the exploitation of the rest of the world. A further dilemma is raised by the need to attain material growth that is ecologically sustainable. Can an acceptable life be achieved in the short run while avoiding long-term setbacks? Will permanent global solidarity require a drastic elimination of differentials in income, wealth, and power in the industrialized nations? Does economic development (q.v.) in less industrialized nations, if it is to be sustainable, first require a redistribution of wealth?

In contrast to the previous concept of the "responsible society" (q.v.), suggested by the Amsterdam assembly in 1948, the JPSS model advocated revolutionary action. Christian faith understands the present contradictions and struggles as a part and a manifestation of a dynamic in history pressing for eschatological fulfillment, thus defending history against both pretension and discouragement. The conviction was expressed that the kingdom of God (q.v.) is already operative in human history as an alternative reality of hope pressing toward fulfillment and that the struggles of the oppressed, in spite of their ambiguities, are pointers to this truth. To give prominence to the JPSS model is not to reject the concerns of the responsible society, but rather to modify and subordinate them to the emphasis of the former. Christian realism cannot be discarded; we live in an imperfect world and have to envision proximate goals, which will be achieved through less then perfect means. It is necessary, however, to move beyond the political pessimism engendered by the concept of the responsible society by using the kingdom perspective inherent in the JPSS model. The kingdom perspective affirms that the ongoing struggles for justice, peace and the integrity of creation are themselves indications that the kingdom of God is already operative in history and, despite their ambiguities, are signs of hope.

The WCC central committee meeting in Kingston, Jamaica, in 1979 rejected the findings of the JPSS advisory committee. The old, unresolved debates on the relationship between the kingdom of God and history that had been with the ecumenical movement since the Oxford conference resurfaced and on the study was relegated to a search for ecumenical ethics. The following reasons are given for this decision: ". . . the distinction between the human and the divine, history and eschatology (q.v.) was not made clearly enough; there was a tendency at times toward an unexamined messianism; the elements of 'sin', 'humility', 'repentance', 'sacrificial servant', etc. were not given sufficient consideration; the use of biblical material should be more carefully treated; a great deal more work needs to be done in order to move from theological categories to political categories". A few years later the concern for justice, peace and the integrity of creation (q.v.) was introduced. *See also* JUSTICE, PEACE AND THE INTEGRITY OF CREATION; RESPONSIBLE SOCIETY.

JUST WAR. A "just" war is totally different from the notion of a "holy" war. The latter has never been defended in Christianity, though perhaps the crusades and wars of religion were in fact holy wars. But for Christians, war was from the beginning basically unholy, and participation in it was considered problematic. The doctrine of the just war, as developed in the thought of St Augustine, Thomas Aquinas and others, was never intended to glorify war or to qualify war as positive, but rather to indicate situations in which the evil of war might or even must be accepted in preference to some greater evil of injustice, oppression or inhumanity that would continue if not eliminated by an act of war.

The ecumenical discussion on just war has not produced a larger agreement, although the efforts have concentrated on the means and the ways to prevent war, a point on which there is no disagreement. As the old distinction between "military" and "civilian" has become blurred and war is increasingly mechanized and automated, the concept of "limited war" has emerged. But the voices of pacifism (q.v.) in an active form and unilateral disarmament have also become stronger. See also PEACE AND DISARMAMENT.

JUSTICE. The concept of justice is connected with divine justice, human justice, economic justice, social justice and international justice. The complete integration of love and justice is the chief characteristic of Christianity. It is through love of God and the neighbor that the kingdom of God (q.v.) is achieved within Christians. Yet, this love cannot be authentic unless they continually attempt to form the external world by the same dynamic force. Only thus do human beings honestly respond to the justice that God has gratuitously bestowed upon them. From a theological point of view, justice among men and women is not primary. The primacy belongs rather to God's own sovereign justice, justifying sinners with utter grace, making them just and simultaneously, with and through gratuitous justice, making them capable of a newer and "better justice". Theologically prior to justice among human beings is the awareness that the "justice" owed to God is a totally free and yet absolutely binding love involving human beings as a whole. In the biblical-theological view, justice among members of the human race deserves the name justice in the full sense only if it is accomplished with a view toward God in that love, thanksgiving and obedience owed to God absolutely.

In this respect biblical thought is fundamentally different from the anthropocentrism of Aristotelian and Stoic thought. The relation of a human being to God is far different from a relation between equals, and it involves far more than a strict equality between giving and receiving. Human beings in their totality, with whatever good there is in them, are a gift of God, a gift in person. And in the life of grace (q.v.) God gives the human being his most personal love. It is therefore the original duty of "justice" that finds expression in the piety and worship of God. "What can I give the Lord for all that he has given me?" (Ps 115:12). The exemplar of justice is Jesus, who in his sacred humanity gave himself up to the Father for the sake of the redemption from the human being's most fundamental injustice, namely sin. Consequently, "we are unprofitable servants; we have done what it was our duty to do" (Lk 17:10). Justice among human beings will become a genuinely Christian virtue only if it is an extension of that grateful justice that is owed to God.

The first major ecumenical missionary conferences were concerned with how to understand the kingdom of God and God's justice in relation to history. The conferences in Edinburgh (1910) and in Jerusalem (1928) implied that the realization of the kingdom of God meant foremost the Christianization of the world. They did not raise questions about justice enhanced by Western civilization, though they were critical of the injustice of the colonial powers. The Oxford conference (1937) pointed out that the Bible offers no direct solutions for contemporary political and social conflicts. It stated that "the laws of justice are not purely negative; they are not merely 'dykes against sin'. The political and economic structure of society is also the mechanical skeleton which carries the organic elements of society". Yet, a

Christian ethics of justice derived from the love commandment must face the reality of evil and the difficulty of direct
application of the commandment of love: In an imperfect
world, justice must be maintained and enforced in face of the
constant threats of injustice, and Christians have a duty to
uphold justice as well as to exercise love.

The WCC (q.v.) faced from the very beginning the question
of international justice, and increasingly the problems of
economic and social justice. The Amsterdam assembly (1948)
was concerned with resisting the pretentions of imperialist
powers, the combat of indifference and despair in the futility of
war, the establishment of just peace treaties, and the churches
promotion of peaceful change and the pursuit of justice. The
Evanston assembly (1954) was concerned that justice requires
the development of political institutions that are humane as
they touch the lives of people, that provide protection by law
against the arbitrary use of power and that encourage responsible participation by all citizens.

From the mid-1960s onward, the ecumenical concerns for
economic and social justice came to the forefront. In our
contemporary age of steadily increasing economic complexity, of countless interrelations and a solidarity that extends
far beyond particular industries, indeed, beyond national
economies, it becomes much more apparent than in the ages
of city economy that the principles of commutative justice
alone are entirely insufficient. There is much more involved
in every transaction than mere exchange between private
parties, for every transaction presupposes countless prior
transactions on the part of society. And ultimately it is not
merely a question of transactions and prior transactions. A
truly realistic view of justice, achieved only gradually in the
present era, envisions above all the community of persons
created by God: the common family of all humanity. Every
form of justice is included in and presupposed by social
justice, but in the latter case it is always a question of rights
and duties that derive from the nature of the human community and the dignity of persons.

Where crushing and unjust power structures are defended by
the rich nations with all the force at their command and are not
subjected to any international effective political control, and

where the poor (q.v.) are increasingly oppressed, it is, besides being biblically justifiable, also realistic to expect justice simply as a result of prophetic appeals to those who are in power. Rather, the churches must be alongside those who are suffering in refusing to countenance injustice. They must themselves begin to practice justice in all its forms as a reality in their own life and thus, as churches of peace and liberation, transcend the majority church model. This was reflected at the Uppsala assembly (1968) when it stated in a section on "economic justice and world order": "The churches must strive more actively and urgently for that reform of will and conscience among the people of the world which alone can inspire the achievement of greater international justice . . . They should also stress that economic justice cannot be achieved without sacrifice and support for the establishment of an international development tax".

To this statement the WCC assembly in Vancouver (1983) added: "So long as economic injustice prevails between nations, lasting international security cannot be achieved, either by collective defence systems or by negotiated weapons reduction alone. Only a common enterprise undertaken by all the nations of the world together can ensure dependable international security". Eight years later the Canberra assembly (1991) struck a sobering note: "The organization of the international market in ways which would promote life and justice for all remains a major challenge. We look for a review leading to more accountable and just economic and monetary structures, within the jurisdiction of the United Nations (q.v.) and the International Court of Justice. The creation of a just world economic order may require the creation of new international organizations".

To sum up: For Christians and churches two realities flagrantly contradict each other. The free market economic system is a global reality and universally endorsed, even by the former leaders and people of socialist societies. It allows for no alternative and shows itself to be unhesitating in sacrificing everything for the sake of profit. In the absence of a competing superpower to check its hegemonic ambitions, it will strengthen systematic structures of injustice, pay no attention to the misery of the poor and the powerless and wreak havoc upon the environment (q.v.). The South could more than ever before lead a life of virtual slavery to the North. On the other hand, Christians believe that it is *God's* justice, the righteousness of the power who is behind and over all other powers they know, the one who has made known his love for all and who as the Holy Spirit (q.v.) is ever active to guide and inspire. It is God's *justice*, which is no simple ideal or merely a slogan, but a steady will and struggle to restore damaged relationships and to enhance the qualities of human living for creativity and love. It is a justice that deserves and demands the fullest and deepest spiritual energies that Christians can command as individuals and communities, just as it deserves and demands the toughest and most costly of the material powers they can devote to it.

JUSTICE, PEACE AND THE INTEGRITY OF CREATION (JPIC). Both the title and its initials, JPIC, are shorthand for a fuller statement: "To engage member churches in a conciliar process of mutual commitment (covenant) to justice, peace and the integrity of creation should be a priority for World Council programs". In issuing this invitation, the Vancouver assembly (1983) was not so much initiating a process as responding to a situation. Vancouver shifted from the position of understanding Christian involvement in world affairs largely as the concern of Christian ethics—to translate the values of the kingdom into achievable social goals (the middle axioms of the responsible society [qq.v]). Instead, it placed the emphasis on confessing the faith (q.v.), which calls for a new understanding of the missionary task of the church at this time. To realize this intention, the assembly envisaged a process that would bring the churches together to take a common stand on the urgent issues concerning the survival of humankind. This is the intention of the phrase "conciliar process of mutual commitment". It expects the process to lead to a council of the church that will take such a common stand and presumably take the churches to a new stage in covenant (q.v.) relationship into which they had entered at the inaugural assembly in Amsterdam in 1948.

But the term "covenant" did more to confuse than to clarify the meaning of "mutual commitment". At least four difficulties were encountered. First, the term is used in common parlance to refer to pacts and alliances between human partners, so that it is not clear what more is meant when it is used as a theological term in conjunction with "mutual commitment". Second, the Bible mentions several types of covenant, each with its own character and emphasis, so that a common biblical understanding of the term cannot be assumed. Third, while the term has ecclesiological significance in some church traditions, it does not in others. This makes the term even more suspect as a way of stating the mutual commitment of all churches to JPIC. Finally, many churches understand God's covenant to have been accomplished "once for all" in Jesus Christ (q.v.). So what does it mean theologically to speak of covenanting?

The Vancouver call touched off a worldwide process to which many national, regional and confessional organizations contributed. There were conferences or assemblies on JPIC in the Pacific (September 1988), Europe (May 1989) and Latin American (December 1989). Other contributions came from Orthoxy (Sofia 1987 and Minsk 1989), Roman Catholicism (Pontifical Council on Justice and Peace, Vatican 1989) and the World Alliance of Reformed Churches (Seoul 1989) (qq.v.). A World convocation on "Justice, Peace and the Integrity of Creation" in Seoul in March 1990 was able to make ten affirmations. Yet, it was honestly added in the introduction to the report that "the convocation underlined the deep differences that still divide us . . . There was a clear tension between local/regional perceptions and global analysis. Equally evident were the differences in preparation for and expectation of the convocation. The term 'conciliar process', used in the Vancouver call, had to be abandoned for theological reasons. In spite of all attempts made, there were still some unresolved differences in the understanding of the word 'covenant' ".

To these observations the following four points of criticism could be added: 1) The term "integrity of creation" has not been defined and begs a basic question: how should God's nonhuman creation interact with the history of God's dealing with his covenant people? 2) The analysis of social powers and trends in the document is unrealistic and undialectical. A black-and-white, good/evil scheme seems to dominate the world as a whole. The tone is exhortative and idealistic, and therefore not very helpful to faithful witness in the real world. 3) The theology of the document, despite some good statements, is vague, sometimes contradictory, sometimes lacking. Forgiveness and grace (q.v.) are missing, nor is anything said about sharing in the redemptive suffering of Jesus Christ. 4) The document lacks an evangelical witness to the saving work of God in human society. God is present as creator, sustainer and other for the poor, but the rest is left to human struggle as defined in a long list of possible actions. There is too much ill-digested law and not enough convincing gospel. The WCC continues to search for the right direction in the JPIC process. *See also* JUST, PARTICIPATORY AND SUSTAINABLE SOCIETY; RESPONSIBLE SOCIETY.

JUSTIFICATION. In classical Protestant theology, the human being is justified by "faith alone" (*sola fide*), or more precisely, by grace (q.v.) alone through faith (q.v.) alone in Christ alone. The word "alone" is meant to exclude all thought of the sinful human being's doing or deserving, as in any way motivating his justification. The theme of the divine righteousness/justice in human salvation (q.v.) is prominent in the Book of Romans, where St Paul explains how God can forgive sinners, be they Jewish or Gentile. Because St Augustine thought of the principle of righteousness being infused in the soul at baptism (q.v.) and of the Christian life being a process of being made righteous in order that, after death, God, for Christ's sake, could pronounce the Christian justified, Paul's teaching was misinterpreted for centuries. The doctrine of justification of St Augustine was confirmed by the Roman Catholic Church (q.v.) at the Council of Trent (1545–1563). All the Protestant churches followed Martin Luther in insisting that the primary meaning of justification is the declaration of God who accounts a sinner to be righteous in his sight for the sake of Jesus Christ (q.v.).

As a result of the 20th-century ecumenical movement, it has been possible for Roman Catholic and Protestant theologians to discuss amicably the doctrine of justification and other doctrines. Although this has not led to entire agreement, it has helped to sort out where there are differences and where they have been, and remain, misunderstandings. During the 1950s and the 1960s many books on justification were written by Roman Catholic scholars from new perspectives. Most important from the dialogues is *Justification by Faith: U.S. Lutheran-Roman Catholic Dialogue* (1983). Also *Salvation and the Church: An Agreed Statement by the Second Anglican-Roman Catholic International Commission* (1987) should be mentioned. In both documents the issues are set out with great clarity and integrity. Curiously, justification by faith has never been a major preoccupation of the Orthodox churches (q.v.). They therefore have no contribution to make to the debate. *See also* FAITH; GRACE; SALVATION.

- K -

KAGAWA, TOHOHIKO (1888–1960). As one of the most outstanding Japanese Christian leaders, born in Kobe as the son of a wealthy businessman and baptized in 1903, Kagawa was disowned by his family and not long after devoting himself to Christian service to the poor and helpless in the slums of Kobe. He studied later at Princeton Theological Seminary (1914–1916) and also became known in the West as a prominent evangelist, distinguished social worker and leader of labor movements and cooperatives of various kinds. His strong views on social and political matters made him an object of suspicion to reactionary and military authorities in Japan. He was twice arrested in 1940 and 1943, but because of his popularity with the people the government judged it wiser not to keep him in prison. After the war he refused the invitation to enter politics and to help rebuild the nation. Japanese Christians tended to be critical of him as a man who started many things he was not able to complete, and who did not always keep his feet firmly on the stable ground of reality. Kagawa was a poet and author of 180 books on religious, social, scientific and other subjects. He was president of the All Japan Farmers' Association, the Japan Cooperative Association, and the *Christian News Weekly*.

KAREKIN II (SARKISSIAN) (1932–). Karekin II is Catholicos of the Armenian catholicessate of Galicia, Antelias, Lebanon, and was vice moderator of the WCC (q.v.) central committee, 1975–1983. He headed the eastern prelacy of the United States and Canada from 1973 and previously was prelate of the Julfa-Isfahan diocese in Iran. Before serving in North America, Karekin II was chancellor and dean of the Armenian Theological Seminary in the catholicossate of Antelias. He lectured in Armenian studies at the American University of Beirut and was president of the Alliance for Theological Education in the Near East. During this period he also served as general secretary for interchurch relations in the catholicossate and was a member of its central committee for religious affairs.

KARRER, OTTO (1888–1976). Karrer was a Jesuit theologian who through his contributions to the study of religions, biblical theology and ecumenics became one of the forerunners of contemporary Catholic theology. He became convinced that everything must be done to avoid Christians injuring one another and to promote the unity (q.v.) of the church. "Controversy from a distance" is questionable and harmful. The real problem of division is neither the doctrine of justification by faith (qq.v.), nor the relation between Bible and Tradition, but the papacy (q.v.), which is not power. Karrer was particularly faithful to Cardinal Newman, whom he regarded as one of the church fathers of modern times. His influence in the realm of theology of religions on the Second Vatican Council (q.v.) was considerable.

KELLER, ADOLF (1872–1963). The term "interchurch aid" (q.v.) can probably be ascribed to Keller. It appears in the title of the European Central Bureau for Inter-Church Aid, the body that he was largely instrumental in founding in 1922, with offices in New York and Geneva, and that carried on until it was merged in the provisional WCC (q.v.) in 1944 as an integral part of the Department of Reconstruction and Inter-Church Aid. From the beginning the first task of the bureau was to help churches, Christian institutions and ministers in distress. Keller was among the initiators who founded the Swiss Federation of Protestant Churches in 1920 and served as its secretary until 1941. In this function he facilitated contacts with the World Alliance of Reformed Churches (q.v.) and became its vice president, 1937–1948. One of the secretaries of the Universal Christian Conference on Life and Work in Stockholm in 1925, he served afterward as one of the three executive secretaries of the Life and Work movement (q.v.). In 1927 he was appointed director of the International Christian Social Institute, a predecessor of the study department of the WCC. Keller visited more than 200 universities and theological schools, in both Europe and America, to lecture and to discuss with the faculties the problem of ecumenical teaching. He also taught social ethics at the Universities of Basel, Zurich and Geneva and held ecumenical seminars that were later continued at the Ecumenical Institute of Bossey (q.v.).

KIMBANGU, SIMON (1889–1951). When the Kimbanguist movement started in Zaire in 1921, it was regarded by the colonial authorities as a political time bomb. Kimbangu, after several healings, suddenly became the center of a vigorous revival movement, which lasted only a few months. He was imprisoned as a dissident for the remaining 30 years of his life. In 1921 a military court sentenced him to death. The sentence was commuted by King Albert I of Belgium into detention for life. Kimbangu was deported to Lubumbashi (2,000 km from his home), where he died. Nearly 100,000 of his followers were exiled between 1921 and 1957, when the movement officially established itself as the Church of Christ on Earth by the Prophet Simon Kimbangu. This church with 5 million members is now active in Zaire, Congo, Angola, Zambia, Sabon, Central African Republic, Burundi, Kenya, France, Belgium and Portugal. It became a member of the WCC (q.v.) in 1969. It recognizes four sacraments: baptism, eucharist, marriage and ordination (qq.v.).

KING, MARTIN LUTHER, JR. (1929–1968). At the age of twenty-seven King took his first step toward greatness when he accepted the leadership of the ensuing boycott of the public buses of Montgomery in protest of racial segregation. His plea for racial equality and his use of the passive resistance tactics of Ghandi and Thoreau made Americans of every race examine their consciences. Later in Birmingham, Selma, Chicago and wherever else bigotry had to be fought, he adhered to his philosophy of nonviolence. In 1957 he summoned together a number of Negro leaders and laid the groundwork for the organization of the Southern Christian Leadership Conference. In 1960 he became co-pastor, with his father, of Ebenezer Baptist Church in Atlanta, Georgia. Three years later his nonviolent tactics were put to the most severe test in Birmingham, Alabama, where he led a mass protest for fair hiring practices, desegregation of department store facilities and the establishment of a biracial committee. King organized, along with other civil rights leaders, the massive "March on Washington", which brought an estimated 250,000 people, many of them white, to the Lincoln Memorial. In 1968 he began planning the Poor Peoples Campaign, in which not only Negroes, but Puerto Ricans, Mexicans, American Indians and poor whites were to march on Washington to dramatize the plight of all the poor people in the USA. On 4 April King was assassinated in Memphis by James Earl Ray. He had been invited to preach the opening sermon at the WCC Uppsala assembly in the summer of that same year.

KINGDOM OF GOD: According to Mark 1:15 Jesus began his ministry with a proclamation including the words ". . . the kingdom of God is at hand". Since Jesus never defined the term, various interpretations are possible. The kingdom could mean: 1) the eternal and invisible reign of God, which is independent of human response or knowledge; 2) the realization of God's reign in groups or individuals who accept his sovereignty; or 3) the eschatological kingdom at the end of history when all will recognize the sovereignty of God. In a broad sense the kingdom serves as a symbol for the will of God, which may be carried out in particular situations through humble obedience, but which is never fully accomplished within the confines of history because of human limitations. Thus, the kingdom "comes", but its final manifestation remains a future hope (q.v.).

In the ecumenical movement the concept of the kingdom, though undefined, played a major role in several contexts. One can say that the notion as an ideal society, characterized by justice (q.v.), equality and freedom has been generally accepted. The WCC Humanum Studies (1969–1975) served as a typical illustration of the growing use of the concept of the kingdom of God in ecumenical documents, emphasizing that "the churches have preached the kingdom of God while being in open and hidden alliance with various exploitative kingdoms of men" and that "the future and fulfilment of humanity does not lie in Christianity but in God". The Faith and Order (q.v.) meeting in Accra (1974) added to these statements: "Hope in Christ is *pain* and *joy* at the same time, *making us restless,* so that we no longer conform ourselves to this enslaved and divided world, but have to strive for liberation and peace, *making us joyful,* because we believe, in spite of frustration and sin, that we are children of God's kingdom".

The theme of the world conference on mission and evangelism (q.v.) at Melbourne (1980) was "Your Kingdom Come". The sections concentrated on: I. Good News to the Poor; II. The Kingdom of God and Human Struggles; III. The Church Witnesses to the Kingdom; and IV. The Crucified Christ Challenges Human Power. Another important context is the present Faith and Order study on "The Unity of the Church and the Renewal of Human Community", focusing on "the church as mystery and prophetic sign". Although the study is still only in its initial stage, the concept plays a major role, as "church" and "human community" are related within the larger perspective of the kingdom. Although the final realization of the kingdom remains solely God's gift, the ecumenical movement rightly insists that human beings are nevertheless liberated to participate actively in establishing at least some signs of the kingdom. *See also* ESCHATOLOGY; HOPE.

KOECHLIN, ALPHONS (1885–1965). In 1923 Koechlin served on the staff of the World Student Christian Federation (q.v.), and from Stockholm 1925 onward became one of the pioneers of the ecumenical movement. He was president of the Basel Missionary Society, 1936–1959, and president of the Federation of Protestant Churches in Switzerland, 1941–1954. He regularly informed George Bell (q.v.) about the developments of the German church struggle, 1933–1945, and during the Second World War assisted W. A. Visser 't Hooft (q.v.) in the activities of the WCC (q.v.) Reconstruction Department. He participated in the preparation for the Amsterdam assembly (1948) and retired from his manifold ecumenical activities at Evanston (1954). His correspondence with George Bell was published in 1969.

KOENIG, FRANZ (1905–). Archbishop of Vienna, 1956–1985, and appointed cardinal, 1958, Koenig was president of the Vatican Secretariat for Non-Believers, 1965–1980. In 1961 he became the first cardinal to visit the ecumenical patriarch of Constantinople since the schism. Founder of Pro Oriente for the promotion of the dialogue between Roman Catholicism and Orthodoxy (qq.v.), he established the first relationship with the Romanian Orthodox Church. In 1974 he convened the colloquium "Koinonia", which paved the way for the official Roman-Catholic-Orthodox dialogue and for five consultations with the Non-Chalcedonian Orthodox churches. Koenig maintained a liaison with Ethiopian and Syrian Orthodoxy. He visited the Evangelical Lutheran Church in Finland in 1978, and the general synod of the Church of England (qq.v.) in 1984.

KOYAMA, KOSUKE (1929–). As a Japanese theologian Koyama has been lecturer in theology, Thailand Theological Seminary, 1960–1968, director of the Association of Theological Schools in Southeast Asia, dean of the South East Asia School of Theology, and editor of the *South East Asia Journal of Theology*, 1968–1974. A member of the Commission on Faith and Order (q.v.), he has participated in many ecumenical conferences. He has greatly promoted an indigenous Asian theology.

KRAEMER, HENDRIK (1888–1965). Kraemer studied Javanese at the University of Leiden and Islam at El Azhar University in Cairo in order to be prepared for his work for the Dutch Bible Society in Indonesia, 1922–1937. He received an honorary doctorate from the University of Utrecht in 1937, and was appointed professor of sociology of religion at Leiden. Shortly after the war, he was a member of a delegation of churches that went to Stuttgart to meet the Council of the Evangelical Church of Germany issuing the Stuttgart declaration of guilt. In preparation for the assembly of the International Missionary Council (q.v.) in Tambaram, India, in 1938, he was commissioned to write what became his best-known book, *The Christian Message in a Non-Christian World*, which influenced subsequent years of missionary theology and practice. Later ecumenical theologians and missiologists have faulted Kraemer for overemphasizing the exclusiveness of the Christian message and its radical discontinuity with other living faiths, thus not doing sufficient justice to God's presence and inspiration in them. Kraemer was director of the Ecumenical Institute in Bossey (q.v.), 1947–1955, and afterward he was active at the Institute "Kerk en Wereld" from where he lectured half of the time abroad and worked the other half of the time for parishes in the Netherlands. His book *Theology of the Laity* (1958) became a classic in the field.

KÜNG, HANS (1928–). Küng studied theology at the Gregorian University in Rome, the Sorbonne and the Institute Catholique in Paris, and in Amsterdam, Berlin, Madrid and London. Ordained in 1954, he became professor of dogmatic and ecumenical theology at the faculty of Catholic theology and director of the institute for ecumenical research at the University of Tübingen, 1963–1980, and afterward full professor of ecumenical theology in Tübingen. He was censured by the Vatican in 1979 for questioning traditional church doctrines. He has also been critical of developments within the ecumenical movement and accused the WCC of not challenging courageously the Roman Catholic Church (qq.v.). His numerous works, translated into many languages, include *The Council and Reunion* and *Infallible? An Enquiry.*

KURIEN, CHRISTOPHER THOMAS (1931–). Kurien made a plenary presentation at the Church and Society conference in Geneva in 1966, and at the Faith, Science and Future conference (MIT) in 1979. He was a member of the WCC (q.v.) Advisory Committee on Technical Services and continues to be associated with the WCC Advisory Group on

Economic Matters. He was director of the Madras Institute of Development Studies, 1978–1988, and is now senior fellow. He was professor of economics at Madras Christian College, 1962–1978, a member of the Indian Council of Social Science Research, and continues to serve on the Panel of Economists of the Indian Planning Commission. He was one of the seven experts invited by the secretary-general of the United Nations (q.v.) to make an independent evaluation of the world food situation.

- L -

LABOR *see* WORK/UNEMPLOYMENT

LAITY. The word is derived from the Greek *laos,* meaning "people". In the New Testament it is used to describe the members of the church as the people of God. During the Middle Ages an elaborate hierarchical structure of priestly offices was developed, with the result that the laity came virtually to be regarded as having no ministerial function at all. The Reformation (q.v.) took certain steps to remedy this situation. Luther's teaching on the vocation of lay Christians made it clear that one could serve God effectively in other ways than in holy orders or in religious communities. But generally the distinction between the ordained clergy and the laity remained in spite of a new emphasis on the priesthood of all believers. Only the 20th century rediscovered the crucial role of the laity in church and world.

The first three WCC assemblies (qq.v.) pointed out the vital concern for lay participation in the ecumenical movement. Amsterdam (1948) stated forcefully: "The laity constitutes more than 99 per cent of the church . . . Only by the witness of a spiritually intelligent and active laity can the church *meet* the modern world in all its actual perplexities and life situations . . . We need to rethink what it means to speak of the church as 'a royal priesthood', 'a holy nation', 'a peculiar people', and as the 'body of Christ' to which every member contributes in his measure". To which Evanston (1954) added: "The laity stand at the very outposts of the kingdom of God (q.v.). They are the missionaries of Christ in every secular sphere''. New Delhi (1961) still further developed the concern for full lay participation in the ecumenical movement. ''In a real partnership between clergy and the laity, the layman must help the theologian to understand the dilemmas of ordinary men and women in a rapidly changing world . . .''. Several meetings of the WCC central committee during the 1960s dealt with questions of the various ministries of the laity.

The WCC Department of the Laity, replacing the former Secretariat for Laymen's Work, functioned within the Division of Ecumenical Action from 1954 to 1971. It sponsored many national, regional and world consultations, engaged in numerous staff visitations and issued, besides the periodical *Laity,* several publications. From the beginning the Ecumenical Institute in Bossey (q.v.) organized many courses and consultations on the laity, open to all except ordained pastors. The institute was in fact originally conceived as an international center for the training of the laity. In the 1950s and 1960s evangelical academies (q.v.) and lay training centers were created in Germany, Sweden, the Netherlands and other European countries to provide new challenges to established ecumenism. They were effective in meeting lay-peoples' spiritual needs, running conference retreats, specializing in courses for politicians, economists, sociologists and trade unionists, discussing the life problems of industrial workers and training lay workers for parishes and schools. Lay institutes spread outside Europe in Japan, Korea, India, Zambia, Australia, Canada, the United States and several other countries.

Also within the Roman Catholic Church (q.v.) significant developments took place. The Dogmatic Constitution on the Church of Vatican II (q.v.), adopted in 1964, contained a chapter on the laity. It stated: ''The laity are called in a special way to make the Church present and operative in those places and circumstances where only through them can she become the salt of the earth''. The Decree on the Apostolate of the Laity was proclaimed in 1965. The WCC Department on the Laity was involved in the World Conference of Catholic International Organizations and helped plan the World Congress on the Apostolate of the Laity in 1967.

The ecumenical preoccupation with the role of the laity in church and society diminished considerably from the early 1970s onward. In the new WCC three-unit program structure there was no more a specially designated department on the laity. In the functions of Unit III, Education and Renewal, reference is made only to "processes of Christian nurture of children, youth and adults, relevant to life in contemporary society". Significantly the Vancouver assembly (1983) deplored that "participation by laity becomes impossible: 1) when the laity is excluded from the decision-making structures of the church; 2) when the laity is not effectively equipped or encouraged for ministry in the world. We affirm that the laity has a special opportunity to share and interpret the gospel creatively and sensitively in the home, in the community, and in all areas of daily work, especially in the field of science, and in local congregations". Since the word "laity" has almost disappeared from ecumenical documents, a new sense of ecumenical learning and vocation of every ordinary Christian has to be regained.

LANGE, ERNST (1927–1974). His mother came from a Jewish family in East Prussia, and in 1937 took her own life in desperation. Lange learned to hope, and determined to live for that hope. Participating in the life of a storefront church in the slums of East Harlem, New York, he began to see the oikoumene as creating a state of emergency of faith (q.v.). In 1960 he took part in the ecumenical youth conference in Lausanne, and filled with shame, he joined many others in breaking out of the limits of "an ingrowing world-forgetting church narcissism". In 1963 he became professor of practical theology at the church seminary in Berlin. From 1968–1970 he served as the first German theologian to be the director of the Division of Ecumenical Action of the WCC and in this capacity was one of the associate general secretaries. In his short life Lange made a lasting contribution to the whole ecumenical movement because of his extraordinary gift of understanding and interpretation of the most complicated issues. His thinking, his writing and his work centered on the renewal of preaching and teaching, and the renewal of the church in general. Stating that "contemporary man is living in a planetary world with a parochial conscience'', he came to the sobering conclusion that the capacity of the churches to learn and to act would remain extremely small, unless church members would be stimulated to mental awareness. After participating in the 1971 meeting of the Commission on Faith and Order (q.v.) in Louvain, Lange wrote an unusual and sharp report of this gathering (*And Yet It Moves: Dream and Reality of the Ecumenical Movement*), which had an inestimable effect in rousing public opinion.

LARNACA 1986 *see* INTERCHURCH AID

LATIN AMERICAN COUNCIL OF CHURCHES. Historically, Latin America has for centuries been the home of a dominant Roman Catholicism (q.v.) closely linked in many instances with traditional political and economic centers of power. It is also a continent where a strong minority of the leadership in the Roman Catholic Church is now involved in a far-reaching *aggiornamento.* Protestantism (q.v.) is largely the outcome of missions, chiefly from North America, which, on conservative theological grounds, are hostile to, or lack sympathy with, the ecumenical movement. Many Christian groups are opposed to common worship (q.v.), service and witness. Only four larger churches are members of the WCC (q.v.): The Evangelical Pentecostal Church "Brazil for Christ'', the Church of the Lutheran Confession in Brazil, the Methodist Church of Brazil, and the Pentecostal Church of Chile. There are 14 smaller churches that are also members of the WCC.

From the Panama Missionary Conference (1916) onward, a number of councils and federations of churches were created under the influence of North American mission boards and churches. Several of these organizations were related to the International Missionary Council (q.v.) and to the USA Committee on Cooperation in Latin America (CCLA). In 1941 the Ecumenical Youth Movement in Latin America (ULAJE) was created. Church and Society in Latin America (ISAL) was born in 1961, which related to the Church and Society concerns of the WCC, specifically to the program of study on the church in rapid social change.

The Movimiento por Unidad Evangélica Latinoamericana (UNELAM), founded in a provisional form in 1965, was not a council of churches, but a loose alliance of Christian communities and organizations to promote cooperation and greater unity. It was preceded by two Latin American Evangelical Conferences in Buenos Aires in 1949 and in Lima in 1961. During the Fourth Latin American Protestant Conference (IV-CELA) in Oaxtepec, Mexico, in 1978, representatives of 110 churches and ten continental ecumenical organizations accepted the proposal of UNELAM to create a Latin American Council of Churches (CLAI)—which was officially constituted in Lima, Peru, in 1982. Continuous efforts are made to strengthen relationships with churches that are now members of the CLAI and to contact other churches in Latin America to bring them into its fellowship. The CLAI includes Methodists, Lutherans, Presbyterian and Reformed, Anglicans, Pentecostalists, Baptists, Moravians (qq.v.), Waldensians, united churches, independent and Orthodox (q.v.) churches. In ecumenical fellowship all these Christian communities and associated or fraternal ecumenical bodies recognize the doctrinal basis of the CLAI, i.e., the confession of "Jesus Christ (q.v.) as God and Savior according to the scriptures". In unity they are trying to "fulfill together their common calling to the glory of God, Father, Son and Holy Spirit (q.v.)".

LAUBACH, FRANK CHARLES (1884–1970). A Congregational educator and evangelist, in 1929 Laubach began an educational project of teaching reading by phonetic symbols and pictures, eventually developing literacy primers for some 300 languages and dialects in over 100 countries and localities in Asia, Africa and Latin America. As originator of the "Each One Teach One" concept of adult literary instruction, he founded Laubach Literacy in 1955, with headquarters in Syracuse, New York, but with branch offices and centers in many parts of the world. He was professor at the Manila Union Theological Seminary, dean of Union College in Manila, dean of the College of Education at Manila University and director of Maranaw folk schools. He also served as special counselor to the Committee on World

Literacy and Christian Literature of the Division of Foreign Missions of the National Council of the Churches of Christ in the USA (q.v.).

LAUSANNE 1927 *see* INTRODUCTION, FAITH AND ORDER

LAUSANNE COMMITTEE FOR WORLD EVANGELIZA-TION. This committee was created after the International Congress on World Evangelization, held in Lausanne, Switzerland, in 1974. The congress was sponsored by the Billy Graham Evangelistic Association. Linked with the Lausanne Covenant and a shared vision, the 75-member committee seeks to be a catalyst and facilitator for world evangelization through conferences, publications and networking. Its members come from a wide denominational background, with the majority from the Third World. Its international office is located in Singapore. The committee convened a second International Congress on World Evangelization in Manila in 1989. *See also* MISSION.

LAY TRAINING CENTERS *see* ECUMENICAL INSTITUTES

LEIPER, HENRY SMITH (1891–1975). A leading authority on religious activities in countries overrun by Nazism, and an advocate of world peace (q.v.) and detente between the nations having different ideologies, Leiper was associate general secretary of the WCC (q.v.), 1938–1952. He served previously as a missionary in China, 1918–1922, as executive secretary of the American section of the Universal Christian Council on Life and Work, as ecumenical and then foreign secretary of the Federal Council of Churches (q.v.), 1945–1948, and as executive secretary of the Congregational Christian Church's mission council, 1952–1959. He ardently defended the WCC against its critics in the 1940s and the 1950s. Leiper was editor of *Ecumenical Courier,* 1948–1952.

LEISURE/TOURISM. Following the encouragement of the Uppsala assembly (1968) that the WCC do studies in "Changing Concepts of Work and Leisure", the Laity staff of the Division on Ecumenical Action arranged a world consultation on leisure and tourism at Tutzing, Germany, in 1969. The report, *Leisure—Tourism, Threat and Promise,* was widely circulated. There have been follow-up conferences in several areas, including the Caribbean, the Pacific, East Africa, Korea, Japan and Sri Lanka. The topic appeared again as a major concern at a consultation in Crete of the Ecumenical Association of Directors of Academies and Lay Centers in Europe in 1973. Until the 1970s the churches had shown little interest in tourism, beyond the marginal concern related to pilgrimages and holy places. That situation rapidly changed. Several regional church groups initiated consultations to deal with aspects of tourism and the responsibility of the churches. These culminated in an international workshop on tourism held in Manila, Philippines, in 1980. *Third World Stopover: The Tourism Debate,* by Ron O'Grady, was published in 1981. It explored the negative effects of tourism in poor countries, and reflected the concern of Third World Christians over the exploitation of people and the undermining of their culture, which tourism encourages. It also discussed how tourism may be salvaged and become a force for human development.

A particular concern has been sex tourism, including child prostitution, which enslaves children. It is estimated that a million Asian children today are lured into prostitution or sold into it by poor parents in countries such as Thailand, Sri Lanka, Philippines and Taiwan. Ecumenical programs have pointed to the evils of prostitution, the threat of AIDS and other sexually transmitted diseases and the links with drugs. Other programs have focused on alternative approaches to tourism that enable tourists to see the actual life-styles and cultural traditions of people. As a result the Ecumenical Coalition on Third World Tourism was formed in 1982 with headquarters in Bangkok. As is often the case, the ecumenical program on leisure/tourism was not officially continued.

LIBERATION THEOLOGY *see* THEOLOGY, LATE 20TH CENTURY TRENDS IN

LIBERTY, RELIGIOUS *see* RELIGIOUS LIBERTY

LIFE AND WORK. At a conference of the World Alliance for Promoting International Friendship through the Churches (q.v.) in The Hague in 1919, Nathan Söderblom (q.v.) launched the idea of an ecumenical council of churches "which should be able to speak on behalf of Christendom on the religious, moral and social concerns of men". Other international church leaders collaborated with Söderblom at a meeting in Geneva in 1920 to prepare for the Universal Christian Conference on Life and Work in Stockholm in 1925. Their task was an urgent one because of the great catastrophe of the First World War for humanity and Christianity. Yet, despite the sense of urgency and the serious preliminary studies, the great hopes for a bold Christian program for world order and social reconstruction were disappointing in Stockholm. The postwar situation seemed hardly more promising, as the spirit of vengeance and nationalism prevented cooperation in the rebuilding of destroyed societies and the establishment of world peace (q.v.). Yet, like Roman Catholic social movements at the end of the 19th century, Protestant, Anglican and Orthodox (qq.v.) leaders had committed themselves to a new involvement in the world in the interest of social justice (q.v.). They perceived that the spirit of pious individualism that predominated at that time was no answer to the problems of industrial revolution and international conflict. They sought to construct a new ecumenical concern based upon the inspiration of various Christian social movements of the day.

In 1930 a continuation committee was reconstituted as a permanent body, the Universal Christian Council for Life and Work. The principal objective of the council, according to its constitution, was "to perpetuate and strengthen the fellowship between the churches in the application of Christian ethics to the social problems of modern life". Noteworthy was the stipulation concerning the five sections: "The sections shall be the constituent bodies of the Council, and shall be in each case responsible for their own organization; the sections shall be composed of representatives of the churches". Though not strictly a responsibility of Life and Work, the European Central Bureau for Inter-Church Aid began its work under the patronage of the Federal Council of the Churches of Christ in America (q.v.) and the Federation of Swiss Protestant Churches, later joined by other European churches. At a conference in Copenhagen in 1922, the bureau was officially established with offices in New York and Geneva, and with Adolf Keller (q.v.) as director. By setting up its headquarters in Geneva, Life and Work established contacts with other international Christian organizations, the League of Nations and the International Labor Office. An International Christian Social Institute developed from the late 1920s onward an extensive and ever-growing program of ecumenical study and education (q.v.). It dealt with developments in international social work, relations of religion and labor and social endeavors within the churches. A network of correspondents in various countries was created; their first assignment was to supply data for an international survey on the social work of the churches.

The 1937 Conference on Church, Community and State in Oxford, like the 1925 Stockholm conference, can be understood only against the background of the economic and political situation and the changing attitudes within the church regarding its task in society. The world economic and social situation had steadily worsened during the 1930s. The effects of the economic depression in the great industrial nations had spread around the whole world, and the social tensions they produced convulsed practically every society. The ideologies (q.v.) of totalitarian communism in the Soviet Union and of National Socialism in Germany had succeeded in keeping these nations under absolute control. In contrast to Stockholm 1925, Oxford 1937 argued that a Christian social ethic cannot be developed directly from the love commandment or the kingdom of God (q.v.), since these, because of human sinfulness, are in contradiction with the world. Therefore, "in as far as the kingdom of God is in conflict with the world and is therefore still to come, the Christian finds himself under the necessity of discovering the best available means of checking human sinfulness and of increasing the possibilities and opportunities of love within a sinful world". The task of the Christian is to make use of the "principle of justice", as the relative expression of the commandment of love in any critique of economic, political and social institutions''.

Ecumenical discussion of sociopolitical questions was interrupted by the Second World War, but churches in various regions struggled to prepare themselves for the postwar period by their discussions of the conditions of peace and postwar reconstruction. Their debates now focused on the issues of state planning and the welfare society, as alternatives to capitalism (q.v.) and communism, and this came to be the main social issue in the debates of the first assembly of the WCC (qq.v.) in Amsterdam in 1948. Within the WCC Study Department, an inquiry on ''Christian Action in Society'' was started, and in 1949 Paul Abrecht (q.v.) was invited to direct this program.

LIFE-STYLES *see* NEW STYLES OF LIVING.

LILJE, HANNS (1899–1977). Lilje received his ecumenical education as vice president of the World Student Christian Federation (q.v.) and as general secretary of the Student Christian Movement in Germany, 1924–1934. He was one of the founders of the Lutheran World Federation (q.v.) in Lund in 1947, was its president, 1952–1957, and a member of the executive committee, 1947–1970. Lilje was involved in the German church struggle from 1933 onward and instrumental in the establishment of the Evangelical Church of Germany after the war. He was bishop of the Evangelical Lutheran Church in Hanover from 1947 until his retirement in 1971, and presiding bishop of the United Evangelical Lutheran Church in Germany, 1955–1969. He became a president of the WCC from 1968 until 1975.

LIMA LITURGY. This liturgy (q.v.) was first celebrated at the conclusion of the meeting of the Commission on Faith and Order in Lima, Peru, in 1982. It incorporates convergencies expressed in the text on *Baptism, Eucharist and Ministry* (q.v.), whose maturity was unanimously approved in Lima for the reception of the churches, and includes liturgical elements from various Christian traditions. Subsequently the liturgy was celebrated in Geneva in 1982, as closing worship at the meeting of the WCC (q.v.) central committee. The liturgy was drawn up by Max Thurian (q.v.) and can be followed in English, French, German and Spanish. It has become clear that there is an obvious desire among the people of God to see emerging doctrinal convergencies become embodied and rooted in the liturgical life of the church.

LITURGY. In the narrow sense the Greek word *leitourgia* (a public work) is used as a synonym for the eucharist (q.v.) as the church's corporate and official act par excellence. In a wider sense it covers all the church's public formal worship (q.v.), in contrast to the private devotions of individual Christians and less formal public services such as prayer-meetings, though the line cannot be very sharply drawn. During the first three centuries of the Christian era, the rite of the church was comparatively fluid, based on various accounts of the last supper. In the 4th century the various traditions crystallized into four liturgies, the Antiochene or Greek, the Alexandrian, the Roman and the Gallican, from which all others have been derived.

Liturgical renewal in the second half of this century focused on a return to the worship principles of the early church. The new interest in patristics among Orthodox, Roman Catholics and Protestants (qq.v.) is tending toward common forms of worship—restoring the importance of both Word and sacraments (q.v.), simplifying the church year, renewing interest in art and architecture, and recovering the entire treasury of music. New prayer books and revised liturgical materials are becoming available. By the end of World War II a new liturgical movement spread widely in Europe and America. In Asia and Africa the churches began to search for expressions of local worship drawn from the indigenous cultures and to probe the missionary implications of liturgical renewal.

When Vatican II (q.v.) convened, the first order of business was the liturgical constitution, which had already been in the making for a considerable time. *De sacra liturgia* was passed by an overwhelming majority and promulgated by Pope Paul VI (q.v.) in 1963. This document is the most important liturgical document of the 20th century, not only because it reflects more than a century of change, but because it is ecumenical in scope, providing principles of worship and objectives for renewal applicable to all the churches. The most pronounced change in Protestant churches can be seen in the liturgy of the Church of South India, a liturgy that is in keeping with the liturgical movement and widely relevant to the Christians of South India. The Taizé community (q.v.) in France also has had a great impact on Protestant worship through its common liturgical life, music, and widespread ecumenical practice. Other Protestant bodies, notably mainline Lutherans, Presbyterians, Methodists and Disciples of Christ (qq.v.), all issued new liturgical books for congregational worship in the 1970s and 1980s. The influence of the liturgical movement also shows new initiatives among evangelical (q.v.) and charismatic churches.

In Orthodox churches (q.v.) three liturgies are approved and used throughout the year. These are the liturgies of St James (used on the Feast of St James) and the liturgy of St Basil the Great (used on Christmas Eve, Eve of Epiphany, Feast of St Basil, Sundays of Lent and Thursday and Saturday of Holy Week): the liturgy of St John Chrysostom is celebrated at all other times. The Byzantine liturgies have not changed substantially. Some Orthodox liturgists have called for new life to be breathed into the liturgy, not so much through change but through the rediscovery of the original gospel meaning of the liturgy.

In the Roman Catholic Church the reform, embodied in the *Constitution on the Liturgy* of 1963, returns to sacramentality, wherein the liturgy is seen as the action of Christ through the signs of the Word and table mediating to the worshipping people and beyond them to the world, the benefit of Christ's saving death and resurrection. The communal-celebration sharing among worshippers is restored through singing, praying, hearing the Word, passing the peace, and receiving the bread and the wine. The centrality of the Word proclaimed is also reintroduced. The priest now faces the people, and the church year is reorganized around the paschal mystery. Preaching has returned, and because participation is vital, the Mass is now celebrated in the vernacular.

New rites appeared in the Anglican churches (q.v.) in the

New Book of Common Prayer in America (1979), Australia (1978), England (1980), Ireland (1984) and Canada (1984). The *Lutheran Book of Worship* (1978) was published in the USA following a ten-year trial use. While some Western churches follow a relatively fixed order and texts (particularly Roman Catholic, Anglican and Lutheran), other Reformed, Methodist, Baptist and Free churches remain more experimental. An understanding in greater depth of the various liturgical traditions is decisive for future ecumenical progress. *See also* WORSHIP.

LOCAL COUNCILS OF CHURCHES *see* COUNCILS OF CHURCHES, LOCAL, NATIONAL, REGIONAL

LOCAL ECUMENISM. The gap between the ecumenical movement at its numerous conferences and in the places where it has to be lived out day by day is considerable; but it cannot be so large that there is no longer any connection between a world conference and a local church. On the one hand, the insights and challenges of the conferences are dependent on what is alive to a certain extent in the churches and at the parish level. On the other hand, ever since the ecumenical movement started, it has realized that "the universal must be local to be real". At its conferences, therefore, attention was constantly drawn to the importance of the local church for the witness, service, and unity (q.v.) of the church. The life of the local Christian community—in the parish or congregation—is at the heart of the renewal (q.v.) of the church. It is within the congregation that the great majority of Christian worship (q.v.) and witness and sharing and confessing takes place. This centrality of the local is reflected in the very name of the WCC (q.v.) subunit formed after the 1975 assembly to address these concerns: Renewal and Congregational Life. To be sure, an indispensable condition for and consequence of renewal in the congregation is a breakdown of "parochial" attitudes and a deepened recognition of the church of Jesus Christ (q.v.) beyond its own walls. The various statements on unity, which were approved by the assemblies (q.v.) of the WCC since New Delhi (1961), focus on the local church as the basic unit for unity.

New Delhi speaks of a unity that "is being made visible as all in each place who are baptized . . . are brought . . . into one fully committed fellowship . . . and are united with the whole Christian fellowship in all places and all ages". The fourth world conference on Faith and Order (q.v.) (1963) decided to have a whole section on the ecumenical importance of the local congregation, "All in Each Place: the Process of Growing Together". The unit formula of New Delhi was taken up and used in the formulation of the theme. It stated: "We acknowledge that many of God's gifts to his whole church cannot be shared by us in our local churches until we recognize ourselves as the one people of God in each place, and are prepared to embody this fact in new and bold ventures of living faith (q.v.) today". The Nairobi assembly (1975) saw the one church "as a conciliar fellowship of local churches which are themselves truly united", emphasizing that "each local church possesses, in communion with the others, the fullness of catholicity".

The documents of Vatican II (q.v.) also reflected the revitalization of the local church and of the growth of universal networks of communion. *Lumen gentium* revives the insight that episcopal ministry and the celebration of the eucharist (q.v.) determine the very being of the church, rather than specific local characteristics. Similarly *Baptism, Eucharist and Ministry* (q.v.) insists that "eucharistic celebrations always have to do with the whole church, and the whole church is involved in each local eucharistic celebration" (E19). Although the words local church still need a precise ecumenical definition, there is considerable common agreement on the intimate local-universal relationship. *See also* UNITY.

LORD'S PRAYER, THE. Whatever Jesus' intent, the Lord's Prayer has become a part of public worship (q.v.) in almost every branch of the church. The prayer may come early in the service, but also later on, perhaps at the close of the pastoral prayer, if the order calls for that exercise. In the Lima liturgy (q.v.) the Lord's Prayer, the peace, the breaking of the bread and the Agnus Dei immediately precede communion. The emotion was intense when at the inaugural assembly of the World

Council of Churches (q.v.) in Amsterdam in 1948 all participants were invited to pray the Lord's prayer, each in his or her
own language. This had not happened since the Reformation
(q.v.). After some decades it has now become a rather traditional and routine exercise, also during the Week of Prayer for
Christian Unity (q.v.). French-speaking people have a common
and identical Lord's prayer for Catholics, Protestants and
Orthodox (qq.v.). The Lord's prayer has been paraphrased by
Christian communities for times of adversity, oppression and
anguish, as, for example, in Chile and Nicaragua (*see With All
God's People: the New Ecumenical Prayer Cycle*).

LORD'S SUPPER *see* EUCHARIST

LOUVAIN 1971 *see* FAITH AND ORDER

LUBAC, HENRI-MARIE-JOSEPH SONIER DE (1896–). A
champion of the "new theology", particularly among
French theologians, Lubac joined the Jesuits in 1913, and in
1930 was appointed professor of fundamental theology and
of theology of religions at the Catholic faculty in Lyon. In
1960 John XXIII chose him as a consultant to the theological
commission preparing for the Second Vatican Council (q.v.)
and as an expert during the Council. From 1974 onwards he
was a consultant to the Vatican Secretariats of Non-
Christians and of Unbelievers. Insisting on his continuing
dedication to "traditional Catholicism", Lubac pleaded at
the same time for a modern theology that has to come to
terms with the contemporary world. With his fellow Jesuits
Jean Daniélou and Claude Mondesert, he undertook the
direction of *Sources chrétiennes,* an annotated collection of
well over 300 volumes on Christian antiquity, in which he
himself published several volumes. Particularly his *Corpus
mysticum* illustrated how the content of a theological formula changes in the course of time.

LUBICH, CHIARA (1920–). In 1943 Lubich founded and
became president of the Focolare movement, based on an
intensive experience of living the word of God in a great
variety of situations. The movement, now involving some 2

million adherents in over 180 countries, seeks to promote the realization of the prayer of Jesus that "they may all be one" (John 17:21); it was officially approved by the Vatican in 1962. Lubich participated as an auditor in the bishop's synods on the Second Vatican Council (1985) and on the Laity (1987). In 1977 she was awarded the Templeton prize for progress in religion and received as well the medal of St Augustine from Archbishop Runcie and the Byzantine Cross from Patriarch Dimitrios I. In 1981 she spoke to 10,000 Buddhists of the Risho Kosei-kai movement about her Christian experience.

LUND 1952 *see* FAITH AND ORDER

LUTHERAN CHURCHES. The teaching of Martin Luther found early expression in several confessions and formulations, which were brought together in the *Book of Concord* of 1580. In these the Scriptures are affirmed to be the sole rule of faith, to which all the creeds (q.v.) and other traditional statements of belief are subordinated. The principal Lutheran tenet is justification (q.v.) by faith alone. Redemption consists in the justification of human beings by faith in Christ, by reason of which, though in fact they were great sinners before, they are now accounted righteous in the sight of God without any initiative on their part. In the later 16th and early 17th centuries Lutheran doctrines were elaborated in a scholastic mold, which gave them a severely intellectual cast. Against this scholarly "Orthodoxy", the Pietism of the later 17th century strongly reacted.

The worship (q.v.) varies from country to country, but its principle feature is always the sermon set in the framework of the vernacular liturgy (q.v.). Lutheranism has favored a sound elementary and secondary religious education as well as theological and biblical studies. There is only one order of clergy, examined and provided for by the government in certain places. Both clergy and laity are organized in synods. Apart from Germany, where Lutheranism had been accepted by the majority of the population before the end of the 16th century, it also became the official religion in Scandinavian countries. The Evangelical Church in Germany (EKD) embraces Lutherans, Calvinists and "United" and was formally constituted in 1948. The varied backgrounds of the Lutherans who came to the USA, together with the different dates of their arrival, led to a proliferation of Lutheran bodies in that country; gradually, and particularly during this century, there have been mergers among American Lutheran communities.

Most Lutheran churches of the world were loosely affiliated in 1923 in the Lutheran World Convention, which in 1947 developed into the Lutheran World Federation (LWF). In its doctrinal basis the LWF "acknowledges the holy scriptures of the Old and New Testament as the only source and infallible norm of all church doctrine and practice, and sees in the three ecumenical creeds and in the confessions of the Lutheran Church, especially in the Unaltered Augsburg Confession and Luther's Small Catechism, a pure exposition of the word of God".

LWF assemblies have been held in Lund (1947), Hanover (1952), Minneapolis (1957), Helsinki (1963), Evian-les Bains (1970), Dar es Salaam (1977), Budapest (1984) and Curitiba, Brazil (1990). The last assembly adopted a new constitution and authorized a new LWF structure. Headquarters for the LWF secretariat are in the Ecumenical Center, Geneva, with about 100 staff members. Approximately 5,000 persons are employed in LWF world service projects throughout the world. Lutheranism and the LWF program continue to emphasize the theological contributions Lutherans can make to the entire ecumenical movement. This includes official dialogue with Anglicans, Methodist, Orthodox, Reformed and Roman Catholic churches (qq.v.). The Institute for Ecumenical Research in Strasbourg, France, sponsored by the Lutheran Foundation for Interconfessional Research, contributes to the fulfillment by the Lutheran churches of their ecumenical responsibility in the area of theological research. The LWF has today over 100 member churches representing 54 million faithful. There are some 16 million Lutherans not represented in the LWF, particularly the Lutheran Church-Missouri Synod in the USA.

LUTHERAN WORLD FEDERATION *see* LUTHERAN CHURCHES

- M -

MACFARLAND, CHARLES STEDMAN (1866–1956). General secretary of the Federal Council of the Churches of Christ in America (q.v.), 1912–1931, Macfarland was untiring in personal contacts with officials of churches and of countries and in service to the worldwide ecumenical movement. His audacity, tenacity and willingness to take risks went far toward making the Council what it became. He was one of the close collaborators of Nathan Söderblom (q.v.) in preparing for the Stockholm conference in 1925 and was an interpreter of the Life and Work movement (q.v.) to the American churches. During the war he tried to persuade Hitler to compromise on the Jewish question and on the church struggle. For over fifty years Macfarland served the churches in America and Europe as teacher, pastor, creative administrator and author.

McGILVRAY, JAMES C. (1911–1993). From 1968 to 1976 McGilvray served as the first director of the WCC's (q.v.) Christian Medical Commission. He was born and educated in the United Kingdom, and began his career as hospital superintendent for the Christian Medical College in Vellore, India. Later, he worked as a hospital administrator in the United States, and then in the Philippines he organized the first agency for coordination of planning and action of church-related health programs. Returning to the United States, he conducted a world survey of church-related medical programs. McGilvray used its findings to critique existing approaches and help develop the concepts of primary health care propagated at the 1978 meeting of the World Health Organization in Alma Ata, Kazakhstan.

MACKAY, JOHN ALEXANDER (1889–1983). Chairman of commission 5 on "The Universal Church and the World of Nations" of the Oxford conference, 1937, Mackay was a member of the provisional committee of the WCC (q.v.), 1946–1948, chairman of the International Missionary Council (IMC) (q.v.), 1947–1957, a member of the WCC central committee, 1948–1957, chairman of commission 2 on "The

Church's Witness to God's Design'' of Amsterdam 1948, chairman of the Joint Committee of the IMC and WCC, 1948–1954, and president of the World Presbyterian Alliance, 1954–1959. Mackay was secretary for Latin America and Africa, Board of Foreign Missions, Presbyterian Church in the USA, 1932–1936, and then president and professor of ecumenics at Princeton Theological Seminary. See *The Ecumenical Era in Church and Society: A symposium in Honor of John A. Mackay.*

MALINES CONVERSATIONS. These conversations are a historic series of semiofficial discussions between Anglican and Roman Catholic (qq.v.) church leaders. On the basis of the Appeal to All Christian People of the Lambeth conference of 1920, the Anglo-Catholic leader Lord Halifax proposed to Cardinal Mercier (q.v.) of Malines (Mechelen) discussions to explore the possibility of Anglican-Roman Catholic reunion. With the formal approval of the pope and the archbishop of Canterbury, four conversations were held at Malines in 1921–1925. The fourth conversations dealt with the crucial question of papal supremacy both theologically and canonically. Fundamental differences as well as possible hopes of understanding were explored when Mercier's death put an end to the series. A fifth conversation was held in 1927 merely to draw up a report. From 1950 onward unofficial meetings of Anglican and Roman Catholic scholars took place both in England and on the continent. The first visit to Rome by an archbishop of Canterbury was made by Archbishop Geoffrey Fisher (q.v.) to Pope John XXIII in 1960.

MANIKAM, RAJAH BHUSHANAM (1894–1969). As executive secretary of the National Christian Council of India from 1937 onward, Manikam participated in the International Missionary Council's (IMC) (q.v.) assemblies in Tambaram 1938, in Whitby 1947 and in Amsterdam 1948. In 1951 he became the joint-Asian secretary of the committee on the integration of the WCC and the IMC and traveled widely. He played a leading role in the formation of the East Asian Christian Conference and was its secretary from 1951–1956. Manikam advocated the union between the Church of South

India and the Lutheran churches, being the president of its federation in 1954. In this capacity he was also a key figure in the growth of the Lutheran World Federation (q.v.). In 1956 he was appointed bishop of Tranquebar. His whole life was filled with initiatives and plans "to participate more fully in the life of the ecumenical Church". *See* Carl G. Diehl and T. Bachmann, *Rajah Bushanan Manikam: A Biography.*

MARRIAGE, MIXED AND INTERFAITH. The term "mixed marriage" refers to the wedlock of two Christians who belong to different churches, denominations or confessions. The term "interfaith marriage" is used for the marriage of two persons who belong to different religious traditions, such as Christianity and Islam, etc. While in the Bible no clear justification or condemnation of intermarriage, but only a discussion of the duties of the faithful in marriage with partners of other religions, can be found, the church cannot approve any law against racial or ethnic intermarriage, for Christian marriage involves primarily a union of two individuals before God, which goes beyond the jurisdiction of the state or of culture. Interfaith marriages, and particularly mixed marriages, are very common in the contemporary multi-religious and multicultural world and far from being a problem for a religiously mixed minority.

Until the middle of the 20th century the position on confessionally mixed households did not change. Those who contracted a mixed marriage usually had to accept the disapproval of their families and in most cases of their churches. As a result, one of the two partners would renounce his or her membership in the church. The progress made in ecumenism has altered the situation, though not in all circumstances and in all countries. Although the *motu proprio* on mixed marriages by Pope Paul VI (q.v.) has eliminated some of the obstacles that in the past made relations difficult, and left important details to the decision of the episcopal conferences—which interpreted the *motu proprio* as generously as possible in formulating their rules—the WCC (q.v.) central committee in 1972 expressed its concern that in some situations there had been hardly any change. According to the 1983 code of canon law, the Roman

Catholic partner must "do all in his or her power in order that the children be baptized and brought up in the Catholic church".

Nevertheless, ecumenical celebration of marriages are increasingly taking place. A minority of mixed couples who are believers often practice a lively faith together and with their children. Ecumenical celebrations of baptism (q.v.) and common catechesis are indications that the children of mixed couples experience a situation quite similar to that of their parents; they are engaged in dual membership and participation in the life of two churches. It should be added that the majority of mixed couples, at least in Europe and North America, are indifferent to religion, but not more so than couples of the same tradition. There is reason to rejoice that groups of mixed couples are the driving force of ecumenism. They organize the Week of Prayer for Christian Unity (q.v.), help bring two different Christian communities together and launch and support interconfessional social and charitable work, a variety of ecumenical publications, and so on. Common participation in the eucharist (q.v.) remains the most serious difficulty for mixed couples and their children. It is not possible when one of the partners is Orthodox. In some places "eucharistic hospitality" is tolerated rather than accepted.

The fact that Christian marriage is founded on the full recognition of the human personality of the wife, as a partner whose rights are equal to those of the husband, poses the greatest difficulty in interfaith marriages, because the woman is considered a creature of lower rights and religious inferiority in other religions. In interfaith marriages, and especially in polygamous marriage, there is no opportunity for the full development of the personality of the woman or for the exchange in full measure of giving and receiving. Her major vocation is to lift part of the burden of work from her husband and to be the willing object of his sexual desires. The churches have carried on a long and often unsuccessful campaign against bride-price and polygamy. The method most widely used was that of the legalistic application of church discipline; but this has either led to hypocrisy or made it impossible for a polygamist to become a Christian, since the dismissal of his excessive wives would have led to their social ruin.

The question of interfaith marriages has also been an issue in other faith traditions. Within the Jewish community anxiety over mixed marriages has to do primarily with the depletion of the community. Traditionally, Islam has permitted the marriage of a Muslim male to a woman of Jewish or Christian faith. There is no obligation for the female partner from another faith to become a Muslim, but in actual practice social pressures result in most women embracing the Muslim faith. Hindus and Buddhists have been more open to interfaith marriages, but there is considerable resistance to the Christian or Muslim insistence on conversion, the use of the Christian or Muslim religious rites for the marriage ceremony and the insistence of raising the children in the Christian or Muslim tradition. Since the Roman Catholic Church made at Vatican II (qq.v.) a thorough evaluation of the problematic situation in various parts of the world, the baptism and Christian education of children is now required of only the Catholic partner. The Orthodox (q.v.) tradition, which also holds marriage as a sacrament, continues to insist that it is valid only in case the two persons are baptized. Protestantism (q.v.) has also generally rejected interfaith marriages as contrary to the church's theology and practice. Often churches would have nothing to do with mixed-faith marriages, thus forcing the partners to engage in a civil ceremony or a ceremony according to the other faith tradition involved. Since interfaith marriages are increasing steadily in modern societies, there is a great need to examine more fully the pastoral dimension of the issue.

MARXIST-CHRISTIAN DIALOGUE. From 1948 onward, when the WCC (q.v.) was inaugurated in Amsterdam until his death, Josef Lukl Hromádka (q.v.) has been the chief promoter of the Christian-Marxist dialogue and a spokesman of modern socialism with a human face in the ecumenical movement struggling to find the right direction in sociopolitical ethics. As a promoter of the dialogue Hromádka was and still is the irreplaceable person who without sparing himself traveled, spoke, pleaded, wrote and prayed for unceasing conversion and for repeated meeting. Be it in the name of the WCC or his own movement, the Christian Peace Conference (q.v.), he was always there to draw people together and insist on breaking through isolation, suspicion, prejudice and bigotry—all archenemies of the ecumenical movement. During the 1960s a series of gatherings of Marxists and Christians were held in East and West Europe. The international congresses in Salzburg (1965), Herrenchiemsee (1966) and Marianske Lazne (Marienbad, 1967), organized by the Paulus Gesellschaft, became particularly well-known. A variety of issues were on the agenda: atheism (q.v.), transcendence, death, alienation, the individual and the community, Marxist and Christian eschatology (q.v.), the search for the meaning of life, personal and collective standards of morality.

Many Marxists openly admitted that religion is not always the "opium of the people" (Marx), or the "opium for the people" (Lenin), and that the Christian religion, in particular, has sometimes been and can still be a protest against injustice, oppression and exploitation. They conceded that socialism is by no means a magical leap from alienation to a de-alienated society. Since the contradictions of human social life cannot be erased by one act of liberation, communists must constantly criticize dehumanizing tendencies in whatever form they arise and they must seek radical change as a ferment in even advanced socialist societies. For their part, Christians pointed out that Marx and Feuerbach, in stressing that God is an idea of humanity, ignored the fact that God is a necessary idea, deeply rooted in all human beings. They expressed their conviction that human efforts at social improvement can never make the gospel of Jesus Christ (q.v.) superfluous, and that even in the most advanced and ideal communist society there would be new questions that would not find answers from within the system. Only the Christian faith (q.v.) can provide an adequate response to new disillusionments and perplexities. Yet, Christians can cooperate with Marxists without embracing communism as the only true vision for a human future.

After the Warsaw Pact forces invaded Czechoslovakia to suppress the liberal Marxist movement led by Alexander

Dubcek, the Marxist-Christian dialogue declined. Until that year there had been a staggering output of literature in English, French, German, Italian, Spanish and other languages. The main contributors from the Marxist side were R. Garaudy, V. Gardavsky, M. Machovec, E. Bloch, L. Kolakowski and A. Schaff. On the Christian side were such theologians as J. Hromádka, G. Casalis, A. Dumas, H. Gollwitzer (q.v.), J. Smolik (q.v.), G. Girardi, K. Rahner and J. M. Gonzalez-Ruiz. In the USA, H. Cox, C. West, P. Lehmann, T. Ogletree and J. L. Adams took interest in the dialogue.

After the dramatic political changes in Central and Eastern Europe, witnessing to the collapse of the Marxist ideology, it has become clear that both capitalist and socialist ideologies continue to cover up their imprisonment in structures of economic, political and military power, which divide and spoil the potential well-being of the world community. All nations suffer visibly from conceit, hypocrisy and imposture. No single nation eager to advance either justice or freedom, or both, can claim to be out in the forefront of rendering society truly participatory, sustainable and human. The ecological crisis sharpens even more the notion of sin as human pride and revolt against God, the Creator of both human beings and nature. Human superiority to a soulless nature has nourished the desire of humankind to draw the whole world into itself. The undialectical emphasis on the human and its creativity reveals itself as a destructive untruth and causes the loss of the human itself in an aggressive, acquisitive and possessive civilization, even if justice and equality are emphasized. The anthropocentric dimension of both the Judeo-Christian tradition and of Marxism has hindered the correction of the concept of dominion over nature and postponed a thorough reinterpretation of human stewardship in God's precious creation.

Christianity has dismally overlooked that even God-centered religion and morality can become the occasion for a new pride in which believers thank God that they behave more responsibly than unbelievers. After Auschwitz, Hiroshima, Bhopal and Chernobyl, churches can no longer endorse traditional theology's all-wise, all-powerful and an all-merciful God. Similarly, still practicing Marxists are interrogated on their cherished doctrines of dialectical and historical materialism if the systematic rape of nature continues in their technocratic enterprises. Outlining that in a classless society human beings will raise cattle in the morning, fish in the afternoon and discuss human matters in the evening, without ever becoming professional cattle raisers or fisher people, Karl Marx clearly showed himself a child of his prescientific and pretechnological era. Even a desire for collective profit and the establishment of the power of the people today can ignore the "commonwealth" of the world as one single and interdependent reality, ambiguous and fragile in all its dimensions, including both the religious and ideological ones. *See also* IDEOLOGY AND IDEOLOGIES.

MARY, VIRGIN. The role of Mary in the salvation (q.v.) of the world is generally problematic in the ecumenical movement. Ecumenical dialogue, to be fruitful, must not seek to reduce the various faiths to a low common denominator, but rather must lead Christians to deeper theological reflection on their disunity. It is significant that the title "virgin" or "mother" is never attributed to Mary by the gospels in a triumphalist manner. On the contrary, her virginity appears as a unique consecration to the Lord, and her motherhood is presented as an ever-faithful response to the divine call. It is with a focus on these aspects that a theology of Mary can most effectively contribute to ecumenical dialogue. She is for all the churches, including Protestant and Orthodox (qq.v.), a model of the believer.

Yet, in 1950 the doctrine of the bodily assumption of Mary was solemnly promulgated in the Roman Catholic Church (q.v.). For the first time since Vatican I (q.v.) a pope had clearly spoken *ex cathedra.* Quite apart from the fact that a belief had thereby been proclaimed that the vast majority of non-Roman churches did not share and that even in the view of most Roman Catholic theologians could not be established from holy Scripture and certainly not from Scripture alone, it seemed clear from this act that the Roman Catholic Church was unwilling to take account of the fellowship that had come into being as the result of the ecumenical movement. The disappointment this caused was such that in many places initially promising contacts were broken off. Reactions were frank and explicit and many non-Roman Catholics saw their picture of Rome confirmed. The Orthodox churches also joined in the criticisms, indeed, they often expressed themselves much more forcibly. For them mariology remains an integral part of soteriology and Christology (qq.v.). The only dogmatic title they apply to Mary is *theotokos* (mother of God). In spite of all this, many leaders of the ecumenical movement openly expressed the hope that ultimately even fellowship with the Roman Church might become possible. The Nairobi assembly struck a conciliatory note when it stated: ''As the mother of Jesus, Mary embodies particular significance for Christian women and men. Her openness and willingness to respond to the call of God, in ways that were totally unexpected, proclaim to all people their responsibility to be free from any preconceived understandings as to how God works in and through people''.

Mary now appears in new realms of ecumenical discussion, e.g., in liberation theology (q.v.) and feminist theology. Devotion to Mary is often intensively practiced among the world's poor and oppressed. The story of Mary, rejected by the innkeeper, fleeing from violence, quietly raising her son, then witnessing to his suffering and agony, yet sharing in his victory, inspires the imagination and hope of many. Already Martin Luther recognized the Magnificat for its reversal of the world's values. Similarly, feminism finds encouragement in Mary as representative of the powerless and as a unique example of human behavior.

MATTHEWS, ZACHARIAH KEODIRELANG (1901–1968). Matthews made a significant contribution to the ecumenical movement. He participated in the Cottesloe declaration (1960) and was the first area secretary for Africa within the WCC (q.v.) Division of Inter-Church Aid, Refugee and World Service. His report, *Africa Survey,* opened the eyes of the United Nations (q.v.) to the extent and the gravity of the refugee situation on that continent. He was during this period associated with the All Africa Conference of Churches (q.v.), at whose founding in 1963 he was chairperson of the constitutional committee. In 1966 he was appointed ambassador of Botswana to the United Nations and the USA. He developed close associations with future political leaders such as Albert Luthuli and Alphaeus Zulu (q.v.). He joined the African National Congress (ANC) in 1940 and served on the Native Representative Council. He proposed "a national convention of all races . . . to draw up a freedom charter for the democratic South Africa of the future". His draft of the charter was adopted in part by the congress of the people in 1955 and also by the ANC as part of its policy from 1956 onward. For such activity he was charged with high treason, but was acquitted in 1962.

MAURY, PIERRE (1890–1956). Secretary of the World Student Christian Federation (q.v.), 1930–1934, and president of the Reformed Church of France, 1950–1953, Maury was a member of the WCC (q.v.) central committee and of the Commission on Faith and Order. He participated actively in the Oxford conference, 1937, and in the Evanston assembly, 1954, where he pleaded for the cause of the Jewish people. Pastor in Ferney-Voltaire (near Geneva), 1925–1930, he became a close friend of W. A. Visser 't Hoft (q.v.) and a pastor of his family, and professor at the Protestant Faculty of Theology in Paris, 1943–1950. As a member of the ecumenical delegation to the Evangelical Church in Germany, which prepared for the reception of the Stuttgart declaration, 1945, Maury suggested the delegation should say: "We have come to ask you to help us to help you". Influenced by Karl Barth (q.v.), he had great qualities of understanding and conciliation. Together with Marc Boegner (q.v.) he made an impact on the involvement of the Protestant churches in France in the ecumenical movement.

MEAD, MARGARET (1901–1978). Mead was a specialist in education and culture, cultural aspects of nutrition problems, mental health, family life, national character, cultural change and culture building. After having lived for many years with South Seas people and having learned seven indigenous languages, she was a member of the WCC (q.v.) working committee on Church and Society, 1961–1975. At the World Conference on Church and Society in 1966, she chaired the section on "Man and Community in a Changing Society". She also attended the Church and Society conference of the National Council of the Churches of Christ in the USA (q.v.) in Detroit in 1967. During the 1950s and 1960s she returned to the Admiralty Islands to restudy the life of their inhabitants. Mead was president of the American Association for the Advancement of Science, curator emeritus of ethnology at the American Museum of National History in New York, adjunct professor of anthropology at Columbia University and chairman of the social sciences division at Fordham University. Her books were best-sellers and brought anthropology to the attention of the English-speaking world.

MEDICAL MISSIONS see HEALTH, HEALING AND WHOLENESS

MEHL, ROGER ADOLPHE (1912–). Mehl was a member of the WCC (q.v.) central committee, 1968–1975, and of the Faith and Order (q.v.) commission, 1961–1975. He addressed the Geneva conference in 1966. Ordained in the Eglise reformée d'Alsace et de Lorraine in 1947, he occupied the chair of Christian ethics at the Theological Faculty in Strasbourg, 1956–1981, where he founded the Centre de sociologie du protestantisme in 1969. He served on the council of the Fédération protestante de France, 1955–1981, and was president of the commission on ecumenical studies, 1956–1980. As vice president of the Marc Boegner (q.v.) Foundation, he published a biography on the French church leader.

MELBOURNE 1980 see MISSION

MELITON (HACIS) (1913–1989). Meliton studied theology at Halki. In 1938 he became under secretary of the holy synod of the Patriarchate of Constantinople, from 1943 onward in charge in Greek parishes in Manchester and in Liverpool. As metropolitan of Chalcedon he was a member of the WCC (q.v.) central committee, 1961–1968, its vice president,

1968–1975, and a member of the WCC committee on Church and Society. As representative of the Ecumenical Patriarchate at WCC assemblies and the principal collaborator of Athenogoras I (q.v.) and Dimitrios I, he promoted the activities of the WCC, was deeply engaged in the Pan-Orthodox conferences of Rhodes and Chambésy, and helped with the rapprochement between the WCC and the Roman Catholic Church (q.v.).

MENNONITES. The community is the oldest Protestant Free Church. The Mennonites are followers of Menno Simons (1496–1561). At one time parish priest in Dutch Friesland, he renounced his connections with the Roman Catholic Church (q.v.) in 1536 and joined the Anabaptists, then suffering severe persecution after the attempted kingdom of saints in Munster. For twenty-five years he shepherded and reorganized the stricken communities in Holland and neighboring territories. His views put stress on believers' baptism (q.v.), a connectional type of church organization with an emphasis on the responsibilities and the rights of the local congregation, a rejection of Christian participation in the magistracy and nonresistance.

The common ground for the different Mennonite communities later became the rejection of church organization, infant baptism and the doctrine of the real presence in the eucharist (q.v.). Every congregation is independent and the Lord's supper is administered by elders chosen by the community. Both men and women may preach. Most Mennonites refuse military service, the taking of oath and any public office. On the other hand, they recognize no common doctrine so that some of them are practically Unitarian (q.v.) in their views while others hold to the doctrine of the Trinity (q.v.). Originally the movement had a strong sense of mission, which suffered considerably during many decades of persistent persecution, resulting in the withdrawal of the group into isolated areas in various countries. One of the characteristics that Mennonites share with Quakers, the Church of the Brethren (qq.v.), and some other groups, is their peace (q.v.) witness, which led them during the two World Wars to accept alternative service, and to do relief work in war-stricken countries, under the auspices of the Mennonite Central Committee. The general conference of the Mennonite Church united with the Federal Council of the Churches of Christ in America (q.v.) in 1908, but reluctantly withdrew in 1917 because of the positive attitude to war that seemed to characterize so many American Christians at that time.

By the end of 1987 world membership for Mennonite and related churches surpassed 800,000 in sixty countries. Smaller communities live in Holland, Germany, the USSR, Canada and Mexico. The largest community is in the United States. The Dutch and German communities were founding members of the WCC (q.v.) in 1948. American Mennonitism is yet to arrive at an agreement of joining the WCC. The first Mennonite World Conference was held in Basel in 1925. A global assembly—without executive powers and open to anyone who wishes to attend—convenes regularly; Assembly eleven met in Strasbourg (1984), and Assembly twelve in Winnipeg (1990). The organization maintains a permanent secretariat, currently based in Strasbourg. Among the aims of the conference are mission and evangelism, *diakonia* (qq.v.) and worldwide service, Christian and theological education. The first part of Article I of the constitution of the Mennonite World Conference states: "The purpose of the Conference is to bring together in fellowship the Mennonites, Brethren in Christ, and related bodies of the world. By its activities under the leadership of the Holy Spirit, it seeks to deepen faith and hope (qq.v.), to stimulate and aid the church in its ministry to the world, and to promote the kingdom of God in greater obedience to the Lord Jesus Christ (qq.v.)". The general council meets at least once between assemblies and during the assembly sessions.

MERCIER, DÉSIRÉ (1851–1926). Mercier had a decisive influence on the "Malines Conversations" between Anglicans and Roman Catholics (qq.v.). He was professor of philosophy at Malines (1877) and at Louvain (1882), archbishop of Malines (1906) and cardinal (1907). The Malines conversations were a continuation of contacts made between Roman Catholics and Anglicans by Lord Halifax (1839–1934) and

Abbé Portal (1855–1926). It was Mercier's conviction that the mistakes of the past could be corrected only by an unpolemical new beginning. He undoubtedly influenced the meeting of Paul VI with archbishop Michael Ramsey (qq.v.) in 1966 and the creation of the Anglican-Roman Catholic International Commission (ARCIC).

MERTON, THOMAS (1915–1968). Trappist monk, poet and author, Merton was imbued with a strong social sense, which led him simultaneously to espouse basic charity and to test an attraction to monasticism. He became a Catholic in 1938, and in 1941 entered the Trappist abbey of Our Lady of Gethsemane in Kentucky. He greatly emphasized the ecumenical relevance of monastic renewal. He was one of the first, and among the few in his time, to rediscover the primary value of the contemplative life and to ground it in sound scholarship and social concern. As perhaps the most famous monk in the contemporary world, and while investigating the resources of Far Eastern spirituality, he died suddenly in Bangkok, Thailand, apparently of accidental electrocution.

METHODIST CHURCH. Methodism is the form of Christian belief and practice adopted by the followers of John and Charles Wesley who tried to bring a greater spiritual enthusiasm to the life of the Church of England in the 18th century. Their efforts were successful, but proved unacceptable to the Anglican (q.v.) clergy, so that a separate church was ultimately established. From his high church days, John Wesley carried over the optimistic Arminian view that salvation (q.v.) was possible for all human beings, in contrast to the Calvinistic ideas of election and predestination that were accepted by most Nonconformists. He also stressed the important effect of faith (q.v.) on character, and that perfection in love is possible in this life.

The Methodist Church considers itself part of the church universal, believing in the priesthood of all believers and following in organization the principles laid down by Wesley for the pastoral oversight of the societies of Methodists, which had grown up as a result of his preaching. The weekly class meeting for "fellowship in Christian experience" has from the beginning been a valuable institution. By tradition Methodism has an active concern for both evangelism (q.v.) and social welfare, and by means of its centralized organization it is able to make coordinated efforts in this direction. The Methodist faith became as popular in the USA as in Great Britain, but later there were secessions and splinter movements. American Methodism became primarily episcopal without claiming episcopal orders in a Roman Catholic sense. Movements toward reunion began in the late 19th century and gathered momentum in the 20th. Serious discussions began in England in 1955 for reunion with the Anglican Church, but the proposals agreed on by the Methodist Conference were rejected for a second time by the Church of England in 1972. A third attempt in 1982 also failed.

The first World Methodist Conference—then called the Ecumenical Methodist Conference—was held in 1881 in London. Conferences were then held every ten years until the Second World War. At the first meeting after the war in 1947, it was decided in principle to establish a permanent structure, and since 1951, when a new constitution was adopted, the Council has met every five years. The Council is composed of approximately 500 persons elected to serve for a five-year period. From the Council the executive committee is named, with at least one member from each member church. Its permanent secretary has offices in Lake Junaluska, North Carolina, and a Geneva secretary works out of the Ecumenical Center there. While the paid staff is small, several hundred volunteers do effective work as members of the executive and of fifteen other committees and related organizations.

Among the purposes and activities of the Council, the following may be specially mentioned:

—It has regular program committees on evangelism; ecumenical conversations; social and international affairs; worship and liturgy; theological education; youth; family life; publishing and communication; and exchange of ministers.

—Two important affiliated organizations—the World Federation of Methodist Women and the World Methodist Historical Society—function as supporting bodies of the Council.

—The Oxford Institute of Methodist Theological Studies meets every four years, bringing theologians from around the world to deal with specific theological themes.

—The Council is engaged in bilateral dialogues with the Roman Catholic Church (q.v.) and, since early in the last quinquennium, with the Lutheran World Federation (q.v.). Steps have been taken to seek bilateral conversations with the Orthodox (q.v.).

There are over sixty-five member churches, active in ninety countries around the globe. They have some 20 million communicant members and a total membership of some 50 million people. Today thirty-one national Methodist churches are WCC (q.v.) members. Of the five WCC general secretaries, two have been Methodists—Philip Potter and Emilio Castro (qq.v.).

MEXICO CITY 1963 see MISSION

MEYENDORFF, JOHN (1926–1992). Chairman of the Commission on Faith and Order, 1967–1976, and member of the WCC (qq.v.) central committee, 1975–1983, Meyendorff was ordained priest in Paris, 1959. From 1951 to 1959 he was assistant professor of church history, Orthodox Theological Institute in Paris. In 1959 he became professor of church history and patristics, St Valdimir's Orthodox Theological Seminary, New York, and in 1984 dean of the seminary. He was chairman of the Department of External Affairs, Orthodox Church in America, and adviser to the holy synod as well as editor of the monthly *The Orthodox Church* and *St Vladimir's Theological Quarterly.*

MICHELFELDER, SYLVESTER CLARENCE (1889–1951). Michelfelder was representative of the National Lutheran Council to the reconstruction department of the WCC (q.v.) in Geneva. There he founded the material aid division for postwar reconstruction. In 1945 he was appointed executive secretary of the Lutheran World Convention, which he helped to reorganize as the Lutheran World Federation (q.v.) in 1947. He then served this body as its executive secretary, 1947–1951. Prior to that Michelfelder was superintendent of the Pittsburgh Inner Mission Society, 1926–1931, minister of Trinity Lutheran Church, Willard, Ohio, 1913–1926, and of St. Paul's Lutheran Church, Toledo, Ohio, 1931–1945.

MICKLEM, NATHANIEL (1888–1976). Micklem was professor of Old Testament at the Selly Oak Colleges, Birmingham, 1921–1927, professor of New Testament at Queen's Theological College, Kingston, Ontario, 1927–1931, and principal and professor of dogmatic theology, Mansfield College, 1932–1953. He was also president of the Liberal Party, 1957–1958. Greatly responsible for creating a new attitude among Congregationalists (q.v.) toward their theology, church policy and public worship, he combined a loyalty and responsibility for his own denomination with a Catholic vision of the unity (q.v.) and the mission of the church in all places and through all ages. He insisted on the reform of the whole church and the renewal of all humanity.

MIDDLE AXIOMS. Much thought was given to the principles of Christian action in society at the Oxford conference in 1937; the result was the establishment of the so-called "middle axioms". The term was coined by J. H. Oldham (q.v.). These are less comprehensive than is the command of love in its fullest realization, yet they too are an expression of love, and appeal at the same time in the "intuition of the individual conscience". The report on "Church, Community and State" outlined: "Such, 'middle axioms' are intermediate between the ultimate basis of Christian action in community, 'thou shalt love they neighbor as thyself', and the unguided intuition of the individual conscience. They are at best provisional and they are never unchallengeable or valid without exception for all time; for it is in a changing world that God's will has to be fulfilled. Yet as interim principles they are indispensable for any kind of common policy".

Love as the criterion of Christian action must be translated in practice into justice (q.v.) even where it cannot be realized in its full dimensions. Justice, in the sense of the ideal of a harmonious relationship between human beings, must be helped to assert itself in all social settlements and arrangements, in economic planning and political systems. It ought to provide the individual with his or her appropriate place in society in the face of favoritism and exploitation, discrimination and victimization. However, it ought also to draw attention to the responsibility of the individual toward others and demand sacrifices of him or her in so far as they may be required for the sake of the "harmony" of society as a whole. In order to attain these objectives, justice needs discipline to prevent human beings from asserting their own destructive inclinations. Disciplinary measures are "dykes against sin". They may themselves become the source of new evils and must therefore be under constant control. They are the lowest rung in the ladder of social order into which philanthropy must be translated. They are the framework within which love in the widest sense may be applied to the creation of social relationships and institutions.

The concept of middle axioms has influenced a considerable number of studies in social ethics in the ecumenical movement. They found a more definite formulation in the context of the concept of the "responsible society" (q.v.), developed during and after Amsterdam 1948. *See also* SOCIAL ETHICS.

MIDDLE EAST COUNCIL OF CHURCHES (MECC). Linking Asia and Africa lies the region of the Middle East. It is the cradle of Judaism, Christianity and Islam. Among the characteristics of this immensely diverse region, from Morocco to Iran and from Turkey to central Sudan, are the dominance of Islam, the Arab-Israeli tension, political instability, oil and poverty. Christians form a small minority; among them are various ancient Eastern churches, Roman Catholics and numerous Protestant (qq.v.) bodies. Political divisions and the unresolved refugee problem have created an atmosphere of mistrust in which cooperation and common worship, study and action are not easy.

In 1948 the Near East Christian Council for Missionary Cooperation was created. It later became the Near East Christian Council, then the Near East Council of Churches, and more recently the Middle East Council of Churches. The Council has over 25 members. It has maintained its head office in West Beirut, Lebanon, throughout the long period of civil war. This has symbolized the determination of the MECC to be a bridge between communities and to emphasize the solidarity of the churches of the region with the people as a whole, irrespective of religion. Liaison offices that facilitate the working together of the churches on the local and national levels are established in Cyprus, Egypt, Syria and Bahrain.

The main concerns of the Middle East Council of Churches are: 1) continuity of Christian presence through the difficult, challenging and radically changing situation in the region; 2) church renewal—or deepening the spiritual quality of the Christian communities and helping them to transcend their sociocultural identities; 3) Christian unity beyond ethnic, cultural and structural differences as the churches are called to witness together as one body of Jesus Christ (q.v.); 4) witness through various ways including proclamation, life style, *diakonia* (q.v.), justice (q.v.) and service.

MIGRANTS *see* REFUGEES/MIGRANTS

MIGUEZ-BONINO, JOSÉ (1924–). Observer at Vatican II (q.v.) for the United Methodist Church, Miguez-Bonino has been a member of the Commission on Faith and Order, and the WCC (qq.v.) central committee. From 1975 to 1983 he was a president of the WCC. Professor of systematic theology and ethics at the Faculdad Evangélica de Teología, Argentina, 1954–1969 (president, 1960–1969), he then was professor and dean of graduate studies at the Instituto Superior Evangélico de Estudios Teológicos (ISEDET), 1969–1985. Miguez-Bonino was a founding member and president of the Permanent Commission for Human Rights, Argentina, and has been visiting professor at several seminaries and theological faculties in the USA, England, France and Italy. He is an expert in ecumenical ethics and Marxist philosophy.

MILITARISM. A consultation on militarism organized by the WCC's Commission of the Churches on International Affairs in Glion, Switzerland, in 1977 stated: "Militarization should be understood as the process whereby military values, ideology and patterns of behavior achieve a dominating influence on the political, social and economic affairs of the state and as a consequence the structural, ideological and behavioral patterns of both the society and government are militarized''. To which a conference on disarmament, organized by the same commission at the same place in 1978, added: ''Today's arms race is an unparalleled waste of human and material resources; it threatens to turn the whole world into an armed camp; it aids repression and violates human rights; it promotes violence and insecurity in place of the security in whose name it is undertaken; it frustrates humanity's aspirations for justice and peace; it has no part in God's design for His world; it is demonic''.

Evidence of rampant global militarism is provided by statistics dating from the 1980s. Some 36 million men were under arms with another 25 million in reserves and 30 million civilians in military-related occupations. Fully one half of the world's engineers and scientists working at research and development focused all their attention on military inventions and production. The world spent US $1 million per minute on military forces and weapons; that translates into about $400 billion per year. World military spending was double that of the gross national product of the continent of Africa and equal to that of Latin America. In the industrialized world much greater attention was paid to the development of still more destructive arsenals than to the reduction of the economic disparities that persist between developed and developing nations. Three quarters of the international arms trade involved Third World recipients. Developing nations, despite severe food shortages, used five times as much foreign exchange for the imports of arms as for agricultural machinery. In developing countries there was one soldier for every 250 inhabitants, while there was one doctor for every 3,700. Since 1945 there have been more than 130 wars involving more than 70 countries of the Third World. More than 20 million people have been killed in these wars.

The Christian churches have a prophetic task to denounce both the structure of injustice which promotes and sustains militarism in the world, and those who misuse the power they have acquired to maintain those structures. They must be bold enough to imagine new forms of struggle against the evils of militarism, and new alternatives to replace the perverse options for "national security" and peace offered by a militaristic system. They can envision a future in which national security is seen in terms, not of the maintenance of the privileges of the few, but in equal distribution of wealth and power in society. In his address to the United Nations (q.v.) Special Session on Disarmament, the fourth WCC general secretary, Philip A. Potter (qq.v.), spoke in this way of world militarism: "In face of the catalogue of accelerated insecurity, the churches cannot remain spectators and inactive. On the basis of their faith in a God who in Jesus Christ wills that we should have life and have it in all its fullness, and in his purpose that the earth should be replenished and used for the well-being of all, Christians are called to bring new perspectives to bear on the issues of militarism and the arms race". *See also* PEACE AND DISARMAMENT.

MINEAR, PAUL SEVIER (1906–). Minear was moderator of the Commission on Faith and Order (q.v.), 1963–1967. He taught as a biblical scholar at the Hawaii School of Religion, 1933–1934, and was professor of New Testament at Andover Newton Theological School, 1944–1956, and at Yale University Divinity School, 1956–1971, during which time he was also professor of biblical theology. Among several works, his *Images of the Church in the New Testament* (1960) made a significant ecumenical impact.

MINISTRY. In order to fulfill its mission, the church needs persons who are publicly and continually responsible for pointing to its fundamental dependence on Jesus Christ (q.v.), and thereby provide, within a multiplicity of gifts, a focus of its unity (q.v.). The ministry of such persons, who since early times have been ordained, is constitutive for the life and witness of the church. All members of the believing community, ordained or lay, are interrelated. But the community needs ordained ministers. Their presence reminds the community of the divine initiative, and of the dependence of the church on Jesus Christ, who is the source of its mission and the foundation of its unity. He is the unique priest of the new covenant, as his life was given as a sacrifice for all.

Derivatively, the church as a whole can be described as a priesthood. All members are called to offer their being "as a living sacrifice" and to intercede for the church and the salvation (q.v.) of the world. The chief responsibility of the ordained ministry is to assemble and build up the body of Christ by proclaiming and teaching the Word of God, by celebrating the sacraments (q.v.), and by guiding the life of the community in its worship, its mission (q.v.) and its caring ministry. The ordained ministry, however, has no existence apart from the community. Ordained ministers can fulfill their calling only in and for the community. They cannot dispense with the recognition, the support and the encouragement of the community.

The threefold ministerial pattern of bishops, presbyters and deacons has been and remains a central theme in the ecumenical discussion on the nature of the church and its ministry. Although the content of the threefold ministry has varied considerably, *Baptism, Eucharist and Ministry* (q.v.) affirms that this pattern is an instrument of continuity and order, making modest claims that this ministry "may serve today as an expression of the unity we seek and also as a means for achieving it" (M22). Yet the threefold ministry offers little guidance as to how such ministries can be affirmed as genuinely apostolic. There are, moreover, other full-time ministries that have traditionally fallen outside the threefold pattern, such as teachers, evangelists, persons of prayer, etc. Another complicating factor is that ministries can be regarded as utilitarian or organic. Although persuasive, it may be doubted that the utilitarian point of view can be found in the New Testament, where matters of external polity and organization are not simply treated as questions of expediency, and further it has to justify itself against the historical fact that it was hardly thought of before the Reformation (q.v.). Generally speaking, the organic view of ministry regards it as an organ of the body that, because essential to the functioning of the body, cannot operate apart from it. Roman Catholicism (q.v.) has taken another step by separating the ministry from the church in the sense that it regards the former as primary and standing over against the latter. Hence possession of so-called valid orders, in the Roman sense of orders within the apostolic succession (q.v.) sacramentally interpreted and conveying an indelible character, is regarded as guaranteeing whether or not a particular group of Christians is within the Catholic church. The consequence of this kind of ecclesiology (q.v.) was that the idea of the church as the people of God (q.v.) was compromised and the nonordained became known as the laity (q.v.) and as inferior members of the body. This idea of the ministry being a dominant exercise of authority has been challenged in the ecumenical movement as the notion of the ministry of the laity has been gradually rediscovered. But the church is constantly threatened by a seemingly uncontrollable process of clericalization.

Ministry has been a central issue in some eight bilateral dialogues (q.v.). Texts relevant to the problem of ministry can be consulted in *Growth in Agreement: Reports and Agreed Statements of Ecumenical Conversations on a World Level* (1984). They concern the following dialogues: Anglican-Lutheran, Anglican-Orthodox, Anglican-Roman Catholic, Baptist-Reformed, Lutheran-Roman Catholic, Methodist-Roman Catholic, Old Catholic-Orthodox and Reformed-Roman Catholic (qq.v.). In these dialogues questions have been raised about the following issues: 1) What is the distinction between the ministry of the ordained and other ministries of the church? Is ordained ministry a gift to the community, or the community's own choice of leadership? 2) What is the relation between episcopacy (q.v.) and other ordained ministries? Is the distinction between the episcopate and the presbyterate mainly one of jurisdiction among those holding the same order, or is the episcopal order a distinctive and essential one? 3) Is apostolic succession the exclusive possession of those who receive it in a tangible chain of ordinations claiming to have been practiced from the earliest times? Or does this notion embrace a wider tradition of the church's life through the centuries? 4) What is the status of the ordination of women (q.v.)? This issue has surfaced only more recently and causes much disagreement among Orthodox, Roman Catholic and Protestant churches. 5) What is the relation between traditional ministries and several new, contextually responsive ministries and forms of ministerial practice; this problem arises, for example, in the context of Latin American church-based communities (q.v.). Because of a general shortage of priests, can unordained persons who often are leaders of these communities preside at the eucharist? There is at least one general agreement that New Testament patterns and practices do not settle the issues of today. *See also* ORDINATION; ORDINATION OF WOMEN; UNITY.

MISSIO DEI. The concept *missio Dei* (mission of God) has been used in Roman Catholic theology to describe those activities within the divine Trinity (q.v.) itself by which the way of mission (q.v.) is prepared. The Father sends the Son; the Father and the Son send the Holy Spirit for the salvation (qq.v.) of humankind. The concept appeared in the development of a theological basis for the missionary enterprise, especially in Anglican-Protestant circles within the International Missionary Council (q.v.) in the 1950s. The phrase was adopted by the missionary conference held in Willingen in 1952 in order to bring the missionary activity of the church into the closest relationship to the missionary activity of God himself. The church cannot really be the church of God unless it takes its share in the mission of God's Son. J. C. Hoekendijk (q.v.) has criticized the church-centered orientation of the missionary enterprise becoming too easily narrow in scope through ''defining the whole surrounding world in ecclesiological categories . . . The world has almost ceased to be the world and is now conceived as a sort of ecclesiastical training-ground''. On the other hand, Roman Catholics and Orthodox (qq.v.) cherished the concept of *missio Dei* because they judged the Trinitariam approach to mission as the only valid alternative to excessive Christocentrism in Protestant missionary thinking and piety. The church must always remain the self-revelation of the Triune God in Jesus Christ.

MISSION AND EVANGELISM. The opinion that missions were simply the spiritual and cultural aspect of western colonialism has often been expressed. Careful historical study, however, shows that the facts are far more complex than this simple statement allows. Nevertheless, it is true that by and large the colonial systems of the Western powers provided the political and cultural framework within which missions operated in most parts of what is now called the Third World during the century and a half prior to 1947. That year, in which the Indian subcontinent became independent of British rule, may be taken as the starting point of the process of decolonization, which has been completed within less than 20 years. A change so profound and rapid, which removed within two decades the framework within which missions had been operating for two centuries, could not fail to shake profoundly the whole missionary movement, even though discerning missionary leaders had for many years been advocating and preparing for the liberation of dependent peoples, and even though the work of missions was itself one of the most powerful forces preparing for that liberation.

Mission and evangelism have been a primary concern of the 20th-century ecumenical movement. This movement is generally reckoned to have begun at the world missionary conference in Edinburgh in 1910. Two of the principal architects of this conference were John R. Mott and Joseph H. Oldham (qq.v.). John R. Mott remains chiefly known for his zealous propaganda on behalf of missions, based upon his watchword "the evangelization of the world in our generation". The Edinburgh conference led to the establishment of the International Missionary Council (IMC) (q.v.) in 1921, with the aim "to help coordinate the activities of the national missionary organizations of the different countries and to unite Christian forces of the world in seeking justice in international and inter-racial relations". To achieve this goal a whole series of world missionary conferences followed. From 1939 onward the IMC worked closely with the WCC (while the latter was "in process of formation"). Then in 1961, after the third WCC assembly (qq.v.) in New Delhi, the IMC became the Division of World Mission and Evangelism. It had taken several decades to realize that the unity (q.v.) of the church and the mission of the church are but two sides of the same coin. From 1954 to 1961 the Department on Evangelism and the Department of Missionary Studies in the WCC Division of Studies supplemented the work of the IMC Research Department. In 1967 the Department on Evangelism and the Department of Missionary Studies were integrated into the Department on Studies in Mission and Evangelism.

The Jerusalem 1928 conference of the International Missionary Council marked noteworthy advances beyond Edinburgh 1910. The preparation was carefully developed through seven volumes of comprehensive studies. The growing worldwide threat of secularism to Christianity was given major attention. Missions were thus seeking to touch life from more angles than in earlier years. The larger place of the younger churches at Jerusalem was partly due to their rapid growth in numbers and leadership. To follow up the concerns of the problems of industrialization, the meeting authorized what came to be known as the Department of Social and Economic Research and Counsel. Larger in numbers and more representative than Jerusalem, Tambaram 1938 dramatized the fact that the church had become a truly worldwide company. The representatives of the younger churches constituted slightly more than half of the official delegates. The younger churches, while mostly minorities in their countries, were now strong enough to assume more of the burden not only of their own support and direction but also the evangelization of their nations. The first section was considerably reinforced by a preliminary book *The Christian Message in a Non-Christian World,* written at the request of the IMC by Hendrik Kraemer (q.v.).

The theme of Whitby 1947 (Canada) was "Christian Witness in a Revolutionary World". Even during the terrible period of the Second World War, the IMC had been able to maintain to a remarkable degree the fabric of cooperation, especially through the vast program of support for "orphaned missions". The title of the report of the meeting, *Renewal and Advance,* well indicated the dominant mood of the conference. It had not yet become clear, however, how drastic the changes were that the world had undergone as a result of the convulsions of the war years. The complete extinction of the colonial pattern, most dramatically in China, but also the rest of Asia and Africa, was still in the future. The extent of the spiritual damage that Christianity had suffered could not yet be assessed. Nevertheless, "expectant evangelism'' and ''partnership in obedience'' were the two slogans of the gathering. The meeting in Willingen 1952 (Germany) was widely judged to have failed in its major task. But subsequent history has shown how significant it really was. Two issues dominated the section that was preparing a statement on the missionary obligation of the church. On the one hand, a sharp attack was launched, primarily by J. C. Hoekendijk (q.v.) of the Netherlands, against the church-centered view of missions that had dominated the thinking of the IMC since Tambaram. On the other hand, and closely related to the first, a strong effort was made, especially by the North American study group that had prepared for the conference, to relate the missionary task to the signs of Christ's present sovereignty in the secular world. While the Willingen meeting could not achieve an acceptable reconciliation of the theological tensions, its work proved fruitful in subsequent years.

An important item on the Accra 1958 conference agenda was the draft plan of integration of the IMC and the WCC that the joint committee of the two bodies had prepared. There were serious reservations about this plan, and a great deal of further discussion was needed. The conference accepted a statement on ''Christian Mission at this Hour'' which took as its starting point ''the Christian world mission is Christ's, not ours''. The statement affirmed that the distinction between older and younger churches was no longer valid or helpful because it obscured the fact that every church, because it is a church, has the same missionary calling. Preparations were made to set up a Theological Education Fund (q.v.), which over the years was to bring about a considerable change in quality and strength of theological education at various seminaries and schools in the world. The meeting in Mexico City 1963 was the first one of the Division of World Mission and Evangelism of the WCC, since the integration of the IMC into the WCC in 1961. With its main theme ''Witness in Six Continents'', it broke new ground by paying attention to the specific problems of mission in Europe and North America. Section 4 advocated advance in the direction of more international and ecumenical action in the field of mission. Throughout the meeting there was a vigorous debate about mission in the context of six continents. The Department on Studies in Evangelism, following the New Delhi assembly (1961), had launched a worldwide study on "The Missionary Structure of the Congregation" (q.v.); it raised radical questions concerning the nature of the church and evangelism. The aim of mission is not primarily the qualitative growth of the church but *shalom* for the world. "Realization of the full potentialities of all creation and its ultimate reconciliation in Christ" is the goal of *missio Dei* (q.v.).

The Bangkok 1973 conference faced the theological theme of liberation, affirmed the right of every Christian and church to cultural identity, and urged them to formulate their own response to God's calling in a theology, a liturgy (q.v.), a praxis, and a form of community that were rooted in their own culture. The Africans, especially, attacked the West's imperialism over theology. The meeting drew attention to the indissoluble connection between the individual and social aspects of salvation (q.v.): to respond to Christ and his missionary call means to be involved in the struggle for social justice, peace (q.v.), and fully human life. The conference debated at length the question of missionary relationships that would reflect genuine equality between partners. Proposals ranged from a temporary moratorium to new forms of cooperation between the churches. Bangkok 1973 was undoubtedly one of the most contextual and interdisciplinary ecumenical missionary conferences. The Orthodox churches (q.v.) were involved both in the preparation and holding of the Melbourne 1980 conference, and many Roman Catholic (q.v.) theologians, as at the Bangkok conference, participated in the meeting. The main findings were, first, that the kingdom that Christians pray for is the reign of the one who died outside the gates. Jesus Christ (q.v.) affirmed his centrality by giving it up. He moved toward the periphery in order to seek the marginalized and the downtrodden. Second, the poor challenge missionary criteria. Jesus established a visible link between the coming of the kingdom and the proclamation of the good news to the poor. Third, evangelism takes place in the midst of human struggles. There is no evangelism without involvement, and no Christian involvement without evangelism. Fourth, at the center of church life is the eucharist (q.v.), pilgrim bread and missionary food, for the people on the march. The eucharist is a powerful example of self-emptying.

Under the theme "Your Will Be Done: Mission in Christ's Way", San Antonio 1989 (Texas, USA) was marked by a great diversity of participants, including, for the first time, consultants of other faiths. It was planned not to feature authoritative ecumenists instructing the delegates, but to create a context in which persons active in mission could address one another. Its two significant trends, said the conference message, were "the spirit of universality (Catholicity) of the gathering, and its concern for the fullness of the gospel", holding "in creative tension spiritual and material needs, prayer (q.v.) and action, evangelism and social responsibility, dialogue and witness, power and vulnerability, local and universal". Especially extensive were discussions of the tension between dialogue (q.v.) and witness that, a section report said, "we appreciate . . . and do not attempt to resolve".

Slowly but increasingly it has been realized in the ecumenical movement that mission and dialogue are intimately related in structure, method and content. After a long history of separate developments the time has come for the combination of the WCC Sub-unit on World Mission and Evangelism and its Sub-unit on Dialogue into one Sub-unit on Mission and Dialogue. True dialogue is never opposed to witness. Lynn de Silva of Sri Lanka underlined this fact when he wrote: "Fears have been expressed that dialogue blunts proclamation. (But) how can we proclaim the love of God if we do not love our neighbors? If we are not prepared to listen to what people of other faiths have to say, how can we expect them to listen to what we have to say to them?" It is only in person-to-person dialogue that mission and evangelism have any meaning. The integrity of response to the witness of the risen Lord depends solely on the unlimited power of the Holy Spirit and never on the correctness of the biblical testimony by influential individuals or impressive Christian establishments only blocking profound person-to-person encounters beyond the church space.

MISSION BOARDS AND SOCIETIES. All churches are to some extent missionary, but for the most part their missionary activity is exercised in their own immediate neighborhood. The planning of missionary work on a larger scale and at a greater distance has been a later development, coming at a time at which the churches have developed a considerable measure of stability and self-consciousness. The Protestant world mission has been distinguished by a strong sense of unity from the beginning, and union societies were early evidence of it. They were generally inspired by the example of the London Missionary Society, founded in 1795 for united action by evangelicals in Independent, Presbyterian and Anglican churches (qq.v.). In the USA the New York Missionary Society was established the next year, 1796, by pastors and laypeople of the Reformed Dutch, Presbyterian (q.v.) and other churches. Other missionary societies included the Church Missionary Society (1795), Dutch Mission (1799), American Board of Commissioners for Foreign Missions (1810) and Edinburgh Medical Missionary Society (1814). The example of the London Missionary Society had a profound effect on the continent of Europe. Although a denominational Reformed organ, the Netherlands Missionary Society, was founded in 1797 to cooperate with the London Missionary Society, early societies were mostly joint Lutheran and Reformed (qq.v.) organizations. These union societies included the Basel Evangelical Missionary Society (1815), the Berlin Missionary Society (1824), the Renish Missionary Society of Barmen (1828) and the North German Missionary Society of Bremen (1836).

Overseas mission work by European Roman Catholics (q.v.), almost exclusively undertaken by religious communities, collapsed by the 1800s. Beginning in the mid-1810s, the scene began to change, and the revival of missionary activity eventually became a priority church concern. The old communities reorganized themselves, such as the Jesuits, Franciscans, Dominicans, Benedictines, Capuchins, Holy Spirit Fathers and Lazarists. Unlike the Protestant societies, the Roman Catholic ones were composed of clergy, religious brothers and sisters, assisted by a rather small percent of laypeople, married or unmarried. And unlike most Protestant societies, the Roman Catholic bodies were dependent on church control. Protestant policies of comity did not involve Roman Catholics. Since the mid-1960s, the Roman Catholic Church has experienced a process of drastic reduction of male and female vocations to religious communities in Western Europe and North America, but in Asia, Africa and Latin America a steady increase of new members in older religious communities and new indigenous ones took place. Due to ecumenical understandings close cooperation has developed on the world level, for example, between SEDOS (Servizio de Documentazione e Studi) in Rome and the WCC's Commission on World Mission and Evangelism.

In the Orthodox church (q.v.) organized missionary activity was confined almost exclusively to Russian initiatives. Missionary unions that supported the work of missionaries were, for example, the Society for the Restoration of Orthodox Christianity in the Caucasus (1860) and the Missionary Society for the Promotion of Christianity among the Heathen (1865), which was later absorbed into the Orthodox Missionary Society, founded in 1870. The world federation of Orthodox youth, Syndesmos, created in 1953, places foreign mission work high on its agenda. The present situation in a unified world has compelled missionary science to take up the problem of missionary activity on ''all six continents''.

MISSIONARY STRUCTURE OF THE CONGREGATION. The title of a study program carried out by the WCC (q.v.) Department on Studies in Evangelism between the New Delhi assembly (1961) and the Uppsala assembly (1968). After more than a decade of debate on evangelism it was noted that the average congregation poses a serious problem for the accomplishment of contemporary evangelistic tasks, and that the renewal (q.v.) of the church is intimately related to not only spiritual regeneration but also to organizational changes. The study involved a wide range of theological considerations. Of particular importance was the need to clarify the relationship between ''church'' and ''gospel'' and the meaning of the ''kingdom of God'' (q.v.). The study was carried out in several parts of the world by regional working groups, such as Europe, North America, South America, Asia, Africa, Oceania and Australia.

The findings of the study were presented as follows: a) Not only in its missionary activities but also in its entire life the church participates in the mission of God, and therefore mission (q.v.) is an obligation for every congregation; b) The churches' structures must be as flexible as is demanded by the ways and actions of God's mission; c) As history shows, all organizational structures of the Christian communities are temporary. Missionary congregations exist in their very essence in different forms in order to meet different situations. Churches must be ready to recognize officially new congregational structures; d) Especially in areas of industrialization and urbanization, churches find themselves living in new localities. Social changes have widely enlarged the traditional parish and the field of mission.

The Uppsala assembly (1968) discussed the direction and emphasis that had been taken by the study on the missionary structure of the congregation and proposed a further stage of the study under the title: "Missionary Participation in Human Institutions". That study drew less enthusiasm than the previous one.

MOELLER, CHARLES (1912–1986). Moeller was the first secretary of the Vatican Secretariat for Promoting Christian Unity (q.v.). He studied theology and philosophy at Malines and Louvain, was appointed professor of poetry at the Institute Saint-Pierre in Jette, 1941–1954, and later became professor at the University in Louvain in 1956. An outstanding scholar and humanist who was widely versed in ecumenism, he was one of the leading experts on the theological commission of the Second Vatican Council (q.v.), 1962–1965, and under secretary of the Congregation on the Doctrine of the Faith, 1966–1973. Moeller served as rector of the Institute for Advanced Ecumenical Studies at Tantur (q.v.) (near Jerusalem) from 1969–1973. He was a member of the Royal Academy for French Language in Belgium. He wrote numerous articles and several books, particularly on 20th-century literature.

MOLTMANN, JÜRGEN (1926–). Moltmann served as pastor in a Reformed congregation in Bremen, 1953–1958, and then became professor of systematic theology at the Wuppertal Kirchliche Hochschule, 1958–1963, at Bonn University, 1963–1967, and since 1967 at the University of Tübingen. He has also been professor at Duke University, Durham, North Carolina, and at Emory University, Atlanta. He was a member of the Faith and Order Commission, 1963–1983, and a member of the Klingenthal conferences on the filioque (q.v.) clause. Author of numerous books, many of which were translated into English, he was also editor of *Evangelische Theologie* and chairperson of the Gesellschaft für Evangelische Theologie.

MONOD, WILFRED (1867–1943). Pastor of the Reformed Church in France and from 1909 onward professor of practical theology in the Protestant faculty of the University of Paris, Monod in 1912 became president of the Union des Eglises reformées de France. He was one of the leading personalities in the Life and Work movement (q.v.) and its continuation committee, and in the World Alliance for Promoting International Friendship through the Churches (q.v.). He expressed his conviction that the forthcoming world conference on Faith and Order in Lausanne, in 1927, would be successful to the extent it proclaimed the "non-possumus" opposed by all prophetic religion to all clerical and sacramental religion. Monod never wavered in his commitment to the ideal of true ecumenicity. He called upon the worldwide church to give a soul to the League of Nations, and was among those who desired in 1937 the closest possible coordination between the Faith and Order (q.v.) and Life and Work movements.

MONTREAL 1963 *see* FAITH AND ORDER

MORAVIANS. These Christians belong to a community, called the Unity of the Church, also known as *Unitas Fratrum,* or Moravian Church. It traces its origins as a distinct branch of the church in Bohemia to 1457. It developed out of the national renewal of religion in Czechoslovakia, of which John Hus

(1373–1415) was a prominent figure. In the 1720s a few families from Moravia, Bohemia, Silesia and Poland, who had kept the traditions of the *Unitas Fratrum*, emigrated to Saxony where Nicolaus Ludwig von Zinzendorf (1700–1760) was offering them religious freedom. They built a village, which they named Herrnhut. Under Zinzendorf, who quickly became their leader, the community became a renewed church. Within the next decade the church established relations with evangelical Christians in Western Europe and America.

The *Unitas Fratrum* is strongly missionary oriented and basically Presbyterian in polity. It has retained from its earliest days the threefold order of ministry: bishop, presbyter and deacon. Among the traditions handed down by Zinzendorf is the personal devotional book *Daily Texts*, published annually and now available in 34 languages. The total membership of the Moravian Church (1984) is almost half a million. It is a charter member of the WCC (q.v.).

MOTT, JOHN R. (1865–1955). Mott was a unique promotor of the modern ecumenical movement. "The evangelization of the world in our generation" was for him more than just a watchword. As an American Methodist layman he met Nathan Söderblom and Wilfred Monod (qq.v.) in 1890 and left the USA for the first time in 1891 to attend a conference of the World's Young Men's Christian Associations in Amsterdam. His influence on the founding of the World Student Christian Federation (q.v.) was decisive; he served it, as general secretary from 1895 and as chairman from 1920, for 33 years. When the International Missionary Council (q.v.) was created at Lake Mohonk, New York, in 1921, Mott became its moderator and he was associated with the Council for the rest of his life. Both at Oxford and Edinburgh 1937 he was among those who spoke forcefully in favor of the proposal to establish a world council of churches. He was a member of the committee charged with the planning of the structure of the emergent WCC (q.v.). He preached, then in his eighty-third year, at the opening service of the inaugural assembly of the WCC in Amsterdam in 1948, and became the honorary president of the Council. He was awarded the Nobel peace prize in 1946.

MUELDER, WALTER G. (1907–). Muelder actively participated in several WCC assemblies (qq.v.), including Evanston, New Delhi and Uppsala. He was the chairman of the Faith and Order study commission on Institutionalism, which presented its report to the Montreal meeting in 1963. He has criticized neo-orthodox theologians for separating faith and reason and for their everly pessimistic anthropological views. His emphasis on nonviolence strongly influenced one of his students, Martin Luther King, Jr. (q.v.). Following seminary, Muelder studied at the University of Frankfurt. He taught at Boston University School of Theology and served as its dean during much of his career. He is an expert on Ernst Troeltsch's philosophy of history.

MULTILATERAL DIALOGUES. While a few multilateral church unions have taken place at a national or regional level (notably the Church of South India in 1947 and the Church of North India in 1970), at the international level the WCC (q.v.) has been the principal instrument of the churches for multilateral dialogue. In particular, Faith and Order (q.v.) has supplied the forum for the most sustained and cumulative treatment of doctrinal problems. The interchurch dynamics of multilateral dialogue vary with the issues under discussion. Progress is slow and considerable patience required as the attempt is made to clarify the manifold positions of the churches, to develop a convergence, from many different points of view, and to keep the greatest number of participants in a state of positive engagement for the furthest possible advance.

Multilateral dialogue tends to focus on central themes of the Christian faith (q.v.), since these are shared by the widest range of partners, and it is on these that it is crucial to reach an agreement in confession and interpretation. The reward will be the maturity that is, for example, widely recognized in the Lima text (1982), which resulted from 55 years of attention to questions of *Baptism, Eucharist and Ministry* (q.v.) in Faith and Order. Also the current study *Towards the Common Expression of the Apostolic Faith Today* is a sign of a fruitful outcome of multilateral conversations. Under the auspices of Faith and Order and the officers' conference of

Christian World Communions (q.v.), five forums (1978, 1979, 1980, 1985 and 1990) have enabled the tendencies and results of the various bilateral dialogues (q.v.) to be compared multilaterally. *See also* BILATERAL DIALOGUES.

MUNBY, DENIS (1919–1976). Exerting a considerable influence on ecumenical social thought, Munby was a consultant at Evanston 1954, and was active in the study on "Rapid Social Change" in the 1950s. Editor of one of the preparatory volumes *Economic Growth in World Perspective* for the world conference on Church and Society in Geneva, 1966, his volume on *World Development* gathered the report and the papers from the Conference on Development in Beirut, 1968, organized by the WCC (q.v.) and the Pontifical Commission Justice and Peace. Munby for 20 years was a member of the WCC working committee on Church and Society. An Anglican layman and an Oxford economist, he was a reader in transportation economics at Nuffield College, Oxford, and lectured at Union Theological Seminary, New York.

MUSLIM-CHRISTIAN DIALOGUE *see* DIALOGUE WITH PEOPLE OF LIVING FAITHS

- N -

NAIROBI 1975 *see* WORLD COUNCIL OF CHURCHES ASSEMBLIES

NATIONAL COUNCIL OF THE CHURCHES OF CHRIST IN THE USA (NCCC). North America is the only continent that has no regional council of churches, but two national councils of churches, namely the National Council of the Churches of Christ in the USA and the Canadian Council of Churches. Whenever necessary these two councils consult with each other and collaborate. The absence of a regional body has not excluded North American regional initiatives. The North American Ecumenical Youth Assembly in Ann Arbor in 1961, and the North American Faith and Order

Conference in Oberlin in 1957, for instance, have shown what can be done regionally even without an established regional organization.

The National Council of the Churches of Christ in the USA was established in 1950, succeeding the Federal Council of the Churches of Christ in America (q.v.), which was created in 1908. Its aims, functions, main concerns and activities in collaboration with the churches are spelled out as follows: 1) further their vocation to proclaim Jesus Christ as Savior and Lord; 2) engage in ecumenical worship and in biblical and theological study; 3) challenge and counsel one another in mutual accountability as a witness to the unity (q.v.) of the church; 4) share resources for unity and mission (q.v.); 5) strive for peace and justice (qq.v.) in the social, political and economic order; 6) advocate careful stewardship of God's creation; 7) act as responsible servants to people in need; 8) foster education about and for ecumenism and engage in all educational efforts from an ecumenical perspective; 9) nurture ecumenical life through relationships with: a) local, regional, national and world ecumenical bodies, and b) groups and movements of Christians seeking renewal and unity; 10) cultivate relationships and dialogue with people of other faiths and ideologies.

The NCCC's program is formulated and carried out through unit committees of the divisions and commissions, which are composed of representatives of the member communities. Council staff, under the direction of the general secretary, the six associate and ten assistant general secretaries, serve as a secretariat of these bodies. The thirty-one member communions nominate approximately 260 representatives to the Governing Board, which meets twice yearly to decide Council policy and organization and to speak on societal issues. The work of the Governing Board is also carried out through Standing Committees. The Executive Committee oversees operational work of the Council and functions for the Governing Board between its meetings. The Council has an annual budget of about US $40 million, 75 percent contributed and 25 percent earned income. Approximately 35 percent comes from the member churches.

The following Christian communities are members of the

NCCC: African Methodist Episcopal Church, African Methodist Episcopal Zion Church, American Baptist Churches in the USA, Antiochian Orthodox Christian Archdiocese of North America, Armenian Church of America, Christian Church (Disciples of Christ), Christian Methodist Episcopal Church, Church of the Brethren, Coptic Orthodox Church in North America, Episcopal Church, Friends United Meeting, General Convention, Swedenborgian Church, Greek Orthodox Archdiocese of North and South America, International Council of Community Churches, Lutheran Church in America, Moravian Church in America, Northern and Southern Province, National Baptist Convention of America, National Baptist Convention, USA, Inc., Orthodox Church in America, Patriarchal Parishes of the Russian Orthodox Church in USA, Philadelphia Yearly Meeting of the Religious Society of Friends, Polish National Catholic Church of America, Presbyterian Church (USA), Progressive National Baptist Convention, Inc., Reformed Church in America, Serbian Eastern Orthodox Church, Syrian Orthodox Church of Antioch, Ukrainian Orthodox Church in America, United Church of Christ, United Methodist Church. *See also* FEDERAL COUNCIL OF THE CHURCHES OF CHRIST IN AMERICA; UNITED STATES OF AMERICA.

NATIONAL COUNCILS OF CHURCHES *see* COUNCILS OF CHURCHES, LOCAL, NATIONAL, REGIONAL

NATURAL LAW. The conviction that there are certain precepts or norms of good and right conduct, discoverable by all members of the human race, is the broadest significance of natural law. By their own reason human beings can gain knowledge of the ethically good without any reference to God's revelation. Natural law designates those rules of justice that may be found written in the human heart or conscience. The long tradition in Roman Catholicism (q.v.) which is structural and rational, has been that of natural law, conceived and developed by Thomas Aquinas. Scriptural references that inspire Christian ethics were not used and integrated in Roman Catholic teaching. Yet, even Thomas Aquinas, and more convincingly later theologians, have insisted that the limitations of imperfect human moral knowledge must be supplemented and perfected by God's special revelations, notably the gospel of Jesus Christ (q.v.), and that grace is necessary to observe the prescriptions of natural law in its entirety.

In his book *The Social Thought of the World Council of Churches,* Edward Duff stated that the "ethic of ends" and the "ethic of inspiration" express the deepest differences on the subject of social philosophy in the ecumenical community. The whole viewpoint of the "ethic of ends", or natural law approach, supposes in men a capacity to apprehend the general pattern of correct personal moral existence and of a just social organization. The whole viewpoint of the "ethic of inspiration", or the new Reformation (q.v.) theology approach, rejects any continuity between man's sin-wrecked powers and the fulfillment of his ultimate responsibilities. Both the temptation of Protestantism to emphasize radical breaks with the past and the temptation of Roman Catholicism and Orthodoxy (qq.v.) to emphasize continuity with it have their pitfalls. The ecumenical movement needs to become more comprehensive. The concept of natural law has certainly been badly used by those most attached to it, but it is hard to do without it in some form.

In spite of religious opposition to it, natural law has gained support in secular thought in general and in legal thought in particular. This does not mean, however, that the meaning of natural law should not ever be newly interpreted. Since we are living in an advanced era, the fundamental elements of Thomism must be translated to suit the demands of new social problems. There is a necessity of consolidating the unshakable rock of moral law by appeals to divine revelation and to authoritative teaching of the church. The Roman Catholic Church moves slowly but steadily in this direction. The World Council of Churches (q.v.) and its constituency, on the other hand, need to examine critically its fondness for moving from the Bible to a judgment about the modern world without any intermediate steps in thought being made clear. In the past appropriate biblical comments have been made on the serious predicament of society, but in more recent times suitable texts from the Bible have been sought as pegs on which to hang Christian blame and condemnation. Biblical thinking, to be sure, is dynamic. The world is not a more or less well-ordered cosmos, but the field of God's ever new creative activity. The world process and its continuity are not due to the stability of a given order, but to God's faithfulness that he never forsakes his own creation. Yet, the natural law makes possible communication with other believers and nonbelievers on a just society and common norms of conduct.

This last point has often been overlooked or inadequately handled in the ecumenical movement, precisely because of its conviction of having the biblical-prophetic voice at its disposal in matters of peace, justice (qq.v.) and the safeguarding of creation. Saying that these concerns are not just Christian—they are universal concerns—forbids ecumenical Christianity to invite people of other living faiths just as guests and observers to international gatherings. The concept of natural law, despite its ambiguity and complexity, not only relates to issues for a Christian ethics that intends to be relevant to human reality, but to the common response of all people to the problems of humanization of existence in a multireligious, multicultural and multi-ideological world. While a common search for the healing of the world's ills is the best meeting point for religions in our time, that meeting can also surface what is most problematic about religions themselves. *See also* GRACE.

NAUDÉ, CHRISTIAN FREDERICK BEYERS (1915–). On accepting the directorship of the Christian Institute of South Africa, Naudé was discharged from his ministry in the Nederduitse Gereformeerde Kerk in 1963. The institute, which he had helped to establish, worked with Christians of all races on all issues of church and society in South Africa and was the most outspoken organization against apartheid in that country. He served the institute until 1977, when both the paper he edited and the institute were banned by the government. A banning order during seven years severely curtailed his freedom of movement. Serving as general secretary of the South African Council of Churches, 1958–1987, he continued to oppose the policy of apartheid and to counsel various organizations in South Africa, which assisted disadvantaged people in educational and other spheres. From 1940–1963 he served seven congregations of the Nederduitse Gereformeerde Kerk.

NEILL, STEPHEN CHARLES (1900–1984). After studies at Cambridge University, Neill served as principal of a theological college before becoming bishop of the Anglican (q.v.) diocese of Tinnevelly, South India, in 1939. He was a delegate at the Tambaram assembly of the International Missionary Council in 1938 and much involved in the formation of the Church of South India. He was professor of mission (q.v.) and ecumenics at the University of Hamburg, 1962–1969, and professor of philosophy at the Department of Religious Studies, University of Nairobi, 1970–1973. He was associate general secretary of the WCC (q.v.), responsible for its study program, 1948–1950. Neill became well-known as general editor of the World Christian Books series, a program of basic Christian literature of some 30 translations, and as editor of *The History of the Ecumenical Movement, 1517–1948,* together with Ruth Rouse (q.v.).

NELSON, J. ROBERT (1920–). Nelson was executive secretary of the Commission on Faith and Order (q.v.), 1953–1957, and chairman of its working committee, 1967–1976. Professor of systematic theology at Vanderbilt Divinity School, 1957–1960, Oberlin Graduate School, 1962–1965, Boston University School of Theology, 1965–1984, and visiting professor in India at Bangalore and Jabalpur, 1961–1962, in 1968–1969 he became the first non-Catholic to teach at the Pontifical Gregorian University, Rome. Nelson was president of the American Theological Society and of the North American Academy of Ecumenists, vice president of the Société européenne de cultures, and is a fellow of the American Academy of Arts and Sciences. He is active in many programs of the National Council of Churches of the Churches of Christ in the USA (q.v.) and of the United Methodist Church.

NEW DELHI 1961 *see* WORLD COUNCIL OF CHURCHES ASSEMBLIES

NEW RELIGIOUS MOVEMENTS (NRMs). During the past few decades societies around the world have .experienced a tremendous spiritual ferment, which has had a far-reaching impact upon the social, cultural and religious life of the people. This spiritual ferment has manifested itself in the form of innumerable "new religious movements". Many observers of this phenomenon consider that the explosive proliferation of such religious movements in recent years is historically unprecedented. While there has been a great deal of publicity about new religious groups in Western countries, the phenomenon is not confined to the West. There is ample evidence of new movements proliferating in Africa, South America, Asia (most notably in Japan, India, Korea) and in such regions as Melanesia and the Caribbean.

The term "NRMs", in its newly developed usage, refers to a plurality of new kinds of religion or religiosity, which in earlier terminologies were identified as "sects", "cults", "heresies" or "deviations". These earlier terms were found to be problematic and inadequate to describe the contemporary expressions of the phenomenon; not only were they judgmental and carried pejorative connotations, they were also very much tied to the framework of Christian heritage and therefore could not adequately accommodate the new religious groups originating from non-Christian and non-Western sources. The term NRMs has thus emerged as a convenient expression to designate a collective phenomenon, a pattern of religiosity that has become highly visible in the West.

The mainline churches in many Western countries, already preoccupied with concerns of combating the growing "secular" outlook in their societies, were literally caught unaware by the sudden mushrooming of alternative forms of religion in the 1960s. The phenomenon was indeed baffling at first sight and was thought to be a by-product of the youth counterculture. But the persistence of many of these movements into recent times has forced the churches to pay attention to the spiritual change occurring in their midst. Although they have begun to take seriously the challenge of the NRMs, it will not be easy to forge a coherent response. In face of widespread "spiritual illiteracy" in many Western countries, they are faced with the enormous task of educating their members in the Christian faith. There is no point in being simply alarmed about young people joining the NRMs when they themselves have been unable to meet their spiritual needs. The solution to this lies not in naively emulating certain "surface characteristics" of NRMs, like introducing meditation or some Christianized forms of yoga in their midst. Rather, the churches need to recover lost elements of their experiential tradition that may once again become relevant in today's context. But there is no guarantee that this will counter the influence and success of NRMs. Some of the movements are demonstrably fraudulent. In such cases churches should certainly confront them and minister to the victims and families affected. But there may be some things that the Christian community might want to learn from other NRMs, and its attitude toward certain NRMs should therefore shift from fear to an attempt to understand, from anathema to dialogue.

To comply with a request from their member churches, the World Council of Churches and the Lutheran World Federation (qq.v.) sponsored an international consultation, involving Christians who are knowledgeable about and/or involved with NRMs, at the Free University of Amsterdam in 1986. The report is entitled *New Religious Movements and the Churches*. It deals with: 1) movements originating from within Christianity; 2) movements bearing the imprint of Western psychology and therapeutic subculture; and 3) movements derived from Asiatic religions. A number of NRMs are assuming a competitive attitude toward Christianity and other religions, and aim at conversion, which usually results in the convert leaving the church. Other movements are claiming .a complementary function. The present religious situation is highlighted by the fact that NRMs center around a new messiah or avatar and are expected to bring about religious unity, thus succeeding where others have failed.

NEW STYLES OF LIVING. Already the world conference on Church and Society in Geneva (1966) spoke of "the world-wide search for new cultural and spiritual foundations for new societies". The Uppsala assembly (1968) included Section VI on "Towards New Styles of Living" in which it was stated: "Christian life requires a willingness to be changed, and to change the world which has not yet attained the goal set for it by God. Christians have often resisted change. On the other hand they have been themselves the agents of change. Each age has called for fresh discernment. In our time Christians are called to leave familiar territory and venture out toward unknown horizons". In an appendix to the report it was emphasized that Section VI is not a complete or an authoritative outline of a Christian style of living today. It represents the beginning of what can be hoped will become a worldwide debate on this issue. Any statement from a world conference obviously reflects inadequately the particular concerns arising from different regions.

When the Laity Council was constituted in Rome in 1967, the Joint Working Group between the Roman Catholic Church and the World Council of Churches (q.v.) suggested that its partner in the WCC should be the Division of Ecumenical Action. The Laity Council collaborated in the program on "Participation in Change", which was a follow-up to the Uppsala Section VI report "Towards New Styles of Living". The WCC central committee in 1974 outlined "the importance of discovering alternative life styles which give new expression to the role of spirituality in society characterized predominantly by rationality". Again the central committee in 1976 recommended "to assist local congregations and other Christian communities in their authentic forms of worship, new styles of Christian spirituality and styles of life, and also help discover the richness in old forms of worship for the enrichment of Christian life". In the late 1970s, the question of new life-styles in the WCC's Commission on the Churches' Participation in Development was grounded in the concern about the quality of life in view of the ecological problem and about perceived life-styles of the rich and the poor. Several reports of the Vancouver assembly (1983) made reference to new styles of living without elaborating on them. It is a fact that many millions of Christians are living a life fully committed to simplicity and a gradual reform of modern civilization. They are, moreover, eager to learn from one another. *See also* RENEWAL.

NEWBIGIN, JAMES EDWARD LESSLIE (1909–). Educated at Westminster College, Newbigin was ordained in 1936 and appointed by the Church of Scotland as a missionary in India. He took a major part in the church union negotiations of the Church of South India and in 1947 was appointed bishop in Madurai and Ramnad. In 1958 he was elected moderator, and one year later general secretary of the International Missionary Council (q.v.). He promoted the integration of the IMC into the WCC (qq.v.) in 1961 and became director of the Division of World Mission and Evangelism of the WCC, 1961–1965, when he returned to South India as bishop of Madras until 1974. Afterward he was professor of missions at the Selly-Oak Colleges in Birmingham, England. Newbigin has rendered valuable services to the ecumenical movement in the realms of unity, mission and renewal (qq.v.). He supported the rapprochement with the Orthodox and the conservative Evangelicals (qq.v.) who were close to his heart. He has been critical of modern liberal theologies, which have been influential during recent decades.

NICENE-CONSTANTINOPOLITAN CREED *see* CREEDS

NICODIM (BORIS GEORGIVICH ROTOV) (1929–1978). In 1960 Nicodim became the leader of the foreign office of the Russian Orthodox Church, in the same year bishop of Jaroslavl, in 1961 archbishop, in 1963 metropolitan of Minsk, and in 1963 of Leningrad. He had to leave the foreign office in 1972. He was elected president of the WCC (q.v.) in 1975. Nicodim contributed considerably to the improvement of the relationship with the Roman Catholic Church and greatly admired Pope John XXIII (qq.v.). He was the driving spirit behind the Moscow patriarchate when it decided in 1961 to join the WCC and remained a loyal supporter of the Council until the end of his life. He died of a heart attack during an audience with Pope John Paul I (q.v.).

NIEBUHR, REINHOLD (1892–1971). Educated at Eden Theological Seminary and at Yale University, Niebuhr undertook pastoral duties in Detroit, Michigan, where the labor movement came to his attention. His involvement in its struggles was the basis for his later work in Christian social ethics (q.v.). At first a pacifist, he shared the optimism of the Social Gospel movement. However, by 1932, with the publication of *Moral Man and Immoral Society,* he argued against the Social Gospel that the law of love would never lead to social perfection. He emphasized in particular the doctrine of original sin; human pride is everywhere at work and especially in the political order with the temptations of power (q.v.). Niebuhr was professor of applied Christianity at Union Theological Seminary in New York, 1928–1960, and influential at Oxford 1937, at Amsterdam 1948, and also at the world Christian youth conferences in Amsterdam (1939) and Oslo (1947). He wrote a considerable number of important and widely read works, particularly on the ecumenical movement.

NIEMÖLLER, MARTIN (1892–1984). Ordained in 1924 a minister of the Protestant Church in Westphalia, Niemöller was appointed pastor at Berlin-Dahlem in 1931. His anti-Nazi religious activities and support of the Confessing Church (q.v.) led to his arrest in 1937 and confinement in the concentration camps of Sachsenhausen and Dachau until the end of the war. He participated in the writing of the Stuttgart declaration of guilt in 1945 and became head of the foreign relations department of the Evangelical Church in Germany, 1945–1956, and president of the territorial church of Hessen and Nassau, 1947–1964. He opposed the creation of the Federal Republic of Germany in 1949, and was equally opposed to any crusade against communism and the US war in Vietnam. Niemöller was a member of the provisional committee of the WCC (q.v.) 1946–1948, a member of the central and executive committees, 1948–1961, and a president of the WCC, 1961–1968.

NILES, DANIEL THAMBIRAJA (1908–1970). After being educated in his native Jaffna, Ceylon, Niles studied theology in Bangalore, India, 1929–1933. Being involved in the Student Christian Movement, he became its national secretary in 1933 and participated in the meeting of the general committee of the World Student Christian Federation (q.v.) in Sofia. He became chairman of the Federation in 1953. He served as general secretary of the National Christian Council of Ceylon, 1941–1945, as chairman of the WCC's (q.v.) Youth Department, 1953–1959, as executive secretary of the WCC Department of Evangelism, and from 1957 onward as general secretary (later as president) of the East Asia Christian Conference (q.v.). Already at the first assembly of the WCC he was one of the main speakers and he was invited to preach the opening sermon at the Uppsala assembly in 1968. At this assembly he was also elected to the presidium. He was chairman of the northern district of the Methodist Church in Sri Lanka, 1954–1964, and continued to be greatly involved in the work of the WCC, including its assemblies in Evanston and New Delhi. Niles remains remembered for his passion for mission (q.v.) and evangelism in an ecumenical context. Central to his life was the giving and receiving of friendship. He was an intimate friend of W. A. Visser 't Hooft (q.v.).

NISSIOTIS, NIKOS ANGELOS (1925–1986). After studies in Athens, Basel, Zurich and Louvain (where he obtained a doctorate) Nissiotis soon became a bridge builder between Orthodoxy (q.v.) and Western theology. He served as general secretary of the Student Christian Movement in Greece, was active in the World Student Christian Federation (q.v.), addressed the New Delhi assembly in 1961 on the role of the Orthodox churches in the ecumenical movement and was a WCC observer at Vatican II (q.v.), 1962–1965. Nissiotis served as director of the Ecumenical Institute in Bossey (q.v.) 1966–1974, was a member of the WCC central committee, 1975–1983, and moderator of the Commission on Faith and Order (q.v.), 1976–1983. He taught at the theological faculty of the University of Athens. As a member of the International Olympic Committee, he lectured often on the philosophy of Olympic sport to young athletes.

NOLDE, O. FREDERICK (1899–1972). Nolde was a longtime director of the WCC (q.v.) Commission of the Churches on International Affairs, and served as professor and dean of the Graduate School at the Lutheran Theological Seminary in Philadelphia. He was a member of the Department of

International Justice and Goodwill, of the Commission to Study Origins of Peace, and of the executive committee of the board of trustees of the Carnegie Endowment for International Peace. At a few hours notice he was prepared to go anywhere in the world to try to solve a conflict situation. He helped moderate a conference between American and East Asian church leaders over the tragedy in Vietnam. Nolde was devoted to the United Nations (q.v.) and the principles it serves. In the days of the Joint Committee on Religious Liberty, he clarified the main elements of religious freedom and related rights and prepared himself for drafting and defending the key formulation in the Universal Declaration of Human Rights. His book *Free and Equal* was an important document on both the ideas and the history of the effort to build international safeguards for the inherent rights and dignity of human beings.

NONTHEOLOGICAL FACTORS OF CHURCH UNITY *see* SOCIOLOGY OF THE ECUMENICAL MOVEMENT

NORTH, FRANK MASON (1850–1935). North was instrumental in organizing the Methodist Federation for Social Service and the Federal Council of the Churches of Christ in America (q.v.). To the latter, at its founding in 1908, he presented a report on the Church and Modern Industry, which became the historic "Social Creed of the Churches". After chairing the commission on the Church and Social Service (with such colleagues as Walter Rauschenbusch [q.v.], Shailer Mathews and Jesiah Strong), he was elected chairman of the executive committee of the Federal Council in 1912, and president of the Council, 1916–1920. North attended the Edinburgh missionary conference of 1910, served on the continuation committee, and chaired the drafting committee for the constitution of the International Missionary Council (q.v.), adopted in 1921.

NYGREN, ANDERS THEODOR SAMUEL (1890–1978). Nygren was a delegate to Lausanne, 1927, Oxford 1937, Edinburgh 1937, Amsterdam 1948, and Lund 1952. He played a leading role in the formation of the WCC (q.v.), advocating a confessional basis for the Council. He was the first president of the Lutheran World Federation (q.v.), 1947–1952, and then was chairman of the Faith and Order (q.v.) commission on Christ and the Church, 1953–1963. From 1924 onward he was professor of systematic theology at Lund, and served as bishop of Lund from 1949 until his retirement in 1958. Nygren became particularly known for his view on the uniqueness of the Christian idea of (God's) love (*agapē*) as opposed to *eros* (human love), stressing that *agapē* is the essential feature of Christianity.

- O -

OLD CATHOLIC CHURCH. Old Catholics are a group of national churches that at various times separated from Rome. The term "Old Catholic" was adopted to mean original Catholicism. Old Catholic Christians are composed of three sections: 1) the Church of Utrecht, which originated in 1724 when its chapter maintained its ancient right to elect the Archbishop of Utrecht, against opposition from Rome; 2) the German, Austrian and Swiss Catholic Churches, which refused to accept the dogmas of the Infallibility and the universal ordinary jurisdiction of the pope, as defined by the Vatican Council (q.v.) of 1870; 3) smaller groups of Slav origin. National church movements among the Poles in the USA (1897) and the Croats (1924) have resulted in the establishment of the National Polish Church with four bishoprics in America and one in Poland, and of the Yugo-slav Old Catholic Church. The Philippine Independent Church established sacramental communion with Old Catholics in 1965.

The doctrinal basis of the Old Catholic churches is the Declaration of Utrecht (1889). The Old Catholics recognize the same seven Ecumenical Councils as the Eastern Orthodox (q.v.) churches, and those doctrines accepted by the church before the Great Schism of 1054. They admit seven sacraments and recognize apostolic succession (qq.v.). They also believe in the real presence in the eucharist (q.v.), but deny transubstantiation, forbid private masses and permit the reception of the eucharist under one or both elements. Bishops, as well as the rest of the clergy, are permitted to marry. All services are in the vernacular. From the start, Anglicans (q.v.) have been close to Old Catholics. They participated in an international conference of theologians, convened in Bonn by Old Catholics in 1874, to discuss the reunion of churches outside Rome. Old Catholics recognized Anglican ordinations in 1925. Since 1932 they have been in full communion with the Church of England. Old Catholic-Orthodox dialogues (q.v.) have taken place since 1931. Since the Second Vatican Council (q.v.) the Old Catholic churches have been in conversation with the Roman Catholic Church (q.v.). A limited agreement on church communion was reached in 1974. An international Old Catholic congress has met regularly since 1890. The international Old Catholic bishops' conference is the main instrument for maintaining the ties of the communion. It not only decides on internal church matters but serves to promote relationships with various other churches. The president of the conference is the Archbishop of Utrecht. Old Catholics number over 400,000.

Old Catholic involvement in the ecumenical movement began with the participation of a Swiss and a Dutch bishop in the Faith and Order (q.v.) conference in Lausanne in 1927. Since then Old Catholics have never missed a Faith and Order gathering. They also participate in other activities of the WCC (q.v.) and national councils of churches. Old Catholics believe the unity that the ecumenical movement seeks for the churches is one that needs to exist as a reconciled diversity of all, rooted in the common faith and discipline of the ancient church of the first ecumenical councils and their statements of faith (q.v.).

OLDHAM, JOSEPH HOULDSWORTH (1874–1969). Educated at Cambridge and Oxford, where he met John R. Mott (q.v.) and became his friend, Oldham was founder and organizer of more significant ecumenical initiatives than any other Christian of his generation. He was executive secretary of the world missionary conference in Edinburgh in 1910, became secretary of the continuation committee in 1911 and secretary of the International Missionary Council (q.v.) in 1921.

He launched and was the editor of the *International Review of Missions,* 1912–1927. He was appointed chairman of the research committee of the Universal Council on Life and Work in 1934, and chief organizer of its conference on "Church, Community and State" in Oxford in 1937. In 1938 he prepared with others the meeting in Utrecht, which drew up the constitution and made final plans for the creation of the WCC (q.v.). He was made honorary president at the Council's first assembly in Amsterdam in 1948. In 1946 he became vice chairman of the study commission on "The Church and the Disorder of Society" in preparation for the assembly. In 1924 he published what many call his most influential book: *Christianity and the Race Problem.* Other works in the 1930s greatly clarified and strengthened the world Christian community as it faced the rise of National Socialism, the threat of the totalitarian state and problems of economic justice and political order. At his memorial service in London, W. A. Visser 't Hooft (q.v.) said: "Ecumenical history is full of examples of new development which he started, but which others carried to their conclusion. I have no hesitation in saying that the ecumenical movement owes more to him than any other of its pioneers".

ORDINATION. The word is derived from the Latin *ordinare,* which means to organize or to set in order; in ecclesiastical usage it is the act of separating and commissioning a person for a role of special ministerial or priestly service, either for a specified mission or for life. The act of ordination traditionally centers in the laying on of hands by a bishop in episcopal church government, by those already ordained to the ruling or teaching eldership in the presbyterian form, and by ordained pastors, elders and/or deacons in the congregational form. The doctrinal interpretation of the action admits of a greater variety, but two main positions are held: according to one, ordination is a sacrament (q.v.) whereby something is conveyed; according to the other, it is not a sacrament and is primarily an act of authorization.

In the ecumenical discussion, questions such as by whom should ordination be performed?, and what rites of unification can be found for a mutual recognition of ministries between churches?, are still not settled. The 16th-century reformers looked for a ritual that gives priority to God's call to ministry (q.v.), places the ministry in relation to the priesthood of all believers and avoids priestly or sacramental interpretations of order. The ecumenical consensus document *Baptism, Eucharist and Ministry* (q.v.) suggests that all churches restore the laying on of hands as the primary ordination rite, as a sign of the gift of the Spirit for ministry. It also proposes that all churches restore the threefold ministry of bishop, presbyter and deacon. As far as mutual recognition of ministries is concerned, for the Roman Catholic Church (q.v.) issues of validity should first be resolved, involving episcopal succession and the understanding of which ordinations are to be performed. For Orthodox churches (q.v.), recognition of ministry has to take place within the recognition of churches. For several Protestant (q.v.) churches, a common faith (q.v.) has to lie at the foundation of such acceptance. The corollaries of the sacramental and authoritarian positions are that whereas ordination in the first sense is to the priesthood of the whole church, in the second sense it is only to the ministry to a specific body of Christians and, in a state of divided Christianity, is necessarily limited. *See also* EPISCOPACY; MINISTRY; SACRAMENTS.

ORDINATION OF WOMEN. The 1982 Lima document on *Baptism, Eucharist and Ministry* (q.v.) does not treat the ordination of women in the main part of the text on ministry (q.v.) but presents the issue in a commentary (to M18), which gives a short description of those churches that ordain women as ministers and of those that do not. It notes that churches that ordain women do so on the basis of the conviction "that the ordained ministry of the church lacks fulness when it is limited to one sex. This theological conviction has been reinforced by their experience during the years in which they have included women in their ordained ministries"—and no such church has ever reversed its decision. While an increasing number of theologians, including Roman Catholics (q.v.), see no theological issue here, the sociological and psychological issues are by no means

insignificant. Already in 1965 Faith and Order (q.v.) published a study *Concerning the Ordination of Women.* The
study on "The Community of Women and Men in the
Church" produced in 1980 a book entitled *Ordination of
Women in Ecumenical Perspective.*

The arguments for the ordination of women run as follows: All ministry is to be understood in the light of him who
came "not to be served, but to serve" (Mark 10:45). In
describing the nature of the church, the witness of the
historical community around Jesus should not be bypassed.
Contemporary Christians have recognized anew the radical
nature of the fellowship around Jesus. This fellowship broke
through traditional social barriers. It included women as well
as men in unconventional ways. This implies that the church
contains an enduring insight into the nature of the redeemed
humanity in Christ that is a constant source for the renewal
(q.v.) of the church. As previously justified inequalities are
nullified in Christ, all baptized Christians, including women,
can seek ordination.

The same commentary of the Lima text continues to
outline: "On the other hand, these churches which do not
practice the ordination of women consider that the force of
nineteen centuries of tradition against the ordination of
women must not be set aside. They believe that such a
tradition cannot be dismissed as a lack of respect for the
participation of women in the church. They believe that there
are theological issues concerning the nature of humanity and
concerning Christology (q.v.) that lie at the heart of their
convictions and understanding of the role of women in the
church". While such differences hinder the mutual recognition of ministries, the text says, they do not prevent further
efforts toward such recognition. "Openness to each other
holds the possibility that the Spirit may well speak to one
church through the insights of another. Ecumenical consideration, therefore, should encourage, not restrain, the facing of
this question".

Most Roman Catholic, and all Orthodox (q.v.) theologians, argue that the incarnation of God in the male Jesus
requires the representation of Christ to be through a male
priesthood. By the gift of the Holy Spirit (q.v.) the church

participates in the unique priesthood of the Son of God incarnate. This unique priesthood conditions the meaning of priestly ordination (q.v.) and of the special grace (q.v.) it confers. The universal priesthood of all believers and the sacramental priesthood both derive from the unique priesthood. The bishop and the priest only actualize, by the grace of the Holy Spirit in time and space, the unique and eternal priesthood of the High Priest. This argument would continue that, on the basis of biblical anthropology, men and women are different and at the same time one both in accordance with the order of creation and the order of redemption. This unity/diversity can be signified in the reconciled new creation, which is beginning in the church here and now, through the presence at the altar of a man and a woman, both ordained to ministries of equal importance and dignity, though of different symbolic significance.

The fact that the several Protestant churches ordain women to the ministry (q.v.), and Anglican and Methodist (qq.v.) churches even ordain women as bishops, has become a considerable new obstacle in the search for church unity (q.v.). The reconciliation of ministries between the Roman Catholic Church and the Church of England has become complicated in a new way. It is as if Christians moved back to the year 1916 when Anglican William Temple (q.v.) expressed a view that many committed ecumenists still share today: ''I would like to see women ordained; . . . desirable as it would be in itself, the effect might be (probably would be) to put back the re-union of Christendom—and re-union is more important''. Here the condition of unity is conceived in a static and ahistorical perspective.

Because the Incarnation dictates the radical historicity of the church, it must always seek to be contemporary in its understanding of its task, and therefore of its ministry. When the circumstances of the church change, its inherited patterns of ministry need reformulation and reshaping; there is the continual need for the ministry to incarnate itself in the culture in which it finds itself. Such obedient adaptation is made more difficult when the previous historical experience of the church is ''absolutized'' and regarded as normative for all time, or even given an ''ontological'' rationale. Jesus did not in fact include any women or Gentiles among the Twelve, and there were understandable reasons for that. But it is quite another matter to assert, on this ground, that women are by nature physically, personally and ontologically incapable of receiving the grace (q.v.) and responsibility given in ordination. Churches that ordain women have found that women's gifts and graces are as wide and varied as men's, and that their ministry is fully as blessed by the Holy Spirit as the ministry of men. But even churches that already ordain women must guard against discriminatory tendencies, since a real ambiguity can be observed in these churches— the women ordained have usually been given positions of juridical and pastoral inferiority. *See also* ORDINATION; MINISTRY.

ORIENTAL ORTHODOX CHURCHES. These churches have histories that go back to the Nestorian and Monophysite controversies during the 4th and 5th centuries over the one or two natures of Jesus Christ (q.v.). Two Ecumenical Councils—Ephesus in 431 and Chalcedon in 451—dealt with these Christological disputes. The Oriental churches constitute a group of communities, peoples and nations that in terms of race, language and culture display a wide diversity. They are present not only in the Middle East but also on the African continent (Ethiopia) and in South India. The Oriental Orthodox churches are not in communion with the Eastern Orthodox (q.v.) but are generally held to belong to the family of Eastern churches. They are also referred to as Ancient Oriental, Lesser Eastern, and Pre- or Ante-Chalcedonian churches. The First Pan-Orthodox Conference, held in Rhodes in 1961, discussed the relations between the Eastern Orthodox and the Oriental Orthodox churches.

The Syrian Orthodox Church has its center in the Patriarchate of Antioch (now Damascus, Syria). It is spread over Syria, Iraq, Lebanon, Jordan, Turkey and other countries in the Middle East. The Syrian Orthodox Church in India is situated in the state of Kerala. The Coptic Orthodox Church in Egypt has gone through a series of persecutions. Outside Egypt there are Coptic dioceses in Jerusalem, in the Sudan and in South Africa. The Ethiopian Orthodox Church, having lived for many centuries under the influence of the Coptic Church, has been autonomous and autocephalous since 1959. Considerable segments of the Armenian Church are spread all over the world from the Middle East to the Far East, from Canada to Australia and from Europe to Transcaucasia, its homeland being Armenia, part of which is under Soviet rule and part under the Turks. These five churches together have an estimated membership of 23 million. They all have contributed leaders to the ecumenical movement. Paulos Gregorios (q.v.) of the Orthodox Syrian Church (Malankara) has been president of the WCC (q.v.) from Vancouver to Canberra and was also moderator of the Sub-unit on Church and Society from 1975–1983. Patriarch Shenouda and the late Bishop Samuel of the Coptic Church, Patriarch Ignatius Zakka of the Syrian Church and V. C. Samuel of the Malankara Church have done signal service for the ecumenical movement. Aboon Theophilus, patriarch of Ethiopia, was one of the presidents of the WCC from 1954–1961; Armenian Catholicos (Antelias) Karekin Sarkissian was vice moderator of the central committee from 1975 to 1983.

ORTHODOXY. Eastern Europe and the Middle East are the geographical areas where Christian churches known as Orthodox, Greek Orthodox, Eastern Orthodox (q.v.) or Orthodox Catholic are found. Fifteen of these churches are known as "autocephalous", meaning self-governing. Ranking first in honor are the ancient patriarchates: Constantinople, Alexandria, Antioch and Jerusalem, in that order. The members adhering directly to these patriarchates total fewer than three million. In addition, churches that refer to themselves as Oriental Orthodox churches (q.v.) have histories that go back to the Nestorian and Monophysite controversies over the one or two natures of Christ of the 4th and 5th centuries. The Orthodox Church does not have an external center of authority, like the office of Pope within the Roman Catholic Church (q.v.). The Ecumenical Patriarchate in Constantinople is accepted by all Orthodox churches as *primus inter pares,* which gives it the right of initiative in calling Pan-Orthodox conferences and in some matters affecting relations with other churches. In the last three decades the relations between the Orthodox churches and the Roman Catholic Church have undergone a great change for the better. The Pan-Orthodox conferences of 1961, 1963 and 1964 discussed the relations of Orthodoxy and Roman Catholicism. Popes John XXIII and Paul VI and the ecumenical patriarch Athenagoras I (qq.v.) were major factors in the changing climate.

Since the majority of church divisions is within the Protestant (q.v.) family, ecumenism is often regarded as a Protestant phenomenon (and the WCC a Protestant body). Yet the World Council of Churches (q.v.) that came into being in 1948 closely resembled an idea first put forward by the Orthodox churches nearly 30 years earlier. The 1920 letter of the synod of the Church of Constantinople (the Ecumenical Patriarchate) "to all the churches of Christ everywhere", calling for formation of a "league of churches", was the first official proposal by a church for an institutional expression of worldwide ecumenical collaboration. Although Orthodox representatives were active in all the streams that flowed into the WCC, not all Orthodox churches joined the Council at the beginning. Just a month before the Amsterdam assembly (q.v.) a meeting of Orthodox leaders in Moscow discouraged participation in the WCC. Despite its recommendations (largely based on a misunderstanding of what the WCC aimed at), some 40 Orthodox delegates were present at the first assembly. In the years after 1948 the WCC maintained contacts with other Orthodox churches—especially with the Russian Orthodox Church, largest of the nonmembers. The 1950 Toronto Statement (q.v.) allayed the fears of a "super-church" that Orthodox had feared. Ecumenical relief and development aid attested to the tangible values of solidarity within the WCC. Slowly, the obstacles were overcome and, at the third assembly in New Delhi (1961), all the Orthodox churches in the world that were not WCC members joined.

The Orthodox presence in the WCC has undoubtedly been mutually enriching, though by no means always smooth. To understand the place of the Orthodox churches in the ecumenical movement requires recognizing their particular historical experience as well as their theological convictions. The 1920 encyclical of the Ecumenical Patriarchate was a response to their emergence from centuries of isolation, suffering, persecution and martyrdom under the just-defeated Ottoman empire. Since the end of World War II some Orthodox churches have endured the difficulties of life under Marxist governments committed to atheism (q.v.) and unwilling to allow the church any public role except conducting worship services (and often making that very difficult). Others have the experience of being minority churches in predominantly Muslim countries. Still others, especially in North and South America, have coped with the difficulties of being immigrant churches in diaspora (q.v.).

Fundamental to the Orthodox participation in the ecumenical movement is the belief that unity in faith (qq.v.) is a condition for the reunion of the divided churches. Church unity must be unity in the apostolic truth, not just an external structure for common action. "Ecumenism of space", Christian unity in every part of the world, cannot be separated from "ecumenism in time", faithfulness to the apostolic and patristic teaching of the ancient undivided church. They see their vocation in the WCC as holding up the universality and continuity of the Holy Tradition (q.v.). In line with this understanding the Orthodox, even before the founding of the WCC, often issued separate statements on important issues, highlighting their divergencies from Protestant theology. More recently, they have sought to bring Orthodox perspectives into ecumenical discussion earlier in the process through consultations before major WCC conferences and assemblies (q.v.). It is no doubt in theology and liturgy (qq.v.) that the presence of the Orthodox churches in the World Council has been most influential. Renewed ecumenical appreciation of the trinitarian character of Christian theology, which many see as enriching the strongly Christocentric tones of the earliest years of the WCC, owes much to the Orthodox presence. As ecumenical worship has evolved, the Orthodox influence has made itself felt (not least through the many sung liturgical responses that have become familiar around the world). As ecological concern has reawakened ecumenical interest in the theology of creation, Orthodox theology has provided rich resources. And the model of unity as "a conciliar fellowship of local churches which are themselves truly united"—articulated by the fifth assembly in Nairobi (1975)—mirrors in many ways the relationship of the independent and self-governing local (national) Orthodox churches, which are themselves united in a "conciliar fellowship".

Orthodox leaders have acknowledged that they have also gained from ecumenical participation. In some cases it has been practical assistance—aid to refugees (q.v.) and victims of natural disaster, support to help restore their monasteries or build theological institutes, opportunities to send their members abroad for training or to participate in ecumenical meetings. The WCC has also been a vehicle for introducing other Christians to the often unknown world of Orthodoxy, the richness of its spirituality and the depth of its theology. Membership in the WCC has also had consequences for internal Orthodox relations, especially building the contacts between Eastern Orthodox and Oriental Orthodox. And, particularly in connection with recent changes in the Soviet Union and Eastern Europe, Orthodox leaders have attested to the value of what they have learned in the WCC about the role of the church in society—a role that many of them were unable to play for many years.

Inevitably, tensions remain, Orthodox churches are not comfortable with the WCC's structures. They have voiced concern that the search for doctrinal consensus might lead to a situation in which delicate matters concerning "unity in faith" could be put to a vote and decided by a majority. (WCC "rules of debate" thus allow members of governing bodies to request that an issue that they believe goes against the self-understanding of their church not be put to a vote.) They remain unconvinced that the WCC's style of work and of making theological statements really allows room for the Orthodox perspective to come through, or that the way the WCC is organized allows sufficient attention to the priorities of their churches. Orthodox churches have expressed a consistent concern about their under-representation on WCC staff and governing bodies.

On two specific issues considerable tension remains. One was already mentioned in the 1920 encyclical attempts by Western Christians in traditionally Orthodox countries to make Protestants of their members. WCC statements have repeatedly reaffirmed ecumenical opposition to proselytism (q.v.), but the issue continues to surface—even though most of the Western groups accused of doing this kind of mission in traditionally Orthodox countries are not affiliated with the WCC or any other ecumenical organization. Another controversial issue is the ordination of women to the ministry (qq.v.). The Orthodox insist that the exclusively male sacramental priesthood in their churches is rooted in the Tradition and does not in any way imply that women are inferior to men. They agree on the need to discuss a wider role for women in the service and spiritual work of the church (including, some have said, the renewal of the institution of deaconesses in the church).

The theological understanding that lies behind this view is not shared by many Protestant churches (including some that do not themselves ordain women). Some Protestant churches have in fact moved in the direction of suggesting that opening all church offices to both men and women is a core issue of the faith. A related controversy has arisen over ecumenical attempts to make the language used in worship "inclusive" of all, for example, by replacing the traditional Trinitarian formula "Father, Son and Holy Spirit" with names for God that do not suggest masculine gender or attributes (such as "Creator, Redeemer, Sustainer"). While not objecting in general to the use of different names for God, Orthodox churches have argued that the traditional formula must be retained at certain points in the liturgy.

Regarding the challenges of Orthodox participation in the ecumenical movement, Boris Bobrinskoy from Paris has said: "In its confrontation with the churches of Rome and of the Reformation (q.v.), contemporary Orthodoxy, forced out of its many centuries of isolation, is rediscovering its universal dimensions and is compelled to answer in new terms the question: What is the message of Orthodoxy? It is in terms of plenitude, of experience of trinitarian life, of the divine life radiant in Christians through eucharistic communion that this answer must be built up''. He concluded by saying that the substance of the message of Orthodoxy is inseparable from an attitude of humility and penitence. *See also* EASTERN ORTHODOX CHURCHES.

OSLO 1947 *see* YOUTH

OUTLER, ALBERT COOK (1910–). Outler is a Methodist (q.v.) ecumenist with a special interest in the problem of scripture and tradition (q.v.). He was a delegate to the Lund conference in 1952, a member of the Faith and Order (q.v.) working committee, 1953–1974, cochairman, Faith and Order study commission on Tradition and traditions, 1954–1963, vice chairman of Montreal 1963, and a delegate to New Delhi 1961, and to the Consultation on Church Union (COCU) (q.v.), 1969–1976. Involved in union negotiations between Methodist, Evangelical and United Brethren churches, he was also appointed delegate-observer by the World Methodist Council to the Second Vatican Council (q.v.), 1962–1965. He was professor of theology successively at Duke, Yale and Southern Methodist universities. He is regarded as one of the foremost 20th-century interpreters of John Wesley.

OXFORD 1937 *see* INTRODUCTION; LIFE AND WORK

OXNAM, GARFIELD BROMLEY (1893–1963). President of the Federal Council of Churches of Christ in America (q.v.), 1944–1946, and a president of the WCC (q.v.), 1948–1954, and later a member of the central committee, Oxnam was also chairman of the general board of education of the Methodist Church (q.v.), 1939–1944, and chairman of the general board of missions, 1944–1952. He was elected bishop in 1936 with episcopal assignments in Omaha, Boston, New York and Washington, D.C., wielding considerable influence as secretary of the council of bishops, 1939–1956. Oxnam transformed the periodic meetings of church leaders into a real council. He originated the plan that requires bishops to visit foreign fields so as to gain firsthand knowledge of world conditions.

- P -

PACIFIC CONFERENCE OF CHURCHES (PCC). The vast area of the Pacific, more water than land, comes within the orbit of the Pacific Conference of Churches, another well-established regional expression of the ecumenical movement. The discussion, initiated by the London Missionary Society (the pioneer mission in the area) with some of the churches and missions in the Pacific in 1959, resulted in a request that the International Missionary Council (q.v.) take responsibility for convening a regional gathering. After a period of intense preparation within the area itself, a conference was held in Samoa in 1961. All the main island groups, such as Fiji, Solomon Islands, Tahiti, Tonga, New Caledonia and the New Hebrides (Vanuatu), as well as Papua New Guinea, Australia and New Zealand, were represented. The meeting recognized the need to overcome isolation and to consult on common problems.

It is therefore not surprising that, at what was convened as an ad hoc consultation in Samoa, the decision was taken to form a more permanent regional organization. This was formally constituted five years later in an inaugural assembly in Lifu, New Caledonia, in 1966. Other assemblies followed in different places. The basic concerns of the Pacific Conference of Churches are related to the ministry (q.v.), its nature, training and employment; the unity (q.v.) of the church, especially in a region where geographical isolation has combined with denominational insularity to harden separation; the nature of a Christian society and its implication for tribal communities; the special pressures and problems that have become universal in the aftermath of the Second World War and through the spread of a worldwide technological culture.

Currently over 20 churches and the Episcopal Conference of the Pacific (including ten Roman Catholic (q.v.) dioceses) are members of the PCC. Its offices are in Suva, Fiji. Since 1982 the programmatic growth has been slower and more selective, but the conference has explored new ways of serving the region. The PCC and the WCC (q.v.) have close links. Much energy has been spent speaking out against nuclear testing and in favor of national independence.

PACIFISM. There has always been a minority tradition of Christian pacifism based on the Sermon on the Mount. Mennonites, Quakers and Brethren (qq.v.)—called the "historic peace churches"—have subscribed to a consistent nonviolent position. Mahatma Gandhi used pacifist methods, including civil disobedience, in the movement to liberate India from British colonial rule. From Gandhi the line of influence passes through the struggles of the US civil rights movement, led by Martin Luther King (q.v.). World wars and the technological developments culminating in the nuclear bomb led to increasing recognition of the pacifist position around the world. Pacifist groups were especially active and powerful between the two world wars (1919–1939), as pacifism became linked with isolationism in the USA. Despite the unpopularity of their position during World War II, conscientious objectors were recognized by law in the USA and in England. Instead of facing imprisonment as was common during World War I, pacifists were allowed to do alternative service. However, some objected on principle even to conscription for nonviolent service and refused to participate.

The popularity of pacifism as a religious ideal or a philosophy of life declined during World War II and the Cold War, but in the USA the Vietnam conflict led to a resurgence. Churches that advocated the new pacifism were greatly influenced by those who defended a total repudiation of war. A primary argument has been that St Augustine's position on just war (q.v.) had been rendered absurd by the potential for nuclear annihilation. Pacifism, therefore, appeared to be the most realistic theological position available to Christians. Ironically, at the same time pacifism was resurfacing in the church, a new theology (q.v.) justifying · armed conflict also arose. This "theology of revolution" (afterward "theology of liberation"), espoused by many theologians, supported guerrilla warfare as a means to remedy political and social injustices.

The ecumenical debate has reflected these shifts in the world scene. At its first assembly in Amsterdam in 1948, the WCC stated that "war as a method of settling disputes is incompatible with the teaching and example of our Lord Jesus Christ". The final document of the European Ecumenical Assembly in Basel in 1989 stated: "There are no situations in our countries or on our continent in which violence is required or justified". It is a measure of the injustice in the countries of the Third World that there are no comparably clear statements from other continents, or at the world level. The WCC's (q.v.) world convocation on Justice, Peace and the Integrity of Creation (q.v.) in Seoul in 1990 spoke, however, of the need to overcome the necessity of war and continued the clear denunciation of the possession and use of weapons of mass destruction. But the debate on the Gulf war at the seventh WCC assembly in Canberra in 1991 revealed again the deep differences within the ecumenical movement over classic questions about the justifiability of war. Even those who believe in nonviolence cannot agree how far this teaching is universally applicable. *See also* JUST WAR; MILITARISM; PEACE AND DISARMAMENT; VIOLENCE AND NONVIOLENCE.

PANIKKAR, RAIMUNDO (1918–). Born in Barcelona, Spain, to a Hindu father and a Spanish Roman Catholic mother, Panikkar has been a controversial theologian and philosopher of interfaith dialogue, particularly of the Hindu-Christian dialogue (q.v.). In his earlier work *The Unknown Christ of Hinduism* (1964), he claimed that the genuine Hindu is saved by Christ through the sacraments of Hinduism. He was a follower of the fulfillment theology of John N. Farqhar and agreed with Karl Rahner's (q.v.) concept of "anonymous Christian". In a second much revised and enlarged edition of his book (1981), Panikkar admitted that his position had become much more radical and that four rivers, the Hindu, Christian, Buddhist and secular, flowed through his life. He dared to characterize Western Christianity as "ancient paganism, or to be more precise, the complex of Hebrew-Hellenic-Greek-Latin-Celtic-modern religions converted to Christ more or less successfully". He has been professor of comparative philosophy and history of religions at the University of California, Santa Barbara, since 1971.

PANNENBERG, WOLFHART (1928–). Pannenberg was successively professor of systematic theology at Wuppertal

(1958–1961), Mainz (1961–1968) and Munich, at the Protestant Faculty of Theology (1968–). He has been a member of the Commission on Faith and Order (1983). Contending that he is a Christian, he has set himself the controversial task of demonstrating the reasonableness of Christian faith (q.v.) in the modern world. In the early 1960s he developed a theology in which history, including intelligible history, was itself revelation: the events of scriptural history were not to be seen as different in kind from other historical happenings, and the rationality of faith required a foundation in such authentic occurrencies. He went on to produce an influential essay in Christology (q.v.), *Jesus: God and Man,* and a programmatic study of the foundations of the philosophy of science in relation to Christian theology. More recently he has written extensively on ethics and the doctrine of human nature (*Anthropology in Theological Perspective*). In Pannenberg's view, the growth in understanding of the biblical figure of God has "actually the form of a syncretistic process". In his estimation, "Christianity affords the greatest example of synoretic assimilative power; this religion not only linked itself to Greek philosophy but also inherited the entire religious tradition of the Mediterranean world". The majesty of God should be interpreted in terms of the future rather than in terms of the past: God is the attractant power of the things to come.

PAPACY/PRIMACY. The title "pope" (*papa*-father) was in the early Western church given to any important bishop and in the Eastern church to the bishop of Alexandria. During the 3rd century the title became restricted to the bishop of Rome. His moral authority became partly based on his political preeminence and partly on the fact that both St Peter and St Paul had been martyred in that city. During the following centuries Leo I (440–461), Gregory VII (1073–1085) and Innocent III (1198–1216) claimed increasing power and authority. The climax was reached with Beniface VIII (1294–1303), who in his bull *Unam Sanctam* declared that both the spiritual and temporal power were in the power of the church and the latter was subject to the former and concluded that it is necessary for the salvation (q.v.) of every human being to be subject to the Roman pontiff. One of the essential functions of the bishop of Rome was to convene an ecumenical council, to preside over it (personally or through his delegates) and to approve it. The Orthodox churches (q.v.) developed the view that a council is in fact ecumenical only if the whole church accepts its decisions.

The primacy of the papacy has been emphasized in different ways. Vatican Council I's (q.v.) constitution *Pastor Aeternus* made it clear that the primacy belongs to the *church* of Rome and that it takes effect in the *bishop* of Rome through the exercise of a genuinely episcopal authority that does not restrict the authority of other bishops over their own flock. Vatican Council II (q.v.) argued in a very similar way that in the Roman Catholic Church (q.v.) bishops exercise authority only in union with the Roman pontiff, who "has full, supreme and universal power over the whole church, a power which he can always exercise unhindered . . . Together with their head, the Supreme Pontiff, and never apart from him, the bishops have supreme and full authority over the universal church; but this power cannot be exercised without the agreement of the Roman Pontiff" (*Lumen gentium* 22).

The Orthodox churches have historically always rejected the Roman Catholic doctrine of the primacy of the pope as extraneous to their tradition and to the practice of earlier centuries. The Reformation (q.v.) churches remain alien to the idea of jurisdiction, which attributed to the church an instrumental role in the domain of salvation. Reformed/Presbyterian (q.v.) tradition is less tied to a territorial understanding of the church and stresses instead the relative independence of the ministerial "college". Local synods and national assemblies attended by both clergy and lay delegates are concerned with issues of common interest and exercise varying degrees of authority ever the smaller units. Many congregational traditions such as Baptists (q.v.) have abandoned almost all traditional offices and developed structures like those employed by modern business corporations. The Anglican (q.v.) communion has always sought to be a *via media,* but its "comprehensiveness" covers in fact a very complex situation. It includes trends close to the Roman Catholic conception (high church) and others close to Reformation ecclesiology (evangelical). Anglicanism has always shown itself ready to accord to the pope a primacy of honor (but not jurisdiction) as head of the church in the West, much as the archbishop of Canterbury is accorded a primacy of honor in the Anglican communion.

Although most non-Roman Catholic Christians still today find the historical papacy and its claims uncongenial, not only on the ground that they cannot find satisfactory justification in Scriptures and tradition, but also because this seems to allow for churchly self-aggrandizement, difficult to reconcile with the humility of Jesus Christ (q.v.), many of them are more than before inclined to accept the papal primacy as a pastoral primacy of spiritual responsibility, of charismatic leadership, of moral guidance and active provision for the welfare of the church as a whole. What is important about the Petrine ministry of leadership is not the historical evidence of a line of succession, but a succession in spirit: that is, in the Petrine mission, testimony and service, for the cause of Jesus Christ. Pope John XXIII (q.v.), in the view of leaders of non-Roman Catholic communions, has given the right example. Also, the relationship of "collegiality" (q.v.) that all bishops enjoy toward the pope as a fellow-bishop, without ostensibly affecting his historic claims to be the bishop of bishops and to exercise power over all bishops, should be increasingly strengthened after Vatican II pointed in the right direction. *See also* AUTHORITY; INFALLIBILITY.

PARLIN, CHARLES COOLIDGE (1898–1981). Lawyer, educated at Harvard Law School, financier, and dedicated layman in the ecumenical movement, Parlin was a president of the WCC (q.v.), 1961–1968, and an elected delegate to seven Methodist general conferences, 1940–1964. He was president of the World Methodist Council (q.v.), 1970–1971, secretary of the Methodist Commission on Church Union, 1948–1964, and first vice president of the National Council of the Churches of Christ in the USA (q.v.). He was also chairman of the committee in the USA that raised money for the foundation of the WCC. Parlin attended the first four assemblies of the WCC, was a member of the WCC finance committee, 1948–1968, and chairman of the working committee of the WCC Department of Information. He was a director of the First National City Bank of New York and of other corporations, as well as trustee of Union Theological Seminary, Drew University, American University, Bethune Cookman College and the American Bible Society.

PARMAR, SAMUEL L. (1921–1979). Parmar was a member of the Church of South India. As a brilliant economist and an expert in matters of development he participated in numerous ecumenical conferences. He was chairman of the working committee on Church and Society, member of the Commission of the Churches on International Affairs, vice chairman of the World Student Christian Federation (q.v.), vice chairman of the Student Christian Movement in India, chairman of the Christian Institute for the Study of Religion and Society, Bangalore, member of the executive committee of the National Council of Churches of India, WCC representative on the Committee for Society, Development and Peace, and associate director of the Ecumenical Institute in Bossey (q.v.). He taught international economics at Allahabad University College.

PARTICIPATION. Among the priority areas for WCC programs, the Vancouver assembly (1983) outlined the following priority: "The development of a community of healing and sharing within the WCC and the member churches where women, men, young people and children, able and disabled, clergy and laity (q.v.), *participate fully* and minister to one another should be another priority. Participation implies encounter and sharing with others, working and making decisions together in styles that enhance inclusiveness, and living together as people of God. The Council should continue to examine the roles of both laity and clergy in the churches' mission and witness in the world . . . Laity and disabled (q.v.) persons should be given more opportunities for participation in decision-making bodies of the WCC".

An important issue is, indeed, how to provoke dialogue of the whole people of God on every area of ecumenical concern. In every activity the WCC organizes, it is obliged to confront questions like "how many youth?", "how many women?", "how many laypeople?". When churches select delegates to an assembly (q.v.), they are asked to incorporate all categories as far as possible. That in itself is an educational process. It forces churches to be aware that the ecumenical movement is a matter of the whole people of God, not just a sector representing the rest of the people. There has been improved participation, but it is not enough. It is still believed that not all the right persons out there in that pool of hundreds of millions of members in the member churches are found. Others would say that what has been achieved is not sufficiently positive because they still do not have a chance to participate fully.

Pressure for adequate representation of all kinds of people—also indigenous people as well as the marginalized should be included—has raised questions about the aim of WCC gatherings. The success of the participatory process has been accompanied by new problems and frustrations that were never envisaged when 145 member churches first assembled in Amsterdam in 1948. Many complications surface today whenever the WCC has to allocate assembly seats, appoint members of a presidium or a central committee, compile subunit commissions and working groups or choose staff. The participatory process, demanding that various categories be fully represented, can overshadow the stated aim of the activity or gathering itself. Participation risks becoming engulfed in a sheer computer-process arithmetic. Participation depending on different kinds of events often requires expert knowledge and personal competence. Last but not least, much more work has to be done to involve local pastors and parish priests. If one looks at who takes part in ecumenical activities, one sees bishops and church executives and a fairly wide variety of laypeople. But very few local pastors are ecumenically involved at the international level. This is a very serious weakness. Those pastors are the ones who are in the front line of interpreting the ecumenical ideal to the grass roots. A further complication is the geographical and cultural dynamics and the structural injustices built into the contemporary world, which make people from poor and barely educated countries suspicious and envious of those from rich and well-educated countries. The division here is not between clergy and laity but between advantaged and disadvantaged. *See also* DISABLED; LA-ITY; WOMEN IN CHURCH AND SOCIETY; YOUTH.

PATON, WILLIAM (1886–1943). After six years active as secretary of the World Student Christian Federation (q.v.), 1911–1917, where he met John R. Mott and William Temple (qq.v.), Paton spent a year in India in the service of the YMCA. He served afterward as secretary of the National Council of Churches of India, and in 1927 became secretary of the International Missionary Council (q.v.) preparing for its conferences in Jerusalem (1928) and in Tambaram (1938). His policy of encouragement of full participation of the so-called younger churches was of great significance. His diplomatic skill and organizing ability came into full prominence when, with W. A. Visser 't Hooft (q.v.), he became associate general secretary of the WCC in process of formation in 1938. Paton was deeply involved in the British scene with refugees, Jews, internees and peace aims, where he was an ally of bishop George Bell (q.v.). In his theology he moved from the missiology of the era of John R. Mott to a more confessional ecumenism.

PAUL VI (GIOVANNI BATTISTA MONTINI) (1897–1978). A pattern of moderate progressivism has marked the pontificate of Paul VI as he led the Roman Catholic Church into the post-Vatican II (qq.v.) era. After spending his first years seeing the Council through to its conclusion in 1965, he has devoted himself to making its work effective in the life of the church. He promoted ecumenism, social justice (q.v.), peace (q.v.), liturgical reform, internal change of church structures and general strengthening of church life throughout the world. At the same time, he has warned against radicalism in matters of birth control (*Humanae vitae*, 1968), priestly celibacy (*Sacerdotalis caelibatus*, 1967), the eucharist (q.v.) (*Mysterium fidei*, 1965) and non-ordination of women (q.v.). Paul VI was called "progressive" for his appeals for social justice in developing countries (*Populorum progressio*, 1967), for his teaching on urbanization, racial discrimination, environment (q.v.) and the evolution of Marxism (e.g., *Octogesima adveniens*, 1971) and evangelization of the modern world (*Evangelii nuntiandi,* 1975). Following up his 1964 visit to the holy land and his historic meeting there with the spiritual leader of Eastern Orthodoxy, Athenagoras I (q.v.), he visited Istanbul in 1967 for another meeting with the patriarch and received him at the Vatican later the same year. In 1965 they mutually nullified the anathemas issued by their predecessors against each other in 1054. In 1969 Paul VI visited Geneva to participate in ceremonies marking the 50th anniversary of the International Labour Organization and to visit the headquarters of the WCC (q.v.). He sent a message of commendation to the WCC in 1973 when it observed the 25th anniversary of its founding. He approved of the creation of the Joint Working Group (q.v.) between the Roman Catholic Church and the World Council of Churches in 1965. In carrying out the teaching of Vatican II on collegiality (q.v.), in 1965 he established the Synod of Bishops in Rome, which met in 1967, 1969 and 1971, when it decided to meet every three years. Each time it has received close personal attention from Paul VI.

PAYNE, ERNEST ALEXANDER (1902–1980). Payne studied theology in London, Oxford and Marburg and was ordained pastor in 1928. He was active in the Baptist Missionary Society and was general secretary of the Baptist Union of Great Britain and Ireland, 1951–1967, vice president of the United Society for Christian Literature and of the British and Foreign Bible Society, and chairman of the executive committee of the British Council of Churches, 1962–1971. He served the WCC (q.v.) central committee as vice moderator, 1954–1968, and was a president of the Council, 1968–1975. He functioned as moderator of the committee for the reformulation of the basis of the WCC from 1954 onward. He defended the controversial Program to Combat Racism in his own church. Payne had extensive knowledge of church history and the history of different confessions.

PEACE AND DISARMAMENT. Hardly any other theme and concern has been more constantly, widely and intensively discussed in the ecumenical movement and in the WCC (q.v.) since 1948 than peace and disarmament. The involvement of the various ecumenical constituencies and of many committed individuals has been progressive and staggering. The recognition of this fact leads to the following paradoxical statement. The incessant search of ecumenical Christianity for the solution to the problems of peace and disarmament is encouraging and discouraging, impressive and depressive, comprehensive and eclectic, fearless and fearful, universal and parochial, selfless and selfish, heartwarming and heartbreaking. The more Christians become aware of the intricacies of disarmament and peace, the more they have great difficulty in finding lasting answers in the realms of liberation and reconciliation.

The more the need is felt for a truly united and universal stand of the churches on the burning issue of peace, the more Christians in local situations everywhere need to respond to the challenges of poverty, oppression and survival. The "universal" can become artificial and crushing when the "local" is not authentic and outspoken. The stronger and more convincing the voices of the Christian communities become in all matters of injustice, and of conventional and nuclear war, the more they must express modesty, humility and proportion. The wider the disastrous effects of racism (q.v.), classism and sexism are recognized, the more they are to be related to the healing powers of baptism, eucharist and ministry (qq.v.). The ecumenical movement is still greatly split on this issue. It is extremely difficult to admit that all church's divisions are an integral part of the world's divisions. The absence of justice (q.v.) and peace in the church is an adumbration of the absence of justice and peace among the nations.

There is no developed theology of peace. The worldwide absence of peace and the many forms of injustices are so real that biblical and theological approaches to justice and peace cannot but have a provisional value, particularly in the eschatological kingdom perspective. The Hebrew word *shalom* for the word "peace" designates not only the elimination of conflict but rightness and wholeness—not only peace but justice. The same root is properly translated as liberation, salvation (q.v.). It denotes things as they should be and shall be in the divine purpose. The vision of Isaiah 2 and Micah 4 promises that peoples will "no longer learn war" because "the oracle of Yahweh will go out from Jerusalem".

The first WCC assembly in Amsterdam in 1948 included such affirmations as "war is contrary to the will of God" and "peace requires an attack on the causes of conflict between the powers". The assembly could not reach an agreement, however, on the question of whether war can be an act of justice. The Evanston assembly in 1954 emphasized the relation of justice and peace at the national and international levels and encouraged "a continuing effort to reach agreement on outstanding issues, such as the peace treaties and disarmament" and "readiness to submit all unresolved questions of conflict to an impartial international organization and to carry out its decisions". During this period of the ecumenical movement, many rather general, diplomatic and consensus statements on peace were issued. The armaments race was acknowledged, yet it was rather superficially analyzed. An incredible escalation in arms production and distribution was not anticipated.

It was only from the late 1960s onward that it was increasingly realized that the tensions and conflicts between East and West, and North and South, are intimately related to one another and condition each other. There can be no peace without justice, and there will be no justice without peace. The powerful and the powerless nations are both caught in the web of defense and exploitation. Domination and destruction are two sides of the same coin. There is no peace where justice is not maintained. The Uppsala assembly in 1968 was preoccupied with the concentration of nuclear weapons in the hands of a few nations. Only in the Vancouver assembly was the rejection of nuclear war to find clear expression in ecumenical documents.

The Churches as Peacemakers?—An Analysis of Recent Church Statements on Peace, Disarmament and War (1988) notes that numerous public pronouncements on war and peace are so different in style, structure and contents that they render a methodological convergence quite impossible. All positions, to be sure, are for the prevention of atomic war, a mutual and verifiable halt to the testing, production and deployment of nuclear weapons as a necessary step toward disarmament, a new international order based on justice for all and within every nation, an encouragement to establish nuclear free zones in various parts of the world. Furthermore, many churches see the urgent need for deeper reflection on the possibilities of nonviolent resistance and nonviolent use of civil disobedience. Recommendations to provide for educational peace programs rank high on church agendas. There is an insistence on establishing a theology and ministry of peace-making on many levels.

But all these serious intentions and lofty proposals are conditioned by inertia and illusion since the two main sub-traditions of Christian ethical thought—pacifism and just war (qq.v.) doctrine—are much divided by the dilemma of nuclear deterrence. The just war theory became part of Christianity 1,500 years ago as a consequence of the Constantinian settlement of the roles of church and state (q.v.). Still today, the more structured and institutional churches, like the Roman Catholic, Anglican, Lutheran and Reformed churches (qq.v.) claim, to some extent at least, their traditional attachment to the just war doctrine. The reality of sin residing both in human hearts and in human institutions has made the use of coercive force at times in history morally justified, as a lesser evil. The conviction that war is possible and justified on moral grounds, even necessary in the name of justice, remains intact. The first use of nuclear weapons and retaliatory action indiscriminately wiping out innumerable innocent lives, to be sure, are condemned. But the acceptance of deterrence on strict conditions and as a temporary expedient leading to progressive disarmament is still a widely accepted view in many Christian camps.

There are also the more or less pacifist voices of churches, which reject the idea of nuclear deterrence, though they may differ in attitudes toward a defensive war with conventional weapons and should not be synchronized with the position of historical peace churches, such as Mennonites and Quakers (qq.v.). The traditional just war doctrine for a number of Christian communities has become totally invalid. By supporting the present irrational arms race Christians are guilty of sin and disobedience to God and invite his judgment upon the world. The attitude toward weapons of mass destruction should be solely determined by the Christian faith. It is a question of affirming or denying the gospel itself. By 1990 a world consensus against nuclear armaments seemed stronger than any pacifist movement had been in world history. This was, however, despite the cheerleading from many Christians, totally a secular pacifism. Today national civil wars and destructive rivalries between ethnic majorities and minorities, again reinforced by different religious allegiances—as in ex-Yugoslavia—and the impotence of nations and churches to intervene in monstrous massacres, are the order of the day. In the ecumenical movement the present system of cooperating and competing confessional bureaucracies cannot channel the shared commitments to the restored vision of wholeness that *shalom* demands. *See also* INTERNATIONAL ORDER; JUST WAR; JUSTICE; MILITARISM; PACIFISM; VIOLENCE AND NONVIOLENCE.

PENTECOSTAL CHURCHES. The Pentecostal movement began in the first years of the 20th century among believers who sought a baptism in the Holy Spirit (qq.v.) accompanied by speaking in tongues along the lines recorded in Acts. The movement spread rapidly. It received its greatest impetus in the British Isles between 1925 and 1935 under the fervent preaching of Welsh evangelists Stephen and George Jeffreys. It attained its greatest dimensions in North America, South America, especially Brazil and Chile, and Scandinavia. The total world membership is over 7 million.

Pentecostal Christians are characterized by a distinctive emphasis on sanctification that includes a conversion (q.v.) process in which an adult makes a decision or has a conversion experience, a cleansing from sin, or justification, and a renewal of the gifts of Pentecost consequent to baptism, especially the climatic charismata of glossolalia and faith healing. The Bible is the sole doctrinal authority. Some of the Pentecostal churches celebrate the Lord's supper (q.v.), but allow a free interpretation of its significance. Many practice foot washing as part of divine ordinances. Good works, as part of the spirit-filled life and as a preparation for the coming of the Lord, are urged on all Pentecostalists. These include visiting the sick, strengthening the weak, encouraging the fainthearted and pointing out the way of salvation (q.v.). The Pentecostal ethos prescribes a strict abstinence from indulgence in worldly pleasures and the support of the church through tithes. Members are discouraged from participating in war, destroying property or injuring human life. Worship is informal rather than ritualistic or liturgical, and freedom is encouraged. Government is generally along the lines of congregational polity, although in some instances the organization of the church includes district conferences, annual conferences and a general conference. Missionary (q.v.) work is vigorously carried on at home and in many foreign countries under the guidance of local or denominational missionary boards.

Differences between the various Pentecostal churches made it difficult to establish international community. The first Pentecostal World Conference was held in Zurich in 1947. During the second World Conference in Paris in 1949 the idea of a permanent world organization was rejected. The conferences in London, 1952, and in Stockholm, 1955, showed greater openness to other churches. Now held every three years, the conferences are largely celebratory occasions that center on worship, testimonies and inspirational preaching, without any forum for public debate.

Pentecostals have generally been hostile to the ecumenical movement, which they perceive as embracing the apostate, and stigmatize it as merely human efforts to organize institutional unity. This opposition has been less marked in Latin America, with two Chilean Pentecostal churches joining the WCC (q.v.) in 1961, followed in 1969 by the large Evangelical Pentecostal Church "Brazil for Christ". The vision of baptism in the Spirit promoting Christian unity (q.v.), found among some early Pentecostals, has been kept alive especially by David Du Plessis (q.v.) who attended all the WCC assemblies from Evanston onward and constantly labored to gain official denominational support for the international Catholic-Pentecostal dialogue (q.v.). As a matter of fact, since 1972 conversations with the Roman Catholic Church (the Secretariat for Promoting Christian Unity)

(qq.v.) have taken place. *See also* CHARISMATIC MOVE-
MENT.

PEOPLE OF GOD. In the Old Testament, "people of God"
designates the calling and mission of Israel as the people
elected by God from among all the peoples. The people is not
a collective entity in which the individual completely loses
his identity; but neither is each single member an "individual" who is only interested in his or her salvation (q.v.). The
Old Testament conception of the relationship between people and individual can be appropriately described neither by
the term "collectivism" nor by that of "individualism": at
most it can be described as "solidarity". Furthermore, the
people of God is not a static organization, but an organism
that is constantly developing, renewing itself, at times too, it
must be admitted, becoming sick and transforming itself, but
in the last analysis immortal by reason of the promises made
to it. For, even when the visible Israel of the Old Covenant
has vanished, the ideal Israel still remains, the holy
"remnant" of those who will come through judgment and
penance to receive life from God and to experience the
fulfillment of the promises brought by the Messiah, the
mediator and servant of God par excellence. Thus the
Christian community is the "true" people of God of the end
times, founded by the self-offering of Jesus Christ (q.v.) and
united by the Spirit of God.

The image of the church as the "people of God" has a
clear ecclesiological advantage over other images of the
church. It views the nature of the church in its historical
setting, determined by its relation to the kingdom of God. The
image of the people of God presupposes the active participation of all members of the church, while also pointing to the
unity of the church and finally of all humankind. One can
quite well envisage the possibility of calling humanity itself
the people of God. It is not just the natural substratum of the
people of God, in whatever sense one takes this term.
Humanity is a unity by reason of its origin and its destiny. It
has only one history, to which Jesus Christ belongs. All
human beings are comprised in the universal salvific will of
God. Hence humanity as a unity and a totality, prior to the

personal decision of the individual and prior to the formation
of the church, is something constituted by the gracious act of
God in Jesus Christ.

According to Vatican II (q.v.), membership of the church
can be at various levels, and thus the notion of the church
admits degrees. It can be taken in a broad or narrow sense. If
one speaks of the "church" without qualification, one might
confine oneself to the strictest and fullest sense of the word
"church". This is the Roman Catholic usage, as reflected in
Lumen Gentium (8), where it is said that *the church* "subsists" in the Catholic Church. It is therefore desirable to use
the term "people of God" to designate the further implications of the notion of church, taken in its widest sense. But
then the question remains as to whether baptism (q.v.) must
be included among these necessary factors, or whether
justification (q.v.) is sufficient, this being possible without
baptism of water.

Facing various ecumenical ecclesiological questions, the
WCC (q.v.) has likewise adopted "people of God" as an
image of the church. In *Baptism, Eucharist and Ministry*
(q.v.), the understanding of ministry (q.v.) is developed on
the basis of the opening declaration that "God calls the
whole of humanity to become God's people" (M1). The
mission of the church to proclaim the kingdom of God (q.v.)
in the world is founded on this calling. Missionary movements have often neglected to invite people of other faiths
and no faith to become part of the people of God, which
would enable them to become Christian without social
dislocation, while remaining in full contact with their non-
Christian relatives, thus enabling other groups of that people
(tribe, caste or section of society) across the years, after
suitable instruction, to confess Jesus Christ and be formed
into sound churches. What really should take place is
multi-individual mutually interdependent conversion. Each
member of the group becoming Christian participates in the
decision to follow Christ, while observing others of his or her
kin making similar decisions at the same time. Thus, the
church as the people of God will not be locked up in many
geographic, linguistic and denominational pockets.

Several WCC programs are not related to the role, the

condition and the struggles of "the people", particularly in countries where they are dominated and exploited. The phrase "theology by the people" was coined at the WCC assembly in Vancouver (1983). This slogan arises from the rediscovery of the church as the people of God. The clericalization of the church has been the model for a long time. The sentence that the church is "a chosen race, a royal priesthood, a holy nation, God's own people, that you may declare the wonderful deeds of him who called you out of darkness into his marvellous light" (1 Peter 2:9) has gained a new significance. The term "theology by the people" carries some new assumptions and implications. If Holy Scripture is the source of revelation, it is also claimed that people's experiences can be a source of revelation. While a relevant and authentic theology may reflect a particular temporal situation, it must nevertheless retain the biblical as well as the transcendental dimension as a frame of reference. *See also* LAITY; MINISTRY; VATICAN COUNCIL II.

PHILIP, ANDRE (1902–1970). Philip was one of the main speakers of the Geneva Church and Society conference (1966), the Montreux conference on development (1970), and Uppsala (1968). He was professor of law in Lyons. In 1941 he joined De Gaulle in London and held the post of commissioner of the interior. After the war he became the minister of national economy in the first new French government, leaving the Socialist party when the war broke out in Algeria. In 1958 Philip was appointed professor of economics at the Sorbonne in Paris and became one of the leaders of the European movement for unification as the chairman of the ecumenical committee on European cooperation. He was president of the commission on international affairs of the Federation of Protestant Churches in France.

PITTINGER, NORMAN (1905–). Pittinger taught for thirty-three years at General Theological Seminary in New York City before going to England where he became senior resident at King's College, Cambridge University, from which he is now retired. He was chairman of the North American section on Christ and the Church, which submitted its report to the fourth world conference on Faith and Order in Montreal (1963). Author of more than 75 books, Pittinger is particularly noted for his works on the eucharist and Christology (qq.v.) and for his interest in process theology. This process orientation resulted in a strong emphasis on the development of Christian doctrine through the centuries and on the need to reformulate these doctrines in each new age.

PLURALISM, RELIGIOUS. For centuries it has been customary in the West to accept the authority of only one religion in one country. This kind of attitude was due to the continuous spread of Christianity throughout Europe until the whole continent professed the Christian religion. There were some religious minorities, but these were hardly tolerated, and even persecuted. In the East, however, religions have coexisted for a long time. In India Hindu, Muslim, Jain, Sikh communities and Christian minorities tolerated one another. In China Confucianism, Taoism and Buddhism coexisted and mutually influenced one another. In Japan religious tradition was based both on Shintoism and Buddhism. This multi-religious situation is referred to today as "religious pluralism", which has become a normal phenomenon in many countries. Obviously the question of the inter-relationship of various religions is raised. A dominant religion can no more exercise authority over the rest. The plurality of religious traditions must be seen as both the result of the manifold ways God relates to peoples and nations and a manifestation of the richness and diversity of humankind. As never before all world religions have no other choice than to speak of the paradox of the certainty of universal salvation (q.v.). On the one hand, it seems impossible to know of universal salvation without some absolute principle of certainty, and yet, on the other hand, it seems impossible to have universal salvation once such a principle is adopted.

Although the WCC (q.v.) continues to work out a fresh approach to a theology of religious pluralism, and although Vatican II (q.v.) emphasized the recognition of a religious plurality, by replacing compulsion with freedom, Christianity is still often afraid or reserved to cross the frontier of its own religion and civilization. This should not come as a surprise as for almost two millenia Christians have been engaged in a religious monologue. In a consultation in Baar, Switzerland, in 1990, sponsored by the WCC Sub-unit on Dialogue with People of Living Faiths, Orthodox, Roman Catholic and Protestant (qq.v.) theologians discussed the theological significance of the other world religions. The consultation issued a statement: "Religious Plurality: Theological Perspectives and Affirmations". "We affirm that God has been present in the seeking and finding (of other religions), that there is truth and wisdom in their teachings, and love and holiness in their living, this like any wisdom, insight, knowledge, understanding, love and holiness that is found among us in the gift of the Holy Spirit. We also affirm that God is with them as they struggle, along with us, for justice and liberation". It remains to be seen how the challenge of religious pluralism and the praxis of dialogue (q.v.) will become part of the context in which Christians search for fresh understandings, new questions and better expressions of their faith and commitment. *See also* DIALOGUE WITH PEOPLE OF LIVING FAITHS.

PNEUMATOLOGY *see* HOLY SPIRIT

PONTIFICAL COMMISSION JUSTICE AND PEACE. In the 1967 *motu proprico* "Catholicam Christi ecclesiam", Pope Paul VI (q.v.) established the Pontifical Commission for Justice and Peace. In the document, the pope stated the general purpose of the commission: "Its aim shall be to arouse the People of God (q.v.) to full awareness of its mission at the present time, in order on the one hand, to promote the progress of needy nations and encourage international social justice, and on the other, to help underdeveloped nations to work for their own development". Initially the Pontifical Commission Justice and Peace was set up for a five-year period, with Cardinal Maurice Roy of Quebec City as its president and Joseph Gremillion (q.v.) as its secretary. During this period, the commission, with a full-time staff and twenty-five members and consultants, defined its wide-ranging task aided by the encyclical *Populorum progressio.*

The Pontifical Commission is an advisory, not a deliberative agency, and makes as such recommendations to the pope through the Vatican secretary of state. In addition, it has developed a close liaison with superiors general of major religious orders and congregations of men and women for whom social action in their pastoral programs has a high priority. The commission, jointly with the WCC (q.v.), established the exploratory Committee on Society, Development and Peace (SODEPAX) (q.v.), thus highlighting the importance of issues such as development, peace and human rights (qq.v.) for the ecumenical movement. In 1980 this joint venture came to an end.

PONTIFICAL COUNCIL FOR PROMOTING CHRISTIAN UNITY see SECRETARIAT FOR PROMOTING CHRISTIAN UNITY

POOR/POVERTY. It is only from 1968 onward that the worldwide phenomenon of the poor suffering from extreme poverty and its possible eradication has become a major concern in the ecumenical movement. Before the WCC Uppsala assembly (qq.v.) the slogan "the rich are becoming richer and the poor are becoming poorer" could not have been coined and would have fallen on deaf ears. The whole debate on development of the last twenty-five years must be seen in the light, or rather in the darkness, of the churches' endorsement of colonialism and neocolonialism, and its divorce from the agricultural and working classes, which go hand in hand. They did not draw the consequences from their estrangement of the masses of the poor and the exploited for more than two centuries. Christianity clearly did not succeed in taking adequate account of the demands made on it by the unexpected development of new economic and social conditions and adjust its mission and ministry (qq.v.) accordingly.

Throughout the period of Western industrialization of the 19th century, the structures of the church institutions, with minor adjustments, continued to be those of the preindustrial world. Instead of listening to the pleas of the underprivileged classes, the churches stood aside and remained isolated from the radical developments that were taking place. The gulf between the growing marginal population and the Christian middle-class institutions widened. The loss of memory has led the Christian communities too easily and too quickly to believe that they have caught up with their questionable past and now do behave as a kind of avant-garde for the sake of the poor and marginalized. It remains a striking fact that in spite of many ecumenical documents the WCC central committee never engaged in a thorough discussion of poverty. Only after 28 meetings in 1976 did it adopt a report of the review committee in which world poverty was mentioned among the words of injustice, waste and deprivation. The Ecumenical Institute in Bossey (q.v.), which sponsored numerous consultations and seminars, never sponsored a conference on worldwide poverty and its disastrous consequences.

In the third report, *Towards a Church of the Poor,* published by the Commission on the Churches' Participation in Development, a number of disturbing questions come forcibly to the fore: Do the verbs align, develop, support, activate and commit still not connote a past paternalistic and condescending attitude? Are not other agencies than the churches' organs better equipped to practice a solidarity with the struggles of the poor? How did unjust structures of society come into being? Who contributed to them and who prolonged them? Are the churches not jointly guilty? Do the poor need the alignment of the churches with their fate? Can they have confidence in the effectiveness of the churches' networks? Are liberation movements of poor and exploited people not manipulated or threatened by powerful leftist or rightist regimes with which churches tacitly identify? These and other questions show that it is very difficult to speak of relations and interactions between the institutional churches and millions of poor people wherever they are to be found. They are in fact often unrelated to one another and seldom truly serve each other in spite of the rediscovery of the liberating force of the Bible and God's clear preferential option for the poor.

A vital and natural link between *Baptism, Eucharist and Ministry* and the concept of the ''church of the poor'' still needs to be established. It has become increasingly clear that the sacraments of baptism and the eucharist (qq.v.) are effective antidotes against all status distinctions and against the separation of the communities of the powerful and the powerless in the church and in the world. Baptism makes living and dignified people out of poor and starving people. Their baptism in the dying and risen Lord takes place in order that their righteousness may be revealed. Baptism is the prerequisite for freely joining liberation movements and church-based communities (q.v.) in order that more justice (q.v.) be obtained and genuine personhood and authentic humanity in Christ become visible. The eucharist is the sacrament through which all sins are forgiven, all human weaknesses are healed and all frustrations of poverty are overcome. Eating Christ's body and drinking his blood puts an end to the indulgence in the life to come of the rich and kindles a spirituality of the poor. At the Lord's table it becomes clear that the unity (q.v.) of the church is only cheap grace when rich and poor come together remaining affluent and destitute. The Lord's supper rules out all unrestrained profit-centered economy. It is the banquet of both the spiritually and materially poor. "The eucharist celebration demands reconciliation and sharing among all those regarded as brothers and sisters in the one family of God and is a constant challenge in the search for appropriate relationships in social, economic and political life" (BEM, M20).

The precarious language of "the church in solidarity with the poor" and "the church of the poor" has never been tested in the ecumenical dialogue with people of other living faiths and ideologies (q.v.). No bilateral or multilateral dialogue (qq.v.), sponsored by the WCC, has made poverty and the fate of the poor a subject of inter-religious discussion. No attempt has been made to discuss with Marxists their key concept of the "dictatorship of the proletariat", the necessary length of that dictatorship, and the ecumenical rediscovery of the ministry of the poor. The absence of the poor in inter-religious and secular encounters indicates that the ecumenical movement is not ready yet to draw some fundamental theological consequences from its present predicament. When Christians confuse "alienation from the church" with "separation from God", they deny both the reality and the efficacy of Christ's cross and resurrection.

God in Christ has once and for all laid claim to the world, and shown the extent of his love for it, especially for those who are in dire need. Nothing can be placed beyond the range of his redemption (q.v.), neither by the greed and lust for power of human beings nor by the indifference of Christians.

The complex, creative and urgent character of ecumenical reflection on poverty has become abundantly clear. This debate rests on differing analyses and assumptions, whether economic, political, anthropological or sociological. But ecumenical documents in the final examination reveal that the issues of the poor and their poverty ultimately entail a moral, spiritual and theological debate as well. *See also* DEVELOPMENT.

POPULATION POLICY. Population growth has been a growing concern in the ecumenical movement from 1950 onward. The WCC Evanston assembly (qq.v.) (1954) stated, "Many underdeveloped countries, especially in Asia, are very densely populated in relation to their resources. Redistribution of population nationally and internationally, family planning and birth control are burning questions. The profound ethical, political and social issues which they raise need to be courageously examined and guidance should be given by the churches". In his book, *The Population Explosion and Christian Responsibility* (1959), Richard M. Fagley (q.v.), on the staff of the Commission of the Churches on International Affairs, was the first to address the problem of population growth from an ecumenical perspective. Subsequent world gatherings considered various aspects of the population question. The world and the church, it was said, must consider realistically the fact that for the year 2000 the world population is projected at from 5.5 to 7.5 billion, depending on the extent to which birth rates are reduced. The problem of feeding and employing these people must be faced. The very specter of hunger and of the waste of human resources has become ever present. Hence there is an urgent need for the rapid dissemination of birth control information and techniques.

The Uppsala assembly (1968) fully addressed the challenge of the population problem, emphasizing the enormous task facing the nations. The church must always put its work in this field in the context of responsible parenthood, and not simply that of the limitation of families. Overemphasis on the technical aspects of population control can result in dehumanization. It was regretted that some specialized agencies of the United Nations (q.v.) do not speak and act more openly on the whole issue, and that many developing countries have been slow to seek such international assistance as is available. Churches should challenge people and organizations to support private groups giving assistance with the population problem. They should also continue their study and research in this field and be prepared to act where others can or will not do so. The WCC central committee received in 1973 the report of an international study of the related problems of population policy, social justice and the quality of life. This report was submitted as the WCC's contribution to the UN-sponsored world population conference in Bucharest in 1974, and remains the most important statement of the WCC on the population issue. From Nairobi (1975) onward WCC assemblies did not do much more than mention the problem in relation to economic development (q.v.) and the sustainability of society.

Since most of the programs involve methods of family planning regarded in Roman Catholic (q.v.) teaching as illicit, opposition from Catholic governments and religious groups has been strong; increasingly, however, there have been many signs of greater accommodation with regard to public policies, which reflect differing religious and ethical points of view. The types of intergovernmental assistance that are coming forth are largely those not immediately related to family planning: help in the statistical field, medical research and training, support for public health and education programs. Emphasis on such forms of indirect aid decreases the dangers of international misunderstanding and helps to reduce religious controversy. Nevertheless, the problem remains whether particular families, regions, tribes or nations and their future are not being sacrificed in the search for an overall solution to the general and universal human problem. If one policy is needed for the world as a whole, should worldwide attempts be made to enforce such a policy?

POTTER, PHILIP ALFORD (1921–). Potter was a Methodist lay preacher and a lawyer in the Caribbean, 1940–1943, studied theology in Jamaica and London and participated in the second world conference of Christian youth in Oslo in 1947. He was a staff member of the WCC (q.v.) Youth Department, 1954–1958, and became its director in 1958. He was president of the World Student Christian Federation (q.v.), 1960–1968. As a Methodist Missionary Society overseas secretary, he was active in the International Missionary Council (q.v.) during integration with the WCC, and in 1967 he was appointed director of the WCC Division of World Mission and Evangelism. He succeeded Eugene C. Blake (q.v.) as third general secretary of the WCC, 1972–1984. Potter was an outspoken representative of churches in the Third World, an advocate of justice (q.v.), the combat of racism (q.v.) and the promotion of the role of women in church and society. An eloquent and forceful speaker and leader of Bible studies, he was honored with a doctors degree by the University of Hamburg and several other honorary degrees and awards. A central committee resolution honoring Potter on his departure identified some main thrusts the WCC owed to his leadership: "the insistence on the fundamental unity of Christian witness and Christian service which the gospel commands and makes possible, the correlation of faith and action, the inseparable connection between the personal spiritual life of believers and their obedient action in the world".

POWER, ECUMENICAL PERSPECTIVES ON. Christian theology has often made the mistake of assuming that any exercise of power is sinful; sin has to be more with the manner in which power is exercised. Power undoubtedly corrupts, but the unwillingness or inability to use power also corrupts. By using power human beings order common life, determine the goals of society and become responsible for the distribution of its goods. Not to share in this power implies not to share in the life of the community. Since sharing in the commonwealth is an indispensable condition for human life, misusing or being deprived of power reduces human beings to less than being human. The problem of power has long been a key issue for theological ethics. There is no single biblical view of state power. In the Old Testament royal power without qualification was not applied to the kings of Israel and Judah. Kings were appointed and dethroned by the will of the people and the army, often on the basis of prophetic initiative. In the New Testament Luke and Acts accept the legitimacy of the power of the Roman empire almost uncritically. There have been many misinterpretations of Romans 13. St Paul clearly argued that Christians, who claimed to be exonerated from obeying the state, because Jesus alone was their Lord and King, were wrong. They should obey the secular authorities and laws as all other citizens. In Revelations 13 the Roman state becomes the servant of the dragon (the devil) and takes on the appearance of a horrible beast. But its days are numbered because God will not permit his apostate servant to reign for a long time.

Among the modern theologians, Reinhold Niebuhr (q.v.) attempted to grasp the complexity of the issue of power in its religious and secular context. Power is good and necessary as the response of human ingenuity to its Creator, he said. But it is also the source of evil in the world as "the will to live becomes the will to power", which knows no limits to its desire for domination and exploitation. The first task of human society is, therefore, to avert the judgment of God and human destruction by balancing power against power in order to achieve a relative justice. History will be, until its very end, the history of various forms of political, economic, religious and military power struggling to achieve tentative forms of justice (q.v.), but at the same time new forms of domination will arise, subject to new counter power and change, challenged and humbled by the mercy of God in the servanthood and sacrifice of Jesus Christ (q.v.). Niebuhr laid a valid foundation for an ecumenical understanding of power by criticizing both the assumed continuity between divine and human power in liberal Christianity and the dualism of orthodox theology, which had a traditional dialectical understanding of sin and grace (q.v.) in the human power struggles.

In the framework of the "responsible society" (q.v.) the Amsterdam assembly (q.v.) (1948) stated: "It is required that the people have freedom to control, to criticize and to change their governments, that power be made responsible by law and tradition, and be distributed as widely as possible through the whole community''. Therefore "any denial to the human being of an opportunity to participate in the shaping of society'' must be condemned. Quoting the Oxford conference on Church, Community and State in 1937 that "there can be for the Christian no ultimate authority but very God'', the Evanston assembly in 1954 outlined that "justice requires the development of political institutions which are humane as they touch on the lives of people, which provide by law against the arbitrary use of power''. The Geneva world conference on Church and Society in 1966 dealt extensively with power in a subsection "Power and the State—Especially in Developed Countries''. "We see that 'direct democracy'—in the sense that complicated decisions may be made by a referendum of citizens—is increasingly obstructive of decisionmaking, even in the best educated societies. Yet we cannot indulge in an idolatry of experts. The necessity of delegation of power, so obvious in our world, makes it all the more important that the few who make decisions, should be held accountable to the people, who themselves retain the ultimate right of decision over their destinies''.

Section VI of the Nairobi assembly was entitled: "Human Development: Ambiguities of Power, Technology and Quality of Life''. In it the assembly called the churches to a serious self-criticism of their economic, political and ideological role in their own societies. They should examine their interest in and concern for: 1) social justice; 2) peaceful coexistence of nations; 3) participation in people's organizations; 4) participation in an educational process that will develop critical awareness in order to shape the features of a new society. An international consultation on political ethics, held in Cyprus in 1981, and organized by the Commission on the Churches' Participation in Development, concentrated in particular on questions of people's power, legitimacy and power, people's participation in politics, structures of participation and action. It noted that "people's power becomes decisive when it grows to the point of a consolidated people's organization based on awareness of the unjust situation, clarity of goals and commitment to structural corporate action . . . Through the pooling of forces, powerlessness can become meaningful political power''.

A high sensitivity has grown in the ecumenical movement that the incontrollability, irrationality and inhumanness of concentrated political, economic, technological and military power conditioning internationally one another in the contemporary world needs a very careful analysis and evaluation. As the concept of national security depends increasingly on a system of keeping the power of the enemy in check and eventually destroying the enemy with all possible means, political systems thriving on hostility and attack and justifying the concentration of power in the hands of a few need to be critically examined. Contrary to what many affirm, apocalyptic faith is not exclusively pessimistic, dualistic or escapist. The tradition of the faith is realistic because it reveals that within and behind the power struggles there are cosmic powers at work. Only God's judgment and a new act of creation can change the state of this world.

In his book *The Contradiction of Christianity,* David E. Jenkins (q.v.) deals with aspects of power in the perspective of radical spirituality and radical politics and in a discussion on the contradiction of violence. ''Radical repentance, radical change and radical distribution of power and privilege are overwhelmingly required by the realities of the kingdom of God (q.v.) and the possibilities of being human . . . If we are ever to get a state of equilibrium in which we are all fulfilled in each other and can enjoy all (a creative Kingdom of love) than there must be a power at work which will *absorb* powerful power rather than *counter* power with power . . . To build any creative human society (and not one which is just a repetition of an old power-structure with the components arranged differently) it is *literally* necessary to love your enemy in class struggle, the revolution, the schism''. And Charles C. West (q.v.), who wrote *The Power to Be Human,* admonishes the ecumenical movement with the following words: ''The power of God is self-limited by covenant with the people of God (qq.v.), implicitly with the whole creation as well. It is an open-ended covenant filled with promise, a covenant redeemed even when human beings in their power struggles seek to destroy it. Under the risen Christ and looking to his coming, it is a promising covenant fulfilled in the service of one another and appreciative use of creation around us. The exercise of power in this responsibility is an ecumenical art we are only beginning to learn''.

PRAYER. Since the earliest days of Israelite religion prayer was spontaneous and natural, however formalized it may have become in later Judaism. The Psalms exemplify the direct approach of Israel to God. Whether individually or corporately, Jews poured out all their concerns to God. Such spontaneous address was possible only because God was essentially ''Thou'', the one who expects a response from those to whom he revealed himself. Jesus and his disciples inherited this long tradition of intimate personal dialogue with God. But Jesus introduced an even more direct relationship as he made use of the most private family address, *Abba*-Father. The seven petitions included in the prayer that he taught his disciples indicate what he considered to be the seven most important things about which Christians should pray.

The World Day of Prayer, founded in the USA in 1887 in response to needs following the Civil War and for prayer for missions overseas, has developed over the years into a worldwide movement, composed mainly of women, who engage in ''informed prayer and prayerful action'' on behalf of the needs of the whole world. The worship of early ecumenical conferences and assemblies remained traditional as the various church leaders shared their own denominational treasures. It was not until 1968 that the WCC Uppsala assembly (qq.v.) faced the reality of the ever-changing world situation and demanded a realignment of prayer and theology. It stated: ''Since the church should make clear its solidarity with the world, corporate worship and prayer alike should draw into themselves, with thanksgiving and faith, all the joys and sorrows, the achievements, doubts and frustrations of mankind today''. Churches were invited to observe Monday, July 15, as ''a day of prayer and fasting as a symbol of commitment to sacrificial action in a world where millions of fellow human beings are hungry and starving''. The wide-reaching changes initiated at Vatican II have allowed considerable participation of Roman Catholics (qq.v.) in ecumenical prayer, wherever it is appropriate.

There is wide agreement today that if the expression of solidarity worldwide is a "horizontal" image of the WCC's vocation, its inseparable counterpart is intercession. As a fellowship of solidarity moving toward unity (q.v.), the churches need to discover and to support each other. What better way to grow into such unity than bearing one another's burden first of all in prayer? Unless the church is the place of intercession for the entire world, its prayer can be selfish. Prayer vigils are vital to the ecumenical movement. Today, the annual Week of Prayer for Christian Unity (q.v.) is the oldest manifestation of ecumenical concern that systematically reaches toward all Christian congregations (and the most substantial endeavor in which the Roman Catholic Church is fully involved with the WCC). Recognizing the importance of interceding specially for individual churches, the WCC's *Ecumenical Prayer Cycle* provides brief information about the churches in every nation and a weekly schedule by which Christians all around the world can pray for those in the same single geographical area at the same time. The prayer cycle is both a fruit of ecumenical solidarity and an instrument to root that solidarity more deeply. *See also* SPIRITUALITY; WEEK OF PRAYER FOR CHRISTIAN UNITY; WORSHIP.

PRESBYTERIAN AND REFORMED CHURCHES. The term is sometimes taken to include all the Protestant churches that have accepted the principles of the Reformation (q.v.), but in a narrower and more accurate sense it is used specifically of the Calvinist bodies, as contrasted especially with the Lutherans (q.v.). All adhere, with some variation, to a form of ecclesiastical polity wherein the church is governed by presbyters. Its proponents in the 16th and 17th centuries did not regard it as an innovation but as a rediscovery of the apostolic model found in the New Testament. According to Calvin the primitive church had four different offices: pastor, doctor or teacher, deacon, and presbyter or elder. He recognized, however, that other offices might be adopted. Synods consist of members of several presbyteries within a large area. The general assembly is the supreme legislative and administrative body.

The primary presupposition of the Reformed churches is that the risen Christ is the only head of the church. He rules his people by his word and Spirit. Thus, there is no stress on a special elite group that has received through direct revelation or by the laying on of hands extraordinary powers of authority (q.v.). Doctrines are traditionally Calvinistic. Worship (q.v.) is simple, orderly and dignified, with an emphasis upon the preaching and hearing of the word of God. Only a few churches have weekly celebration of the eucharist (q.v.); monthly celebration or four times a year is not uncommon. The level of education required for the Presbyterian minister is traditionally long and high. Churches in Holland, France, Switzerland, Hungary and other European countries carry the name "Reformed". In Anglo-Saxon countries the name "Presbyterian" is more common. There are large Presbyterian churches in South Africa, New Zealand, Australia, Indonesia and Korea. After the Roman Catholic Church (q.v.), the Reformed churches are the most widely spread throughout the world.

Twenty-one Reformed and Presbyterian churches meeting in London in 1875 officially constituted "The Alliance of the Reformed Churches throughout the World holding the Presbyterian System". At that time, it was mainly a grouping of European and North American churches. In 1949 the International Congregational Council (q.v.) was formally established. At Nairobi in 1970, the two organizations, Reformed and Congregational, came together in the new World Alliance of Reformed Churches (WARC). At the time of this merger the Alliance had 114 member churches in 70 countries. It currently includes 175 churches in 84 countries with an estimated 70 million communicant members. Nearly two-thirds of the churches are in Africa, Asia and Latin America; most are minority churches. About forty churches of the WARC member churches are engaged in union negotiations. Leaders of the Reformed family of churches were among the pioneers of the WCC (q.v.). Ecumenism has shaped the work and witness of the Alliance. Broadly speaking, the Reformed ethos considers that every church is a particular expression of the one universal church of Jesus Christ (q.v.); each community of faith contributes to the life of the whole. This underlying principle has led succeeding executive committees and staff to promote ecumenism and church unity (q.v.) wherever possible. Regional needs and growing membership have given rise to area organizations within the Alliance. Two areas are structured—the European and North American. The central offices of the WARC are located in the Ecumenical Center in Geneva. Besides the general secretariat, the secretariats of the two departments on theology, and cooperation and witness, are also housed here.

PRIBILLA, MAX (FRIEDRICH ALBERT) (1884–1956). A Jesuit, Pribilla made a single and significant contribution to the early ecumenical movement, by studying its origins and manifesting a sympathetic interest in the theology of reunion. A pioneer in the Una Sancta movement (q.v.), Pribilla was a spokesman of resistance to National Socialism. He was professor of ethics at Munich, 1908–1909, and then in Valkenburg (the Netherlands). Due to his convictions of freedom and responsibility, and his service as a chaplain in the First World War, he became interested in interconfessional approaches to social ethics. His death prevented him from exercising an influence on the Second Vatican Council (q.v.). He was editor of *Die Eine Kirche.*

PRIMACY *see* PAPACY/PRIMACY

PROGRAM ON THEOLOGICAL EDUCATION *see* THEOLOGICAL EDUCATION FUND

PROSELYTISM. The word proselyte comes from the Greek word *proselutos* meaning "one who has come over" and consequently a convert to a faith not originally his or her own. In the New Testament it referred to a Gentile who had been converted to Judaism by Jewish missionary activity and became a Jew by undergoing circumcision. Proselytism ended in Judaism by the beginning of the 2nd century, when Roman law forbade the Jews the right to make converts. The word proselytism is now used almost entirely in a derogatory sense to express any form of missionary activity that enforces conversion (q.v.) on the other person instead of permitting a free response to the gospel. It can be applied both to people changing their religion or to those changing their denominational allegiance within the Christian faith. Proselytism is often difficult to define but it can typify aggressive self-assertion, destructive attack on other faiths and practices, and the use of various forms of coercion and seduction. Whenever a church presents itself as something foreign, because its message is wrapped in an alien dress and is allied with an alien culture and change in style of life, evangelism (q.v.) does not amount to more than a proselytizing program. It is as the church becomes indigenous and "baptizes" the local culture into Christ that conversion will appear not as a sedition or a rejection of one's own culture, but a free surrender to the power of God who radically changes the life of human beings.

The WCC (q.v.) has made several attempts to ensure that its member churches behave honestly and decently toward one another. The New Delhi assembly (q.v.) (1961) commended a study document on "Christian Witness, Proselytism and Religious Liberty" to the churches. The Joint Working Group between the Roman Catholic Church (qq.v.) and the WCC issued a document *Common Witness and Proslytism* in 1970. Both reports point to the contrast between genuine witness and eager proselytism. The perversion of evangelism into proselytism depends on the intention and the means used. Every attempt to divide another church or to alienate members from it constitutes inducement to not a better but to a sectarian faith. To offer material or social advantages is simply to proselytize. Unfortunately, the ecumenical consensus does not bind all Christian communities. Proselytism remains a serious problem. During very recent years, i.e., because of the confusions and uncertainties in Eastern Europe, evangelical groups, particularly from the United States, continue to disturb Orthodox churches (qq.v.) by claiming that their soul-saving conversions of Orthodox Christians is according to the will of the saving activity of God. They still demonstrate a lack in the power of the Holy

Spirit (q.v.) and a lack of respect for the uniqueness of every human being, which is implicit in the doctrine of creation. *See also* CONVERSION; RELIGIOUS LIBERTY.

PROTESTANTISM. All denominations, groups, religious associations and sects that developed out of the Reformation (q.v.) are grouped together under the collective name "Protestantism". The word "Protestants" was applied in political circles to the Lutheran (q.v.) signatories of the protest made at the Diet of Speyer, in 1529, against the annulment of the decision of the Diet of 1526 by which, until a church council should meet, the governments of individual states were to regulate religious affairs. The term was seen applied to Lutherans in general and later to all adherents of the Reformation, including Anglicans (q.v.). In the 20th century "Protestantism" became more a cultural and ethical concept, particularly after a number of conservative Protestant denominations started to identify themselves as "evangelical" rather than Protestant, since they wished to emphasize the preaching of the pure gospel in preference to the negative idea of protesting against the errors of the Roman Catholic Church (q.v.). The term "Protestantism" should, however, be maintained if one refers to the influence exerted by the Reformation on modern civilization, institutions and intellectual activities. Protestantism has always shown great variety and radical changes. Sharp internal controversies and many secessions on points of theology or conscience have been characteristic from the very beginning; but this trend was indirectly conducive to the tolerance and a recognition of necessary variety. Protestant churches as a significant minority in world Christianity are still divided, although they increasingly admit to share in a substantial theological basis and in closely related forms of worship (q.v.).

Today the great majority of Protestant churches throughout the world are members of the WCC, and belong to the large Christian world communions, such as the World Alliance of Reformed Churches, the Lutheran World Federation, the Anglican communion, the Baptist World Alliance, and the World Methodist Council (qq.v.), in which they continue to be engaged in common activities and dialogues concerning church unity (qq.v.). Various unions of Protestant churches have already taken place. The first one was the United Church of Canada in 1925. Later church unions followed between various Protestant communities, such as the Church of South India and the Church of North India, and the Uniting Church of Australia. In Europe most Lutheran, Reformed and United churches approved the Leuenberg agreement (1973), which established a complete table and pulpit fellowship. In the USA, the Consultation on Church Union (q.v.) has been under way for more than 30 years. Protestant churches are also members of national and regional councils of churches (q.v.), to which they delegate responsibility for taking common measures in ethics or sociopolitical life, and common charitable activities. This whole process of ecumenically growing together will continue.

The ecumenical movement of this century has felt a strong impulse from Protestant missions and missionaries and their organizations; but it is also a revival of the largely frustrated unitive projects and efforts of the Reformers and their 17th-century followers. Cooperation among Protestant missions grew, notably through the world missionary conference in Edinburgh (1910) and the International Missionary Council (q.v.), which arose from it. The two world wars of the 20th century curtailed the resources of the missionary societies in Great Britain and Europe and by the mid-20th century the Protestants of the USA were carrying the major share of the burden for Protestant missions, both financially and in personnel. By that time about half the personnel from the USA was contributed by societies that did not cooperate with the International Missionary Council and its successor, the Division of World Mission and Evangelism of the WCC. The rising tide of revolt against Western imperialism and colonialism was accompanied by greater self-reliance of the churches that had arisen from Protestant missions and their mounting share in the Protestant missionary movement.

Ecumenical Protestantism and Orthodoxy (q.v.), particularly since 1961, have close relations with each other and remain in continuous contact with the Roman Catholic Church. It remains to be seen how far this surprising development can be considered as a prelude to a veritable transformation of Christianity in its structures, forms of worship and functions in relation to the world society and the world religions. The theologies that relate to the indigenization of Christianity are still in their infancy, and the so-called theologies of liberation (q.v.) (which are only partly Protestant) are exciting ethical calls that must be heard, but probably because of their one-sidedness they have so far not succeeded in really renewing Protestant thinking.

- Q -

QUAKERS *see* RELIGIOUS SOCIETY OF FRIENDS

- R -

RACISM. The race problem of humanity has been on the ecumenical agenda since the very beginning. Already at the Stockholm conference (1925), a report on the race question was introduced and discussed. This report, like subsequent documents, was marked by a naive optimism. The churches and their faithful believed that by preaching the brotherhood of human beings and by spreading modern education race prejudice would soon be eliminated. The International Missionary Council (q.v.), meeting in Jerusalem in 1928, adopted a statement demanding "worldwide inter-racial unity". Two years earlier, J. H. Oldham (q.v.) had published a voluminous book entitled *Christianity and the Race Problem.* This pioneer in the ecumenical movement was far ahead of his time by stressing the fundamental unity of humanity, the white race's responsibility and the church's obligation to be in the mainstream of the world's life. The Oxford conference (1937) included in its report a section on "The Church and Race", in which it was stated: "The sin of man asserts itself in racial pride, racial hatred and persecutions, and the exploitation of other races. Against this in all its forms the church is called by God to set its face implacably and to utter its word unequivocally, both within and without its own borders".

In the postwar period, WCC (q.v.) statements on various occasions urged the member churches to eliminate racist practices in their own ranks, to recognize their involvement in racial and ethnic tensions in the world, and to denounce the violation of human rights (q.v.) through discrimination on grounds of race, color and culture. Very soon the policy of apartheid in South Africa became a central issue. At almost every meeting of the WCC central committee since 1949 the appropriate action to be taken was debated. Yet, only in 1960, a secretariat on Racial and Ethnic Relations was set up within the Department on Church and Society. This should have been done much earlier. Confronted with grave racial conflicts the churches trusted too much the immediate impact of ecumenical assembly and conference pronouncements. It has now become clear that the history of 20th-century ecumenical preoccupation with worldwide racism falls into two parts: before and after 1968. Before that year Christians spoke against race prejudice and racial discrimination. Their declarations and documents dealt with problems of inter-racial relations. During and after the Uppsala assembly (1968) terms such as "change of racist structures of society" and "combat of white racism" were used for the first time. Not only did ecumenical statements become considerably more passionate and concrete; increasingly words were matched by action.

Calling upon the WCC to take a number of steps to struggle against racism, the stormy Notting Hill Consultation on Racism (1969) formulated the last step as follows: "That all else failing, the church and churches support resistance movements, including revolutions, which are aimed at the elimination of political or economic tyranny which makes racism possible". A few months later the WCC central committee at Canterbury recommended an ecumenical program to combat racism and outlined its five-year activities. It made a profound prophetic statement: "Our struggle is not against flesh and blood. It is against the principalities, against the powers of evil, against the deeply entrenched demonic forces of racial prejudice and hatred that we must battle. Ours is a task of exorcism. The demons operate through our social, economic and political structures. But the root of the problem is as deep as human sin, and only God's love and man's dedicated response can eradicate it. The World Council's program is but part of that response. It is God's love and not the hatred of man that must ultimately triumph. By God's love, by the power of His Spirit, some day, soon, we shall overcome". Not only the first general secretary of the WCC has been in the forefront of the battle against racism. His successors, Eugene Carson Blake and Philip A. Potter (qq.v.), have valiantly maintained their witness for racial justice.

On the same theological ground as the central committee at Canterbury, a consultation organized by the Commission on Faith and Order and the Program to Combat Racism (PCR) spoke in 1975 of the gospel of forgiveness and the confession of collective sin. It clearly stated that "the demonic pervasiveness of racism compels us to speak of collective sin. 'None is righteous, no not one' (Rom 3:10). We are thrown together in the solidarity of sin. We are not free to dissociate ourselves self-righteously from this evil" Armed with this deep insight into the wickedness of human nature the consultation went on to assert: "Repentance-action will not be unambiguous nor safe from misinterpretation. We could wish it were otherwise but the sad fact is that all our actions will inevitably bear the mark of the histories and structures in which we live and will therefore still sometimes have racist elements. There will always be a risk of making ourselves vulnerable on all sides".

A world consultation on "The Churches' Response to Racism in the 1980s" was held in the Netherlands in 1980. The consultation considered how to continue the various struggles against racism in view of the profound changes that had taken place in the past ten years. Two concerns were high on its agenda: 1) to find out from one another in different regions and situations what qualitively new aspects of racism—overt and covert—were emerging both within the churches and in society that need to be taken into serious consideration; 2) how to deal with these forms of racism on a local, national, regional and worldwide level, taking into consideration the experiences already gained, the questions raised and the criticism made over the past period.

Indeed the WCC's Program to Combat Racism has been

passionately attacked and rejected from the very beginning. This program was created out of the WCC's conviction that the victims of racism must undertake their own liberation, with outsiders playing only a supportive role. Bitter criticisms and disagreements have arisen when this support took the form of grants from the PCR Special Fund to organizations engaged in armed struggle against white-minority rule in Southern Africa—the Patriotic Front in Zimbabwe (then Rhodesia) in the 1970s, the African National Congress (ANC) in South Africa and the South-West Africa People's Organization (SWAPO) in Namibia. The WCC has insisted on making such grants "without control of the manner in which they are spent", seeing such trust as essential to the solidarity with the victims of racial injustice they are meant to express. Moreover, the organizations receiving money were well known ecumenically, and each year approval of grants to them was preceded by extensive consultation, especially with WCC member churches in the region. Applications for a grant had to specify the purpose for which the money will be used; and the organizations were aware that any evidence of misusing the money would mean the end of ecumenical support.

Nevertheless, the accusation has often been made that the WCC, through the Special Fund grants, is in effect "buying guns for terrorists". Even those who acknowledge that there has never been a shred of evidence for this still express opposition to or unease about ecumenical support for such organizations. The fact that only money specifically designated for the Special Fund—and no general WCC funds—is used for the grants has not quieted this unease or opposition. Nor are opponents of the grants impressed by the observation that the size of the Special Fund grants could hardly make a significant contribution to buying weapons. They contend that the decision of a liberation movement to take up arms to achieve its goals should make it ineligible for church support, no matter what the money is used for, no matter how worthy these goals are. Despite these misgivings, the WCC has held before all Christians the costly imperative of working for justice (q.v.) and reconciliation. Hence its insistence, in South Africa, on economic sanctions and disinvestment as peaceful means to end the injustice of apartheid. Hence its challenge to Christians who reject all use of violence to assume on themselves the suffering of the oppressed and to acknowledge responsibility to remove structures of oppression. PCR has given considerable attention to racism in education. A study was made on racism in school textbooks in 1978, while it sponsored a consultation in Toronto in 1990 on racism in education and the mass media, with particular reference to North America. While Southern Africa has remained a priority, PCR has also focused for several years on the struggle of indigenous people and land rights. In 1990 PCR was much involved in discussions on the resurgence and new forms of racism in Europe. It prepared a new working program to support emancipation in India and extended its support work with minority groups in Asia and Latin America. There is no doubt that the WCC through its activities to combat racism has become more relevant to a majority of Christians and even to people of other faiths. Concrete action against racism has severely tested the ecumenical fellowship, but has not torn it apart. *See also* ANTI-ECUMENISM; VIOLENCE AND NONVIOLENCE.

RAHNER, KARL (1904–1984). Rahner joined the Jesuit order in 1922 and was ordained in 1932. He studied philosophy and theology in Pullach, Valkenburg and Freiburg. He taught Catholic dogmatics in Innsbruck, 1939–1945, in Vienna, 1945–1948, in Pullach, 1948–1964, in Munich, 1964–1967, and in Munster, 1967–1971. His main works were collected in 16 volumes of "Schriften zür Theologie". Together with Heinrich Fries (q.v.) he published *Unity of the Churches: An Actual Possibility* (1984). Rahner was one of the most influential Roman Catholic (q.v.) theologians of our time; he made original contributions to the ecumenical dialogue from his particular theological perspective. He also greatly influenced the Second Vatican Council (q.v.). He believed that ecumenism is an achieved reality at the level of ordinary Christians, though it continues to be debated in the ranks of the churches' hierarchies. He coined the phrase "anonymous Christian", a concept that depends on the offer of salvation and grace (qq.v.) by God to all human beings throughout history.

RAISER, KONRAD (1938–). A Lutheran pastor and theologian, Raiser became general secretary of the WCC (q.v.) in 1993. After theological studies in Tübingen, Bethel, Heidelberg and Zurich, and studies in sociology and social psychology at Harvard University, he worked as an assistant for practical theology in the Protestant theological faculty in Tübingen from 1967–1969. From there he went to Geneva, where he served for four years as study secretary for the Commission on Faith and Order (q.v.). In 1973 he was named deputy general secretary of the WCC, including after 1979 responsibilities as staff moderator for the Program Unit on Justice and Service. In 1983 Raiser was appointed professor of systematic theology and ecumenics in the Protestant theological faculty of the Ruhr-University in Bochum, and director of the ecumenical institute of the theological faculty there. A member of several academic, church and ecumenical committees, including the presidium of the German Protestant *Kirchentag,* he was WCC staff member responsible for the program of the fifth and sixth assemblies (1975 and 1983), an adviser at the ecumenical assembly in Basel 1989, the conference in Seoul in 1990 and a delegate of the Evangelical Church in Germany to the WCC's seventh assembly in Canberra in 1991.

RAMSEY, ARTHUR MICHAEL (1904–1988). After theological studies, Ramsey was ordained a priest, bishop of Durham, 1952–1956, archbishop of York, 1956–1961, and archbishop of Canterbury, 1961–1974. He was professor of divinity at Durham University, 1940–1950, and Regius professor of divinity, University of Cambridge, 1951–1952. He promoted church union negotiations between the Anglican (q.v.) church and other churches in the Third World. He visited patriarch Athenagoras I (q.v.) in Constantinople in 1962 and received patriarch Alexis (q.v.) of the Russian Orthodox Church in London in 1964. He met with Pope Paul VI (q.v.) in Rome in 1966. Ramsey was a president of the WCC, 1961–1968.

RANSON, CHARLES WESLEY (1903–1988). Ranson was secretary of the National Christian Council of India, Burma and Ceylon, 1943–1945, and general secretary of the International Missionary Council (q.v.) from 1948 onward. He was skeptical of the worldwide confessional bodies as they "tend to project themselves across the world and to fasten upon the younger churches those leading strings from which we have been trying to free them for many years". In 1958 he became director of the Theological Education Fund (q.v.), and was president of the Methodist Church in Ireland, 1961–1962. He was professor of theology and ecumenics at Hartford Seminary Foundation, 1968–1972.

RAUSCHENBUSCH, WALTER (1861–1918). Pastor and theology professor, Rauschenbusch was ordained a minister of the second German Baptist Church in New York City in 1886, where he became aware of social problems in a depressed neighborhood. With others he founded a society of Jesus later expanded into the brotherhood of the kingdom. In 1897 he joined the faculty of Rochester Theological Seminary, and in 1902 became professor of church history. Among several works he wrote, *A Theology for the Social Gospel* should be mentioned. Believing that the kingdom of God (q.v.) required social as well as individual salvation and demanding "a new order that would rest on Christian principles of equal rights and democratic distribution of economic power", he gained recognition as the major spokesman of the social gospel (q.v.) movement. The Federal Council of Churches of Christ in America (q.v.) adopted at its constituent meeting in 1908 "The Social Creed of the Churches", the most significant of American church pronouncements on Christian social principles.

RECEPTION. There is hardly any disagreement today that theological convergences and agreements need to be officially "received" by the churches on all levels of their life in order to facilitate steps toward unity (q.v.). The spiritual dimension of unity should be affirmed by all; and at the same time the role of so-called non-theological factors (q.v.) in facilitating or preventing closer fellowship is also generally recognized.

The idea of reception as a process of appropriation and mutual critical testing of different traditions along the lines of the faith (q.v.) of the church through the centuries was seriously discussed at two consultations, organized by Faith and Order (q.v.), in Crêt-Bérard in 1977 ("Towards an Ecumenical Consensus on Baptism, the Eucharist and the Ministry") and in Odessa in the same year ("How Does the Church Teach Authoritatively Today?"). Already at its meeting in Louvaine in 1971, the Faith and Order Commission insisted that the process of reception is multiplex and may last several centuries. "Even after the formal conclusion of such a process and the canonical reception of a council's doctrinal formula, reception continues in some way or other as long as the churches are involved in self-examination on the basis of the question whether a particular council has been received and appropriated properly and with justification. In this sense we can say that in the ecumenical movement the churches find themselves in a process of continuing reception or re-reception of the councils".

The consensus document on *Baptism, Eucharist and Ministry (BEM)* (q.v.) was sent to the churches in 1982, and over 190 churches (member or not of the WCC) replied. This marked a new significant stage in the ecumenical movement. It has become clear that official reception means different things in different churches. While the process of reception is relatively simple for some churches it is very complicated in others. The difference needs to be acknowledged and respected. Despite this, it has become possible to build into the reception process appropriate forms of mutual accountability. The responses have indicated some rather radical new insights and learnings that churches have received through BEM, and many churches have stated that these insights will have important consequences for their own faith and practice.

REDEMPTION *see* SALVATION

REES, ELFAN (1906–1978). In 1947 Rees was called to become the second director of the refugee division of the WCC, where his ecumenical career formally began. Growing up in a Congregational church environment, he witnessed the struggle of Welsh miners at close hand. In the early 1950s he took up the post of permanent representative in Europe of the Commission of the Churches on International Affairs, and in that capacity, as well as through his work as a senior adviser to the WCC Division of Inter-Church Aid, continued his efforts on behalf of refugees by helping the United Nations (q.v.) equip itself for work in this field. Rees was one of the founders and served as one of the first presidents of the conference of nongovernmental organizations in consultative status with the Economic and Social Council of the UN, and was president of the standing conference of voluntary agencies working for refugees. In 1958 he became chairman of the international committee for the World Refugee Year. In the reports he sent on a daily basis from the UN General Assembly to the WCC general secretary, Rees analyzed the changes occurring both in the UN and in the world as a result of the entry of the newly independent nations of the Third World into membership. He pleaded at an early stage for the WCC to revise its policies and its approach to the UN to keep pace with this new reality.

REFORMATION. The 16th-century Reformation in European Christianity was the result of social, religious and educational conditions of the age, preceded by the Renaissance. The commanding leadership of Martin Luther and the faithful services of many gifted, competent and committed scholars, preachers and organizers made the Reformation succeed. The general deterioration in the church and the abuses connected with penance and indulgencies offered the point of passionate departure in 1517. Besides Martin Luther, John Calvin, Huldreich Zwingli, Heinrich Bullinger, John Knox and other eminent Reformers were men who had passed through an inward struggle to an earnest and undoubting assurance of a biblical and evangelical faith. The Reformers were also a company of particularly able men, thoroughly versed in the Bible (q.v.) and familiar with the church fathers.

The Reformation gained its advances principally by persuasion rather than force. While the whole Bible was the arsenal in assailing the Roman Catholic (q.v.) system, it was from the Pauline letters that the most effective arguments were drawn. The doctrine of justification by faith (qq.v.) was based on the thought of St Paul, as was also that of the priesthood of all believers. The Reformation brought a new dimension to the religious practice of common people. By spreading the Bible to them, it made every human being a potential participant in Scripture-centered theology. The Reformation did, however, shatter the unity that Western Christianity had enjoyed, and did introduce divisions graver and more intractable than any that had entered in since the early days of the church.

No one at the time set out with the idea of producing divisions; all the Reformers proclaimed their desire for only a sincere and thoroughgoing inward reformation of the church. Nor did it seem likely at the start that they would succeed in producing any permanent divisions; everything suggested that these "heresies", like others in the past, would be crushed by the combined weight of church and state, and that outward unity would be reestablished, as it had been in previous centuries. It was not very long, however, before it became evident that what would satisfy the Reformers could not be carried out within the framework of the existing church, and that, in the peculiar political conjuncture of the 16th century, strong forces would be available to protect the reforming movements from the destruction with which they seemed to be threatened. Consequently schism and disruption followed in the wake of the Reformation and the process has greatly multiplied the number of autonomous units in non-Roman Christianity, all claiming the legitimacy of their teachings, church structures, liturgy and ethics on the authority of the Bible.

Critical observers of this trend during four centuries have often drawn the conclusion that Protestantism (q.v.) has at its heart a divisive principle by which it is irresistibly driven to disintegration. Many Protestants have acquiesced in this view, justifying it on the ground of an unqualified religious individualism, which they have professed to derive from the teaching of the Reformers. On the other hand, those who have seriously studied Reformation sources have found in them a consistent affirmation of the reality of the one holy catholic church and a clear avowal of the principle of ecumenical unity (q.v.). Those Protestants who recognize the validity of the latter judgment are, nevertheless, embarrassed by the historical record of failure to embody the principles espoused; while those who regard Protestantism as historically bound for disunity are challenged by the 20th-century impressive upsurge of ecumenical interest and unitive efforts.

Although theologians during the 17th century were preoccupied with questions of church unity in doctrine, and during the 18th century concerned with unity in life, piety and the organization of Christian community, a new era in the ecumenical reevaluation of the Reformation was only inaugurated at the end of the first half of the 20th century. It was the Roman Catholic historian Joseph Lortz who, in his two volume study *The Reformation in Germany* (1939–1940), challenged the old Catholic tradition of scholarship that blamed the misfortune of the Reformation on Luther's imbalanced character and excessive religiousness. He was even ready to defend against Roman Catholic critics, like Heinrich Denifle who, in his work *Luther and Lutheranism in Its First Development* (1904), claimed that Luther's critique of Roman Catholic theology was based to a large extent on his ignorance of the valid tradition he rejected, the unusual position that Luther was a profound and sound Christian theologian, whose theology of the cross and salvation (q.v.) was based on the very themes of the gospel. Another new note in the Roman Catholic reappraisal of the Reformation was sounded by Otto Pesch who argued that Luther and Thomas Aquinas had similar understandings of divine grace (q.v.). During the 1950s and the 1960s numerous Roman Catholic scholars wrote in affirmative ways on the Protestant doctrine of justification by faith. During the last few decades Protestant, Roman Catholic and secular historians have equally positively evaluated the insights of the Reformation. On the other hand, it remains quite difficult to explain to the Orthodox churches (q.v.) why the Reformation and the Counter-Reformation took place at all, and why the principle of *ecclesia semper reformanda* (the church continuously to be reformed) is an indispensable part of Protestant doctrinal teaching. The question is still wide open as to whether the Holy See will some day revoke the excommunication of Martin Luther.

REFORMED CHURCHES *see* PRESBYTERIAN AND RE-FORMED CHURCHES

REFUGEES/MIGRANTS. So vast and complex was the refugee problem in postwar Europe that churches at the national level were unequipped to deal with it. Consequently, the WCC set up a centralized refugee service within its Division of Inter-Church Aid, Refugee and World Service, which carried out projects for refugees unable to find a country of resettlement. As soon as feasible, these projects were turned over to local churches or ecumenical agencies. The Commission of the Churches on International Affairs was also involved in refugee issues at intergovernmental levels. When the Office of the United Nations High Commissioner for Refugees was established in Geneva in 1951, the CCIA supported the formation of a voluntary International Assistance Fund, which in turn made it possible for agencies like the WCC and Inter-Church Aid and Lutheran World Relief to extend their humanitarian services. Improvement in the European situation was accompanied by new refugee problems in the Near East, and later in Africa and Asia. The WCC became increasingly involved in the problems of Palestine refugees and many new homeless from the Korean War.

When the refugee situation seriously worsened in the 1970s and 1980s and assumed global dimensions, the WCC refugee service developed into a worldwide network of churches and ecumenical agencies working closely together for the protection and assistance of refugees. The great majority of today's 15 million refugees live in the countries of the southern hemisphere. As these countries can least afford to carry the burden in hosting and helping refugees, they stress the need for greater burden-sharing by the northern hemisphere. Growing concerns on assisting refugees have led together with Roman Catholic (q.v.) churches to the formation of an international ecumenical consultative group on refugee protection, a forum for joint reflection and action. The fact that most refugees today are of other religious traditions has opened up new possibilities of dialogue (q.v.). As millions of refugees fall outside the scope of the mandate of the United Nations High Commissioner for Refugees, the Christian churches, not bound by official definitions of who is a refugee, carry particular responsibilities. This had led to a deeper awareness of the root causes of refugee conditions, more effective advocacy on behalf of their rights, alertness with regard to xenophobic and racist trends, the sharing of objective information and the granting of sanctuary to refugees.

A distinction should be made between refugees and migrants. Refugees are also migrants, who for security reasons cannot return home. Migrants are those who have left their country in search of economic survival, looking for a viable future for themselves and their children. Their departure is often a voluntary choice. The growth of migration within Europe and outside led to increased ecumenical attention. In 1957 a joint study on "The Role of the Churches in Migration" by the Commission of the Churches on International Affairs and the Division of Inter-Church Aid prepared the way for a conference on migration held in Leysin, Switzerland, in 1961. This was followed by the establishment of the Secretariat on Migration within the Division of Inter-Church Aid, which publishes a periodical *Migration Today.* A European conference likewise created a secretariat for migrant workers. It remains a major problem whether migrant people should become integrated in their new society or whether they should prepare to return eventually to their country of origin.

REGIONAL COUNCILS OF CHURCHES *see* ALL AFRICA CONFERENCE OF CHURCHES, CARIBBEAN CONFERENCE OF CHURCHES, CHRISTIAN CONFERENCE OF ASIA, CONFERENCE OF EUROPEAN CHURCHES, LATIN AMERICAN COUNCIL OF CHURCHES, MIDDLE EAST COUNCIL OF CHURCHES, PACIFIC CONFERENCE OF CHURCHES

RELIGIOUS LIBERTY. During the 20th century religious liberty has gained its widest acceptance among human individuals and groups of any century since its initial advocacy during the 17th century. Yet, paradoxically, the 20th century has witnessed more victims of maintaining the Christian faith than all other centuries in the history of Christianity combined. In 1948, forty-eight members of the United Nations (q.v.) signed the Universal Declaration of Human Rights, article 18, which declares: "Everyone has the right to freedom of thought, conscience and religion; this right includes freedom to change his religion or belief, and freedom, either alone or in community with others and in public or private, to manifest his religion or belief in teaching, practice, worship and observance". From 1946 to 1948, alongside governmental representatives, Frederick Nolde (q.v.), the first director of the WCC Commission of the Churches on International Affairs (CCIA), participated in the drafting of the Universal Declaration, serving especially as a consultant on religious liberty and freedom of conscience.

The emphasis with regard to the concept of human rights (q.v.) has undergone an evolution in the succeeding decades. In 1948 there was a tendency to regard the rights of the individual as a prerequisite for the rights of the whole society. Collective rights were thought of as an accumulation of individual rights. The "Declaration of Religious Liberty", adopted by the inaugural assembly in Amsterdam in 1948, reflected this position. In 1949–1950, at the request of the World Council the CCIA undertook a study on "Religious Freedom in Face of Dominant Forces" and submitted "a comprehensive plan for promoting the observances of religious freedom". The CCIA lacked, however, the extensive resources required for a firsthand investigation of situations in which fundamental rights are denied. A Secretariat on Religious Liberty, established by the WCC within its Division of Studies in 1958, brought "A Christian Statement on the Nature and Basis of Religious Liberty" to the central committee in 1960. It promoted various consultations among specialists and ecumenical leaders in several parts of the world and published a considerable number of reports. During Vatican Council II (q.v.) the Secretariat pointed out that the main features of the Roman Catholic position should meet the expectations of other churches and Christians. After 1965 it was concerned to promote a correct interpretation and implementation of Vatican II's "Declaration on Religious Freedom", which stated that every person has a right "to immunity from coercion" in religious matters. The church itself utterly repudiates coercion in religion. Christians must respect religious freedom even more consciously than others.

By the time of the Nairobi assembly (1975), the conviction had grown that a church seeking the realization only of its own rights is neither credible nor true to the gospel mandate. The right to religious freedom was therefore integrated into a comprehensive catalog as one of the basic human rights, but no longer given any exclusive predominance. In a 1979 statement, the WCC Executive Committee put it even more succinctly: "The realization has grown in the ecumenical movement that religious liberty cannot be divorced from other aspects of human rights, and that the church is not credible if it fights for its own rights isolated from a concern for all rights of all people". Although welcoming the adoption of the UN Declaration on All Forms of Intolerance and Discrimination based on Religion or Belief, the Vancouver assembly (1983) feared that this instrument, over 16 years in drafting, did not go far enough to protect religious communities. The CCIA has been active in devising means to strengthen the Declaration, as through its recommendations to the 1986 Session of the UN Commission on Human Rights on the mandate of a special rapporteur.

Recently governments feel greater responsibility to the international community regarding religious tolerance in their countries. It has been proposed to work out a more binding instrument such as a convention, because there are three reasons that deeply influence the contemporary situation with regard to religious liberty: religious resurgence enforced by fundamentalism and fanaticism, changes in the policies of several formerly socialist states, and increasing conflict between politics and religion over the sociopolitical manifestations of religion. In several countries this has resulted in inter-religious conflict and the introduction of laws based on the tenets of the majority religion, leading in turn to infringement of the religious liberty of minorities. The introduction of Islamic shari'a in such countries as Iran,

Libya, Pakistan, Syria and Turkey is a clear example. Current developments in countries like Russia and the People's Republic of China seem to lead to greater religious liberty, but it has yet to be seen whether there is a fundamental change in policy. One thing is quite obvious: the more churches are involved in struggles for religious liberty in certain countries, the more freedom risks being curtailed and minorities being suppressed. *See also* HUMAN RIGHTS

RELIGIOUS SOCIETY OF FRIENDS. The community of Quakers, later called the Religious Society of Friends, originated about 1650 under the leadership of George Fox and other voluntary itinerant preachers. Within a short time their message spread throughout Great Britain and Ireland, Northern Europe, the British colonies on the American seaboard, and to the West Indies. Because of their rejection of compulsory church attendance, their refusal to take up military service and their deliberate disregard of minor social conventions, such as deference to superiors and judicial oaths, the Quakers met vigorous opposition nearly everywhere. In 1682 William Penn founded the Quaker community in Pennsylvania.

The central doctrine of the Society of Friends is the "Inner Light". Its possession consists chiefly in the sense of the divine and direct working of Christ in the soul, by which human beings are freed from sin, united to Christ and enabled to perform good works. Among its visible effects are a moral character, simplicity, purity and truthfulness. From the paramount importance given to the Inner Light is derived the rejection of the sacraments, the ministry (qq.v.) and all set authority of church, creed (q.v.) or Bible. The Friends have thus retained their emphasis on continuing firsthand religious experience. A belief in spiritual baptism (q.v.) and spiritual communion is maintained. The Friends' devotion to social and educational work—and especially in the 20th century to international relief—has earned them very widespread respect.

Though there is no formal ministry, the Society recognizes certain officers with specific duties, including "elders" responsible for the pastoral care of the congregation. From the beginning women have had an equal role in all aspects of the

Quaker movement. The total community has some 400,000 members. The early simple organizations consisting of local meetings were grouped into progressively larger units called respectively monthly, quarterly and yearly meetings. They are largely autonomous. Larger groupings of yearly meetings came into existence in America in 1902: the Friends General Conference and the Five Years Meeting of Friends. The first Friends World Conference was held in 1920.

Quakers were founding members of the WCC (q.v.). They had an accredited observer at Vatican II (q.v.) (1962–1965). Two were delegates to the 1963 Faith and Order (q.v.) conference in Montreal. Quakers participate in the Faith and Order commission of the National Council of the Churches of Christ in the USA (q.v.). Evangelical Friends are active in the World's Evangelical Alliance and other evangelical groupings.

The Friends World Committee for Consultation, which started its activities in 1937, has met every three years. As its name indicates the Committee has no executive power over its constituent yearly meetings. Its aim is to promote deeper understanding between Friends in various nations, and to engage in dialogue (q.v.) with people of other Christian communities and also of other faiths. The Committee further endeavors to strengthen the spiritual life of Quaker groups throughout the world and their efforts to work for peace (q.v.). In 1948 the Friends World Committee was recognized by the Economic and Social Council of the United Nations as a nongovernmental organization with consultative status.

RENEWAL. Although renewal is vital to the activities of the WCC (q.v.), and although there is general agreement about the importance of the Council's support for the ministry of the laity (q.v.), the community of women and men, the place of youth (q.v.) in the church, sharing the worship (q.v.) and ecumenical learning, the fact remains that these aspects of the WCC's work are often eclipsed—in terms of public attention and funding—by its official engagement in unity, mission, justice (qq.v.) and service. There are several explanations why fostering the renewal of the church is an awkward function for the WCC.

1) The various ways in which Christians understand renewal may not lead them to see it as an ecumenical priority. International ecumenical youth programs, for example, may have difficulty attracting due attention and financial support because many churches consider ministry (q.v.) with young people to be a "domestic" matter. Some traditions emphasize the divine origin of the church as a perfect society that cannot be changed or improved; renewal, as they see it, can take place only in the lives of individual Christians. Those who believe that renewal will only come with the new heaven and the new earth complacently accept the ecclesiastical status quo, while others, who believe that a perfect church can be realized on earth may see "renewal" as a process of separating oneself from the sin and imperfection of existing churches.

2) The Life of the local Christian community—in the parish or congregation—is at the heart of the renewal of the church. It is within the congregation that most of the Christian worship, witness, sharing and confessing takes place. This centrality of the local is reflected in the very name of the WCC Sub-unit formed after the Nairobi assembly (1975) to address these concerns: Renewal and Congregational Life. An indispensable condition for and consequence of renewal in the local congregation, to be sure, is a breakdown of "parochial" attitudes and a deepened recognition of the church of Jesus Christ (q.v.) beyond its own walls. Yet, the structure of the WCC allows very little contact between it and local congregations, quite apart from the practical impossibility of reaching from Geneva into more than a very small percentage of these hundreds of thousands of member church congregations. Even a national church headquarters—with which the WCC does relate—may have limited influence on its affiliated congregations, from which it may in turn be separated by several levels of judicatories.

3) Much of the dynamism for renewing the church comes from movements and groups that feel a specific vocation that takes shape outside institutional church structures. House churches and prayer cells coming together in someone's home, charismatic (q.v.) renewal groups, Pentecostal churches (q.v.) with an independent and congregational

structure, evangelical (q.v.) caucuses within WCC member churches, intentional communities, Christian action groups that band together to campaign for disarmament or the end of apartheid or a new life-style—all these may represent creative efforts to live out the faith (q.v.) across the boundaries that have historically divided Christians. The WCC has always prized its contacts with such groups, recognizing that the ecumenical movement is something more than the sum of the institutional bodies that affiliate through membership with a council of churches. At the same time, these groups and movements, which do not "fit" the organizational structures of the WCC, may be isolated from the ecumenical process, thus limiting their contribution to the ecumenical renewal of the church.

4) As Christians seek the coming of the kingdom of God (q.v.), they quite naturally emphasize different aspects of their obedience to the call of the Holy Spirit (q.v.). Often, mutual suspicion divides Christians active in struggles against injustice, those who focus on liturgical life, and those who stress conversion and personal holiness. Indeed, the stronger the convictions that animate their engagement in one or another of these realms, the greater the tension is likely to be between them and other Christians. Each group is tempted to see its own priority as non-negotiable and other forms of Christian living as optional extras. The result is that the overall force for renewal of the church is diminished rather than enhanced by the presence of these different accents. Even if the call for renewal of the church is not a call to abandon cherished convictions and traditions, it is an appeal for change; and any call for change, especially from a body like the WCC, which may seem remote from the concrete reality of any local situation, will meet at least the inertia of the status quo if not the outright resistance of those who have a stake in maintaining it.

Despite the limitations and shortcomings of the WCC, just enumerated, continuing reflection on the concepts of "renewal" and "congregation" has made it possible for the Sub-unit on Renewal and Congregational Life (RCL) to agree on certain characteristics common to all forms of genuine renewal. Renewal is the gift of the Holy Spirit. It requires in those who work for it an attitude of dependent expectation toward the One who said: "Behold I make all things new". Therein lies the ground of the hope that inspires God's people in their search for renewal. Renewal requires an attitude of creative faithfulness toward authentic tradition (q.v.) as well as toward the concrete situation in which faith is lived out. It is therefore not necessarily experienced as something new but can happen through the revitalizing of the old. No actual expression of renewal is final, since renewal has its focus in the future toward which God is always leading his people.

Renewal that is of the Spirit will lead to struggle in terms of the personal, social, political and economic realities faced by individuals and communities in their day-to-day life. The pattern of this renewal is to be found in the Lord Jesus Christ. In him God has taken on our nature, our condition, and transformed it. Any genuine "sign of renewal" will express this same mystical reality of the fusion of the human and the divine. The renewing activity of the triune God is always marked by a loving dynamism that radiates outward— growing, expanding, always opening persons toward their neighbors and creating communities open to the world. Worship is clearly central to all renewal. From it Christian visions are born, and hopes stirred. In it their failure is confessed and they are emboldened to offer to God once again their schemes, programs and endeavors. Through worship they are delivered both from that despair and from that presumption, which are the greatest barriers to the renewal to which God is ever calling his people.

The most widespread impact on the liturgical life of the churches was probably made by the publication of *For All God's People,* an ecumenical prayer cycle prepared jointly with the Sub-unit on Faith and Order in 1978. The book became available in twenty languages. In 1989 a new edition appeared under the title *With All God's People.* The demand for shared liturgical material continues to be great. The RCL has initiated a series of seminars and consultations on a spirituality for our times. "Spirituality in Interfaith Dialogue" was the theme of a joint consultation with the WCC Subunit on Dialogue in Kyoto in 1987. A seminar on "Renewal through

Iconography'' (Chevetogne, Belgium, 1988) has underlined the value of artistic and visual expressions such as icons (q.v.), symbols and paintings for liturgical renewal and as an essential aspect of ecumenical spirituality.

RESPONSIBLE SOCIETY. Already before the Amsterdam assembly (1948) several ecumenical pioneers were involved in the discussion of the best term to express the responsibility of the church in society. Various phrases had been suggested such as the ''free society'', the ''open society'', and the ''free and responsible society''. In the end the term ''responsible society'', coined by J. H. Oldham (q.v.), was adopted and used in subsequent years. A responsible society was defined by the Amsterdam assembly as ''one where freedom is the freedom of men who acknowledge the responsibility to justice (q.v.) and public order, and where those who hold political authority or economic power (q.v.) are responsible for its exercise to God and the people whose welfare is affected by it''. John Foster Dulles described communism as the greatest obstacle to world peace (q.v.). Josef L. Hromádka (q.v.) pleaded for a sympathic understanding of it as a force embodying much of the social impetus the church and Western civilization should represent but had largely lost. Amsterdam said: ''Each has made promises which it could not redeem. Communist ideology puts the emphasis on economic justice, and promises that freedom will come automatically after the completion of the revolution. Capitalism (q.v.) puts the emphasis upon freedom, and promises that justice will follow as a by-product of free enterprise . . . It is the responsibility of Christians to seek new, creative solutions which never will allow either justice or freedom to destroy the other''.

The concept of the responsible society proved to be durable as it became clear that it provided a flexible guidance because its mild language had considerable strength. It clearly opposed totalitarianism of any kind, and spoke both to East and West, but not in a strong ideological language one heard from governments and the press. It exposed people to various social evils and gave them a basis of approach to the major faiths of scientism and materialism. At the second assembly in Evanston (1954) the term responsible society was broadened and its meaning as a guide for action further clarified: "Responsible society is not an alternative social political system, but a criterion by which we judge all existing social orders and at the same time a standard to guide us in the specific choices we have to make. Christians are called to live responsibly, to live in response to God's act of redemption in Christ, in any society, even within the most unfavorable social structures". In contrast to the first assembly (q.v.), the second assembly pointed to the great changes in economic and social policy that had come about in many countries in the postwar years: "These developments suggest that disputes about 'capitalism' and 'socialism' disguise the more important issues in the field of social and economic policy. Each word is applied to many different social forms and economic systems. It is not the case that we have merely a choice between two easily distinguishable types of economic organization . . . The concrete issues in all countries concern the newly evolving forms of economic organization and the relative roles of the state, organized groups and private enterprises".

The evidence shows that the concept of the responsible society evolved as it was applied to the problems arising in the changing world situation since the WCC was founded. Thus, it was able to express the preoccupations of the changing constituency of the Council and contributed to making the political and social witness of the ecumenical movement a force for justice and peace in these years. Nevertheless, by the late 1950s the world political and economic situation had greatly changed. Also, the countries in North America and Western Europe had to face demands for radical social change, emanating especially from the younger generation dissatisfied with life in societies organized and dominated by a technological and exploitative approach to life and, indeed, to all of nature. Under these circumstances it became clear that there was need for a review of ecumenical social thought and its applicability to the new social situation. *See also* JUST, PARTICIPATORY AND SUSTAINABLE SOCIETY; JUSTICE, PEACE AND THE INTEGRITY OF CREATION

REVOLUTION. Christian theology recognizes the kingdom of God (q.v.) as a radical transformation of historical societies. But in much of the history of the church that kingdom has been located at the end of human history; it thus has little meaning for present social and economic life. Christianity can be interpreted as a divinely ordained social order—certainly imperfect, but God's will for a sinful world. Nevertheless, from the 12th century onward a qualified right to overthrow a tyranny in extreme cases has been occasionally advocated. Social revolution has become a frequent theme in ecumenical theology, though it raised many controversies. During the world conference on Church and Society in Geneva in 1966 addresses and discussions discovered a revolutionary spirit in the Bible and recognized a revolutionary ferment in the contemporary world. Some participants called for a "theology of revolution". A few years later the word revolution was replaced by the word liberation. The report of section II, "The Nature and Function of the State in a Revolutionary Age", recommended nonviolent methods of change but raised the question "whether the violence which sheds blood in planned revolutions may not be a lesser evil than the violence which, though bloodless, condemns whole populations to perennial despair". A year after the Uppsala assembly (1968), the WCC launched the Program to Combat Racism (q.v.), one that led to controversies when its Special Fund made grants for nonviolent educational and humanitarian activities to organizations that in other activities resorted to violence.

The encyclical *Populorum progressio* (1967) of Paul VI (q.v.) noted the grave social ills, including the economic bondage of some newly independent nations. While warning against utopian messianism and totalitarian ideologies, the pope stated: "A revolutionary uprising—save where there is manifest, longstanding tyranny which could do great damage to fundamental personal rights and dangerous harm to the common good of the country—produces new injustices, throws more elements out of balance and brings new disasters". That statement obviously warned against revolution and at the same time for the exception that justifies revolution. At the Latin American bishops' conference (CELAM) in Medellin, Colombia, in 1968 a call was issued for political and economic reforms, for liberation from neocolonialism. The conference affirmed that justice is a prerequisite for peace (qq.v.). It strongly urged nonviolent change but also pointed out the reality of "institutional violence" in existing systems. "We must obey God rather than men" (Acts 5:29) is a better guide than "let every person be subject to the governing authorities" (Rom. 13:1).

One of the most deliberately reasoned theological approaches to the problem of Christianity and revolution has been the theology of liberation, designed to frame a response to grave injustices within Latin American society. The theology was used, with some adjustments, in other Third World contexts and the American civil rights movements from the late 1960s onward. Basically liberation theology (q.v.) taught that authentic Christian practice (called praxis) is founded on Christ's love by liberating the oppressed. Strongly anticipating God's kingdom, the church should strive to create that kingdom by destroying the sin of domination and disruption. While the theology of liberation was developed within Roman Catholicism (q.v.) it had a great impact on the WCC and the mainline churches from the late 1960s through the 1980s. By 1990 its black theology (q.v.) counterpart was waning in the USA and elsewhere, and the active participation of theologians, priests and laypeople dampened public support when new governments in the Third World became oppressive themselves.

Revolution raises some very difficult questions for Christian social ethics. Is revolution, in intention and action, truly aimed at justice? How does ideology (q.v.) impinge on theology? How does the revolutionary relate to eschatology? Does revolution maximize the possibilities of nonviolent action and restrain violence as far as possible? Roger L. Shinn (q.v.) said: "Only an idolatry of the status quo can discourage all revolution. Yet revolution can itself become an idol. The distinction between God and idols is a constant issue for the ecumenical church throughout its history and as far ahead as anyone can see". *See also* RACISM; THEOL-

OGY, LATE 20TH CENTURY TRENDS IN; VIOLENCE AND NONVIOLENCE.

RICHTER, JULIUS (1862–1940). Member of the Edinburgh continuation committee and delegate to the Oud Wassenaar conference (1919) of the World Alliance for Promoting International Friendship through the Churches (q.v.), Richter was influential in the ecumenical approach to missions through many works, travels and contacts. First professor of missions at Berlin, 1920, and president of the missionary conference of Brandenburg, of the German Evangelical missionary council and of the society of missionary studies. He wrote over 30 books and numerous essays and articles on the development of missions in all continents.

ROMAN CATHOLIC CHURCH (RCC). The Roman Catholic Church with over 700 million members rightly claims to be the truly universal Christian church. It is geographically spread throughout almost every nation of the world, in contrast to all other churches. A pilgrimage to St Peter's cathedral in Rome conveys the origins of the Christian community; two millennia of church history find a visible expression in the "eternal city". It remains the unique center of worldwide Christianity. Roman Catholicism presents itself as a structured hierarchy of bishops and priests with the pope as its head. This institution has been built up during centuries and rests its claims on the powers entrusted by Jesus Christ (q.v.) to his apostles in general, and to St Peter in particular, as whose successors the popes are regarded. The primary aim of this impressively large Catholic community still remains the sanctification of its millions of members and the conversion (q.v.) of many other souls.

In Roman Catholicism the church's subordination to the Word of God takes the form of being bound to Holy Scriptures and tradition (q.v.). The Bible contains all the truth necessary for salvation (q.v.). Tradition is not an external addition to Scripture. It bears witness to the one gospel that is written by the Holy Spirit, not just on parchment, but also in the hearts of the faithful. Authentic interpretation of Scripture and tradition is carried out by the teaching ministry of the church with a special charisma, i.e., the totality of the episcopate (q.v.) together with the pope. The sacred Magisterium of the church is appointed to the divine commission and ministry of guarding and interpreting both the Word of God and the whole body of subsequent doctrines and disciplines throughout the centuries.

The specific features of Roman Catholic theology that above all distinguish it from the theologies of other churches are the particular way in which it is rooted in the universal church and the way in which it is practiced as a discipline. Since theology is faith (q.v.) in search of understanding it is not limited to the church. Its dimensions concern the whole of humanity. St. Thomas Aquinas (1225–1274) in particular became a norm for the practice of Roman Catholic theology as a special discipline, on the one hand through his distinction between theology and philosophy, and on the other, through the utilization of human knowledge for the theological exploration of faith. The doctrine of the analogy between faith and knowledge sets the theology of the Roman Catholic Church apart from the insistence on renewal (q.v.) in Protestant theology and, though not so fundamentally, from the tradition of Orthodoxy (q.v.), which has more the character of wisdom stamped by liturgy (q.v.) and doxology. Many forms of constriction and isolation, as a result of dialogue with the world religions, modern science, art and culture, modern philosophies, ideologies (q.v.), and in particular modern atheism (q.v.), are a distinctive feature of Roman theological reflection.

The remaining part of this entry deals with the impact of the Roman Catholic Church since it joined the ecumenical movement. To appreciate the nature and extent of the change brought about by the Second Vatican Council (q.v.), the frustrations of the first half of the 20th century should be recalled. The RCC had refused to take part in the first world conference on Faith and Order (q.v.), which met in Lausanne in 1927. It also refused to send observers to the first WCC assembly (qq.v.) in Amsterdam in 1948. The WCC Toronto statement (1950) (q.v.), recognizing that membership in the council "does not imply a specific doctrine concerning the nature of church unity" or that "each church must regard the other member churches as churches in the true or full sense of the word'', made unofficial Roman Catholic contacts with the WCC easier. In 1960 Pope John XXIII created the Secretariat for Promoting Christian Unity (qq.v.).

During the post-Vatican decades there have been several examples of structured cooperation between the RCC and the WCC. Among them is the Joint Working Group (1965) (q.v.), which regularly reviews matters of mutual and overall interest. There is a significant number of Roman Catholic theologians in the membership of the Faith and Order Commission—which makes that commission the most representative theological body in the Christian world. Roman Catholic missionary religious orders have a close consultancy participation in the Commission for World Mission and Evangelism (q.v.). A group representing both the RCC and the WCC is responsible for the annual preparation of the Week of Prayer for Christian Unity (q.v.). The joint commission for society, development and peace (SODEPAX) (q.v.) was active from 1968 to 1980. Roman Catholic consultants have served on the staff of the WCC's Commission on World Mission and Evangelism, the Christian Medical Commission and the Ecumenical Institute in Bossey (q.v.). Apart from such instances of ongoing cooperation, the WCC assemblies since New Delhi (1961) and major ecumenical conferences have profited by the presence of Roman Catholic advisers, consultants and observers. The visits of Paul VI (q.v.) in 1969 and John Paul II (q.v.) in 1984 to the Ecumenical Center in Geneva were concrete expressions of a growing understanding between the RCC and the WCC.

All this has been made possible by the theological work of Vatican II (1962–1965), which not only led to a renewal in worship (q.v.) and life of the RCC but benefited the whole church of Jesus Christ and the ecumenical movement. The Decree on Ecumenism was basically an expression of the RC Church's new commitment to the ecumenical movement. It saw the non-Roman churches in a new perspective and recognized in some measure their true ecclesiality. The Dogmatic Constitution on Divine Revelation highlighted the authority of the Holy Scriptures and led to a new emphasis within the RCC on the Bible and the proclamation of the Word. The document made use of some of the findings of the fourth world conference on Faith and Order on "Scripture, Tradition and Traditions" (Montreal, 1963). The Constitution on the Sacred Liturgy stimulated the renewal of worship and liturgy (q.v.) within the RCC. The reverberations were clearly felt in many non-Roman churches as well, and there was a movement toward liturgical renewal in many parts of the world.

The Dogmatic Constitution on the Church, with its interpretation of the church as God's people, was seen by many as correcting an ecclesiology (q.v.) that had for long appeared excessively hierarchical. "The lay apostolate", it declared, "is a participation in the saving mission of the church itself". The emphasis on common witness and the missionary task of the whole people of God (q.v.) made possible, however indirectly, the publication of the study document entitled *Common Witness* by the RCC-WCC Joint Working Group. The Pastoral Constitution on the Church in the Modern World developed the understanding of the church as a sign and sacrament of God's coming kingdom. It emphasized the church's responsibility for the oikoumene, the whole inhabited earth, and it projected the ideal of the serving church. The Declaration on the Relationship of the Church to Non-Christian Religions was of vital importance in the search for a theology of religious pluralism and for a human community committed to "pro-existence" beyond mere "co-existence". The section of the report from the Uppsala assembly (1968) entitled "The Holy Spirit and the Catholicity of the Church" evidently profited from its insights. Both the Decree on the Pastoral Office of Bishops in the Church and the Decree on the Apostolate of the Laity (q.v.) reinforced the understanding of the church as a movement of God's people. The detailed discussion of collegiality (q.v.) led to the establishment of regional bishops' conferences and ensured wider participation in decision making. The Declaration on Religious Freedom also contributed to better understanding between the RCC and other churches. The commitment to religious freedom and human dignity that it embodied has provided invaluable support in the various struggles of people.

Yet, in spite of all these new sources of inspiration and an impetus for renewal for churches everywhere, there have been and still are times since Vatican II that have given rise to disappointments, both within and outside the RCC. The promises made and the expectations generated were too many and too momentous. Immediately following Vatican II, the pace of change appeared too fast, and in later years too slow, so that the vision floundered. But despite setbacks there have also been concrete achievements, chief among which is the new realism that marks current relationships. If the present situation gives the impression of an impasse, it is at least an informed impasse. But it need not really be taken as an impasse, because there are always tasks that are ecumenically possible and necessary, to which Christians can address themselves. Only through dialogue based on trust and mutual respect can each church tradition, including the Roman Catholic, come to understand itself in greater depth, purify itself of imperfections and shortcomings, and contribute finally to the fullness of the unity (q.v.) of the church for which Jesus prayed. *See also* FAITH AND ORDER; UNITY; VATICAN COUNCIL II.

ROMERO Y GALDAMES, OSCAR ARNULFO (1917–1980). Romero was archbishop of El Salvador and was assassinated in his cathedral at the hands of an unknown assailant, after repeated threats to his life, because he fearlessly condemned the violent actions of government armed forces, right-wing groups and leftist guerrillas involved in his nation's tragic conflict. A champion of the poor (q.v.) and the oppressed and an outspoken advocate of implementing human rights (q.v.) he was nominated by a number of US congressmen and members of the British parliament for the 1979 Nobel peace prize. He courageously denounced the dictatorship of General Carlos Humberto Romero (no relation) and the brutal activities of the national guard, and refused to support the military-civilian junta that succeeded the deposed dictator. For his biography, see J. R. Brockman, *The Word Remains: A life of Oscar Romero.*

ROUSE, RUTH (1872–1956). A member of the World's YWCA (q.v.), 1906–1946, and its president, 1938–1946, Rouse was editor of the *Student Volunteer,* 1895–1897, traveling secretary of the North American Student Volunteer Movement for Foreign Missions, 1897–1898, secretary of the College YWCA in the USA, 1898–1899, and member of the Missionary Settlement for University Women in Bombay, also working through the Student Department of the YWCA, 1899–1901. She returned to England because of ill health. Appointed traveling secretary of the World Student Christian Federation (WSCF) (q.v.) in 1905, she visited 65 countries, some of them several times. She worked in close cooperation with John R. Mott (q.v.), often also accompanying him on his travels for the WSCF. She was secretary of the executive committee of the WSCF, 1920–1924, and during these years she gave a great deal of her time to European Student Relief, which she had initiated. Later she served as educational secretary of the Missionary Council of the National Assembly of the Church of England, 1925–1939. She wrote *The World Student Christian Federation: A History of the First Thirty Years,* and together with Stephen C. Neill (q.v.) edited *A History of the Ecumenical Movement, 1517–1948.*

RUNCIE, ROBERT ALEXANDER KENNEDY (1921–). As archbishop of Canterbury, 1980–1991, Runcie marked the growing together of Anglicanism and Roman Catholicism by welcoming Pope John Paul II (qq.v.) on a historic visit to Canterbury cathedral in 1982, symbolizing the great strides taken in recent years to overcome the estrangement between the two traditions, which dates to the 16th century. In 1989 Runcie visited the pope in Rome. The two also met in Accra, and twice in 1986, in Bombay and in Assisi. He traveled more widely than any of his predecessors, visiting virtually all parts of the Anglican world, and many parts of the ecumenical world. He presided over Anglicanism during a period when its unity was tested by a growing consciousness of cultural and linguistic plurality, and by the ordination of women (q.v.) as priests and bishops in some parts of Anglicanism, and resistance to such ordinations in others. During the 1970s Runcie was particularly involved in the dialogue with Orthodox churches (q.v.).

- S -

SABEV, TODOR (1928–). In 1979 Sabev was appointed WCC (q.v.) deputy general secretary and staff moderator of the program unit on faith and witness until 1992, when, under a new WCC structure, he became deputy general secretary for relationships, giving particular attention to the Roman Catholic Church, Orthodox Churches and Christian World Communions (qq.v.). For the past 30 years he was involved in ecumenical work on the national, regional and global levels. From 1954–1979 he taught church history, first at his church's theological seminary in Plovdiv, then at the academy in Sofia, where he became full professor in 1966. In 1974 he founded an institute of church history and archives in Sofia. He helped organize several WCC meetings in Bulgaria and facilitated study in Western Europe for many young Bulgarian theological students. He was a member of the WCC central and executive committees, 1968–1975, and served on the Council's commissions on interchurch aid, refugee and world service (1969–1975) and churches' participation in development (qq.v.) (1976–1979).

SACRAMENTS. The New Testament does not speak of sacraments as such, although the Greek word later used for this concept, *mysterion*, does occasionally occur in reference to the gospel. The word was used in its modern sense from the 4th century onward. The Latin word *sacramentum* means "oath" (taken by soldiers) and has an older history. In medieval theology the two concepts were fused, and the signs were regarded as proofs of God's presence and his grace (q.v.) at work. Theologians of all major traditions would agree that, though the sacraments are institutional forms within the structures of the church, their importance consists of what God is doing in and through them. The convictions of those who receive the sacraments are subjective and theologically secondary. Nor are the sacraments dependent for their validity as means of grace upon the worthiness of the celebrating minister. Jesus Christ (q.v.) is the only one and true celebrant of the sacraments. The objectivity of the sacraments is guaranteed by God's covenant and promise.

During the centuries there has been much controversy about the number of valid sacraments. The Orthodox churches do not recognize any fixed number, but in practice give special prominence to the eucharist and to baptism (qq.v.). The Roman Catholic Church (q.v.) formally acknowledged seven sacraments at the Council of Florence in 1439. They are divided into two categories: baptism, confirmation (q.v.), the eucharist, penance and extreme unction, on the one hand, and holy orders and matrimony, on the other. In practice this division is not universally practiced even in the Roman Church, which admits married priests in the Eastern rite and recently in the Western rite as well, in the case of converts from the already married Protestant clergy. Protestant churches generally recognize only two sacraments, namely baptism and the eucharist, though some denominations grant that the other five accepted by Rome have some sacramental value. Marriage is almost universally accepted as a valid ordinance among Protestants, and most denominations have an ordained ministry (q.v.). Confirmation in one or another form is also widespread.

Due to the progress in the ecumenical movement, and especially to a wide acceptance of the consensus document *Baptism, Eucharist and Ministry* (BEM) (q.v.), different churches recognize the validity of one another's baptism. Baptists (q.v.) and others who reject infant baptism are increasingly willing to accept a confession of faith from a person who was baptized as an infant instead of insisting on rebaptism. This position is not taken by a majority of sectarian groups, however, which practice rebaptism on a wide scale. Intercommunion (q.v.), or better eucharistic hospitality, is less common on the whole but it too is gaining wide acceptance as the barriers between denominations slowly break down. Still further mutual recognition of sacramental practices of different traditions will take place if the sacraments are seen in the context that is fully Trinitarian, Christological, anthropological, soteriological and eschatological. *See also* BAPTISM; EUCHARIST.

SALVATION. The entire story of Israel in the Old Testament (OT) is the history of God's activity in saving his chosen people from all their enemies, material and spiritual. Accordingly, all the institutions, practices and ideas of Israel originate in saving acts of God. Salvation appears in passages that recount events of deliverance and liberation and speak of blessings granted and promised, of peace and life. In the Prophets salvation is that which God has in store for the future—the glorious age of the Messiah, a regenerated cosmos, perfect fellowship between God and his people, and a kingdom of harmony, righteousness and love. In the ministry of Jesus salvation is used again of God to make people whole. Jesus cures physical and mental diseases and restores people to a right relationship with God. His healing, miracles, exorcisms, and works of mercy are all signs of the wholeness that lies in the provision of salvation by God. However, we see in the teaching and acts of Jesus that salvation also involves the removal of the barrier of sin, which lies between human beings and their Creator: Jesus saw himself as the ransom and sacrifice by which this barrier would be everlastingly removed and thus the new and living way opened to God for repentant human beings. He went to the cross as the suffering servant, the lamb of God, the obedient Son, in order to make salvation possible as a gift from God to humankind. What the OT sacrifices had imperfectly achieved, he perfectly accomplished. He was gloriously vindicated in his resurrection from the dead and exaltation into heaven. No wonder his disciples proclaimed that God's salvation now comes to humankind in no other name than in the name of Jesus.

At the beginning of the 1970s a new understanding of salvation began to emerge in the ecumenical movement. Salvation, it was pointed out, can involve (especially in OT terms of the temporal blessings experienced by the covenant people of God) freedom and deliverance from oppression, injustice, poverty and disease in the present world and age. Further, since the future age of the kingdom will be wholly free of evil and sin, it may also be claimed that God wills at all times and in all places the removal of all sinfulness and evil. This is the general usage that is found in much contemporary ecumenical theology (q.v.) and explains the involvement of the churches in matters of peace and justice (qq.v.) in this world. Particularly the conference of the WCC Commission on World Mission and Evangelism in Bangkok in 1973, debating the theme "Salvation Today", stated that "salvation works in the struggle for economic justice against the exploitation of people by people and in the struggle for human dignity against political oppression of human beings by their fellow men". God's all-embracing salvation for the whole person frees human beings for their own total salvation. This emphasizing of the earthly and social dimensions of salvation did of course provoke criticism from various churches, including the Orthodox and evangelical (qq.v.) communities. They admitted that recognizing moves for justice and peace in this world as possible signs of God's care and love for the human race, the church is to support and encourage all that which truly dignifies human beings as creatures of God made in his image and likeness. The signs are not, however, God's salvation as such. They are indicators that ought to turn people to God in Christ's name, looking for his full and final salvation beyond history.

The Nairobi assembly (1975) deemed it necessary to distinguish between earthly well-being and eschatological salvation. It stressed that the reality of salvation must be proclaimed where earthly, social well-being has not yet been achieved. "We regret that some reduce liberation from sin and evil to social and political dimensions, just as we regret that others limit liberation to private and eternal dimensions . . . We pray in the freedom of the Spirit and groan with our suffering fellow human beings and the whole groaning creation until the glory of the Triune God is revealed and will be all in all". On the other hand, the world conference on mission and evangelism in Melbourne in 1980, with "Your Kingdom Come" as its theme, stressed again the social dimension of salvation, especially with regard to the poor (q.v.). The poor "accept the promise that God has come to their rescue, and so discover in his promise their hopes for liberation and a life of human dignity". The discussion on the meaning of mission (q.v.), which equates salvation and human wholeness, remains problematic. *See also* MISSION; THEOLOGY, LATE 20TH-CENTURY TRENDS IN.

SALVATION ARMY (SA). So far as the ecumenical movement is concerned, the Salvation Army is regarded as a church, so it is represented in meetings of the Christian World Communions (q.v.). The SA was a founding member of the WCC (q.v.) in 1948, but since 1978 the Army has been in the revised status of fraternal relationship. This status is more suited to the Army's polity of a single representative for all its worldwide constituents. The SA continues to play a significant role in the WCC, as well as in other movements such as the Lausanne Committee for World Evangelization (q.v.). It works in 70 countries and has more than 19,000 officers (ministers) who preach the gospel in 146 languages through over 17,000 preaching stations. It publishes 139 periodicals with a circulation of over 2 million. It conducts social service programs through 2,000 social centers, 69 hospitals and over 800 day schools. Its primary aim is "to proclaim the Gospel of the Lord Jesus Christ to men, women and young people untouched or uninfluenced by the Gospel and to develop its membership into a fighting force of God". The headquarters of the SA is in London, where its work began in 1865 under the leadership of William and Catherine Booth in the East end slums of the city. Relationships between the Army and the historic churches are marked by free and friendly cooperation. It is a long established rule with the Army not to proselytize and not to criticize the doctrine, worship and organization of other churches. The SA is led at present by General Eva Burrows, elected in 1986, and the movement's second woman leader. From its early days the Army has given equal opportunities to men and women.

SAMARTHA, STANLEY JEDIDIAH (1920–). Samartha studied at Madras University, United Theological College, Bangalore, Union Theological Seminary, New York, and Hartford Seminary Foundation, where he obtained a Ph.D. degree. He was a lecturer at Karnataka Theological College in Mangalore, 1947–1949, and became its principal from 1952 onward. Afterward he became principle of Serampore

College, West Bengal, and consultant to the Christian Institute for the Study of Religion and Society in Bangalore. Samartha was the first director of the WCC Sub-unit on Dialogue with People of Living Faiths and Ideologies (qq.v.), 1970–1981. In this capacity he significantly promoted the inter-religious dialogue in the ecumenical movement and was an able organizer of bilateral and multilateral dialogues (qq.v.) within the setting of the WCC. Samartha is now visiting professor at the United Theological College in Bangalore and also active in the South Asia Theological Research Institute.

SAN ANTONIO 1989 *see* MISSION

SANTIAGO DE COMPOSTELA 1993 *see* FAITH AND ORDER

SCHILLEBEECKX, EDWARD CORNELIUS ALFONSUS (1914–). An influential Roman Catholic (q.v.) theologian whose views brought him into conflict with the hierarchy of his church, Schillebeeckx developed a contemporary sacramental theology and a modern Christian ethics; indeed, his entire work aims at making faith (q.v.) for modern human beings a vibrant, personal venture. He entered the Dominican order in 1934 and was ordained priest in 1941. He was professor of dogmatic theology at Louvain, 1943–1957, and professor of dogmatic theology, history of theology and hermeneutics at the University of Nijmegen, 1957–1982. He received the European Erasmus Prize for Theology in 1982. His book *Jesus: An Experiment in Christology* (1974) received acclaim in the wider theological world, but the disapproval of the Vatican. His controversial *Ministry* (1981) caused even greater concern.

SCHLINK, EDMUND (1903–1984). Schlink was a delegate to Amsterdam 1948, addressed Evanston 1954, attended New Delhi 1961, and Uppsala 1968. He addressed the third world conference on Faith and Order (q.v.) in Lund (1952), and was a member of the Division of Ecumenical Studies and of the Commission on Faith and Order, 1949–1975, and an official observer of the Evangelical Church in Germany at the Second Vatican Council (q.v.), 1962–1965. In 1934 he became professor at Giessen, in 1935 at Bethel, and from 1946 onward professor of systematic theology at the University of Heidelberg. Founder of the Ecumenical Institute in Heidelberg, 1957, in 1971 he joined the board of trustees of the Ecumenical Institute at Tantur (q.v.) (near Jerusalem). He was involved in several synods of the Confessing Church (q.v.) in Germany and participated in several bilateral dialogues (q.v.). His ecumenical influence on his nation was considerable. He wrote, among many works, *The Coming Christ and the Coming Church.*

SCHUTZ-MARSAUCHE, ROGER (1915–). Brother Roger is the founder and prior of the ecumenical community of Taizé, near Cluny, in France. In 1940 he arrived alone at the site in Burgundy and in 1949 seven brothers took monastic life vows with him. He wrote *The Rule of Taizé* in 1952 and *The Office of Taizé* in 1962, which is of careful ecumenical liturgical balance attracting all kinds of Christians eager to experience spiritual renewal in their life. Pope John XXIII received him at the Vatican in 1958 and invited him later to attend the second Vatican Council. Since the early 1970s Taizé has received many thousands of young people from Europe and all over the world. An international council of youth took place in 1974. Schutz addressed the WCC Vancouver assembly in 1983. He received the Templeton prize in 1974, the peace prize in Germany in 1974, and the UNESCO prize for peace education in 1988.

SCHWEITZER, WOLFGANG (1916–). Schweitzer was secretary of the WCC (q.v.) Department of Studies, 1946–1952, member of the consultative committee of the Christian Peace Conference (q.v.), 1964–1980, and secretary of the theological conferences of representatives of the Church of England (q.v.) and the Evangelical Church in Germany. He became professor at the University of Heidelberg in 1951, and professor of systematic theology at the Kirchliche Hochschule, Bethel, Bielefeld, 1955–1980. He was editor of the *Zeitschrift für evangelische Ethik.*

SCIENCE AND RELIGION. This vast topic merits a much longer treatment than is provided in this short article. There was no science in the modern sense of natural or experimental science until the late Middle Ages. The domination of European thought by Greek philosophical notions delayed the rise of modern science until the age of Copernicus, Kepler and Galileo. It took a long time to work the lingering traces of Aristotelianism out of the European mind and to develop methodical atheism, that is, never to resort to God as a principle of explanation. This does not involve, however, the view that natural science is atheistic in its conclusions; science as such is not concerned with explanation beyond the range of natural phenomena, and there cannot be an ultimate conflict between science and religion. It was in the past—for example, at the conflict over Darwin's theory of evolution—that old-fashioned and untenable theological interpretations about the nature of biblical revelation gave rise to the widespread assumption that there is an inherent incongruity between religion and science. There can be conflict only where false theological theories are held, since natural science itself provides no answers to ultimate questions.

Another problem of discontinuity between faith and science in the field of ethics has also plagued human minds and is only slowly being solved today. In its beginning modern science depended on the moral and philosophical assumptions of Christian Europe. But more recently, in view of its achievements, science has become a self-authenticating activity and is hardly anymore dependent on prior moral conditioning. Misplaced trust is eventually exposed, and the overwhelming weight of scientific success acts to reinforce the values of the scientific community. In fact, so widely accepted are these values that the original relationships between ethics and science have been turned upside down, and made scientific success the criterion of value: what promotes the scientific attitude is good; what denies or stultifies it is bad.

The assembly of the WCC (qq.v.) in Uppsala in 1968 was influential in becoming a turning point for ecumenical concern about science and technology (q.v.). It recommended that "the WCC give particular attention to science and the problems of world-wide technological change in its study program, in cooperation with the Roman Catholic Church and in dialogue with secular ideologies''(qq.v.). Out of this recommendation a new study program was undertaken by Church and Society under the title "The Future of Man in a World of Science-based Technology". An exploratory conference in Geneva in 1970 proposed the "end of the faith-science divorce" and had a great impact in the following years. Together with scientists and sociologists several consultations were held that examined specific issues such as nuclear energy and alternative energy technologies, genetics and the quality of life, limits to growth, humanity, nature and God, science, ideology and theology, genetic engineering and science education. A second critical conference on "Faith, Science and the Future" was held at the Massachusetts Institute of Technology in 1979, which published a two-volume report, *Faith and Science in an Unjust World.* A range of inter-related concerns came onto the agenda, calling for challenging the contemporary rational technological worldview and broadening the discussion, both among experts and the general public, of ethical issues raised by the various sciences. At the insistence of a large number of scientists, some of whom had themselves worked on developing nuclear weapons, "Science for Peace" was a topic added to the agenda. The conference also urged a five-year moratorium on building new nuclear power plants. The plea for a halt to the nuclear arms race resulted in the proposal that the WCC organize an international public hearing on nuclear weapons and disarmament (q.v.), which took place in Amsterdam in 1981.

The debate on the relation between science and religion will undoubtedly continue in the ecumenical movement. Both must explore in greater depth the questions of what science is and what theology is and how they can serve each other. Particularly important are the unresolved issues of a theology of nature and a less anthropocentric or biocentric ethic. The results can be rewarding since both sides have become more open to each other. *See also* BIOTECHNOLOGY AND BIOETHICS; TECHNOLOGY.

SCOTT, EDWARD WALTER (1919–). Scott was educated at the University of British Columbia and the Anglican Theological College in Vancouver. He became active in the Student Christian Movement in Canada and was for five years its general secretary. He was appointed associate secretary of the National Council for Social Services until he was elected bishop of Kootenay in 1966. As an active supporter of ecumenical concerns and with particular gifts for prayer and reconciliation he served the WCC as the moderator of its central and executive committees, 1975–1983.

SECRETARIAT FOR PROMOTING CHRISTIAN UNITY (SPCU). Both in its status and in the range of its activities the SPCU has undergone significant transformation since it was originated by Pope John XXIII (q.v.) in 1960. From a preparatory commission for Vatican Council II (q.v.) it became a conciliar commission in 1962. In 1966 its permanent character was confirmed by Pope Paul VI (q.v.). The Apostolic Constitution on Reform of the Roman Curia, issued in 1967, established its place among the other curial departments that assist the pope in the guidance of the church. In 1989 it became the Pontifical Council for Promoting Christian Unity. The Secretariat has a dual role. One is to assist other curial departments and local churches in the development and coordination of their ecumenical task. The other is to serve as a point of contact between the Roman Catholic Church (q.v.) and representatives of other churches and the Jewish people. The first president of the SPCU was Augustin Cardinal Bea, succeeded by Jan Cardinal Willebrands (qq.v.). The latest president is Edward Cardinal Cassidy. The membership of the Secretariat is composed of more than 30 cardinals and bishops both from other departments of the Curia and from dioceses around the world, who normally meet annually in plenary session to review the work of the Secretariat. The staff is composed of two sections: one to relate with other churches of the East and one to relate with Reformation (q.v.) and post-Reformation churches.

Since Vatican II the SPCU has published several normative documents, such as the *Directory for Ecumenical Mat-*

ters, Parts I and II (1967 and 1969). Another category of documents is advisory. This includes such statements as *Reflections and Suggestions Concerning Ecumenical Dialogue* (1970) and *Ecumenical Cooperation at National, Regional and Local Levels* (1975). The SPCU has been cosponsoring international theological dialogues with the Lutheran World Federation (1965), the Anglican Communion (1966), the World Methodist Council (1966), the Old Catholic churches (1966), the World Alliance of Reformed Churches (1968), the Pentecostals (1972), the Disciples of Christ (1977), the Evangelicals (1977), the Orthodox church (1979) and the Baptist World Alliance (1984) (qq.v.).

SECULARIZATION. The word "secular" is derived from the Latin *saecularis,* "belonging to the particular age". In medieval Latin "secular" came to be used for "this present age" as contrasted with the "age to come". As in modern times "secularization" increased, while "sacred" or religious activity has been progressively confined to a narrow ecclesiastical realm and personal piety. Consequently, the churches have lost a great deal of their former significance and influence in society. Dietrich Bonhoeffer (q.v.) described secularization as a movement "towards the autonomy of man, in which I would include the discovery of the laws by which the world lives and deals with itself in science, social and political matters, art, ethics and religion". He developed a positive theology of secularization. Christ confronts the world, according to Bonhoeffer, not in its weakness and dependence on religious worldviews but at the strong points of human ingenuity and responsibility. Similarly Friedrich Gogarten linked secularization directly to the faith of the Reformation (qq.v.). Justified by grace (q.v.) alone, Christians are free to participate in the sonship of Jesus Christ (q.v.). Because of their creatureliness human beings receive the world to rule over responsibly. Karl Barth (q.v.) rejected Bonhoeffer's and Gogarten's understanding of humanity as mature in its secularity apart from faith. He criticized every attempt to emancipate from transcendent absolutes.

Some would emphasize that ours is an age of rampant secularization; others that we are witnessing an unprecedented revival of religion. In the 1950s and 1960s ecumenical theologians predicted that secularization, inspired by the gospel, is the wave of the future. During these decades, focus on human responsibility for this world was at the root of much ecumenical enthusiasm for and even celebration of the secular, seen in terms of the liberating potential of the "truly human". Some spoke of the need for a "secular ecumenism", taking its point of departure in a thorough engagement of the church in the world. Yet, religious revivals have arisen in reaction to the ongoing technological logic and power of the secularization process. Many new religious movements (q.v.) have become attractive to the younger generation. Charismatic movements (q.v.) thrive in many nations and disturb the churches.

The different senses in which the words "secular", "secularization" and "secularism" are used makes it difficult to specify the implications of growing secularity for the churches and the ecumenical movement. Sometimes, "secular" is used to describe a political system in which no religion is favored over any other—an arrangement generally welcomed by Christian minorities and congenial to what the ecumenical movement has said about freedom of religion. To be sure, the political power of the religious majority may erode such constitutional guarantees of religious neutrality; and laws are sometimes proposed that seek to ensure harmony in such a "secular" society by forbidding conversion (q.v.) from one religion to another, which violates one element of ecumenical understanding of religious liberty (q.v.). "Secular" is also used in an apparently descriptive way to refer to that which is religiously neutral. For example, holidays whose origins are not in religious commemorations are sometimes called "secular holidays". But already at this point difficulties appear, for some will say that determining what is "secular" in this sense is seldom an "objective" decision.

"Secularization" is further used more specifically to describe or explain the decline of "traditional" church life, especially in Europe and North America. This decline has implications for the WCC (q.v.) because it is from such churches that the Council has historically drawn the bulk of its financial support. When membership of these churches declines, their income dwindles, making less money available for the WCC itself. But the danger of "secularization" in this sense is not just financial. Lower membership figures usually mirror diminishing interest in the church; and if fewer people are committed to or even interested in the local congregation, that will mean less interest in national church structures and even less interest in international ecumenical structures built from these churches.

Whether one emphasizes secularity or revival, it is clear that the global religious context in which the ecumenical movement lives and works at the end of the 20th century is much different from what was taken for granted by those who attended the Edinburgh conference in 1910 or who came to Utrecht in 1938 to shape a world council of churches or who founded the WCC in Amsterdam in 1948. Exactly what it means for how the WCC is organized and how it helps the churches to fulfill their "common calling" remains to be seen. Neither secularization nor religiosity, but authentic faith is the decisive factor. See also UNITY OF THE CHURCH AND THE RENEWAL OF HUMAN COMMUNITY.

SEOUL 1990 see JUSTICE, PEACE AND THE INTEGRITY OF CREATION

SEXUAL ETHICS. The ecumenical movement has not contributed significant new insights into ethical issues that were of importance in the concerns of the churches in the past, such as marriage, family and sexual ethics. The traditional consideration of these subjects under the so-called "mandates" or the "orders of creation" or, in the Roman Catholic tradition of "natural law" (qq.v.), was considerably alien to the Christological perspective of the ecumenical movement for several decades. But agreed classical issues are now newly challenged, partly because of changes in culture related to social, economic and political developments, partly because of new human possibilities opened by science and technology (qq.v.), both resulting in the erosion of old patterns of behavior, tacitly or explicitly accepted and supported by the churches. The debates about abortion, birth control and homosexuality cannot be postponed. Traditional issues of divorce and euthanasia demand the taking up of new positions. The ecumenical movement finds it difficult to develop a coherent theological approach and clear ethical criteria for facing such controversial issues but it will undoubtedly have to deal with them in the future.

Contemporary Christian sexual ethics in general gives more emphasis to love as a norm, and less to procreation. In the light of post-Freudian psychology, sexuality is seen as a profound stratum of the personality, not to be equated with genital activity. The ability to experience sexual desire and pleasure is seen as a positive good and an avenue of love and commitment. This emphasis on the affective and enjoyable aspects of sex has implications for moral criteria. Procreation is widely seen as valuable but not essential. To the extent that the affective and interpersonal dimensions of sex have replaced procreation and marriage as its morally defined criteria, it has become possible to reevaluate previously sexual expressions.

Abortion. Views of abortion vary greatly among Christian churches. Although the weighing of fetal, maternal, familial and social values does not depend on specifically religious premises, Christianity's doctrines of creation and redemption sustain biases in favor both of preserving human iife and of enhancing its quality. The symbols of sin, cross, forgiveness and reconciliation provide a perspective on moral decisions in which are recognized human finitude, the brokenness of the human condition and the need to make difficult choices that achieve at best the lesser evil.

Roman Catholicism tends to place a high value on the unborn, even in early pregnancy, but shows increasing sensitivity to the difficulties that pregnancy can cause for women and their families. The mainstream Protestant (q.v.) traditions diverge from the Catholic by placing more weight on the unique circumstances of each abortion decision and on the responsibility to decide of those involved, especially the woman. Often the conflict inherent in abortion is acknowledged by calling abortion tragic and ambiguous, even when morally wanted. For Orthodoxy (q.v.) the choice between prohibitions and permissions has more to do with legalism and bureaucracy than with the love of God. The Eastern churches in their teaching on sexuality have put more emphasis upon love both human and divine, and this understanding is beginning to be appreciated by Western Christians.

The feminist critique of Christianity begins from women's experience of oppression and exclusion from power (q.v.) within the history of the Christian religion and the patriarchal institutions that it has endorsed. A central target is the subordination of women within the family and the confinement of the female influence to the domestic sphere. Christian feminists aim for shared male and female responsibility within domestic, economic, religious and ecclesiastical realms. As a precondition, many view it as necessary to enhance the autonomy of women in matters of reproduction, freeing them from the burden of unplanned or unwanted pregnancy.

Although the Christian tradition yields a generally negative view of abortion, contemporary Christians are divided on whether it can be justified in some exceptional cases, and if so, what these cases are. Abortion as an option receives broader support when the pregnancy has resulted from a clear injustice to the mother, for example, in the case of rape or incest, or when it gravely threatens her physical or mental health, or when the fetus is seriously abnormal; and when the abortion can be performed during early pregnancy. All these conditions have to be responsibly considered.

Birth control. The progressive development of generally safe and widely available methods of contraception has increased opportunities to liberate couples from conceiving unwanted children and the attendant burden of anxiety. In the beginning churches saw in this several complications: that of disobeying God, the actual giver of children, by artificial intervention in the natural mystery of procreation, that of family selfishness and that of growing immorality as sexual relations became free of risking conception. Increasingly, these timid attitudes were at odds with the aspirations of couples and above all women, scientific possibilities and social needs.

The official Roman Catholic Church teaching has consistently opposed contraception by artificial means. In his encyclical *Humanae Vitae* Paul VI (q.v.) wrote that "the church, calling men back to the observance of the norms of the natural law as interpreted by constant doctrine, teaches that each and every marriage act must remain open to the transmission of life". Besides this reasoning from natural law, the encyclical stressed that any kind of artificial birth control has such consequences as conjugal infidelity, general lowering of morality, corruption of youth and loss of respect for women. The encyclical drew negative responses in some Catholic quarters. A number of European and North American bishops conferences noted the primacy of conscience, the need to be understanding and forgiving and the judgment that Catholic Christians who cannot follow the church's teaching are not thereby separated from the love of God.

The relationship of artificial means of birth control to population policy is also a controversial issue. In 1960, Richard M. Fagley (q.v.) published *The Population Explosion and Christian Responsibility,* in which he as a Protestant argued for voluntary family planning, and urged an ecumenical conception of responsible parenthood. The broad consensus for which he pleaded has been realized, except for Roman Catholic opposition to the use of contraceptives.

Homosexuality. Churches have adopted different positions concerning the issue, which range from a rejecting-punitive position to a full acceptance of homosexual orientation, with homosexual acts themselves to be evaluated by the same standards used for heterosexual acts. It is contended that same-sex relationships can fully express God's central purpose for sexuality, the unitive. Thus, affirming homosexual as well as heterosexual orientation, this position holds that all sexual acts ought to be evaluated by their relational qualities. In addition to the general theological-ethical question of homosexuality, a number of more specific moral issues now face the churches. A major issue is the support of civil rights and social justice for lesbians and gay men, an issue on which most major church bodies now publicly agree. More divisive are those that directly affect the internal life of the church. These include the acceptance of gays and lesbians into full church participation, the provision of adequate pastoral care, the ordination (q.v.) of publicly affirmed lesbians and gay men, the liturgical blessing of gay or lesbian unions and the support of legal rights for gay or lesbian unions analogous to the legal rights of heterosexual marriages.

The World Council of Churches has not directly discussed ethical, theological and ecclesiological issues raised by homosexuality. The Vancouver assembly in 1983 simply encouraged churches "to examine and study for themselves and with one another the question of homosexuality, with special stress on the pastoral responsibility for the churches everywhere for those who are homosexual".

SHERRILL, HENRY KNOX (1899–1980). A president of the WCC (q.v.), Sherrill raised the initial funds for the Episcopal Church Foundation and the new headquarters of the WCC. He was president of the National Council of the Churches of Christ in the USA (q.v.), 1950–1952. He served as rector of the Church of Our Savior, Brookline, Massachusetts, 1919–1923, Trinity Church, Boston, 1929–1930, bishop of Massachusetts, 1930–1947, and presiding bishop, 1947–1958. Sherrill appealed for World Relief Funds after the war and the ecumenical One Great Hour of Sharing. In 1945 he was named chairman of the Army and Navy Commission. He was executive secretary (1935–1938) and president of the American Association of Theological Schools (1938–1940), and the author of numerous books.

SHINN, ROGER LINCOLN (1917–). Consultant to the WCC (q.v.) working group on Church and Society, 1971–1976, and member of this group, 1976–1983, Shinn was involved in the conference on Church and Society, Geneva, 1966, and in the conference on Faith, Science and the Future, Boston, 1979. He was cochairman of the consultation on church and state, Bossey, 1976, and of the North American-European conference on the Technological Future of the Industrialized Nations and the Quality of Life, Pont-à-Mousson, France, 1973. Shinn traveled extensively through Asia, Africa, and Eastern and Western Europe, studying issues of the relations between technology and social ethics. (qq.v.). He chaired the National Council of Churches' task force on human life and the new genetics. From 1959 to 1985 he was Reinhold Niebuhr Professor of Social Ethics at Union Theological Seminary, New York, and he also taught at Columbia University, Jewish Theological Seminary of America, and New York University Graduate School of Business Administration. Shinn was active in the United Church of Christ.

SIEGMUND-SCHULTZE, FRIEDRICH (1885–1969). A pioneer of the ecumenical movement, Siegmund-Schultze helped found and until 1948 was secretary of the World Alliance for Promoting International Friendship through the Churches (q.v.). He also founded the International Covenant of Peace and was its president until his death. He published the journal *Die Eiche,* 1913–1933, and the church newsletter *Ekklesia.* Expelled from Germany during the Second World War, he became a student pastor in Switzerland and developed an international church relief board for refugees. In 1957 he founded and chaired the central office for justice and protection of conscientious objectors (q.v.) and in 1959 developed extensive ecumenical archives in Soest, which were later transferred to Berlin.

SIMATUPANG, TAHI BONAR (1920–1990). After being educated at the Dutch royal military academy, Simatupang was a key figure in organizing the war against the Netherlands after Indonesia had claimed its independence in 1945. After early retirement as chief of staff of the armed forces, he became much involved in the ecumenical movement at local, regional and international levels. He was president of the East Asia Christian Conference (q.v.), 1973–1977, and president of the National Council of Churches in Indonesia, 1967–1984. He served as a member of the WCC (q.v.) central and executive committees, 1968–1975, and as a president of the WCC, 1975–1983.

SITTLER, JOSEPH (1904–). Chairman of the Commission on Worship of Faith and Order in North America, Sittler delivered a major address on "Called to Unity" at New Delhi 1961. Ordained to the ministry of the United Lutheran Church in 1930, he was professor of theology, Lutheran Theological Seminary, Maywood, Illinois, 1930–1943, and professor of theology, Chicago University, in 1957.

SKYDSGAARD, KRISTEN EJNER (1902–). Skydsgaard was professor of dogmatic theology at the University of Copenhagen and has significantly contributed to the dialogue with Roman Catholic theology. As a member of the Commission on Faith and Order (q.v.) he devoted much of his attention to the question of "Scripture and Tradition", and became an observer for the Lutheran World Federation (LWF) at the Second Vatican Council (qq.v.). In 1957 he was appointed to the commission of ecumenical research of the LWF and became actively involved in the establishment of the Institute for Ecumenical Research in Strasbourg; he served its board as vice president, 1964–1974. Skydsgaard was also a member of the official group of dialogue between the Lutheran churches and the Roman Catholic Church (qq.v.).

SLACK, KENNETH (1917–1987). Slack was an English minister, ecumenist and writer. Ordained in 1941 in the Presbyterian Church of England, he became a Royal Air Force chaplain (1942–1946), was minister of St James', Edgware (1946–1955), general secretary of the British Council of Churches (1955–1965), minister of St Andrew's, Cheam (1965–1967), minister of the City Temple (1967–1975), director of Christian Aid (1975–1982), and minister of Kensington United Reformed Church (1982–1987). He was moderator of the Free Church Federal Council (1983–1984) and a well-known religious journalist and broadcaster. He edited the WCC Uppsala report (1968) (qq.v.).

SMITH, JOHN COVENTRY (1903–1984). Member of the WCC (q.v.) central committee, 1961–1968, and a president of the WCC, 1968–1975, Smith played a leading role in facilitating the integration of the International Missionary Council (q.v.) and the WCC. Missionary to Japan, 1929–1943, and US Presbyterian mission executive, 1948–1970, he served as general secretary of the Commission on Ecumenical Missions and Relations of the United Presbyterian Church in the USA and as moderator of the 180th United Presbyterian assembly. Smith was also active in the National Council of the Churches of Christ in the USA (q.v.), 1963–1966, the US civil rights movement and theological education issues. He was a trustee of several theological seminaries in the USA and in Asia, and wrote *From Colonialism to World Community*.

SMOLIK, JOSEF (1922–). Smolik was a member of the WCC (q.v.) central committee, 1975–1991, and of the Faith and Order (q.v.) Commission, 1961–1991. He was also a member of the theological commission of the Christian Peace Conference (q.v.), 1961–1968, and has been active in strengthening ecumenical relations in Central and Eastern Europe, and deepening them between East and West Europe. He has been professor of theology and dean of the Comenius Faculty in Prague from 1950 onward. He has been a foremost interpreter of the life and work of Josef L. Hromádka (q.v.).

SOCIAL ETHICS. Through long and painful experiences, the ecumenical movement has learned that there is no structure of society, no system of human power and security, that is perfectly just. There is no divinely ordained social order, but there is the judgment of God under which every social system falls, to be transformed into one that is more just. There can be no self-protecting status quo in the light of the judgment, that is the crucifixion of Jesus Christ (q.v.): it is, indeed, continuously challenged by the church that in its essence is the pilgrim people of God and that can therefore never harden into a status quo. This must lead to corresponding thought and action with the aim of bringing about an effective social change whereby the poor and oppressed will receive their share of justice (q.v.). If it comes to revolution, Christians owe the revolutionary freedom from hatred, freedom to build a new world in which also the enemy will find a just place, and freedom from self-righteousness—freedom to accept the give-and-take that modifies even revolutionary plans and powers. For revolutions are also under the judgment when they make their cause absolute and promise final salvation.

Even after some 70 years of various international endeavors an evaluation of ecumenical social ethics can be only groping and provisional because of its complex and demanding nature. Perhaps the next generation will be in a position to spell out more systematically and convincingly to what extent Christian churches have succeeded in wrestling with the multiple problems of humanity. At this stage no one can deny that in the realm of social, economic and political policy the ecumenical movement has lost some of its credibility. Its effectiveness on the international scene is less obvious than might have been expected at a time when religion (including Christianity) is once again playing an important role. The fact that the discovery has been made that the slogan "doctrine divides, service unites" of the earlier decades was misleading and had to be replaced by the opposite slogan "doctrine unites, service divides" speaks for itself. The overburdened and unfinished agenda of ecumenical social ethics becomes even more complicated because of innate tensions and continuous conflicts between the Roman Catholic, Orthodox, Protestant and evangelical (qq.v.) components of the ecumenical movement. All ecumenical organizations, including the World Council of Churches (q.v.), are as much potentially guiding and enabling, as factually fragile and vulnerable entities. All statements, positions and resolutions regarding sociopolitical reflection and action are subject to reserve and disagreement and often lead to new divisions and dissensions. It should not be a surprise that the World Council of Churches in the realms of social and political ethics has been the target of constant and passionate criticism from the very beginning.

Surveying for the first time together the needs of contemporary society, the 1920s were marked by a social idealism and generated a mood of optimism that reflected the spirit of the post-First World War period. The discovery of an international Christian fellowship that transcends denominational divisions and national antagonisms and the obligation of the churches "to apply the gospel in all realms of industrial, social, political and international life" inspired the Life and Work movement (q.v.) with great hope and confidence. It perceived that the ethos of pious individualism that predominated at that time was no answer to the problems of industrial revolution and world conflicts. Consequently, it sought to construct an ecumenical ethic based on the inspiration of various Christian social movements of the day. These were progressive movements, movements of indignation and protests against social evils, movements of reform and action. Although the Stockholm conference of 1925 endorsed many ideas of the social gospel (q.v.) movement in the Anglo-Saxon world and in several European countries, it remained critical of several of the conclusions that adherents of the social gospel drew from their insights.

During the 1930s the ecumenical movement found itself in an increasingly alarming international situation, which was to lead inexorably to the Second World War. The industrial countries were plagued by economic depression and social upheaval. Mussolini's Italy, Hitler's Germany and Stalin's Soviet Union became the typical forms of a society and a government where all aspects of personal and social life were subordinated to the absolute authority of a demonic center of power. An exclusive value was attributed to the state, the national community and the dominant class. The struggle in the ecumenical movement was particularly fierce where groups of Christians and even churches supported their government and tried to justify it theologically.

The Oxford conference of 1937 clearly saw that totalitarianism becomes an idolatry by claiming for the state, the nation or the race a total allegiance that is owed to God alone. This ideology reduces human beings, created in the image of God, to mere objects of the social system and prevents them from participating in the building up of a responsible and democratic society, thus denying their fundamental rights and a demand that God makes of them. But the maturing Life and Work movement did even more than challenge outright the elimination of all existing political institutions, laws and traditions and the organized and large-scale violence in the nations just mentioned. Experiencing the breakdown of prevailing liberal theology and the optimism of the social gospel, the delegates at Oxford were forced to lay a solid basis for the social and political responsibility of the churches in matters of the state, international relations and the economic order. They managed to reach a consensus on ethical approach and methodology.

On the other hand, by emphasizing the provisional character of all Christian efforts at social and economic policy-making, the Oxford conference helped to avoid the dangers of churches making ecclesiastical/theological commitments to contemporary social-ideological fashions. By its emphasis on cooperation with the social sciences and on the contribution of the Christian laity (q.v.), it helped to prepare the way for a new type of Christian social thinking, avoiding the kinds of ecclesiastical pontification and moralizing on social issues and economic problems that so often in the past characterized the churches' thought and action. Foreshadowing the developments of the last 50 years it is essential to confirm the fact that as much as the weakness of the Stockholm conference recurred in the history of the ecumenical movement, as much the strength of the Oxford conference has periodically disappeared. Churches and Christian groups have indulged in an overconfidence of having the right ethical answers to the horrendous problems of modern society, thereby failing to profit from the analytical and sobering experiences of the social sciences. Theological experimentalism, extreme contextualism in social ethics, and the total commitment to particular activist recipes of social justice have fragmented the ecumenical movement and hindered fruitful dialogue between the so-called "experts" and the so-called "people". Opting for a radical program of political activism weakens an effective witness to the world at large. An influential and convincing option for ecumenical social thought can be worked out only in and through the mutual challenge of different theological-ethical views.

From its inception, the World Council of Churches amplified and applied the teachings of Oxford as it sought to establish the marks of a political and economic order compatible with Christian ethics, to transcend the East-West conflict and to speak to both sides permanent words of peace (q.v.) and justice. It also faced the new challenges of the postwar world such as a new arms race, the support of the

United Nations (q.v.), various race conflicts and the problems of newly independent nations. At WCC assemblies, issues of social ethics were part of the agenda along with issues of faith and order, mission and evangelism (qq.v.), and so on. They were not given full-time consideration as at Stockholm and Oxford. Nevertheless, every intensive preparatory study was done both for the Amsterdam and Evanston assemblies, and social questions received their share of attention.

Even in the absence of the churches of China, the articulate delegates from Africa and Asia provided a constant reminder that hundreds of millions of people on those continents had awakened and were demanding recognition. Not surprisingly, in the late 1950s the churches moved from an overemphasis on the concerns of the western world to an equal concern for the eastern and southern parts of the globe. Unfortunately the ecumenical movement did not really come to grips with the problems of these areas until the decolonization process was well under way; this was partly due to the fact that prior to this time few churches in Third World countries were members of the WCC. Their contact with the ecumenical movement was largely through the International Missionary Council (q.v.), a world body of missionary agencies. When the urgent need was felt to develop an independent regional consciousness, Asian churches led the way in this respect, and churches in Africa and Latin America followed their example.

Another outstanding feature of the late 1940s and the 1950s was the conviction that a common approach to the Bible would not only bring Christians nearer to one another, but would enable them to make a common witness to their faith (q.v.) in the social and political realms. The contributions to *Biblical Authority for Today* are a prominent example of an attempt to read and interpret Holy Scripture together in order to learn how "the church gets from the Bible to the modern world". In this diligent ecumenical exercise not only the old liberal-orthodox antithesis was considerably modified but a consensus was reached on the Lordship of Christ whose universal sway over all earthly and heavenly powers is part of the central message of the gospel. It is in his name that the crumbling social structures of modern society are to be reconstructed and re-Christianized.

Two distinctive trends marked the period of the 1960s. The WCC became more truly universal in its membership, for it added more churches from the Third World and from the communist countries to its roster. And the ecumenical movement was directly confronted with the world issues of development (q.v.), revolution, technology and secularism (qq.v.). When many Orthodox and younger churches joined the Council, bringing along different viewpoints, the tensions and conflicts of the world became reflected in the social thinking of the WCC itself. The time was gone when earlier theological and ethical consensus was possible because the ecumenical movement had been predominantly Western and predominantly Protestant. From now on, the WCC was undertaking a more complicated task than in the previous decades, and increased tensions were accompanied by increased challenges. At the same time the theological perspective known as Christian realism fell into decline. Though there was no clear unifying pattern in the 1960s, a new humanism or a theology of secularization came into considerable prominence; the church was asked to take a positive stand toward the world. While the 1930s and 1940s stressed the dangers of secularism, especially the totalitarian forms, the 1960s emphasized the positive aspects of secular society. While in the earlier phase the primary emphasis was placed on the concern for freedom and order, the central notion from the mid-1960s onward became justice in its economic, social and political dimensions, and the concern for freedom was now expressed in terms of human dignity. A clear transition from study to action, translating consolidated consensus into specific commitments resulted in a stress on the gospel-based bias toward the poor (q.v.) and the oppressed and the political necessity of their participation in the decision-making processes.

Reading the signs of the time, the World Conference on Church and Society in Geneva (1966) and the fourth WCC assembly in Uppsala (1868) recognized that deep changes in world economic and political structures are required if global human justice and economic growth are to be achieved. The

Geneva gathering focused on the right way in Christian social ethics to relate biblical and theological traditions to the fast-changing conditions of the modern world, the ambiguity of the necessity of "revolution" and the need for a clearer statement of the theological ideas that underlie a positive and critical response to the various demands for revolutionary change. The Uppsala assembly forcefully stated: "If our false security in the old and our fear of revolutionary change tempt us to defend the status quo or to patch up with half-hearted measures, we will all perish". Pope Paul's encyclical *Populorum progressio* (1967) supported similar goals of world development as were espoused at Geneva, and opened the door to new possibilities of common Christian action. Continued and effective cooperation was assured through the formation of SODEPAX (q.v.)—the exploratory Committee on Society, Development and Peace.

During this period there were changes in ethical thinking. Contextual or situation ethics received wide support while the ethics of principles, including middle axioms (q.v.), declined in influence. According to contextual ethics, the Christian community needed to find what God was doing in each historical situation and to respond to his actions. It would be difficult to find general principles valid for all parts of the world. Thus, the proximate theological and ethical consensus of the previous period seemed to dwindle. Polarization was taking place between people of rich nations and people of poor nations, members of black and members of white races, advocates of reform and espousers of revolution, believers in situation ethics and believers in principle ethics, theologians with traditional perspectives and theologians with contemporary ones. It was apparent that ecumenical social thought had moved in the past half century from a Western-oriented to a universal movement; from cooperation without agreement on theological foundations to cooperation with considerable agreement, then back to cooperation with only limited agreement; from a somewhat humanistic social gospel to an orthodox theological foundation and back in the direction of humanism; from an optimistic view about the world to rather bleak views of secularism and back to more hopeful views of the secular world; from a responsible society (q.v.) to a responsible world society; from nonparticipation of the Roman Catholic Church in the ecumenical movement to dialogue (q.v.) and a close working relationship.

Although it is more difficult to evaluate the trends of the following period because of the closeness to it and the debates surrounding it, the 1970s and the 1980s can be characterized by both a continuation of and a compromise with the previous decade as well as some new contributions to Christian thinking on social issues. Internally the WCC and its constituency continued the earlier pattern of gathering together, discussing urgent issues and engaging in new policy-making. But a growing degree of routine and repetitiousness in procedures can be detected. Not only did the agenda of successive WCC assemblies become ever more overcrowded and difficult to survey; the debates on sociopolitical and economic problems tended to be more general and diffusive and the reports descriptive and open-ended. The annual meetings of the central committee were even more concerned with structural, operational and administrative matters than with new attempts to concentrate and reflect in greater depth on theological-ethical issues, as had been the case in the early beginnings of the Council. The decision-making process was almost entirely left to cumbersome and self-perpetuating committees and commissions in which every member had an opinion and a voice but in which there was no persuasive opinion and no clear voice. As independent, self-confident and visionary leaders were less and less available, ecumenical discussions often ended up in complexity, indecisiveness and mediocrity.

No human mortal will dare to predict in what direction ecumenical social ethics will move before and after the year 2000. The recent unexpected collapse of the communist part of the world, for example, is an unmistakable reminder that future developments in the world's affairs are and remain unpredictable and are in God's hands, not in ours. But it is not too difficult to observe that the ecumenical movement, including the WCC, is clearly at a crossroads and in dire need of a reorientation and reformulation. The recently adopted four-unit program structure of the Council was no distinctive advance over the former three-unit program structure. The social and economic programs of the WCC, which it inherited from the Uppsala assembly in 1968, have, despite some modifications and adaptations, virtually remained the same for almost twenty-five years and should have been cast in a new mold in order to meet the new situation of the shaken and desperate world. Their permanency should also be questioned in the light of the accusation that as the Council has not made sufficient progress in the realms of church unity and world mission (qq.v.) it was unable to resist the temptation to excel instead in social endeavors. There is further no reason to bewail the fact that recent Roman Catholic social pronouncements carry considerably more weight than the statements of the World Council of Churches and that the firm stand of the present pope on moral and ethical problems is often in the limelight.

The ever new starting point of Christian social ethics is the response of the historical Christian community to the God whom it recognizes in Christ and whose guidance it seeks in continuing history. The church *seeks* the kingdom of God (q.v.). It struggles to find ways of faithfulness in a world of conflict. Hence its ethic is not a deductive system, elaborated from a set of given propositions. It is a venturing ethic, the ethic of a people in pilgrimage—and therein lies its grandest possibilities and its perils. Faithfulness sometimes means constancy in the face of temptations; but faithfulness sometimes implies innovation in response to new opportunities. The Christian community at the end of this century, more than in the past, must relate itself to two kinds of reality: the social and the technical. The old realities of sin and grace, of divine and demonic promptings in history, of steadfastness in the faith and loyalty to a kingdom yet to come—these work themselves out in the midst of social and technical realities. Each of these realities requires attention in turn.

Nevertheless, besides facing these realities more than ever before, the question also of the nature and the destiny of the church vis-à-vis the world in regard to the eschatological future cannot be answered in an entirely positive and resolute way. More than ever before, the WCC and its worldwide constituency are freed from the requirement of always being credible and immediately relevant. The ecumenical verbalizing of social truth has to be replaced by the courage not to be universally valid because the world has become permanently multipolitical, multicultural and multireligious. More than ever before, the dictum of Paul Tillich is true that "religion is the substance of culture, and culture the form of religion". As there are many cultures and many religions, a world community of communities can be built up only by constant interaction and mutual correction. The great pressure and test for the ecumenical movement in the years to come is whether it has the wisdom and the capacity to disentangle itself finally from the snare of the superior Christian civilization and its inherent excessive anthropocentrism. Trying to grasp the perplexities of the scientists and the technocrats and listening attentively to the voices of politicians, economists and sociologists, the ecumenical movement may help to balance the dilemma of the destructive forces set in motion. Its message that these forces reduce human beings to their proper place in the commonwealth of creation and keep them accountable to God carries even more weight. In this way it shares with all humanity the unshakable hope that God alone remains the ultimate source of history and its final goal.

SOCIAL GOSPEL. The "social gospel" movement in America was the reaction against the impact of the industrial revolution with its large-scale production, concentration of economic power, urbanization and inequalities in the distribution of wealth and income in the latter part of the 19th century and the beginning of the 20th century. Certain key ideas, rooted in liberal theology, were characteristic of the social gospel. Their leaders explained that at the very center of Jesus' message was the kingdom of God (q.v.), which they understood to be a historical possibility to come on earth in some fullness, to bring with it social harmony and to eliminate gross injustices. Key figures in the movement were Walter Rauschenbusch (q.v.) and Shailer Mathews. Washington Gladden (q.v.) has been called the father of the social gospel, but Rauschenbusch became its outspoken theological advocate. The most systematic work among his numerous writings was *A Theology for the Social Gospel* (1917). The social gospel movement was a strong current in the Federal

Council of the Churches of Christ in America (q.v.), which started its activities in 1908. It declared that the churches must stand for the principles of conciliation and arbitration in industrial dissensions, for the abolition of child labor, for the reduction of hours of labor, for a living wage as a minimum standard in every industry, for the most equitable division of the products of industry as can ultimately be devised and for the abatement of poverty (q.v.).

Social gospel leaders looked for the "real" Jesus, as they believed he could be known by historical scholarship. He greatly emphasized the law of love. God works in and through human beings toward the kingdom of love, a cooperative commonwealth in which socialized and enlightened men and women will work for the good of all. Sin was considered to be primarily selfishness, but human beings can be educated to prefer social good to private advantage. Although sensitive to the facts of the collective transmission of sin through human institutions, the social gospel movement believed that social salvation would come as institutions as well as individuals come under the law of love. Through self-sacrifice Christians are able to become heroes of the coming dawn. Much of the social gospel was pacifistic, especially in its later phases between the two world wars.

During its climax and afterward social gospel theology has been challenged in its view of the human being as over optimistic and in its strategy of preaching the gospel as naive. This neo-orthodox critique was shared among many by W. A. Visser 't Hooft (q.v.) in his early days when he wrote his dissertation *The Background of the Social Gospel in America* (1927) in which he criticized the emphasis on the imminence of God rather than on his transcendence and the misleading belief in the perfectibility of the human being and society. The central idea of the gradual progress of humanity toward higher stages of moral and spiritual development contradicts the realistic biblical affirmation of the sinful predicament of human beings. Yet, at the end of his thesis Visser 't Hooft noticed that "the social gospel is in a sense the first expression of American religious life which is truly born in America itself" and that "this ethic constitutes the one most important attempt to transcend the individualistic notions of the last centuries at a solidaristic conception of social life''. The social gospel has continued to influence the ecumenical movement at several stages. The success of a recent "neo-social gospel", especially visible in the theology of liberation (q.v.), results in a similar passion for justice and in a strong commitment and cooperation to eliminate injustice. But again it makes little sense to decry the faith in unlimited economic growth and never-ending progress, if the inhuman consequences of the capitalist system are not spelled out and corrected.

SOCIALISM. The word "socialism" has a wide range of different meanings. Traditionally and generally it has been used to imply (partly) collective ownership of the means of production, but more recent positions have tended to see the essence of it as being not so much public ownership as public control and planning of the economy and equality of opportunity. Marxist ideology has used the term in a precise meaning as a state in which capitalism (q.v.) has been superseded, but abundance for all has not yet been attained. Karl Marx and Friedrich Engels claimed to have made a science out of socialism by placing it on solid empirical ground rather than dreams and speculations. Stalinism was a simplified, rigid and dogmatic version of socialism, which became the ruling ideology of the USSR and its satellites under the dictator's regime. Maoism emphasized the role of the peasantry as the agents of revolution and asserted that contradictions and thus change will continue even in a communist society. The alternative, non-Marxist strand of socialist thought is often called social democracy or democratic socialism and sees socialism compatible with liberal democracy. Although there is more or less general agreement on the social control of the means of production, there has been marked difference of opinion on the narrower issues of public ownership.

There is a long history of interaction between Christianity and socialism. English Christian socialism was created in the mid-19th century by F. D. Maurice and Charles Kingsley and has been carried on in a variety of movements and groups until today. Some of these Christian socialists mainly opposed the emphasis of capitalism on self-interest and competition. The reaction in America to the industrial order came somewhat later than in England and on the continent of Europe. The first major figure in the so-called "social gospel" (q.v.) movement was Washington Gladden (q.v.). He greatly influenced Walter Rauschenbusch (q.v.), who became the systematic theologian of the movement. By 1890 most of the principles of the social gospel movement had been stated, and in 1908 the Federal Council of Churches of Christ (q.v.) was to sanction them by the adoption of what amounted to its creed, *The Social Ideas of the Churches*. Two Swiss Protestant pastors, Hermann Kutter and Leonard Ragaz, provided the chief impetus for the formation of the Christian socialist movement in Switzerland. Their influence extended far beyond their native country and their time. An ongoing dialogue between theology and socialist ideas profoundly influenced several theologians, in particular Karl Barth (q.v.) and Paul Tillich.

The errors of Marxism and liberal individualism, although in opposition in their concept of society, are on a par and spring from similar roots, according to Roman Catholicism (q.v.). In opposition to both excesses the church presents a balanced order of society: human beings are the foundation, the cause and the end of all human institutions. As social beings they are meant to live and work with others and to contribute to one another's welfare. The principle of subsidiarity, which Pius XI called "a fundamental principle of social philosophy, unshaken and unchangeable", stands in sharp contrast to both individualism and totalitarianism. Against the former it asserts the legitimate role of the state; against the latter it asserts the right of citizens as persons; against both it defends the rights of individuals freely to form associations within the state to promote their legitimate interests. In *Mater magistra,* John XXIII (q.v.) stated that "the right of private property, including that pertaining to goods devoted to productive enterprises, is permanently valid".

The WCC (q.v.) became much involved with the claims of socialism because its member churches lived to a considerable extent in socialist societies. In a more general sense socialism also influenced the ecumenical movement because of its outspoken demands for socioeconomic justice. The first WCC assembly (q.v.) in Amsterdam (1948) tried to steer an independent course by rejecting "the ideologies of both communism and laissez-faire capitalism", as if "these two extremes are the only alternatives". The Evanston assembly (1954) argued that "disputes about 'capitalism' and 'socialism' disguise the more important issues in the field of economic and social policy . . . The concrete issues in all countries concern the newly evolving forms of economic organization, and the relative roles of the state, organized groups and private enterprises".

The encyclical *Centesimus annus* (1991) of John Paul II (q.v.) comes in the most recent time when socialism in Central and Eastern Europe as well as in several nations of the southern part of the world has received a deathblow. Communist parties have collapsed and changed their name to a socialist variant. The anticommunist, prodemocratic and pro-market developments have radical social, historical, ethical and theological significance not only for the world, but also for the church. On the other hand, human community is disabled by consumerism, possessiveness and ecological damage that dehumanizes life in the nonsocialist societies. *Centesimus annus* seeks not only to "manifest the true meaning of church tradition", but also to apply it to "an analysis of some events of recent history". It shows, moreover, seriously secular thinking regarding economics and politics in secular society. In speaking of "structures of sin" it is profoundly biblically oriented. The world ecumenical movement is adjusting to the current profound transformations of socialism whose final outcome is quite unclear.

Although the WCC welcomed the new liberties and democratic processes in Eastern Europe, it called attention to a number of concerns as well: uncritical acceptance of free-market capitalism as the ·solution to the economic malaise created by a generation of state socialism; the danger—heightened by the move toward a single market in Western Europe and the economic competition between the USA and Japan—of a selfish attitude that ignores the poverty (q.v.) and oppression in the rest of the world; and the potential for conflict created by raising ethnic and national consciousness among long-oppressed minority groups. *See also* CAPITALISM.

SOCIETAS OECUMENICA *see* ECUMENICAL INSTITUTES

SOCIOLOGY OF THE ECUMENICAL MOVEMENT. For the first time, the world conference on Faith and Order (q.v.) in Lund (1952) discussed the social, cultural, political and racial elements and so-called nontheological factors in church divisions and church unity. This awareness led to studies on institutionalism (the church as institution) and to the attempt to relate the issue of conflict and unity in the church with that of conflict and community among humankind. Although it has been admitted that the nontheological factors, such as fear of change and institutional inertia, should not be minimized, it has become apparent that quite a number of original reasons for separation and division in the church were indeed "nontheological", that is, contextual, in spite of the fact that intensive theological dialogues between the churches lead to growing agreement.

In recent years social scientists have described typical forms of disunity and conflict. They have distinguished between conflicts that occur within a shared set of values and those that represent ultimately incompatible options. They have considered, moreover, different ways of analyzing and resolving conflict for harmonious social life. Unfortunately, neither the churches nor the ecumenical movement have, on the whole, taken advantage of insights from such studies to deal with their internal conflicts or with those that emerge in their relation with society. There is here a continuous tension between theology and sociology that is very difficult to resolve. The estrangement between the church and the world has in it an element of emanicipation, of a natural affirmation of the autonomy of culture over a church that all too often sought to keep the world under its tutelage. On the other hand, secularism (q.v.) can take an aggressively anti-Christian form and develop ideologies (q.v.) that become practically pseudo-religions. There is another element in the estrangement between the church and the world. It is the new sense of the integrity of the church and the refusal on the part of Christians to accept a coexistence with the world in which Christianity loses its identity. There had to be a ''No'' to a wrong relation between church and world before there could again be a ''Yes'' and a new turning to the world on the basis of a clearer conception of church and world.

The question is whether this context does explain the emergence of the ecumenical movement. Sociologists will be inclined to answer this question affirmatively and to interpret the ecumenical movement as the response of the churches to external challenges, threats and pressures. Theologians will be inclined to deny such sociological conditioning and point out that the movement is fundamentally a rediscovery and reaffirmation of a dimension of truth that is inherent in the very nature of the church from the beginning. W. A. Visser 't Hooft (q.v.) wrote: ''It would seem that there is more truth in the sociological interpretation than most theologians are willing to admit and more truth in the theological understanding than the sociologists accept''. And he adds Roger Mehl's (q.v.) observation that ''to say that the ecumenical movement was born in a given sociological context, to say that its birth and development have been favored, influenced and orientated by a certain number of sociological facts, does not mean at all to pronounce a judgment on the significance of the movement''.

That the theologians have a convincing point can be shown by the fact that the ecumenical movement has not followed what could be called the line of the least cultural resistance. If the movement had been essentially a response to an external threat, it would certainly have organized itself as a movement to defend traditional Western civilization against its enemies inside and outside the camp. But this has not happened. On the contrary, the ecumenical movement has been a critical element in Western culture and sought to find new answers to the problems of relations between the ideological East and the ideological West, or between the traditionally Christian nations and those dominated by other religions, answers that grew out of the Christian faith and world vision rather than out of traditional cultural attitudes. It should also be remembered that the ecumenical movement has shown that it has not been dependent upon the ups and downs of internationalism and that during World War II and during the postwar tensions it has shown that it can transcend sociopolitical forces that drive human beings apart.

On the other hand, the sociologists are surely right if they maintain that the development of the ecumenical movement has been helped and intensified by the historical situation in which the churches find themselves in this period of history. The recall to the universal dimension of the faith has found a wider echo in our time because the church cannot perform its calling in the "one world" if it remains divided and provincial in its outlook. The fundamental significance of the ecumenical movement is ultimately grounded in the common recapturing of the simple biblical truth that the church as the people of God and the body of Christ must manifest in this world how God gathers members of the human race together from all corners of the earth to live as a new humanity. Sociology should appreciate that dialogue is the proper mode of doing theology in the ecumenical movement, over against the apologetic defensiveness of traditional theology. *See also* UNITY OF THE CHURCH AND THE RENEWAL OF HUMAN COMMUNITY.

SODEPAX. The joint Committee on Society, Development and Peace (SODEPAX) was from 1968 to 1980 the co-responsible agency between the Holy See (through the Pontifical Commission Justice and Peace, established in 1967) and the World Council of Churches (qq.v.) (through its Commission of the Churches' Participation in Development, created in 1968, afterward in 1971 through the more embracing Unit II, Justice and Service). Jointly announced as an "ecumenical experiment" with three-year mandates, SODEPAX had a sufficient number of charter documents to support it, including *Gaudium et spes* (1965) of Vatican II (q.v.) and the findings of the WCC assembly in Uppsala (1968). From its inception the joint committee energetically took up its responsibilities, helping to set up local and national groups and launching six programs on social communication, education for development (q.v.), mobilization for peace (q.v.), development research, theological reflection, and engaging in dialogue with people of living faiths (q.v.). It organized several large international conferences, notably on development in Beirut (1968), on the theology and challenge of development in Montreal (1969), and on peace and the international community in Baden, Austria (1970).

The more or less "official" version of the spectacular advance, the long stagnation and the painful liquidation of SODEPAX is that it became the victim of its own successes. It soon needed more staff to respond to demands from several parts of the world, but did not find sufficient outside funding. The two parent bodies reluctantly bore its main costs at the very time when they were worrying about SODEPAX becoming a quasi-independent third entity, due to the diffuse nature of its program and its free style of operation. The joint committee revealed indeed the problems of relations between the Roman Catholic Church (q.v.), a single, large and well-organized church, and the World Council of Churches, not more than a council of churches a few steps removed from (or ahead of) the decision-making structures of its member churches. There was, moreover, an increasing concern about competition between SODEPAX and the Pontifical Commission for Justice and Peace, on the one side, and the WCC's subunit on Church and Society and the Commission of the Churches' Participation in Development, on the other. The disappearance of SODEPAX was also bound up with the larger and still more important and complicated question of the eventual membership of the Roman Catholic Church in the WCC. The hope of an eventual joining of the largest Christian church in the life and activities of the WCC was still vivid in the early 1970s.

The version of the fate of SODEPAX, whose offices were located in Geneva near the WCC headquarters, given by George Dunne, its first general secretary, is quite different from the official story, and likely to be more plausible. The death of SODEPAX in 1980, according to the Jesuit Father, was caused primarily by questionable intrigues and power struggles among church officials from both sides, and less by the malfunctioning of church structures. (See his memoirs *King's Pawn* (1990)). In his recollections he asserts that an uncommon strength and a genuine zeal for service to the churches was lacking. Furthermore, he added, the universal church of Christ is far more vulnerable in suppressing the truth than by frankly admitting it. After 1980 an interim structure was formed by a Joint Consultative Group, linking the WCC Unit II with the corresponding dicasteries in the Vatican, but this group did not yield satisfactory results either.

SÖDERBLOM, NATHAN (1866–1931). Söderblom was one of the most important pioneers of the 20th-century ecumenical movement trying to unite various churches and denominational communions into one common fellowship. After studying theology in Uppsala, he served as chaplain to the Swedish legation in Paris, 1894–1901, where he received a doctorate with a dissertation on ancient Persion religion. He became professor of the history of religion in Uppsala, 1901–1914 (and simultaneously in Leipzig, 1912–1914). His appointment as archbishop of Uppsala in 1914 gave Söderblom an unexpected scope for exercising his ecumenical responsibilities, which was expressed in the first instance in his repeated initiatives for peace during the First World War. In spite of three efforts to bring church leaders in the belligerent countries together in an international church conference, he was able only to draw participants from several neutral countries. His renewed efforts after the war at founding an ecumenical council of churches, which would seek to bring Christian principles to bear on international relations and social, industrial and economic life while deferring consideration of differences of doctrine, were crowned eventually with the Universal Christian Conference on Life and Work (q.v.) in 1925. The success of the conference was almost exclusively due to his personal initiatives and wide breadth of vision. Taking part in the parallel Faith and Order movement (q.v.) as well he chaired the section on the unity of Christendom at its first world conference in Lausanne in 1927. He was awarded the Nobel peace prize in 1930.

SOLOVIEV, VLADIMIR (1853–1900). As theologian, philosopher, poet and ecumenist, Soloviev pleaded for the re-union of his Orthodox Church with the Roman Catholic Church (qq.v.). His attitude toward the Reformation and Protestantism (qq.v.) tended to be negative, though in his later years he did speak of a "super-confessional" Christianity, and even of a "religion of the Holy Spirit" (q.v.). He met a hostile reception in Russia, and the holy synod forbade him to write further on religious subjects. In 1896 he made a confession of faith, confessed to a Roman Catholic priest and received holy communion. The merit of Soloviev was that he tried to clarify the presuppositions that underlie the Catholic doctrine of the church. His ultimate ecumenical vision, so vividly presented in his *Story of the Antichrist,* included the whole of Christianity and the fullness of the Christian tradition—the spiritual insight of the Orthodox East, the authority of Rome, and the intellectual honesty of Protestantism. His true legacy is neither his "Romanism", nor his utopian theocratic dream, but his acute sense of Christian unity (q.v.), of the common history and destiny of the Christian religion, and his firm conviction that Christianity is the church.

SOTERIOLOGY *see* SALVATION

SPIRITUALITY. The ecumenical movement serves as a meeting place for the diverse spiritual traditions of the churches. They are a common treasure, containing as they do the essential ingredients of what can be described as ecumenical spirituality. Spirituality in the ecumenical movement was a force from the very beginning in Edinburgh (1910), and prior to practical and theological ecumenism, as expressed in the conferences of Life and Work (1925) (q.v.) and Faith and Order (1927) (qq.v.). It was the foundation on which the WCC (q.v.) was built (1948). Also in the Roman Catholic Church (q.v.) spiritual ecumenism developed in the 1930s and prepared the way for the changes made by the Second Vatican Council (q.v.). There are various traditional forms of spirituality: Orthodox worship (qq.v.) life, monastic silence, contemplative orders, spiritualities of the Reformation (q.v.). More recently spirituality of liberation, renewal movements, feminist spirituality, new communities and the development of lay ministries have come to the forefront.

Besides coining the phrase "spirituality for combat", the Nairobi assembly (1975) conducted a workshop on spirituality. Among the various statements the following sentences are significant: "Christians are called to live in the likeness of Jesus Christ (q.v.). No authentic spirituality serves simply one's own satisfaction. Christian spirituality means repentance, discipline (*ascesis*), sacrifice, and readiness to be humiliated (Phil. 2:7, 8). The cost of discipleship is high. The door to freedom and inner unity in Jesus Christ is narrow (Matt. 7:14), the path of love thorny, and the cross terrible yet glorious". The WCC Sub-unit on Renewal and Congregational Life sponsored a few workshops on spirituality afterward. At one of these workshops in 1978 it said that spiritual exploration "demands of us all an openness to Christians of other confessions, times, cultures and ideologies, as well as a willingness to contribute to the quest of other Christians as they for their part engage in the same pilgrimage of faith".

There is no doubt that the sixth WCC assembly in Vancouver (1983) was more deeply engaged in worship, prayer (q.v.), intercession and meditation than any other assembly. The liturgical life of this assembly was no accident. It was the culmination of a long pilgrimage of the WCC, always looking with more and more passion to express its real being, its spiritual raison d'être. Behind the worship of the assembly was the recognition that confronting the grave problems of humanity, Christian human resources are utterly inadequate, and that only through a new and radical grounding of their actions in the adoration of God will they continue to have the courage, the patience and the perseverance to be engaged in hard struggles. Without deep and pervasive spirituality there can be no appropriate action.

Another new emphasis, controversial but challenging, is the place of "spirituality" in the dialogue with people of other living faiths (q.v.). Until the 1970s this issue was either avoided entirely or touched upon in a superficial manner. Now it is admitted that religion is more than concepts and rituals. The symbols and signs of prayer, meditation and silence have deep meaning for life in communities of other faiths. Moreover, "the spirituality of the secular" in its thrust for self-transcendence is also part of the human being's request for meaning. In every contemporary dialogue this matter has been present, raising disturbing but searching questions not only for Christians but for people of other faiths as well. The problem is not so much one of definitions or fear of syncretism (q.v.). Rather, it concerns the dimensions of spiritual life 1) in an age of science and technology (qq.v.) when quite a few people, including much of the world's youth (q.v.), are rejecting traditional forms of worship, and 2) at a time when many people, including young people in the West, are turning to forms of Eastern spirituality, such as Yoga, Zen, etc. In the context of inter-religious dialogue the question also involves trying to understand the religious life of the dialogue partner not only through doctrines and academic concepts but through religious symbols, music, art and meditation. The crux is whether the ecumenical movement can show that the spiritual dimension is a vital link between the active and the contemplative, the mystical and the historical, the present and the future. *See also* HOLY SPIRIT; PRAYER; WORSHIP.

STATUS CONFESSIONIS. The concept (Latin for "situation of confession") signifies the borderline between decisions of faith (q.v.) for intermediate questions (*adiaphera*) and confession, and belongs to the latter. It was not literally used in the documents of the Reformation (q.v.). Only recently it entered into the ecumenical vocabulary with some common acceptance. *Status confessionis* in the Barmen declaration (1934) of the Confessing Church (q.v.) in Germany meant that the moment of truth had come to confess the faith in the context of the idolatrous powers of the Nazi ideology. The term was used by the Lutheran World Federation (q.v.) at its assembly in Dar es Salam (1977) condemning apartheid in South Africa. It has also been used by the World Alliance of Reformed Churches (q.v.) rejecting the justification of nuclear war (1982). Medellin (1968) was also a significant synod of Roman Catholic bishops in Latin America, which felt the need for confessing the faith in the face of the fate of millions of poor (q.v.), which destroys human life on a massive scale. There are dangers in taking up a categorical position because there is no guarantee that this will automatically renew the life of the church.

STENDAHL, KRISTER (1921–). Moderator of the WCC (q.v.) committee on the church and the Jewish people, Stendahl participated actively in several consultations of the Sub-unit on Dialogue with People of Living Faiths and Ideologies (qq.v.) and addressed several major ecumenical gatherings. Ordained in 1944 and completing a doctoral thesis on the Dead Sea scrolls and the gospel of Matthew, he was professor of New Testament at the Harvard Divinity School, 1954–1984, and its dean, 1968–1979. In his defense of Jews and women he felt called ''to seek a method of interpretation which can counteract the undesirable side affects of the scriptures''. In 1984 he was consecrated a bishop of the Church of Sweden in Stockholm.

STOCKHOLM 1925 see INTRODUCTION; LIFE AND WORK

STRENOPOULOS, GERMANOS (1872–1951). In 1922 Strenopoulos was elected metropolitan and exarch of the Ecumenical Patriarchate of Constantinople in Western and Central Europe with his see in London, where he remained until his death. He studied at the Theological School of Halki, obtained the degree of doctor of philosophy from the University of Leipzig, and was appointed professor at the Theological School of Halki. He worked diligently in the negotiations between Greek and Anglican churches and in the ecumenical movement for 30 years. The encyclical of the Ecumenical Patriarchate ''Unto all the Churches of Christ wheresoever They Be'' (1920), inviting the churches to establish and promote ''contact and understanding and a League of Churches'', was mainly prepared by the Faculty of Theology of the School of Halki and reflected the thoughts of its members, including those of Dean Strenopoulos. He wrote numerous articles on various subjects in Greek, English, German and Swiss periodicals.

STUDY CENTERS see ECUMENICAL INSTITUTES

SUNDKLER, BENGT (1909–). Sundkler was lecturer in the history of missions, 1945–1949, and in 1949 became professor of church history and the history of missions in Uppsala. In 1961 he was appointed the first bishop of the Lutheran Church in Northwest Tanganyika. In his epoch-making findings in *Bantu-Prophets in South Africa* (1961), he drew attention to the necessary interaction of church and society, thus pointing to ways in which relevant missionary frontiers can be traced and crossed. Within his missiological seminars in Uppsala, these emphases proved very inspiring as guidelines for further missionary research. As faithful heir of the ecumenical legacy of Nathan Söderblom (q.v.)—he wrote a scholarly biography of this ecumenical pioneer in 1968—and Ingve Brilioth (q.v.), he contributed to the WCC Uppsala assembly (qq.v.) in 1968.

SWANWICK 1966 see INTERCHURCH AID

SYNCRETISM. The word refers to the mingling together of different religions or religious philosophies, resulting in hybrid forms of religions or philosophies of religion. If what is drawn from local sources retains its original religious meaning, and is merely amalgamated with certain Christian elements, one can speak of religious syncretism. This is a mixture in which Christ through the Scriptures does not control all elements, and at best is only partly Christian. When the key Christian revelation is in itself interpreted and transformed in another religious direction, it becomes again a foreign religion, although now enriched by Christian borrowings. Examples of extreme syncretism occur where Jesus Christ (q.v.) becomes simply another great teacher or is replaced by a local founder of a new religion as messiah; where ecstatic behavior is the main gift of the Holy Spirit (q.v.) who may also be confused with other spirits; where baptism (q.v.) becomes a purification or a healing ceremony; where Christian conduct is the observance of a set of tabus. There are, however, also forms of cultural syncretism that may lead to genuine indigenization of religion.

The term ''syncretism'' in its negative meaning came into the forefront at the assembly of the International Missionary

Council (q.v.) at Tambaram, South India (1938), which was strongly influenced by Hendrik Kraemer (q.v.). Any indiscriminate mixture, amalgamation or harmonization of the Christian revelation with elements from other religions was, according to him, illegitimate. W. A. Visser 't Hooft (q.v.) in his book *No Other Name: The Choice between Syncretism and Christian Universalism* (1904), followed much the same line. Both owe their theological position to Karl Barth (q.v.) who insisted that religion is nothing but the attempt of a godless and wicked human race to reach up to God. In all their religious acts, human beings worship idols and indulge in a false adoration of God. Only the Christian faith (q.v.) is not a religion because it does not indicate the way to God, but accepts God's coming into the world in Jesus Christ. Surprisingly, the issue of syncretism was again passionately debated at the WCC Canberra assembly (1991), which had as its main theme "Come, Holy Spirit—Renew the Whole Creation". There was considerable confusion in speaking about the Holy Spirit and human spirits, inspired or not by the Holy Spirit. Statements by Orthodox and evangelical (qq.v.) participants in particular stressed the need for serious ecumenical study of syncretism in order to develop criteria for determining the limits of theological diversity in this radically pluralistic age. A "private" spirit, the spirits of the world or other spirits should not be substituted for the Holy Spirit.

It has become quite clear that in the dialogue with people of other living faiths (q.v.) the problem of syncretism as the combination and fusion of various religious beliefs has been resolutely shelved. The inter-religious dialogues (q.v.) of the last few decades have amply proved that humanity is not on its way to produce a syncretistic world religion, a new normative faith for all the members of the world community. Such a combined faith is not only a poor alternative to religious search for truth and an impoverishment of the human race, but it is strongly resisted by any religion defending its own spiritual integrity. Only if a faith dwells explicitly in repentance, trust and hope (q.v.) in the presence of the eternal God can it continue to enact a final dialectic and be creative in the midst of all life. As people manifest an unshakable faith they witness to God's particular presence in history. If Christians make an attempt to keep the purity of the gospel isolated from other world religions, it will lead to an emphasis on the uniqueness of Jesus Christ, which militates against his universality.

SYNDESMOS. The World Fellowship of Orthodox Youth was founded in 1953 at the initiative of Orthodox (q.v.) Christians who were involved in the work of the WCC (q.v.) youth department. *Syndesmos* is the Greek word for "uniting bond". It is a federation of youth movements and theological schools within local Eastern Orthodox churches. At its first congress young people from France, Greece, Finland and the Middle East participated. General assemblies have been held in France, Greece, Lebanon, Sweden, the USA, Switzerland and Finland. This world fellowship has implications for Orthodox witness in general and fosters ecumenical relations, in particular with the World Council of Churches, the Ecumenical Youth Council in Europe, the Conference of European Churches (q.v.) and the Middle East Council of Churches (q.v.).

The functions of SYNDESMOS are: 1) to be a bond of unity between Orthodox Christian youth organizations throughout the world and to set up such organizations wherever possible; 2) to promote among them a deeper understanding of the Orthodox Christian faith and a common vision of the tasks of the Orthodox church in the modern world; 3) to foster relations, cooperation and mutual aid between them in the realization of these tasks; 4) to assist Orthodox youth in their relations with other Christians and people of other faiths; 5) to be an instrument of furthering cooperation and deeper communion with the Oriental Orthodox churches (q.v.) through common youth activities. *See also* YOUTH.

- T -

TAFT, CHARLES PHELPS (1897–1983). Taft was president of the Federal Council of Churches (q.v.), 1947–1948, and an

Episcopal delegate to the WCC Amsterdam assembly (qq.v.), 1948. During the 1950s he served as a member of the WCC central committee, on the general board of the National Council of Churches, and chaired its department on the church and economic life. Having graduated from Yale University, he practiced law in Cincinnati, and served on the city council several times between 1938 and 1977, becoming mayor from 1955 to 1957. He was senior warden of Christ Episcopal Church in that city, and a lay deputy at several triennial conventions of the Protestant Episcopal Church.

TAIZÉ COMMUNITY. The ecumenical community of Taizé was founded by Roger Schutz (q.v.) in 1940 near Cluny in southeastern France. During the Vichy regime Schutz provided shelter to Jews and others at Taizé. In 1942 he was forced to leave and went to Geneva where he made contacts with Max Thurian (q.v.) and others interested in a Protestant monastic movement. By 1944 he had returned to Taizé and by 1947 seven brothers took the vows of celibacy, obedience and common property. The Rule of Taizé was completed in 1952. Today the brothers number ninety and include Roman Catholics, Anglicans and others from various Protestant (qq.v.) backgrounds from twenty countries. The community lives exclusively from its work and refuses donations. Offices are said three times a day. There is a novitiate of two to three years. Once admitted to the order, brothers stay in Taizé or go into many parts of the world to work at one's profession and promote Christian unity (q.v.). Since 1958 Taizé has attracted hundreds of thousands of young people from around the world for weekly meetings. They participate in the daily prayers and reflect together on inner life and human solidarity. Church leaders like John Paul II, archbishops Ramsey and Runcie, Metropolitan Nicodim and many others have visited the community.

TAKENAKA, MASAO (1925–). A graduate of Doshisha University in Japan in 1950, Takenaka received a Ph.D. degree in social ethics from Yale University in 1955. He was professor of Christian ethics and sociology of religion at Doshisha University from 1962 onward, and was visiting professor at

Union Theological Seminary, New York, 1962–1963, at Yale University, 1973, and Harvard University, 1981–1982. Takenaka has been active in the WCC and the Christian Conference of Asia (qq.v.) and has addressed major ecumenical gatherings. He is a specialist in Asian Christian art.

TAMBARAM 1938 *see* INTERNATIONAL MISSIONARY COUNCIL

TANTUR ECUMENICAL INSTITUTE *see* ECUMENICAL INSTITUTES

TAVARD, GEORGES HENRI (1922–). Theologian, ecumenist and historian, and expert at the Second Vatican Council (q.v.), Tavard has won a distinguished place in the ecumenical movement because of his precision of thought, command of intellectual history and original mind. He was professor of theology in Surrey, England, 1948, coeditor of *Documentation catholique* in Paris, 1951, lecturer at Assumption College in Worcester, Massachusetts, 1956, leader of the theological department of Mount Mercy College in Pittsburgh, 1959, and professor of theology at the Methodist Theological School in Ohio. Among various works, he wrote *Two Centuries of Ecumenism.*

TAYLOR, JOHN VERNON (1914–). Taylor studied theology at Oxford, was warden of Bishop Tucker Theological College, Uganda, 1945–1954, and became bishop of Winchester, 1975–1985. He served the International Missionary Council (q.v.) as a research worker, 1956–1959, was Africa secretary of the Church Missionary Society, 1959–1963, general secretary of the same Society, 1963–1974, and vice chairman of the Theological Education Fund (q.v.), 1968–1974. He lectured at the Ecumenical Institute in Bossey (q.v.) in 1955 and 1957 and was a delegate to several ecumenical missionary conferences. He wrote several books.

TECHNOLOGY. The relationship between Christianity and the progressive development of technology has become increasingly complex and ambiguous. On the one hand, the Christian religion and its civilization has done more than any other world religion to associate itself and sustain an ethos in which the purposive control of the natural environment for the attainment of better health, greater comfort, increased prosperity, additional mechanical power and productive knowledge has been considered a privileged human activity. On the other hand, Christians ever more frequently express negative concerns about the consequences of spectacular technological progress and even try to resist it. Technical power is often morally ambiguous, and the art of using it brings about accepting a freedom without becoming enslaved to it. Nuclear energy is a clear example of such ambivalence. The automobile is another: enormously increasing the range of human mobility, it has become a prison of human initiative. The widespread use of fertilizers and insecticides threatens many forms of agricultural and animal life, and human health as well, and raises the same general questions about how far it is both safe and desirable to produce radical changes in the human environment (q.v.). Advances in the biological sciences closely affecting human life itself have scarcely yet begun to make their impact (*see* BIOTECHNOLOGY AND BIOETHICS).

It was only since around 1970 that the ecumenical movement has been increasingly concerned about the social and environmental implications of technology. The WCC Subunit on Church and Society concentrated, moreover, on the important and vexing ethical considerations that arise in connection with the transfer of technology from industrially developed nations to other parts of the globe. It insisted that the Christian faith calls Christians to understand technology as something that intensifies the inequities that exist in the world and widens the gulf between the haves and have-nots. This way of thinking about the role played by technology in the contemporary world was especially evident in the discussions at the world conference on "Faith, Science and the Future", sponsored by the WCC at the Massachusetts Institute of Technology in 1979. In the eyes of the critics technology must be understood as an instrument to be used to liberate people from oppression, to serve the cause of justice (q.v.) and to facilitate widespread participation in the making of decisions that affect their lives.

In the 1980s the Sub-unit on Church and Society not only reacted critically to the disasters in Bhopal and Chernobyl, but reviewed, in the light of the escalating costs of nuclear installations, the lack of any significant progress in waste storage and the slow advance in searching for alternative energy production and transmission technologies, and the ethics of nuclear energy generation in the context of the most recent technology, information, costs and accidents. In other consultations it expressed a critical awareness of the tropical forest crisis leading to soil erosion, loss of fertility, falling water tables, desertification and eventually to climatic change. Perhaps the most serious environmental threat is the rapid deterioration of the atmosphere. The greenhouse effect appears to be caused by the trapping of heat around the earth as a result of the accumulation of a blanket of gases, derived from intensive industrial and agricultural practices and in particular from the consumption of fossil fuels in vehicles, power plants, and so on. These changes are made even more serious by the cumulative impact of acid rain and destruction of the protective ozone layer in the upper atmosphere. As a response to these urgent issues Church and Society has encouraged discussion of these questions with a view to the churches' contribution. The challenge for ecumenical Christianity is to find new ways in which technology can be used to promote the interdependence of the whole of creation and humanity.

Technology has brought obvious and great benefits; it has also created significant problems. Fortunately it has given human beings greater material resources for grappling with social problems, new and old. The problems that they are facing will test more their moral, spiritual and intellectual than their economic resources. *See also* ECOLOGY/ ENVIRONMENT; SCIENCE AND RELIGION.

TEMPLE, WILLIAM (1881–1944). Temple was the most prominent British ecumenist from 1910 to the end of his life. His father was archbishop of Exeter, 1897–1902. The son attended Rugby School and Balliol College, Oxford, taught philosophy at Queen's College, Oxford, 1907–1910, and was ordained in spite of some doubts of his bishop (Paget) over certain doctrinal issues. He was a steward at the Edinburgh conference in 1910 and chairman of the Conference on Christian Politics, Economics and Citizenship in Birmingham in 1924. He came into international ecumenical prominence at the international missionary conference in Jerusalem in 1928 where he drafted the statement of the conference. He was influential at the Faith and Order (q.v.) conference in Lausanne, 1927, drafted the final statement of the Life and Work (q.v.) conference in Oxford, 1937, and was chairman of the Faith and Order conference in Edinburgh in the same year. At the first meeting of the provisional committee of the WCC (q.v.) Temple was elected chairman. It was in 1942 at his enthronement as archbishop of Canterbury—he was appointed bishop of Manchester in 1921 and archbishop of York in 1929—that he referred to the ecumenical movement as "the great new fact of our era". He coined another famous phrase: "Any authority the World Council of Churches will have will consist in the weight which it carries with the churches by its own wisdom". Temple was in the line of Anglican social thinkers, running back through the Christian social union to F. D. Maurice. He combined an incarnational theology with an acute social conscience. His book *Christianity and Social Order* became a well-known work. His early death was a great shock to a war-stricken nation.

THADDEN-TRIEGLAFF, REINHOLD VON (1891–1976). Thadden-Trieglaff was the founder and first president of the German "Evangelischer Kirchentag", 1949–1964, which soon brought together innumerable Protestant and Roman Catholic (qq.v.) laypeople from both Germanies, East and West, and from abroad. Chairman of the German Christian Student Movement, 1928–1939, in 1936 he was appointed vice chairman of the World Student Christian Federation (q.v.). Active in the German church struggle against National Socialism, he was present at the synod in Barmen in 1934 as representative of the church synod of Pomerania. He combined influential work for the students with a relentless opposition to Hitler and was twice arrested by the Gestapo.

He held the senior position in the German army's occupation of Louvain, and received afterward the official thanks of the city for the humane way he carried out his duties. Refusing offers of asylum, in 1945 he returned to Pomerania, whence he was deported to prison camps on the Arctic circle by Soviet troops. In 1946 he returned to Berlin, his health and voice ruined. He was on the staff of the WCC (q.v.) for work among German prisoners of war, 1946–1948, and a member of the WCC central committee, 1948–1961.

THEOLOGICAL EDUCATION FUND (TEF). This Fund was set up at the Ghana meeting of the International Missionary Council (q.v.) in 1957 and completed three mandates until 1977, when it became the WCC (q.v.) Program on Theological Education (PTE). It was concerned with theological education in the non-Western world, and was supported during each phase by funds that totaled about US $4 million. During the first phase, efforts were directed toward the development of textbook programs in local languages and the strengthening of a limited number of strategic institutions. In the second phase there was a more general application of grants for projects aimed at the development of the seminary toward mission. A notable feature of the third mandate was that nearly all of the projects were developed and evaluated in terms of redefining theology in context. Greater emphasis was placed on projects for programs growing out of local attempts to deal with theological education at the "grass roots". A number of these involved continuing education, lay training and education by extension. Senior staff members of the TEF visited regularly various theological schools in the Third World.

The Program on Theological Education is particularly interested, according to its mandate, "to relate with and support the churches' efforts to develop creative theological education and adequate ministerial formation in the fulfillment of their mission". Since the Vancouver assembly (1983) its two special programmatic emphases are: theology by the people, and spiritual, theological and ministerial training. *See also* CHRISTIAN LITERATURE FUND.

THEOLOGY, LATE 20TH-CENTURY TRENDS IN. The history of ecumenical theology in this century can be traced in five overlapping phases:

1) Ecumenical beginnings owed much to the evangelical revival of the 19th century and its reaction against widespread indifference to the gospel. This was largely a nonintellectual and nondenominational theology. There was a more Christocentric approach and at the same time a greater stress on transcendence. In soteriology (q.v.) a return to the idea of atonement by vicarious suffering took place. Yet, the world conference on mission in Edinburgh in 1910, often called the birthplace of the ecumenical movement, deliberately did not discuss doctrinal matters.

2) From the mid-1920s on Protestant liberalism was in ascendancy. This liberalism was characterized by a naturalistic bias, a "low" Christology (q.v.), the interpretation of the Bible as a record of human experience and opinion, an optimistic humanism, speaking of the human being's "fall upward", of sin as maladjustment and of the kingdom of God (q.v.) as an indefinitely improvable system of human society. The Life and Work (q.v.) movement—which, despite its slogan that "doctrine divides, service unites", did a lot of theologizing—reflected many of the impulses associated in the USA with the "social gospel"(q.v.). This term is still used negatively by critics of WCC (q.v.) involvement in economic and political questions.

3) A radical critique of liberalism associated with such theologians as Karl Barth, Reinhold Niebuhr (qq.v.) and Emil Brunner, who insisted that theology depends entirely on God's self-revelation in Scripture, not on human culture, became more and more influential in the ecumenical movement up to the end of World War II. This neo-orthodox theology was characterized by a thoroughgoing insistence on the transcendence of God as opposed to all immanentism, a stress on the radical nature of sin, an interpretation of revelation as being primarily the self-disclose of a person rather than the unveiling of propositions, and a strong emphasis on the importance and necessity of personal decision and commitment.

4) Biblical theology—interpreting the Bible from the

point of view of Jesus Christ as the center of the history of salvation (qq.v.)—dominated ecumenical theology during the early years of the WCC. Although New Testament theology was dominant, interest in Old Testament thought was renewed. Satisfactory synthesis of the scientific and theological approaches remained a problem.

5) The early 1960s saw the waning of the influence of the great systematic theologies of Barth, Tillich and others. The ecumenical movement was coming to rediscover a prophetic tradition of theology, and there was a growing call to make theology relevant by "contextualizing" it, rooting it in its historical and cultural setting. Hence the diversity of theologies within the ecumenical movement today. Alongside continued attempts to produce traditional theologies, on the basis of a Christian confession, and efforts at "consensus theology" acceptable across traditional lines, "genetic theologies" (such as theology of liberation, theology of secularization, theology of the poor and theology of the people) and "adjectival theologies" (such as political theology, black theology, feminist theology and minjung theology), developed.

All these theologies are contextual, for each arises from a given context; their existence within the one ecumenical movement is not in itself a mark of incoherence, but reflects the movement's diversity and vitality. If the WCC is true to the best of its heritage, it will avoid both abstract intellectualism, which does not touch and is not touched by the conditions of people everywhere, and the parochialism of supposing that our talk about God and the church need not inform or be informed by thoughtful reflection on the rest of the world.

Political theology. This theology in its contemporary meaning originated in the 1960s as a movement among Roman Catholic and Protestant scholars to develop a new hermeneutics (q.v.) in Christian thought responsive to the temper and problems of modernity. Stressing the social context and historical character of reflection, political theology is critical of other forms of theological method. It considers the Roman Catholic (q.v.) doctrine of nature and natural law (q.v.) as ahistorical, transcendental Thomism, with its turn toward the subject, as apolitical: Lutheranism (q.v.), with its two-kingdom theory and orders of creation, as dualistic and static; and modern Protestantism (q.v.) (Rudolf Bultmann), and with its existential commitment, as individualistic. The primary proponents of political theology were from Germany (Johannes Baptist Metz, Jürgen Moltmann [q.v.], Dorothee Soelle), but the movement has been influential as well in other European countries, and also in the USA.

According to political theology, the moral critique of society is a fundamental mission of the church. It is a messianic association within society, bearing witness to the two-sided history of suffering and liberation. Through its "dangerous memory" (Metz) of Christ's crucifixion and resurrection, it is a call to identify with forgotten and victimized peoples and to engage in emanicipatory praxis. The church is always political in some sense, but to be true to its mission under modern conditions it must undergo a radical reformation. Internally, it must overthrow its patriarchal tradition and become a church of and for the people. Externally, it must become an effective force representing the meaning of the kingdom of God (q.v.) in history through a critique of prevailing economic, social and cultural idolatries and through a specification of justice (q.v.) and love, the mandates of discipleship. Despite its praxis orientation, political theology has yet to develop a systematic approach to ethics.

Theology of liberation. Christian theology has been predominantly a European affair, with offshoots in North America; and it has also been predominantly an academic affair. By contrast, a new theological approach surfaced in Latin America, a region on the periphery of world politics, and it was the work of theologians deeply involved in the struggle for liberation of their continent. However, these theologians were quick to point out that this was not just a "Latin American" theology. It was not as if European theology were the only theology that could be considered "the theology of the universal church". The theology of liberation developed in Latin America was to be a summons and a challenge to the conscience of all Christians. It was the continent's contribution toward a truly "catholic" theology.

What had been a colonial church was becoming a genuine autochthonous church.

Gustavo Gutiérrez (q.v.) was the first to begin the soundings for a liberation theology, and his starting point was the one great fact of poverty. The Medellin pronouncements on poverty (1968), which were the work mainly of Gutiérrez, are important because of their revelation of the poor (q.v.) as oppressed. A whole new approach to theology was started, epistemologically because of the formulation of the question of dependence, spiritually because of the discovery of the countenance of today's poor. It was along this path that Hugo Assmann, for example, with his grasp of European theology, began his critique of European theologians, showing step by step that that theology was confined to a given horizon to the point of becoming ideology. Other liberation theologians are: Gustavo Segundo, Clodovis Boff, Leonardo Boff, John Sobrino, Julio de Santa Ana, José Miguez-Binono (q.v.) and Rubem Alves.

There is no doubt that the growing participation of priests, ministers and laypeople in the life and struggles of the large poor majorities to overcome the conditions of marginalization, poverty and oppression was inspired by the growth of the church-based communities (q.v.). It is from them that theologians learned that the question of a spirituality (q.v.) related to the quest for liberation is of fundamental importance. Since it remains closely related to the life of the churches, liberation theology is ecumenical in its origin, intention and expression. Although the WCC never explicitly dealt with the theology of liberation in some consultation, the overall concern for liberation has been present in several of its conferences and programs. The Vatican Congregation for the Doctrine of the Faith issued in 1984 an *Instruction on Certain Aspects of the Theology of Liberation,* and in 1986 an *Instruction on Christian Freedom and Liberation.* The first document strongly warned against the danger of the infiltration of Marxist ideology in Christian social ethics and the one-sided interpretation of the Bible by church-based communities. The second document was milder in tone, stating that liberation theology is justified in certain circumstances.

Minjung theology. Minjung is the Korean word for people or masses of people, but it refers especially to the oppressed vis-à-vis the oppressors, or the poor over against the rich and the powerful. Korean theologians focused their attention on minjung, the neglected and suffering people who gain their selfhood through struggles. The irruption of people's histories and cultures into Asian consciousness has brought a critique of the elite-oriented theologies and philosophies of religion. The minjung (not all of whom are Christians) are the theological actors or subjects of theology to the extent in which they struggle against domination. In the 1970s Korea's oppressive military dictatorship silenced nearly all of its political opposition, denying the people their fundamental human rights (q.v.). The place of theology therefore is the human community striving for liberation and life, in which the Spirit is at work.

Minjung theology expresses itself in people's stories—mostly unwritten, articulated in symbols, folk songs, poems, myths, dance and celebration. It further takes seriously the liberation movement of women; Korean feminist theologians argue that women are the ''minjung of the minjungs''. Their theology condemns the sexist exploitation of the poor and the patriarchal systems that discriminate against women, whether in the church or in society. The danger of minjung theology is that it identifies too closely messianic movements or charismatic personages with Jesus of Nazareth. While it is justified in insisting that the suffering minjung must become the protagonists of their own history, it is questionable to say that minjung must achieve their own salvation. A clear distinction should be made between liberation and redemption (q.v.). If the radicality of biblical anthropology is to be preserved, the fact must be emphasized that rulers and ruled are equally alienated from God and that both are in need of the forgiveness and redemption that come through the saving work accomplished in Christ. Furthermore, a distinction should be made between the ''people of God'' (q.v.) and ''people''. God, indeed, cares for the whole of the human race; nonetheless, the *missio Dei* (q.v.) also aims at the gathering of the community.

Feminist theology. This theology begins with the assertion that women's lives are fundamental to the enterprise of theology. It seeks to create theology shaped by the heretofore unacknowledged—in the Christian tradition—experience of women. As a form of liberation theology it questions the very epistemological foundations of theology itself. In that questioning there arises the possibility of transforming theology. Feminist theology is reexamining the Bible and the history and tradition of the church from the perspective and perception of women. It is a contextual and concrete theology that understands daily life to be the place where the manifestation of God occurs. It is marked by humor, joy and celebration, and it is filled with a spirituality of hope (q.v.). It is personal and communal; personal in the sense that it begins with stories of individual women's lives, and communal in the sense that theology arises in response to the shared stories. In feminist theology there is a constant breaking apart of the old patriarchal categories and systems in order that a theology closer to common life may come into being. Indigenous forms of such theology have appeared in Latin America, Asia, Africa and other parts of the world.

From the early 1970s onward it was increasingly recognized that the liberating forces of the gospel pertain as much to women as to men. God's reconciliation breaks down the sinful barriers between the sexes. Discrimination between male and female vocations in the church is not yet healed by the admission of women to the ordained ministry (q.v.). As women are created, like men, in the image of God (Genesis 1:27), and face the new life, offered by the resurrected Christ (Galations 3:28), not only their predicament of subordination needs to be changed, but their full participation in the life of the Christian community is required. When women and men join together, women's demands are no longer felt to be embarrassing and traditional theology is seen to be the real problem. Only both partners of the human race can share in God's intention for unity. The new community of women and men in Christ is called to render a true Christian witness. It releases a new dynamic for the human society, torn apart by discriminatory practices.

Since questions of feminist theology cannot be settled by superficial concessions and friendly accommodations, because the credibility of the church's witness is at stake, and since the question remains whether Christianity does not in fact render a false witness, the problem of procedure is still open and difficult. Many church leaders resist, as do theologians and laypeople (male and female), a thorough reexamination of Christian anthropology and ecclesiology, contaminated by an age-old system of patriarchal and paternalistic values, and the structures of a so-called Christian society. It takes much energy and imagination to communicate a "Copernican turn" in the ecumenical movement. Since women discovered the power of their own thinking and action, the churches and their hierarchies continue to suffer from ignorance, uncertainty, fear, embarrassment and defensiveness. While many new theological and biblical insights have been gained, many psychological, sociological and cultural barriers to the understanding and acceptance of women's full contribution to the church and society remain. Particularly the problem of ordination of women (q.v.) threatens, more than ever before, the very unity and wholeness the churches are seeking.

Black theology. As a type of liberation theology, this theology is rooted in the black experience of slavery and economic exploitation, particularly in the United States of America and South Africa. It is a theological reflection that springs from the experience of people of black pigmentation who are discriminated against and oppressed in diverse manners. In that context, revelation to the blackness is a revelation of black power, which includes black awareness, black pride, black self-respect and a desire to determine one's own destiny. Its components are the black experience, the black theological heritage and the Bible. The perspectives of black peoples at the bottom of the heap become a critical ingredient of theology.

Like liberation theology, black theology has been criticized for being simply politics using a vocabulary of religion and theology, often in the context of a Marxist approach to history. Yet, black theology attempts to speak responsibly about God dealing with his world, and to promote social relations based on justice and love. It believes that God intends that racial identity should become a positive factor in the life of humanity. The races should enrich one another. They should work together for the common good as members of one body, each part of which makes its contribution to the whole. This can happen only if each race develops its identity in full and responsible freedom. Nevertheless, it is an open question whether black theology, instead of playing a decisive role in a situation of apartheid and contributing to the struggle of the masses, is not just an intellectual exercise of elite black theologians to enhance their status in the academic world.

Black church leaders and religious thinkers have become increasingly aware of the pressing needs of American blacks for an organization that can give direction and focus to the emerging interests in black theology. This has led to the establishment of the Society for the Study of Black Religion, founded in Atlanta in 1971. This group explores more fully dimensions of black religious history, black ethics and black systematic theology. It is more academic than ecclesiastical in focus, being the catalytic agent in furthering deeper analysis of black life and the Christian heritage. Indeed, a more profound appraisal of the African tradition is one of the more important tasks for black theology.

THILS, MARCEL-GUSTAVE (1909–). In 1947 Thils became professor of theology at Louvain and later a member of the Vatican Secretariat for Promoting Christian Unity (q.v.), and in 1968 president of the national Catholic commission on ecumenism (Belgium). He contributed several widely consulted works to the ecumenical movement from a Roman Catholic (q.v.) perspective, including *Histoire doctrinale du mouvement oecuménique.*

THIRD WORLD. The Third World is defined as the politically nonaligned and economically developing and less industrialized nations of the world. The emergence of the Third World has been one of the most significant phenomena of the post-World War II world. The countries of the Third World comprise 49 percent of the world's land surface and 51 percent of the world's population. Forty of these countries are the poorest in the world and nearly 1.2 billion of its inhabitants—60 percent of the Third World's population—subsist in chronic poverty (q.v.). The stress on self-reliance stems from the desire of the developing nations to fashion economic and political policies according to what they see as their own needs, problems and historical experiences. It is also an expression of their frustration with conventional strategies and policies of the developed world that they regard as exploitative. Despite the growing importance of the Third World, the basic issues in the relationships between rich and poor countries and the problems afflicting the poorer countries are only dimly perceived. Many in the West fail to understand the real nature of the social and economic processes at work in the Third World and their possible impact on their own societies.

The gap between the developed countries and the developing ones remains substantial. Average life expectancy is still sixteen years lower than in developed countries and infant mortality is five times as high. Despite dramatic breakthroughs in education, only 52 percent of the people of the Third World can read and write as compared with 99 percent in the developed world, and average educational expenditures are only US $18 per capita as against US $286 per capita in the developed world. About 850 million have no access to schools and rarely go beyond the primary grades. Only one quarter of the population of the Third World have access to safe water and only one half the urban households have minimally adequate housing. Economically, the Third World is bearing a crushing burden of debt (q.v.), which amounts today to over US $282 billion. But the greatest failure of the Third World has been its inability to halt the uncontrolled growth in population. By the year 2000, developing countries (including China) will account for 79.4 percent of the world's population.

From 1955 to 1960 the WCC's Department on Church and Society undertook a study on "Our Common Christian Responsibility Towards Areas of Rapid Social Change", which culminated in an international study conference on rapid social change in Thessalonica, Greece, in 1959. From 1966 onwards the WCC has increasingly concentrated on North-South relations, instead of East-West relations. Development of the Third World became one of its primary concerns, sometimes to such an extent that the Council was criticized for its leftist outlook and its one-sided political orientation. It later entertained the notions of "God's preferential option for the poor" and "the church of the poor". The encyclical *Populorum progressio* of Paul VI (qq.v.) was the first Roman Catholic document that called attention to the grave problems of the Third World. The ecumenical movement continues to press for a "new international economic order" that would include nondiscriminatory and preferential treatment of manufactured goods from the Third World in the markets of industrialized countries, more stable and higher prices for their commodities, renegotiation of their external public debt, codes of conduct for the activities of transnational corporations, more transfer of technologies (q.v.) to less developed countries—the First World (and Japan) has a monopoly on 97 percent of scientific and technological progress—and a greater voice in the management of the world's monetary system.

THOMAS, MADATHETHU ABRAHAM (1913–1993). A priest of the Mar Thoma Church, he worked in his early days for the Inter-Religious Student Fellowship and the Student Christian Movement. He was the founder of the Ecumenical Christian Center in Whitefield, near Bangalore, and its director until 1979. Concerned about human rights (q.v.) violations and sensing an erosion of democratic traditions, Thomas founded the Vigil India Movement after President Indira Ghandhi's declaration of emergency in 1975. A secular movement, it developed a network of groups in many parts of India. Under his leadership it participated in struggles for justice (q.v.) and worked to build awareness of human rights issues. He served as president of the Indian section of Amnesty International and of the Association of Christian Institutions for Social Concern in Asia. He preached many ecumenical sermons that contributed to the growth of ecumenical norms in the Indian Church's search for unity.

THOMAS, MADATHILPARAMPIL MAMMEN (1916–). M. M. Thomas is a member of the Syrian Mar Thoma Church of

Malabar. He studied chemistry at the University of Madras, afterward social ethics, one year at Union Theological Seminary, New York. He received an honorary doctor's degree from the University of Seramporc, India, and the University in Leiden, 1975. He was much involved in the three Christian youth conferences in Oslo (1947), in Kottayam (1952) and in Lausanne (1960). He was secretary and later vice chairman of the World Student Christian Federation (q.v.). He became director of the Christian Institute for the study of Religion and Society in Bangalore, 1962–1975. Thomas has lectured widely in North America, Europe and Asia on Christian social ethics and the dialogue of Christians with people of other living faiths (qq.v.). He was visiting professor at Union Theological Seminary, at Princeton Theological Seminary and at Perkins School of Theology. He served as chairman of the world conference on Church and Society in Geneva in 1966 and was the moderator of the WCC central committee, 1968–1975. In 1990 he was appointed governer of Nagaland in India. He published numerous works, including *My Ecumenical Journey* (1990).

THURIAN, MAX (1921–). After meeting Roger Schutz (q.v.) in 1942, Thurian became the theologian and liturgist of the Taizé community (q.v.). He has made a fresh approach to some of the most difficult problems in the Roman Catholic-Protestant dialogue (q.v.) from a biblical basis: celibacy, confession, confirmation (q.v.), intercommunion, the eucharist (q.v.) and devotion to the Virgin Mary (q.v.). Together with Roger Schutz he was personally invited by Pope John XXIII to be an observer at the Second Vatican Council (qq.v.). Thurian was instrumental in preparing the concensus document on *Baptism, Eucharist and Ministry* (BEM) (q.v.) (1982), and served the secretariat on Faith and Order (q.v.) from 1970 to 1987. He was responsible for editing six volumes of official responses of the churches to the BEM document: *Churches Respond to BEM* (WCC, 1986–89). In 1987 he became a priest of the Roman Catholic Church in Naples.

TILLARD, JEAN M. ROGER (1927–). Tillard was a theological expert at the Second Vatican Council (q.v.) and since then has been engaged in much ecumenical work. He is consultant to the Vatican Secretariat for Promoting Christian Unity, vice moderator of the Commission on Faith and Order, and was involved in preparing the consensus document on "Baptism, Eucharist and Ministry" (qq.v.) and now in "Towards the Common Expression of the Apostolic Faith Today". A member of the Anglican-Roman Catholic International Commission (I and II), and the International Commission on the Dialogue between the Orthodox Churches and the Roman Catholic Church (qq.v.), Tillard is also involved in the dialogue with the Disciples of Christ (q.v.). A member of the Dominican Order, he is professor of dogmatic theology at the Dominican Faculty at Ottawa and a regular lecturer at Fribourg (Switzerland) and Oxford, and has previously taught at Geneva, Lincoln and Nottingham.

TING, K. H. (DING GUANGXUN) (1915–). Educated at St John's University in Shanghai and Union Theological Seminary and Columbia University, New York, Ting was ordained as an Anglican (q.v.) priest in 1942, and made a bishop in 1955. He was secretary of the YMCA, 1938–1946, secretary of the Student Christian Movement in Canada, 1946–1947, secretary of the World Student Christian Federation (q.v.), 1948–1951, and general secretary of the Christian Literature Society, Shanghai, 1952–1953. He became principle of Nanjing Theological Seminary in 1953, and vice president of Nanjing University in 1979. Since 1981 he has been president of the China Christian Council and the National Three-Self Movement. He became vice moderator of the National People's Consultative Conference in 1989. Ting was at the WCC assembly (qq.v.) in Canberra in 1991 where the China Christian Council became a member of the WCC.

TOLEN, AARON (1937–). Tolen is a president of the WCC (q.v.), and has been a member of the WCC central and executive committee, 1983–1991, and also a member of the executive committee of the Commission of the Churches on International Affairs, 1969–1975, and moderator of the Commission on the Churches' Participation in Development,

1976–1983. He was active in the World Student Christian Federation (q.v.) China Project, 1964–1967, and was permanent representative to UNESCO, 1966–1969, co-secretary for Africa and Madagascar, 1969–1974. He addressed the assembly of the All Africa Conference of Churches (q.v.), Abidjan 1969, was international secretary of the Christian Peace Conference (q.v.), 1967–1970, and a member of the Committee of the Société des missions évangéliques de Paris, 1967–1969. In 1972 Tolen became executive secretary of the Department on Development of the Fédération des Eglises et missions évangéliques du Cameroun. He studied political science, law and economics in Bordeaux and in 1966 obtained a doctor's degree in history from the Faculté des lettres et des sciences humaines in Bordeaux.

TOMKINS, OLIVER STRATFORD (1908–1992). After being active in the Student Christian Movement in Great Britain and in a parish in Sheffield as an Anglican (q.v.) priest, Tomkins became WCC (q.v.) associate general secretary in charge of its London office from 1945 to 1953. He served as secretary of the Commission on Faith and Order (q.v.) from 1948–1953 and as chairman of the Faith and Order working committee from 1953–1967, during which period he also chaired a study committee on the ''Future of Faith and Order''. He was the moderator of the Faith and Order Commission, 1952–1968, in which function he presided over the fourth world conference in Montreal in 1963. He was a member of the WCC central committee, 1968–1975, and a member of the Joint Working Group (q.v.) during the same period. Tomkins had an extensive knowledge of the history of the Russian Orthodox Church (q.v.). He observed that ''today we dare not speak of the unity (q.v.) of the church without also speaking of its renewal (q.v.)''. He was the bishop of Bristol, 1953–1975.

TORONTO STATEMENT. The full title of the statement is: ''The Church, the Churches, and the World Council of Churches (q.v.)'', with an explanatory subtitle: ''The Ecclesiological Significance of the World Council of Churches''. It was adopted by the WCC central committee meeting in

Toronto in 1950. Its major contents is: "The World Council of Churches is not and must never become a super-church" (III.1). Its competence does not even cover union negotiations; its purpose is "to bring the churches into living contact with each other" (III.2). The WCC has no ecclesiology (q.v.) of its own (III.3), therefore no church is obliged to change its ecclesiology (III.4) nor to accept "a specific doctrine concerning the nature of church unity (q.v.)" (III.5). The basis for fellowship in the WCC is merely "the common recognition that Christ is the divine head of the body" (IV.1). Admittedly the churches belonging to the WCC recognize "that the membership of the church of Christ is more inclusive than the membership of their own church body" (IV.3); but this does not imply "that each church must regard the other member churches as churches in the true and full sense of the word". But "they recognize one another as serving the one Lord" (IV.4). Moreover, they "recognize in other churches elements of the true church" (IV.5). It is on this basis that they seek "a common witness before the world" (IV.6), "render assistance to each other in case of need, and refrain from such actions as are incompatible with brotherly relationships" (IV.7). "The member churches enter into spiritual relationships through which they seek to learn from each other and to give help to each other in order that the body of Christ may be built up and that the life of the churches may be renewed" (IV.8).

All this sounds very cautious and reserved. Clearly it was intended more to describe the existing situation than to point toward a future goal, in order that all the member churches might participate and cooperate. It was noted that "we can live beyond Toronto, but we cannot formulate beyond Toronto". Evidently a majority of churches had not reached the point in their own thinking that could enable them to formulate in precise terms their understanding of the nature of their membership in the World Council. In some cases, however, this reserve may have been motivated by the fear that they would have to draw practical conclusions from recognizing the theological significance of the WCC, that is, to concede it greater power and authority (qq.v.). The Toronto Statement still remains basic and relevant. It has rightly been described as more of a milestone than a stumbling block. It has served the churches in many ways for more than 40 years, though it obviously needs revision. But those undertaking that revision "will need the wisdom of Solomon, the patience of Job, and the grace of the gospel and, beyond all, the guidance and presence of the Holy Spirit". *See also* ECCLESIOLOGY; WORLD COUNCIL OF CHURCHES.

TOURISM *see* LEISURE/TOURISM

TRADITION AND TRADITIONS. A distinction must be made between Tradition (with a capital T) and tradition(s) (with a small t). By Tradition is meant the gospel itself, transmitted from generation to generation in and by the church. Christ is always present in the life of his people. The word tradition(s) stands for the whole of Christianity, considered as a complex of doctrines, practices, norms of behavior, religious experience, rituals and cult, handed down from the early church onward. It can also be used to mean a particular strand of doctrine or of practice—as in the tradition of teaching about the atonement, or the tradition of celebrating the eucharist (q.v.), or the Reformed tradition of preaching. Even Protestant (q.v.) churches claiming the Bible as the sole source of faith (q.v.) cannot live without tradition, because they have also taught the Christian faith. To exist without tradition is to establish a tradition of dispensing with tradition. Conservative evangelical communities live on the tradition of prescribing a particular gospel diet in order that their faithful will be rescued through a particular pattern of salvation (q.v.).

Tradition should not be rejected; it holds the company of faithful together. The trouble came when one tradition absolutized itself and rejected all other traditions. The history of the church is the sour story of many confessional positions competing with one another. It has led to condemnations, schisms and excommunications. Yet, Tradition is essential and deserves considerable attention from many theologians of different church traditions. In particular, the role of Tradition in the interpretation of Scripture is of capital importance for both Roman Catholics (q.v.) and Protestants. That which creates a sense of unity between differing confessions in spite of their divisions, and has made possible the ecumenical movement, is not the awareness of a common allegiance to Scripture, but the sense of sharing a common Tradition deriving from the period of the early church.

The fourth world conference on Faith and Order (q.v.) in Montreal in 1963 devoted a section to "Scripture, Tradition and traditions". It noted that, while on the Roman Catholic side, tradition has generally been understood as divine truth not expressed in the Bible alone, but orally transmitted, the Protestant position has been an appeal to Scripture alone, as the infallible and sufficient authority in all matters pertaining to salvation, to which all human traditions should be subjected. "For a variety of reasons, it has now become necessary to reconsider these positions . . . Historical study and not least the encounter of the churches in the ecumenical movement have led us to realize that the proclamation of the Gospel is always inevitably historically conditioned. We are also aware that in Roman Catholic theology the concept of tradition is undergoing serious reconsideration". For the Orthodox churches (q.v.) the Tradition is not only the act of God in Jesus Christ, who comes by the work of the Holy Spirit (qq.v.) to save all human beings who believe in him; it is also the Christian faith itself, transmitted in wholeness and purity, and made explicit in unbroken continuity through definite events in the life of the catholic and apostolic church from generation to generation.

Since Vatican II (q.v.) many Roman Catholic theologians agree that Tradition and Scripture, while different in form, are identical in content, so that Tradition is only formally, but not materially, independent of Scripture. The notion of a hierarchy of truths (q.v.), invoked in the *Decree on Ecumenism,* points to the fact that certain elements in Tradition are nearer than others to the central core of the gospel of salvation; Tradition should not be understood in strictly monolithic terms.

Today radical changes in social structure are taking place in many parts of the world. The church is thus faced with a dual responsibility. The Tradition has to be simultaneously transmitted in diverse ways; on the one hand, in popular everyday language; on the other hand, in terms of the complex and critical contemporary thought. The seriousness of this extraordinary situation cannot be easily exaggerated. Just as there are inherent dangers, there are also enormous potentialities for good. When the churches take the Tradition to new peoples in new nations, it is necessary that the essential content should find expression in new cultures. They have to face the serious problem of how the new churches may become truly indigenous, finding the Tradition among many old and new traditions, without falling into syncretism (q.v.).

TRANSNATIONAL CORPORATIONS (TNCs). At the WCC Nairobi assembly (qq.v.) (1975) the influence of transnational business in our time of world trade, technological transfer, social structures and political events was pointed out. There was an agreement that the international impact of transnational corporations (TNCs) cannot be ignored by the churches and the ecumenical movement. A task force on TNCs was organized at the level of WCC staff of representatives of several Subunits, with the Commission on the Churches' Participation in Development responsible for the coordination and implementation of the work. Several consultations were organized at regional levels (Latin America, Western Europe, Eastern Europe, Asia, Pacific, Australia and New Zealand), and in 1981 an international consultation was held in Bad Boll, Federal Republic of Germany, where church representatives, economists, social scientists, business people and community organizers from many countries and all regions of the world came together. The most relevant points can be summarized as follows.

1) The myth of TNCs as omnipotent institutions that manage the modern economic, political and cultural world, subverting, destabilizing or preserving nation-states must be confronted with the reality of TNCs as changing entities, which are central components of the unstable and changing system that gave birth to them. TNCs, therefore, cannot be fully understood outside the context of the world market system, which articulates production, finance, trade and

information on a global scale, and of which transnational forms and banks are the integrative force.

2) Awareness has developed among churches that TNCs are important not only because they are the most powerful and mobile economic institution in today's world, but also because their logic of unlimited growth, hierarchical decision-making, global expansion and profit maximization has imposed itself and become a dominant force in the world economy. National logic, both state and private in this "free market" world, including in TNCs' countries of origin, is increasingly subordinated to the global logic of TNCs. This TNC worldview considers people as objects of history of their elites, accumulation of wealth as the central purpose of development, and the world as the arena for the realization of capital itself.

3) TNCs have brought certain positive contributions to the world economy and all their potentials should be explored in the search for full human development. However, TNCs singly and collectively represent a major focus of unconstrained power (q.v.), whose primary concern is profit and growth. As such, they are alien to moral imperatives such as socioeconomic justice, accountability and participatory democracy. Churches are called upon to work closely with and to support all social forces seeking new ways to organize human society, through which the human being is brought to the center of economic development (q.v.)—i.e., urban and rural labor unions, women's groups, minorities' and migrants' organizations, consumer groups and governments committed to the needs and rights of their people.

4) In the world led by TNCs, capital and money are often viewed as human goals, and human freedom is seen as a consequence and by-product of price and market freedom. This monetary "mystique" denies the subjectivity of the human being and personifies the market as the paradigm of justice. Human progress is identified with economic growth and unlimited accumulation of wealth. The economy becomes dominant over the life of society and each individual. Churches and the ecumenical movement today are confronted with the tremendous challenge of listening to the voice of the poor (q.v.) and all those deprived of justice and human dignity.

The WCC program of critical examination has not been brought to an end because of its inherent complexity.

TRINITY. The doctrine of the Trinity has not been explicitly formulated in the New Testament, but is an attempt to draw out the implications of the biblical revelation of God— Father, Son and Holy Spirit (q.v.)—as it takes the history of salvation (q.v.) as a starting point: the fact of Jesus Christ (q.v.) incarnate, crucified and risen and the coming of the Spirit at Pentecost and his continuing impact on the church and the world. The structure of the New Testament is basically triadic and is verified in the three aspects of the Christian experience of God, linked to the decisive moments of revelation—God over us, God with us and God in us. The doctrine expresses the mutuality or reciprocity of indwelling whereby the love that is God passes and repasses between Father, Son and Holy Spirit. Such fullness of differentiated personal Being, it can be claimed, represents the nearest approach that the human mind is able to reach to the ineffable mystery of God.

The beginning of the formulation of the doctrine of the Trinity took place at the end of the 2nd century by the Cappadocian fathers because the truth of the gospel had to be protected from the misunderstandings of the ancient world: Christ interpreted as a semi-divine being, the fact of the incarnation interpreted as a myth that merely reflects eternal reality, and the Holy Spirit seen as one of the varieties of religious experience. Fully formulated by the fathers of the church in the Nicene (325) and Constantinopolitan (381) creeds (q.v.) and at the Council in Chalcedon (451), the unity of God was successfully preserved, not as an abstract arithmetical or quantitative kind of unity that makes God an eternal solitude, but the Trinitarian unity as the eternal, indivisible and life-giving communion of the three consubstantial, equal and yet distinct persons, avoiding any separation, subordination and confusion among them. In subsequent centuries the doctrine of the Trinity has been very differently and often controversially interpreted. Among many Christians the doctrine has been reverently ignored. Unitarianism (q.v.), tracing its history back to Michael

Servetus, who was burned at the stake in Geneva in 1553, finds no sound basis for the doctrine in Scripture.

The expanded Basis of the WCC (q.v.) (1961) reads: "The World Council of Churches is a fellowship of churches which confess the Lord Jesus Christ as God and Savior according to the Scriptures and therefore seek to fulfill together their common calling to the glory of the one God, Father, Son and Holy Spirit". The final doxological formula, by setting the Christocentric affirmation in a Trinitarian setting, adds a celebrative element to the fact of and aspiration for unity (q.v.). This unity was fully spelled out by the same New Delhi assembly as follows: "The unity which is given is the unity of the one Triune God from whom and through whom and to whom are all things. It is the unity which he gives to his people through his decision to dwell among them and to be their God. It is the unity which he gives to his people through the gift of his Son, who by his death and resurrection binds us together in him in his Sonship to the one Father. It is the unity given to his people through his Spirit, and through all the gifts of the Spirit which enliven, edify and empower the new humanity in Christ".

The Trinitarian perspective concerning the unity of God and the unity of the church also marked to some degree the deliberations of the Second Vatican Council (q.v.) in its teaching on revelation and the mystery of the church. Also the Faith and Order (q.v.) world conference in Montreal (1963) showed interest in the Trinitarian dimension in its understanding of worship (q.v.) as a "service to God the Father by men redeemed by his Son, who are continually finding new life in the power of the Holy Spirit". Furthermore, the study of the Faith and Order Commission on the ecumenical significance of the filioque (q.v.) controversy ended in 1979 with the recommendation that the meaning of faith in God, Father, Son and Holy Spirit be more fully examined "so that the Holy Trinity may be seen as the foundation of Christian life and experience". Finally, some bilateral dialogues concentrated on the meaning of the Trinity. The first theme of the international dialogue between Orthodox churches and the Roman Catholic Church (qq.v.)

was "The Mystery of the Church and the Eucharist in the Light of the Mystery of the Holy Trinity". In Orthodox-Reformed and Anglican-Orthodox dialogues (qq.v.) an agreement was reached that faith in the Trinity is a necessary presupposition for a common vision of church unity. The Trinitarian approach to the gospel is of primary importance as well for Christian mission (q.v.). Jesus Christ cannot be introduced to people of other faiths and no faith simply as God, but must be proclaimed as the Son of the Father. The sovereign freedom of the Holy Spirit in the church and in the world is the basic source of all renewal (q.v.). The church's mission to humanity is subject to the Father who overrules all things according to his will. *See also* HOLY SPIRIT; JESUS CHRIST; UNITY.

TUTU, DESMOND MPILO (1931–). Tutu was general secretary of the Nairobi-based All Africa Conference of Churches (q.v.) from 1987 onward, and was re-elected as general secretary of this ecumenical body in 1992. He served from 1978 to 1985 as general secretary of the South African Council of Churches and was earlier assistant director of the WCC Theological Education Fund (q.v.), 1972–1975. He was a main speaker at the Vancouver assembly (1983). He served as a member of the chaplaincy staff of the University of Fort Hare (1967–1969) and was a lecturer in the department of theology of the University of Botswana, Lesotho and Swaziland (1970–1972). He was the dean of Johannesburg (1975–1976), bishop of Lesotho (1976–1978), bishop of Johannesburg (1985–1986) and since 1986 arch-bishop of Cape Town. Throughout his whole life he was a strong opponent of apartheid and political violence (q.v.). Apartheid is intrinsically evil, he repeatedly stated, and must therefore use equally evil and violent methods to perpetuate itself. In a sermon preached in 1992, he said: "We must proclaim loud and clear that we are created freely for freedom, that it is our inalienable right to be able to choose freely without being intimidated or coerced, to choose freely from various political options available". He is undoubtedly one of the most charismatic Christians of South Africa.

- U -

UNA SANCTA MOVEMENT. This movement was part of an ecumenical awakening in Germany, France and the Netherlands during the years 1933–1945, and after the Second World War. It gave a sense of a common heritage in peril to Roman-Catholic-Protestant (qq.v) relations in these countries and a depth of fellowship in Christian witness that had never existed before. In Germany, Roman Catholics and Protestants suffered and died together in prisons and concentration camps; together they sometimes served the agonizing Jews and refugees; friendships were made that only death could unbind. The Una Sancta movement, which was founded by Max Joseph Metzger (1887–1944), who was executed by the Nazis for high treason in 1944, became a means of close devotional contacts with Protestants, and the Roman Catholic liturgical movement had an influence welcomed by many Lutherans (q.v.). In France, similar sufferings and similar friendships led to new depths of mutual understanding and respect; Roman Catholics and Protestants participated together in the hazardous publications of the resistance. In Holland, during the Nazi occupation, pastoral letters were signed jointly by Roman Catholic bishops and leaders of the Reformed churches; thus the cooperation was often public and official to a degree unknown before or since. After Vatican II, the movement in Germany merged largely into new ecumenical bodies, which from the Roman Catholic side were cofounded by the ecumenical institute (q.v.) of Niederalteich. The biennial German Roman Catholic laity (q.v.) congresses and the Protestant *Kirchentage* of the 1950s, and particularly the Una Sancta event at the eucharistic congress in Munich in 1960, made clear how far the ecumenical movement had caught the commitment of the grass roots in the church.

UNIATE CHURCHES. These churches emerged during the great schism in 1054 to overcome the rupture between Rome and Constantinople. The search for unity (q.v.) actually produced further schisms. Within national churches some believers allied with Rome while others, usually the great majority, refused to do so. Sometimes called "Eastern Catholics", the churches of the Byzantine rite are in full communion with the papacy and acknowledged parts of the Roman Catholic Church (q.v.), though retaining their own Eastern liturgical traditions and, indeed, such Eastern traditions as a married priesthood. The Catholic Church is not, in Roman teaching, confined to Latin Christianity. The bishop of Rome claims jurisdiction not only over all Latin Christians as patriarch of the West, but also over all Christians in the East as supreme pontiff.

Officially, Eastern Catholics—the name is preferred to Uniate churches because of its pejorative connotation—are divided into five major rites, four of which are further subdivided into national churches: 1) the Byzantine rite includes Ukrainians, Russians, Greeks, Bulgarians, Italo-Greeks, Melkites of Syria and a few others; 2) the rite of Antioch includes Syrians, Maronites and Malankarese; 3) the Alexandrian rite includes Coptic and Ethiopian Catholics; 4) the Chaldean rite includes Chaldeans and Malabarese; 5) the Armenian rite. "Rite" refers to the entire system of church discipline, covering more than simply the patterns of worship (q.v.). In the 20th century a complex process has been under way to create a single code of canon law (q.v.) to govern all Uniate churches. As political and social changes in Central and Eastern Europe since the late 1980s have brought greater religious freedom, their resurgence has been a source of conflict and in some cases even bloodshed.

Complicating the recent situation is a particular problem over the relationship of Ukrainian Orthodox to the Russian Orthodox Church. A group has been organized that claims to be an autocephalous (independent) Ukrainian Orthodox Church, though it is not recognized by any Orthodox Church (q.v.). Heading this group, which has about 6 million members (about 10.5 percent of the republic's population) is a US-based archbishop Mstislav Skrypnyk, who has been declared patriarch of Kiev. In the Western Ukraine the autocephalous group has some 1,600 churches. The Russian Orthodox Church vigorously disputes the charge of oppressing the Greek Catholic Church in the years after 1946, when under communist rule this church with all other Uniate churches was formally liquidated and its parishes incorporated in the Orthodox Church. Patriarch Alexy II argues that a whole generation has grown up since then and that an automatic return to its former status is for the time being not possible. More than 90 percent of clergy and laity, moreover, oppose it. The Roman Catholic Church is accused of proselytism (q.v.).

UNITARIANISM *see* UNIVERSALISM/UNITARIANISM

UNITED AND UNITING CHURCHES. The search for unification of churches has been an integral aspect of the ecumenical movement that proceeded quite independently of its varied organizational forms. Little causal connection can be drawn between, for instance, Life and Work, Faith and Order, or the WCC (qq.v) on the one hand, and the unions that have been achieved. Between 1925 and 1945, 19 united churches were formed, involving 57 churches. More than 60 churches have taken a leap of faith into "organic" union since the Second World War. Some churches have already gone through more than one union. That this movement is worldwide is indicated by the fact that the unions took place on all six continents and included a great number of countries.

Among most of the churches that have already joined, or will be joining, doctrinal issues do not appear all-important. This is especially true for developing countries where many church leaders have argued that overcoming confessional differences through corporate union should not be their primary agenda. The major challenges before the church, they maintain, are political and social injustice or threats to peace (q.v.), and the deepest source of division between Christians is not their denominational identity but their differing responses to such issues. The tremendous effort expended on uniting would thus be better spent on the struggles against domination, exploitation, racism (q.v.), hunger and want or militarism (q.v.). Where doctrinal differences do exist among church people negotiating for union, such differences often do not follow denominational lines.

They are differences that exist within all churches. The Church of South India, which in 1947 brought together Anglican, Methodist and Reformed (qq.v) traditions, was certainly the most celebrated among the "early" church unions, though far from unique. During one five-year period from 1965–1970, united churches were ushered in in Zambia, Jamaica and Grand Cayman, Madagascar, Papua New Guinea and the Solomon Islands, Belgium, North India, Pakistan and Zaire. These have been the source of genuine ecumenical hope—and a good deal of surprise.

During the past two decades fewer unions have been consummated than in previous decades. One of the unions that has taken place involved the Protestant Church of Belgium, which underwent its second union in ten years in 1978. The year 1977 saw the birth of the Uniting Church in Australia, a church with a membership of 2 million Christians. These are hardly insignificant achievements. The two major issues are the unification of ministries and the order of the united church. The first is highlighted in negotiations like the one in Great Britain between Anglicans and Methodists, where the proposed "Service of Reconcilation" between ministries and memberships has been a crucial issue. The other was devised in the course of discussions in North India. Nevertheless, bishops of the united church have received into their jurisdiction ministers of uniting churches with the laying on of hands and prayer A related issue in the discussion of ministry (q.v.), which has sometimes impeded church union in some parts of the world, is that of the ordination of women (q.v.). Increasingly negotiations are under way between churches that have ordained women presbyters and those that so far refuse ordination to women.

Advanced negotiations aimed at church union are currently taking place in several countries. These negotiations often reveal a willingness to learn from past efforts. There is a positive desire that the new church should be as healthy as possible at the time of birth. Many ecumenically committed Christians have wanted to set organic union as the final goal, and they are disappointed when the new churches have to struggle for unity (q.v.) after union. Such negotiations are not easy. But many of the current conversations seem to point to the existence of a genuine basis for unity. United churches must always be uniting churches, constantly seeking a deeper and broader unity in Christ. Present developments are indeed encouraging. A more recent development in India, for instance, is the setting up of a joint council by the Church of South India, the Church of North India and the Mar Thoma Church. Representatives of the three churches, working through the Joint Council, have reached a great measure of agreement on matters of faith, ministry and sacraments (q.v.). The goal is organic-cum-conciliar union, and negotiations have reached the point for the United Church that would do justice to their separate past, distinctive emphases at present and common future.

Many of the union developments have received focused attention at a series of Faith and Order (q.v.) consultations, which involve representatives of united and uniting churches around the world. Five such meetings between 1967 and 1987 exchanged information, sought solutions to common problems, lifted up the vision of church union and strengthened relations between these churches. There is broad agreement that visible unity must be realized "in stages". Several union efforts (for example, the Commission of the Covenanted Churches in Wales and the Consultation on Church Union (COCU) [q.v.]) have established or are trying to establish "covenants" (involving such agreements as the mutual recognition of members, regular eucharistic sharing and common mission) as a way of moving toward deeper fellowship. Church union, in other words, is viewed not as an all-or-nothing, one-time achievement, but as a process of gradual growth that allows the churches to strengthen their commitment to one another through interim steps. The staff of the Faith and Order secretariat compiles biennially a "Survey of Church Union Negotiations", which is published in the *Ecumenical Review*. *See also* ECCLESIOLOGY; UNITY.

UNITED BIBLE SOCIETIES *see* BIBLE SOCIETIES

UNITED NATIONS (UN). The primary objective of the United Nations is to resolve or attempt to resolve the problems that threaten peace (q.v.) and international security, to develop friendly relations among the nations and to promote and encourage respect for human rights (q.v.) and fundamental freedoms. It can take initiatives only when conflicts and problems are submitted formally by the states involved in disputes. Its effectiveness is further limited by the fact that the necessary emergency enforcement agencies have not been organized on a permanent basis. For each crisis, funds must be voted and volunteer forces recruited from among the member states. The UN officially was established on 24 October 1945, when the Charter had been ratified by China, France, the UK, USSR, USA and a majority of other signatories at the conference. That Charter has remained unchanged. Today the UN has a membership of over 160 nations. The Security Council has five permanent members: People's Republic of China, France, the USSR, UK and USA. The remaining ten members are elected by the General Assembly for two-year periods.

Despite its limitations the UN has worked effectively to promote international cooperation in solving problems of an economic, social, educational and humanitarian nature. The achievements of the UN Educational, Scientific, and Cultural Organization (UNESCO) are especially important, in the areas of scientific research, education, and the wide diffusion of cultural programs. The World Health Organization (WHO) has fought against disease all over the world and has helped member states to protect the health and physical welfare of their people. The Food and Agriculture Organization (FAO) has carried out important studies aimed at improving crops, both in quality and in yield, and has helped to increase agricultural production. Other important agencies are the International Labour Organisation (ILO), the UN High Commissioner for Refugees (UNHCR), the UN Children's Fund (UNICEF) and the UN Development Program (UNDP).

The WCC's (q.v.) Commission of the Churches on International Affairs, which has consultative status with the Economic and Social Council of the UN (and with all major specialized agencies), represents the WCC in the UN system. It played an important role in the formulation of the article on "religious liberty" (q.v.) in the Universal Declaration of Human Rights and in the establishment of the UN Commission on Human Rights. During the second half of the 1950s, and in the early 1960s, the Third Committee of the UN General Assembly gave extensive and detailed consideration to the texts of two draft covenants, one on "Economic, Social and Cultural Rights", and the other on "Civil and Political Rights". By this time, numerous newly independent developing countries had joined the UN, and agreement on wording for the final text became complicated because of divergent cultural, political, ethical and religious factors and of differences in constitutional and legal systems and the unequal ability of governments to observe the provisions once they were agreed upon. There was also a feeling that the Universal Declaration of Human Rights had given more prominence to liberal conceptions of human rights (q.v.) than to socialist conceptions. The covenants were meant to redress this imbalance.

The UN provides several instruments for the promotion of disarmament (q.v.). It is a unique public forum for the debate of proposals of disarmament before the world community. It has the capacity to monitor arms-limitation agreements. There have been conferences, sponsored by the UN, on human environment (q.v.) and world population. On the occasion of the 40th anniversary of the UN, the WCC central committee reaffirmed its support for the UN activities, calling this international organization the principle instrument of the community of nations "in defence of the common good of humankind". The Vatican as a non-member state has a permanent observer status at the UN.

In a very real sense the UN's functional objectives and developmental directions are set and shifted by the operation of its political process, in which the clash and consensus of the aims of the member states determine the choices made among the possibilities provided by the general state of the international system at any given point in time. Thus, we are confronted not with the question of believing in the UN as a sacred cause, but with the necessity of recognizing it as an agency subject to manipulation by states for such purposes as they may jointly decide to pursue or competitively succeed in imposing on it. The UN can, at best, facilitate the balancing of power against power (q.v.), and mobilize the resources of political adjustment. In the long run it is inevitably more affected by the circumstances of international relations than effective in altering them. From this also follows that the ideals of the UN Charter cannot be taken too literally. Their fulfillment depends on how responsibly the sovereign states exercise their membership. In practice they may use the United Nations for a variety of ends, some of which do not figure in the Charter and in fact militate against it.

In spite of all these realities, the WCC central committee in 1985 affirmed that "therefore, more than at any other time, it is necessary to reaffirm the hopes and ideals which led to the founding of the United Nations and to work incessantly for their realization". In an annex to its statement the central committee added: "Over the past four decades, the United Nations has lived through an unprecedented period of turbulent change: the rapid transformation of society by science and technology (qq.v) as well as the aspirations of the people to equality, participation and dignity; the doubling of the world's population; the tripling of its membership as over 700 million people emerged from colonial rule; the threat of global nuclear destruction and the widening disparities between affluence and poverty (q.v.) among and within nations. Sitting in the vortex, the UN has demonstrated itself to be indispensable, unique in its hopes, achievements and potential". *See also* INTERNATIONAL ORDER AND LAW.

UNITED STATES OF AMERICA. There is no other society in which Christians are so separated in competing communities as the USA. Resulting from mobility and freedom of choice, American believers belonged to almost 300 denominations, which were divided by ecclesiastical and doctrinal tradition, sectionalism, ethnic or social ties, or styles of religious experience. Many waves of immigrants since colonial days had contributed to this religious mixture. Opinionated leaders often formed new, independent church bodies, or even launched fresh movements that promoted a different theological outlook. Still today over 250 separate Christian churches exist, some large and some very small, each with its independent authority and organization. The most prominent mainline churches are the Baptists, Methodists, Presbyterians, Lutherans, Congregationalists (qq.v.) and Episcopalians.

The proliferation of divided denominations was countered, however, by an equally dramatic movement toward unity (q.v.). Especially important was the US branch of the Evangelical Alliance (1867), a fellowship within the World Evangelical Alliance (q.v.), founded in London in 1846. The alliance championed Christian unity, religious liberty for minorities, the Week of Prayer for Christian Unity, arbitration for peace and international mission (qq.v.). In this last field Protestant leaders in America and other countries recognized that the world missionary movement demanded interdenominational teamwork. Impetus for cooperation came particularly from the leadership of John R. Mott (qq.v.) in the Student Volunteer Movement, founded in 1886. His watchword was "the evangelization of the world in this generation". Before 1930 more than 20,000 missionaries were sent overseas. In 1908 the Federal Council of Churches (q.v.) was created to foster unity among American denominations. The rise of local, state, national and international councils (q.v.) signaled Protestant efforts to deal with a divided Christianity. The Federal Council was greatly influenced by liberal theology. In simplified terms it became designated as the social gospel (q.v.), which interpreted Jesus not as the divine Savior of sinners but as the great moral teacher pointing the way to social justice. Among the prominent spokesmen of the social gospel were Washington Gladden, Walter Rauschenbush (qq.v.) and Harry Emersen Fosdick.

In 1950 the movement toward Christian unity took another major step with the formation of the National Council of the Churches of Christ in the USA (NCCC) (q.v.). The Federal Council of Churches had represented only a segment of cooperative activity among the churches. In 1981 the NCCC changed its mandate and character from a cooperative agency of the churches to a community of Christian communions. Already in 1962 the most important and far-reaching movement toward church unity in the USA was the formation of the Consultation on Church Union (COCU) (q.v.). COCU was the result of a sermon preached two years earlier at Grace Cathedral, San Francisco, by Eugene Carsen Blake (q.v.), stated clerk of the United Presbyterian Church in the USA. Considerably beyond the reconciliation of historic church divisions, COCU continues to illustrate a new ecumenism by confronting the divisions of the church in the light of one baptism, one eucharist and one ministry (qq.v.).

Denominational mergers also characterized the drive for unity. In 1957 the Congregational Christian Churches joined with the Evangelical Reformed Church to become the United Church of Christ. The next year 96 percent of all Lutherans belonged to either the American Lutheran Church, the Lutheran Church in America or the Lutheran Church—Missouri Synod. The Methodists, North and South, and the smaller Methodist Protestant Church had unified in 1939, and subsequently joined with the Evangelical United Brethren in 1968. Standing outside the ecumenical movement, numerous smaller, conservative denominations formed the National Association of Evangelicals in 1943. The Southern Baptists Convention, operating independently, continued as the largest single Protestant denomination. Its membership by 1980 approached 14 million. Roman Catholicism comprises the largest single Christian constituency in the nation. By the middle of the 20th century anti-Catholic prejudice subsided. Practice and reflection were strengthened by a new emphasis on biblical studies by the laity (q.v.) and liturgical renewal, which soon included the vernacular Mass. The election of Pope John XXIII (q.v.) in 1958 and of Roman Catholic John F. Kennedy as president in 1960 signaled the coming of a new age in America.

For several decades the churches in the USA have been the major financial supporters of the World Council of Churches (q.v.). They contributed almost 75 percent of its total budget. The decline is not due to less generous giving, but to the considerable devaluation of the dollar. The following American churches are either founding members of the WCC or joined the Council at a later date: African Methodist Episco-

pal Church (2,500,000 members), African Methodist Episco-
pal Zion Church (1,500,000 members), American Baptist
Churches in the USA (1,617,000 members), American Lu-
theran Church 2,352,430 members), Christian Church (Dis-
ciples of Christ) in the United States (1,217,750 members),
Christian Methodist Episcopal Church (700,000 members),
Church of the Brethren (164,680 members), Episcopal
Church (3,025,000 members), Hungarian Reformed Church
in America (11,110 members), International Council of
Community Churches (175,000 members), International
Evangelical Church (168,100 members), Lutheran Church in
America (3,052,000 members), Moravian Church in Amer-
ica (Northern and Southern Province) (56,000 members),
National Baptist Convention of America (3,500,000 mem-
bers), National Baptist Convention, USA, Inc. (6,500,000
members), Orthodox Church in America (1,000,000 members), Polish National Catholic Church (100,000 members),
Presbyterian Church (USA) (3,132,000 members), Progressive National Baptist Convention, Inc. (521,700 members),
Reformed Church in America (350,000 members), Religious
Society of Friends: Friends General Conference (26,200
members), Religious Society of Friends: Friends United
Meeting (69,400 members), United Church of Christ
(1,702,000 members), United Methodist Church (9,840,475
members).

All these churches have contributed many able leaders to
the ecumenical movement who were prominent in WCC
assemblies, conferences and consultations. They also participated actively in many bilateral and multilaterial dialogues
(q.v.) between the churches.

UNITY. Unity is the primary goal of the ecumenical movement. It
is also the raison d'être of the World Council of Churches
(q.v.). The word has been used in a wide sense in the context
of the unity of humankind (related to the unity of the church)
and in various other contexts such as unity and mission;
unity, cooperation; unity, experienced in the ecumenical
movement; unity, God's gift; unity, God's will; unity, nontheological factors; unity, models of; unity of all in each
place; unity, organic; unity, uniformity and diversity; unity,

union negotations; unity, visible; unity, ways to, the unity we seek, and in yet other combinations of concepts and words. This entry briefly refers to the history and meaning of most of the ecumenical terms. The WCC Commission on Faith and Order (q.v.) has sponsored a great number of consultations on the various topics, been engaged in many study projects and issued many publications.

The Commission has invested much of its energies in taking soundings on the theme "Unity of the Church—Unity of Humankind", later changed to "The Unity of the Church and the Renewal of Human Community". The profound influence of the idea of the unity of humankind came from the WCC assembly in Uppsala in 1968, which stated: "The church is bold in speaking of itself as the sign of the coming unity of humankind. However well founded the claim, the world hears it sceptically, and points to 'secular catholicities' of its own. For secular society has produced instruments of conciliation and unification which often seem more effective than the church itself". The first phase of studies reached its provisional conclusion in a report entitled *Unity in Today's World* (1978). It specified that the unity of humankind is a theological term for the eschatological promise of the coming of the kingdom of God (q.v.). Explicating "the church as mystery and prophetic sign" and probing two major problems as issues of church unity—the community of women and men, and the search for justice (q.v.)—a progress report was submitted to the WCC Canberra assembly in 1991, which noted that a tension between those who are concerned with the unity of the church and those concerned with the desperate need for justice, peace (q.v.) and reconciliation in the human community persists.

During the first fifteen years of the WCC a strong emphasis was placed on the shame of the churches for not recognizing one another as part of the one, holy, catholic and apostolic church and on the nontheological factors (q.v.) of unity and disunity. No advance toward unity can be made if cultural, social, political and psychological components of the life of the churches are not painstakingly analyzed and evaluated. Many unconscious and unavowed prejudices and false presuppositions are too often treated as essentially in harmony with the gospel and not as the conditioning by a particular culture and society. The history of the churches and their divisions is to a large extent reflected in the history of civilizations and political systems. The Christian communities experience, as did its incarnate and sinless Lord, the consequences of the broken relationship between the Creator and his creatures. Division is a universal reality. Although it has later been stressed that in a sinful world the bonds of mutual love, understanding and sharing in the churches are repeatedly challenged by human divisions, and that the pluralism (q.v.) of cultures and societies is the pluralism of churches and their people, more recent documents and statements on ecclesiology (q.v.) have not sufficiently grasped the possibilities and implications of historical diversity taken absolutely seriously in the context of the ecumenical activities of God. An example is the consensus document *Baptism, Eucharist and Ministry* (BEM) (q.v.) (1982). Although this text, based on the three basic ecclesial conditions of the church, succeeds in summing up corporate Christian life and gives it coherence and continuity, it is still a Western document, rooted in the old cultural traditions of Roman Catholicism, Orthodoxy and Protestantism (qq.v.) of the European continent.

Consequently, it should not come as a surprise that the question of church unity has been largely absent in the churches of the Third World. Only from the middle of the 1960s onward do reports of assemblies of regional conferences of churches occasionally contain a few references to the problem of unity. But the emphasis in this context is far more on church cooperation, living together a common life for the sake of a united witness, not creating a common front for the protection of minority rights, universality to strengthen the missionary movement, the breaking out of the church's captivity to power and security, the church as an instrument of transformation of the whole society and the identification with the millions of poor (q.v.) and oppressed than on confessional ecclesiology, internal ecclesiastical matters and the important role of the WCC in the ecumenical movement. Therefore Asian and African theologians had little part in the drafting of the BEM document, and the responses of missionary churches to BEM did not break out of the mold of the mother churches, with few exceptions.

The New Testament refers to a great variety of ways to the unity of the church as the fundamental characteristic of its being. This unity is grounded in and reflects the unity of the Trinity (q.v.). As there is only one God, one Lord, one Holy Spirit (q.v.) and one communion among them, there can be only one church: the one people of God, the one body of Christ, the one temple of the Holy Spirit. This God-given unity is continuously sustained by the proclamation of the one gospel, the celebration of the one baptism (q.v.) as incorporation into the one body, and the eucharistic communion with Christ in the Holy Spirit and with one another. The first constitutional function of the WCC is "to call the churches to the goal of visible unity in one faith and in one eucharistic fellowship expressed in worship and in common life in Christ, and to advance toward that unity in order that the world may believe". Since 1948 the Council has assisted various churches to enter into radically changed relationships with one another, to reach agreements and convergencies in basic matters of faith and order, and to develop forms of solidarity and common witness. Since the Roman Catholic Church entered the ecumenical movement at the time of Vatican Council II (q.v.), the search and efforts for unity now includes all the major Christians traditions.

Organic unity is the historical goal of the Faith and Order movement, which has envisioned "a church so united (that) the ultimate loyalty of every member would be given to the whole body and not to any part of it". This unity would be that "of a living organism, with the diversity characteristic of the members of a healthy body". The New Delhi assembly (1961) stressed that the institutional price of such unity would "involve nothing less than a death or rebirth of many forms of church life as we have known them". This has meant the end of denominational identities and the creation, instead, of new "local" (that is, national) churches expressing the fullness of Christ's body in that place. Though no such local union has yet encompassed all churches in any one place, this vision has been most fully embodied in the some sixty united churches (q.v.) that have come into being in the past in all regions of the world. The New Delhi assembly in fact formulated for the first time the goal of unity: ''We believe that the unity which is both God's will and his gift to the church is being made visible as all in each place who are baptized into Jesus Christ and confess him as Lord and Savior are brought by the Holy Spirit into one fully committed fellowship, holding the one apostolic faith, preaching the one gospel, breaking the one bread, joining in common prayer, and having a corporate life reaching out in witness and service to all, and who at the same time are united with the whole Christian fellowship in all places and all ages in such ways that ministry and members are accepted by all, and that all can act and speak together as occasion requires for the tasks to which God calls his people''.

The Uppsala assembly (1968) emphasized the global dimensions of unity and expressed the hope that ''the members of the WCC, committed to each other, should work for a time when a genuinely universal council may once more speak for all Christians''. This vision of a ''genuinely universal council'' was taken up at the next meeting of the Faith and Order Commission in Louvain (1971). In a statement ''Conciliarity and the Future of the Ecumenical Movement'', a vision of unity was sketched in the form of a ''conciliar fellowship of churches''. There were reasons for this change in emphasis. The growing role of the Orthodox (q.v.) churches in the life and activities of the WCC gave wider recognition to the importance of ecumenical councils in the history of the church. And the massive presence of the Roman Catholic Church in the ecumenical movement from the Second Vatican Council onward had shifted emphasis from local schemes of union to bilateral dialogues between the Christian world communions (qq.v.). It was obvious that the Roman Catholic Church as a single world communion should find its partners in the world confessional families.

The Vancouver assembly (1983) reaffirmed the Nairobi statement and sought to develop it further through a search for a common understanding of the apostolic faith, through mutual recognition of baptism, eucharist and ministry (q.v.), and through common ways of decision-making. The Canberra assembly noted that, although cooperation between the churches is increasing, the processes of unity are slowing down. The question of the Roman Catholic Church's inclusion in a world ecumenical structure—whether the present WCC or whatever new body would be created to facilitate this integration—is no longer a pressing issue. The problem is more serious than just a loss of enthusiasm for unity between ecclesiastical centers. It looks as though, with the growth of the means of communication and an increasingly conscious option for plurality, church divisions are more and more accepted as an inevitable fact of life. It is taken for granted that Christians cannot get beyond their confessional differences. Clearly no single way to unity is sufficient in and of itself. Therefore, it is the ever new responsibility of Christians to pursue the search for visible unity through all the ways open to them, with ever new energy and ever new ingenuity. Any application of the concept of "reconciled diversity" should show that genuine Christian unity can only be a fully committed fellowship in life, witness and service, which must lead beyond mere peaceful coexistence. *See also* APOSTOLICITY/APOSTOLIC SUCCESSION; ECCLESI-OLOGY; UNITED AND UNITING CHURCHES.

UNITY OF THE CHURCH AND THE RENEWAL OF HUMAN COMMUNITY. This theme has been on the working agenda of the Commission on Faith and Order (q.v.) since its meeting in Louvain in 1971. The theme was originally formulated as: "Unity of the Church—Unity of Humankind". Ever since, many Christians have warmly welcomed the fact that the aspect of the unity of humankind has at last been recognized as an important topic for the ecumenical movement. They regard reflection on the "unity of the church" in isolation as an anachronistic ecclesiocentric provincialism and are eager to see all ecumenical resources concentrated on achieving long-overdue progress in the problems facing humanity. On the other hand, many conservative Christians regard the theme of the "Unity of the Church and the Renewal of Human Community" as a betrayal of the real task of the ecumenical movement. The mission (q.v.) to unbelievers and the task of gathering the true children of God from all the kingdoms into the kingdom of God (q.v.) has been lost from view, and consequently the WCC (q.v.) has become an instrument serving the eschatological activities of the Antichrist.

Both have an important point; yet neither faces the ultimate question. Those who say that the program of Faith and Order on "Baptism, Eucharist and Ministry" and "Confessing the Apostolic Faith Today" are not simply intra-Christian debates, but contain the deepest source of hope and, at least, a partial renewal of a broken humanity, still have to demonstrate why this is so. Christians gathered around the eucharistic table proclaim the Lord's death until he comes. But does that imply that human communities can grasp that the cross is the judgment of their false dreams, and the resurrection the hope for human unity? Those who say that the church is first of all a servant community struggling for the values of the kingdom in human community fail to ask whether the world actually appreciates the church services. Humanity can and does suspect that the church wishes to be engaged in the struggle for the poor (q.v.) and the oppressed as a starting point for the attainment of its own unity.

The Vancouver assembly (1983) stressed that a "single vision unites our two profoundest ecumenical concerns: the unity and the renewal (qq.v.) of the church and the healing and destiny of the human community. Church unity is vital to the health of the church and to the future of the human family. Moreover, it is a response of obedience to God's will and an offering of praise of God's glory". It recommended that Faith and Order take up a study "The Church as Mystery and Prophetic Sign" in line with the affirmation of the Uppsala assembly (1968) that "the church is bold in speaking of itself as the sign of the coming unity of humankind". It is only a church that goes out from its eucharistic center, strengthened by word and sacrament and thus strengthened in its own identity, resolved to become what it is, that can take the world on to its agenda. There will never be a time when the world, with all its political, social and economic issues, ceases to be the agenda of the church.

At its Stavanger meeting (1985) the Faith and Order commission adopted this study document, intended as a statement of theological orientation in the study on "The Unity of the Church and the Renewal of Human Community". The report describes the relation between church and world in an eschatological perspective, that is, in light of the kingdom of God, which is related both to church and world in judgment and grace (q.v.). The church is seen as that part of humanity that acknowledges the truth of the coming kingdom. That is the church's inalienable identity; but this identity implies the recognition that what is gathered, reconciled and renewed in the church is in fact "world"; what takes place in the church refers back to the world and forward to its final redemption (q.v.). Both aspects of the church— "mystery" and "prophetic sign"—must be understood in this eschatological framework. The Canberra assembly (1991) greatly welcomed the continuing work on the study by Faith and Order, "through which the relations between the two basic concerns of the ecumenical movement are examined from the overall perspective of the promise of the kingdom of God and hopefully can be convincingly illuminated for everyone".

Since the study on the "Unity of the Church and the Renewal of Human Community" has been developed for a quarter of a century, it remains to be seen whether it does promote the wholeness and the oneness of the WCC and whether the so-called advocates of the unity of the church and the so-called advocates of the unity of humankind can be truly reconciled. Only the more radical questions with regard to the survival of the human race and the sustainability of life on the planet can ultimately lead away from the Christocentric missionary paradigm that has tended to dominate ecumenical thinking until recently. A new ecclesiology (q.v.) emerging from the long study must ultimately lead to a different kind of WCC basis, clearly including the kingdom perspective. The strength of the ecumenical movement is tested by such a daring new orientation. *See also*, ECCLESIOLOGY; KINGDOM OF GOD; SOCIOLOGY OF THE ECUMENICAL MOVEMENT.

UNIVERSALISM/UNITARIANISM. The doctrine of universalism holds that hell is temperative and purgative and that in the end all beings—angels, human beings and devils—will be saved and will share ultimately in the grace (q.v.) of God. This view can be found in some liberal Greek fathers, in particular in Origin (c.185–c.254). St Augustine strongly opposed the doctrine and it was condemned at Constantinople in 543. Unitarianism holds that God is one person only, denies the doctrine of the divinity of Christ and of the Holy Spirit (q.v.) (as distinct from the person of God), and therefore also the doctrine of the Trinity (q.v.). Though unitarian ideas were not unknown in the early church, the main developments of the doctrine occurred after the Reformation (q.v.). Unitarians do not profess any formal creed (q.v.) or confessional statement.

The International Association for Liberal Christianity and Religious Freedom was founded in 1930 as a continuing body to function between congresses, which were held since 1910. It represents twenty-three member groups in seventeen countries and individual members in all parts of the world. As this association does not and cannot accept the trinitarian basis of the World Council of Churches (q.v.), it has no official relationship with the Council. In the United States Universalist churches were denied admission to the Federal Council of Churches (q.v.); on the other hand, many individual "liberal" churches are included in state and local councils (q.v.), especially in the northern and Eastern states.

UPPSALA 1968 *see* WORLD COUNCIL OF CHURCHES ASSEMBLIES

URBAN INDUSTRIAL MISSION *see* URBAN RURAL MISSION

URBAN RURAL MISSION. From the mid-1960s onward Urban Industrial Mission (UIM) was located in the WCC Commission on World Mission and Evangelism (CWME) (qq.v.). It has taken seriously the Bible's demands for faithful witness to the gospel among urban people of low economic and social status. Clergy and laypeople who have been engaged in urban and industrial mission activities have in many places of the world suffered physical abuse, harrassment, imprisonment, loss of jobs and even exile. The Commission on World Mission and Evangelism has tried to provide a framework for international exchange of information and mutual encouragement of the some 500 local UIM groups on all six continents through regional contact groups and an international advisory group. The emphasis on Urban Industrial Mission inevitably led to the concern for the mission of the church in a rural and agricultural setting. A desk for Rural Agricultural Mission was established in 1973 with the purpose of assisting the churches in their involvement in rural community organization and in fulfilling their pastoral role in a changing rural scene.

In 1978 the Urban Industrial Mission and Rural Agricultural Mission Desks of the CWME were integrated to form the Urban Rural Mission. This integration recognizes the fundamental inter-relationship between urban and rural issues and has stimulated solidarity among Christian groups working in both areas. URM is a decentralized operation. Major policies and strategy decisions, as well as program implementation, are the responsibility of the regional contact groups. Besides funding of much of the work, the activities of URM include leadership development and training, providing support for the involvement of the churches in the efforts of the poor (q.v.) to organize themselves, biblical and theological reflection on the meaning of Christian obedience in concrete situations (particularly through listening to the stories of people) and theological discussion of the evangelistic vocation of the Christian community. Considerable work has involved supporting the victims of political oppression. Three significant publications are *Mission and Justice: Urban and Industrial Mission at Work* (1977), *Struggle to be Human* (second edition 1977) and *People are the Subject* (1980). In addition, the Institute on the Church in Urban-Industrial Society in Chicago has been monitoring a great number of publications of URM-related groups. A high point of URM activities was reached in Manila in 1987 with the "Celebration and Challenge" event, bringing together 120 community organizers and others from all parts of the world to mark the 25th anniversary of URM concerns within the WCC.

- V -

VAN DUSEN, HENRY PITNEY (1897–1975). President of Union Theological Seminary in New York, Van Dusen was appointed in 1934 to the advisory council on research of the Universal Christian Council for Life and Work. In 1938 he became chairman of the study commission of the WCC (q.v.) provisional committee and remained a member of that committee until 1948. The year before, he delivered a major address to the International Missionary Council (IMC) (q.v.). He chaired the study department committee in preparation for Amsterdam 1948 as well as the joint committee of the WCC and the IMC, 1954–1961. He criticized the Toronto statement (q.v.) of 1950 for leaning too far in support of more extreme ''Catholic'' churches.

VANCOUVER 1983 *see* WORLD COUNCIL OF CHURCHES ASSEMBLIES

VANIER, JEAN (1928–). In 1964 Vanier, a Canadian citizen, founded communities of l'Arche, an ecumenical network of communities (now numbering ninety throughout the world) with and for people who have a mental handicap (q.v.). He also began Faith and Light, an ecumenical movement of groups (now with 600 around the world) where people with a mental handicap, their families and friends meet for a time of sharing, celebration and prayer. He gave a main address at Vancouver 1983 on ''The Poor, a Path to Unity'', and continues to animate ecumenical retreats in North America, Europe, India and Japan.

VASSADY, BÉLA (1903–1992). Vassady was a member of the Provisional Committee responsible for the organization and orientation of the WCC (q.v.) prior to its Amsterdam assembly in 1948. He taught theology in Sarospatak and at the University of Debrecen in Hungary during the 1930s. After a post-World War II lecture tour in the USA, Vassady was appointed guest professor at Princeton Theological Seminary and decided in 1948 not to return to his country because of his US connections and the deterioration of US-Soviet relations. He published his memoirs *Limping Along* in 1985.

VATICAN COUNCIL I. The Council convened from 8 December 1869 until 18 July 1870; the closure of the third session was precipitated by the withdrawal of French troops from Rome, due to the outbreak of war between France and Prussia, and by the occupation of the city by Italian troops. The key figure in the Council was Pope Pius IX himself who pursued a reactionary policy during his long reign. The composition of the Council helped the pope's ambitions. The 276 Italian bishops outnumbered the 265 from the rest of Europe. The 195 nondiocesan bishops were particularly dependent on the pope. Many of the bishops were theologically mediocre and so were open to the pressures of the majority party. The constitution *Pastor aeternus,* dealing with papal primacy and infallibility (qq.v.), was passed on 13 July 1870. The decree was resisted on various grounds—that it was unbiblical and unhistorical, that it denied the status of bishops, that it made future councils redundant, that it was inopportune—this last objection coming from the Eastern Catholics from Orthodox lands and those from the Protestant (qq.v.) nations. The dogmatic definitions of Vatican I present a major problem today to the new Roman Catholicism (q.v.).

VATICAN COUNCIL II. This Council was the twenty-first ecumenical council of the Roman Catholic Church (q.v.) and a major turning point in its history. In office only ninety days, Pope John XXIII (q.v.) suddenly and unexpectedly, at the "motion of the Holy Spirit", announced his intention to convene an ecumenical council. Leo XII, Pius XI and Pius XII had evidently entertained the idea, but nothing had come of it. The Council opened on 11 October 1962, with 2,540 voting delegates present. Paul VI (q.v.), having succeeded John XXIII in June 1963, opened session two, promulgated its acts, and closed the council on 9 December 1965. More than 100 non-Catholic Christians were observers at one time or another. A message on 14 November 1960 told the preparatory committees that the proclamation of new dogmas would not be a principal end. The official language was Latin, the only tongue that all the participants shared.

The acts of Vatican II consisted of sixteen documents of three different types: constitutions, decrees and declarations. Of the four constitutions, two on the church and divine revelation, were entitled dogmatic, and it is therefore in these two documents that the doctrinal teaching of the Council can be primarily discovered. But theological issues arose in many other documents, in particular in the Constitution on the Divine Luturgy, and on the Church in the World of Today, and in the Declaration on Religious Liberty. The main emphases of Vatican II were: 1) *Aggiornamento* (updating) of the church was to be achieved by a continuous return to the sources of Christian life in revelation, tradition (q.v.) and adjustment to the "changed conditions of the times". 2) For the first time in the history of councils, the Roman Catholic Church in an opening message addressed not merely its faithful, but "all men and nations". A new universal orientation for the church was being signaled. 3) The new orientation was demonstrated in new social ministries and awareness, such as showing concern for the poor (q.v.), and condemning discrimination. The Council expressed a more generous view on salvation (q.v.); it stated: "Whoever fears God and does what is right is acceptable to God". It also fostered broader religious freedom. 4) There was a new understanding of the church. The crucial role of the laity (q.v.) was emphasized by, among others, the later John Paul II (q.v.). The ecclesiastical notion of the church being the "body of Christ" was not abandoned, but it was supplemented by a concept of the church as the "people of God" (q.v.).

The promise of a new era is especially evident in the new way in which the Decree on Ecumenism speaks of non-Catholic Christians. No one can read it without being impressed by the respect shown for those outside the Roman obedience and by the care that is taken to understand their position and to state it fairly. Moreover, instead of dogmatically insisting on their return to Rome as the only possible movement toward unity (q.v.), the Decree is concerned with a movement toward Christ. From non-Catholic angles, this fresh orientation is of high consequence and pregnant with creative possibilities. The Decree's recognition of the "truly Christian endowments" that are to be found among the non-Roman bodies is crucial. The ecumenical dialogue (q.v.) is lifted to a new level when it is acknowledged that they "have by no means been deprived of significance and importance in the mystery of salvation" and that the work of God's grace (q.v.) in them could result in "a more ample realization of the very mystery of Christ and the Church" (4). The assumption that the Holy Spirit (q.v.) is at work in "ecclesial communities" outside the Roman Catholic Church is very different from the previous way of treating non-Roman Christians merely as individuals and ignoring their corporate life and structure.

Another seminal point is the emphasis on the task of "renewal (q.v.) and reform" as essential to ecumenical advance. To Protestants it is especially gratifying to read that "Christ summons the Church, as she goes on her pilgrim way, to that continual reformation of which she has always need" (6). The decision that "in certain special circum-stances" it is "allowable, indeed desirable", that Roman Catholics "join in prayer with their separated brethren" (8) has had a far-reaching influence. Yet, while clearly commit-ting the Roman Catholic Church to ecumenical dialogue and action, the Decree wisely warns against "a false conciliatory approach" (11). Such an approach, it is rightly affirmed, would be "foreign to the spirit of ecumenism". With this in mind, it is obvious that the Decree does not really reconcile its ecumenical outlook with its assumption that the Roman Catholic is the only true church. This assumption is explicit in the statement that "it is through Christ's Catholic Church alone, which is the all-embracing means of salvation, that the fullness of the means of salvation can be obtained" (3). Associated with this is the further assumption of the primacy of Peter and of his jurisdiction over the whole Church. These assumptions seem to indicate that the Roman Catholic understanding of ecumenism is unchangeably Rome-centered. The question is still unanswered whether the center of ecumenism is solely the person of Jesus Christ (q.v.).

Nevertheless, the Catholic theologian Karl Rahner (q.v.),

writing of the enduring significance of Vatican Council II, was right when he observed that it was the Roman Church's first reflection on the justification of having pluralism (q.v.) within the church: ''The importance of bishops in dogmatic developments, and the autonomy of dioceses, are becoming clear: The *de facto* abolition of Latin as the language of worship, the growing importance of national conferences, the autonomy of many churches which has developed through external political circumstances—these and many other symptoms show that the age in which uniformity prevailing within the Latin Church was taken for granted is over''.

VICEDOM, GEORGE FRIEDRICH (1903–1974). Vicedom attended the conference of the International Missionary Council (q.v.) in Ghana, 1957–1958 and New Delhi, 1961. In 1958 he was lecturer at the Bossey Ecumenical Institute (q.v.), and in 1968 president of the Commission on Mission of the United Evangelical Lutheran Church in Germany. He was a missionary in New Guinea, 1929–1939, and traveled widely in Asia, Africa and North America. He was professor of missiology at Neuendettelsau, 1947, and professor of missions at the University of Erlangen.

VILLAIN, MAURICE (1900–1977). A close collaborator of Abbé Paul Couturier (q.v.) and an apostle of prayer for Christian unity (qq.v.), Villain had an outstanding influence on French Roman Catholic-Protestant relationships and on deeper contacts with the Anglican communion (qq.v.). He participated in the creation of the Groupe des Dombes, and was its copresident, 1953–1974. An expert at the Second Vatican Council (q.v.), 1962–1965, he wrote many articles and contributed to the Decree on Ecumenism. In 1919 he entered the Order of the Marist Fathers in La Nellyere (near Lyons) and was ordained priest in 1927. He was professor of ecclesiology (q.v.) and church history at the University of Lyons, 1932–1948 and lectured widely, establishing many new contacts in his quest for spiritual unity.

VINAY, VALDO (1906–). Vinay was a member of the Commission on Faith and Order, 1963–1974, and of the theological commission in Europe of the World Alliance of Reformed Churches (qq.v.). He studied theology in Rome, Leipzig and Bonn, and was professor of church history and practical theology at the Facoltà Valdese di Teologia in Rome, 1940–1976, and guest lecturer at the Pontificio Ateneo Sant' Anselmo in Rome, 1969–1981. He published widely on the history of the Waldensian church and on the developments of Protestantism in Italy.

VIOLENCE AND NONVIOLENCE. In the early 1970s a two-year study on the problems and potentialities of violence and nonviolence in the struggle for social justice (q.v.) was undertaken by the WCC Sub-unit on Church and Society. In the report to the central committee meeting in Geneva in 1973 it dealt with the dilemmas of violence and nonviolence. On the one hand, there are forms of violence in which Christians may not participate and which the churches must condemn; but, on the other hand, there are situations of violence in which Christians already find themselves and have no other choice than to participate. It was noted that far too little attention had been given to methods and techniques of nonviolence in the struggle for a just society. Nonviolent action can be highly political and extremely controversial. The report, *Violence and Non-violence in the Struggle for Social Justice,* said: "Violence should not be equated with radicalism and revolution, or nonviolence with gradualism and reform, nor vice versa. Either or both forms of struggle may be used with a wide range of intention, from the revolutionary over-throw of a whole system to relatively minor alterations within a social system".

In 1983 a consultation was convened in Ballycastle (Northern Ireland), hosted by the Corrymeela community and sponsored by the Commission of the Churches on International Affairs, to review and assess the continuing debate on violence and nonviolence in the light of new issues that had emerged since 1973. In this debate it became quite clear that Christian churches still have great difficulty in facing the complexity of the international situation and in understanding the actual experience of people who justify the use of violence for political ends. It called for a continuous reappraisal of the ways Christians and their communities can and should be involved in intricate political affairs. The report, *Violence, Nonviolence and Civil Conflict,* was considerably less optimistic about the results of struggle for justice and peace (q.v.) than the 1973 report. It stated: ''For the churches the question becomes how to articulate the gospel in such a way that we may be delivered both from the illusion of facile optimism and the paralysis of faithless pessimism''. In the context of militarism (qq.v.), weapons of mass destruction and revolutionary conflict, both pacifism and the just war (qq.v.) theory become ever more problematic and ecumenical alternatives are difficult to find. *See also* JUST WAR; PACIFISM.

VISCHER, LUKAS (1926–). Vischer studied theology and history at the Universities of Basel, Strasbourg, Göttingen and Oxford and obtained a Ph.D. degree from the University of Basel in 1952. Ordained to the ministry in 1950, he became pastor of the Reformed Church in Herblingen, near Schaffhausen in Switzerland. Vischer was secretary of the secretariat of the Commission on Faith and Order (q.v.) from 1961 onward and became its director, 1965–1979. He was a WCC observer at the Second Vatican Council (q.v.), 1962–1965, and moderator of the theological department of the World Alliance of Reformed Churches (q.v.), 1982–1989. He directed an Ecumenical Institute in Bern and taught ecumenical theology at the University of Bern.

VISSER 'T HOOFT, WILLEM ADOLF (1900–1985). Visser 't Hooft was the first general secretary of the WCC, 1938/1948–1966, and from 1968 onward its honorary president. He was active in the Student Christian Movement in the Netherlands, became secretary of the World's YMCA in Geneva in 1924, and was the youngest participant in the Stockholm Life and Work (q.v.) conference in 1925. The doctoral dissertation that he presented to the University of Leiden in 1982 was entitled *The Background of the Social Gospel in America.* In 1931 Visser 't Hooft became secretary, in 1933 general secretary and in 1936 president of the World Student Christian Federation (q.v.). He was actively engaged in the preparation and the leadership of the conferences in Oxford and Edinburgh in 1937, and appointed as general secretary of the WCC (q.v.) in process of formation at the meeting of the provisional committee in Utrecht in 1938. During the war he maintained contacts with churches and their leaders from his office in Geneva. In 1945 Visser 't Hooft traveled with an international delegation to Stuttgart where the Evangelical Church in Germany issued a declaration of guilt. As WCC general secretary he visited many countries around the world, making a vast number of personal contacts, lecturing and speaking on behalf of the Council and attending hundreds of meetings. The bibliography of his literary output contains over 1,300 titles. He was honored by several Festschriften, numerous honorary degrees and awards. He published his *Memoirs* in 1973 and was from 1948 onward the editor of the *Ecumenical Review,* which was well-planned and of outstanding theological quality.

During his retirement Visser 't Hooft remained a memorable initiator and observer and contributed his impatient wisdom to numerous debates in the central and executive committee meetings. As the shrewd parent of the ecumenical movement he received Pope Paul VI at the Council's headquarters in 1969, and questioned Pope John Paul II on the problem of the "hierarchy of truths" (qq.v.), when he visited Geneva in 1984. Paul Abrecht (q.v.) wrote after his death that without Visser 't Hooft's "combination of gifts the WCC might never have existed. No other person in the leadership of those days possessed the acumen, imagination, statesmanship, experience, daring, energy and languages necessary to bring it into being". In 1987 the WCC central committee adopted a proposal to set up a "Visser 't Hooft endowment fund for ecumenical leadership development" and commended this endeavor and its success to the churches and the public for the strengthening of the ecumenical movement and its future.

VRIES, EGBERT DE (1901–). De Vries was actively involved in the work of the WCC Department on Church and Society, serving as chairman of its rapid social change study, 1953–

1966. His book *Man in Rapid Social Change* became a classic example of descriptive analysis of the social sciences, and was translated into many languages. Senior officer and adviser of the International Bank for Reconstruction and Development, 1950–1956, De Vries was rector of the Institute for Social Studies, The Hague, 1956–1966, and professor of international development, University of Pittsburgh, 1966–1983.

- W -

WARD, BARBARA *see* JACKSON, LADY

WARNECK, GUSTAV (1834–1910). Warneck was the founder of scientific missiology. He studied for the ministry, served six years on the staff of the Barmen (Rhine) Mission, 1871–1877, and then devoted the rest of his life to academic endeavors. His first great contribution was the creation of the journal *Allgemeine Missionszeitschrift* in 1874 whose aim was the objective and scholarly discussion of missionary subjects. His *Sketch of the History of Protestant Missions from the Reformation to the Present Day* (1892) was reprinted ten times. Warneck also wrote *Evanglische Missionslehre,* which appeared in five volumes between 1892 and 1903. His linking of the Bible with experience, and the understanding of mission (q.v.) in terms of divine education, are derived from the fact that the task of mission is held both to be "the extension of the kingdom of God"(q.v.), and also "the founding of the church", which is not to be understood simply as "the invitation addressed to individuals to become believers". He insisted that "the Christian faith does not destroy but transfigures the particular character of a people". Warneck had a considerable influence on the deliberations of the world missionary conference in Edinburgh (1910) and the formation of the International Missionary Council (q.v.).

WARNSHUIS, ABBE LIVINGSTON (1877–1958). Warnshuis was an American missionary in China and an ecumenical pioneer. He had a leading role in educational programs in

Fukien Province and in the preparations that led to the formation of the Church of Christ in China. Under the pressure of John R. Mott (q.v.) in 1916 he became national evangelistic secretary of the body that developed into the National Christian Council of China. In 1920 he moved to London to serve as secretary, associated with Joseph H. Oldham, of the International Missionary Council (IMC) (qq.v.). He opened the New York office of the IMC in 1925 and served jointly as a secretary of the Foreign Missions Conference of North America, 1925–1942. His retirement in 1942 was only the prelude to a further long period of service, first as foreign counselor of the Church Committee on Overseas Relief and Reconstruction on behalf of the European churches, and then in the extension of this relief and rehabilitation work to Asia. He became the chief architect of Church World Service, the service agency of the American churches.

WARREN, MAX ALEXANDER CUNNINGHAM (1904–1977). General secretary of the Church Missionary Society (CMS), 1942–1963, and canon and subdean of Westminster Abbey, 1964–1974, Warren had a great influence on the development of the ecumenical missionary movement in arguing for ''an entirely new type of missionary activity to be developed alongside the traditional modes''. The Willingen conference of the International Missionary Council (q.v.) in 1952 called for action to follow up the call of Canon Warren to shape Christian mission (q.v.) to a new cultural, political and religious environment. He also greatly contributed to the fusion of the WCC (q.v.) and the IMC in New Delhi in 1961. Warren became a CMS missionary to Nigeria in 1927, and was vicar of Holy Trinity Church, Cambridge, and secretary of the Cambridge pastorate, 1936–1942. Among several works, he wrote *The Christian Mission.*

WATTSON, PAUL JAMES FRANCIS (1863–1940). In 1886, with Mother Mary Lurana White, Wattson founded in Graymoor, New York, the Society of the Atonement, comprising Franciscan friars and sisters of the atonement who worked and prayed for this objective. In 1903 he began publishing

The Lamp in which he defended papal infallibility and urged all Anglicans (qq.v.) to return to Rome. To this end, in 1909, he inaugurated an eight-day period of prayer called the Church Unity Octave, held each year from 18–25 January. While he remained a Roman Catholic in loyalty and doctrine, the evangelical ethos of his witness often struck an unexpectedly ecumenical note. Later a Graymoor Ecumenical Institute—which publishes *Ecumenical Trends*—was established, and ecumenical work further expanded with the creation of the Centro pro Unione in Rome and the Catholic Central Library in London. The Center in Rome has been greatly active in collaborating with the WCC in preparing the material for the Annual Week of Prayer for Christian Unity (q.v.). It has also issued valuable bibliographical publications on the numerous bilateral church dialogues (q.v.). See Charles Angell and Charles LaFontaine, *Prophet of Reunion: The Life of Paul of Graymoor.*

WEBER, HANS-RUEDI (1923–). Ordained a pastor of the Swiss Reformed Church in 1947, Weber served as a missionary in Central Celebes and East Java. He received a Ph.D. degree from the University of Geneva in 1966. He was director of the WCC Department on the Laity, 1955–1961, associate director of the Ecumenical Institute Bossey (qq.v.), 1961–1971, and director of biblical studies at the WCC, 1971–1988.

WEDEL, CYNTHIA CLARK (1908–1986). Wedel received a Ph.D. in psychology from George Washington University, Washington, D.C., was associate general secretary of the National Council of the Churches of Christ in the USA (q.v.), 1960–1969, and president, 1969–1972, as well as director of the Center for a Voluntary Society, and executive director of the Church Executive Development Board until her retirement in 1973. Wedel was president of Church Women United, 1955–1958, and served as observer at the second Vatican Council (q.v.). She was also a member of the WCC commission on the cooperation of men and women in church, family and society, and of the committee on the laity (q.v.), 1961–1968. She was a WCC president, 1975–1983.

WEEK OF PRAYER FOR CHRISTIAN UNITY. The contemporary week of prayer for Christian unity (qq.v.) finds its origin in the Association for the Promotion of the Unity of Christendom, founded in 1857 in England, in which Anglicans, Roman Catholics and Orthodox (qq.v.) prayed for the unity of the church with the pope in its center. Pope Leo XIII fixed the days between Ascension and Pentecost as special days for the prayer of unity of the church. Paul Wattson (q.v.), an Anglican priest who became a Roman Catholic, proposed in 1908 a "church unity octave", to be held from 18–25 January every year, which was Roman Catholic in intention. Abbé Paul Couturier (q.v.) broadened this exercise by calling in 1935 for a Universal Week of Prayer for Unity, a unity to be achieved as "Christ wishes and by the means which he desires". From 1957 onwards a common booklet of prayers has been prepared by the Commission on Faith and Order (q.v.) and the Roman Catholic ecumenical agency Unité chrétienne in Lyons, France. Since 1966 the week of prayer for church unity has become a joint project of the Faith and Order Commission and the Vatican Secretariat for Promoting Christian Unity (q.v.). Observances are widely organized in some 75 countries throughout the world, through WCC member churches, Roman Catholic bishops conferences, national councils of churches (q.v.), ecumenical institutes (q.v.), etc. In some countries, as in Germany, the week of prayer for Christian unity is not observed in January but in the week before Pentecost.

WENDLAND, HEINZ-DIETRICH (1900–). Wendland participated in the Oxford conference in 1937, was a member of the preparatory committee for section 3 at Evanston 1954, and contributed an essay on the responsible society (q.v.) in one of the preparatory volumes of the Geneva conference in 1966 and gave a keynote address there. In 1929 he was appointed docent in Heidelberg. In 1937 he became professor at Kiel, and in 1955 professor of Christian social ethics (q.v.) at Münster. Focusing on the exegetics of the New Testament as well as on the field of social ethics, Wendland became an influential Lutheran and ecumenical theologian in Germany.

WEST, CHARLES CONVERSE (1921–). West was an assistant director of the Ecumenical Institute of Bossey (q.v.), 1956–1958, and associate director, 1958–1961. He was a member of the WCC working committee on mission and evangelism (qq.v.), 1961–1968 (chairman 1965–1968), and consultant to the office of studies in Church and Society, 1961–1980. He served as a missionary teacher and pastor in China, 1947–1950, and as a fraternal worker of the Presbyterian Church USA to the Evangelical Church in Germany, 1950–1953. In 1961 he became professor of Christian ethics at Princeton Theological Seminary.

WHITBY 1947 *see* INTERNATIONAL MISSIONARY COUNCIL

WILLEBRANDS, JOHANNES GERARDUS MARIA (1909–). After studies in philosophy and theology at the Theological Seminary in Warmond, Willebrands was ordained in 1934. He obtained a doctorate from the Angelicum in Rome with a dissertation on J. H. Newman, was chaplain to the Begijnhof-Church in Amsterdam, 1937–1940, and afterward became professor of philosophy in Warmond. In 1946 he was appointed president of the Society of St Willibrord, a Roman Catholic movement for the promotion of ecumenism. In 1960 he was named secretary of the Secretariat for Promoting Christian Unity (q.v.). In this capacity Willebrand was responsible for the participation of observers from other churches and ecumenical bodies in the Second Vatican Council (q.v.) and for the drafting of the documents on ecumenism, religious liberty (q.v.), the relation of the church to other religions, and an important part of the Dogmatic Constitution on Divine Revelation. In 1969 he was named a cardinal and in 1975 archbishop of Utrecht while Pope Paul VI made him the successor of Cardinal Bea (qq.v.) as president of the secretariat.

WILLINGEN 1952 *see* INTERNATIONAL MISSIONARY COUNCIL

WILSON, LOIS MIRIAM (1927–). Ordained a minister of the United Church of Canada in 1965, Wilson shared several pastorates with her husband in Ontario, 1965–1980. She was visiting lecturer on mission and evangelism (q.v.) in several theological colleges in Canada, and at the Ecumenical Christian Institute in Bangalore, India, in 1975. She was a president of the WCC (q.v.), 1983–1991, president of the Canadian Council of Churches, 1976–1979, and moderator of the United Church of Canada, 1980–1982.

WOMEN IN CHURCH AND SOCIETY. A worldwide study of the place and work of women in the churches was sponsored by the WCC (q.v.) following the 1948 assembly meeting. Kathleen Bliss's (q.v.) interpretation of the survey is one of the most complete analyses of the status of women in the churches. Fundamentally, women's status is a question of the relationship between men and women, a relationship that is never entirely fixed. Christianity recognizes both an order of creation in which God created male and female, and the order of redemption (q.v.) in which there is neither male nor female. A wide divergence of opinions has found expression in the churches from both doctrines. The church's concept of women and their relationship with men is, moreover, affected by society. In the contemporary world of continuous social change the question of the status of women in the churches has become a vital issue in many denominations. Persons in modern society face a complex of questions regarding the changing pattern of family life. These changing patterns are interwoven with emerging new attitudes toward sex and sexual (q.v.) morality. The participation of men and women in the socioeconomic and political spheres of life raises questions about the roles of both in the policy-making and the decision-process in society and the Christian community.

The Bible has no direct answers for the specific questions raised in our time. In the creation story there is no sex-conscious distinction in man and woman. Only in the story of the Fall is the result of disobedience that women are to bear children in pain and should be in subjection to husbands who are to rule over them. In the Old Testament the place of women is strongly influenced by the prevailing patriarchal form of family life. Behind the new status given to women in the New Testament is the attitude of Jesus himself. He deals with women as persons, worthy to be listened and talked to, in need of salvation (q.v.) equally with men. All four gospels testify that Jesus Christ (q.v.) made women the first witnesses of his resurrection. St Paul takes up a twofold position. He is eager for women to submit themselves to the accepted customs of their time, as a matter both of dignity and decency. On the other hand, he expresses the fundamental equality of women and men by stating that in Christ there is neither male nor female.

Throughout the history of Christianity women have been engaged in two major tasks—nurture and education of the young and the care of the sick, the poor and the aged. The avenues that have been available to women for carrying out these tasks have varied in the periods of church history, reinforcing the fact that the status of women in the church and the use of their gifts and talents has never been entirely static and settled. It was by the beginning of the 20th century that such movements as the Young Women's Christian Association (q.v.), the Women's World Day of Prayer, the various auxiliaries for the support of women missionaries and sisterhood movements were pioneering ecumenical relations across the denominations. As said at the beginning of this entry the WCC was ahead of most churches in giving serious attention to the problem of the status of women. The WCC Department on the Co-operation of Men and Women in Church, Family and Society, created in 1954, extended its scope of work from the consideration of the role of women in the church to the whole complex of man-woman relationships in every aspect of society. Madeleine Barot (q.v.), the department's first executive secretary, emphasized the need for the churches to reflect theologically on the status of women within their own traditions (q.v.). At the same time she developed relations with secular organizations, such as the United Nations (q.v.), which were also increasingly concerned about the role of women in all spheres of life.

It was not until the late 1960s that the word "feminism" became a key word for a new women's movement. While the earlier women's movement was chiefly concerned with improving the position of women in society, emancipation, economic independence and work, the issues for the feminist movement became replacement of the age-old patriarchal order, raising consciousness of the disastrous effects of the division between woman/nature and man/intellect, and the adoption of female rather than male guiding principles. In this connection a "a feminist theology" developed that takes seriously the criticisms and conclusions of contemporary feminism. It entails the self-conscious adoption of a critical feminist hermeneutic (q.v.), which is applied to the various disciplines of theology. Under the heading of feminist theology is to be found work on Scripture, church history, doctrine, philosophy of religion and ethics. It is a theological method, rather than a branch of theology or area of study.

Not until 1974, at an international women's consultation on "Sexism in the 1970s" in Berlin, sponsored by the WCC, were the structures of an "exclusively masculine environment" fundamentally challenged. The conference found a new kind of community and renewed its commitment to work for change to end all those things that deny their humanity, and above all the creative purposes of God, for an end not only to sex discrimination but to all forms of oppression. The problem of sexism within the church was dealt with in greater depth in the following years through a Faith and Order (q.v.) study "The Community of Women and Men in the Church", which culminated in an international conference in Sheffield, England, in 1981. The preliminary study material had an unprecedented popular reception, involving more local groups in discussion and response than any other study initiated by the WCC. The Sheffield message proved to be both controversial in its challenge to the long tradition of male domination, and normative in its encouragement to both women and men to seek the mutual enrichment coming through fuller partnership. The Vancouver assembly in 1983 gave clear evidence that the ecumenical process begun has prompted widespread concern for fuller representation of women in all the deliberative councils of the churches and for women's voices to be heard on all the major issues. The proportion of women elected during the assembly rose to 29 percent. In 1988 a special decade for women was launched.

Language that is carefully chosen, ensuring that both vocabulary and content include all people, is called inclusive language. Women have become increasingly sensitive to the fact that a language in which a masculine noun or pronoun is used to denote membership of both sexes reflects a culture in which the male is normative. Language that includes only male metaphors of God ignores the female images of the divine. Such language, particularly in English, has begun to change. As women emerge from subordination, inclusive language has started to make them visible. There is no doubt that feminist theology is one of the most dynamic and creative fields of scholarship within contemporary theology. *See also* ORDINATION OF WOMEN; THEOLOGY, LATE 20TH-CENTURY TRENDS IN.

WORK/UNEMPLOYMENT. The question of work and the problem of unemployment have been two concerns of the ecumenical movement. From 1948 onward the inquiry on "Christian Action in Society" included an examination of the "Meaning of Work", based on an introductory booklet *Work in Modern Society,* by J. H. Oldham (q.v.). In a section on "The Christian Understanding of Work", the Evanston assembly (1954) stated: "Because work is a divine ordinance for human life, there is an obligation upon society to provide all its members with opportunity to work. Unemployment is not only a problem for economists but for all Christian people . . . All work honestly done, whether undertaken for the sake of earning a livelihood, or for the sake of the community, or out of spontaneous joy in creative effort, has genuine value and meaning in the purpose of God". It was noted that a strong tendency for human beings exists to become simply the tools of production, a tendency that is found not only among workers but also among other classes of employees including those with academic training. Influenced by the great depression in the 1930s, the Oxford conference (1937) already noticed that the threat of unemployment "produces a feeling of extreme insecurity in the minds of masses of people. Unemployment, especially when prolonged, tends to create in the mind of the unemployed person a sense of uselessness, or even being a nuisance, and to empty his life from any meaning''.

Roman Catholic documents, such as *Gaudium et spes* (1965) and *Laborem exercens,* the encyclical of John Paul II (qq.v.) (1981), are very emphatic about labor issues, the rights of workers and the principle of priority of labor over capital. In contrast to the 1960s when the issue of unemployment received less ecumenical attention because of the relatively high employment levels, the WCC Sub-unit on Church and Society and the Commission on the Churches' Participation in Development organized several consultations in the 1970s and 1980s and published reports on the problem of unemployment seen from a global perspective. The WCC continues to face a grave dilemma. On the one hand, a long list of ''proper working conditions'' has been worked out in more than a century of labor movements and have gone some way to securing long-term benefits for managers, owners, workers, clients and citizens alike: securing safe and healthy working conditions, the right to collective bargaining, a liveable family wage, health benefits, equal opportunities for women and differently abled people, adequate redundancy pay and opportunities for retraining when needed, and so on. Even the partial achievement of these goals has helped to revitalize human freedom and dignity. On the other hand, the technological society rendering work more and more automatic and meaningless and the international market system are in need of thorough reform. Yet, there is widespread confusion about the way forward and the ecumenical debate on these issues is also influenced by uncertainty. New issues of labor, unemployment and under-employment, particularly in the Third World (q.v.), demand fresh analyses, but it will take time for such new analyses to mature. Christians are likely to be in for a long period of reflection and experimentation.

WORLD ALLIANCE FOR PROMOTING INTERNATIONAL FRIENDSHIP THROUGH THE CHURCHES. Two members of the British parliament, the Quaker J. Allen Baker and the Anglican Willoughby H. Dickinson, were prompted by two peace (q.v.) conferences of various churches at The Hague in 1899 and 1907 to promote peaceful relations between Christian communities in Great Britain and Germany by a large-scale exchange of visits of representatives. A German church delegation, led by Friedrich Siegmund-Schultze (q.v.), visited England in 1908, and the next year an English delegation went to Germany. The Federal Council of the Churches of Christ in America (q.v.) also played an important role in working for closer understanding between churches in the USA and in Europe. In 1914 Protestant, Roman Catholic and Jewish organizations founded the Church Peace Union. It received US $2 million from the industrialist Andrew Carnegie, and this money served to finance most of the activities of the World Alliance. Created a day after the First World War erupted, the World Alliance started functioning through national councils in the United States, Canada, India, Japan and several European countries. At a postwar conference in Oud Wassenaar near The Hague in 1919, the German delegates made a declaration to the effect that they personally considered Germany's violation of Belgian neutrality an act of moral transgression. This declaration produced a profound impression and made trustful cooperation within the World Alliance possible for the national committees. A 1929 peace conference in Prague of 500 delegates was the most significant gathering the World Alliance sponsored.

Throughout its existence until 1948 the World Alliance attempted to help substitute reason and arbitration for war as a means of settling international disputes. It conducted seminars, published books, pamphlets, and the *World Alliance News Letter* (with a circulation of 14,000); cooperated with the United Nations (q.v.), with some 80 different secular agencies, with churches, schools, colleges and other groups working for the attainment of collective security and a just and abiding peace; and developed projects to help establish among nations, in their dealings with one another, the moral and ethical principles that stem from their religions. It further encouraged the churches to support wholeheartedly the work of the League of Nations, and later the United Nations.

From 1931 to 1937 the World Alliance for Promoting

International Friendship through the Churches and the Universal Christian Council for Life and Work (q.v.) were closely related through common offices in Geneva, a joint general secretary, joint youth work and a common bulletin: *The Churches in Action*. In 1938 the World Alliance decided to remain ''an autonomous movement which serves the churches'' rather than to join Faith and Order and Life and Work, in forming ten years later the World Council of Churches (qq.v.). It was in 1946 replaced by the WCC Commission of the Churches on International Affairs.

WORLD ALLIANCE OF REFORMED CHURCHES *see* PRESBYTERIAN AND REFORMED CHURCHES

WORLD ALLIANCE OF YOUNG MEN'S CHRISTIAN ASSOCIATIONS. In the decade following the founding of the first YMCA in London in 1844, YMCAs spread rapidly among workers and students in Europe and America. Jean Henri Dunant in Geneva—later instrumental in founding the Red Cross—and others urged a world movement of YMCAs. Thus was founded in Paris in 1855 the World Alliance of WMCAs. It united those who regard ''Jesus Christ as their God and Savior according to the Holy Scriptures''. That basis, later adopted by the WSCF, the World YWCA and the WCC (qq.v.), represents one of the many contributions of the World Alliance of YMCAs to the ecumenical movement. Encouraging close relations with the church and seeking to produce for its ministry young men with vision for a meaningful world, it has always insisted on lay control and encourages lay witness. Its missionary thrust, especially in Asia, has been notable. It has worked chiefly among non-students—soldiers, sailors, railwaymen, young men in business and industry, and rural youth. Other major endeavors included prisoners of war, displaced persons and refugees (q.v.), migrants, literacy programs, physical education and boys' work. Strong Protestant evangelical and missionary concern produced the World Alliance, but later in the 20th century members included Roman Catholics, Orthodox (qq.v.), and also people of other faiths.

During the 1980s the world YMCA has been searching, in

the context of contemporary social realities, for a deeper understanding of its Christian mission, through action-oriented studies related to the issues of justice and peace (qq.v.). It has also tried to come to grips with increasing secularization and the new climate of religious pluralism (qq.v.), which affect its self-understanding to a considerable degree.

WORLD ASSOCIATION FOR CHRISTIAN COMMUNICATIONS (WACC). The origins of this international organization go back to 1950 to a conference of Christian broadcasters from several national broadcasting corporations in Europe in Chichester, England. A new constitution was drawn up at a gathering in Limuru, Kenya, in 1963, providing for the rules for a new World Association of Christian Broadcastings (WACB). Corporate membership included several countries throughout the world; there were approximately 200 personal members. In 1968 another group, the Coordinating Committee for Christian Broadcasting, merged with the WACB, to form the WACC. Its concerns now include all forms of media available in the ecumenical movement to proclaim the gospel and their relevance to life and the building up of a just and peaceful society. It promotes its policies and principles through studies in theology and communication (q.v.), training and publications. It publishes a quarterly journal *Media Development,* and *Action,* a monthly newsletter, carrying news of events and trends in communication worldwide. The WACC also sponsors the publication of books by subsidizing researchers, in particular from the Third World (q.v.).

There was an intensive debate during the 1970s on the problems of international communication, most of which was initiated by the nonaligned movement of communication specialists working for nongovernmental organizations. This resulted in a call for a "new international information order", which greatly influenced the future course of the international organization. The call emphasized the continuing and increasing dependence of the Third World countries on the rich industrialized countries for nearly all of their communication equipment, technology, skills and even software; the overwhelming imbalance in the flow of news, TV programs, films, magazines, books and other cultural software between the rich and the poor countries, whereby the one dominate the other with alien models and values, making national development goals almost impossible to realize; the quite irreversible concentration of power (q.v.) in the hands of the rich nations achieved through computer data banks and globe-spanning computer networks owned by multinational corporations primarily to their own commercial advantage.

The WACC comprises some 600 corporate church agencies and communication organizations and individual members. Some 500 persons from 70 countries attended its first world congress in Manila in 1989, discussing the theme "Communication for Community". It remains an ecumenical agency that is participatory and liberating and prophetic, promoting solidarity and respecting people's cultures. *See also* COMMUNICATION.

WORLD CONFERENCE ON RELIGION AND PEACE. This international inter-religious organization has representatives from most of the world's religious traditions—Buddhist, Christian, Confucian, Hindu, Jain, Jewish, Muslim, Shinto, Sikh, Zoroastrian, the traditional cultures of African and North America and others. Its first world conference took place in Kyoto, Japan, in 1970. Subsequent world assemblies have been held in Louvain (1974), Princeton (1979), Nairobi (1984) and Melbourne (1989). The conference is convinced that through struggle it is able to build trust. It insists that differences of culture and religion, far from being a threat to one another, are a treasure. Its multiplicity is a source of strength. It bears the testimony of experience that a world community of communities is possible. From its diversity of traditions, the conference is united in faith and hope, and in its common pursuit of human dignity and world peace (q.v.). The WCRP has consultative status with the United Nations (q.v.) as a nongovernmental organization. It has regular contacts with such organizations as the World Council of Churches, the Christian Peace Conference (qq.v.) and International Pax Christi.

WORLD CONVENTION OF THE CHURCHES OF CHRIST
(DISCIPLES) *see* CHRISTIAN CHURCH (DISCIPLES OF
CHRIST)

WORLD COUNCIL OF CHRISTIAN EDUCATION (WCCE). A
decisive element in the process of ecumenical education
(q.v.) was the World Council of Christian Education, which
traced its history even further back than the Faith and Order
and Life and Work (qq.v.) movements. It began with Sunday
school conventions in the 19th century and was formally
organized in Rome in 1907 as the World Sunday School
Association. Successive assemblies, held every four years,
met in all parts of the world: Toronto, Tokyo, Belfast,
Nairobi and Lima. From the late 1940s onward the WCCE
became the common instrument for its interdependent world
constituency for enlisting and providing resources in
thought, personnel, counsel, material, finances, training
events and cooperative projects wherever needed for the
development of more effective educational programs and
competent leadership.

During the 1960s the WCCE moved its headquarters to
Geneva and increasingly shared in many activities with the
WCC (q.v.), chiefly in youth (q.v.) work and education. Joint
appointments of youth staff were made, and the WCCE
shared in sponsoring major youth meetings in collaboration
with the WCC, the World Student Christian Federation, the
World Alliance of Young Men's Christian Association and
the World Young Women's Christian Associations (qq.v.).
In 1964 a WCC/WCCE joint study commission on education
was appointed, which presented its report to the Uppsala
assembly in 1968. The Office of Education was established
within the WCC on the basis of that report, as well as the
accompanying survey of church engagement in general and
religious education in many parts of the world. The basic task
of this effort was to direct the churches' attention to education in the widest sense. In 1968 a joint negotiating committee went to work and in 1971, at its assembly in Lima, Peru,
the WCCE voted to integrate with the WCC. Thus, a long
tradition and lengthy experience of work with children,
youth and adults in education was added to the Unit's already

wide constituency, known as the Unit on Education and Renewal.

WORLD COUNCIL OF CHURCHES (WCC). The plan to establish a World Council of Churches was worked out at a gathering of 35 leaders of several sections of the ecumenical movement just before the two world conferences of Life and Work in Oxford and of Faith and Order (qq.v.) in Edinburgh in 1937. It was widely felt that these two movements should be brought together since the issues of unity (q.v.) and those of witness in face of the needs of the world were closely related. At the same time, the situation was ripe to give a more definite shape to the ecumenical work of the churches and to create a body that would be truly representative of the participating member bodies. The two world conferences approved the plan in principle. Thus, it became possible to call a conference in Utrecht in 1938 to elaborate a draft constitution. This constitution, together with a letter of invitation, was sent to the churches. It was hoped to hold the first official assembly in 1941, but this proved impossible because of the Second World War. In the meantime the provisional committee of the WCC (in process of formation) had to take responsibility for the ongoing ecumenical work to which were added the new tasks due to the war—prisoners of war, refugees, interchurch aid (q.v.). The inaugural assembly took place in Amsterdam in 1948, and approved the constitution worked out at Utrecht. This entry deals with the structures, basis, authority, nature and functions, membership, finance and relations of the WCC. Several other entries are devoted to developments in ecumenical thinking and activities that the WCC has initiated and stimulated through its programs and staff.

WCC structures. Constitutionally, the "supreme legislative body governing the WCC" is the assembly (q.v.). Meeting about every seven years, it is made up of delegates appointed by member churches. The number of delegates to which each church is entitled is determined by its size (every member church may send at least one delegate), with allowance made in the allocation of delegates for balancing confessional, cultural and geographical representation.

Member churches select their own delegates to the assembly. But they are urged to do so in a way that will ensure a good distribution of church officials, parish ministers and laypeople, men and women and persons under the age of 30. Moreover, to improve the balance of the assembly or to provide special knowledge and experience, up to 15 percent of the delegates may be persons proposed by the WCC central committee, which then asks their churches to name them as additional delegates. Also present at each assembly is a wide range of nonvoting participants—advisers, representatives and observers from nonmember churches or other ecumenical organizations and guests (including, since the fifth assembly in Nairobi in 1975, persons of other faiths). Since WCC assemblies are too large and infrequent to make detailed decisions, they are rather an occasion to look at the larger ecumenical picture: evaluating the work of the WCC since the previous assembly, seeking a common assessment of which current issues demand ecumenical attention and specifying in broad terms what the Council should focus on until the next assembly. The assembly also elects the presidents of the WCC and, from delegates present, the 150 members of the central committee.

This functional description hardly does justice to the actual experience of a WCC assembly. Considerable effort is made to bring together as wide as possible a group of participants in the actual assembly deliberations; and in recent assemblies extensive programs have been organized for accredited visitors. Worship and Bible study give the assembly spiritual and theological rootage. Small group sessions allow for building friendships and community across all kinds of boundaries. Visits to local parishes help to anchor the global experience in local realities. The presence of several hundred journalists from around the world helps to give the assembly something of the character of a "media event". Indeed, there is sometimes a tension between the assembly as business meeting and the assembly as Christian festival. Each assembly has a main theme and several sections or issues related to the theme. The seven assemblies so far have been quite different in outlook and thrust, partly due to the rapidly changing times of the world.

The central committee is responsible for implementing the policies adopted by the assembly. It meets annually in different places, but often in Geneva, to review and supervise WCC activities, approve new programs and adjust priorities as necessary. The central committee elects the WCC general secretary, appoints senior staff, takes responsibility for finances and names people to the committees, boards, working groups and commissions working directly with specific programs. The central committee elects fourteen to sixteen of its members to the executive committee (central committee officers and WCC presidents are automatically members). Meeting twice a year, the executive committee's role in policy-making is limited to matters specifically referred to it by the central committee, though in emergencies it may take provisional decisions. Most program staff appointments (except for directors) are made by the executive committee and it supervises the budget approved by the central committee. More specific guidance concerning day-to-day operations of WCC programs comes from advisory bodies, which the central committee appoints.

From 1954 to 1971 the WCC operated within a structure of divisions: the Division of Studies, the Division of Interchurch Aid, the Division of World Mission and Evangelism and the Division of Ecumenical Action. Each division had several departments. From 1971 to 1992 the WCC operated within a three-unit program system: Unit I, Faith and Witness; Unit II, Justice and Service; Unit III, Education and Renewal. Proposals for the work of each unit and its subunits came from unit committees. Each subunit had a working group or commission of representatives of member churches with expertise in its area of work. In the new program structure there are four program units: I. Unity and Renewal; II. Life, Education and Mission; III. Justice, Peace and Creation; IV. Sharing and Service.

Day-to-day operations to carry out the policies set by the governing bodies are conducted by the WCC staff. Subject to what the rules describe as "the primary need of competence" (and "dedication to the aims and spirit of the WCC" among personnel responsible for programs), an attempt is made to recruit staff "on as wide a geographical and confessional basis as possible and without distinction as to race and sex''. Given that the number of staff responsible for programs is fewer than 100, most WCC churches have no member on the WCC staff. Other factors also make it difficult to achieve the desired balance: dependence on member churches as a pool (many churches, for example, have appointed few women to positions that would provide the experience for WCC staff work); differences between the WCC structures and that of many member churches (the Council has no staff positions that could make use of the talents of some of their leaders); the virtual necessity for facility in the English language to carry out WCC staff work; and the reluctance of churches, especially small and poor ones, to ''lose'' their leaders to the international ecumenical movement. A staff executive group, consisting of the general secretary, the deputy and assistant general secretaries, directors and other staff invited to secure adequate representivity, meets weekly or biweekly to advise the general secretary on policy implementation. It sets up coordinating staff groups for specific activities, such as relations with churches in each region, relations with the Roman Catholic Church and evangelicals (qq.v.) and certain overall WCC concerns.

WCC Basis. The Amsterdam assembly (1948) declared: ''The World Council of Churches is a fellowship of churches which accept the Lord Jesus Christ (q.v.) as God and Savior''. Soon this formulation of the basis gave rise to questions, inquiries and requests for a clearer definition of its Christocentricity, a more explicit expression of the trinitarian faith and a specific reference to Holy Scriptures. The result was the formulation adopted by the third assembly in New Delhi in 1961 stating: ''The World Council of Churches is a fellowship of churches which confess the Lord Jesus Christ as God and Savior according to the Scriptures and therefore seek to fulfill their common calling to the glory of the one God, Father, Son and Holy Spirit''.

This basis is not a full confession of faith (q.v.) but rather a foundation for the Council defining its nature and clarifying the limits of its membership. Since the WCC is not itself a church, even less a superchurch, it passes no judgment upon the sincerity with which member churches accept the basis. The member churches themselves must remind one another that membership is meaningless if commitment to the basis disappears. Some very conservative churches judge the basis not biblical enough; some liberal churches do not accept the trinitarian formula. How seriously the great number of churches take their membership in the world body is not a matter that can be legislated; as archbishop William Temple (q.v.) said: "Any authority the Council will have consists in the weight which it carries with the churches by its own wisdom".

WCC's authority. Authority (q.v.) was a major point of discussion in the early negotiations that led to the merging of various streams of united Christian endeavor into a world council of churches, for the churches themselves have widely different notions of authority. Two passages in the WCC constitution and rules address the question of authority. Article IV of the constitution states: "The World Council shall offer counsel and provide opportunity for united action in matters of common interest. It may take action on behalf of the constituent churches only in such matters as one or more of them may commit to it and only on behalf of such churches. The World Council shall not legislate for the churches, nor shall it act for them in any manner except as indicated above or as may hereafter be specified by the constituent churches". Article IX of the rules describes the authority of WCC public statements: "While such statements may have great significance and influence as the expression of the judgment or concern of so widely representative a Christian body, yet their authority will consist only in the weight which they carry by their own truth and wisdom, and the publishing of such statements shall not be held to imply that the World Council as such has, or can have, any constitutional authority over the constituent churches or right to speak for them".

In some church traditions, these limitations of the WCC's authority will seem so obvious as scarcely to warrant mentioning. The idea that the WCC does not exercise binding authority over member churches will strike many people as a consequence of the belief that no church body may bind the conscience of its individual members. At the same time, some churches have stayed out of the WCC precisely because it claims no authority to ensure that all its member churches in fact adhere to the theological affirmations of the WCC Basis. But to emphasize only this negative side of what the WCC constitution and rules say about authority is to overlook a more dynamic understanding, which reflects the Council's heritage as a *movement* toward Christian unity. This dynamic understanding of the WCC's significance and influence presupposes several attitudes and convictions on the part of its member churches. When these are present, the WCC can and does exercise a kind of authority—not, to be sure, authority *over* them, but authority *through* them.

WCC's nature and functions. The WCC has sought to define its own nature in a statement adopted by the Central Committee in Toronto (q.v.) in 1950. This statement makes clear that the Council is not a new or a special church and does not promote one particular conception of church unity to the exclusion of others. The WCC seeks to bring the churches into living contact with one another and to deepen their fellowship. It believes that conversation, cooperation, common witness and common action must be based on the common recognition that Jesus Christ is the divine head of the body. The member churches of the Council believe, on the basis of the New Testament, that the church of Christ is one, and consider it a matter of Christian duty for each church to do its utmost for the manifestation of the church in its oneness. They therefore recognize their solidarity with one another, seek to learn from each other and to give help to one another in order that the body of Christ be built up and the life of the churches may be renewed. The latest formulation of the functions and purposes of the WCC can be found in its constitution and rules, revised by the Canberra assembly in 1991.

WCC membership. The first assembly in Amsterdam was constituted by invitation, but since then membership of the WCC has been by application. The assembly and the central committee have from time to time formulated criteria for membership other than acceptance of the basis. These criteria include autonomy, stability, size, and relationship with other churches. The third assembly in 1961 decided that as a rule no church with an inclusive membership of less than 10,000 should be admitted, and authorized the creation of a special category of associated churches for Christian communities that satisfy the criteria except the one concerning size. The minimum requirement of 10,000 members was raised to at least 25,000 members at the fifth assembly in 1975. An associate church, having at least 10,000 members, may participate in all the activities of the Council, and has the right to speak, but not to vote at an assembly.

The number of member churches at Amsterdam was 147 churches; at Evanston 161; at New Delhi 197; at Uppsala 235; at Nairobi 285; at Vancouver 301; at Canberra 317.

WCC finances. The WCC budget mirrors its activities. About 75 percent of the income is given by member churches and their mission and aid agencies. About 96 percent of that income comes from 13 countries, the USA and Germany being the principal donors. Between the Vancouver and the Canberra assembly, the program budget expenses were SFr. 307.5 million. A substantial amount of money is channeled through the Council every year en route to ecumenically supported programs and projects for relief and development (q.v.) throughout the world. Money for certain projects comes from secular or governmental organizations and foundations. There is no fixed membership fee; churches are encouraged to contribute what they feel they can. Churches whose giving is limited by currency restrictions make contributions other than money. A systematic internationalization of the Geneva staff and salary structure was started in 1972. The 1990 payroll for the 359 people on the total staff was around SFr. 26.4 million. The total income of the WCC from all sources in 1991 was SFr. 125 million.

WCC relations. The WCC maintains relationships with numerous councils of churches (q.v.), national and regional, and with other national and international bodies, such as the Christian world communions (q.v.). There are 35 national councils of churches associated with the WCC. Forty-six national councils are affiliated with the WCC Conference on World Mission and Evangelism. Thirty-five Christian councils are in a working relationship, though not in association, with the WCC. An annual meeting of representatives of

Christian world communions takes place in Geneva. Of the twelve international confessional organs, the Lutheran World Federation, the World Alliance of Reformed Churches and the World Methodist Council (qq.v.) have their offices with the WCC in the Ecumenical Center. There are further a variety of relationships with European ecumenical institutes (q.v.) that make scholarly contributions to ecumenical theology, social ethics, and spirituality, and with Asian and African study and dialogue centers that deepen the understanding of the Christian faith in a multireligious environment. The WCC is further in working relations with various evangelical academies and lay training centers and is regularly represented at the *Kirchentag* in Germany. The Commission of the Churches on International Affairs is in close working relation with the NGOs. A New York office at 475 Riverside Drive maintains relations with various churches in the USA and the National Council of the Churches of Christ in the USA (q.v.).

The WCC is not the definitive answer to the problem of Christian unity. It is rather an instrument that helps the churches to move forward on the road to full unity and, as long as that unity does not exist, to act together in all matters except those in which deep differences of conviction compel them to act separately.

WORLD COUNCIL OF CHURCHES ASSEMBLIES. The assembly is constitutionally the supreme legislative body governing the World Council and ordinarily meets every seven or eight years. It is composed of official representatives of the member churches. The number of delegates to which each church is entitled is determined by its size (every member church can send at least one delegate). The Assembly has the following functions: 1) to elect the presidents of the World Council; 2) to elect not more than 145 members of the central committee from among the delegates that the member churches have elected to the assembly; 3) to determine the policies and programs of the World Council and to review programs undertaken during the last seven or eight years; 4) to delegate to the central committee specific functions, except to amend the Constitution and to allocate the membership of the central committee granted by the Constitution to the assembly exclusively.

Assembly	Delegates	Churches
1. Amsterdam 1948	351	147
2. Evanston 1954	502	161
3. New Delhi 1961	577	197
4. Uppsala 1968	704	235
5. Nairobi 1975	676	285
6. Vancouver 1983	847	301
7. Canberra 1991	842	317

Besides the delegates a great number of nonvoting advisers, representatives and observers from nonmember churches or other ecumenical organizations and guests (since the fifth assembly, also persons of other faiths) are present. There are, moreover, several hundred press and media persons and in recent assemblies extensive programs have been arranged for accredited visitors. Assemblies are magnificent occasions for worship (q.v.) and celebration, but too large and infrequent to make detailed decisions. They can only evaluate the wider ecumenical picture of the past and project some general guidelines for the future. A brief overview of each assembly is provided in this entry.

Amsterdam 1948. Main theme: Man's Disorder and God's Design. Sections: 1. The Universal Church in God's Design; 2. The Church's Witness to God's Design; 3. The Church and the Disorder of Society; 4. The Church and the International Disorder.

Dr. John R. Mott (q.v.) was named honorary president. The first presidents of the WCC were: Rev. Marc Boegner (q.v.), Archbishop Geoffrey Fisher, (q.v.) Professor Tsu-Ch'en Chao (succeeded in 1951 by Mrs. Sarah Chakko [q.v.]), Bp. G. Bromley Oxnam (q.v.), Archbp. Germanos of Thyateira (q.v.) (succeeded in 1951 by Archbp. Athenagoras of Thyateira [q.v.]), Archbp. Erling Eidem (succeeded in 1950 by Bp. Eivind Berggrav [q.v.]). The Bishop of Chichester, George A. K. Bell (q.v.), served as moderator of the central committee. Vice Moderator: Dr. Franklin Clark Fry (q.v.).

The first assembly was attended by 351 delegates representing 147 churches from 44 countries. Only 30 churches came from Asia, Africa and Latin America. Five churches from China were present. Among the oldest churches represented were the Church of Ethiopia and the Orthodox Syrian Church of Malabar. Several of the youngest were also present, such as the Old Catholic Church and the Salvation Army (qq.v.).

The message expressed the fact that churches themselves assumed responsibility for the ecumenical movement as follows: "Here at Amsterdam we have committed ourselves afresh to Him, and have covenanted with one another in constituting the World Council of Churches. We intend to stay together". The "nature of the Council" was more closely defined in a separate statement. It was stated that the churches had decided to make common cause in accordance with the will of the Lord of the Church. Where this common way would lead them was unforeseeable. "We acknowledge", the Report of Section I emphasized, "that He is powerfully at work amongst us to lead us further to goals which we but dimly discern".

In Section II the indissoluble connection between unity and inner renewal (qq.v.) was expressed: "We pray for the churches' renewal as we pray for their unity. As Christ purifies us by His Spirit we shall find that we are drawn together and that there is no gain in unity unless it is unity in truth and holiness". It was also realized for the first time that evangelism is the common task of all the churches, and that "the present day is the beginning of a new epoch of missionary enterprises". As mission (q.v.) and evangelism belong together and condition each other, the distinction between "Christian" and "non-Christian" nations must be discarded. The question of the training of the laity (q.v.) was examined by a special committee, which took as its starting point the experience of the Ecumenical Institute in Bossey (q.v.).

In Section III the ecumenical concept of the "responsible society" (q.v.) emerged as an alternative to laissez-faire capitalism (q.v.), on the one hand, and totalitarian communism, on the other. "Each has made promises which it could not redeem. Communist ideology puts the emphasis upon economic justice, and promises that freedom will come automatically after the completion of the revolution. Capitalism puts the emphasis upon freedom, and promises that justice will follow as a byproduct of free enterprise; that, too, is an ideology which has been proved false. It is the responsibility of Christians to seek new, creative solutions which never allow either justice or freedom to destroy the other''. It was also agreed that ''no civilization, however 'Christian', can escape the radical judgment of the Word of God, and none therefore is to be accepted uncritically''.

The fact that Section IV included such divergent positions as those of Josef L. Hromádka (q.v.) and John Foster Dulles and was able to support them both showed the strength of a fellowship like that of the newly formed Council and put it to the test for the first time. Two points that arose in this Section and were significant for the assembly as a whole as well as for the future of the WCC were: a) the rejection of war in principle (''war is contrary to the will of God''), but also the inability to accept unanimously this attitude within Christianity; b) the concern that every kind of tyranny and imperialism is a call for opposition and struggle, and for efforts to secure human rights (q.v.) and basic liberties, especially religious freedom.

The first assembly adopted the Constitution of the WCC— which has been revised at successive assemblies—laid down the conditions for membership, outlined the programs of the Council's departments and secretariats, described relationships with other existing ecumenical bodies and addressed a message to the churches—a practice repeated by the following assemblies. A statement on ''The Church, the Churches and the World Council of Churches'', adopted by the central committee in Toronto in 1950, defined in greater detail the ecclesiological significance of the Council.

Evanston 1954. Main theme: Christ—the Hope of the World. Sections: 1. Faith and Order; Our Oneness in Christ and Our Disunity as Churches; 2. Evangelism: The Mission of the Church to Those Outside Her Life; 3. Social Questions: The Responsible Society in a World Perspective; 4. International Affairs: Christians in the Struggle for World Community; 5.

Intergroup Relations: The Churches Amid Racial and Ethnic Tensions; 6. The Laity: the Christian in His Vocation.

Dr. John R. Mott continued to be honorary president until his death in 1955 and on Bp. Bell was bestowed the same title. Presidents for the next period were: Principal John Baillie (q.v.), Bp. Sante Uberto Barbieri, Bp. Otto Dibelius, Metrop. Juhanon Mar Thoma, Archbp. Michael (succeeded in 1959 by Archbp. Iakovos) and Bp. Henry Knox Sherill (q.v.). Moderator of the central committee: Dr. Franklin Clark Fry, Vice Moderator: Dr. Ernest A. Payne (q.v.) (until 1968).

The motto of Evanston was: "We dedicate ourselves to God anew, that He may enable us to grow together". It was this deep sense of belonging together and of the responsibility which it implied that enabled the assembly to tackle the main theme, theologically an extremely difficult one. Compared with Amsterdam the theme clearly represented a turning toward the center, which linked together all the churches belonging to the WCC. The very theme, however, gave rise to differing interpretations. The concept of the Christian hope (q.v.) held by the European churches tended to be eschatological, whereas the concept of North American churches was more optimistic and more concerned with the Christian hope in this world here and now. The statement of the report of the advisory committee on the main theme, in which eminent theologians had cooperated for three years, said that "sharp differences in theological viewpoint were expressed" in the discussions. A discordant note was introduced by the reference of the hope of Israel (Rom. 9–11), which was finally omitted after a heated debate. Many did not wish to recognize that the Jewish people occupy a special place in the history of salvation (q.v.).

The phrase "the responsible society" was more clearly defined than at Amsterdam; it was made clear that it did not indicate "an alternative social or political system", but "a criterion by which we judge all existing social orders and at the same time a standard to guide us in the specific choices we have to make". As at Amsterdam, Evanston devoted in its Report several pages to "The Church in Relation to Communist—Non Communist Tension". Priority in Sections III and IV were given to "the social and economic problems in the economically underdeveloped regions", a question to which the WCC paid increasing attention. The assembly affirmed its responsibility for international peace and justice (qq.v.), and issued an appeal to governments urging the prohibition of all weapons of mass destruction, and abstention from aggression. Also statements on religious liberty (q.v.), and on "inter-group relations", insisting on racial equality, were issued. In continuation of Amsterdam, the missionary task of the laity was even more strongly stressed. It "constitutes more than 99 percent of the Church", "bridges the gulf between the Church and the world", and "stands at the very outposts of the Kingdom of God".

The so-called younger churches, except those in China, were much better represented than at the first assembly, and their presence was felt in many ways, especially when discussing the unity of the church in the form of an impatient urge for action. The missionary dimension of the churches' task, which had been so characteristic of Amsterdam, was missing at the second assembly. On the other hand, it showed that the WCC was penetrating more deeply into the Word of God, which was helping it to become clearer theologically in many spheres, and helping the churches to discover their common heritage.

New Delhi 1961. Main Theme: Jesus Christ, the Light of the World. Sections: 1. Witness; 2. Service; 3. Unity.

Dr. Joseph H. Oldham (q.v.) became honorary president. Presidents: Archbp. Arthur M. Ramsey (q.v.), Sir Francis Ibiam (q.v.), Archbp. Iakovos, Dr. David G. Moses, Dr. Martin Niemöller, Dr. Charles C. Parlin. Moderator of the Central Committee: Dr. Franklin Clark Fray, Vice Moderators: Dr. Ernest A. Payne and Dr. J. Russell Chandran (1966–1968).

Of the twenty-three new member churches, eleven came from Africa, five from Asia and two from South America. Only five were from Europe and North America. The two Pentecostal churches from Chile formed a bridge to evangelical churches, most of which dissociated themselves from the WCC, and still do so. The main theme continued the

Christocentric line of the Council, extending it now into the sphere of the other world religions. It was liable to misinterpretation in view of the fact that light is one of the symbols that appears in Asian religions. In order to avoid being misunderstood as syncretism (q.v.), the theme therefore had to be worked out with great care on its biblical basis. It was, however, not given prominence, as it had been the case at Evanston; it was merely regarded as a guiding principle.

The adhesion of the large Orthodox (q.v.) churches in Eastern Europe was rightly regarded as "the opportunity to ensure that a real spiritual dialogue shall take place between the Eastern churches and the churches which take their origin in the West. If we accept this opportunity our ecumenical task will not become easier, but we shall surely be greatly enriched". Out of some 400 million Christians today—the total membership of the churches represented in the WCC—almost 140 million are Orthodox. With the act of integration, whose preparation took some 15 years, the International Missionary Council (q.v.) ceased to exist as a separate entity and was replaced by the WCC Division on World Mission and Evangelism. The assembly approved an extension of the existing form of the Basis of the WCC adding a reference to the Scriptures and the trinitarian formula.

In Section I a theological problem arose that has continued to preoccupy the WCC ever since: the influence of Christ in other religions, that is, to what extent God's action in other religions is in accordance with the Christian faith, and what possibilities arise from it. By relating the concept of "solidarity" to God's love for human beings, a distinction was drawn between Christian service and mere philanthropy. Yet, it lacked a substantial and valid theological foundation, and among many different kinds of churches it was impossible to achieve a consensus. The primary aim of Section II was to face the problems of political, economic and social change, and thus help the churches in the Third World (q.v.) in their situation. The unity of the church in Section III was conceived of as "one fully committed fellowship, holding the one apostolic faith, preaching the one gospel, breaking the one bread, joining in common prayer, and having a corporate life reaching out in witness and service to all and who at the same time are united with the whole Christian fellowship in all places and all ages . . .''.

At New Delhi 1961 the WCC had become more and more the mouthpiece of the member churches. This was shown in a renewed stand on religious liberty, a resolution on anti-Semitism, a common stand on the international crisis, a message to Christians in South Africa and in an "Appeal to all Governments and Peoples''. The WCC had assumed increasing responsibility for relief to people in distress, refugees (q.v.) and victims of human-made or natural catastrophes all over the world. The churches' desire to stay together (Amsterdam) and to grow together (Evanston) had developed into joint progress in assuming new tasks (New Delhi).

Uppsala 1968. Main theme: Behold, I Make All Things New. Sections: 1. The Holy Spirit and the Catholicity of the Church; 2. Renewal in Mission; 3. World Economic and Social Development; 4. Towards Justice and Peace in International Affairs; 5. Worship; 6. Towards New Styles of Living.

Honorary Presidents: Dr. Joseph H. Oldham and Dr. W. A. Visser 't Hooft (q.v.). Presidents: Patriarch German, Bp. Hanns Lilje (q.v.), Dr. Daniel T. Niles (q.v.), Dr. Kiyoko Takeda Cho (q.v.), Dr. Ernest A. Payne, Dr. John Coventry Smith (q.v.), Bp. Alphaeus H. Zulu (q.v.). Moderator: Dr. M. M. Thomas (q.v.), Vice Moderators: Ms. Pauline Webb and Metrop. Meliton (q.v.).

The fourth assembly marked the end of an era in the ecumenical movement and also a new beginning. It was the most activist and politically oriented assembly in the history of the WCC. Stating that "the Church is bold in speaking of itself as the sign of the coming unity of mankind", it also noted that "secular society has produced instruments of conciliation and unification which often seem more effective than the Church itself''. Therefore, "churches need a new openness to the world in its aspirations, its achievements, its restlessness and its despair''. The unity and the catholicity of the church was set in God's activity in history. For the first time "a genuinely universal council", able to speak for all Christians, was articulated. It was agreed that all the structures of the church from local to world level must be examined to see whether they enable the church and its members to be a mission, or obstruct them from it. More dialogue with the world and more effective proclamation of the good news are equally needed.

The reality that the rich become richer and the poor (q.v.) poorer dominated the discussion of all sociopolitical and economic issues. The assembly recommended to the churches that they should set aside 1 percent from their total income for development aid, and should appeal to their governments to invest the same percentage from their GNP. The figure should be considerably increased in the following years. The central issue in development (q.v.) is the criterion of the human. Public opinion must be persuaded to support deep changes in both developed and developing nations. "If our false security in the old and our fear of revolutionary change tempt us to defend the *status quo* or to patch it up with half-hearted measures, we may all perish".

In the realm of worship (q.v.) four major points were made: a) worship is dependent upon symbols that are cognitively and emotionally understood; b) all Christians should be open to learn from the practices of worship of other Christians—uniformity and freedom, the universal and the local, continuity and change are all valuable; c) segregation by race or class must be rejected in Christian worship; d) God, through the Holy Spirit (q.v.), is the one who alone can quicken our worship and make it alive. We need to pray to be enabled to pray. It was recommended "that all churches consider seriously the desirability of adopting the early Christian tradition of celebrating the Eucharist (q.v.) every Sunday". Finally, it was stressed that worship "is ethical and social in nature and can never be true worship unless it is orientated towards the social injustices and divisions of mankind".

Discussing new styles of living, the assembly grappled with the problem of how Christians truly make ethical decisions. Social and cultural differences make a single style of Christian life impossible and even wrong. Refusing to choose between "contextual" and "rules", the gathering pressed for the position that individual moral choices can be made only in community, held together by biblical insight and the communion table.

Youth (q.v.) was visibly present and highly critical of the ecumenical establishment. It staged demonstrations in the forms of sit-in, stand-up, walking-out, picketing and boycott as it was not satisfied with its place in the assembly. Its concrete proposals for change in many realms of faith and life were, however, neither better nor more "radical" than the proposals officially introduced into the assembly. In his address, Roberto Tucci made reference to the possibility of membership of the Roman Catholic Church (q.v.) in the WCC, which was seriously discussed in the following years. Also, closer relations with national and regional councils of churches were high on the agenda.

Uppsala added several new subunits to the WCC: the Program to Combat Racism (PCR), the Commission on the Churches' Participation in Development (CCPD), the Christian Medical Commission (CMC), the Dialogue with People of Living Faiths and Ideologies (DFI) and the Sub-unit on Education. Unit II, Justice and Service, became from 1971 onward the largest unit of the Council.

Nairobi 1975. Main theme: Jesus Christ Frees and Unites. Sections: 1. Confessing Christ Today; 2. What Unity Requires; 3. Seeking Community; The Common Search of People of Various Faiths, Cultures and Ideologies; 4. Education for Liberation and Community; 5. Structures of Injustice and Struggles for Liberation; 6. Human Development: Ambiguities of Power, Technology and Quality of Life.

Honorary President: Dr. W. A. Visser 't Hooft, Presidents: Hon. Mrs. Justice Annie R. Jiagge, Prof. José Miguez-Bonino (q.v.), Metrop. Nicodim (q.v.) (succeeded in 1979 by Patriarch Iliya II of Georgia), General Tahi B. Simatupang (q.v.), Archbp. Olof Sundby, Dr. Cynthia Wedel (q.v.). Moderator of the Central Committee: Archbp. Edward W. Scott (q.v.), Vice Moderators: Mrs. Jean Skuse, Archbp. Karekin Sarkissian (q.v.).

The WCC initially had three "official languages"— English, French and German—to which were added de facto Russian and Spanish. At Nairobi there was also some interpretation into and from Portuguese and Swahili. The assembly has been called a gathering of consolidation. There was not much especially new in the way of ideas. The insights and causes were still for the most part those that had erupted at Uppsala and before. But they were stated less shrilly and more firmly, and they were understood more theologically. Nairobi raised religious and sociopolitical issues in one breath by stating that faith in the triune God and sociopolitical engagement, the conversion to Jesus Christ and the active participation in changing economic and social structures, belong together and condition each other. Yet, there were a number a contentious issues. A difficult moment came when an appeal for support by the WCC of two Soviet dissidents was discussed, and the Russian Orthodox Church protested being singled out as representing a nation violating human rights (q.v.). The assembly did not polarize between the Third World and the North Atlantic or between East and West.

The task of evangelism, debated in Section I, was seen as relating spirituality to involvement—the influence of the World Missionary Conference in Bangkok in 1973 and of the World Congress for Evangelism in Lausanne in 1974 was visible. It was stressed that Christian mission that does not liberate human beings from crushing poverty, vile working conditions and evil tyranny is largely irrelevant today. As unity requires a commonly accepted goal, a fuller understanding of the context and companionship in struggle and hope, it was proposed in Section II to ask the churches to transmit their responses to the three agreed statements on "Baptism, Eucharist and Ministry", compiled by the Commission on Faith and Order (qq.v.). The document appeared in a final version in 1982.

As there were serious objections to the Report of Section III, the document was referred back to the section for reconsideration before it was voted in plenary. Objections of delegates in the West were that the report was weak and uncommitted and would be understood as a spiritual compromise and as opposition to mission. Representatives of Asia stressed that dialogue in no way diminishes full commitment to one's own faith, that dialogue, far from being a temptation to syncretism, is a safeguard against it, and that it is a creative interaction that liberates a person from a closed religious system. Too much arrogance, aggression and negativism of evangelistic crusades have obscured the gospel and caricatured Christianity as an authentic religion.

The assembly stood firmly behind the Uppsala positions and the actions since 1968. There was no weakening on the issues of the Program to Combat Racism and the Special Fund. But it was also emphasized that this commitment to action on behalf of the weak and the oppressed must be understood in a more evangelical way. The search for a "just, participatory and sustainable society" (qq.v.) became a major undertaking. Programs on faith, science and technology (qq.v.), militarism and disarmament (q.v.), ecology (q.v.) and human survival, the crucial role of women in church and society, and renewal and congregational life—all received a new emphasis. A beginning was made in the discussion of the concern of "sharing of ecumenical resources".

After the assembly, the central committee, at the recommendation of the assembly's Program Guideline Committee, laid down four "program thrusts" for the Council until the next assembly:

1) The expression and communication of our faith in the triune God.

2) The search for a just, participatory and sustainable society.

3) The unity of the Church and the renewal of human community.

4) Education and renewal in search of true community.

Vancouver 1983. Main theme: Jesus Christ—the Life of the World. Issues: 1. Witnessing in a Divided World; 2. Taking Steps Toward Unity; 3. Moving Toward Participation; 4. Healing and Sharing Life in Community; 5. Confronting Threats to Peace and Survival; 6. Struggling for Justice and Human Dignity; 7. Learning in Community; 8. Communicating Credibly.

Honorary President: Dr. W. A. Visser 't Hooft (died in 1985). Presidents: Dame R. Nita Barrow (q.v.), Dr. Marga Bührig (q.v.), Metrop. Paulos Mar Gregorios (q.v.); Bp. Johannes W. Hempel, Archbp. W. P. Khotso Makhulu, Dr.

Lois M. Wilson (q.v.). Moderator of the central committee: Rev. Dr. Heinz-Joachim Held, Vice Moderators: Metrop. Chrysostomos of Myra, Dr. Sylvia Talbot. The assembly was a greatly representative world gathering. More than 4,500 people a day, on average, found themselves taking part one way or another in the various sessions. Of the delegates 30.46 percent were women, 13.46 percent under the age of 30 years, and 46.3 percent laypeople. Leadership by women, prominent as never before, was welcomed for the obvious competence of those providing it. Canada's cultures and concerns made a strong impact on the gathering. The quality of work done by most of the issue groups left a lot to be desired. The stress was on a participatory assembly; but this experience should not be repeated, if the price includes a mediocrity in the written texts "commended to the churches for study and appropriate action".

The worship services in a large tent drew thousands of people every day and penetrated the whole assembly. Celebrating the Lima (q.v.) order of worship—the order used by the Faith and Order Commission meeting in Lima, Peru, in 1982—many Christians joyfully rediscovered the sacramental depth of the Church and the divine blessing of its age-long liturgy (q.v.). A vigil commemorating the tragedy of the bombing of Hiroshima and Nagasaki was maintained throughout the night. At Vancouver, Amsterdam and Uppsala appeared to have come to terms with each other. It was a "re-integrated" assembly.

Churches were requested to respond officially to the document on "Baptism, Eucharist and Ministry" by the end of 1986. The fifth report of the Joint Working Group (q.v.) between the RCC and the WCC was received, and future steps of collaboration outlined. In the realm of evangelism, wide attention was drawn to Christian witness in the contexts of culture, worship, the fate of the poor, the life of children and the pluralistic world of living faiths. Concentrating on education, the assembly urged member churches "to take seriously the ecumenical dimension of learning and include it in all educational activities and programs. In particular we urge the revision of curricula of schools and seminaries and the activities of congregations to provide for ecumenical perspective''. Emphasizing the central importance of language and culture in ecumenical education, churches were encouraged to experiment with alternative forms of communication (q.v.).

Concentrating on sociopolitical responsibilities, the sixth assembly showed growth in maturity in dealing realistically with sharp divisions and tragic conflicts in the world without allowing them to destroy the ecumenical fellowship. The relevance of ''realized eschatology'' (q.v.) in the face of the oppressive powers and the web of domination and injustice in the world was recognized. The assembly can be considered a climax in the process of linking peace to justice. ''There is no peace in the world without justice, and there will be no justice without peace''. Hostilities and clashes between East and West, and between North and South, are deeply related to one another. Society is a single reality. It was recommended ''to engage member churches in a conciliar process of mutual commitment (covenant) to justice, peace and the integrity of all creation'' as a priority of the WCC. ''The foundations of this emphasis should be confessing Christ as the life of the world and Christian resistance to the demonic powers of death in racism (q.v.) sexism, caste oppression, economic exploitation, militarism (q.v.), violations of human rights, and the misuse of science and technology''. The central committee in 1987 approved the proposal that a ''world convocation'' on Justice, Peace and the Integrity of Creation (q.v.) be held in 1990 in conjunction with the next assembly of the WCC in 1991.

The Program Guidelines Committee suggested that the following priority areas should inspire all WCC activities for the next seven years: 1. Growing Toward Unity; 2. Growing Toward Justice and Peace; 3. Growing Toward Vital and Coherent Theology; 4. Growing Toward New Dimensions of the Churches' Self-understanding; 5. Growing Toward a Community of Confessing and Learning.

Canberra 1991. Main theme: Come, Holy Spirit—Renew the Whole Creation. Sections/sub-themes: 1. Giver of Life—Sustain Your Creation; 2. Spirit of Truth—Set Us Free; 3. Spirit of Unity—Reconcile Your People; 4. Holy Spirit—Transform and Sanctify Us.

Presidents: Dr. Anne-Marie Aagaard, Bp. Vinton R. Anderson, Bp. Leslie Boseto, Mrs. Priyanka Mendis, Patriarch Parthenios, Rev. Eunice Santana, Pope Shenouda, Dr. Aaron Tolen (q.v.). Moderator of the central committee: Archbp. Aram Keshishian, Vice Moderators: Rev Nélida Ritchie and Ephorus Dr. Soritua Nababan.

Christians from the Peoples' Republic of China attended a WCC assembly for the second time since Amsterdam 1948, and the China Christian Council (a united church in process of formation) was one of the seven churches welcomed as a new member. Another new milestone was the presence of observers from the Dutch Reformed Church in South Africa, a first since it left the council in the 1960s. As at Vancouver, delegates from member churches made up only about a fifth of those present; other participants included 10 guests from other faiths, about 1,500 visitors and over 200 observers from nonmember bodies.

The main theme was not only a departure from earlier assemblies in that it concentrated on the third person of the Trinity (q.v.) but that the theme was formulated in the form of a prayer. Frequent remarks in assembly sessions, however, showed that while the pneumatological emphasis opens new perspectives on ecumenical concerns, it can also be the cause of much new controversy. There was a repeated emphasis on linking Jesus Christ (q.v.) to the Holy Spirit. It was the first assembly when a global war took place in the world. Painful and long discussion about a statement on the Gulf War revealed the deep differences within the WCC over the old question of a just war (q.v.) and participation in it. The crisis and conflict in the Middle East overshadowed other situations of tension and oppression in the world and highlighted growing difficulty in the ecumenical movement itself to distinguish between global and local concerns. A statement that defended the rights of Australian aboriginals was not unanimously endorsed.

Assembly debates and worship services made clear that despite recent ecumenical convergence on several theological matters, questions of the ordained ministry, the nature of the eucharist and different understandings of the church continued to be real stumbling blocks to full communion.

The Orthodox churches insisted that the goal of the WCC must remain the restoration of the unity of the church and to that effect Faith and Order must continue as the priority program of the Council. The last sentence of their message was: "Has the time come for the Orthodox churches and other member churches to review their relations with the World Council of Churches"?

The Program Policy Committee recommended that the following program policies should undergird and inspire all WCC programs in the coming years: A. Renewal through Reconciliation; B. Renewal through Freedom and Justice; C. Renewal through a Right Relationship with Creation; D. Renewal through Enabling the Full Participation of Women; E. Renewal through an Ecumenical Spirituality for Our Times.

For an extensive bibliography on the first six WCC assemblies consult *The Ecumenical Advance: A History of the Ecumenical Movement,* vol. 2: 1948–1968. Ed. by Harold E. Fey. Geneva: WCC, 1986. 3rd ed.

WORLD DAY OF PRAYER. This annual international prayer, founded in 1887 by Mary Ellen James, president of a US Presbyterian women's home mission board, in response to needs following the Civil War and for prayer for mission (qq.v.) overseas, has developed over the years into a worldwide movement, composed mainly of women, who engage in "informed prayer and prayerful action" on behalf of the needs of the whole world. It is still prepared annually by women of different countries and highlights each year the particular needs of the country responsible for the theme. In response to the growth of the world day of prayer, an international committee was created to carry overall responsibility for this movement. Since 1967 representatives of national committees have met every four years in a different region to share in the experience of the international exercise and select themes and writers for forthcoming services in view of developments in the world.

WORLD EVANGELICAL FELLOWSHIP (WEF). The Evangelical Alliance was founded as a world body in London in 1846 by leaders from fifty-two branches of churches in Europe and North America. It functioned for more than a century as a number of alliances in various countries but in 1951 formed the World Evangelical Fellowship to strengthen its global dimension, especially through the work of its theological commission. Until the 1960s membership was on an individual basis, but it is now open to local evangelical fellowships, societies, denominations and individual churches that are in agreement with its doctrinal basis and its stated aims. These aims have been somewhat indefinite, not going much further than the cultivation of mutual love and the promotion of common purposes. One of its best-known activities has been the sponsoring of a united week of prayer throughout the world, traditionally during the first week of January. During the 19th century the alliance convened international conferences that were important because of their size, character and wide representation of evangelical Christianity (such as London, 1851, and New York, 1873). It disseminated a vast amount of information through these conferences, which included detailed surveys of the religious scene worldwide.

In 1952 the WEF opened the first of several hostels for overseas students in London, and in 1954/1955 sponsored the first Haringey Billy Graham (q.v.) crusade. In 1958 it formed the Evangelical Missionary Alliance, which links nearly 100 evangelical missionary societies and training colleges. Subsequently it launched a magazine, *Crusade* (later renamed *Today*), and established a relief fund, the TEAR Fund (1967), which by the mid-1980s raised as much as £11 million annually. In 1989 the WEF counted 60 national evangelical fellowships, 80 percent of them from the Third World (q.v.). Several internationally constituted commissions spearhead its programs. Consultations and general assemblies and various publications give voice to the concerns of the WEF's worldwide constituencies. Representatives of the WEF, the Lausanne Committee for World Evangelization and the WCC (qq.v.) participated in 1989 in an international consultation on evangelism (q.v.).

WORLD FELLOWSHIP OF ORTHODOX YOUTH *see* **SYNDESMOS**

WORLD METHODIST COUNCIL *see* METHODIST CHURCH

WORLD STUDENT CHRISTIAN FEDERATION (WSCF). The WSCF was established in 1895 at Vadstena Castle, Sweden, by students and student leaders from ten countries in Europe and North America. Among its key founders was John R. Mott (q.v.). Through this organization the student Christian movements (SCMs) of each nation express their universality. The WSCF was a primary pioneer of the modern missionary and ecumenical movement; it has nurtured many missionary and ecumenical leaders for the church. Its ecumenical vision and commitment emphasized the necessity of continuous communication, cooperation and challenge with the established churches. It was instrumental in the creation of the International Missionary Council (1921) and the World Council of Churches (qq.v.) (1948). Since its inception, the WSCF has drawn most of its membership from Protestant students, although Roman Catholic (qq.v.) students have also been members, especially in Latin America and in some parts of Asia. The Orthodox (q.v.) joined the federation as the result of a conference in Constantinople in 1911. Until the late 1960s the international staff of the WSCF was based in Geneva. Afterward a major structural change decentralized the federation into six regions: Africa, Asia/Pacific, Europe, Latin America, Middle East and North America. The Geneva headquarters became the inter-regional office.

Over the years WSCF emphases have changed, sometimes dramatically. By the First World War concern for social action had expressed itself. In the 1930s new interest centered on the Christian message for the world. By the Second World War the meaning of the university was a prime question, and the mission in the university was a strong concern. By the 1950s in the era of increased secularization (q.v.), when old ecclesiastical structures appeared inadequate, the "life and mission of the church" came to the fore. At a world "teaching conference" in Strasbourg in 1960, some of the ablest speakers did their best to pass on the ecumenical vision, but the audience was restless. There seemed to be too much speaking about the life of the church; what students wanted was action in their world. And there seemed to be too much mission; what students wanted was a welcome to this world. Subsequent conferences were stormy and controversial. Gradually the WSCF tilted to the left; its theme in the 1970s—Christian Witness in the Struggle for Liberation—points to its political commitment. The debates were painful, sometimes divisive. Now there is a strong new interest in theological reflection, honoring contextual theologies as well as seeking global visions. The greatest contribution of the WSCF to the worldwide church remains in those it has trained and projected into major leadership. Various biographies in this volume should be consulted. A striking example was W. A. Visser 't Hooft (q.v.), who was the WSCF's general secretary in the 1930s.

WORLD VISION INTERNATIONAL. One of the largest Christian humanitarian organizations, founded in 1950 as a Protestant evangelical agency to help Korean war orphans. By the late 1980s World Vision had international headquarters near Los Angeles, California, and regional centers in Canada, Great Britain, Finland, Netherlands, Australia, Switzerland, West Germany, Africa, Hong Kong, New Zealand and Singapore. Recently it ministered to nearly 400,000 children and their families through developing community and family resources in 80 nations, and provided emergency aid to victims of natural disaster, famine and war in more than 100 disaster projects. Its Missions Advanced Research and Communications Center gathered and interpreted current information to aid mission agencies, and national churches plan effective evangelism (q.v.) strategies. By the end of the 1980s its annual budget was well over US $100 million and its staff was about 3,000 nationals working in their own countries.

WORLD YOUNG WOMEN'S CHRISTIAN ASSOCIATIONS (WORLD YWCA). This organization, founded in 1894, with headquarters in Geneva, endeavors "to build a worldwide fellowship through which women and girls may come to know more of the love of God as revealed in Jesus Christ for themselves and for all people, and may learn to express that love in responsible action". The movement is concerned with the whole of the life of female persons, and this broad conception leads it into many kinds of different activities: into concerns like education and vocational training, leadership development, the struggle against discrimination, international understanding of peace (q.v.), the eradication of illiteracy; and into undertakings such as the setting up of hostels, clubs, nurseries, camps, refugee (q.v.) and emergency services. A number of YWCA projects receive support from Inter-Church Aid and Technical Aid sources.

The interdenominational character of the World YWCA was a distinctive form from its beginning and led to its playing a leading role in the early stages of the ecumenical movement. Working today in 92 countries, the World YWCA has a federated structure of 79 national affiliates that in turn direct thousands of local branches. It has consultative status with the United Nations (q.v.) and its specialized agencies, and cooperates with many ecumenical and nongovernmental organizations. It has developed from Protestant origins into a fully interconfessional body. Roman Catholics, Orthodox and Protestants (qq.v.) of various denominations now work together in the legislative and executive bodies of the World YWCA. Women have emerged as prominent leaders struggling for women's rights, for international peace and for development with justice (qq.v.) for all.

WORSHIP. Christian worship is the worship of God the Father through Jesus Christ in the power of the Holy Spirit (q.v.). Christians do not need to persuade human beings to worship God. The fact that they are worshipping beings is one of the fundamental facts about humanity. That fact at once establishes the unity of humankind and holds out the possibility that all human beings become one in worship, which is worship in Spirit and in truth. Christians are not concerned to deny that worship other than Christian worship is a genuine activity of the human spirit; still less are they concerned to deny that God will hear and accept all prayer addressed to him, whatever an idea of God a human being may have. No Christian is entitled to impose limits on the mercy and loving-kindness of God. It is the task of the church through its worship to help fellow human beings to discover God as revealed in Jesus Christ. The Greek word for worship is *latreia*. In its basic meaning it refers to any occupation by which one earns one's daily bread. All one's life is therefore meant to be full of worship. All life has to be related to the Giver of life.

The recognition of the priority of worship over doctrinal formulation is of great theological importance. The normal order of things is that worship precedes credal definition and theology. The early Christians found themselves worshipping Christ before they had reached any formal theological formulation of his person and nature. The earliest Christian confessions of faith (q.v.) had their origin in worship, as, for example, in the Christ-hymn in Phil. 2:5–11, which was not composed by St Paul but was quoted by him from a familiar act of Christian worship. Worship is primary; theology is secondary. Worship, moreover, as adoration, reverence and praise of God is closely connected with Christian witness and service. This was the concern of the WCC Amsterdam assembly (qq.v.) (1948) when it stressed that "a worshipping group of individuals is not necessarily a community". It is essential that each group become a real fellowship, through acceptance by all of full Christian responsibility for mutual service, and by breaking down the barriers of race and class.

In preparation for the third world conference on Faith and Order (q.v.) in Lund, 1951, a whole volume on *Ways of Worship* was published in 1951. An international theological commission had started to work on such a book as early as 1939. The report is divided in three parts: the elements of liturgy (q.v.); the inner meanings of word and sacraments (q.v.); liturgy and devotion (all three parts deal with Roman Catholic, Orthodox, Anglican, Reformed (qq.v.) and other traditions). It struggled with several unresolved problems in the areas: 1) differences of opinion as to the relation of word and sacrament; 2) the blessing of the eucharistic elements; 3) the difficulty of defining precisely "liturgical" and "non-liturgical" forms of worship; 4) worship led by any member of the congregation or by the ordained minister; 5) the sacrificial aspect of the eucharist (q.v.); 6) the distinction between "saints" and "blessed saints". The report also concentrated on the intimate relation between faith and cultural tradition, and on nontheological (q.v.), that is, on social and psychological, factors that prevent "the development of liturgical forms suitable to the age in which we live". Among several recommendations it was suggested that "a more detailed exploration, theological, metaphysical and psychological, of mystery in relation to worship" should be undertaken.

The WCC New Delhi assembly in 1961 reiterated the importance of the intimate relationship between worship and service. The worship of God is an end in itself and at the same time serves to strengthen Christians for witness and service. In worship they offer to God the work, the concerns for the people of this world, and then return again as Christ's servants into everyday life. In worship they confess their sins and receive forgiveness and courage for the old and new daily tasks. Worship helps them to regain their perspective and gives them a certain freedom from the pressures of this world. The report *Worship and the Oneness of Christ's Church* of the fourth world conference on Faith and Order in Montreal (1963), in contrast to Lund, which had maintained that worship is no less essential to the church's life than faith and order, called worship "the central and determinative act of the church's life" and pressed for an examination of worship as one of the primary tasks of ecumenical dialogue. It clearly recognized the fundamental ecclesiological significance of worship. The original title of the section "The Worship of God in a Secular Age" of the Uppsala assembly (1968) was changed to "Worship", because protest was voiced against too much emphasis by Western theologians on secular theology. A reconciliation between "secularizing radicals" and "heavenly conservatives" became impossible. The section noted wide divergencies of practice, resistance to change and the corrosive effects of secularization, (q.v.) which make the church a strange and alien atmosphere for many contemporary people.

At Vancouver in 1983 the skillful leadership of worship in a large tent became the assembly's focus and symbol, creating vivid images of an inclusive and worldwide community for whom worship was at once a serious activity and joyful celebration. The worship service that attracted the most attention was no doubt the celebration of the eucharist according to a liturgy that highlighted the convergencies in the text on Baptism, Eucharist and Ministry (q.v.), which the WCC's Faith and Order Commission had submitted to the churches after its meeting in Lima (q.v.) in 1982. The Archbishop of Canterbury presided, joined by six ministers from other traditions and parts of the world. Those who read Scripture and led prayers at the service included Roman Catholic and Orthodox Christians whose official norms generally preclude them from receiving the bread and wine of the communion under ecumenical auspices. The entire service was thus a vivid reminder of the divisions that still remain in the church as well as a hopeful foretaste, as one of the prayers put it, "that we may soon attain the visible communion in the Body of Christ, by breaking the bread and blessing the cup around the same table".

There is a need for further reflection on the dialectical and dynamic relation between penitence, adoration and political action. From Nairobi 1975 onward the slogan "spirituality for combat" has caught ecumenical attention. In Orthodox circles the expression "the liturgy (q.v.) after the Liturgy" has become popular. These terms are a reminder that desperate struggles against racism (q.v.), classism and sexism must become part of Christian spirituality (q.v.) and liturgy. The process of building modern ecumenical theologies of worship should continue. Doxology is the ground of all striving for unity (q.v.). *See also* HYMNOLOGY; LIMA/LITURGY; PRAYER; SPIRITUALITY.

- Y -

YOUNG MEN'S CHRISTIAN ASSOCIATIONS *see* WORLD ALLIANCE OF YOUNG MEN'S CHRISTIAN ASSOCIATIONS

YOUNG WOMEN'S CHRISTIAN ASSOCIATIONS *see* WORLD YOUNG WOMEN'S CHRISTIAN ASSOCIATIONS

YOUTH. Christian youth has participated in the ecumenical movement and even preceded that movement. It became organized and was active in the YMCA, the YWCA, the World Student Christian Federation (WSCF), the World Alliance for Promoting International Friendship through the Churches and the Life and Work (qq.v.) movement. The Ecumenical Youth Commission (later the World Christian Youth Commission) organized the first world conference of Christian youth in Amsterdam in 1939. Almost 1,500 Christian youth gathered there to share together in "the growing concerns of the whole ecumenical movement" and "to hear and to follow the clear call of God". Looking back to the international gathering soon after the war, S. Franklin Mack wrote: "*Christus Victor* came to stand as a supreme symbol of oneness; youth had brought this about, Christian youth; youth undismayed by the bigness of the undertaking, undeterred by the imminent threat of war in Europe, confident that every problem has a Christian solution".

The second world conference of Christian youth in Oslo in 1947 could not repeat Amsterdam 1939. But it was the first major postwar gathering of youth from all parts of the world and it marked the beginning of another stage in the involvement of youth in the ecumenical movement. Oslo was marked by a spirit of forgiveness, reconciliation and solidarity. Not surprisingly a delegation of 100 young people attended the first assembly of the WCC (qq.v.) in Amsterdam in 1948, participating in the plenary sessions and organizing an intensive program on its own. The timely decision to set up a joint youth department committee of the WCC and the World Council of Christian Education (q.v.) and Sunday School Association had far-reaching consequences, in particular for close and regular cooperation between North America and Europe.

A third period of development and change in the consciousness and concerns of youth began with Evanston 1954. Active after the second WCC assembly within the Division of Ecumenical Action, the Youth Department now tried out a new style of work. Not only did it continue to deepen ecumenical fellowship among Christian young people and to strengthen the youth work of the churches around the world, but it followed up its mandate "to keep before the churches their responsibility for the evangelization of young people and their growth in the Christian faith". The overall study theme "The Integration of Youth in the Life and Mission of the Church" served as a guiding principle of orientation and action.

Increasingly, however, questions were debated among youth as to what kind of life and fellowship the church offers. Slowly the very concept of the integration of youth in the church was challenged. Integration within the existing ecclesiastical structures is only an invitation to conform. No possibility is offered to youth to be at the same time relatively distant from and deeply involved in the Christian community in order that they become critical participants in it. The crisis in ecumenical youth work came to a head in the early 1960s. A widespread underground movement, ignored for the most part by the majority of experienced church leaders, now came to the surface. Both the ecumenical youth assembly in Lausanne and the world teaching conference in Strasbourg in 1960 inaugurated a new period of rapid and radical change. Youth became increasingly caught up in its own agonies, dilemmas and aspirations. Forced into restless encounters with Christian and secular communities it searched on its own for meaning in the gospel of reconciliation.

Throughout the 1960s young people were destined to press too hard for solutions and to overshoot the marks, as they underestimated the influence of tradition and prejudice in the churches and the innumerable complexities of an emerging interdependent world society. The problematic of the politization of youth became more and more visible, particularly at the WCC assembly in Uppsala in 1968. Young people had developed their own new methods of involvement to hammer home the urgency of common service to the suffering, the exploited and the poor (q.v.). The sharing of the bread in the eucharist (q.v.), they felt, must be directly related to the pursuit of international justice (q.v.). The divisions of the churches aggravate human conflicts and the struggles in the world perpetuate the polarization of the churches. The gulf between the affluent and the destitute cuts across all denominational and confessional lines. Nevertheless, the youth participants in the assembly were as vulnerable as the adult delegates. In spite of their effective new style of communication, their proposals and recommendations were not more to the purpose than the official decisions in the world gathering. They grasped only imperfectly that identification with the victims of racial discrimination, economic and ideological oppression involved more than the staging of demonstrations and the shouting of slogans.

The present era has been marked by even more far-reaching changes and unforseeable developments in the orientation, behavior and commitment of youth. The WCC's youth office, just like the World Student Christian Federation, struggled with the problems of the right balance between centralization and decentralization, the attention to be paid to overall as against specific concerns, and the gap in communication between the international headquarters in Geneva and the different youth networks and constituencies throughout the world. Many national and regional youth organizations were satisfied with their particular achievements and resisted interference in their internal affairs. Plans to hold a world youth conference in 1981 did not materialize. The YMCA, the YWCA and the WSCF felt threatened by the prospect of such a major event. The YMCA argued that it had full Roman Catholic participation and could not take part in a world conference unless there was full Catholic involvement. The WSCF was still sorting out its domestic problems and was seriously short of funds.

The countercultures of the young have posed a fundamental challenge to the Western cultural tradition. Profoundly alienated from adult church and adult society, youth went its own way, leaving it to adults to tackle the world's problems. The older generation itself clung to its traditional attitude, since the youth searching for new norms, values, social structures and life-styles was apparently a small portion of the total youth population. Facile generalizations, instead of a careful assessment of contemporary youth, were deemed sufficient in view of the transient and limited character of the deviation and dissent. Also the assumption that the countercultures had a wordly orientation and were militantly secular, added to the reservations of the church hierarchy. In actual fact they were, with a few exceptions, deeply religious, though not in the sense in which evangelical church leaders would define religion. Their quest for the sacred was an odd amalgam of the Eastern and the Western, yet another sign of how deeply alienated from the immediate cultural traditions the countercultures were.

There is now a minority of young sociopolitical activists passionately engaged in movements for the preservation of nature and for lasting harmony and peace in the world. Ecological pressure groups vary in their character from country to country. In some Western nations they are well organized as political parties. There are also ecological movements of young people in the Third World (q.v.). There are, moreover, several peace movements of young people in many countries of the First World; but those in the Netherlands and in Germany are the strongest and the most outspoken. Their radical antiwar activism has greatly increased as they know the futility of the reliance on force.

The issues raised here have bearings on the present and future youth work in the ecumenical movement. It is true that adult Christians tend to escape from the present into defensive justifications of the past. And young people tend to escape from the past into Utopian projections of the future. Both risk ignoring the quality of newness that the present always possesses and that changes the understanding of both as to where they came from and where they are to go. They both, therefore, are called to catch a few glimpses of the wholeness of the oikoumene.

There are over 500 Christian youth movements and organizations that are of major significance at national and wider levels. Among the Roman Catholic bodies are the Grail (International Movement of Catholic Laywomen), the Legion of Mary (Association of Lay Roman Catholics), the International Catholic Youth Federation (ICYF) and Pax Romana (International Movement of Roman Catholic Students). Young Christian Students (YCS) and Young Christian Workers (YCW) were created in Belgium in 1925. Mention should be made of the Focelare movement, which from 1944 onward, under the guidance of Chiara Lubich (q.v.), has spread to many parts of the world. Its aim is to promote Christian unity, particularly among the young. Youth for Christ International (YFCI) was organized in the United States in 1945. There are at least thirty youth organizations in Great Britain and twenty-eight youth organizations in the USA. There is indeed no lack in Christian bodies ministering to the needs of youth throughout the world. But the question may be raised as to whether their traditions and structures hinder rather than help them in developing a new sensitivity to the ever-changing aspirations of the younger generation. Their outlook and function can become as anachronistic and irrelevant as those of adult institutions unless they face the challenges of the time.

- Z -

ZANDER, LEO (1893–1964). Zander participated in the conferences of Edinburgh 1937, Oslo 1947 and Amsterdam 1948, as well as the central committee meeting in Toronto in 1950. He taught philosophy in Perm in 1918, and in Vladivostok, 1919–1922, and from 1925 onward was professor of philosophy and confessional studies at the Russian Orthodox St Serge Institute in Paris. He founded an annual seminar of liturgical experience held during the Eastern period in the Ecumenical Institute of Bossey (q v) and in Paris. As secretary of the Orthodox student Christian movement, he carried out an indefatigable lifelong activity dedicated to encouraging an ecumenical approach by the Orthodox church to the Western churches. A follower of Sergius Bulgakov (q.v.) he was much interested in contributing to an alternative form of Orthodoxy (q.v.) in the West.

ZANKOV, STEFAN (1881–1965). A Bulgarian Orthodox pioneer in the ecumenical movement, Zankov was one of the leaders of the Faith and Order and Life and Work movements, the World Alliance for Promoting International Friendship through the Churches and the World Student Christian Movement (qq.v.). He lectured several times at the annual ecumenical seminar in Geneva, sponsored by the

Universal Christian Council of Life and Work. In the triangular relation between Roman Catholicism, Protestantism and Orthodoxy (q.v.) he emphasized the close relation between the last two. He was also an active participant in the world Christian youth movement and a cofounder of the Christian Peace Conference (q.v.). He acted as vice chairman of the holy synod of the Bulgarian Orthodox Church, 1905–1908, was professor of church history and Christian sociology at the University of Sofia, 1923–1950, and at the Orthodox Theological Academy of Sofia, 1950–1961.

ZERNOV, NICOLAS (1898–1980). Zernov was secretary of the Russian Student Christian Movement in exile, 1925–1932, and was honorary secretary of the youth commission of the World Alliance for Promoting International Friendship through the Churches and the Life and Work (qq.v.) movement, with the Orthodox countries as his special field, 1934–1939. Secretary of the Fellowship of St Alban and St Sergius (q.v.), 1933–1947, and lecturer at the School of Slavonic Studies in London, 1936–1939, he was also professor of Eastern Orthodox culture at the University of Oxford, 1947, and afterward was associated with an Orthodox college in Kerala, India, 1953–1954. Zernov promoted ecumenism in the Orthodox churches and was in the forefront evaluating ecumenical relations between East and West.

ZULU, ALPHAEUS HAMILTON (1905–1988). Educated at St Peter's Anglican theological college, Zulu was ordained a priest in 1942. He was appointed assistant curate at St Faith's mission in Durban, 1940–1960. He was consecrated assistant bishop of St John's diocese in the Transkei in 1960, and in 1968 he became bishop of Transkei. His spiritual mentor was Albert Luthuli to whom he became a great friend. He refused to condone any form of violence. Zulu was a president of the WCC (q.v.), 1968–1975, a member of the executive committee of the Christian Council of South Africa, 1945–1958, of the South African Institute of Race Relations, 1943–1984, and of the African National Congress, 1942–1960.

THE BIBLIOGRAPHY

Introduction

The library of the World Council of Churches, established in Geneva in 1946, has over 40,000 titles of printed ecumenical literature in various languages (books, pamphlets and periodical articles). Since 1986 it has provided a computer service to churches, ecumenical bodies and individuals. The library also houses the archives of the 20th-century ecumenical movement, including some 3 million typewritten or mimeographed documents (see Ans. J. van der Bent "Historia Oecumenica", *Ecumenical Review,* vol. 35, no. 3, 1983). Students and scholars have direct access to most of the archival records.

The following bibliography of printed literature is obviously a selection of the bulk of ecumenical publications. With a few exceptions only books in English, or translated into English are listed. Yet, it is a reliable working bibliography of primary and most important sources. For more detailed information other bibliographies should be consulted. In the United States of America several libraries have a limited, but significant, collection of ecumenical literature, including Union Theological Seminary and General Theological Seminary in New York, Pacific School of Religion, Berkeley, California, and the Divinity School of the University of Chicago. The Yale Divinity School Library has an important collection on ecumenical missions.

Table of Contents

BIBLIOGRAPHY

Bent, Ans J. van der. *A Guide to Essential Ecumenical Reading*. Geneva: WCC, 1984.

Classified Catalogue of the Ecumenical Movement, 2 vols. Boston: G. K. Hall, 1972, 1st suppl., 1981. (Contains the collections of ecumenical literature in the WCC library in Geneva)

The Ecumenical Advance. A History of the Ecumenical Movement, vol. 2, 1948–1968. Ed. by Harold E. Fey. Second ed. with updated bibliography. Geneva: WCC, 1986. pp. 451–553.

The Ecumenical Movement: A Bibliography Selected from ATLA Religion Data-base. Chicago: American Theological Library Association, 1983. (Author and subject index)

A History of the Ecumenical Movement, vol. 1, 1517–1948. Ruth Rouse and Stephen C. Neill eds., 3rd ed. Geneva: WCC, 1986. (Bibliography: pp. 747–801)

International Ecumenical Bibliography (Internationale ökumenische Biliographie), 1962–1979, 18 vols. Munich: Kaiser Verlag; Mainz: Matthias-Grünewald-Verlag, 1967–1992.

Répertoire bibliographique des institutions chrétiennes. Strasbourg: Centre de recherche et de documentation des institutions chrétiennes (CERDIC), 1968–, (Annual volumes and special subject volumes indexed by computer)

Handbooks, Dictionaries and Encyclopedias

Bent, Ans J. van der. *Six Hundred Ecumenical Consultations, 1948–1982*. Geneva: WCC, 1983.

————. *Vital Ecumenical Concerns: Sixteen Documentary Surveys.* Geneva: WCC, 1986.

Corpus Dictionary of Western Churches. Ed. by T. C. O'Brien. Washington, DC: Corpus Publications, 1970.

Dictionary of the Ecumenical Movement. Nicholas Lossky, José Miguez Bonino, John Pobee, Tom Stransky, Geoffrey Wainwright, Pauline Webb eds. Geneva: WCC; Grand Rapids: William B. Eerdmans, 1991.

Handbook of Member Churches: World Council of Churches. Ed. by Ans J. van der Bent, rev. ed. Geneva: WCC, 1985.

Index to the World Council of Churches Official Statements and Reports, 1948–1978. Pierre Beffa and Ans J. van der Bent eds. Geneva: WCC, 1978.

Ökumene Lexikon: Kirchen, Religionen, Bewegungen. Hanfried Krüger, Werner Löser and Walter Müller-Römheld eds. 2nd ed. Frankfurt am Main: Otto Lembeck, 1987.

Ökumenische Theologie: Ein Arbeitsbuch. Ed. by Peter Lengsfeld. Stuttgart: Kohlhammer, 1980.

Orientierung Ökumene: Ein Handbuch. Im Auftrag der Theologischen Studien-abteilung beim Bund der Evangelischen Kirchen in der DDR. Hans-Martin Moderow and Matthias Sens eds. Berlin: Evang. Verlagsanstalt, 1982.

World Christian Encyclopedia: A Comparative Study of Churches and Religions in the Modern World, AD 1900–2000. Ed. by David B. Barrett. Nairobi: Oxford UP, 1982.

Major Current Ecumenical Journals and Serial Publications in English

CCIA Background Information, Geneva, 1975–

CCPD Documents, Geneva, 1983–

Christian Century: An Ecumenical Weekly, Chicago, 1884–

Christianity and Crisis, New York, 1941–

Concilium, Edinburgh, 1965–

Current Dialogue, Geneva, 1980–

Ecumenical Press Service, Geneva, 1933–

Ecumenical Review, Geneva, 1948–

Ecumenical Trends, Garrison, NY, 1972–

Ecumenism, Quebec, 1965–

Ecumenist: A Journal for Promoting Christian Unity, Ramsey, NJ, 1962–

Episkepsis, Chambésy-Geneva, 1970–

Information Service, Secretariat for Promoting Christian Unity, Rome, 1967–

International Bulletin of Missionary Research, New Haven, 1950–

International Review of Mission, Geneva, 1912–

Journal of Ecumenical Studies, Philadelphia, 1964–

Mid-Stream: An Ecumenical Journal, Indianapolis, IN, 1961–

One in Christ: A Catholic Ecumenical Review, London, 1965–

One World, Geneva, 1974–

PCR Information: Reports and Background Papers, Geneva, 1979–

Pro Mundi Vita Bulletin, Brussels, 1964–

WSCF Journal, Geneva, 1979–

Ecumenical Conferences and Assemblies

EDINBURGH 1910

World Missionary Conference, 1910. 9 vols. Edinburgh: Oliphant, Anderson and Ferrier, n.d.

STOCKHOLM 1925

The Stockholm Conference 1925: Official Report of the Universal Christian Conference on Life and Work held in Stockholm, 19–30 August 1925. Ed. by G.K.A. Bell. London: Oxford UP, 1925.

LAUSANNE 1927

Faith and Order: Proceedings of the World Conference Lausanne, August 3–21, 1927. Ed. by H. N. Bate. London: SCM, 1927.

JERUSALEM 1928

Report of the Jerusalem Meeting of the International Missionary Council, March 24–April 8, 1928. (The Jerusalem series, 8 vols.). London: Oxford UP, 1928.

OXFORD 1937

The Church, Community and State Series, 7 vols. London: George Allen and Unwin, 1937–1938.

The Churches Survey Their Task: The Report of the Conference at Oxford, July 1937, on Church, Community and State. London: George Allen and Unwin, 1937.

EDINBURGH 1937

The Second World Conference on Faith and Order held at Edinburgh, August 3–18, 1937. Ed. by Leonard Hodgson. London: SCM, 1938.

TAMBARAM-MADRAS 1938

International Missionary Council Meeting at Tambaram, Madras, December 12–29, 1938. (Tambaram-Madras Series, 7 vols.). Oxford: Oxford UP, 1939.

AMSTERDAM 1939

Christus Victor: Report of the World Christian Youth Conference, Amsterdam, July 24 to August 2, 1939. Ed. by Denzil G. M. Patrick. Geneva: Conference Headquarters, 1939.

OSLO 1947

The Report of the Second World Confernce of Christian Youth, Oslo, Norway, July 22–31. Ed. by Paul G. Macy. Geneva: WCC, 1947.

WHITBY 1947

International Missionary Council. *Minutes of the Meeting at Whitby, 1947.* London: IMC, 1947.

Latourette, Kenneth Scott and Hogg, William Richey. *Tomorrow is Here:* The Mission and Work of the Church as Seen from the Meeting of the International Missionary Council at Whitby, Ontario, July 5–24, 1947. New York: Friendship Press, 1948.

AMSTERDAM 1948

Man's Disorder and God's Design. (Amsterdam Assembly Series, 5 vols.) London: SCM, 1948. Especially vol. 5, *The First Assembly of the World Council of Churches . . . Amsterdam, August 22 to September 4, 1948.* Ed. by W. A. Visser 't Hooft.

WILLINGEN 1952

Minutes of the Enlarged Meeting and the Committee of the International Missionary Council, Willingen, Germany, July 5–21, 1952. London: IMC, 1952.

LUND 1952

The Third World Conference on Faith and Order, Lund, August 15–28. Ed. by Oliver S. Tomkins. London: SCM, 1952.

TRAVANCORE 1952

Footprints in Travancore. Report of the Third World Conference of Christian Youth, Dec. 11–26, 1952. Coonoor, Nilgiris: India Sunday School Union, 1953.

EVANSTON 1954

The Evanston Report: The Second Assembly of the World Council of Churches, 1954. London: SCM, 1955.

ACCRA, GHANA 1958

The Ghana Assembly of the International Missionary Council, 28 Dec. 1957 to 8 Jan. 1958. London: Edinburgh House Press, 1958.

NEW DELHI 1961

The New Delhi Report: The Third Assembly of the World Council of Churches, 1961 London: SCM, 1962.

MEXICO CITY 1963

Witness in Six Continents: Records of the Meeting of the Commission on World Mission and Evangelism, Mexico City, Dec. 8–19, 1963. Ed. by Ronald Kenneth Orchard. Geneva: WCC, 1964.

MONTREAL 1963

The Fourth World Conference on Faith and Order, Montreal 1963. The Report. Ed. by P. C. Rodger and Lukas Vischer. New York: Association Press, 1964.

GENEVA 1966

Christians in the Technical and Social Revolutions of Our Time: World Conference on Church and Society, Geneva, July 12–26, 1966: The Official Report. Geneva: WCC, 1967.

SWANWICK 1966

Digest of the 1966 World Consultation on Inter-Church Aid at Swanwick, Great Britain. Geneva: WCC, 1966.

BRISTOL 1967

New Directions in Faith and Order, Bristol, 1967: Reports, Minutes, Documents. Geneva: WCC, 1968. (Faith and Order Paper, no. 50)

UPPSALA 1968

The Uppsala Report 1968: Official Report of the Fourth Assembly of the World Council of Churches, Uppsala, July 4–20, 1968. Ed. by Norman Goodall, Geneva: WCC, 1968.

MONTREUX 1970

Fetters of Injustice: Report of an Ecumenical Consultation on Ecumenical Assistance to Development Projects, Montreux, 26–31 Jan. 1970. Ed. by Pamela H. Gruber. Geneva: WCC, 1970.

LOUVAIN 1971

Faith and Order: Louvain 1971. Study Reports and Documents. Geneva: WCC, 1971. (Faith and Order Paper, no. 59)

BANGKOK 1973

Bangkok Assembly 1973: Minutes and Reports of the Assembly of the Commission on World Mission and Evangelism, 31 Dec. 1972 and 9–12 Jan. 1973. Geneva: WCC, 1973.

BUCHAREST 1974

Science and Technology for Human Development: The Ambiguous Future and the Christian Hope. Report of the 1974 World Conference in Bucharest, Romania. In: *Anticipation, no. 10.*

ACCRA 1974

Uniting in Hope: Reports and Documents from the Meeting of the Faith and Order Commission, 23 July–5 August 1974, University of Ghana. Geneva: WCC, 1975. (Faith and Order Paper, no. 72)

NAIROBI 1975

Breaking Barriers, Nairobi 1975. The Official Report of the Fifth Assembly of the World Council of Churches, Nairobi, 23 Nov.–10 Dec. 1975. Ed. by David M. Paton. London: S.P.C.K., 1976.

CHIANG MAI 1977

Faith in the Midst of Faiths: Reflections on Dialogue in Community. Ed. by S. J. Samartha. Geneva: WCC, 1977.

BANGALORE 1978

Sharing in One Hope. Reports and Documents from the Meeting of the Faith and Order Commission, 15–30 August 1978, Bangalore, India. Geneva: WCC, 1978. (Faith and Order Paper, no. 92)

MIT 1979

Faith and Science in an Unjust World. Report of the WCC Conference on Faith, Science and the Future, Cambridge, MA, 12–24 July, 1979. Vol. 1: Plenary Presentations. Ed. by Roger L. Shinn; Vol. 2: Reports and Recommendations. Ed. by Paul Abrecht. Geneva: WCC, 1980.

MELBOURNE 1980

Your Kingdom Come: Mission Perspectives. Report of the World Conference on Mission and Evangelism at Melbourne, Australia, 12–25 May, 1980. Geneva: WCC, 1980.

LIMA 1982

Towards Visible Unity: Commission on Faith and Order, Lima 1982. Vol. I: Minutes and addresses; Vol. II: Study Papers and Reports. Ed. by Michael Kinnamon. Geneva: WCC, 1982. (Faith and Order Paper, nos. 112 and 113)

VANCOUVER 1983

Gathered for Life. Official Report, Sixth Assembly of the World Council of Churches, Vancouver, Canada, 24 July–10 August, 1983. Ed. by David Gill. Geneva: WCC, 1983.

STAVANGER 1985

Faith and Renewal. Reports and Documents of the Commission on Faith and Order, Stavanger, Norway, 13–25 August 1985. Ed. by Thomas F. Best. Geneva: WCC, 1986. (Faith and Order Paper, no. 131)

LARNACA 1986

Called to be Neighbours—Diakonia 2000. Official Report, World
Consultation on Inter-Church Aid, Refugee and World Service,
Larnaca, 1986. Ed. by Klaus Poser. Geneva: WCC, 1987.

EL ESCORIAL 1987

Sharing Life. Official Report of the World Consultation on Koinonia:
Sharing Life in a World Community, El Escorial, Spain, Oct. 1987.
Ed. by Huibert van Beek. Geneva: WCC, 1989.

SAN ANTONIO 1988

The San Antonio Report: Your Will be Done: Mission in Christ's Way.
Ed. by Frederick R. Wilson. Geneva: WCC, 1990.

BUDAPEST 1989

*Faith and Order, 1985–1989: The Commission Meeting at Budapest
1989.* Ed. by Thomas F. Best. Geneva: WCC, 1990.

SEOUL 1990

*The Final Document on Justice, Peace and the Integrity of Crea-
tion, Seoul, Republic of Korea, 5–12 March, 1990.* Geneva: WCC,
1990.

CANBERRA 1991

Signs of the Spirit. Official Report Seventh Assembly, Canberra, Australia, 7–20 February 1991. Ed. by Michael Kinnamon. Geneva:
WCC, 1991.

General Surveys

Bilheimer, Robert S. *Breakthrough: The Emergence of the Ecumenical
Tradition.* Geneva: WCC, 1989.

Boyer, Charles. *Christian Unity and the Ecumenical Movement.* London: Burns and Oates, 1962.

Brown, William Adams. *Toward a United Church: Three Decades of Ecumenical Christianity*. New York: Scribner, 1946.

Church History in an Ecumenical Perspective: Papers and Reports of an International Consultation held in Basel, October 12–17, 1981. Ed. by Lukas Vischer. Bern: Evangelische Arbeitsstelle Ökumene Schweiz, 1982.

"Commemorating Amsterdam 1948: 40 Years of the World Council of Churches". *Ecumenical Review*, vol. 40, nos. 3–4, July–October, 1988.

Conord, P. *Brève histoire de l'oecuménisme*. Paris: Les bergers et les mages, 1958.

Documents on Christian Unity. Ed. by G.K.A. Bell. London: Oxford UP, 1924–1958. 4 vols.

The Ecumenical Advance: A History of the Ecumenical Movement, vol. 2, 1948–1968. Ed. by Harold E. Fey. Geneva: WCC, 1986. 2nd ed.

Ecumenical Documents 1930–1983, collected by Nils Ehrenström. A Bibliography. Uppsala: Nordiska Ekumeniska Institutet, 1987.

From Uniformity to Unity, 1662–1962. Geoffrey Nuttall and Owen Chadwick eds. London: S.P.C.K., 1962.

Gaines, David P. *The World Council of Churches: A Study of Its Background and History*. Peterborough, VT: Richard R. Smith, 1966.

Goodall, Norman. *The Ecumenical Movement: What It Is and What It Does*. London: Oxford UP, 1961.

———. *Ecumenical Progress: A Decade of Change in the Ecumenical Movement, 1961–1971*. London: Oxford UP, 1972.

A History of the Ecumenical Movement, 1517–1948. Ruth Rouse and Stephen Ch. Neill eds. Geneva: WCC, 1986, 3rd ed.

Latourette, Kenneth Scott. *Christianity in a Revolutionary Age: A History of Christianity in the Nineteenth and Twentieth Centuries*. Vols. III and V. New York: Harper, 1961–1962.

Macfarland, Charles S. *International Christian Movements.* New York: Fleming H. Revell, 1924.

————. *Steps Toward the World Council: Origins of the Ecumenical Movement as Expressed in the Universal Christian Council for Life and Work.* New York: Fleming H. Revell, 1938.

McNeill, John T. *Unitive Protestantism: The Ecumenical Movement and its Persistent Expression.* Richmond, VA: John Knox Press, 1964.

Neill, Stephen Ch. *The Church and Christian Reunion.* London: Oxford UP, 1968.

Nelson, John Robert. *Overcoming Christian Divisions.* Rev. ed. New York: Association Press, 1962.

O'Brien, John A. *Steps to Christian Unity.* Garden City, NY: Doubleday, 1964.

Scheele, Paul-Werner. *Alle eins: Theologische Beiträge II.* Paderborn: Verlag Bonifatius, 1979.

Schlink, Edmund. *The Coming Christ and the Coming Church.* Edinburgh: Oliver and Boyd, 1967.

Tavard, Georges. *Two Centuries of Ecumenism.* London: Burns and Oates, 1960.

Thils, Gustave. *Histoire doctrinale du mouvement oecuménique.* Louvain: E. Warny, 1962.

Towards Christian Unity: A Symposium. Ed. by Bernhard Leeming. London: G. Chapman, 1968.

Villain, Maurice. *Unity: A History and Some Reflections.* London: Harvill, 1963.

Wainwright, Geoffrey. *The Ecumenical Movement: Crisis and Opportunity for the Church.* Grand Rapids, MI: Wm. B. Eerdmans, 1983.

Whale, J. S. *Christian Reunion: Historic Divisions Reconsidered.* London: Lutterworth, 1971.

Interpretative Introductions

Against the World for the World: The Hartford Appeal and the Future of American Religion. Peter L. Berger and Richard J. Neuhaus eds. New York: Seabury Press, 1976.

Bent, Ans J. van der. *Major Studies and Themes in the Ecumenical Movement.* Geneva: WCC, 1980.

Boegner, Marc. *The Long Road to Unity.* London: Collins, 1970.

Bridston, Keith R. and Wagoner, Walter D. *Unity in Mid-Career: An Ecumenical Critique.* New York: Macmillan, 1963.

Brown, Robert McAfee. *Frontiers for the Church Today.* New York: Oxford UP, 1973.

Castro, Emilio. *A Passion for Unity.* Geneva: WCC, 1992.

Cavert, Samuel McCrea. *On the Road to Christian Unity: An Appraisal of the Ecumenical Movement.* New York: Harper, 1961.

Christianity and the Wider Ecumenism. Ed. by Peter C. Phan. New York: International Religious Foundation, 1990.

Duchrow, Ulrich. *Conflict over the Ecumenical Movement: Confessing Christ Today in the Universal Church.* Geneva: WCC, 1981.

Edwards, David L. *The Futures of Christianity.* London: Hodder and Stoughton, 1987.

The Future of Ecumenism. Ed. by Hans Küng. New York: Paulist Press, 1969. (Concilium, 44).

Henderson, Ian. *Power without Glory: A Study in Ecumenical Politics.* London: Hutchinson, 1967.

Horton, Walter M. *Christian Theology: An Ecumenical Approach.* Rev. ed. New York: Harper, 1958.

Jackson, Eleanor M. *Significant Developments in the History of "Organized Ecumenism" 1910–1968.* Birmingham: Un. of Birmingham Dept. of Theology, 1972.

Küng, Hans. *Theology for the Third Millennium: An Ecumenical View.* Garden City, NY: Doubleday, 1988.

Lambert Bernard. *Ecumenism: Theology and History.* London: Burns and Oates, 1966.

MacKay, John A. *Ecumenics: The Science of the Church Universal.* Englewood Cliffs, NJ: Prentice Hall, 1964.

Macquarrie, John. *Christian Unity and Christian Diversity.* London: SCM, 1975.

Mascall, Erich L. *The Recovery of Unity: A Theological Approach.* New York: Longmans, Green, 1958.

Newbigin, Lesslie. *The Other Side of 1984: Questions for the Churches.* Geneva: WCC, 1983.

Outler, Albert C. *The Christian Tradition and the Unity We Seek.* New York: Oxford UP, 1957.

Post-Ecumenical Christianity. Ed. by Hans Küng. New York: Herder and Herder, 1970. (Concilium, 54)

Potter, Philip A. *Life in All Its Fulness.* Geneva: WCC, 1981.

Raiser, Konrad. *Ecumenism in Transition.* Geneva: WCC, 1993. 2nd ed.

Roux, Hébert. *De la désunion vers la communion: Un itinéraire pastoral et oecuménique.* Paris: Le Centurion, 1978.

Sartory, Thomas: *Ecumenical Movement and the Unity of the Church.* Oxford: Blackwell, 1963.

Schüttke-Scherle, Peter. *From Contextual to Ecumenical Theology? A Dialogue between Minjung Theology and "Theology after Auschwitz".* Frankfurt am Main: Peter Lang, 1989.

Sheerin, John B. *A Practical Guide to Ecumenism.* New York: Paulist Press, 1967.

Smith, John Coventry. *From Colonialism to World Community: The Church's Pilgrimage.* Philadelphia: Westminster Press, 1982.

Tavard, George. *The Church Tomorrow*. London: Darton, Longman and Todd, 1965.

Thomas, M. M. *Risking Christ for Christ's Sake: Towards an Ecumenical Theology of Pluralism*. Geneva: WCC, 1987.

Till, Barry. *The Churches Search for Unity*. Harmondsworth: Penguin Books, 1972.

Torbet, R. G. *Ecumenism: Free Church Dilemma*. Valley Forge, PA: Judson Press, 1968.

Torrance, T. F. *Conflict and Agreement in the Church*. London: Lutterworth Press, 1959–1960. 2 vols.

Visser 't Hooft, Willem Adolf. *Has the Ecumenical Movement a Future?* Belfast: Christian Journals Ltd., 1974.

———. *The Meaning of Ecumenical*. London: SCM, 1953.

———. *Memoirs*. London: SCM, 1973.

———. *The Pressure of Our Common Calling*. Garden City, NY, Doubleday, 1959.

Voices of Unity. Essays in Honour of Willem Adolf Visser 't Hooft on the Occasion of His 80th Birthday. Ed. by Ans J. van der Bent. Geneva: WCC, 1981.

Wainwright, Geoffrey. *Doxology: The Praise of God in Worship, Doctrine and Life: A Systematic Theology*. London: Epworth, 1980.

Whale, John S. *Christian Reunion: Historic Divisions Reconsidered*. London: Lutterworth, 1971.

Zander, L.A. *The Essence of the Ecumenical Movement*. Geneva: WSCF, 1937.

World Council of Churches

And So Set Up Signs: The World Council of Churches First 40 Years. Geneva: WCC, 1988.

Bell, G.K.A. *The Kingship of Christ: The Story of the World Council of Churches.* Harmondsworth: Penguin Books, 1954.

Bent, Ans J. van der. *What in the World is the World Council of Churches?* With an Interview with Philip Potter. Geneva: WCC, 1978. 4th printing 1983.

"Commemorating Amsterdam 1948: 40 Years of the World Council of Churches", *Ecumenical Review,* vol 40, nos. 3–4 (July–October 1988).

The Ecumenical Future and the WCC: A Dialogue of Dreams and Visions. Geneva: WCC, 1991.

The Ecumenical Movement Tomorrow: Suggestions for Approaches and Alternatives. Marc Reuver, Friedhelm Solms, Serrit Huizer, eds. Kampen: Kok; Geneva: WCC, 1993.

Ecumenical Terminology. Geneva: WCC, 1983.

Faith and Faithfulness: Essays on Contemporary Themes: A Tribute to Philip Potter. Ed. by Pauline Webb. Geneva: WCC, 1984.

The First Six Years 1948–1954. Geneva: WCC, 1954.

Handbook of Member Churches. World Council of Churches. Ed. by Ans J. van der Bent. Geneva: WCC, 1982. rev. ed. 1985.

The Humanum Studies 1969–1975. A Collection of Documents, World Council of Churches, Portfolio for Humanum Studies. Geneva: WCC, 1975.

Reports of the central committee to the next assembly, all published by the WCC:

Evanston to New Delhi, 1961

New Delhi to Uppsala, 1968

Uppsala to Nairobi, 1975

Nairobi to Vancouver 1983

Vancouver to Canberra, 1990

Rules, By-Laws, Mandates and Programmes—World Council of Churches. Comp. by Ans J. van der Bent. Geneva: WCC, 1987.

The Ten Formative Years 1938–1948. Geneva: WCC, 1948.

Van Elderen, Marlin. *Introducing the World Council of Churches.* Geneva: WCC, 1990.

Visser 't Hooft, Willem Adolf. *The Genesis and Formation of the World Council of Churches.* Geneva: WCC, 1982.

Whither Ecumenism? A Dialogue in the Transit Lounge of the Ecumenical Movement. Ed. by Thomas Wieser. Geneva: WCC, 1986.

The World Council of Churches and the Churches. By Anna Marie Aagaard, Johannes M. Aagaard and others. Aarhus: IDOC, 1969.

The World Council of Churches: Its Process of Formation. Geneva: WCC, 1946.

Biographies and Festschriften

COLLECTIVE BIOGRAPHIES

Chirgwin, A. M. *These I Have Known.* London: London Missionary Society, 1964.

Foster, John. *Men of Vision.* London: SCM, 1967.

Great Christians. Ed. by R. S. Forman. London: Ivor Nicholsen and Watson, 1933.

Italiaander, Rolf. *Partisanen und Profeten: Christen für die eine Welt.* Erlangen: Evang. Luth. Mission, 1972.

Neill, Stephen Ch.: *Men of Unity.* London: SCM, 1960.

Ökumenische Gestalten: Brückenbauer der einen Kirche. Ed. by Günter Gloede. Berlin: Evang. Verlagsanstalt, 1974.

Ökumenische Profile: Brückenbauer der einen Kirche. Ed. by Günter Gloede. Stuttgart: Evang. Missionsverlag, 1961–1963. 2 vols.

Ökumenische Profile: Gestalten der einen Kirche in aller Welt. Berlin-Hermsdorf: Heimatdienst Verlag, 1954–1960. 6 vols.

Pioniere und Plätze der ökumenischen Bewegung. Pioneers and Places of the Ecumenical Movement. Ed. by Günter Gloede. Hamburg: Herbert Reich, 1974.

Simpfendörfer, Werner: *Ökumenische Spurensuche: Poträts.* Stuttgart: Quell Verlag, 1989.

Wegbereiter der Oekumene. Stuttgart: Verlag "Junge Gemeinde", 1954.

INDIVIDUAL BIOGRAPHIES

Peter Ainslie, 1867–1934

Idleman, Finis S, *Peter Ainslie: Ambassador of Good Will.* Chicago: Willet, Clark, 1941.

Athenagoras I, 1886–1972

Clement, Oliver: *Dialogues avec le Patriarche Athenagoras.* Paris: Fayard, 1969.

Georghiu, Virgil: *La vie du Patriarche Athenagoras.* Paris: Plon, 1969.

Ohse, Bernhard. *Der Patriarche Athenagoras I von Konstantinopel: Ein ökumenischer Visionär.* Göttingen: Vandenhoeck und Ruprecht, 1968.

Vedanayagam Samuel Azariah, 1874–1945

Graham, Carol. *Azariah of Dornakal.* London: SCM, 1946.

Hodge, J. Z. *Bishop Azariah of Dornakal.* Madras: Christian Literature Society, 1946.

Karl Barth, 1886–1968

Keller, Adolf. *Karl Barth and Christian Unity: The Influence of the Barthian Movement Upon the Churches of the World.* London: Lutterworth, 1932.

Willems, B. A. *Karl Barth: An Ecumenical Approach to His Theology.* Glen Rock, NJ: Paulist Press, 1965.

Augustin Bea, 1881–1968

Augustin, Kardinal Bea. *Wegbereiter der Einheit. Gestalt, Weg und Wirken in Wort, Bild, Dokument.* Augsburg: Verlag Winfried-Werk, 1972.

Schmidt, Stepan. *Augustin Cardinal Bea: Spiritual Profile: Notes from the Cardinal's Diary with a Commentary.* London: Geoffrey Chapman, 1971.

George Allen Kennedy Bell, 1883–1958

Jasper, Ronald C. D. *George Bell, Bishop of Chichester.* London: Oxford UP, 1967.

Slack, Kenneth. *George Bell.* London: SCM, 1971.

John Coleman Bennett, 1902–

Theology and Church in Times of Change: Essays in Honor of John Coleman Bennett. Edward L. Long and Robert T. Handy eds. Philadelphia: Westminster, 1970.

Eivind Berggrav, 1884–1959

Johnson, Alex. *Eivind Berggrav: Mann der spannung.* Göttingen: Vandenhoeck und Reprecht, 1960.

Eugene Carson Blake, 1906–1985

Brackenridge R. Douglas. *Eugene Carson Blake: Prophet with Portfolio.* New York: Seabury, 1978.

Maertens, Malene. *Eugene Carson Blake: Der zweite Generalsekretär des Ökumenischen Rates.* Berlin: Lettner Verlag, 1966.

Marc Boegner, 1881–1970

Boegner, Marc. *The Long Road to Unity: Memories and Anticipations.* London: Collins, 1970.

Dietrich Bonhoeffer, 1906–1945

Bethge, Eberhard. *Dietrich Bonhoeffer.* Munich: Chr. Kaiser Verlag, 1967.

Bonhoeffer, Dietrich. *Ökumene—Briefe—Aufsätze—Dokumente 1928 bis 1942.* Munich: Chr. Kaiser Verlag, 1958.

Charles Henry Brent, 1862–1929

Things That Matter: The Best of the Writings of Bishop Brent. Ed. with a biographical sketch by Frederick Ward Kates. New York: Harper, 1949.

Zabriskie, Alexander C. *Bishop Brent: Crusader for Christian Unity.* Philadelphia: Westminster, 1948.

Samuel McCrea Cavert, 1888–1976

Schmidt, William J. *Architect of Unity: A Biography of Samuel McCrea Cavert.* New York: Friendship Press, 1978.

Sarah Chakko, 1905–1954

Slater, Mary Louise. *Future-Maker in India: The Story of Sarah Chakko.* New York: Friendship Press, 1968.

Thomä, H. *Sarah Chakko—eine grosse Inderin.* Stuttgart: Evang. Missionsverlag, 1955.

Yves Congar, 1904–

Jean Puyo interroge le Père Congar: une vie pour la vérité. Paris: Le Centurion, 1975.

Jossua, J. P. *Le père Congar.* Paris: Cerf, 1967.

Paul Couturier, 1881–1953

A la mémoire de l'Abbé Paul Couturier. (Several contributions.) Lyons E. Vitte, 1954.

Allchin, M. *The Abbé Paul Couturier, Apostle of Christian Unity.* Westminster: Faith Press, 1960.

Curtis, Geoffrey. *Paul Couturier and Unity in Christ.* London: SCM, 1964.

Villain, Maurice. *L'Abbé Paul Couturier: Apôtre de l'unité chrétienne: Souvénirs et documents.* Tournai: Casterman, 1957.

Otto Dibelius, 1880–1967

Dibelius, Otto. *In the Service of the Lord:* The Autobiography of Bishop Otto Dibelius; translated from the German by Mary Ilford. London: Faber and Faber, 1964.

Otto Dibelius: Sein Denken und Sein Wollen. Ed. by R. Stupperich. Berlin: Christliche Zeitschriften, 1970.

Suzanne de Diétrich, 1891–1981

"Reconnaisance à Suzanne de Diétrich", special issue of *Foi et Vie*, May 1971.

Geoffrey Francis Fisher, 1887–1972

Purcell, William. *Fisher of Lambeth: A Portrait from Life*. London: Hodder and Stoughton, 1969.

Franklin Clark Fry, 1900–1968

"Franklin Clark Fry: A Palette for a Portrait". Ed. by Robert H. Fischer. Suppl. no. of the *Lutheran Quarterly*, vol. 24, 1972.

Norman Goodall, 1896–1985

Goodall, Norman. *Second Fiddle*. London: S.P.C.K., 1979.

Kenneth Grubb, 1900–1980

Grubb, Kenneth. *Crypts of Power: An Autobiography*. London: Hodder and Stoughton, 1971.

Joseph Lukl Hromádka, 1889–1969.

Hromádka, Josef L. *Thoughts of a Czech Pastor*. London: SCM, 1970.

Neumärker, Dorothea. *Josef L. Hromádka: Theologie und Politik im Kontext des Zeitgeschehens*. Munich: Chr. Kaiser Verlag, 1974.

John XXIII, 1881–1963

Bianchi, Eugene C. *John XXIII and American Protestants*. Washington: Corpus Books, 1968.

Hebblewaite, P. *John XXIII: Pope of the Council*. London: Chapman, 1984.

Martin Luther King, 1929–1968

Branch, Taylor. *Parting the Waters*. New York: Simon and Schuster, 1988.

Garrow, D. *Bearing the Cross*. New York: Morrow, 1986.

Alphonse Koechlin, 1885–1965

Espine, Henri d' *Alphonse Koechlin: pasteur et chef de l'Eglise*. Geneva: Labor et Fides, 1971.

Hendrik Kraemer, 1888–1965

Leeuwen, A. Th. van. *Hendrik Kraemer: Pionier der Oekumene*. Basel: Basileia Verlag, 1962.

Frank Charles Laubach, 1884–1970

Mason, D. E. *Frank C. Laubach: Teacher of Millions*. Minneapolis: Denison, 1967.

Hans Lilje, 1899–1977

Lilje, Hans. *Memorabilia: Schwerpunkte eines Lebens*. Stein: Laetare, 1973.

Charles Stedman Macfarland, 1866–1956

Macfarland, Charles S. *Across the Years.* New York: Macmillan, 1936.

John Alexander Mackay, 1889–1983

The Ecumenical Era in Church and Society: A Symposium in Honor of John A. Mackay. Ed. by Edward J. Jurji. New York: Macmillan, 1959.

Rajah Bushanam Manikam, 1894–1969

Diehl, Carl Gustav. *Rajah Bushanam Manikam: A Biography.* Madras: Christian Literature Society, 1975.

John Raleigh Mott, 1865–1955

Fisher, Galon M. *John R. Mott: Architect of Co-operation and Unity.* New York: Association Press, 1952.

Hopkins, C. Howard. *John R. Mott, 1865–1955: A Biography.* Geneva: WCC, 1979.

Mathews, Basil. *John R. Mott: World Citizen.* New York: Harper, 1934.

James Edward Lesslie Newbigin, 1909–

Newbigin, Lesslie. *Unfinished Agenda: An Autobiography.* Geneva: WCC, 1985.

Reinhold Niebuhr, 1892–1971

Durkin, K. *Reinhold Niebuhr.* London: Chapman, 1989.

Martin Niemöller, 1892–1984

Davidson, Clarissa Start. *God's Man: The Story of Pastor Niemöller.* New York: Ives Washburn, 1959.

Schmidt, Dietmar. *Pastor Niemöller.* London: Odhams Press, 1959.

Daniel Thambyrajah Niles, 1908–1970

A Testament of Faith, compiled by Dayalan Niles. London: Epworth, 1972.

William Paton, 1886–1943

Jackson, E. M. *Red Tape and the Gospel: A Study of the Significance of the Ecumenical Missionary Struggle of William Paton.* Birmingham: Phogiston Publ. Co., 1980.

Sinclair, Margaret. *William Paton.* London: SCM, 1949.

Ernest Alexander Payne, 1902–1980

West, W.M.S. *To Be a Pilgrim: A Memoir of Ernest A. Payne.* London: Lutterworth, 1983.

Philip A. Potter, 1921–

Gentz, William H. *The World of Philip Potter.* New York: Friendship Press, 1974.

Müller-Römheld, Walter. *Philip Potter: Ein ökumenisches Lebensbild.* Stuttgart: Evang. Missionsverlag, 1972.

Arthur Michael Ramsey, 1904–1988

Chadwick, O. *Michael Ramsey: A Life.* Oxford: Clarendon, 1990.

Simpson, James B. *The Hundredth Archbishop of Canterbury*. New York: Harper, 1962.

Oscar Arnulfo Romero y Galdames, 1917–1980

Brockman, J. R. *The World Remains: A Life of Oscar Romero*. Maryknoll, NY: Orbis Books, 1983.

Nathan Söderblom, 1866–1931

Curtis, Charles J. *Söderblom: Ecumenical Pioneer*. Minneapolis: Augsburg Publishing House, 1967.

Sundkler, Bengt. *Nathan Söderblom: His Life and Work*. London: Lutterworth, 1968.

William Temple, 1881–1944

Fletcher, Joseph. *William Temple: Twentieth-Century Christian*. New York: Seabury, 1963.

Irenmonger, F. A. *Willlam Temple: Archbishop of Canterbury: His Life and Letters*. London: Oxford UP, 1948.

Willem Adolf Visser 't Hooft, 1900–1985

"Für Willem A. Visser 't Hooft zum 80/Geburtstag". *Reformatio*, Band 29, no. 9, September 1980.

No Man is Alien: Essays on the Unity of Mankind in Honour of Willem Adolf Visser 't Hooft. Ed. by J. Robert Nelson, Leiden. Brill, 1981.

Oecumene in 't vizier aangeboden aan W.A. Visser 't Hooft. W. F. Golterman and J. C. Hoekendijk eds. Amsterdam: W. Ten Have, 1960.

The Sufficiency of God: Essays on the Ecumenical Hope in Honour of W.A. Visser 't Hooft. Robert C. Mackie and Charles C. West eds. London: SCM, 1963.

Visser 't Hooft, Willem Adolf. *Memoirs.* London: SCM, 1973.

Voices of Unity: Essays in Honour of W.A. Visser 't Hooft. Ed. by Ans J. van der Bent. Geneva: WCC, 1981.

Paul James Francis Wattson, 1863–1940

Angell, Charles and LaFontaine, Charles. *Prophet of Reunion: The Life of Paul of Graymoore.* New York: Srabury, 1975.

Regional, National and Local Councils of Churches and Ecumenism

All Africa Conference of Churches. *Directory of AACC Member Churches.* Kenya: AACC, 1981.

All Africa Council of Churches. *Assemblies, 1963–.* Nairobi: AACC.

Benignus, Emma. *All in Each Place: A Guide to Local Ecumenism.* Cincinnati: A Forward Movement Publication, 1966.

Caribbean Conference of Churches. *Assemblies, 1973–.* Kingston: CCC.

Cavert, Samuel McCrea. *The American Churches in the Ecumenical Movement, 1900–1968.* New York: Association Press, 1968.

———. *Church Cooperation and Unity in America: A Historical Review, 1900–1970.* New York: Association Press, 1970.

"Christian Councils: Some Appraisals", *One in Christ,* vol. VIII, no. 2, 1972.

Christianity in Asia. Ed. by T. K. Thomas. Singapore: Christian Conference of Asia, 1979.

Conciliar Fellowship. A Study of the Commission on Faith and Order of the National Council of the Churches of Christ in the USA. Indianapolis: COCU, 1982.

Conference of European Churches. *Assemblies, 1957–.* (The first eight assemblies took place in Nyborg, Denmark.) Geneva: CEC.

Conference of European Churches. *Why is it? What is it? Who is it?* Geneva: CEC, 1971.

Davies, Rupert E. *In All Places and All Ages.* London: British Council of Churches, 1964.

Directory of Christian Councils. Geneva: WCC, 1st ed. 1971; 2nd ed. 1975; 3rd ed. 1980; 4th ed. 1985.

Directory of Ecumenical Conference Centres. Geneva: WCC, 1990.

The Ecclesiological Significance of Councils of Churches. New York: National Council of the Churches of Christ in the USA, 1963.

Garrett, John. *To Live Among the Stars: Christian Origins in Oceania.* Geneva: WCC; Suva: Institute of Pacific Studies, 1982.

Goodall, Norman. *The Local Church: Its Resources and Responsibilities.* London: Hodder and Stoughton, 1966.

Grassroots Ecumenicity: Case Studies in Local Church Consolidation. Ed. by Horace S. Sills. Philadelphia: United Church Press, 1967.

Handbook of Churches in the Caribbean. Ed. by Lisa Bessil-Watson. Bridgetown: CEDAR Press, 1982.

Horgan, Thaddeus and Gouthro, Arthur, *Parish Ecumenism.* Garrison: Graymoor Ecumenical Institute, 1977.

Horner, Norman A. *Rediscovering Christianity Where It Began: A Survey of Contemporary Churches in the Middle East and Ethiopia.* Lebanon: Heidelberg Press, 1974.

Hoyer, H. Conrad. *Ecumenopolis USA: The Church in Mission in Community.* Minneapolis: Augsburg Publishing House, 1971.

International Ecumenical Congress of Theology. *The Challenge of Basic Christian Communities.* Papers from the International Ecumenical Congress of Theology 20 Feb.–2 March 1980, Sao Paulo. Sergio Torres and John Eagleson eds. Maryknoll, NY: Orbis Books, 1981.

Macfarland, Charles S. *Christian Unity in the Making: The First Twenty-Five Years of the Federal Council of the Churches of Christ in America.* New York: FCCCA, 1948.

Middle East Council of Churches. *Assemblies,* 1974–. Nicosia, Cyprus: MECC

Modras, Ronald E. *Paths to Unity: American Religion Today and Tomorrow.* New York: Sheed and Ward, 1968.

M'Passou, Denis. *Mindolo, a Story of the Ecumenical Movement in Africa.* Kabulong, Lusaka: Multimedia Publications, 1983.

National Council of the Churches of Christ in the USA. *Biennial and Triennial Reports, Annual Division Reports.* New York: NCCC, 1952–

———. *A Guide to the NCCC Archives 1950–1972.* Donald L. Haggerty and Alan Thomson eds. Philadelphia: Presbyterian Historical Society, 1984. 2 vols.

Pacific Conference of Churches. *Assemblies,* 1966–. Suva: PCC.

———. *The Fourth World Meets.* Suva: PCC, 1972. *Salvation–Development—Liberation.* Nairobi: AACC, 1972.

Secretariat for Promoting Christian Unity. *Ecumenical Collaboration at the Regional, National and Local Levels.* London: Catholic Truth Society, 1975.

Short, Frank. "National Councils of Churches", *The Ecumenical Advance: A History of the Ecumenical Movement, vol. 2, 1948–1968.* Philadephia: Westminster, 1970. pp. 93–114.

La situation oecuménique dans le monde. Etudes du Centre international d'Information et de Documentation sur l'Eglise conciliare. Paris: Ed. du Centurion, 1967.

There is No End. Checklist of EACC-CCA Publications and Other Related Asian Ecumenical Documents 1948–1981. Comp. by Dorothy M. Harvey. Singapore: Christian Conference of Asia, 1982.

Vanderwerf, Nathan H. *The Times Were Very Full: A Perspective on the First 25 Years of the National Council of the Churches of Christ in the USA, 1950–1975.* New York: NCCC, 1975.

Weber, Hans-Ruedi. *Asia and the Ecumenical Movement 1895–1961.* London: SCM, 1966.

———. "Out of All Continents and Nations: A Review of Regional Developments in the Ecumenical Movement". *The Ecumenical Advance: A History of the Ecumenical Movement, vol. 2, 1948–1968.* Philadelphia: Westminster, 1970. pp. 63–92.

Whalen, William J. *Separated Brethren:* A Survey of Protestant, Anglican, Eastern Orthodox and Other Denominations in the USA. Huntington: Our Sunday Visitor, 1979.

Will, James E. *Must Walls Divide? The Creative Witness of Churches in Europe.* New York: Friendship Press, 1981.

Williams, Colin W. *For the World: A Study Book for Local Churches.* New York: NCCC, 1965.

Faith and Order

Apostolic Faith Today: A Handbook for Study. Ed. by Hans-Georg Link. Geneva: WCC, 1985. (Faith and Order Paper, no. 124)

Baptism and Eucharist: Ecumenical Convergence in Celebration. Max Thurian and Geoffrey Wainwright eds. Geneva: WCC, 1984. (Faith and Order Paper, no. 117)

Baptism, Eucharist and Ministry. Geneva: WCC, 1982. (Faith and Order Paper, no. 111)

Baptism, Eucharist and Ministry 1982–1990. Report on the Process and Responses. Geneva: WCC, 1990. (Faith and Order Paper, no. 149)

Beyond Unity-in-Tension: Unity, Renewal and the Community of Women and Men. Ed. by Thomas F. Best. Geneva: WCC, 1988. (Faith and Order Paper, no. 138)

The Bible: Its Authority and Interpretation in the Ecumenical Movement. Ed. by Ellen Flesseman-van-Leer. Geneva: WCC, 1980. (Faith and Order Paper, no. 99)

Called to be One in Christ: United Chuches and the Ecumenical Movement. Michael Kinnamon and Thomas F. Best eds. Geneva: WCC, 1985. (Faith and Order Paper, no. 127)

Cantate Domino: An Ecumenical Hymn Book. New ed. Published on Behalf of the World Council of Churches. Basel: Bärenreiter, 1974.

The Challenge to Reunion: The Eugene C. Blake Proposal under Scrutiny. Robert McAfee Brown and David H. Scott eds. New York: McGraw-Hill, 1963.

Church and State: Opening a New Ecumenical Discussion. A Colloquium held at Bossey, 19–25 August, 1976. Geneva: WCC, 1976. (Faith and Order Paper, no. 85)

Church and World: The Unity of the Church and the Renewal of Human Community. Ed. by Thomas F. Best. Geneva: WCC, 1990 (Faith and Order Paper, no. 151)

The Church is Charismatic. Ed. by Arnold Bittlinger. Geneva: WCC, 1981.

Church, Kingdom, World: The Church as Mystery and Prophetic Sign. Ed. by Gennadios Limouris. Geneva: WCC, 1986.

The Church, the Churches and the World Council of Churches: The Ecclesiological Significance of the World Council of Churches. New York: WCC, 1950.

Churches Responding to BEM: Official Responses to the "Baptism, Eucharist and Ministry" Text. Ed. by Max Thurian. Geneva: WCC, 1986–1988. 6 vols.

The Common Catechism: A Christian Book of Faith. Johannes Feiner and Lukas Vischer eds. London: Search Press, 1975.

Concerning the Ordination of Women. Geneva: WCC, 1964. (World Council Studies, 1)

Confessing Our Faith Around the World. Geneva: WCC, 1980–1985. 4 vols. (Faith and Order Papers, nos. 104, 120, 123, 126)

Confessing the One Faith: An Ecumenical Explication of the Apostolic Faith as it is Confessed in the Nicene-Constantinopolitan Creed. Geneva: WCC, 1991.

Conflicting Ways in Interpreting the Bible. Hans Küng and Jürgen Moltmann eds. New York: Seabury, 1979. (Concilium, vol. 138)

Davies, Horton. *Bread of Life and Cup of Joy: Newer Ecumenical Perspectives on the Eucharist.* Grand Rapids, MI: Wm. B. Eerdmans, 1993.

De Groot, Alfred T. *Checklist, Faith and Order Commission: Official Numbered Publications.* Series 1, 1910–1948; Series 2, 1948–1962. Fort Worth, TX: 1958; Geneva: WCC, 1963.

A Documentary History of the Faith and Order Movement, 1927–1963. Ed. by Lukas Vischer. St. Louis: Bethany Press, 1963.

Does Chalcedon Divide or Unite? Towards Convergence in Orthodox Christology. Paulos Gregorios, William H. Lazareth and Nikos A. Nissiotis eds. Geneva: WCC, 1981.

An Ecumenical Confession of Faith. Hans Küng and Jürgen Moltmann eds. New York: Seabury Press, 1979. (Concilium, vol. 118)

Episkopé and Episcopate in Ecumenical Perspective. Geneva: WCC, 1980.

The Eucharist in Ecumenical Dialogue. Ed. by Leonard J. Swidler. New York: Paulist Press, 1976.

Eucharist, International Bibliography 1975–1984. Strasbourg: CERDIC Publications, 1985.

Faith and Order 1985–1989. The Commission Meeting at Budapest 1989 Ed. by Thomas F. Best. Geneva: WCC, 1990. (Faith and Order Paper, no. 148)

Faith and Renewal: Commission on Faith and Order Stavanger 1985. Ed. by Thomas F. Best. Geneva: WCC, 1986. (Faith and Order Paper, no. 131)

Fuerth, Patrick W. *The Concept of Catholicity in the Documents of the World Council of Churches 1948–1968.* Rome: Editrice Anselmiana, 1973.

Gassmann, Günther. *Documentary History of Faith and Order, 1963–1993.* Geneva: WCC, 1993.

Giving Account of the Hope That is in Us. Geneva: WCC, 1975.

Giving Account of the Hope Today. Geneva: WCC, 1976. (Faith and Order Paper, no. 81)

Giving Account of the Hope Together. Geneva: WCC, 1978.

Growing Together Into Unity: Texts of the Faith and Order Commission on Conciliar Fellowship. Ed. by Choan-Seng Song. Madras: Christian Literature Society, 1978.

Growth in Agreement: Reports and Agreed Statements of Ecumenical Conversations on a World Level. Harding Meyer and Lukas Vischer eds. Geneva: WCC, 1984.

Houtepen, Anton. *Bibliography on Baptism, Eucharist and Ministry: Lima Text, 1982–1987.* Utrecht: Interuniversity Institute on Missiology and Ecumenics, 1988.

How Does the Church Teach Authoritatively Today? Report of the Odessa Consultation. Geneva: WCC, 1979.

Icons: Windows on Eternity. Ed. by Gennadios Limouris. Geneva: WCC, 1990. (Faith and Order Paper, no. 147)

Institutionalism and Church Unity. N. Ehrenström and W. S. Muelder eds. London: SCM, 1963.

Intercommunion Today, Being the Report of the Archbishop's Commission on Intercommunion. London: Church Information Office, 1968.

International Bilateral Dialogues 1965–1991: List of Commissions, Meetings, Themes and Reports. Compiled by Günther Gassmann. Geneva: WCC, 1991.

Jones, Hywel R. *Gospel and Church: An Evangelical Evaluation of Ecumenical Documents on Church Unity.* Bryntirion: Evangelical Press of Wales, 1989.

Kinnamon, Michael. *Truth and Community: Diversity and Its Limits in the Ecumenical Movement.* Geneva: WCC, 1988.

Lange, Ernst. *And Yet It Moves: Dream and Reality of the Ecumenical Movement.* Geneva: WCC, 1979.

Lausanne '77. Fifty Years of Faith and Order. Geneva: WCC, 1977.

Lazareth, William H. *Growing Together in Baptism, Eucharist and Ministry: A Study Guide.* Geneva: WCC, 1985. 7th printing. (Faith and Order Paper, no. 114)

Lewis, Christopher A. *A Sociological Approach to "Faith and Order": Methods of Reaching Unity.* n.p., 1973.

Living Today Towards Visible Unity. Report of the Fifth International Consultation of United and Uniting Chuches. Ed. by Thomas F. Best. Geneva: WCC, 1988. (Faith and Order Paper, no. 142)

Lochman, Jan Milic. *The Faith We Confess: An Ecumenical Dogmatics.* Philadelphia: Fortress Press, 1984.

Minear, Paul. *Images of the Church in the New Testament.* London: Lutterworth, 1961.

The Ministry of Deacons. Geneva: WCC, 1965. (World Council Studies, 2)

Mudge, Lewis S. *The Sense of a People: Toward a Church for the Human Future.* Philadelphia: Trinity Press International, 1992.

The Nature of the Unity We Seek. Official Report of the North American Conference on Faith and Order, Sept. 3–10, 1957, Oberlin, Ohio. Ed. by Paul S. Minear. St. Louis: Bethany Press, 1958.

One God, One Lord, One Spirit: On the Explication of the Apostolic Faith Today. Ed. by Hans-Georg Link. Geneva: WCC, 1988. (Faith and Order Paper, no. 139)

Orthodox Perspectives on "Baptism, Eucharist and Ministry". Gennadios Limouris and Nomikos M. Vaporis eds. Brookline, MA: Holy Cross Orthodox Press, 1985. (Faith and Order Paper, no. 128)

Outler, Albert Cook. *That the World May Believe: A Study of Christian Unity*. New York: Board of Missions of the Methodist Church, 1966.

Pigault, Gérard. *Eucharist and Eucharistic Hospitality*. International Bibliography 1971–1973 Indexed by Computer. Strasbourg: CERDIC, 1974.

Reumann, John H. P. *The Supper of the Lord: The New Testament, Ecumenical Dialogues, and Faith and Order on the Eucharist*. Philadelphia: Fortress Press, 1985.

The Roots of Our Common Faith. Faith in the Scriptures and in the Early Church. Ed. by Hans-Georg Link. Geneva: WCC, 1984. (Faith and Order Paper, no. 119)

The Sacraments, an Ecumenical Dilemma. New York: Paulist Press, 1966. (Concilium, 24)

Simonson, Conrad. *The Christology of the Faith and Order Movement*. Leiden: Brill, 1972.

Skoglund, J. E. and Nelson, J. R. *Fifty Years of Faith and Order: An Interpretation of the Faith and Order Movement*. St. Louis: Bethany Press, 1964.

Sobrepena, Enrique C. *That They May Be One*. Manila: United Church of Christ in the Philippines, 1964.

Spirit of God, Spirit of Christ: Ecumenical Reflections on the Filioque Controversy. Ed. by Lukas Vischer. Geneva: WCC, 1981. (Faith and Order Paper, no. 103)

Steady, Leo J. *Intercommunion in the Faith and Order Movement 1927–1952*. Ottawa: University of Ottawa, 1964.

Survey of Church Union Negotiations, 1957–. (Appears every two years in the *Ecumenical Review*)

The Three Reports of the Forum on Bilateral Dialogues. Geneva: WCC, 1981. (Faith and Order Paper, no. 107)

Thurian, Max. *The Mystery of the Eucharist: An Ecumenical Approach.* London: A. R. Mowbray, 1983.

————. *Visible Unity and Tradition.* Baltimore: Helicon Press, 1965.

Towards an Ecumenical Consensus on Baptism, the Eucharist and the Ministry. Geneva: WCC, 1977. (Faith and Order Paper, no. 84)

Towards Visible Unity. Commission on Faith and Order, Lima 1982. Vol. II Study Papers and Reports. Ed. by Michael Kinnamon. Geneva: WCC, 1982.

Unity Begins at Home: A Report from the First British Conference on Faith and Order, Nottingham, 1964. London: SCM, 1964.

Unity in Each Place-In All Places: United Churches and the Christian World Communions. Ed. by Michael Kinnamon. Geneva: WCC, 1983. (Faith and Order Paper, no. 118)

Unity in Today's World. The Faith and Order Studies on: "Unity of the Church-Unity of Humankind". Ed. by Geiko Müller-Fahrenholz. Geneva: WCC, 1978. (Faith and Order Paper, no. 88)

The Unity of the Church and the Renewal of Human Community. Geneva: WCC, 1981.

Watley, William D. *The African American Church and Ecumenism.* Geneva: WCC, 1993.

What Kind of Unity? Geneva: WCC, 1974. (Faith and Order Paper, no. 69)

What Unity Requires. Papers and Report on the Unity of the Church. Geneva: WCC, 1976. (Faith and Order Papers, no. 77)

With All God's People: The New Ecumenical Prayer Cycle. Geneva: WCC, 1989. 2 vols.

Christian World Communions

Creeds of the Churches. Ed. by J. H. Leith. New York: Doubleday, 1963.

Ehrenström, Nils and Gassmann, Günther. *Confessions in Dialogue: A Survey of Bilateral Conversations Among World Confessional Families 1959–1974.* Geneva: WCC, 1975. 3rd rev. and enlarged ed.

Empie, Paul C. "Dilemmas of the World Confessional Groups with Respect to Engagement in Mission and Unity". *International Review of Missions,* vol. LV, no. 218, 1966. pp. 157–170.

Fey, Harold E. "Confessional Families and the Ecumenical Movement". *The Ecumenical Advance: A History of the Ecumenical Movement, vol. 2, 1948–1968.* Philadelphia: Westminster Press, 1970. pp. 115–142.

Fifth Forum on Bilateral Conversations: International Bilateral Dialogues. Ed. by Günther Gassmann. Geneva: WCC, 1992.

Growing Towards Consensus and Commitment. Report of the Fourth Consultation of United and Uniting Churches, Colombo, Sri Lanka. Geneva: WCC, 1981. (Faith and Order Paper, no. 110)

Ishida, Yoshiro, Meyer, Harding and Perret, Edmond. *The History and Theological Concerns of World Confessional Families.* LWF Report, August 1979.

Minutes of the Meetings of Representatives of World Confessional Groups, held in Geneva, 1957–. (In Archives of the WCC Library)

Mudge, Lewis S. "World Confessionalism and Ecumenical Strategy" *Ecumenical Review,* vol. XI, no. 4, July 1959. pp. 379–393.

Puglisi, James F. and Voicu, S. J. *A Bibliography of Inter-Church and Interconfessional Theological Dialogues.* Rome: Centro Pro Unione, 1984.

Schmidt-Clausen, Kurt. "The World Confessional Families and the Ecumenical Movement". *Lutheran World,* vol. X, no. 1, 1963. pp. 35–44.

World Christian Handbook. H. W. Coxill and K. Grubb eds. London: Lutterworth, 1968. 5th ed.

Mission and Evangelism

Bühlmann, Walbert. *The Coming of the Third Church: An Analysis of the Present and Future of the Church.* Slough: St. Paul Publications, 1976.

Castro, Emilio. *Freedom in Mission: The Perspective of the Kingdom of God.* An Ecumenical Inquiry, Geneva: WCC, 1985.

Confessing Christ in Different Cultures. Report of Colloquium held at the Ecumenical Institute Bossey, 16–22 June 1978. Ed. by John S. M'Biti. Bossey: Ecumenical Institute, 1977.

Davis, J. Merle. *New Buildings on Old Foundations: A Handbook on Stabilizing the Younger Churches in Their Environment.* London: International Missionary Council, 1945.

Directory of Study Centres. Geneva: WCC, 1982.

"Edinburgh to Melbourne". *International Review of Mission,* vol. 67, no. 27, 1978. pp. 249–396.

Evangelization and Mission: International Bibliography 1975–1982. Strasbourg: CERDIC Publications, 1982.

Fung, Raymond. *Evangelistically Yours: Ecumenical Letters on Contemporary Evangelism.* Geneva: WCC, 1992.

Go Forth in Peace: Orthodox Perspectives on Mission. Ed. by Ion Bria. Geneva: WCC, 1986.

Hoekendijk, Johannes C. *The Church Inside Out.* London: SCM, 1967.

Hogg, William Richey. *Ecumenical Foundations: A History of the International Missionary Council and Its Nineteenth Century Background.* New York: Harper, 1952.

Kraemer, Hendrik. *The Christian Message in a Non-Christian World.* Grand Rapids: Kregel Publications, 1956. 3rd ed.

McGavran, Donald. *The Conciliar-Evangelical Debate: The Crucial Documents 1964–1976.* South Pasadena, CA: William Carey, 1977.

Margull, Hans-Jochen. *Hope in Action: The Church's Task in the World.* Philadelphia: Muhlenberg Press, 1962.

Martyria-Mission: The Witness of the Orthodox Churches Today. Ed. by Ion Bria. Geneva: WCC, 1980.

Mission and Evangelism: An Ecumenical Affirmation. A Study Guide compiled by Jean Stromberg. Geneva: WCC, 1983.

Mission and Justice: Urban Industrial Mission at Work. George Todd and Bobbi W. Hargleroad eds. Geneva: WCC, 1977.

Mott, John R. *Addresses and Papers.* New York: Association Press, 1946–1947. 6 vols.

Neill, Stephen Charles. *Christian Missions.* Harmondsworth: Penguin Books, 1964.

New Directions in Mission and Evangelization: Basic Statements 1974–1991. Ed. by James A. Scherer. Maryknoll, NY: Orbis Books, 1992.

Newbigin, James Edward Lesslie. *The Gospel in a Pluralist Society.* Geneva: WCC, 1989.

Niles, Daniel Thambirajah. *Upon the Earth: The Mission of God and the Missionary Enterprise of the Churches.* London: Lutterworth, 1962.

Orchard, Ronald Kenneth. *Missions in a Time of Testing.* London: Lutterworth, 1964.

Orthodox Consultation on Confessing Christ Through Liturgical Life of the Church Today. Report of the Orthodox Consultation at Etchmiadzine, Armenia, 16–21 Sept. 1975. Geneva: WCC, 1975.

Protestant Crosscurrents in Mission: The Ecumenical-Conservative Encounter. Ed. by Norman A. Horner. Nashville: Abingdon, 1968.

Ranson, Charles Wesley. *A Missionary Pilgrimage.* Grand Rapids: Wm. B. Eerdmans, 1988.

Re-Thinking Missions: A Layman's Inquiry after One Hundred Years. Ed. by William Ernst Hocking. New York: Harper, 1932.

Sharing One Bread, Sharing One Mission: The Eucharist as Missionary Event. Ed. by Jean Stromberg. Geneva: WCC, 1983.

Sider, Ronald J. *Evangelism, Salvation and Social Justice.* Bramcote: Grove Books, 1979.

Sundkler, Bengt. *The World of Mission.* London: Lutterworth, 1965.

Warren, Max A. C. *The Christian Mission.* London: SCM, 1951.

What is CWME? A Brief History of the Commission of World Mission and Evangelism. Geneva: WCC, 1984.

Witnessing to the Kingdom: Melbourne and Beyond. Ed. by Gerald H. Anderson. Maryknoll, NY: Orbis Books, 1982.

Your Kingdom Come: Mission Perspectives. Report of the World Conference on Mission and Evangelism at Melbourne, Australia, 12–25 May 1980. Geneva: WCC, 1980.

Your Will Be Done: Orthodoxy in Mission. Ed. by George Lemopoulos. Geneva: WCC, 1989.

Dialogue with People of Living Faith and Ideologies

Ariarajah, S. Wesley. *The Bible and People of Other Faiths.* Maryknoll, NY: Orbis Books, 1989.

Bent, Ans J. van der. *Christians and Communists: An Ecumenical Perspective.* Geneva: WCC, 1980.

————. *The Christian-Marxist Dialogue.* A Comprehensive and Partly Annotated Bibliography. Geneva: WCC, 1992.

Brown, Stuart. *The Nearest in Affection: Towards a Christian Understanding of Islam.* Geneva: WCC, 1992.

Christian Mission and Inter-Religious Dialogue. Paul Mojzes and Leonard Swidler eds. Lewiston: Edwin Mellen Press, 1990.

Churches Among Ideologies. Report of a Consultation and Recommendations to Fellow Christians, 15–22 Dec. 1981, Grand Saconnex, Switzerland. Geneva: WCC, 1982.

Cracknell, Kenneth. *Towards a New Relationship: Christians and People of Other Faith.* London: Epworth Press, 1986.

Dialogue and Syncretism: An Interdisciplinary Approach. Ed. by Jerald Gort (et al.). Grand Rapids: Wm. B. Eerdmans, 1989.

Dialogue between Men of Living Faiths. Papers Presented at a Consultation Held at Ajaltoun, Lebanon, March 1970. Ed. by Stanely J. Samartha. Geneva: WCC, 1971.

Dialogue in Community: Essays in Honour of Stanley J. Samartha. Ed. by Constantine D. Jathanna. Bangalore: Karnataka Theological Research Institute, 1982.

Ecumenical Considerations on Christian-Muslim Relations. Geneva: WCC, 1991.

Faith and Ideologies: An Ecumenical Discussion. Cartigny, Geneva, May 1975. Geneva: WCC, 1975.

Faith in the Midst of Faiths: Reflections on Dialogue in Community. Ed. by S. J. Samartha. Consultation at Chiang Mai, 1977. Geneva: WCC, 1977.

Gollwitzer, Helmut. *The Christian Faith and the Marxist Critique of Religion.* Edinburgh: St Andrew Press, 1970.

Guidelines on Dialogue with People of Living Faiths and Ideologies. Geneva: WCC, 1979.

Hallencreutz, Carl F. *Dialogue and Community: Ecumenical Issues in Inter-Religious Relationships.* Geneva: WCC, 1977.

Küng, Hans, Stietencron, J. van and Bechert, J. von. *Christianity and World Religions: Paths to Dialogue with Islam, Hinduism and Buddhism.* Mary Knoll, NY: Orbis Books, 1993.

Living Faiths and Ultimate Goals: A Continuing Dialogue. Ed. by Stanley J. Samartha. Geneva: WCC, 1974.

Man in Nature, Guest or Engineer? A Preliminary Enquiry by Christians and Buddhists into the Religious Dimensions in Humanity's Relation to Nature. Stanley J. Samartha and Lynn de Silva eds. Colombo: Ecumenical Institute for Study and Dialogue, 1979.

Meeting in Faith: Twenty Years of Christian-Muslim Conversations Sponsored by the WCC. Ed. by Stuart Brown. Geneva: WCC, 1989.

Ministerial Formation in a Multi-Faith Milieu. Sam Amirtham and S. Wesley Ariarajah eds. Geneva: WCC, 1986.

My Neighbour's Faith-And Mine: Theological Discoveries through Interfaith Dialogue: A Study Guide. Geneva: WCC, 1989. 3rd printing.

New Religious Movements and the Churches. Alan R. Brockway and J. Paul Rajasbekar eds. Geneva: WCC, 1987.

Primal World Views: Christian Dialogue with Traditional Thought Forms. Ed. by John B. Taylor. Ibadan: Daystar Press, 1976.

Religious Issues and Inter-Religious Dialogues: An Analysis and Sourcebook of Developments Since 1945. Charles Wei-h-sun Fu and Gerhard E. Spiegler eds. Westport, CT: Greenwood Press, 1989.

Samartha, Stanley J. *Courage for Dialogue: Ecumenical Issues in Inter-Religious Relationships.* Geneva: WCC, 1981.

The Theology of the Churches and the Jewish People: Statements by the World Council of Churches and Its Member Churches. Geneva: WCC, 1988.

Towards World Community: The Colombo Papers. Ed. by Stanley J. Samartha. Geneva: WCC, 1975.

Wingate, Andrew. *Encounter in the Spirit: Muslim-Christian Dialogue in Practice.* Geneva: WCC, 1991.

Worship and Ritual in Christianity and Other Religions. Rome: Gregorian University Press, 1974.

Church and Society

Abrecht, Paul. *The Churches and Rapid Social Change.* New York: Doubleday, 1961.

Between the Flood and the Rainbow. Interpreting the Conciliar Process of Mutual Commitment (Covenant) to Justice, Peace and the Integrity of Creation. Geneva: WCC, 1992.

Bock, Paul. *In Search of a Responsible World Society: The Social Teachings of the World Council of Churches.* Philadelphia: Westminster Press, 1974.

Burning Issues. The New International Economic Order, Transnational Corporations and World Disarmament. Ed. by Paulos Gregorios. Kottayam: Sophia Centre Publication, 1977.

Christian Faith and the World Economy Today. A WCC Study Document. Geneva: WCC, 1992.

"Church and Society: Ecumenical Perspectives: Essays in Honour of Paul Abrecht". *Ecumenical Review,* vol. 37, no. 1, Jan. 1985. pp. 1–163.

The Common Christian Responsibility Toward Areas of Rapid Social Change. Second statement. Geneva: WCC, 1956.

C.O.P.E.C. Commission Reports. Conference on Christian Politics, Economics and Citizenship, at Birmingham, April 5–12, 1924. London: Longmans, Green, 1924–1925. 12 vols.

Dilemmas and Opportunities: Christian Action in Rapid Social Change.

Report of an International Study Conference, Thessalonica, Greece, July 25–August 2, 1959. Geneva: WCC, 1959.

Duchrow, Ulrich. *Europe in the World System 1492–1992*. Geneva: WCC, 1992.

Duff, Edward. *The Social Thought of the World Council of Churches*. London: Longmans, Green, 1956.

Economics: A Matter of Faith. Geneva: WCC, 1988.

Ehrenström, Nils. *Christian Faith and the Modern State: An Ecumenical Approach*. London: SCM, 1937.

Ellingsen, Mark. *The Cutting Edge: How Churches Speak on Social Issues*. Geneva: WCC, 1993.

"Fifty Years of Ecumenical Social Thought". *Ecumenical Review*, vol. 40, no. 2, April 1988. pp. 129–286.

From Here to Where? Technology, Faith and the Future. Report of an Exploratory Conference, Geneva, 28 June–4 July, 1970. Ed. by David Gill. Geneva: WCC, 1970.

Genetics and the Quality of Life. Charles Birch and Paul Abrecht eds. Elmsford: Pergamon Press, 1975.

Granberg-Michaelson, Wesley. *Redeeming the Creation. The Rio Earth Summit: Challenge for the Churches*. Geneva: WCC, 1992.

Gustafson, James M. *Protestant and Roman Catholic Ethics: Prospects for Rapprochement*. Chicago: Chicago Univ. Press, 1978.

The Kindness That Kills: The Churches' Simplistic Response to Complex Social Issues. Ed. by Digby C. Anderson. London: S.P.C.K., 1984.

Küng, Hans. *Global Responsibility: In Search for a New World Ethic*. London: SCM, 1991.

Lee, Robert. *Social Sources of Ecumenicity: An Interpretation of the Social History of the Church Unity Movement in American Protestantism*, New York: Abingdon, 1958.

Mehl, Roger. *The Sociology of Protestantism*. London: SCM, 1970.

Miguez Bonino, José. *Toward a Christian Political Ethics*. Philadelphia: Fortress Press, 1983.

Muelder, Walter G. *Foundations of the Responsible Society*. Nashville: Abingdon, 1959.

Nelson, Claud D. *Religion and Society: The Ecumenical Impact*. New York: Sheed and Ward, 1966.

The New Faith-Science Debate. Probing Cosmology, Technology and Theology. Ed. by John M. Mangum. Geneva: WCC, 1989.

Norman, Edward. *Christianity and the World Order*. Oxford: Oxford UP, 1979.

Nuclear Energy and Ethics. Ed. by Kristin Shrader-Frechette. Geneva: WCC, 1991.

Paulos Mar Gregorios. *The Human Presence: An Orthodox View of Nature*. Geneva: WCC, 1978.

Preston, Ronald H. *The Future of Christian Ethics*. London: SCM, 1987.

———. *Religion and the Ambiguities of Capitalism*. London: SCM, 1991.

Ramsey, Paul. *Who Speaks for the Church? A Critique of the 1966 Conference on Church and Society*. Nashville: Abingdon, 1967.

Rauschenbusch, Walter. *A Theology for the Social Gospel*. New York: Macmillan, 1917.

Religion and Society: The First Twenty-Five Years 1953–1978. Ed. by Richard W. Taylor. Madras: Christian Literature Society, 1982.

Science and Our Future. Ed. by Paulos Gregorios. Madras: Christian Literature Society, 1978.

Statements of the World Council of Churches on Social Questions. Geneva: WCC, 1956. 2nd ed.

Suggate, Alan M. *William Temple and Christian Social Ethics Today.* Edinburgh: T. and T. Clark, 1987.

Technology and Social Justice. An International Symposium on the Social and Economic Teaching of the World Council of Churches from Geneva 1966 to Uppsala 1968. Ed. by Ronald H. Preston. London: SCM, 1971.

Temple, William. *Christianity and Social Order.* Harmondsworth: Penguin Books, 1943.

Third World Liberation Theologies: a Reader. Ed. by Deane William Ferm. Maryknoll, NY: Orbis Books, 1986.

Thomas, M. M. *Towards a Theology of Contemporary Ecumenism.* Geneva: WCC, 1978.

Turnbull, John W. *Ecumenical Documents on Church and Society 1925–1953.* Geneva: WCC, 1954.

Utopia and Liberation: Towards a Human World. Summary, Reports and Comments on the Seminar held in Berlin, 17–22 Nov. 1991. Ed. by Israel Batista. Geneva: WCC, 1992.

Visser 't Hooft, Willem Adolf. *The Background of the Social Gospel in America.* Haarlem: T. Willink, 1928, (Reprinted by Bethany Press, St. Louis, 1962)

Visser 't Hooft, Willem Adolf and Oldham, Joseph H. *The Church and Its Function in Society.* Chicago: Willet, Clark, 1937.

———. *The Kingship of Christ: An Interpretation of Recent European Theology.* New York: Harper, 1948.

Vries, Egbert de. *Man in Rapid Social Change.* Garden City, NY: Doubleday, 1961.

Will the Future Work? Values for Emerging Patterns of Work and Employment. Howard Davis and David Gosling eds. Geneva: WCC, 1985.

Peace and Disarmament

Before It's Too Late: The Challenge of Nuclear Disarmament. The Complete Record of the Public Hearing on Nuclear Weapons and Disarmament, Amsterdam, 1981. Paul Abrecht and Ninan Koshy eds. Geneva: WCC, 1983.

Booth, Alan R. *Not Only Peace: Christian Realism and the Conflicts of the Twentieth Century.* London: SCM, 1967.

Churches as Peacemakers? An Analysis of Recent Church Statements on Peace, Disarmament and War. By Friedhelm Solms and Marc Reuver. Rome: IDOC, 1985.

Conflict, Violence and Peace. A Report of a Consultation on "Alternatives to Conflict in the Quest for Peace", 1969. Ed. by Anwar M. Barkat. Geneva: WCC, 1970.

A Council for Peace. Hans Küng and Jürgen Moltmann eds. Edinburgh: T. and T. Clark, 1988.

Duchrow, Ulrich and Liedke, Gerhard. *Shalom: Biblical Perspectives on Creation, Justice and Peace.* Geneva: WCC, 1989.

Facing up to Nuclear Power: A Contribution to the Debate on the Risks and Potentialities of the Large Scale Use of Nuclear Energy. John Francis and Paul Abrecht eds. Edinburgh: Saint Andrew Press, 1976.

Justice, Peace and the Integrity of Creation: Insights from Orthodoxy. Ed. by Gennadios Limouris; Geneva: WCC, 1990.

Macfarland, Charles S. *Pioneers for Peace through Religion, Based on the Records of the Church Peace Union, 1914–1945.* New York: F. H. Revell, 1946.

Niles, Preman. *Resisting Threats to Life: Covenanting for Justice, Peace and the Integrity of Creation.* Geneva: WCC, 1989.

Pattern for Peace: Catholic Statements on International Order. Ed. by Harry W. Flannery. Westminster: Newman Press, 1962.

Peace and Disarmament. Documents of the WCC presented by the

Commission of the Churches on International Affairs, and of the Roman Catholic Church presented by the Pontifical Commission Iustitia et Pax. Geneva: WCC; Rome: Pontifical Commission Iustitia et Pax. 1982.

Peace with Justice: European Ecumenical Assembly. The Official Documentation of the European Eucmenical Assembly, Basel, 15–21 May 1989. Conference of European Churches and Council of the European Bishops' Conference. Geneva: CEC, 1989.

Regehr, Ernie. *Militarism and the World Military Order.* A Study Guide for Churches. Geneva: WCC, 1980.

"Report on the Conference on Disarmament, Glion, Switzerland, 9–15 April, 1978", *CCIA Background Information,* no. 4, 1978.

"Report on the Consultation on Militarism, Glion, Switzerland, 13–18 Nov., 1977", *CCIA Background Information,* no. 2, 1977.

Reuver, Marc. *Christian Peace Movements 1925–1940.* Göttingen: Vandenhoeck and Reuprecht, 1991.

————. *Christians as Peace Makers: Peace Movements in Europe and the USA.* Geneva: WCC, 1988.

The Security Trap: Arms Race, Militarism and Disarmament: A Concern for Christians. Ed. by José Antonio Viera Gallo. Rome: IDOC, 1979.

Violence, Nonviolence and Civil Conflict. Geneva: WCC, 1983.

"WCC Statements on Nuclear Weapons and Disarmament 1948–1981". Prepared for the Public Hearing at Amsterdam, 23–27 Nov. 1981. Geneva: WCC, 1981.

International Affairs

Behind the Mask: Human Rights in Asia and Latin America: An Inter-Regional Encounter. Ed. by Erich Weingärtner. Geneva: WCC, 1988.

Bennett, John C. *Foreign Policy in Christian Perspective*. New York: Scribner, 1966.

Bent, Ans J. van der. *Christian Response in a World of Crisis: A Brief History of the WCC's Commission of the Churches on International Affairs*. Geneva: WCC, 1986.

The Churches in International Affairs. Reports 1979–1982; 1983–1986; 1987–1990. Geneva: WCC.

Derr, Thomas Sieger. *The Political Thought of the Ecumenical Movement 1900–1939*. Ann Arbor: University Microfilms, 1972.

Fonseca, Glenda Da. *How to File Complaints of Human Rights Violations: A Practical Guide to Intergovernmental Procedures*. Geneva: WCC, 1975.

Hudson, Darril. *The Ecumenical Movement in World Affairs*. London: Weidenfeld and Nicolson, 1969.

———. *The World Council of Churches in International Affairs*. Leighton Buzzard: Faith Press, 1977.

Human Rights: A Challenge to Theology. Ed. by Marc Reuver. Rome: IDOC International, 1983.

Human Rights and Christian Responsibility. Report of the Consultation in St. Pölten, Austria, 21–26 Oct. 1974. Geneva: WCC, 1974.

International Affairs: Christians in the Struggle for World Community. An Ecumenical Survey Prepared under the Auspices of the WCC. London: SCM, 1954. (Evanston Surveys, 4).

Koshy, Ninan. *Religious Freedom in a Changing World*. Geneva: WCC, 1992.

Kramer, Leonard J. *Man Amid Change in World Affairs*. New York: Friendship Press, 1964.

"Militarism and Human Rights. Reports and Papers of a Workshop at Glion, Switzerland, 10–14 Nov. 1982". *CCIA Background Information*, 1982, no. 3.

Nolde, O. Frederick. *The Churches and the Nations*. Philadelphia: Fortress Press, 1970.

———. *Free and Equal: Human Rights in Ecumenical Perspective*. Geneva: WCC, 1968.

Religious Freedom: Main Statements by the World Council of Churches 1948–1975. Geneva: WCC, 1976.

Religious Liberty and Human Rights in Nations and Religions. Ed. by Leonard J. Swidler. Philadelphia: Ecumenical Press, 1986.

Toward World-Wide Christianity. Ed. by O. Frederick Nolde. New York: Harper, 1946.

Weingärtner, Erich. "Human Rights on the Ecumenical Agenda: Report and Assessment". *CCIA Background Information*, 1983, no. 3.

Interchurch Aid, Refugee and World Service

Bouman, Pieter. *Tears and Rejoicing: The Story of European Inter-Church Aid 1922–1956*. Pieter Bouman, 1983.

Called to Be Neighbours—Diakonia 2000. Official Report, World Consultation of Inter-Church Aid, Refugee and World Service, Larnaca, 1986. Ed. by Klaus Poser. Geneva: WCC, 1987.

Churches Committee on Migrant Workers in Europe Documents 1964–1972. Geneva: Churches Committee on Migrant Workers in Western Europe, 1972.

Contemporary Understandings of Diakonia. Report of a Consultation, Geneva, 22–26 Nov. 1982. Geneva: WCC, 1983.

Digest of the 1966 World Consultation on Inter-Church Aid at Swanwick, Great Britain. Geneva: WCC, 1966.

Ferris, Elizabeth. *Beyond Borders: Refugees, Migrants and Human Rights in the Post-Cold War Era*. Geneva: WCC, 1993.

Hope in the Desert: The Churches' United Response to Human Need, 1944–1984. Ed. by Kenneth Slack. Geneva: WCC, 1986.

In a Strange Land. A Report of a World Conference on Problems of International Migration and the Responsibility of the Churches held at Leysin, Switzerland, June 11–16, 1961. Geneva: WCC, 1961.

Jacques, André. *The Stranger within Your Gates: Uprooted People in the World Today.* Geneva: WCC, 1986.

Migrant Workers: A Test Case of Human Relationships. Consultation on Migrant Workers in Western Europe, Bossey, May 29–June 4, 1965. Geneva: WCC, 1965.

The Orthodox Approach to Diaconia. Consultation on Church and Service, Orthodox Academy of Crete, 20–25 Nov. 1978. Geneva: WCC, 1980.

The Role of the Churches in Social Service: An International Perspective. Reporting a Consultation held at Mülheim, Germany, July 16–20, 1962. New York: National Council of Churches, 1963.

Sharing Life. Official Report of the World Consultation on Koinonia: Sharing Life in a World Community, El Escorial, Spain, Oct. 1987. Ed. by Huibert van Beek. Geneva: WCC, 1989.

Within Thy Gates. A Report of the Conference on Migrant Workers in Western Europe held at Arnoldshain, Western Germany, June 10–15, 1963. Geneva: WCC, 1963.

Christian Medical Commission

Granberg-Michaelson, Karin. *Healing Community.* Geneva: WCC, 1991.

Healing and Wholeness: The Churches' Role in Health. The Report of a Study. Geneva: WCC, 1990.

The Healing Church: The Tübingen Consultation 1964. Geneva: WCC, 1965.

Health, the Human Factor. Readings in Health, Development and Community Participation. Guest ed. Susan B. Rifkin. Geneva: WCC, 1980.

Hellberg, J. H. *Community, Health and the Church.* Geneva: WCC, 1971.

MacGilvray, James C. *The Quest for Health and Wholeness.* Tübingen: German Institute for Medical Missions, 1981.

The Principles and Practice of Primary Health Care. Geneva: WCC, 1979.

The Search for a Christian Understanding of Health, Healing and Wholeness. A Summary Report on the Study Programme of the Christian Medical Commission of the World Council of Churches, 1976–1982. Geneva: WCC, 1982.

Development

Churches and the Transnational Corporations: An Ecumenical Programme. Geneva: WCC, 1983.

Dickinson, Richard D. N. *To Set at Liberty the Oppressed: Towards an Understanding of Christian Responsibilities of Development/ Liberation.* Geneva: WCC, 1975.

Ecumenical Reflections on Political Economy. Ed. by Catherine Mulholland. Geneva: WCC, 1988.

Elliott, Charles. *Patterns of Poverty in the Third World.* A Study of Social and Economic Stratification. London: Praeger, 1975.

Fagley, Richard M. *The Population Explosion and Christian Responsibility.* New York: Oxford UP, 1960.

Fetters of Injustice. Report of an Ecumenical Consultation on Ecumenical Assistance to Development Projects, Montreux, 26–31 Jan. 1970. Ed. by Pamela H. Gruber. Geneva: WCC, 1970.

The International Financial System: An Ecumenical Critique. Report of the Meeting of the Advisory Group on Economic Matters, Geneva, 1–4 Nov. 1984. Ed. by Reginald Green. Geneva: WCC, 1985.

Justice and Development. Asian Forum on CCA-WCC-CCPD, Singapore, 26–30 Nov. 1984. Ed. by Kim Yong-Bock. Seoul: Yang Seo Press, 1985.

Munby, Denis. *World Development.* Washington, DC: Corpus Books, 1969.

Perspectives on Political Ethics: An Ecumenical Enquiry. Ed. By Koson Srisang. Geneva: WCC, 1983.

Pury, Pascal de. *People's Technologies and People's Participation.* Geneva: WCC, 1983.

Rudersdorf, Karl Heinrich. *Das Entwicklungskonzept des Weltkirchenrates.* Saarbrücken: Verlag der SSIP-Schriften, 1975.

Santa Ana, Julio de. *Good News to the Poor: The Challenge of the Poor in the History of the Church.* Geneva: WCC, 1977.

Separation Without Hope? Essays on the Relation Between the Church and the Poor During the Industrial Revolution and the Western Colonial Expansion. Ed. by Julio de Santa Ana. Maryknoll, NY: Orbis Books, 1980.

Towards a Church of the Poor. The Work of an Ecumenical Group on the Church and the Poor. Geneva: WCC, 1979.

Traitler, Reinhild. *Leaping Over the Wall: An Assessment of Ten Years' Development Education.* Geneva: WCC, 1982.

We Cannot Dream Alone: A Story of Women in Development. Ed. by Ranjini Rebera. Geneva: WCC, 1990.

Several numbers of *CCPD Documents* deal with specific problems and concerns.

Racism

Adler, Elisabeth. *A Small Beginning: An Assessment of the First Five Years of the Programme to Combat Racism.* Geneva: WCC, 1974.

Breaking Down the Walls: World Council of Churches Statements and Actions on Racism 1948–1985. Ed. by Ans J. van der Bent. Geneva: WCC, 1986.

Churches Responding to Racism in the 1980s. Noordwijkerhout, Netherlands: 16–21 June, 1980. Geneva: WCC, 1980.

Cone, James H. and Wilmore, Gayraud. *Black Theology: A Documentary History.* Vol. I: 1966–1979. Vol. II: 1980–1992. Maryknoll, NY: Orbis Books, 1993.

Ecumenical Statements on Race Relations: Development of Ecumenical Thought on Race Relations 1937–1964. Geneva: WCC, 1965.

From Cottesloe to Cape Town: Challenges for the Church in a Post-Apartheid South Africa. Report of the WCC visit to South Africa, October 1991. Geneva: WCC, 1991.

Kitagawa, Daisuke. *Race Relations and Christian Mission.* New York: Friendship Press, 1964.

Mutambirwa, James. *South Africa: The Sanctions Mission.* Report of the Eminent Church Persons Group. Geneva: WCC, 1989.

Oldham, Joseph H. *Christianity and the Race Problem.* London: Student Christian Movement, 1926.

Racism in Theology and Theology Against Racism. Geneva. WCC, 1975.

Rogers, Barbara. *Race: No Peace Without Justice: Churches Confront the Mounting Racism of the 1980s.* Geneva: WCC, 1980.

Sjollema, Baldwin. *Isolating Apartheid.* Geneva: WCC, 1982.

The Slant of the Pen: Racism in Children's Books. Ed. by Roy Preiswerk. Geneva: WCC, 1980.

Vincent, John J. *The Race Race, London, Notting Hill, 1969.* London: SCM, 1970.

Witvliet, Theo. *The Way of the Black Messiah: Hermeneutical Challenge of Black Theology as Theology of Liberation.* London: SCM, 1987.

Several numbers of *PCR Information* deal with specific concerns, problems and conflicts.

Education

Alive Together: A Practical Guide to Ecumenical Learning. Geneva: WCC, 1989.

Christians and Education in a Multi-Faith World: Considerations on Christian Participation in Education in a Multi-Faith Environment. Geneva: WCC, 1982.

Doing Theology in Different Contexts: Latin American and Eastern/ Central Theologians in Dialogue. A Report of a Programme on Theological Education Consultation in Prague, June 1988. Ofelia Ortega and Diana Chabloz eds. Geneva: WCC, 1988.

Education for Effective Ecumenism. A Report on a Workshop held at the Ecumenical Institute Bossey, 20–29 June, 1982. Geneva: WCC, 1982.

Encuentro: New Perspectives for Christian Education. Geneva: WCC, 1971.

Finding the Way Together: Education for Ecumenical Understanding and Action. Ed. by Barbara Stephens. Singapore: Christian Conference of Asia, 1986.

Freire, Paulo. *Education for Critical Consciousness.* New York: Seabury Press, 1973.

———— and Faundez, Antonio. *Learning to Question: A Pedagogy of Liberation.* New York: Continuum Books, 1989.

————. *Pedagogy of the Oppressed.* New York: Herder and Herder, 1970.

The Invitation to the Feast of Life: Resources for Spiritual Formation in Theological Education. Samuel Amirtam and Robin Pryor eds. Geneva: WCC, 1991.

Kennedy, William Bean. *Education for Liberation and Community.* New Haven: Religious Education Association, 1975.

Learning Community. A Consultation on Evaluating the Sunday School Contribution to Church Education in Europe Today, Glion, Switzerland, 24–28 Sept. 1973. Geneva: WCC, 1973.

Ministry by the People: Theological Education by Extension. Ed. by F. Ross Kinsler. Maryknoll, NY: Orbis Books, 1983.

Opting for Change: A Handbook On Evaluation and Planning for Theological Education by Extension. F. Ross Kinsler and James H. Emery eds. Pasadena, CA: William Carey Library, 1992.

Orthodox Theological Education for the Life and Witness of the Church. Report on the Consultation at Basel, July 4–8, 1978. Geneva: WCC, 1978.

Palmer Martin. *What Should We Teach?* A Book about Christians and Education in a Pluralist World. Geneva: WCC, 1992.

Resources for Spiritual Formation in Theological Education. Samuel Amirtham and Robin Pryor eds. Geneva: WCC, 1989.

Richey, Russell E. *Ecumenical and Interreligious Perspectives: Globalization in Theological Education.* Nashville, QR Books, 1992.

Seeing Education Whole. Geneva: WCC, 1970.

Stories Make People: Examples of Theological Work in Community. Ed. by Samuel Amirtham. Geneva: WCC, 1989.

The Teaching of Ecumenics. Samuel Amirtham and Cyrus H. Moon eds. Geneva: WCC, 1987.

Tradition and Renewal in Orthodox Education. Report of the Consultation . . . held in the Neamt Monastery, Romania, 6–12 Sept. 1976. Ed. by Maurice Assad. Geneva: WCC, 1977.

Weber, Hans-Ruedi. *Experiments with Bible Study.* Geneva: WCC, 1981.

———. *Jesus and the Children: Biblical Resources for Study and Preaching.* Geneva: WCC, 1979.

———. *Power: Focus for a Biblical Theology.* Geneva: WCC, 1989.

Laity

Bucy, Ralph D. *The New Laity between Church and World.* Waco: Word Books, 1978.

Centres for Renewal and Study and Lay Training. Geneva: WCC, 1964.

Congar, Yves M. J. *Lay People in the Church: A Study of the Theology of the Laity.* London: Bloomsbury Publ. Co., 1957.

Director of Lay Training Centres, 2 vols. Geneva: WCC, 1962–1963.

Gibbs, Mark and Morton, Ralph. *God's Frozen People: A Book for and about Ordinary Christians.* London: Collins, 1965.

Grubb, Kenneth G. *A Layman Looks at the Church.* London: Hodder and Stoughton, 1964.

Kraemer, Hendrik. *A Theology of the Laity.* London: Lutterworth, 1958.

Laici in Ecclesia: An Ecumenical Bibliography on the Role of the Laity in the the Life and Mission of the Church. Geneva: WCC, 1961.

The Layman in Christian History. Stephen Charles Neill and Hans-Ruedi Weber eds. London: SCM, 1963.

Löffler, Paul. *The Layman Abroad in the Mission of the Church.* Geneva: WCC, 1962.

Thurian, Max. *Consecration of the Layman: New Approaches to the Sacrament of Confirmation.* Baltimore: Helicon Press, 1963.

Voices of Solidarity: A Story of Christian Lay Centres, Academies and Movements for Social Concern. Geneva: WCC, 1981.

Weber, Hans-Ruedi. *Salty Christians: A Handbook for Leaders of Lay Training Courses.* Geneva: WCC, 1962.

Wentz, Frederick K. *The Layman's Role Today.* Garden City, NY: Doubleday, 1963.

World Congress for the Lay Apostolate. *The Laity in the Renewal of the Church.* Rome: Permanent Committee for International Congresses of the Lay Apostolate, 1967.

Women in Church and Society

Bührig, Marga. *Women Invisible.* London: Burns and Oates, 1993.

The Community of Women and Men in the Church. A Report of the WCC's Conference, Sheffield, England, 1981. Ed. by Constance F. Parvey. Geneva: WCC, 1983.

Gnanadason, Aruna. *No Longer A Secret: The Church and Violence Against Women.* Geneva: WCC, 1993.

Half the World's People. A Report of the Consultation of Church Women Executives, Glion, Switzerland, Jan. 1977. Geneva: WCC, 1978.

Herzel, Susannah. *A Voice for Women: The Women's Department of the World Council of Churches.* Geneva: WCC, 1981.

In God's Image: Reflections on Identity, Human Wholeness and the Authority of Scripture. Janet Crawford and Michael Kinnamon eds. Geneva: WCC, 1983.

Katoppo, Marianne. *Compassionate and Free: An Asian Woman's Theology.* Geneva: WCC, 1981.

Melton, J. Gordon. *Women's Ordination.* Official Statements from Religious Bodies and Ecumenical Organizations. Detroit: Gale Research Co., 1991.

Oduyoye, Mercy Amba. *Who Will Roll the Stone Away? The Ecumenical Decade of the Churches in Solidarity with Women.* Geneva: WCC, 1990.

Office of Family Education. *Oaxtepec, Mexico, Jan. 1980.* Geneva: WCC, 1980.

———. *Report of a Consultation on Humanity and Wholeness of*

Persons with Disabilities, Sao Paulo, Brazil, 23–30 Nov. 1981. Geneva: WCC, 1982.

Orthodox Women: the Role and Participation in the Orthodox Church. Report of the Consultation of Orthodox Women, 11–17 Sept. 1976, Agapia, Romania. Geneva: WCC, 1977.

The Power We Celebrate: Women's Stories of Faith and Power. Musimbi R. Kanyoro and Wendy S. Robins eds. Geneva: WCC, 1992.

Ruether, Rosemary Radford. *Gaia and God: An Ecofeminist Theology of Earth Healing.* London: SCM, 1993.

Sexism in the 1970s: Discrimination Against Women. A Report of a World Council of Churches Consultation West Berlin 1974. Geneva: WCC, 1975.

Study on the Community of Women and Men in the Church. Geneva: WCC, 1979.

Thompson, Betty. *A Chance to Change: Women and Men in the Church.* Geneva: WCC, 1982.

Wartenberg-Potter, Bärbel von. *We Will Not Hang Our Harps on the Willows.* Geneva: WCC, 1987.

We Cannot Dream Alone: The Story of Women in Development. Ed. by Ranjini Rebera. Geneva: WCC, 1991.

Webb, Pauline. *She Flies Beyond: Memories and Hopes of Women in the Ecumenical Movement.* Geneva: WCC, 1993.

What is Ordination Coming To? Report of a Consultation on the Ordination of Women held in Cartigny, Geneva, 21–26 Sept. 1970. Ed. by Brigalia Bam. Geneva: WCC, 1971.

Women and Church: The Challenge of Ecumenical Solidarity in an Age of Alienation. Ed. by Melanie A. May. Grand Rapids: Wm. B. Eerdmans, 1991.

Women, Religion and Sexuality: Studies on the Impact of Religious

Teachings on Women. Ed. by Jeanne Becher. Philadelphia: Trinity Press International, 1990.

Youth

Bent, Ans J. van der. *From Generation to Generation: The Story of Youth in the World Council of Churches.* Geneva: WCC, 1986.

Christ the Life: The Report of the Asian Christian Youth Assembly, Silliman University, Dumaguete City, 1964–1965. Ed. by Soritua A. E. Nababan. Damaguete City, 1965.

Christian Youth in a Troubled Society: Ayia Napa, Cyprus, July 13–20, 1978. Geneva: WCC, 1978.

Christus Victor: The Report of the World Conference of Christian Youth, Amsterdam, 24 July–2 August 1939. Geneva: Conference Headquarters, 1939.

Ecumenical Youth Assembly in Europe, Lausanne, 1960. Ed. by Rod French. Geneva: WCC, 1960.

Footprints in Travancore: Report of the Third World Conference of Christian Youth, 11–26 Dec. 1952. Coonoor, Nilgiris: India Sunday School Union, 1953.

The New Creation and the New Generation: A Forum for Youth Workers. Ed. by Albert van den Heuvel. New York: Friendship Press, 1965.

North American Youth Assembly, Ann Arbor, 1961. Ed. by Rod French. Geneva: WCC, 1961.

The Report of the Second World Conference of Christian Youth, Oslo, Norway, 22–31 July, 1947. Ed. by Paul Griswold Macy. Geneva: WCC, 1947.

Youth and the Church. Report to the Continuation Committee of the Stockholm Conference on Life and Work by Its Youth Commission. Basil Mathews, Lucy Gardner and Erich Stange eds. London: Pilgrim Press, 1928.

"Youth in God's World", *Work Book for the Assembly Committees, Uppsala, 1968.* Geneva: WCC, 1968.

Other Ecumenical Bodies and Movements

The Challenge of Basic Christian Communities. Papers from the International Ecumenical Congress of Theology, Feb. 20–March 2, 1980, Sao Paulo. Sergio Torres and John Eagleson eds. Maryknoll, NY: Orbis Books, 1981.

The Churches in Action. Newsletter of the Universal Christian Council for Life and Work and the World Alliance for International Friendship through the Churches. Quarterly. Geneva: 1931–1938.

Directory of Ecumenical Conference Centres. Geneva: WCC, 1990.

Ewing, J. W. *Goodly Fellowship: A Centenary Tribute to the Life and Work of the World's Evangelical Alliance, 1846–1946.* London: Marshall, Morgan and Scott, 1946.

God Calls, Choose Life, The Hour is Late: Christians in Resistance to the Powers of Death, On the Path to Peace and Justice for All. Documents of the Sixth All-Christian Peace Assembly, Prague, July 2–9, 1985. Prague: CPC, 1985.

Gonzalez Balado, José Luis: *The Story of Taizé.* London: A. R. Mowbray, 1980.

Heijke, John. *An Ecumenical Light on the Renewal of Religious Community Life-Taizé.* Pittsburgh: Duquesne UP, 1967.

Howard, David M. *The Dream that Would Not Die: The Birth and Growth of the World Evangelical Fellowship 1846–1986.* Exeter: Paternoster Press, 1986.

Macfarland, Charles S. *Pioneers for Peace through Religion, Based on the Records of the Church Peace Union, 1914–1945.* New York: F. H. Revell, 1946.

Massie, J. W. *The Evangelical Alliance: Its Origin and Development.* London: John Snow, 1847.

Mott, John R. *Addresses and Papers.* New York: Association Press, 1946–1947, 6 vols.

Rice, Anna V. *A History of the World's Young Women's Christian Association.* New York: The Women's Press, 1947.

Rouse, Ruth. *The World's Student Christian Federation: A History of the First Thirty Years.* London: SCM, 1948.

Schutz, Roger. *The Taizé Experience.* London: Mowbray, 1990.

Shedd, Clarence P. *History of the World's Alliance of Young Men's Christian Associations.* London: SPCK, 1955.

———. *Two Centuries of Student Christian Movements.* New York: Association Press, 1934.

Stevenson, Lilian. *Towards a Christian International: The Story of the International Fellowship of Reconciliation.* London: IFR, 1941.

Student World, vols. 1–62, 1908–1969. New York, Geneva: World Student Christian Federation.

Swidler, Leonard J. *The Ecumenical Vanguard: The History of the Una Sancta Movement.* Pittsburgh: Duquesne UP, 1966.

Third World Theologies: Commonalities and Divergences. Paper and Reflections from the Second General Assembly of the Ecumenical Association of Third World Theologians, Dec. 1986, Oaxtepec, Mexico City. Ed. by K-C. Abraham, Maryknoll, NY: Orbis Books, 1990.

Towards a Theology of Reconciliation. Papers presented to the Sixth All-Christian Peace Assembly, Prague, July 2–9, 1985. Ed. by David Omrod. Sheffield: Christian Peace Conference, British Regional Committee, 1985.

World Alliance for Promoting Friendship through the Churches. *Minutes and Reports,* 1914–1946, and *Handbooks,* 1916–1946.

Orthodox Churches in the Ecumenical Movement

Allchin, Arthur M. *The Kingdom of Love and Knowledge: The Encounter between Orthodoxy and the West.* London: Darton, Longman and Todd, 1979.

Bria, Ion. *The Sense of Ecumenical Tradition: The Ecumenical Witness and Vision of the Orthodox.* Geneva: WCC, 1991.

Calian, Carnegie Samuel. *Theology without Boundaries: Encounters of Eastern Orthodoxy with Western Protestantism.* Louisville, KY: Westminster/John Knox Press, 1992.

Declaration of the Ecumenical Patriarchate on the Occasion of the 25th Anniversary of the World Council of Churches. Istanbul: Patriarchal Institute for Patristic Studies, 1973.

Hebly, J. A. *The Russians and the World Council of Churches.* Documentary Survey of the Accession of the Russian Orthodox Church to the WCC, with commentary. Belfast: Christian Journals, 1978.

Hopko, Thomas. *All the Fulness of God: Essays on Orthodoxy, Ecumenism and Modern Society.* Crestwood, NY: St Vladimir's Seminary Press, 1982.

Jesus Christ—the Life of the World. An Orthodox Contribution to the Vancouver Theme. Ed. by Ion Bria. Geneva: WCC, 1982.

Macris, George P. *The Orthodox Church and the Ecumenical Movement during the Period 1920–1969.* Seattle: St Nectarios Press, 1986.

Madey, John. *Ecumenism, Ecumenical Movement and Eastern Churches.* Kottayam, Kerala: Oriental Institute for Religious Studies, 1987.

Meyendorf, John. *Catholicity and the Church.* Crestwood, NY: St Vladimir's Seminary Press, 1983.

———. *The Vision of Unity.* Crestwood, NY: St Vladimir's Seminary Press, 1987.

The New Valamo Consultation: The Ecumenical Nature of the Orthodox

Witness. New Valamo, Finland, 24–30 Sept. 1977. Geneva: WCC, 1978.

Nissiotis, Nikos A. *Interpreting Orthodoxy.* Minneapolis: Light and Live Publ. Co., n.d.

The Orthodox Church in the Ecumenical Movement. Documents and Statements 1902–1991. Ed. by Gennadios Limouris. Geneva: WCC, 1993.

Orthodox Thought. Reports of Orthodox Consultations Organized by the World Council of Churches, 1975–1982. Ed. by Georges Tsetsis. Geneva: WCC, Orthodox Task Force, 1983.

Orthodoxy: A Faith and Order Dialogue. Geneva: WCC, 1960 (Faith and Order Papers, no. 30)

Papers and Discussions between Eastern Orthodox and Oriental Orthodox Theologians: The Bristol Consultation, July 25–29, 1967. D. J. Constantelos, N. A. Nissiotis and P. Verghese eds. Brookline: Holy Cross School of Theology, 1968.

Patelos, Constantin G. *The Orthodox Church in the Ecumenical Movement.* Documents and Statements 1902–1975. Geneva: WCC, 1978.

Schmemann, Alexander. *Sacraments and Orthodoxy.* New York: Herder and Herder, 1965.

The Sofia Consultation: Orthodox Involvement in the World Council of Churches. Ed. by Todor Sabev. Geneva: WCC, Orthodox Task Force, 1982.

Stephanopoulos, Robert G. *Guidelines of Orthodox Christians in Ecumenical Relations.* New York: Standing Conference of Canonical Orthodox Bishops in America, 1973.

Toward a Protestant Understanding of Orthodoxy. New York: Commission on Ecumenical Mission and Relations, 1966.

Waddams, Herbert. *Meeting the Orthodox Churches.* London: SCM, 1964.

Ware, Kallistos Timothy. *The Orthodox Church.* Harmondsworth: Penguin Books, 1967.

You Shall Be My Witness: Mission Stories from the Eastern and Oriental Orthodox Churches. Ed. by G. Lemopoulos. Tertios, 1993.

Zernov, Nicolas. *Orthodox Encounter: The Christian East and the Ecumenical Movement.* London: J. Clarke, 1961.

Roman Catholic Church and the Ecumenical Movement

Baum, Gregory. *Ecumenical Theology.* New York: Paulist Press, 1967.

Bea, Augustinus. *The Way to Unity after the Council.* London: Geoffrey Chapman, 1967.

Boyer, Charles. *Christian Unity.* New York: Hawthorn, 1962. (Twentieth Century Encyclopedia of Catholicism, vol. 138)

Congar, Yves. *Essais oecuméniques: Le mouvement, les hommes, les problèmes.* Paris: Le Centurion, 1984.

———. *Une passion: l'unité.* Reflections et souvenirs 1929–1973. Paris: Ed. du Cerf, 1974.

Derr, Thomas Sieger. *Barriers to Ecumenism: The Holy See and the World Council of Churches on Social Questions.* Maryknoll, NY: Orbis Books, 1983.

Desseaux, Jacques E. *Twenty Centuries of Ecumenism.* New York: Paulist Press, 1985.

The Documents of Vatican II. Ed. by Walter M. Abbott. London: Chapman, 1966.

Dulles, Avery R. *Twenty-Five Years of Ecumenism: Have We Cared Enough?* Mahwah: Paulist Press, 1990.

Girault, René. *L'oecuménisme, ou vont les Eglises?* Paris: Le Centurion, 1983.

Hurley, Denis E. *Catholics and Ecumenism: Prospects and Problems.* Grahamstown: Rhodes University, 1966.

Johannes, Paulus, II. *Addresses and Homilies on Ecumenism 1978–1980.* John B. Sheerin and John F. Hotchkin eds. Washington, DC: U.S. Catholic Conference, 1980.

Küng, Hans. *The Council, Reform and Reunion.* New York: Sheed and Ward, 1962.

Leeming, Bernard. *The Churches and the Church: A Study of Ecumenism.* With a New Postscript. London: Darton, Longman and Todd,1963.

MacDonnell, Kilian. *The World Council of Churches and the Catholic Church.* New York: Edwin Mellen Press, 1985.

Minus, Paul M. *The Catholic Rediscovery of Protestantism: A History of Roman Catholic Ecumenical Pioneering.* New York: Paulist Press, 1976.

L'oecuménisme: Unité chrétienne et identité confessionelle. Paris: Beauchesne, 1985.

Problems Before Unity. J.G.M. Willebrands, Shawn G. Sheehan and Paul Mailleux. Dublin: Helicon Press, 1962.

Rodriguez, Pedro. *Iglesia y ecumenismo.* Madrid: Ediciones Rialp, 1979.

Schütte, Heinz, *Ziel—Kirchengemeinschaft: Zur ökumenischen Orientierung.* Paderborn: Verlag Bonifatius, 1985.

"Theology and Social Ethics: World Council of Churches and Roman Catholic Joint Discussion of Social Questions". *Study Encounter,* vol. 2, no. 2, 1966. pp. 75–102.

They Are in Earnest: Christian Unity in the Statements of Paul VI, John Paul I, John Paul II. Ed. by E. Yarnold. Middlegreen-Slough: St. Paul Publications, 1982.

Todd, John. *Catholicism and the Ecumenical Movement.* London: Longmans, Green, 1956.

Unity of the Churches: An Actual Possibility. Heinrich Fries and Karl Rahner eds. Philadelphia: Fortress Press, 1985.

Vischer, Lukas. "The Ecumenical Movement and the Roman Catholic Church". *The Ecumenical Advance: A History of the Ecumenical Movement, vol. 2, 1948–1968.* Ed. by Harold E. Fey. Geneva: WCC, 1986. pp. 311–352.

Walking Together: Roman Catholics and Ecumenism Twenty-Five Years after Vatican II. Ed. by Thaddeus D. Horgan. Grand Rapids: Wm. B. Eerdmans, 1990.

Willebrands, J. *Oecuménisme et problèmes actuels.* Paris: Cerf, 1969.

Joint Working Group between the Roman Catholic Church and the World Council of Churches

"Catholicity and Apostolicity". *One in Christ,* vol. 6, no. 3, 1970. pp. 452–483.

Clifford, Catherine E. *The Joint Working Group between the World Council of Churches and the Roman Catholic Church: Historical and Ecclesiological Perspectives.* 1987.

Common Witness. A Study Document. Geneva: WCC, 1981. (CWME Series, no. 1)

Official Reports, 1966, 1967, 1971, 1976, 1983, 1991. All published in *Ecumenical Review.*

"Patterns of Relationships between the Roman Catholic Church and the World Council of Churches". *Ecumenical Review,* vol. 24, no. 3, 1972. pp. 247–288.

Towards A Confession of the Common Faith. Geneva: WCC, 1980. (Faith and Order Papers, no. 100)

Committee on Society, Development and Peace (SODEPAX)

The Challenges of Development. A Sequel to the Beirut Conference of 21–27 April 1968 at Montreal 9–12 May, 1969. Geneva: SODE-PAX, 1969.

Church, Communication, Development. Papers from a SODEPAX Consultation, Driebergen, 12–16 March 1970 Geneva: WCC, 1970.

Dunne, Georg Harold. *King's Pawn: Memoirs.* Chicago: Loyola University, 1990.

In Search of a Theology of Development. Papers from a Consultation held at Cartigny, Switzerland, Nov. 1969. Geneva: SODEPAX, 1970.

Partnership or Privilege? An Ecumenical Reaction to the Second Development Decade. Geneva: WCC, 1970.

Peace—the Desperate Imperative. The Consultation on Christian Concern for Peace, Baden, Austria 3–9 April 1970. Sponsored by SODEPAX. Geneva: WCC, 1970.

Towards a Theology of Development. An Annotated Bibliography Compiled by Gerhard Bauer for SODEPAX. Geneva: WCC, 1970.

World Development: Challenge to the Churches. Report of the Conference on Society, Development and Peace held at Beirut, 21–27 April 1968. Washington, DC: Corpus Books, 1969.

Appendix 1.

HISTORICAL AND SIGNIFICANT ECUMENICAL STATEMENTS
(in chronological order)

I. The Relation Between Justice and the Kingdom of God.
In: *The Churches Survey Their Task:* The Report of the Conference at Oxford, July 1937, on Church, Community and State. London: George Allen and Unwin, 1937. pp. 97–98.

II. The Role of the Laity in Church and Society.
In: *The First Assembly of the World Council of Churches, held at Amsterdam August 22nd to September 4th, 1948.* Ed. by W. A. Visser 't Hooft. New York: Harper, 1949. pp. 153–154.
In: *The Evanston Report.* The Second Assembly of the World Council of Churches 1954. London: SCM, 1955. p. 103.

III. The Church, the Churches and the World Council of Churches. The Ecclesiological Significance of the World Council of Churches.
In: *Minutes and Reports of the Third Meeting of the Central Committee of the World Council of Churches, Toronto, July 9–15, 1950.* pp. 84–89.

IV. Decree on Ecumenism (Unitatis Redintegratio). The Introduction.
In: *Documents of Vatican II.* Ed. by Walter M. Abbott. New York: America Press, Association Press, 1966. pp. 341–342.

V. The Progress of Technology.
In: *Christians in the Technical and Social Revolutions of Our Time.* World Conference on Church and Society, Geneva, July 12–26. Geneva: WCC, 1967. p. 80.

VI. Youth in God's World.
In: *Work Book for Assembly Committees, Uppsala 1968.* Geneva: WCC, 1968. pp. 137–152.

VII. Salvation and Social Justice in a Divided Humanity.

In: *Bangkok Assembly 1973:* Minutes and Report of the Assembly of the Commission on World Mission and Evangelism, December 31, 1972 and January 9–12, 1973. pp. 88–90.

VIII. The Role of Women in Church and Society.
In: *Sexism in the 1970s: Discrimination Against Women.* A Report of a World Council of Churches Consultation, West Berlin 1974. Geneva: WCC, 1975. pp. 97–120.

IX. The Importance of Dialogue with People of Living Faiths.
In: *Guidelines on Dialogue with People of Living Faiths and Ideologies.* Geneva: WCC, 1979. 4th printing revised 1990. pp. 5–6 and 22.

X. The Dynamics of Contemporary Militarism.
In: *Faith and Science in an Unjust World:* Report of the World Council of Churches' Conference on Faith, Science and the Future, Massachusetts Institute of Technology, Cambridge, USA, 12–24 July 1979. Vol. 2: Reports and Recommendations. Ed. by Paul Abrecht. Geneva: WCC, 1980. pp. 183–184.

XI. The Challenge of Nuclear Disarmament.
In: *Before It's Too Late:* The Complete Record of the Public Hearing on Nuclear Weapons and Disarmament Organized by the World Council of Churches. Ed. by Paul Abrecht and Ninan Koshy. Geneva: WCC, 1983. pp. 3–34.

XII. *Baptism, Eucharist and Ministry.* Geneva: WCC, 1982. (Faith and Order Paper, no. 111). Parts of the Preface, pp. vii–x.

Appendix 2.

MEMBERSHIP IN THE WORLD COUNCIL OF CHURCHES

Amsterdam, 1948	146 churches
Evanston, 1954	163 churches
New Delhi, 1961	198 churches
Uppsala, 1968	235 churches
Nairobi, 1975	286 churches
Vancouver, 1983	301 churches
Canberra, 1991	317 churches

Appendix 3.

MEETINGS OF THE CENTRAL COMMITTEE

1948	Woudschoten	1971	Addis Ababa
1949	Chichester	1972	Utrecht
1950	Toronto	1973	Geneva
1951	Rolle	1974	Berlin (West)
1952–53	Lucknow	1975	Nairobi
1954	Chicago	1976	Geneva
1954	Evanston	1977	Geneva
1955	Davos	1979	Kingston
1956	Galyatetö	1980	Geneva
1957	New Haven	1981	Dresden
1958	Nyborg Strand	1982	Geneva
1959	Rhodes	1983	Vancouver
1960	St Andrews	1984	Geneva
1961	New Delhi	1985	Buenos Aires
1962	Paris	1987	Geneva
1963	Rochester	1988	Hanover
1965	Enugu	1989	Moscow
1966	Geneva	1990	Geneva
1967	Heraklion	1991	Canberra
1968	Uppsala	1992	Geneva
1969	Canterbury	1994	Johannesburg

ABOUT THE AUTHOR

Ans Joachim van der Bent (Dutch citizen, B.A. in Economics (1943) and MTH (1955), University of Amsterdam and MSLS Simmons College, Boston) was director of the Library and Archives of the World Council of Churches in Geneva (1963–1985) and the Council's ecumenical research officer (1985–1958). He was assistant librarian at the Harvard Business School (1956–1958), assistant librarian at the Harvard Divinity School (1958–1960) and librarian of Bangor Theological Seminary (1960–1963). Ordained as a minister in the United Church of Christ in 1961, he published some 20 books (ecumenical and reference works) and wrote more than 100 articles in ecumenical and theological journals. He was a consultant to university and seminary libraries in various parts of the world and member of several professional societies and associations (on three occasions he gave a major address at the annual convention of the American Theological Library Association). Fluent in English, French, Dutch and German, he has a reading knowledge of Spanish and Russian, and learned Greek, Latin and Hebrew during his classical education. He has a vast memory of the 20th-century ecumenical movement, in addition to this work he has contributed extensively to the *Dictionary of the Ecumenical Movement* published by the World Council of Churches in 1991. He is currently retired in the South of France.